The Legend and Cult of Upagupta

The Legend and Cult of Upagupta

SANSKRIT BUDDHISM IN NORTH INDIA AND SOUTHEAST ASIA

John S. Strong

PRINCETON UNIVERSITY PRESS
PRINCETON, NEW JERSEY

Published by Princeton University Press, 41 William Street,
Princeton, New Jersey 08540
In the United Kingdom: Princeton University Press, Oxford

Library of Congress Cataloging-in-Publication Data

Strong, John, 1948–
The legend and cult of Upagupta : Sanskrit Buddhism in
north India and Southeast Asia / John S. Strong.
p. cm.
Includes bibliographical references and index.
ISBN 0-691-07389-9
1. Upagupta. 2. Buddhism—Asia, Southeastern—History.
I. Title.
BQ992.P34S76 1991 294.3'092—dc20 [B] 91-14434

This book has been composed in Adobe Times Roman

Princeton University Press books are printed on acid-free paper,
and meet the guidelines for permanence and durability of the
Committee on Production Guidelines for Book Longevity
of the Council on Library Resources

Printed in the United States of America

10 9 8 7 6 5 4 3 2 1

In Memory of
U Ko Ko
Eugène Denis
and Maung Maung Gyi
who are in the past
in Mandalay, Bangkok, and Lewiston, Maine

Contents

Figures and Tables

(Photos are by the author unless otherwise noted)

FIGURES

Tables

Preface

When Louis Finot undertook a survey of the libraries of Laotian monasteries in 1917, he discovered that none of them possessed an entire set of the Pali canon. Of the three divisions of the Tipiṭaka, only the "basket of scholasticism"—the Abhidhamma—was complete, but that was because its seven books had important ritual uses at funerals and other ceremonies. The Vinaya—the monastic disciplinary code—was "mostly there," but much of the Sutta piṭaka, purporting to record the words of the Buddha himself, was unknown, and many of its books existed only in the form of anthologies of paritta, texts to be recited for their magical potency.[1]

The situation has not changed much since Finot's time. The volumes of the Pali canon which neatly line the shelves of buddhologists in the West are generally not to be found in the bookcases of Buddhists in Southeast Asia. What *is* there is mostly "extracanonical": jātakas (stories of previous lives of the Buddha), collections of legends from the commentaries, tales of the adventures of saints, accounts of other worlds, ānisaṃsas (stories extolling the advantages of merit making), ritual manuals, anthologies of sermons, secular tales, historical chronicles, grammars, and primers.[2] For most Buddhists, these are the sources that are read and repeated, the texts that best illustrate the Buddha's Teaching. The canon is important for other reasons: for its protective power and magical efficacy, and as an object of refuge and devotion.

I first thought of writing something about the legend and cult of the elder Upagupta—a saint who does *not* appear in the Pali canon—over fifteen years ago, while a graduate student in history of religions at the University of Chicago. My initial impression was that here was a potentially interesting figure who would allow for the investigation in Buddhism of what subsequently has been called, in a different context, that "powerful body of tradition [which] emphasizes not codes but stories, not precepts but personalities, not lectures but lives."[3]

This impression grew stronger and became better grounded during my work on the Sanskrit legends of King Aśoka, in some of which Upagupta is featured in a significant fashion. It was only gradually, however, that I began to understand the full scope of my undertaking, and only after I had embarked on fieldwork and textual study that I discovered the richness and complexity of the written, oral, and ritual traditions about Upagupta, some of which are still to be found in Southeast Asia.

In my view, Buddhism, as it is popularly practiced, consists primarily of deeds done and stories told, that is, of rituals that regulate life both inside and outside the monastery, and of legends, myths, and tales that are recalled by, for, and about the faithful. Encouragingly, in recent years, scholars in various disciplines have become more interested in such "stories,"[4] and concerned more specifically with the study of sacred biographies—the stories told about individual saints.[5] These hagiographies and the lives they feature can be thought of in terms of what Roger Bastide, in a very different context, has called "belvedere phenomena"[6]—compilations of traditions that reveal a broader context, that enable one to see a whole surrounding countryside, in all of its various aspects (doctrinal, sociological, ritual, soteriological).

Many of the stories that will preoccupy us in this book will be Sanskrit Hīnayāna Buddhist tales of a popular bent.[7] In general, buddhology in the West has tended to overlook such sources in favor of Mahāyāna or Pali Theravāda texts. In part, this is due to an understandable bias which inclines us to view the past in terms of the extant present; of all the many and diverse Hīnayāna sects that once thrived in South and Southeast Asia (Sarvāstivādins, Mahāsaṃghikas, etc.), only the Theravādins remain today. As a result, when we do look at Sarvāstivādin or other Sanskrit Hīnayāna works, we tend to view them not in their own light, but in that of other traditions, as complementary to the Theravāda or as precursory to the Mahāyāna. The Sanskrit sources that recount the legend of Upagupta, however, must be understood in their own context. As we shall see, they reflect a popular perspective on Buddhism that is at times significantly different from those of both the Theravāda and the Mahāyāna.

Readers will no doubt detect in the views depicted in this book influences of French buddhologists, inclinations towards anthropology, and imprints of my training in the history of religions. My approach may perhaps best be described, however, as the exegetical exploration of a world of meaning. In this, I have been inspired not only by my mentors at the University of Chicago, but also by the early works of Paul Mus, who, in my opinion, remains exemplary in his treatment of particular texts (or works of art) as focal points for reexamining the broad themes of a given tradition.[8] "Upagupta" is my belvedere, in the way that "Barabuḍur" and the "Buddha paré" were Mus's. The legends, myths, and rituals about him will form the world of our "text," and the effort to understand them will lead us to view not only his "context," but a number of other neglected landscapes in the study of Buddhism.

In what follows, I have tried to be fairly comprehensive, but I cannot pretend to have covered every single aspect of Upagupta's cult and every textual reference to him. Although I was lucky enough to observe and inquire about a number of rites in Thailand and Burma, my time there was limited. Although I believe that I have looked at and dealt with most of the important Buddhist textual references to Upagupta, there are additional sources in Chinese and Tibetan that have not been examined here. And although I have, through translators, consulted both Thai and Burmese works on Upagupta, I know of the existence of manuscripts—in Laotian, Lanna Thai, and Shan (not to mention Sanskrit)—that have remained untouched.

ACKNOWLEDGMENTS

Nothing would be possible, of course, without the help of friends, and thanks are due here to a number of individuals and institutions. Library research in Japan and fieldwork in Thailand and Burma were supported by a fellowship from the National Endowment for the Humanities during 1982–83 and were continued in the summer of 1983 by a grant from the Social Science Research Council. Parts of chapters 4–6 were written in Sri Lanka while I was on a Fulbright fellowship at the University of Peradeniya in 1987, and the rest of the book was more or less completed during a sabbatical leave from Bates College in 1987–88. A Faculty Publications grant from Bates also facilitated the reproduction of some of the photographs.

For initial advice and ideas before this project began, I am grateful to John Ferguson, Charles Keyes, Frank Reynolds, Donald Swearer, and Stanley Tambiah. For support and encouragement in Kyoto, I would like to thank Yoneo Ishii and Hubert Durt. For assistance with Chinese and Japanese sources, I am grateful to Shuo-jen Chen and Sarah Strong. For conversations and help of different kinds, in Chiang Mai and in Bangkok, I am indebted to Charles Archaimbault, François Bizot, John Cadet, Chaveng Yodvong, Sud Chonchirdsin, the late Eugène Denis, John and Fran Hamlin, Sommai Premchit, and Suwasdi Khemakapasiddhi. Most especially, I would like to thank Kitti Keanchampee, former graduate student in anthropology at Chiang Mai University and field assistant extraordinaire; and Louis Gabaude of the Ecole Française d'Extrême-Orient, who unstintingly gave of his time and expert advice, and without whom this project would not have been possible.

For help in Rangoon and Mandalay, I am grateful to Juliane Schober and Mark Woodward, who paved my way; Daw May Kyi Wynn, whose energy and enthusiasm helped me make the most of my time; and the late U Ko Ko of the University of Mandalay, who kindly consented to translate a number of sources for me. For help with other translations, I am also grateful to the late Maung Maung Gyi of Bates College, and, for photos of Burmese Upagupta images, to Steven and Anne Kemper. For support and expertise in Peradeniya, I would like to thank Lily DeSilva and Ratna Handurukande.

Finally, for suggestions and encouraging comments on various drafts of the manuscript, I am grateful to Margaret Case, Reginald Ray, Paula Richman, Sarah Strong, Nancy Trotic, and Donald Swearer.

Lewiston, Maine
25 August 1990

Note and Abbreviations

In citing Sanskrit and Pali sources, I have sought to provide references to original-language editions as well as to English, French, or German translations when available. In dealing with Chinese texts, I have been guided by existing translations in Western languages, but, for the convenience of scholars, I have also included references to originals in the standard Taishō edition (*T.*) of the Chinese canon, even when those translations were based on originals found in other earlier editions. In all cases, editions are cited by abbreviated title (as given below) and translations by the name of the translator (see Bibliography of Works Cited) preceded by an indication of the language of the translation (Eng., Fr., or Ger.). In discussions of Chinese Buddhist texts, I have used reconstructed Sanskrit titles when these are more or less reliable. In this, I have generally followed the forms given in Lancaster (1979).

Abbreviations

A.	*Anguttara Nikāya*
AA.	*Manorathapūraṇī* (Commentary on *A.*)
AbhK.	*Abhidharmakośabhāṣyam*
Aśokāv.	*Aśokāvadāna*
Aṣṭa.	*Aṣṭasāhasrikā-prajñāpāramitā-sūtra*
Avk.	*Avadānakalpalatā*
Avś.	*Avadānaśataka*
Brapaṃsukūla.	*Brapaṃsukūlānisaṃsaṃ*
BuvA.	*Madhuratthavilāsinī* (Commentary on *Buddhavaṃsa*)
Catuṣ.	*Catuṣpariṣatsūtra*
D.	*Dīgha Nikāya*
DA.	*Sumangalavilāsinī* (Commentary on *D.*)
Dāṭh.	*Dāṭhāvaṃsa*
DBK.	*Dasabodhisattuppattikathā*
DhA.	*Dhammapadaṭṭhakathā* (Commentary on *Dhp.*)
Dhp.	*Dhammapada*
Div.	*Divyāvadāna*
Dpv.	*Dīpavaṃsa*
ExtMhv.	*Extended Mahāvaṃsa*
GilgMss.	*Gilgit Manuscripts*
HmanNanY.	*Hman-Nan-Yazawindawgyi*
Itv.	*Itivuttaka*

J.	*Jātaka*
JM.	*Jātakamālā*
Konjaku	*Konjaku monogatari shū*
Kvu.	*Kathāvatthu*
KvuA.	*Kathāvatthuppakaraṇa-aṭṭhakathā* (Commentary on *Kvu.*)
Lakṣacait.	*Lakṣacaityasamutpatti*
Lal.	*Lalitavistara*
LP.	*Lokapaññatti*
M.	*Majjhima Nikāya*
Mhv.	*Mahāvaṃsa*
MhvṬ.	*Vaṃsatthappakāsinī* (Commentary on *Mhv.*)
Mil.	*Milindapañha*
MJM.	*Mahajjātakamālā*
Mkv.	*Mahākarmavibhanga*
MPS.	*Mahāparinirvāṇa sūtra*
MSV.	*Mūlasarvāstivāda Vinaya*
Mtu.	*Mahāvastu*
Pañca.	*Pañcaviṃśatisāhasrikā prajñāpāramitā*
PJāt.	*Paññāsa-Jātaka*
PSK.	*Phra Paṭhamasambodhikathā*
Ratnamālāv.	*Ratnamālāvadāna*
S.	*Saṃyutta Nikāya*
SA.	*Sāratthappakāsinī* (Commentary on *S.*)
Sanghbhv.	*Sanghabhedavastu*
Sās.	*Sāsanavaṃsa*
Saund.	*Saundarananda*
Śāyanāsav.	*Śāyanāsavastu*
Sdmp.	*Saddharmapuṇḍarīka sūtra*
Sdn.	*Saddanīti*
Sīhaḷav.	*Sīhaḷavatthuppakaraṇa*
Śīkṣ.	*Śīkṣāsamuccaya*
Sn.	*Suttanipāta*
SnA.	*Paramatthajotikā II* (Commentary on *Sn.*)
Sumāg.	*Sumāgadhāvadāna*
T.	*Taishō shinshū daizōkyō.* Citations in notes refer to text number, volume, page number, and register (a, b, or c).
T. 99	*Saṃyuktāgama sūtra*
T. 125	*Ekottarāgama*
T. 128	*Sumāgadhavadāna sūtra*
T. 130	*Sumāgadhavadāna*
T. 190	*Abhiniṣkramaṇa sūtra*
T. 200	*Avadānaśataka*

T. 201	*Kalpanāmaṇḍitikā*
T. 202	*Damamūkanidāna sūtra*
T. 203	*Tsa pao tsang ching*
T. 206	*Chiu tsa p'i yü ching*
T. 208	*Chung ching hsüan tsa p'i yü ching*
T. 211	*Dharmapādāvadāna*
T. 213	*Dharmapāda*
T. 310	*Mahāratnakūṭa*
T. 453	*Mi le hsia sheng ching*
T. 456	*Mi le ta ch'eng fo ching*
T. 642	*Śūraṃgamasamādhi sūtra*
T. 643	*Buddhānusmṛti samādhi sūtra*
T. 1262	*Kuei tzu mu ching*
T. 1421	*Mahīśāsakavinaya*
T. 1425	*Mahāsanghikavinaya*
T. 1428	*Dharmaguptakavinaya*
T. 1435	*Sarvāstivādavinaya*
T. 1442	[*Mūlasarvāstivāda*] *Vinayavibhanga*
T. 1448+1450	[*Mūlasarvāstivāda*] *Vinayavastu*
T. 1451	[*Mūlasarvāstivāda*] *Vinayakṣudravastu*
T. 1462	*Samantapāsādikā*
T. 1465	*Śāriputraparipṛcchā*
T. 1507	*Fen pieh kung te lun*
T. 1509	*Mahāprajñāpāramitā śāstra*
T. 1545	*Mahāvibhāṣā*
T. 1634	*Mahāyānavatāra*
T. 1644	*Lokaprajñapti*
T. 1689	*Ch'ing pin t'ou lu fa*
T. 1899	*Chung t'ien chu she wei kuo ch'i yüan ssu t'u ching*
T. 2027	*Chia she chieh ching*
T. 2030	*Nandimitrāvadāna*
T. 2042	*Aśokarājāvadāna*
T. 2043	*Aśokarājasūtra*
T. 2053	*Ta tz'u en ssu san ts'ang fa shih chuan* [of Hui-li]
T. 2058	*Fu fa tsang yin yüan chüan*
T. 2059	*Kao seng chuan* [of Hui-chiao]
T. 2085	*Kao seng fa hsien chuan* [of Fa-hsien]
T. 2087	*Ta t'ang hsi yü chi* [of Hsüan-tsang]
T. 2092	*Lo yang ch'ieh lan chi* [of Yang Hsüan-chih]
T. 2145	*Ch'u san tsang chi chi* [of Seng-yu]
ThagA.	*Paramaṭṭha-dīpanī Therāgātha-Aṭṭhakathā*
Ujishūi	*Uji shūi monogatari shū*

Upasam.	*Upasampadāvidhi*
Vin.	*[Theravāda] Vinayapiṭakam*
VinA.	*Samantapāsādikā* (Commentary on *Vin.*)
VinNid.	*Vinaya Nidāna*
Vsm.	*Visuddhimagga*

The Legend and Cult of Upagupta

Introduction

I SHALL NOT attempt, in this book, to separate fact from fiction in the legendary traditions that surround the Buddhist elder Upagupta. As with many great saints, the stories about him are so filled with the fancies and formulae of later hagiographers that the task of demythologizing these is probably an impossible one. If pressed, I could perhaps say, with a fair degree of accuracy, that historically Upagupta was a Buddhist monk who achieved some fame as a preacher and teacher in the region of Mathurā in Northern India, sometime between the reign of King Aśoka (third century B.C.E.) and the first century of the Christian era. By inclination, he was perhaps a follower of the Sarvāstivādin school. He was probably a forest monk, and he very likely attracted to himself a number of disciples interested in meditation, although this did not stop him from engaging in contact with laypersons.[1] He may have written one book, but this has not survived, and we know almost nothing about it.[2] After his death, his mountain monastery near Mathurā became a center of pilgrimage and remained so at least until the time of the Chinese traveller Hsüan-tsang (seventh century C.E.).[3] Beyond this, however, I would probably not venture to say much, at least not with any confidence.

Fortunately, in this book, we shall not primarily be concerned with the historical Upagupta. Instead, we shall examine his legends as legends and his cult as cult, and both as reflective of the preoccupations and viewpoints of the Buddhist communities that engendered and preserved them throughout the ages. This in itself is a rather formidable enterprise, for the legend and cult of Upagupta have existed for about two thousand years. Not only are there Indian Buddhist stories about him (extant in Sanskrit and, in translation, in Chinese and Tibetan), but, at some point, these traditions were passed on to northern Southeast Asia, where his cult has continued right up to the present and where his tale is still told in Burmese, Thai, and Laotian.

A number of anthropologists have interested themselves in the cult and legend of Upagupta in Southeast Asia; by and large, however, their studies have failed to consider fully the Indian textual traditions about the saint.[4] On the other hand, a number of buddhologists have examined these Indian texts, but they generally have not sought to relate them to the relevant Southeast Asian ethnographic materials.[5] In this book, we shall assume that the overall significance of Upagupta can be understood only by studying both Indian and Southeast Asian sources. We shall also assume that a complete picture of his legend and cult will emerge only with the coordinated consideration of all types of traditions, whether these be textual, oral, ritual, or iconographic. The chapters that follow, therefore, will include translations and exegeses of texts of both Indian and Southeast Asian provenance, descriptions and interpretations of rituals observed in Northern Thailand and Burma, the recounting and evaluation of pertinent oral traditions still being preserved today, and the consideration of images and other representations as these developed in different areas.

One of the most striking things about Upagupta, at least for buddhologists, is that there is no mention of him at all in the Pali canon. Even more remarkably, there are no references to him in the standard Pali commentaries on the canon, and his name appears to have been completely unknown in Sri Lanka.[6] Yet ironically, today, his cult is perpetuated only in Burma, Thailand, and Laos, where the Buddhism that is practiced—at least officially—is that of the Sri Lankan Pali Theravāda school.

There are, of course, historical reasons for this. In Burma, Upagupta figured originally as part of the Buddhist Sanskritic tradition that was initially very influential in that country.[7] When, in the eleventh and twelfth centuries, the Burmese religious milieu was changed by the official establishment of Pali Buddhism from Sri Lanka, saints such as Upagupta suddenly found themselves questioned as no longer quite canonical. This does not mean that his cult was suppressed; instead, it seems to have gone underground and survived as an unofficial remnant of an older Indian Buddhist tradition, but within a new context.

In the process, some interesting transformations appear to have taken place. Today, for instance, the cult of Upagupta is almost the exclusive preserve of Buddhist laypersons. Upagupta himself is thought of as being a monk and is recognized as such both in his iconography and in the details of his cult; but, in parts of Thailand and Laos at least, monks are nonetheless expected *not* to participate in certain rituals involving him. These are carried out instead by leading lay elders.

At the same time, in Southeast Asia generally, Upagupta has become associated with the mythology of nāgas (snake divinities) and of various local guardian deities (although we shall see that these relationships are complex ones). He is thought to still be alive, residing in a brazen palace in the midst of the Southern Ocean. He is invoked primarily as a protective figure, a guardian against disorder. He is also thought to have great magical powers and to be able to intercede in favor of his devotees.

These kinds of transformations raise the issue of syncretism, not only between Buddhism and indigenous religious traditions, but between different types of Buddhism as well. Generally speaking, as Buddhism moved out into non-Buddhist areas, its ideological assimilation of local traditions was asserted by legends telling of the conversion of indigenous divinities to the new faith. These spirits (nāgas, yakṣas, nats, phī) were thus "buddhicized"; they were incorporated into a Buddhist "pantheon" and given roles as protectors of the religion or its followers. At first glance, in the case of Upagupta, it would seem that something of the *reverse* process occurred. Upagupta, a perfectly legitimate and saintly figure in the *Sanskrit* Buddhist tradition, was suddenly found to be lacking a place in the *Pali* scheme of things. Too popular to be dismissed, he was kept on, but his cult was laicized, and he himself was indigenized and associated—though never fully—with local divinities who themselves had become Buddhists—though never completely. At the same time, freed from their Northwest Indian Sanskrit context, the traditions about him were able to expand and develop in all sorts of ways that might not otherwise have been possible. We shall examine the details of this rather complicated process in due course.

Enough has been said to indicate that, in this book, we shall be dealing with materials imbedded in two distinct yet related religiocultural milieux: Northwestern India, where the legend of Upagupta first developed around the beginning of the Christian era; and northern Southeast Asia—especially Burma, Northern and Northeastern Thailand, and Laos—where the traditions about him became established by the twelfth century C.E. (about the time, in fact, that they were dying out in India). In the remainder of this introduction, it may be useful to take an initial look at these two contexts and to survey some of the sources and problems that will occupy us in greater detail later on.

Mathurā and the Sarvāstivādin Tradition

The Indian legends about Upagupta have their origins in the Sanskrit Buddhist traditions of Northwestern India, specifically in the region of Mathurā. Historically, Buddhism seems to have spread to this area in a number of stages. Quite early, perhaps even during the lifetime of the Buddha himself, missionary monks began to wander up the valleys of the Ganges and its tributaries, preaching, converting, and establishing new communities of the faithful as they went. The city of Mathurā on the Yamunā River may well have received their attention from the start.

According to a text that is certainly apocryphal, the Buddha himself is reputed to have visited Mathurā. He arrived there on the day of a festival. The goddess of the city, worried that the Buddha's presence would detract from the celebrations in her honor, sought either to seduce him or to scare him away by appearing before him as a naked woman. He, however, merely declared that clothed females were unattractive; how much more so naked ones! Embarrassed, she went away, and the Buddha then commented to his disciples that Mathurā was a dusty place, plagued by fierce dogs and demons, where there were too many women, the ground was uneven, alms were difficult to obtain, and people (monks?) ate when it was still night.[8] It is clear that, at this point, Mathurā was, in the view of some Buddhists at least, a rather tough mission field and hardly the beacon of the faith that it eventually became.

Nevertheless, there are some stories of successful conversions that are supposed to have taken place even in this early period. A Pali sutta recounts the conversion of a king of Mathurā named Avantiputta by the Buddha's own disciple Mahākaccāna,[9] while a Sanskrit text recalls the story of the honest Brahmin Nīlabhūti, who, all set to condemn the Buddha for his views on caste, quickly found himself overcome by the Blessed One's charisma and willy-nilly breaking out in praise of him instead.[10] Finally, in a sequel to the tale of the Buddha's visit to Mathurā recounted above, the *Mūlasarvāstivāda Vinaya* relates how some devout Mathuran Brahmins subsequently came to the Blessed One to ask him to subdue the yakṣas Gardabha, Śara, and Vana and the yakṣiṇīs Ālikavendā and Timisikā, who had been plaguing the people of the city. The Buddha does so by converting these demonic figures to Buddhism and having the citizens of Mathurā build Buddhist vihāras in their honor.[11] This, as we shall see, is a typical pattern for the implantation of Buddhism in a region.

In any case, by the time of the Council of Vaiśālī, which according to tradition took place one hundred years after the death of the Buddha, Mathurā seems to have become, along with Sāṃkāśya and Kaṇyākubja, one of the centers of Buddhism in the west. As such, it was distinct in a variety of ways from the Buddhist communities of Magadha in the east, where the Buddha had lived and preached.[12] With the reign of King Aśoka in the third century B.C.E., however, Buddhism must have moved into Northwest India as a whole, and in full force. Not only in Mathurā, but beyond it in Gandhāra and Kashmir, new centers of the faith developed where large communities of monks flourished and different schools of thought emerged. Among the sects that firmly established themselves in the region at this time were the Sarvāstivādins, and it is probably to them that we owe our first accounts of the legend of Upagupta.

Indeed, Upagupta himself may have been a Sarvāstivādin; he figures prominently in that school's listing of Dharma masters, and a number of Chinese sources were even willing to credit him with the compilation of the Sarvāstivādin Vinaya.[13] Moreover, the only written work attributed to him, the *Netrīpada śāstra*, would appear to have been a treatise presenting Sarvāstivādin viewpoints.[14]

This is not to say that there were not other sectarian forces operating in Mathurā. Epigraphical evidence shows that, by the second century C.E., at least two other Hīnayānist sects besides the Sarvāstivādins counted adherents there: the Mahāsāṅghikas (forerunners of the Mahāyāna) and the Sammatīyas (another important early group).[15] In addition, early Pure Land notions were developing in the region.[16] By the time the Chinese pilgrim Fa-hsien visited Mathurā about 400 C.E., the city and its environs were clearly religiously pluralistic places.[17] Indeed, as we shall see in chapter 7, not only did various types of Hīnayānists and Mahāyānists flourish there, but there were specialized subgroups within these sects, each devoted to the cult of its own particular patron saint. Moreover, we should not forget that Mathurā was also an important center for Jains and that it was and has remained sacred to Vaishnavites, who see it as the homeland of Kṛṣṇa.

In the midst of all this, however, the Sarvāstivādins, at least in Upagupta's time, still occupied an important position, and we shall, in what follows, focus especially on them. Unlike their Theravādin cousins, who put down their roots in Sri Lanka and recorded their canon in Pali, the Sarvāstivādins preserved their scriptures in Sanskrit. They had their own Vinaya and Sūtra piṭakas, and an Abhidharma that was quite different from that of the Theravādins.[18] In addition, individual Sarvāstivādin scholars soon produced a whole series of commentaries and treatises that established the major scholastic themes for generations of Buddhists in Northern India, Central Asia, China, and Tibet.[19] There is no denying the overwhelming importance of the Sarvāstivādins in the development of Buddhism. Accidents of history have made the Theravādins and their Pali canon better known in modern times, but for centuries Sarvāstivādin monks and their Sanskrit scriptures set many of the standards for thought and practice in large parts of the Buddhist world.

André Bareau has listed 140 theses maintained by the Sarvāstivādins.[20] The first of these is that for which they were best known and to which, in fact, they owed their name: the doctrine that "everything exists" (sarvam asti), that all dharmas (elements of reality) have existence, whether in the past, present, or future.

This assertion must first be understood in the context of the abhidharmic positions of other schools. Early on, some Buddhists painted themselves into a scholastic corner by maintaining the momentariness and fundamental separateness of all dharmas from each other. According to this view, dharmas exist only in the present moment, arising and becoming extinct in an instant. Given this metaphysic, the Sarvāstivādins were worried about the connections and continuities among these theoretically distinct dharmas. Especially, they were concerned about the possibility of perceiving (remembering) things past and perceiving (predicting) things future. Similarly, they wanted to be able to assert, in the context of the doctrine of karma, the reality of past causes and the reality of future fruits.[21]

Given the absence of any ongoing substratum, and given the claim that only existing things could be perceived, once a thing (dharma) was past, how could it be recalled (for instance, by the Buddha in "remembering" someone's previous life) if it did not in some sense still exist? Similarly, if a future thing (for example, the eventual enlightenment of a disciple) did not exist, how could it accurately be foretold? The Sarvāstivādin solution to these problems was simply to affirm the existence not only of present, but also of past and future dharmas. According to them, the past and the future are, like the present, cognizable (jñeya); they "have knowability" (jñeyadharmatā), and it is this knowability that results in their being said to exist, in their having their own real characteristics (svabhāvalakṣaṇa).[22]

This is not to argue that past and future dharmas are in all respects the same as present ones. The manner in which they differ, in fact, became a topic of some debate among various Sarvāstivādin masters.[23] One solution to the problem was to state that they differed in their "activity" or "function" (kāritra). While both a past dharma and a present dharma may be said to exist (since they are cognizable), the latter differs from the former in that, in addition to its cognizability, it is characterized by activity. Similarly, a future dharma lacks activity, though it exists.[24]

This "solution," obviously, is not without its own obscurities and philosophical difficulties, and the Sarvāstivādin theory as a whole was hotly disputed by other Buddhist schools, which tackled these fundamental problems in their own ways. The Theravādins in particular lambasted and ridiculed the Sarvāstivādins, accusing them of propounding heresy.[25]

The Sarvāstivādins themselves, moreover, were by no means free from other kinds of factionalism. By the second century C.E., the "orthodox" Vaibhāṣikas, who claimed that they were the correct interpreters of the Abhidharma along the lines of the *Mahāvibhāṣā* commentary, had become clearly distinguished from the Sautrāntikas, who maintained the sole authority of the sūtras.[26] Later sources also speak of the Mūlasarvāstivādins (Original Sarvāstivādins), who had a separate Vinaya of their own and who thus would appear to have been a distinct sect. Their relative antiquity and relationship to the other Sarvāstivādins are matters of considerable dispute,[27] but their general doctrinal stances do not appear to have been fundamentally different.[28] In what follows, therefore, I shall often lump together sources from these two schools.

Scholars studying the Sarvāstivādins and Mūlasarvāstivādins have generally tended to focus on the abhidharmic and Vinaya issues that distinguished them from their Hīnayānist cousins and from their Mahāyānist successors. But it should not be forgotten that the Sarvāstivādins were by no means just a sect of monks following a certain Vinaya, or a school of scholastic debaters renowned for their Abhidharma. They, and even more so the Mūlasarvāstivādins, were also famous for their collections of popular Buddhist legends (avadānas), which they both incorporated into their canonical texts and preserved as separate anthologies.[29]

Avadānas are stories about the karmic fortunes of individual Buddhists. They tend to emphasize the beneficial effects, in this or a future lifetime, of past or present good deeds and of devout attitudes such as merit making, vow taking, faith, and devotion. Such stories, as well as the jātakas (accounts of the Buddha's previous lives), have always played an important role in Buddhism, especially in the sermons directed towards the laity. But under the

Sarvāstivādins, they seem to have taken on additional importance; they were systematically collected, and, as a genre, they came to be recognized as an official part of the Buddha's Teaching itself.[30]

Indian Sources

The principal sources for our study of the Upagupta legend in India are, in fact, Sarvāstivādin and Mūlasarvāstivādin texts of the avadāna type. These include:

The *Divyāvadāna*, an important anthology of Buddhist legends, which contains in its twenty-sixth and twenty-seventh chapters the fullest extant Sanskrit version of the Upagupta story.[31]

The *Avadānaśataka*, a collection of one hundred avadānas, the last of which mentions Upagupta. It does not actually present much information about him but is important for being perhaps the earliest known reference to him.[32]

Three Chinese versions of the avadāna of King Aśoka: the *Aśokarājāvadāna* (*A-yü wang chuan*),[33] the *Aśokarājasūtra* (*A-yü wang ching*),[34] and several chapters from the *Samyuktāgama sūtra* (*Tsa a han ching*).[35] These have preserved the basic legend of Upagupta more or less as it is found in the *Divyāvadāna* with, in addition, many extra anecdotes about his relationship to his teacher and to his disciples.

The *Mūlasarvāstivāda Vinaya*, an enormous work that has preserved within it many avadānas, including a number of stories about Upagupta. Some of these are available in the original Sanskrit as well as in Chinese and Tibetan translations.[36]

In addition, mention might be made here of a number of other sources that do not necessarily belong to the Sarvāstivādin or Mūlasarvāstivādin schools but whose accounts of Upagupta appear to be based on related sources. These include:

Story no. 54 of the *Kalpanāmaṇḍitikā* (alias *Sūtrālaṃkāra*), an anthology of tales variously attributed to Aśvaghoṣa or Kumāralāta.[37] This story gives an account of Upagupta's conversion of Māra that closely parallels that of the *Divyāvadāna*.[38]

Section 67 of the *Damamūkanidāna sūtra*, an anthology of tales better known by its Chinese title (*Hsien yü ching*) or its Tibetan one (*ḥDsangs blun*), and even more commonly referred to as the "Sūtra of the Wise Man and the Fool."[39] It was compiled by the Chinese monk Hui-chio and his seven companions on the basis of sermons they heard preached in Khotan in 445 C.E.[40]

The memoirs of the Chinese Buddhist pilgrim Hsüan-tsang, who visited India in the late seventh century. He not only recounts in part the legend of Upagupta as he knew it, but also describes sites he visited in Northern India that were associated with him.[41]

The "Upaguptāvadāna," chapter 72 of the *Avadānakalpalatā*, a late collection of

Buddhist legends rewritten and put into verse by the eleventh-century Kashmiri poet Kṣemendra.[42]

The Tibetan histories of Buddhism in India, including most prominently Tāranātha's sixteenth-century *Chos ḥbyung*, which presents the story of Upagupta in its account of the transmission of the Dharma after the death of the Buddha.[43]

A number of late Sanskrit collections of avadānas known as the avadānamālās ("garlands of avadānas"). They present Upagupta as the narrator of the stories, which he tells to King Aśoka and which occasionally add a few details about Upagupta.[44]

A miscellany of other sources preserved mostly in the Chinese Tripiṭaka and containing either variants of basic Upagupta legends or small stories about him not found in other sources.[45]

This list of sources does not pretend to be complete, but it does contain most of the texts to which we shall be referring.

The Mathuran and Aśokan Cycles of Upagupta Legends

Even the most cursory examination of these sources will reveal in them two distinct cycles of stories in which Upagupta appears. In the first cycle, he figures as the hero of his own avadāna. In its fullest form, this avadāna recounts the prediction made about him by the Buddha (which we shall analyze in chapter 1), his past life as a monkey on Mount Urumuṇḍa near Mathurā (see chapter 2), his subsequent birth as the son of a perfume merchant in that city (chapter 3), his encounter with the courtesan Vāsavadattā, his ordination by the elder Śāṇakavāsin, and his fame as a teacher residing at the Naṭabhaṭika monastery (chapter 4). Then it features his victory over Māra (the Buddhist embodiment of evil), an achievement much emphasized in the subsequent tradition (chapter 5), before ending with his death and cremation and with stories of his disciples (chapter 6).

All of these events are presented as taking place in and around the city of Mathurā and so may be said to constitute the Mathuran cycle of stories about the saint. It is because of these stories that it is often thought that Upagupta himself must have been a famous monk of Mathurā, the abbot of the local Buddhist community renowned for his teaching abilities.

The second cycle of stories about Upagupta in these texts is one which associates him with King Aśoka. In these tales (see chapter 7), Upagupta often appears as a sort of spiritual advisor and companion to the great Mauryan monarch. We are told of their meeting in the capital city of Pāṭaliputra and of their joint pilgrimage to all the holy sites of Buddhism in North India.

Jean Przyluski has argued that these stories should also be thought of as part of a Mathuran cycle—that they were made up by Mathuran monks who, eager to enhance the prestige of their hometown abbot, invented the tale of his meeting with the great Mauryan monarch and interpolated it somewhat clumsily into an existing Aśoka legend.[46] Przyluski's argument is an ingenious one, and it has been widely accepted. Nevertheless, the stories connecting Upagupta with Aśoka are distinct from those associating him with Mathurā, a fact that cannot readily be dismissed. For example, in the last chapter of the *Avadānaśataka* (which Przyluski, in his *Légende de l'empereur Açoka*, conveniently ignores), Upagupta is already associated with the Mauryan king, but no mention is made at all of his connections with Mathurā or with Mount Urumuṇḍa. Instead, he is portrayed as residing at the Kukkuṭārāma monastery in Pāṭaliputra, where Aśoka goes to question him.[47] Conversely, in other sources, such as the *Damamūkanidāna sūtra*, Mathurā is very much featured, but no mention at all is made of King Aśoka.[48]

The two cycles of legends, therefore, often appear to have existed independently, side by side, and though various attempts may have been made to join them,[49] each seems to have undergone a separate evolution on its own. Thus, from the Mathuran tradition about Upagupta's cremation at the Naṭabhaṭika hermitage, there arose a whole series of stories about Upagupta's disciples that have nothing to do with Aśoka.[50] Similarly devoid of reference to the Mauryan king was the Mathuran presentation of Upagupta as the fourth (or fifth, depending on the source) Master of the Dharma (dharmācārya)[51] in the Buddhist Sanskrit theory of patriarchal succession. According to this tradition, which is quite different from that of the Pali canon, the Buddha, at the time of his death, committed the Dharma to the keeping of the elder Mahākāśyapa, who, in turn, passed it on to Ānanda; Ānanda then transmitted it both to Śāṇakavāsin and to Madhyāntika, the latter going off to convert Kashmir and the former becoming, in Mathurā, the preceptor of Upagupta.[52]

The Aśokan cycle of Upagupta stories, on the other hand, also gave rise to a number of distinct traditions, including the already-mentioned pattern of his dialogues with the king featured in many late collections of avadānamālās. In these there is no mention of Mathurā. In addition, it was in its descriptions of his relationship with Aśoka that Upagupta's legend was to overlap most significantly with the stories of other great arhats who were reputed to have been associated with the Mauryan monarch. Thus, it is insofar as he encounters Aśoka that Upagupta has been confused with Yaśas, the abbot of the Kukkuṭārāma; with Piṇḍola, a disciple of the Buddha; with Indagutta, another enlightened arhat; and most especially with Moggaliputta Tissa, the president of the Third Buddhist Council in the Pali Theravāda tradition.[53]

Southeast Asia: Texts and Contexts

If the Indian materials about Upagupta are varied and bristling with difficulties, the Southeast Asian sources are no less so. It is not altogether clear when and how the Upagupta tradition was first transmitted to Southeast Asia, but the first two Burmese references to him can safely be dated to the early and mid-twelfth century.

The oldest of these is an inscription found in the Kubyauk-gyi, a temple built around 1113 C.E. at Myinkaba in the ancient Burmese capital of Pagan. The builder of the temple was Rājakumār, son of Kyanzittha, the great king of Pagan, and famed for his unselfish relinquishment of his claim to the throne in an act of filial respect. Gordon Luce has argued that Rājakumār was not only a loyal son to his father, but a remarkable Buddhist scholar as well. Luce claims that the frescoes that covered the walls of his temple at Myinkaba and their accompanying inscriptions testify to the breadth of his familiarity with Buddhist scriptures.[54]

Be this as it may, one of these inscriptions is of particular interest to us here. It states simply: "Tisapagut [Tissa-Upagupta] and King Dhammāsok [Aśoka] discuss the broadcasting of the Religion."[55] We will deal later with the apparent confusion here between Moggaliputta Tissa and Upagupta; suffice it to observe now that, at this point in Burmese history, at least one tradition about Upagupta—that of his association with King Aśoka—must have been known.

The other early reference to Upagupta is a bit different in nature. It is found in the *Saddanīti*, a Pali grammar written in Pagan by the monk Aggavaṃsa in 1154 C.E. As one of the paradigms for the use of the instrumental case, Aggavaṃsa gives the following sentence: "Upaguttena badho Māro" (by Upagutta Māra was bound).[56] This example was not original with him; it appears already in the oldest extant Pali grammar—that of Kaccāyana (fifth and sixth centuries C.E.)[57]—but its inclusion in the *Saddanīti* is significant, for it shows that the tale of Upagupta and Māra, which is part of the Mathuran cycle, must also have been known in twelfth-century Burma. Moreover, it was known in a noteworthy context, for the *Saddanīti* subsequently became one of the most popular of Pali grammars, and one can easily imagine generations of young monks memorizing the Pali paradigm "Upaguttena badho Māro" even if they knew nothing else about the Mathuran saint. Thus, it appears that in Burma, from the time of our earliest datable sources of information (1113 and 1154), both the Aśokan and the Mathuran cycles of stories about Upagupta were known, at least to some extent.

It comes as no surprise, then, to find both of these cycles in the *Lokapaññatti*, a text that was composed or compiled in Burma around the eleventh or twelfth century and that constitutes our most important Southeast Asian source on the legend of Upagupta (see chapter 9).[58] The *Lokapaññatti*, as a whole, is a treatise on cosmology and is usually attributed to one Saddhammaghosa of Thaton in Lower Burma. It is written in Pali but may well have been a reworking of a Sanskrit original, the *Lokaprajñapti*—a version of which is extant in the Chinese Tripiṭaka and bears remarkable affinities to the *Lokapaññatti*, except that it does *not* include the story of Upagupta.[59] Presumably this story was added to the text by Saddhammaghosa on the strength of other Sanskrit traditions.

For all its parallels with the legend of Upagupta as it is found in extant Indian sources, the *Lokapaññatti* version does present a number of interesting divergences. First, the two traditions about Upagupta which we have detected in the Indian sources—the Mathuran and Aśokan cycles—are thoroughly fused for the first time in the *Lokapaññatti*. In the *Divyāvadāna*, the story of Upagupta subduing Māra makes no reference at all to King Aśoka; it belongs exclusively to the Mathuran cycle. In the *Lokapaññatti*, however, the two Indian cycles have been brought together in such a way that they are no longer readily separable: Upagupta subdues Māra at Aśoka's request when the latter is worried that Māra will interfere with his celebration of a festival in honor of the Buddha's relics at Pāṭaliputra.[60]

Second, some new information about Upagupta also appears in the *Lokapaññatti*. Most importantly, he is now said not to have died, but to be dwelling in a brazen palace at the bottom of the ocean. From there he can come to the aid of those devotees who worship him. Here, then, we have an instance of a new kind of tradition developing, syncretistically, in a new situation. In this guise, moreover, Upagutta is also called Kisanāga Upagutta.[61] This, understandably, has led scholars to associate him with the worship of nāgas, or snake spirits, in Southeast Asia, a topic which we shall examine in due time.

Although the *Lokapaññatti* is a key text for the study of the development of the cult of Upagupta, its overall importance in Southeast Asia should not be exaggerated. As a cosmological treatise, it is rather awkwardly organized, and it was soon eclipsed, at least in Thailand, by the better-known *Traibhūmikathā*.[62] But its version of the Upagutta tale (not found in the *Traibhūmikathā*) remained the fountainhead for all subsequent Southeast Asian Upagupta traditions. For example, one of the most popular of the Burmese chronicles, the *Mahāyāzawin-gyi* (the Great Chronicle of the Kings of Burma), compiled by U Kala in 1714, reproduces the whole of the *Lokapaññatti*'s Upagutta story, though it organizes it differently.[63] Likewise, the *Hman-Nan-Yazawindawgyi* (the Glass Palace Chronicle),[64] written in 1829, repeats the tale, although, as we shall see, the committee of scholars that compiled this text saw fit to point out that there was no Pali canonical basis to the story and that the *Lokapaññatti*, as a work, had never been sanctioned by any Buddhist Council.[65]

Despite such official denigration, Upagupta continued to be popular in Southeast Asia, and his story continued to be told. In Burma, it was included in the mid-nineteenth century in the *Maha-win wutthu*, U Kin's retelling of the *Mahāvaṃsa*,[66] even though Upagupta does not appear at all in the Sri Lankan original of that work. It was also incorporated into the *Jinatthapakāsani*, a popular version of the life of the Buddha and history of the early Sangha;[67] and books more or less repeating the Upagupta legend have continued to appear right up to the present time.[68] In Thailand, his story was included in one of the last chapters of the *Phra Paṭhamasambodhikathā*, a widely read life of the Buddha of which there are both Thai and Pali versions.[69] In addition, it has been preserved separately in a number of Northern Thai manuscripts.[70]

The Southeast Asian traditions about Upagupta, however, were not preserved solely or even primarily in written texts, but were kept alive in the practices and beliefs of Buddhist believers (see chapter 10). Today—in Burma, in Northern and Northeastern Thailand, and in Laos—Shin Upago (Burmese) or Phra Uppakhut (Thai, Laotian) is still thought to be alive and living in the ocean, or, alternatively, at the bottom of a nearby river or swamp. In this way, he fits into the cult of those arhats who, somewhat like bodhisattvas, are thought to delay their attainment of parinirvāṇa for the good of the religion until the time of the future Buddha Maitreya (see chapter 11). Just as Aśoka long ago invited Upagupta to come to stop Māra from interfering with his festival in honor of the Buddha's relics, so villagers today invite him to come to their celebrations from a nearby river or swamp to make sure that modern-day Māras do not spoil the festivities by making it rain or by causing drunks to be boisterous or thieves to be active (see chapter 12).

But the Southeast Asian ritual traditions about Upagupta are even more diverse than this. In Burma, where statues of Shin Upago are quite common, he is often depicted as sitting on a raft, floating in the middle of a tank of water (see fig. 1). He has one hand in a begging bowl on his lap, and his head is tilted upwards towards the sky. Two interpretations of this curious posture are commonly given. Some claim that Upagupta is a very strict monk and does not want to violate the Buddhist monastic rules by eating after noon; hence he is looking up to see if the sun has passed the zenith. Others maintain that it is actually already afternoon and that Upagupta is looking skywards because he is using his magical powers to stay the sun in its course so that he can keep on eating.

Whatever the interpretation, such images can be purchased today in almost any pagoda shop, at least in Rangoon, and many people have one at home on their family altar, alongside but subordinate to a statue of the Buddha. Larger images may also be found in special Shin Upago shrines, where people come to make offerings to him. Worship of him is thought to bring to the devotee good luck, protection, and prosperity in this life.

From time to time, especially in Lower Burma, someone decides to float a Shin Upago image on a river down to the ocean. This is meant symbolically to return the saint to his home. It is an occasion for special festivities, at the end of which the statue is installed on a specially constructed raft and towed out to midriver, where it is released. Often, villagers downstream, upon seeing a Shin Upago raft, will intercept it and take it back to their own village, where a whole new cycle of ceremonies in honor of the saint will commence. Then they, too, will put him in the water and send him on his way.

Fig. 1. Upagupta Image from Sagaing, Burma

In Thailand and Laos, on the other hand, statues or other anthropomorphic representations of Upagupta are much less common. There is, to be sure, a large image of him at Wat Uppakhut in downtown Chiang Mai, but this is an iconographic anomaly and totally unlike anything found in Burma. More commonly, the saint is represented in the form of a stone or stones taken from a river bottom or swamp bed (see chapter 12). It is also possible to find in amulet shops small metallic representations of seashells or other marine creatures out of which peers a crudely molded face or in which sits a small figure holding a lotus. These, too, are said to be Phra Uppakhut, and it is thought that, if the shell is immersed in water, it will bring good fortune to the home (see chapter 13).

The obvious connection of Upagupta with water in many of these examples and the Southeast Asian belief that he resides at the bottom of the ocean have spawned a number of popular stories about his origin. In some areas, he is said to be the son of Macchadevī, the foul-smelling fish princess who was born in the stomach of a great fish and later impregnated by a Brahmanical ascetic. Elsewhere, he is known as the offspring of a fish or a nāgī—a female snake divinity—who happened to swallow the Buddha's semen when he ejaculated into a stream![71]

In light of all this, it is not surprising that a number of scholars have concluded that Upagupta, at least in Southeast Asia, should primarily be understood as a spirit connected with water, rain, and fertility. Jean Przyluski, for example, has argued that Shin Upago in Burma was an indigenous demigod, a "king of the waters" of the delta region who was both a nāga and a sort of divinity.[72] As such, Przyluski asserts, he had little real connection with the Upagupta of the Indian legends. Instead, he was a product of the "maritime civilization of the Southeast," a matriarchal "Austroasiatic" culture which, in its myths and rituals, located the source of all magico-religious power in water.[73] Only with the advent of Buddhism to Burma was this indigenous divinity identified with the Indian Buddhist patriarch Upagupta and absorbed into the new religion, "just as in Europe saints were often local heroes predating Christianity but then adopted by the Church."[74]

As we shall see, there are some real difficulties with Przyluski's view. More recent interpretations may be found, however, in the works of Stanley Tambiah and of Richard Davis, who both address the question of Upagupta's identity primarily on the basis of the ethnographic data they collected in the field. For Davis, working in Nan province in Northern Thailand, Upagupta is "a complex and paradoxical figure . . . a 'multivocal' or 'polysemous' symbol, standing for several referents and eliciting a variety of associations depending upon the context."[75] More specifically, he represents a "conjunction of asceticism and piety with virility, sexuality, and natural fecundity."[76]

For Tambiah, working in a northeastern Thai village not too far from the Laotian frontier, Upagupta is also a paradoxical figure, but Tambiah tends more to resolve the various structural oppositions with which he is concerned. Thus, he interprets the story of Upagupta's birth from the union of the Buddha's sperm and the nāgī as reflecting an opposition between nature (the water-dwelling mother) and spiritually endowed humanity (the enlightened father)—an opposition which is bridged by Upagupta, who is somewhat of a hybrid creature.[77] He is a Buddhist monk (that is, a son of the Buddha) and, as such, has subdued his lower nature; but the villagers still identify him with the nāgas, and so with water and rain. The rite of inviting him ("ritually compelling him") to come from the swamp (or river) to protect a Buddhist festival from the incursions of Māra thus represents the taming and conversion of a water spirit to Buddhism. In Tambiah's words, the rite is "an attempt to bring nature under man's metaphysical control," even though "its comprehensiveness must remain partial for man's control over nature is always incomplete."[78]

At the same time, according to Tambiah, this ritual reflects another structural opposition: between society ("human beings in their solidarity") and chaos ("the forces of passion, death and malevolence" represented by Māra). Upagupta resolves this polarity, at least for the duration of the festival, by allying himself with the humans in order to protect them from the Evil One.[79] Finally, in the story of Upagupta's encounter with King Aśoka's elephant (which we shall consider in chapter 9), Tambiah finds a third opposition between spiritual power (Upagupta) and royal power (the elephant) that is resolved in favor of the former when Upagupta easily stops the elephant's charge.[80]

Tambiah's insights here are quite seminal, and we shall try to do greater justice to them later on. Unfortunately, his own ethnographic data did not enable him to explore these structural oppositions fully. He therefore ends his discussion with a limited conclusion that Upagupta is, in the final analysis, a rain spirit which a Buddhist society invites and tries to control in order to ensure the plenitude of the monsoon.[81]

For the village studied by Tambiah, this conclusion may well have been true. There, the invitation of Upagupta occurred only in conjunction with the celebration of Bun Phra Wes, the festival of the recitation of the Vessantara Jātaka, which, in that region, takes place just prior to the advent of the rainy season. It would appear, therefore, that this invitation is timed to help bring on the monsoon. However, when data from a broader region is considered, it is clear that Upagupta can be and is invited at almost any time of the year, and for a host of different celebrations: New Year's, entering the rains retreat, ending the rains retreat, rocket festivals, the festival of lights, dedications of new monasteries or monastic buildings or Buddha images, ordinations of new monks, or, in Burma, boys' initiation ceremonies. As one senior monk in Chiang Mai put it, Upagupta is not necessarily connected with the Vessantara tradition; he can be invited anytime for any festival at all.[82]

Moreover, when laypersons and monks, either in Burma or in Thailand, are asked why Upagupta should be invited to these rituals, usually one of the first answers they give is that he will make sure it does *not* rain, showers being one of the ways in which Māra is thought to spoil a celebration. This seems especially true in Burma, where the mere presence of Upagupta is thought to halt rainfall even in the midst of the monsoon season. As one informant in Rangoon told me, whenever she forgets her umbrella on a cloudy day, she says a little prayer to Upagupta, asking him to see to it that it does not rain on her.[83]

Upagupta, however, is more than just a saint who will protect Buddhist festivals from mishap and who can be called upon to bring good weather for the duration of a celebration. In both Northern Thailand and in Burma, he is also thought to be able to manifest himself in person, suddenly and quite mysteriously appearing in the form of a rather ugly and strange-looking monk on his begging round. In Northern Thailand, he is particularly said to come in this way very early in the morning (at 1:00, 2:00, or 3:00 A.M.) on those few days each year when the full moon falls on a Wednesday.[84] On such days, laypersons should get up before daybreak and offer food to any monks who have gone out on their begging rounds extra early for the occasion. Those who are lucky may actually encounter Upagupta at such times; this is a stroke of good fortune, since food offerings made to him in person are thought to be especially meritorious and to result in great wealth, not just in future rebirths, but in this very lifetime. In fact, stories abound of individuals who struck it rich after encountering Upagupta.[85]

These few remarks will suffice to indicate that the traditions about Upagupta, in Southeast Asia as well as in India, are much more diverse and complex than has generally been realized. It should be pointed out, however, that this book is more than a book about the fame and fortune of a single Buddhist saint, for our investigation of these traditions—our discussion of Upagupta's legend and cult—will lead us to reexamine some fundamental aspects of Buddhism itself in both its Indian and Southeast Asian contexts. Indeed, as we trace Upagupta's hagiography and the rituals attached to it, we shall branch out to explore the legends and practices with which these intersect. In so doing, chapter by chapter, we will be able to reinvestigate a number of basic issues: the liminal situation Buddhists find themselves in in the post-parinirvāṇa period, being contemporaries neither of the now-past Buddha Gautama nor of the still-future Buddha Maitreya (chapters 1 and 2); the role of the lineage of the Masters of the Law (the Sanskrit Buddhist patriarchate) (chapter 3); the nature of the Buddhist Path to arhatship and the places in it of asceticism and ordination (chapter 4); the dynamic structure of image worship and the nature of Buddhist devotionalism (chapter 5); the didactic techniques of Buddhist teachers and the variety of modes of master-disciple relationship (chapter 6); the role of kings and charismatic saints in Sangha-state interactions (chapter 7); the relationship of orthodox and heterodox Buddhist practices within a Theravāda context (chapter 8); the multiple meanings of the word *nāga* (chapter 9); the development of the Buddhist cult of arhats as protectors of the Dharma (chapters 10 and 11); and, finally, the roles of Buddhist saints as facilitators of festivals (chapter 12) and providers of moral and material benefits (chapter 13).

In addressing these questions, our perspective will generally be governed by the popularly oriented Sanskritic sources that we shall be interpreting. In some cases, these will allow us to shed new light on old problems in the study of Buddhism, problems which, for the most part, have been viewed either through the lens of the Pali canon or within the retrospective systems of Mahāyānist philosophers. Hopefully, the largely Sarvāstivādin stories which we shall introduce and analyze in the chapters that follow will help illuminate not only the overall Indian Buddhist milieu in which the traditions about Upagupta originated, but also the contemporary practices of Theravādins in which these traditions have been preserved.

PART ONE

Upagupta in India

CHAPTER ONE

Provisions for the Buddha's Absence

IN MANY of our sources, the Mathuran cycle of Upagupta stories begins with a prediction made by the Buddha while he was on a journey with his favorite disciple Ānanda to the land of Mathurā. Pointing out the mountain called Urumuṇḍa, the Blessed One declares that, one hundred years after his parinirvāṇa, an elder named Upagupta will live there and make many converts. Ānanda then inquires about the karmic history of Upagupta, and the Buddha proceeds to recount the story of the elder's past life as a monkey on that very same mountain. There are thus two distinct episodes to be dealt with here: the prediction the Buddha makes about Upagupta and the account he gives of Upagupta's previous life. Although these are clearly related to each other, for convenience' sake we shall consider them separately, the first in this chapter and the second in chapter 2.

The text of the Buddha's prediction about Upagupta varies a little from one source to another. We shall start by considering that contained in the *Divyāvadāna*:

> When the Blessed One, around the time of his parinirvāṇa, had converted the nāga Apalāla, the potter, the outcaste woman, and Gopalī, he reached the city of Mathurā. There he said to the Venerable Ānanda: "Ānanda, right here in Mathurā, one hundred years after my parinirvāṇa, there will be a perfumer named Gupta. He will have a son named Upagupta, a Buddha without the marks [of a Great Man], who, in those days, will carry on the work of a Buddha. Through his teaching, many monks will rid themselves of all their defilements and experience arhatship—[so many that] they will fill up a cave eighteen cubits long and twelve cubits wide with their tally sticks [śalākā] four inches in length. Furthermore, Ānanda, this same monk Upagupta will be the foremost of all my disciples who are preachers. Ānanda, do you see over there that dark line on the horizon? . . . That is the mountain called Urumuṇḍa. There, one hundred years after my parinirvāṇa, a monk called Śāṇakavāsin will build a monastery and initiate Upagupta into the monastic life. Moreover, Ānanda, in Mathurā, there will be two guild masters, the brothers Naṭa and Bhaṭa. They will build a monastery on Mount Urumuṇḍa; it will be known as the Naṭabhaṭika and will be the best of all my forest hermitages where the beds and seats are conducive to meditation."[1]

Predictions (vyākaraṇa) about the karmic fortunes of individuals abound in Buddhist avadāna literature. Basically, however, they may be said to be of two types. On the one hand, there are those that might be called formulaic predictions of future enlightenment. These tend to be quite stereotyped; the Buddha declares that such and such a person, who has just completed such and such an act of merit, will, as a result of that deed and of his firm resolve, become the Buddha (or the pratyekabuddha or the arhat) so-and-so in such and such a future aeon.[2] Such predictions often cover vast periods of time and look forward to the almost-unimaginable future. Their function seems to be to encourage people to perform acts of merit and devotion, not by showing them their immediate effects, but by more generally guaranteeing their ultimate fruit and giving them a glimpse of what, in the Sarvāstivādin view of things, already exists in the future.

On the other hand, there are those predictions which concern more immediate historical or legendary events and which have the function of legitimizing or aggrandizing an already-known person, place, or event. These "predictions," then, are not actual predictions at all, but have been made up ex post facto and then attributed to the Blessed One in the texts. Thus, when the Buddha, in the *Mūlasarvāstivāda Vinaya*, "predicts" the "future" erection of a stūpa by King Kaniṣka, we naturally assume, as scholars, that the passage in question was written after the Kaniṣka stūpa had, in fact, been built, and that its forecast by the Buddha was made up in order to add to that monument's pedigree and prestige.[3]

Clearly, the prediction about Upagupta is of this second type. It does not concern the distant future, but a more immediate time described as being one century after the Buddha's death. It is not formulaic and general, but quite precise in its forecast—outlining, in fact, a brief hagiography of Upagupta: he will be the son of Gupta, the perfume merchant; he will live in Mathurā one hundred years after the Buddha's death; he will be very much like a Buddha and do the work of a Buddha, though he will not have the thirty-two bodily marks of a Buddha; he will be ordained by the elder Śāṇakavāsin and will dwell at the Naṭabhaṭika monastery on Mount Urumuṇḍa; he will enjoy great renown as a preacher and teacher, leading many disciples to arhatship.

We will consider the significance of each one of these points in due time. Before we do so, however, it is important to examine more fully the context in which the prediction itself appears. In virtually all of our sources, the prediction about Upagupta is introduced by some reference, no matter how slight, to a series of conversions effected by the Buddha prior to his arrival in Mathurā. In the *Divyāvadāna*, as we have just seen, mention is made of the nāga Apalāla, of the potter, of the caṇḍāla woman, and of Gopālī (or Gopāla, the nāga king).[4] Much the same list may be found in the *Samyuktāgama*[5] and the *Aśokarājasūtra*,[6] while the *Aśokarājāvadāna* adds to it some geographical indications: "Of old, when the Buddha was in Udyāna, he quelled the Naga Apalala. In . . . Kashmir he downed and converted [the potter]. In . . . Gandhavatī, he converted Caṇḍāla. In . . . Gandhāra he quelled the ox Nāga. Then he returned to Mathurā."[7]

It has long been recognized that the conversions listed here are among the many performed by the Buddha in the course of his journey to Northwest India prior to his arrival at Mathurā. The account of this trip, like those of so many other voyages the Buddha is reputed to have undertaken—to South India, to Sri Lanka, to Southeast Asia—is, of course, purely apocryphal.[8] For parts of it, at least, the Blessed One is portrayed as flying through the air, converting heretics and conquering demons by means of his magical powers, and predicting the future glory of many sites.

The fullest version of this story is that contained in the *Mūlasarvāstivāda Vinaya*. As Lamotte has shown,[9] the tale may basically be divided into three parts: (1) Accompanied by his disciple Ānanda, the Buddha goes from Hastināpura to Rohitaka via several other towns, converting a number of Brahmins along the way.[10] (2) At Rohitaka, he stays one night in the palace of the yakṣa Hastibala. There, he reflects that he has many conversions left to make before his parinirvāṇa. He summons, therefore, the yakṣa Vajrapāṇi,[11] and together they fly off through the air, cross the Indus River, and go on a great tour of what is now Afghanistan and Kashmir, during which they convert no fewer than seventy-seven thousand beings, including the four that interest us—Apalāla, the potter, Gopāla, and the caṇḍāla woman. Then they return to Rohitaka. Actually, this whole expedition appears to have taken place overnight while the Buddha was in meditation; he is said to have entered samādhi before summoning Vajrapāṇi and to have "returned" to his room before the third watch of the night. The next morning, Ānanda is very surprised to learn that the Buddha has been "away."[12] (3) From Rohitaka, the Buddha and Ānanda then continue on their journey. They proceed first to Ādirajya and Bhadrāsva[13] and then to Mathurā, where the prediction about Upagupta is made.[14]

The stories that will most concern us here all fall in the second and seemingly most supernatural part of the Buddha's journey. Scholars studying this narrative have often assumed that it was an interpolation into existing traditions and must have been made up by Kashmiri or other Northwestern monks seeking to claim that their home communities had actually been visited by the Buddha in person.[15] In making this argument, they have naturally focussed on the geographical indications in the texts and, with the help of modern day archaeology and the reports of the ancient Chinese pilgrims, have sought to identify the sites concerned.[16]

It might be pointed out, however, that only the *Mūlasarvāstivāda Vinaya* and the *Aśokarājāvadāna* actually provide any specific geographical information about this journey. The terser and, in some cases, probably older references to the same trip make no mention of any place-names at all; instead, they focus on the conversions and conquests that took place along the way. In what follows, therefore, we shall be less concerned with the identity of the places the Buddha is supposed to have visited than with the acts he is supposed to have accomplished during his journey. For, however much the *Mūlasarvāstivāda Vinaya* narrative may have been intended to give a pedigree to certain Northwestern sites of pilgrimage, it may also be studied as a capsule account of how Buddhism got established and maintained in a given area. As such, it is interesting not only for the geographical and historical data it contains, but also for the Buddhist ideology of conversion and mission it reflects.

The Conversion of the Nāga Apalāla

The first major conversion the Buddha makes on his midnight expedition with Vajrapāṇi is that of the nāga king Apalāla.[17] The story of this dragonlike monster is found not only in the *Mūlasarvāstivāda Vinaya*, but in a host of other texts as well.[18] According to one version, Apalāla had previously been a Brahmin who managed to put an end to a terrible drought, making it rain by means of his magical powers. When the king and the people failed to recompense him adequately for his timely intervention, he, out of spite, resolved to become a nāga dragon and ravage their crops. He was then reborn as Apalāla.[19]

In the *Mūlasarvāstivāda Vinaya*, when the Buddha and Vajrapāṇi arrive at Apalāla's palace, Apalāla flies up into the air and showers them with hailstones and clods of dirt. The Buddha counters this by using his supernatural powers; he quickly enters into the samādhi of loving-kindness, and the hailstones and clods of dirt are transformed into a cloud of sweet-smelling perfumes. Apalāla then attacks with a shower of weapons, but these are changed into lotus blossoms. He then creates a cloud of smoke, but the Buddha makes an even denser cloud and forces him to retreat to his palace. Then, having successfully defended himself, the Buddha launches his offensive; resolving to give Apalāla a very bad fright, he orders Vajrapāṇi to attack. The latter needs little encouragement; with a few massive blows of his thunderbolt, he destroys the whole mountaintop, crumbling it into Apalāla's lake and forcing him to come out of the water. Before he can flee, however, the Buddha enters into the samādhi of fire and fills the entire region with a mass of flames, leaving only a small space in front of him, right at his feet, free from the conflagration. Apalāla, seeking a cool place, is forced to come there. The Buddha grabs him by the hair and sternly tells him to change his ways: if he repents, he still has a chance to be reborn in heaven, but if he does not, he is destined for hell. Apalāla needs no more convincing. He quickly takes refuge in the Triple Gem and agrees to stop harming the people of the region.[20] In another version of the story, the battle is even more drawn-out, and the Buddha and Vajrapāṇi are assisted by the monk Panthaka, who renders himself invisible and magically blocks up Apalāla's eyes, ears, nose, and mouth.[21]

The violence of this encounter, though at first perhaps somewhat surprising, is actually not atypical in our sources of the Buddha's dealings with non-Buddhists. Similar scenarios occur in other texts. For instance, in different versions of the story of the great tournament of magical powers at Śrāvastī,[22] Vajrapāṇi, acting on behalf of the Buddha, causes a violent hailstorm. He then variously chases the heretics into the river, where they drown;[23] or knocks down their pavilion;[24] or, in a *Divyāvadāna* variant that recalls the tale of Apalāla, works it so that not a single hailstone falls on anyone who stays near the Buddha and honors him. Hundreds of thousands of beings, therefore, run to the Blessed One for shelter and promptly take refuge not only from the storm, but also in him.[25]

Etienne Lamotte has speculated that Vajrapāṇi, in these and other stories, has the function of taking on some of the more aggressive tasks that it would be unseemly for the Buddha (whose commitment is to nonviolence) to perform himself.[26] His point is noteworthy, but it needs some qualification. It is true that the *Mūlasarvāstivāda Vinaya* tries to claim that the Buddha's actions against Apalāla were motivated by loving-kindness and compassion, yet the way in which it does this is not wholly convincing. The fact is that, in the story, the Buddha, compassionate or not, appears to share with Vajrapāṇi the work of attacking the dragon. He is presented as a master of magical means who does not hesitate to use his powers in order to subdue troublemakers and force them to convert. As Alexander Soper has put it, "The Buddha who elsewhere accepts the humility of lesser orders as a matter of course, appears in the North-West in the aggressive role of a conqueror."[27]

Soper goes on to compare the battle between the Buddha and Apalāla with various Vedic and Persian mythic combats between heroes and serpent gods. In particular, he points to the story of Indra and Vṛtra.[28] Apalāla, like Vṛtra, is a watery monster, a symbol of chaos; and the Buddha, together with Vajrapāṇi (with his thunderbolt), seems here to be taking over the role of Indra as slayer of the dragon.[29]

There is one way, however, in which Buddhist ethics have moderated this myth. Unlike Vṛtra, Apalāla is not killed; he is tamed, he is converted, he is forced to change, but he is left alive. The way in which he is conquered, moreover, is distinctly and typically Buddhist. By filling the world with fire, or by causing a violent thunderstorm, the Buddha not only demonstrates his magical powers over the elements; he forces his opponents to realize in very concrete terms the truly intolerable nature of saṃsāra, which becomes for them literally a burning house or a great flood.[30] This, in turn, obliges them to take refuge in him, the Buddha, at whose feet is the only shelter from this world of suffering.

A definite soteriological point, then, is being made in these stories. Salvation, at least for these monsters, comes not through interest in the Dharma or through the charm of the Buddha, but through fear of saṃsāra and realization that the only refuge from it is in the person of the Buddha. Unlike Indra, the Buddha tames his opponents not by defeating them directly in hand-to-hand combat, but by graphically showing them the world as it truly is—an intolerable place of pain.

This raises, in a roundabout way perhaps, an important question: what happens when the Buddha is no longer there, when the refuge is gone? Will the demonic forces subdued by him remain subdued once he departs? Or, in slightly different terms, will the realization of the nature of saṃsāra brought on by the presence of the Blessed One fade after he has left? This question is, of course, much larger than the immediate one of what happens when the Buddha has finished his Northwestern tour. It is more generally the problem of routinization, and it was clearly a major concern to the authors of the *Mūlasarvāstivāda Vinaya*, who were living at a time when, in fact, the Buddha *was* gone, not just from their area of India, but from this world. For despite Buddhism's stress on the acceptance of impermanence, the parinirvāṇa of the Buddha (that is, his absence) was keenly felt by his followers and gave rise to a number of problems for those who were concerned with the spread and continuation of the faith. The legend of Apalāla sets up these questions, but it does not really deal with them. No provision is made for handling the nāga king after his converter is gone, yet the problem is recognized. For the solutions we must turn to the other stories.

The Nāga Gopāla and the Cave of the Buddha's Shadow

Apalāla was by no means the only nāga king subdued by the Buddha in the Northwest. Almost as famous, and equally (though not always so clearly) mentioned in the summary lists of conversions that introduce the prediction about Upagupta, is the figure of Gopāla. The *Mūlasarvāsṭivāda Vinaya* does little more than mention Gopāla in passing.[31] The traditions about him, however, were well known, and for a full version of his story we may profitably turn to three sources: the account given by the Chinese pilgrim Hsüan-tsang (seventh century) in his *Ta t'ang hsi yü chi*;[32] a curious text known as the *Buddhānusmṛti samādhi sūtra* (*Kuan fo san mei hai ching*), translated by Buddhabhadra about 420 C.E.;[33] and the fifty-sixth chapter of Kṣemendra's *Avadānakalpalatā*, entitled "Gopālanāgadamanāvadāna" (The avadāna of the taming of the nāga Gopāla).[34]

The taming and conversion of this dragon is in many ways similar to that of Apalāla. According to Hsüan-tsang, Gopāla was formerly a cowherd (as his name implies) who was once reprimanded by a king for not being able to supply him with milk. Upset, he vowed to become a great dragon and ravage the countryside. He then committed suicide by throwing himself over a cliff and was reborn as the nāga king Gopāla, and he dwelt in a cave in that very same cliff near the town of Nagarahara.[35] According to the *Buddhānusmṛti samādhi sūtra*, he dwelt there along with a host of other nāgas and five rākṣasīs (demonesses), causing famine and epidemics in the area.[36] Fed up with them, the king of Nagarahara called upon the Buddha for help. The Buddha soon arrived together with Vajrapāṇi and five great disciples (Ānanda, Mahākāśyapa, Mahāmaudgalyāyana, Śāriputra, and Mahākātyāyana). Immediately, the nāgas and rākṣasīs caused a violent thunderstorm, which the Buddha countered easily. Vajrapāṇi then attacked Gopāla with his fiery bolt and forced him to take refuge in the coolness of the Buddha's shadow, while Mahāmaudgalyāyana, transforming himself into a great garuḍa bird, obliged the others to submit, take refuge in the Triple Gem, and swear never to molest living beings again.[37]

Thus far, we have more or less a replica of the story of the conversion of Apalāla, but at this point, new developments take place. Gopāla would very much like the Buddha to stay and live in his cave. The Buddha does so for a while, but eventually it comes time for him to leave. This greatly distresses the nāga king. "Blessed One," he cries, "I pray you to remain here always. Why leave me and make it so that I will no longer see the Buddha? I will then surely commit evil deeds and fall into a lower realm of rebirth!"[38] The problem here is clear; despite his faith, or perhaps because of it, Gopāla needs the presence of the Buddha and fears (or threatens) that in the Buddha's absence he will return to his old worldly, destructive, malevolent ways.

At this point in its version of the story, the *Avadānakalpalatā* states rather cryptically that the Buddha then "arranged it so as to always be near [Gopāla's] abode."[39] It does not specify how the Buddha did this, but the common tradition reported by Hsüan-tsang is that he agreed to leave behind in the cave his "shadow" or "reflection," which, because of its power, would stay Gopāla from his evil inclinations.[40]

The importance of shadows as effective substitutes for an actual person is well known in the history of magic and religions. In the Buddhist tradition, one need only recall the fame of the image of the Buddha that was commissioned by King Bimbisāra, who had his artists trace and color in the outline of the shadow which the Buddha projected onto a screen. So potent was the resultant painting of the Blessed One that, when it was sent as a gift to King Udrāyaṇa of Roruka, it was welcomed with great ceremony as though it were the Buddha in person. The image then proceeded to preach the Dharma and to convert the king to the faith.[41] Similarly, at a popular, magical level, the Buddha's shadow in Gopāla's cave *was* the Buddha in his absence.

In this context, the assertion of the *Buddhānusmṛti samādhi sūtra*—that it is the Buddha himself, and not just his shadow, who stays in the cave—becomes more understandable. Indeed, in this version of the story, the Buddha accepts Gopāla's invitation to remain with him always. He then performs various miracles, after which he bodily penetrates into the solid rock wall and stays seated there, his luminescence visible through the stone.[42]

The cave of the Buddha's shadow came to be a famous pilgrimage site in Northwestern India and was an important stop on the itinerary of many of the Chinese pilgrims. These pilgrims, like the *Buddhānusmṛti samādhi sūtra*, consistently describe the shadow itself not as something dark, as one might expect, but as a sort of luminous reflection.[43]

Hsüan-tsang's account is dramatic and well known. According to his biographer, when he arrived at the cave, he was most distressed that he could see nothing. His guide, however, told him to go right in, back away fifty paces from the far wall, and look east. He did so, but still he saw nothing. He then prostrated himself one hundred times, but once again there was nothing. Then, sobbing and reproaching himself for his bad karma, he began reciting sūtras and stanzas, prostrating himself again and again.[44] The rest of the story has perhaps best been told by René Grousset:

> After he had thus made about a hundred salutations, he saw a glow appear on the eastern wall, the size of a monk's alms-bowl, which disappeared in a moment. Filled with joy as well as with sorrow, he recommenced his salutations, and once more he saw a light as large as a basin which gleamed and vanished like a flash. Then, in an ecstasy of ardour and love, he swore never to leave the spot until he had seen the sacred shadow. . . . He continued his devotions and suddenly the whole grotto was flooded with light and the shadow of the Blessed One appeared majestically upon the wall, brilliantly white, as when the clouds part and reveal the marvellous spectacle of the Golden Mountain. A dazzling splendour illuminated his divine countenance. Hsüan-tsang contemplated in joyful ecstasy the sublime and incomparable object of his admiration.[45]

Hsüan-tsang was by no means the only pilgrim to report on the shadow cave. Others claimed to have seen it as well, although their accounts are less personal than Hsüan-tsang's and lay less stress on the need for faith and vision. They all agree, however, that the shadow had a certain miragelike quality such that the closer one got to it, the more it faded away. "From a distance of more than ten paces," declares Fa-hsien, "you seem to see [the] Buddha's real form, with his complexion of gold and his characteristic marks. . . . The nearer you approach, however, the fainter it becomes."[46] Tao-jung gives a similar account. He claims to have seen the shadow from a distance of fifteen feet into the cave. As he drew nearer, it gradually disappeared, and, when he touched the spot with his hand, there was nothing there but the rock wall. As soon as he backed away, however, the image gradually became visible again.[47]

Because of this miragelike quality of the shadow, scholars have supposed that there must have been, in this cave at Nagarahara, some natural phenomenon, some reflective surface on the rock wall which caught the light from certain angles and caused a glow in the depths of the grotto. They are no doubt correct. At the same time, however, this same miragelike quality suggests that the shadow had a very special function as an object of contemplation for those desiring to visualize, or, perhaps better, to remember (smṛtyupasthāna) the Buddha—that is, to remember him with the vivid sense of reality made possible by the Sarvāstivādin notion of the existence of the past (along with the present and the future). As Hsüan-tsang's account makes clear, the very fleeting nature of the image made necessary a certain amount of faith, effort, and meditative discipline for those wishing truly to "see" it. The *Buddhānusmṛti samādhi sūtra*, in fact, confirms this. After describing the way in which the shadow came to be in Gopāla's cave, it goes on to give a detailed set of rules for contemplating it, "for those disciples who, after the Buddha's decease[,] . . . desire to know the Buddha in a sitting posture."[48]

The very unsteadiness of the shadow image seems to have made it a good object of devotion, a good meditation device for remembering the Buddha, for it provided a built-in guard against routinization. It demanded a certain amount of faith and concentration on the part of devotees, who might thus actually see the Buddha in a livelier way, perhaps, than they would with an ordinary static painting or statue of him in front of them.

The miragelike quality of the shadow also brings to mind the reluctance of Buddhist art in its early aniconic period to depict the figure of the Buddha at all. For several centuries, though the Buddha's form was described, his image was not formed, and he was represented only through symbols such as trees, stūpas, empty thrones, etc. This aniconic tradition (perhaps best represented by the bas-reliefs at Sāñcī and Bhārhut) did not imply a denigration of the physical form of the Buddha. Quite to the contrary, Buddhist texts have always been well aware of what the Buddha looked like, often stressing the beauty and splendor of his body and his possession of the thirty-two major and eighty minor physical marks of the Great Man. The avadānas, in particular, are filled with stories of individuals whose faith is aroused by the sight of the Blessed One's body, and the importance of meeting the Buddha face to face is stressed regularly. Upagupta himself, as we shall see, longs to have a vision of the physical form (rūpakāya) of the Buddha and, in fact, asks Māra to display it magically to him.

Students of Buddhist art have tended to see in the various footsteps trees, thrones, and other objects in the friezes of Sāñcī and Bhārhut nonanthropomorphic symbols of the *presence* of the Buddha. They are, however, just as much symbols of his *absence*, graphic gaps which, as Paul Mus has pointed out, are to be filled by the vision and/or visualizations of the faithful.[49] They are, in this sense, meditation devices specifically aimed at combatting routinization; settings where, given a certain amount of faith and concentration, devotees could actually "see" the Buddha while still remembering that he was "gone." The shadow image appears to have functioned in much the same way, though it is located, ideologically (and possibly chronologically), at an intermediate stage between this aniconic tradition and the full development of the representative Buddha image.

In any case, it was this miragelike quality of the image that artists attempting to make copies of the shadow sought to reproduce. Although Fa-hsien declares that artists commissioned to copy the shadow were unable to do so successfully,[50] soon after his time, in the 450s, a Sri Lankan monk named Buddhanandī arrived in China with a painting of the shadow he had made on his way. It had, we are told, the same qualities as the original: from a distance of ten paces, it shone like fire, but the closer one got to it, the more its brightness faded.[51]

Similarly, the famous Chinese monk Hui-yüan, having heard from various pilgrims about the cave of the shadow, resolved to reproduce it at his monastic center on Mount Lu. He, too, strove for the miragelike effect. He had a cave dug out overlooking a stream and commissioned an expert painter to depict within it a "Buddha whose body seemed to shimmer in the air,"[52] whose "colours seemed to have been applied in the void, and [which], when seen from afar, looked like vapour."[53] This image was used by Hui-yüan and his followers for meditative exercises designed to recall vividly the form of the Buddha, and it became the subject of a long hymn of praise by Hui-yüan himself.[54]

It is doubtful, of course, that the Buddha had such visualization exercises in mind for the nāga Gopāla and his five rākṣasī companions. For them, the shadow was what it must have been for the majority of pilgrims who visited the cave: a magically potent reminder of the Buddha and a prop against backsliding. But whether understood simply in this sense or as a meditation device for visualization, the shadow clearly symbolized the ongoing presence of the Blessed One, even though he was no longer there.

The Buddha and the Potter

The stories of the nāga Gopāla and other tales akin to them[55] present one clear solution to the problem of what happens when the Buddha is gone: a powerful reminder of his personal presence—whether that be a shadow, an image, or, by extension, any other relic—is left behind and takes over for him.

A rather different solution to this same problem is presented in the story of the conversion of the potter, which we shall consider next. All of our sources mention, along with Apalāla and Gopāla, the potter (kumbhakāra) in their lists of conversions effected by the Buddha prior to his prediction at Mathurā about Upagupta.[56] Yet the full story of this conversion, contained only in the *Mūlasarvāstivāda Vinaya*, is strikingly different from these other tales. Here is no scenario of cosmic combat, or glorification of the person of the Blessed One; in fact, rather than using his magical powers to magnify himself, the Buddha uses them to conceal his identity. The story is as follows:

> In Naitarī there lived a potter who was [both skillful and] exceedingly infatuated with his art. The pots he made on his wheel were all dry when he took them off. The Buddha, knowing that the time for this man's conversion was at hand, took on the appearance of a potter himself and began talking to him.
>
> "What kind of pots do you make on your wheel?" he asked.
>
> "Dry ones," the other replied.
>
> "I, too, make dry ones," said the Buddha. "We are just the same . . . but I also make ivory ones."
>
> "You are more skillful than I," said the potter.
>
> "Not only ivory ones," the Buddha went on, "but also pots made of gold, silver, cat's-eye, and crystal."[57]

At this point, we are told the potter became favorably disposed (abhiprasanna) to the Teaching of the Blessed One, and the Buddha preached a sermon on the Dharma to him and established him and his family in the Truths.

As a conversion story, this tale is rather intriguing. The potter is a person who appears to have reached the heights of his art. He not only knows how to make good pots, but he has also eliminated the need for drying time: they come off the wheel dry and finished. The Buddha comes along, however, and demonstrates clearly superior skills; when he has finished with a lump of clay, it has become a pot of ivory or of some other precious substance. Impressed by this, the potter can only submit to his mastery. Then the Buddha, having destroyed the potter's pride, preaches the Dharma to him and converts him to the faith.

What is striking is that he does all this not as the Buddha, but in the guise of a potter. Until the very end, the potter-convert does not realize to whom he is talking. There seems to be here a deliberate deemphasis on the charismatic properties of the Buddha's body. The potter is not dazzled and converted, as commonly happens in avadāna literature, by the sight of the physical form of the Tathāgata endowed with all of its magnificent marks and features. Rather, he is converted by one who appears to be a fellow artist but who is saying fantastic things.[58] This, then, is a conversion which could well have been carried out by someone who was not the Buddha—and therefore, at a time when there was no Buddha. We shall see much the same point being made later on: Upagupta, too, converts people without their knowing who he is, for he himself is a Buddha without the marks of a Buddha.

If not the Buddha's personal charisma, what is it then that effectively converts the potter and establishes him and his family in the Truths? Though the text is not altogether clear on this, it seems to be suggesting that it is the Buddha's Dharma that does so, understood here not only as his actual Doctrine, his Teaching; but also, at least initially, as his superior knowledge of the art of pottery.[59]

The potter thinks he knows all there is to know about his craft; the pots he makes are dry when he finishes turning them on the wheel. But another potter arrives and opens up a whole new world of undreamt-of skills; he makes vessels of ivory, or of gold or silver or cat's-eye or crystal. The allegory is not difficult to interpret; Buddhist literature is full of stories of sincere individuals who think they have learned all there is to know, mastered all there is to master, until the Buddha or a Buddhist comes along and reveals to them a new doctrine going beyond what they knew before. These people, then, are converted by the revelation of a new and greater Dharma and not by a sudden surge of devotion for a charismatic master. Similarly, the emphasis in the potter story is not on the person of the Buddha, but on his Teaching.

This conclusion would appear to be warranted by a slightly different version of this story preserved in the Pali canon. There we read of the novice Pukkusāti, who was spending the night in a potter's shed when the Buddha happened by and asked to share his lodgings. Although a Buddhist, Pukkusāti had never seen the Master and so had no idea to whom he was talking. Without disclosing his identity, the Buddha preached the Dharma to Pukkusāti, and he quickly became enlightened.[60] Commenting on this story, Lily DeSilva has remarked, "This episode clearly shows that it is immaterial from whom one learns the truth [i.e., the Dharma]."[61]

These stories, then, suggest another solution to the problem of the Buddha's absence. He does not have to be replaced by shadows or other potent personal substitutes; he can just as effectively be replaced by his Dharma, preached by seemingly ordinary individuals. This solution was sometimes adopted to the exclusion of others by certain Buddhist schools of thought. Some Theravādins, for example, consistently maintained that what was important after the Buddha's death was not his person—his physical form—so much as his Teaching, his embodiment in his Dharma. The body of the Buddha was relegated to the care of kings and laypersons; the Dharma, however, became the preserve and preoccupation of the monks, the elders (thera). Similarly, some followers of the Prajñāpāramitā school, in curious alliance here with the Theravādins, exalted the understanding of the Buddha's Teaching—of his doctrinal body, his Dharmakāya—over that of his physical form (rūpa).[62]

In the Mūlasarvāstivādin account of the Buddha's journey to the Northwest, however, it is important to recognize that there is no such ranking of values. Rather, both of these aspects of the Buddha are emphasized. In the stories of the shadow cave, we saw the ongoing importance of the Buddha's form; but this was not meant to minimize the importance of his Dharma, which is then featured in the tale of the potter. Likewise, we shall find in the story of Upagupta's encounter with Māra an emphasis on both of these aspects. Upagupta has understood, we are told, the Dharma of the Buddha; he has "seen" his Dharmakāya. But this does not prevent him from wanting and obtaining a vision of his physical form (rūpakāya) as well—and this despite his full knowledge of the absence of the Buddha in Nirvāṇa.

The Conversion of Kuntī

The next major story in the *Mūlasarvāstivāda Vinaya*, after the conversions of Gopāla and of the potter (and of the nāgas of Nandivardhana), is the tale of the ogress (yakṣiṇī) Kuntī. The Sanskrit version of the story is as follows:

> Then the Blessed One reached the town of Kuntīnagara. There dwelt a wrathful and fierce yakṣiṇī named Kuntī, who ate all the children born to the Brahmin householders of the town. They, hearing that the Buddha was coming to visit their city and was staying in a certain place [outside of town], gathered together and went out to see him. Drawing near the Blessed One, they bowed down at his feet and then sat down to one side. The Buddha delighted them with a Dharmic discourse. . . .

Then the Brahmin householders, their faith engendered, got up from their seats, put their upper robes over one shoulder, proffered an añjali, and said to the Buddha, "May it please the Blessed One to have a meal tomorrow in our homes, together with the community of monks."

Now [on the following day], when they saw that the Blessed One had finished eating, had washed his hands, put away his bowl, and sat down again, the householders, holding a golden vase, stood up and made this petition: "The Blessed One has converted all sorts of wicked nāgas and yakṣas. Bhadanta, this yakṣiṇī Kuntī, for a long time, has been an enemy of ours, though we have not been one of hers; she does us harm though we do her none! She takes away our children! Oh! May the Blessed One have pity on us and convert the yakṣiṇī Kuntī!"

Now at that moment, the yakṣiṇī Kuntī, who had been seated all along in the midst of that assembly, showed herself [in her true form]. The Blessed One said to her:

"Did you hear, Kuntī?"

"I heard, Blessed One."

"Did you hear, Kuntī?"

"I heard, Sugata."

"Then stop your non-Dharmic evil ways!"

"Bhadanta, I will agree to stop if these householders will build a monastery for my sake."

Then the Blessed One said to the Brahmin householders of Kuntīnagara:

"Did you hear, Brahmin householders?"

"We heard, Blessed One."

"What will you do now?"

"We will build a monastery, Blessed One."

And the Buddha, having thus converted the yakṣiṇī together with her family, went away.[63]

In this story, which is reminiscent of that of the Buddha's conversion of the yakṣas and yakṣiṇīs of Mathurā,[64] we find a situation that initially is analogous to that of the nāgas Apalāla and Gopāla. A monster of some sort is oppressing a group of people, who call on the Buddha for help. Once again, however, the Buddha's method of dealing with the monster is quite different. As in the case of the potter, there is no scenario of cosmic combat here or duel of magical powers; but neither is there a preaching of the Dharma. Instead, the Buddha rather diplomatically arranges a treaty—an agreement between Kuntī and the householders of Kuntīnagara. She will stop eating their children if they will build a Buddhist monastery (vihāra) for her.

Implicit in this agreement is the understanding that, within this monastery, Kuntī will become the object of a cult by the villagers so that her appetite can be ritually assuaged. Where previously she ate children, she now will receive worship and offerings. In return, as we shall see, she also agrees to protect the monastery and the surrounding community from harm.

Of course, not only will the demoness be subdued and converted to Buddhism; the Brahmins of Kuntīnagara, too, will become Buddhists, for their town will now have a vihāra. And Kuntī clearly will not be the only "resident" of this monastery; there will also be images of the Buddha and, perhaps more significantly, monks who will assure the efficacy of her cult.

Unfortunately, we are not given any details about the cult of Kuntī in the *Mūlasarvāstivāda Vinaya.* Her story, however, is strongly reminiscent of that of another, better-known ogress, Hārītī, with whom Kuntī has in fact been identified.[65] The demoness Hārītī was the mother of five hundred young yakṣas and was in the habit of devouring the children of the people of Rājagṛha. The latter implored the Buddha to help them, and he responded by going to Hārītī's abode and hiding the youngest of her sons in his begging bowl. When Hārītī returned and found her youngest missing, she frantically searched for him throughout the universe, from the lowest hell to the highest heaven, but he was nowhere to be found. Desperate with grief, she finally was told by the god Vaiśravaṇa to go and ask the Buddha for help.

The Buddha makes her realize the cruelty of her child-eating ways, and she promises to stop her evil practices. The Buddha then gives her back her child. She takes refuge in the Triple Gem and accepts the five precepts, but then a new problem arises: how are she and her children to feed themselves now that they have given up human flesh? In other words, how are they to avoid backsliding now that they have been converted? The Buddha's answer is noteworthy: Hārītī is not to worry; every day, throughout Jambudvīpa, his disciples, the monks, will make food offerings to her at the end of their own meal. In exchange for this, she is to agree to two things: she will protect all the Buddhist monasteries of Jambudvīpa both day and night and ensure that no harm comes to them or their inhabitants; and, at a more popular level, she will respond to the pleas of childless parents by helping them have offspring.[66] We thus have here some of the ritual details that were missing in our story of Kuntī. Hārītī, the converted ogress, is to be the object of a cult, but within a Buddhist setting where she can be controlled by ritual offerings.

It has long been recognized that Hārītī was, at least originally, a goddess of smallpox.[67] Like other smallpox goddesses of India, she was probably the object of an ambivalent attitude on the part of her worshippers. On the one hand, she was feared as the bringer of the disease and harrier of children. On the other hand, she was worshipped as the one who could spare and, in this sense, give life to those same children; hence her cult, even in Buddhism, as a bringer of offspring.

It is interesting to note here the manner in which the Buddhists assimilated her cult. They allowed its positive side to go on more or less unchanged. Thus, her shrine within Buddhist monasteries remained a popular place with laypersons desiring to have children.[68] On the other hand, they transformed her negative aspects; under the aegis of the Buddhists, Hārītī would no longer devour children, but devour alms given to monks instead.

Buddhism, as a missionary religion, seems to have had a rather loose conversion ideology. It was quite willing to assimilate indigenous beliefs and practices—and this, in fact, was one of the ways in which it managed to impose itself in non-Buddhist areas. This flexibility not only made Buddhism acceptable in a given area, but it also lent continued vitality to the Buddhist faith. Lacking a responsive divinity of their own, Buddhists were able to turn to indigenous deities and draw on the religiosity associated with them. Assimilation of non-Buddhist practices and deities was thus one of the ways in which Buddhism dealt with the problem of the charismatic gap in the post-parinirvāṇa period. Lurking always in the background of Hārītī's cult is the threat that if she is neglected—if the monks fail to give her their leftovers—she may return to her former habit of eating children. The laity should make sure, therefore, that the monks always have enough food and goodwill to give some to Hārītī and thus continue controlling her. What is interesting from our perspective, however, is that here the ongoing control of demonic forces is no longer dependent on the presence of the Buddha himself, but has been taken over by the monks and, secondarily, by the laity. This does not mean that the monks have a full priestly role. They do not intercede and ask for Hārītī's help in granting children to the faithful; the laity can do that for themselves. The monks do, however, agree to control Hārītī's evil inclinations; in this way, her positive side can shine through.

Much the same is true in our story about the ogress Kuntī. No mention is made of a shadow or other powerful substitute for the Buddha, nor even of the preaching of the Dharma. Instead, the householders are told to build a vihāra—a place for Buddhist monks who, given proper support, will take over the function of keeping the demoness in check. The Buddha, of course, will always be present to some extent. The vihāra is his, and in it Kuntī is symbolically subservient to him. But the focus of effective action in this story has nonetheless shifted from the first to the third of the Buddhist refuges; responsibility for doing the Buddha's job has become ritualized and passed on to the Sangha.

Conversions in the Northwest and the Prediction about Upagupta

The stories of Apalāla, Gopāla, the potter, and Kuntī are by no means the only ones narrated in the account of the Buddha's journey to the Northwest. But they are among the most important ones and those consistently listed in our sources as a sort of preface to the prediction the Buddha makes at Mathurā about Upagupta.

It is commonly assumed that this preface is meant only to situate the Buddha's prediction in time and space: it occurred after his journey to the Northwest, when he arrived at Mathurā, around the time of his parinirvāṇa. Our study of the stories referred to in this preface, however, suggests that it is also dealing with a set of problems and a series of solutions that preoccupied the authors of the Upagupta legend.

The compilers of these texts, no matter how firmly they believed the Buddha had visited their home communities in the Northwest, may also have been aware at some level that, in fact, he had not, and that now he could not since he was gone in parinirvāṇa. Their problem, as we have suggested, was that of dealing with this absence of the Buddha. How could their country be converted, how could non-Buddhist forces be controlled, how could the faith be spread and maintained without the Blessed One?

Their solution to these questions, as we have also suggested, revolved around the traditional Triple Gem of Buddhism, but it did so in a particular way. Substitutes for the *Buddha* (shadows, images, etc.) effectively carried on his work by inspiring faith in converts and fear in demons. At the same time, the *Dharma* continued to be in itself enough to attract nonbelievers and to make conversions, even when preached by someone other than the Buddha. Finally, the *Sangha* became the focal point and setting for ritual action that both subsumed and found life in indigenous non-Buddhist forces.

With this understanding of the problems and solutions illustrated in the conversion stories that act as a preface to the prediction about Upagupta, we may at last turn to a point-by-point analysis of the various items in that prediction. (The full text of the prediction as found in the *Divyāvadāna* has been translated at the start of this chapter; it is much the same as that found in the *Mūlasarvāstivāda Vinaya*, with a few exceptions that we shall consider below.)

First, the Buddha predicts that Upagupta will be born as the son of a perfume merchant of Mathurā, one hundred years after the parinirvāṇa of the Buddha.[69] Whatever headaches this statement may have caused scholars interested in dating the life of Upagupta, it is doubtful that we should take it to have any chronological precision at all. It is clear from the context we have been considering that the statement means simply that Upagupta would live in a time well after the Buddha's death, when no one (at least no ordinary human being) who had known the Buddha personally would still be alive. Indeed, the round number—one hundred years—is used in this same stereotypic way to indicate the time of Upagupta's predecessor, Madhyāntika, the patriarch of Kashmir,[70] as well as that of King Aśoka.[71] There is a real sense that, in Buddhist terms, Upagupta has been born too late. He himself, as we shall see, bemoans this fact: unlike Māra, he never saw the Buddha in person. His time, then, frankly embodies the problem that is set for us: the Buddha is gone—what happens now?

Second, the Buddha predicts that Upagupta will do the work of a Buddha. This, in fact, is part of the solution: Upagupta himself will function as the Buddha in the Buddha's absence. He will preach, make converts, and maintain the faith in his region. This function, as we shall see, goes hand in glove with his being a patriarch of the Northern Buddhist tradition, one of the Masters of the Law—who were all, in a sense, Buddhas in their own time. Though no reference is made in the prediction to Upagupta's subduing any nāga kings or other demons, the later account of his battle with Māra has close affinities to that of the Buddha's battle with Apalāla; and, in some Southeast Asian sources, as we shall see, Upagupta takes on much the same role as the shadow left by the Buddha at Nagarahara: he is to stand guard magically at Buddhist festivals against the incursions of demonic forces.

This notion of Upagupta's acting as a substitute for the Blessed One is reinforced in the story of his encounter with King Aśoka. There, as we shall see, the king is quite explicit: "Seeing you today," he tells Upagupta in an ecstatic moment, "I see the Buddha even though he has gone beyond." He later proclaims the same to the people of Pāṭaliputra, urging all those who never saw the Buddha to draw near and look upon Upagupta, who is just like him.[72]

A third point in the Buddha's prediction is that though Upagupta will be a reminder of or substitute for the Blessed One, he will nevertheless not have the thirty-two bodily characteristics of a Buddha and so will not physically resemble him. He will be, predicts the Blessed One, a "Buddha without the marks," an alakṣaṇaka Buddha. This curious epithet appears to have been applied only to Upagupta in the Buddhist tradition and needs some comment here.

The Buddha, it should be remembered, was not the only person endowed with the physiognomic features of a Mahāpuruṣa. Cakravartin kings, too, were said to possess all thirty-two of the signs; and, at least in the Sarvāstivādin tradition, various lesser individuals (mostly members of the Śākya clan and hence relatives of the Buddha) were thought to have a certain number of them. According to the *Sarvāstivāda Vinaya*, the Buddha's half brother, Nanda, had thirty of the marks and was just four inches shorter than the Buddha. Monks, seeing him from a distance, would sometimes confuse him with the Tathāgata and be embarrassed when, upon getting up to greet him, they realized their mistake.[73] Likewise, Devadatta, the Buddha's cousin, is said to have had thirty of the marks despite his evil inclinations.[74]

Does this mean that Upagupta, who is proclaimed as having no marks at all, is further from Buddhahood than Nanda (who was somewhat of a libertine) or Devadatta (a notorious fiend)? It would hardly seem so. The epithet "Buddha without the marks" is clearly intended to have positive connotations. The citizens of Mathurā, as they flock to hear Upagupta's sermons, tell each other excitedly to come quickly, for today a Buddha without the marks is going to preach![75] They are saying, in effect, that Upagupta is just like the Buddha, despite the fact that one would never know it by looking at him.

Ernst Windisch long ago argued that Upagupta's epithet meant that he was not truly a Buddha—who, by definition, had to have the marks of the Great Man.[76] Eugène Burnouf, on the other hand, said it meant that Upagupta *was* a Buddha, but that he was just missing his marks of physical beauty.[77] In their two interpretations lie two rather different understandings of what Buddhahood is all about. Windisch (the editor of one of the oldest Pali texts, the *Itivuttaka*) sees it as achieved only by rare individuals who always have certain physical attributes attained by the accumulation of good karma over aeons of lifetimes. Others may be enlightened, of course, but they are not Buddhas. Burnouf (the translator of the Sanskrit *Lotus Sūtra*) more generously affirms the Buddhahood of all believers, though they may not yet have realized it. Our own view lies somewhere between these two poles.

Traditionally, it was thought that a Buddha accumulated the marks of the Great Man by performing acts of merit during the almost countless rebirths he underwent between the time of his first vow for Buddhahood and that of his final life. Thus, the future Gautama, after making his vow for Buddhahood in the time of the past Buddha Vipaśyi, embarked upon a career of accumulating the marks, a career that is recounted in part in the jātaka stories. It thus seems reasonable to conclude that a Buddha without the marks is someone who has taken a vow and received a prediction of Buddhahood—someone who is on his way, but has not yet finished his meritorious career. In this sense, Upagupta's epithet would mean that he is a "proto-Buddha," one who has within him the elements of Buddhahood, though he has not yet developed them. For Windisch and the Theravādins, this would be no Buddha at all; for Burnouf and the Mahāyāna, this would be a Buddha who had not yet realized his Buddhahood, that is, a bodhisattva.

Our own text inclines perhaps in this Mahāyānist direction; but it does so, it is important to remember, from a somewhat different perspective. Upagupta, as we have seen, is akin to the shadow of the Buddha in Gopāla's cave. He is a living prop, a focal point for the faithful; he can act as the basis for a vision of the Blessed One. In this regard, it is noteworthy that Aśoka's exclamation—that when he looks upon Upagupta, he actually sees the Tathāgata—comes to him only at a moment of heightened faith and devotion, much as does Hsüan-tsang's vision of the form of the Blessed One in the cave of the shadow.

Here we enter once again the fleeting world of magical projection, vision and visualization, that we encountered before—with the difference that Upagupta is not an image or an aniconic symbol, but a living being. We are thus left saying that Upagupta—a Buddha without the marks—both is and is not a Buddha. It is a paradox, perhaps, but one that perfectly reflects his role as a personal substitute for the Tathāgata when the Tathāgata is not there.

Fourth, in addition to being an alakṣaṇaka Buddha, Upagupta will also be, according to the Buddha's prediction in the *Divyāvadāna*, "the foremost of all [the Buddha's] disciples who are preachers." He will convert and lead to arhatship so many persons that they will fill a cave eighteen cubits long and twelve cubits wide with their little four-inch-long tally sticks (śalākā).[78]

We will deal with the traditions about Upagupta's cave and with its fame as a pilgrimage site in Mathurā in chapter 7. For the present, suffice it to focus on his designation as the "foremost of preachers." In the *Mūlasarvāstivāda Vinaya*, in both its Sanskrit and Chinese versions, this prediction states not that Upagupta will be the *foremost* (agra) of all the Buddha's disciples who are preachers, but that he will be the *last* of them (pascimata).[79] These two designations need to be considered.

The epithet "foremost in such and such a category" was reserved for disciples whose chief characteristic was their fame or skill in a particular field. The *Anguttara Nikāya* has a long list of the monks, nuns, laymen, and laywomen, all contemporaries of the Buddha, who were in this way preeminent in one area or another. Thus, the elder Sāriputta was foremost of those monks of great wisdom; the bhikkhunī Uppalavaṇṇā was foremost of the nuns with magical powers; the layman Anāthapiṇḍika was foremost of almsgivers; and the laywoman Sujātā was foremost of those who first took refuge.[80] Inevitably, these epithets, which already reflected certain reputations of these monks and laypersons, became the bases for further legends and elaborations. Upagupta, not being a direct disciple of the Buddha, does not appear in the *Anguttara* list, but this did not detract from the Buddha's declaration about him. His renown was to be as a preacher and teacher of the Dharma, and this is reflected in his legend. His sermons, as we shall see, attracted great crowds in Mathurā; and the *Samyuktāgama* quotes a verse saying that he will be the first of all teachers, renowned in all four directions, and that he will convert an infinite number of living beings.[81] Upagupta, then, was a true successor to the Buddha because, like him, as a preacher, he embodied the Dharma. He was, in fact, a Master of the Dharma (dharmācārya) who had "seen the Dharmakāya" and who, through his sermons and teaching, kept the Dharma alive in his time.

It is in this context only that we can understand the *Mūlasarvāstivāda Vinaya*'s declaration of Upagupta not as the foremost of preachers, but as the last of them. According to a well-established tradition about the transmission of the Dharma, Upagupta was the fourth or fifth patriarch (Master of the Law) in the Northern Buddhist line. Before him, Mahākāśyapa, Ānanda, Śāṇakavāsin, and, in some lists, Madhyāntika had all been entrusted with the preservation and passing on of the Teaching.[82] After Upagupta, however, the line of succession becomes blurred and disputed. This is perhaps best seen in the works of some of the great Chinese masters of the fifth century; they all mostly agree that, up until Upagupta, the Buddha's teachings were perfectly preserved and no divisions occurred in the Sangha. After him, however, the various Vinayas were formed, and five disciples of Upagupta founded five distinct schools.[83] Specifically, according to this tradition, the Vinaya was transmitted without loss up until Upagupta's time; but succeeding generations, being of feeble faculties, could no longer retain it in its entirety.[84]

There is in these sources, then, a definite feeling that Upagupta stands at the end of an era, the end of the golden age of Dharma and Vinaya, and that after him come only degeneration and decline. This tradition reflects a more general theory of the decline of the Dharma, a theory we cannot go into here. What is interesting for our purposes is that, within this context, Upagupta should have been destined to become a sort of final embodiment of the True Dharma, the last of the Buddha's disciples who are preachers, the final fountainhead of the Teaching before the well begins to dry up.

There is one final aspect of the Buddha's prediction about Upagupta that needs to be considered here. He will not only do the work of a Buddha and embody the Dharma in his time, but, predicts the Tathāgata, he will reside at the Naṭabhaṭika monastery, which will be built for him on Mount Urumuṇḍa near Mathurā. He will stay there, moreover, at the head of a great community of monks, eighteen thousand of whom will be enlightened.[85]

Here we have another picture of Upagupta as the leader of a monastic community, a sangha of monks all dwelling at a forest hermitage that the Buddha himself called the best of all places conducive to meditation. We shall deal later with Upagupta's role as a meditation teacher and with his relationship to the forest-dwelling tradition in the Buddhist community. For now, suffice it to state that if Upagupta replaces the person of the Buddha and replicates his preaching of the Dharma, he also, as a monk living at the head of a monastic community, comes to symbolize the third Buddhist refuge, the Sangha. This part of his identity continues to be important, as we shall see when we consider the cult of Upagupta in Southeast Asia. Even today, in Northern Thailand, certain ritual traditions suggest that Upagupta embodies certain monastic ideals and that he still occasionally stands for the Sangha as a whole.

We have suggested in this chapter that in the prediction about Upagupta at Mathurā we may find encapsulated one of the basic themes of the Buddha's journey to Northwest India. This is the concern for the continuation and vitality of the Buddhist faith in the absence of the Blessed One. Buddhism, like all founded religions, had to face a series of important questions after the death of its charismatic leader. For a while, the memory of the deceased Master helped to keep the community together; but, before long, the founder's companions and contemporaries passed away, too, and there was no one left who had seen the Master in person or heard the Teaching from his lips.

It is with these uncertainities—characteristic of a third generation of believers—that the legend of Upagupta attempts to deal. Its treatment of them, as we have seen, appears to revolve around three closely related axes, recalling the

Three Refuges of Buddhism. In this light, as a concluding note to this chapter and a preface to what follows, it may be worth recalling Paul Mus's statement at the beginning of his *Barabuḍur*—that the Buddha, the Dharma, and the Sangha are perhaps the only irreducible factors of the religion and that the unravelling of their meaning and interrelationship is equivalent to the history of Buddhism itself.[86]

CHAPTER TWO

Monk and Monkey: Upagupta's Karmic Past

THE BUDDHA'S prediction about Upagupta is followed in our sources by a more or less elaborate account of Upagupta's previous life as a monkey on Mount Urumuṇḍa. Having just heard the Buddha spell out the future glories of Upagupta, Ānanda "conceives some doubts" and asks the Blessed One to explain in greater detail how it is that Upagupta will do all these things for the benefit of so many persons.[1]

In avadāna literature, such questions amount to a stereotyped call for a previous-life story detailing the past karmic history of the individual in question. The Buddha, therefore, proceeds to narrate the story of Upagupta's past life. This narration has been preserved in several of our sources, but it is given its fullest treatment in the *Mūlasarvāstivāda Vinaya*:

[1] Long ago, O monks, right here on the three slopes of Mount Urumuṇḍa, there dwelt five hundred pratyekabuddhas on one side [of the mountain], five hundred Brahmanical ascetics on another, and five hundred monkeys on a third. Now whenever a baby monkey was born to the head male of the monkey troop, it was customary for him to be put to death. As a consequence, the female monkeys were overcome by sorrow for their offspring and began confabulating: "Listen, sisters, the pack leader kills all the baby monkeys that are born to us. Let's make a plan; the next time one of us becomes pregnant, let's not tell him about it."

Now some time thereafter, one of the female monkeys became pregnant. Accordingly, the others hid her in a secret place and provided her with roots and fruits to eat, and soon she gave birth to a baby boy-monkey. They attended to him in that secret place. They nourished him and raised him, and when he had grown big, he chased the pack leader [his father] away from the troop.

[2] The expelled monkey chief began to wander here and there on Mount Urumuṇḍa, and, in his wanderings, he happened across the five hundred pratyekabuddhas. Once he had become unafraid of their presence, he provided them with roots, leaves, flowers, fruit, and toothsticks.

[3] [a] In return, they threw him some scraps of food. [b] And when, after their meal, they sat down cross-legged in meditation, as was their practice, the monkey imitated their posture and also sat down cross-legged.

[4] After a while, the following thought occurred to those pratyekabuddhas: "We have obtained everything that can be obtained from this body of misery; let us therefore subdue [our selves] and pass into parinirvāṇa." Thus, performing the miracle of

glittering simultaneously with burning flames and showers of water, they entered into the state of Nirvāṇa without remainder . . . and disappeared.

The monkey, [not understanding what had happened and] saddened at no longer seeing them, went to look for them after a while in their cave. There he began to toss about their robes, but the divinities who inhabited that place, thinking a monkey should not thus disturb the robes of pratyekabuddhas, [quickly chased him out] and blocked the entrance to the cave with a big rock. The aggrieved monkey [tried to get back in but was unable to]. Finally, tired and wailing, he went off. He roamed all over Mount Urumuṇḍa, longing for the sounds of humans, but his ever-attentive ears never had that pleasure.

[5] Then one day, he heard some of the five hundred Brahmanical ascetics talking. Like a man who has lost his way [and found it again], he ran towards them along the road. The ṛṣis were engaged in painful ascetic practices. [Some of them held their hands aloft, others stood on one foot. Still others were doing the penance of the five fires. Soon the monkey, unafraid of their presence, provided them with roots, leaves, flowers, fruits, and toothsticks, and they, in return, threw him scraps of food.

This time, however, instead of mimicking the ascetics' postures, the monkey showed them the pratyekabuddhas' meditation position. Chattering at them all the while, he forced those who held their hands aloft to lower them, and he extinguished the fires of those who were practicing the penance of the five fires, and he sat down cross-legged in front of them.

[6] The ṛṣis then spoke to their teacher: "Master, this ape interrupts our asceticism." And they explained the matter fully to him. The teacher replied, "Friends, these apes are endowed with good memories; surely this one must have recently seen some ṛṣis using this posture; you too, therefore, should sit down cross-legged like him." The ascetics thus began sitting in a cross-legged posture, and soon their past roots of merit became manifest, and, without being taught by a teacher [ācārya] or a preceptor [upādhyāya], they gave rise to the dharmas which are the thirty-seven wings of enlightenment, and realized pratyekabodhi. Their faith had been engendered on account of that monkey's constant exposition of the doctrine.

[7] The ṛṣis then began to give to the monkey the first fruits of the fields, and fresh fruit in season which they received on their begging rounds in the region, and only then did they themselves eat. Now after some time, the monkey passed away. The pratyekabuddhas then quested for sweet-smelling wood in the settlements of the whole area, piled it all up, and cremated him.

What do you think, O monks? That monkey who was attended to by those pratyekabuddhas, he is this very same Upagupta. Indeed, at that time, he undertook work for the benefit of many people. So too now I have predicted that he will show compassion for the multitude.[2]

Stories of previous lives such as this one have a number of functions in Buddhist literature. Most prominently, they serve a didactic purpose; they emphasize the importance and tenacity of karma from one life to another and so encourage good deeds and discourage evil ones. They also serve to set the major themes for a person's present life. Even though, theoretically, all events in this life have been conditioned (or at least set up) by karma, the retelling of that karma inevitably singles out certain causes and effects for special attention. Somewhat like predictions, then, previous-life stories help highlight what are considered to be the chief patterns in an individual's life and so act as a sort of hagiographical chart. In this light, the story of Upagupta's life as a monkey is more than just an entertaining tale and deserves to be treated carefully, section by section.

[1] The story begins by describing Upagupta's situation as a monkey-troop leader on Mount Urumuṇḍa at some unspecified time in the past. Somewhat surprisingly for a hagiography, it features first his cruel practice of killing his own offspring—all the infant male monkeys born to the members of his harem. This, however, eventually backfires (as is universally true in such stories), and he ends up being expelled from the troop himself.

It is difficult to know just how to evaluate this episode, which appears to be making a rather negative point about Upagupta in the course of attempting to explain how he, as monkey chief, came to leave his clan. One often-neglected aspect of previous-life stories is that they sometimes allow a tradition to say certain things about a saint that it might not care or dare to otherwise. Simply put, it is easier for repressed feelings about a saint's character to surface in previous-life tales than in his final hagiography. For example, certain negative points are sometimes made about the bodhisattva in jātaka tales that could never be stated about him in his final life as the Buddha,[3] and it may be that we have a similar instance of this in the case of Upagupta.

On the other hand, perhaps we should not view this portion of the story in too human a light; it may be that the authors of the *Mūlasarvāstivāda Vinaya* considered it more or less normal monkey behavior for a troop leader to try to kill off threatening young males and then eventually to be evicted by one of them.

It should also be pointed out that this tale is found only in the Sanskrit text of the *Mūlasarvāstivāda Vinaya*. The *Divyāvadāna*, the *Aśokarājāvadāna*, and the *Aśokarājasūtra* make no mention of it at all. Instead, perhaps embarrassed by the negative moral implications of the infanticide story, they simply say that the monkey chief happened to leave his troop and to come across the pratyekabuddhas.[4]

However we are meant to evaluate this story morally, we should remember that its structure reflects the well-known Indian pattern of the sannyāsin. According to the classic Brahmanical formulation of the four stages of life (āśrama), a man, after being a celibate student (brahmacārin), becomes a householder (gṛhastha) and raises a family. When his own sons grow up, however, he leaves home to become first a forest dweller (vānaprastha) and then a hermit (sannyāsin). This final stage involves not only the complete giving up of worldly life and family attachments; it is even preceded by the ritual performance of the sannyāsin's funeral rites. In this light, the important thing about the Upagupta story is not the monkey chief's infanticidal tendencies, but his departure from the troop, an event that marks his wandering forth—at a relatively advanced age—to a homeless life, the start of a religious quest.

As is well known, however, there developed in Buddhist and other circles, an important variant of this stages-of-life scenario. This was the pattern of the śramaṇa (Pali: samaṇa) according to which it is not the father but the son who wanders forth to a homeless life, abandoning his family for the religious quest. This, of course, was the pattern of the Buddha ("the samaṇa Gotama") and of many other Buddhist monks as well.

In this light, it is noteworthy that, in the Chinese version of the *Mūlasarvāstivāda Vinaya*, it is not the monkey chief who is expelled from the troop, but his son, the young monkey who survives to reach adulthood. Far from staging a successful coup d'état, the latter is the one who is forced to wander off; he then meets the pratyekabuddhas and, in a subsequent life, becomes Upagupta.[5] This version has the advantage not only of exonerating our hero from possible accusations of infanticide, but also of having him follow a more typically Buddhistic śramaṇa pattern. At the same time, it brings the story as a whole more in line with Chinese sentiments of filiality.[6]

In any case, the remainder of the tale, in both its Sanskrit and Chinese versions, may be read as reflecting the various stages in the career of a Buddhist quester—a career which, as we shall see, Upagupta was to follow again in his later human life in Mathurā.

[2] To start off this career, the expelled monkey first becomes a sort of lay devotee; he meets the pratyekabuddhas and, when he becomes used to them, practices dāna. He makes offerings of roots, leaves, flowers, fruit, and toothsticks—all legitimate gifts, but especially easy for monkeys to obtain. It is important to realize that, in avadāna literature, such offerings often mark a layman's initial step onto the path that eventually leads to enlightenment. The *Avadānaśataka*, for instance, is full of stories of devotees who meet a Buddha or pratyekabuddha, make offerings to them of a flower or toothstick or some other seemingly insignificant object, and thereby attain Buddhahood, pratyekabuddhahood, or arhatship themselves in a future lifetime.[7]

More immediately, these same acts can lead to better rebirth through the accumulation of good karma. Upagupta's offering recalls that of another famous Mount Urumuṇḍa monkey—one who made a gift of honey to the Buddha. This story, which became well known in the Buddhist world, was variously recalled at different pilgrimage sites in Northern India—most notably at Vaiśālī and Śrāvastī, but it was also connected to Mathurā. Hsüan-tsang, for one, visited the "stūpa of the gift of honey" right after leaving Upagupta's hermitage. As the Chinese pilgrim tells the story, the monkey, delighted that his gift to the Buddha was accepted, frolicked about so that he fell out of his tree, died, and was instantly reborn in heaven due to his merit.[8] In this context, our own monkey's actions on Mount Urumuṇḍa must be seen not just as playful simian antics, but as the planting of seeds of merit that will eventually ripen into a better rebirth and lead to his own enlightenment.

Pratyekabuddhas (Pali: paccekabuddha)—the field of merit in this story—have been described as Buddhist ascetics, "private" or "selfish" Buddhas who attain enlightenment on their own, but then do not preach the Dharma to others.[9] They spend their time in meditation and are renowned for their mastery of supernatural powers. In the present context, however, it is important to realize several other things about them. First of all, they appear only at times and in places in which there are no bona fide Buddhas. As the *Divyāvadāna* puts it, "When there is no Buddha alive in the world, pratyekabuddhas are born."[10] To some extent, then, pratyekabuddhas serve as fields of merit in the absence of the Buddha; they fill a charismatic gap that occurs prior to the advent of a Tathāgata or after his parinirvāṇa. We have already seen that one of the thrusts of the Upagupta legend as a whole is to deal with the problems caused by the absence of the Buddha. It is appropriate, then, that even in this tale of his previous life, Upagupta should not meet the Blessed One; here, too, he is living in a Buddhaless time.

There is another way in which pratyekabuddhas function as fields of merit. Not only are they "Buddhas" in the absence of the Buddha, but they are also bhikṣus—monks—in the absence of a regular Sangha.[11] Pratyekabuddhas are often described in Pali texts as solitary figures who "live alone like the horn of a rhinoceros."[12] In some cases, however, especially in the Sanskrit tradition, they may be seen to follow a more communal life-style and to live in groups. The *Abhidharmakośa*, for example, distinguishes two types of pratyekabuddhas: those who "are like a rhinoceros" (khaḍgaviṣāṇakalpa), and those who "live in groups" (vargacārin). Significantly, as an instance of the latter, it refers to the pratyekabuddhas in the very story we have been considering (without, however, identifying Upagupta by name): "In former times, it is said, five hundred ascetics were practicing severe austerities on a mountain, when a monkey who had dwelt with some pratyekabuddhas arrived. He showed them their correct posture, and they fully realized pratyekabodhi."[13]

[3] Having made meritorious offerings of roots, fruits, toothsticks, etc. to this proto-Sangha of vargacārin pratyekabuddhas, the monkey then takes the next step in his spiritual development: he actually joins their community. There are two stages in this process, indicated by two events in the text: [a] the pratyekabuddhas share their food with him, and [b] he joins them in meditation.

[a] Our story is explicit in saying that the pratyekabuddhas, after they have eaten, give the monkey their leftovers, the "scraps from their begging bowl" (pātraśeṣam).[14] On the one hand, this act reflects their kindness and compassion towards a hungry animal who has become a sort of monastery pet. On the

other hand, the sharing of food, especially of food left over in one's own bowl, has always been, in India, an act fraught with significance.

The disposal of leftovers was (and remains) an important preoccupation in Buddhist monastic communities. Generally speaking, it was the rule in Indian monasteries that whoever came back last from the alms round was supposed to take care of any food that remained. That monk could, if he so desired, eat it; alternatively, he could take it and throw it away "in a place where there is but little green grass" (that is, on a dump where no crops or vegetation were growing) or into "water where there are no living creatures."[15]

The reason for this disposal of potentially edible food has been much debated, but ultimately it appears to be connected to a sort of taboo, discouraging those who are not members of the Sangha from consuming bhikṣus' leftovers. Although, as we shall see, distinctions are sometimes made between food that is offered to the Buddha and food that is given to ordinary monks, that which is offered to the Sangha generally becomes sacred, and what is left over cannot, therefore, be indiscriminately given away. Indeed, it may be dangerous for others to consume it.[16]

One example of this will suffice here. In the *Suttanipāta*, the Brahmin Kasibhāradvāja makes an offering of milk-rice to the Buddha to thank him for a sermon. The Buddha cannot accept it, however, because he does not eat "that which is acquired by reciting stanzas" (that is, he is not like a Brahmin priest). The food, having already been offered, has technically become "left over," and so Kasibhāradvāja asks what he should do with it. The Buddha tells him to throw it away in a place "where there is little grass" or into some water "where there are no living creatures," but this time he gives a reason. "In the whole world," he declares, "amongst men and gods and Māras[,] . . . samaṇas and brāhmaṇas, there is no one by whom this milk-rice can be properly digested except for the Tathāgata or for a disciple of the Tathāgata."[17]

Buddhaghosa, in his commentary on this passage, tries to explain why this should be so. Just as Kasibhāradvāja was making his offering, he claims, the gods added to it a subtle nutritive essence.[18] Because of this divine essence, the meal becomes undigestible by ordinary human beings, but because it still contains gross human food as its base, it is also undigestible by gods. Hence only the Buddha (neither an ordinary human nor a god) and fully enlightened disciples of the Buddha can consume it.[19]

Whatever one thinks of this explanation, the special nature of this food is clearly emphasized in the *Suttanipāta* story. As soon as Kasibhāradvāja disposes of the milk-rice by throwing it into some "water where there are no living creatures," it immediately "hisses and bubbles" (ciccitāyati citicitāyati) and steams and smokes, as though it were a red hot ploughshare suddenly immersed in a stream.[20] Obviously, such potent "hot" food should not be consumed by mere mortals, and any leftovers had best be disposed of carefully.[21]

In actual practice in India, monks did not always dispose of their leftover food in this manner. But this does not mean that they stored it for future consumption. I-ching, in his description of Sarvāstivādin monastic practices in India in the seventh century, agrees that it is highly improper to save leftovers. "It is not right," he declares, "to eat next morning the soup and vegetables that have been left or to partake later of the remaining cake or fruits." And he mocks, not without malice, the uncouth habits of some visiting Mongolians, who, unfamiliar with Indian ways, preserved their food in a jar. "Remaining food," I-ching states, must be given to "those who may legally eat such."[22]

Much the same point is made in the Pali Vinaya, in the story of the sugar merchant Belattha Kaccāna. This man offers some sugar to the Sangha; he gives a jar of it to the Buddha and then asks what he should do with the rest. The Buddha tells him to distribute it to the monks. When the monks have taken as much as they want (more, in fact, since they are said to fill their bowls and bags, even their water strainers, with sugar) there is still some left. Kaccāna inquires again what he should do with it, and this time the Buddha's answer is noteworthy: he should give what is left to "those who eat the remains of [bhikkhus'] food."[23]

Who are these beings who are legally entitled to eat monks' leftovers? The Belattha Kaccāna story clearly has in mind certain kinds of laypersons, but unfortunately does not specify which. Generally speaking, most laypersons could not touch anything that had been offered to the Sangha, but occasional exceptions were allowed. The Buddha, for instance, several times appears to let monks pass on food they have gotten on their alms rounds to their aged parents.[24] Such practices, however, were clearly controversial, and sometimes steps are taken to "incorporate" such lay recipients of almsfood into the Sangha, even if only symbolically. Thus, in one tale preserved in the *Dhammapada Commentary*, a certain pregnant laywoman eats the excess food of the monks in order to fortify herself, but she does so only after dressing herself up in yellow robes.[25] Similarly, in the *Mūlasarvāstivāda Vinaya*, rather than permit Ānanda to continue feeding two young orphans (his nephews), the Buddha tells him to ordain them as novices and agrees to a lowering of the ordination age so that this can be done.[26]

If we turn to present-day Thailand, at least two kinds of laypersons can often be seen consuming food that is left over after the monks have been served. First, there are the so-called degwads, young servant boys who attend to the various needs of the monks, especially in what concerns the preparation of their food.[27] These boys are technically not novices, but schoolchildren who live at the wat (monastery) and whose lay status, in fact, is important to their function as helpers of the monks. They always eat after the monks. Second, on festival occasions, certain devout, usually older, laypersons who stay at the wat after most of the congregation has gone home may also eat any excess food not wanted by the monks.[28]

I-ching, however, seems not to be thinking of laypersons or even human beings at all, for he goes on to specify that those who may legally eat leftovers are departed spirits—that is, pretas (hungry ghosts)—birds, and other animals.[29] This is not the place to embark upon a discussion of the Buddhist monastic practice, in India and elsewhere, of feeding hungry ghosts; but a few comments may be made about the feeding of animals, since, in our story, Upagupta was a monkey.

It is clear from I-ching's text that crows, pigs, dogs, and other animals abounded in Buddhist monasteries in ancient India, especially around meal times, and that although monks avoided them while eating, it was considered legitimate to give them any leftovers. To this day, throughout much of Buddhist Asia, individual monks can be seen giving scraps to pets or to strays that hang around monasteries. The animals are thus part of a pecking order that extends down to them (but not usually to laypersons!) from the upper reaches of the Sangha.

More generally, we may say that all these examples point to the existence in Buddhism of what might be called a "commensal community." Larger than the bounds of the everyday Sangha (which comprises only novices and monks), it is nonetheless clearly hierarchical. It includes in its upper reaches the Buddha and the figures of certain arhats, such as Piṇḍola, who are thought to be invisibly present and protecting the assembly. At its lower end, it includes certain kinds of laypersons (degwads, devout elders), monastery animals, and, in ritual contexts, demons and demonesses (such as Hārītī) and spirits of the dead (such as the hungry ghosts). It is this commensal community that Upagupta joins as a monkey when he receives scraps of food from the pratyekabuddhas.[30]

[b] After receiving food from the pratyekabuddhas, the monkey (Upagupta) sits down with them in a cross-legged posture of meditation. Buddhist monks in ancient India (and elsewhere) formally sat in order of seniority, with the most senior monks at the "elders' end" (vṛddhānta) and the youngest novices at the "newcomers' end" (navānta).[31] The *Mūlasarvāstivāda Vinaya* does not tell us where the monkey sits down, but the *Divyāvadāna* makes it explicit: "When the pratyekabuddhas sat down to meditate, the monkey prostrated himself in front of the elders and then went to the novices' end where he sat down cross-legged himself."[32] There could hardly be a clearer statement of Upagupta's intention. At one level, he is still a monkey just mimicking the monks; at another level, he is joining the Sangha as a novice and beginning the practice that will mark his career as a teacher and eventually result in his own enlightenment.

[4] As a result of their meditations, the pratyekabuddhas attain enlightenment and promptly pass into parinirvāṇa. They do this in a way that is quite typical of Buddhist saints in legendary literature: they perform the miracle of emitting fire from one half of their body and water from the other half. This

is the Buddhist magical display par excellence, and it demonstrates utter mastery over the elements. It was featured in the Buddha's great show of magical powers at Śrāvastī and is often a prelude to the parinirvāṇa of great saints, who pass away from the world in this manner. What is emphasized here is the monkey's reaction to this event; he is distressed by the sudden disappearance of his masters. Bewildered, he does not know what to do. He looks for them in their cave, but access to it is soon blocked by its guardian deities. The monkey, unable to break in, now wanders off.

[5] Eventually, he comes across the five hundred Brahmanical ascetics and tries to enter into the same kind of relationship with them as he had established with the pratyekabuddhas. He makes offerings to them, and they, too, respond by feeding him. But then, instead of joining their community as a junior ṛṣi and doing what they do, he becomes their teacher. He takes over, in fact, the role of his own deceased masters and demonstrates to the ṛṣis the proper pratyekabuddha way of meditating. The episode, of course, is humorous and pokes fun at Brahmanical ascetic practices, which are often the target of ridicule in popular Buddhist literature. Chattering and gesticulating, the monkey disrupts the ṛṣis' various ascetic endeavors and urges them to sit down cross-legged instead.

[6] His actions are ultimately effective, for, after consulting with their own teacher, the ṛṣis decide to imitate the imitator. They sit down in meditation and soon attain pratyekabodhi. It is noteworthy that, in this process, no new Dharma is imparted to the ṛṣis, who appear to attain enlightenment without ever realizing that they have been converted to Buddhism! Indeed, their own Brahmanical master tells them to do what the monkey is doing because he assumes this to be the practice of some other ṛṣis which the ape must have seen. The hint is thus dropped that conversion to Buddhism may not involve such a drastic change of views and life-style as might be thought, something that was sure not to go unnoticed in the religiously pluralistic society of Northwest India.

Pratyekabuddhas are supposed to attain enlightenment by their own efforts, without being taught by a teacher or a preceptor—that is, without undergoing the upasampadā ordination of a bhikṣu. This, in fact, is one of the things that make them akin to Buddhas and different from disciples (śrāvakas). This does not mean, however, that they receive no assistance whatsoever. Indeed, the ṛṣis in our story realize that they would never have become pratyekabuddhas had it not been for the monkey, and they recognize him, therefore, as their master.

[7] Now, instead of giving the monkey scraps and leftovers, the ṛṣis offer him the best of foods, and they do so before partaking of their own meal. In terms of the hierarchical pecking order described above, they now treat him as though he were an arhat or a senior elder of the community. When he dies, they hold a grand funeral for him, foreshadowing his cremation in his future life as Upagupta. The previous-life story of Upagupta as a monkey thus traces out the major phases of Upagupta's later life as a monk—from layman and

member of a commensal community, to novice, to effective and respected teacher cremated by his disciples. What is curious, however, is that all of this happens without the monkey quite realizing what is going on. He is simply doing what comes naturally to him as an ape. He is not motivated by conscious faith and thought-out devotion, yet he makes effective offerings to a field of merit. He does not make a momentous decision to enter the Sangha and start meditating; he just sits down cross-legged. He knows nothing of the Dharma; but he has learned more than he knows, and he becomes a great teacher.

This lack of conscious motivation is understandable in view of his simian nature, but it may, in fact, reflect fairly accurately the career pattern of many Buddhist monks—more so, perhaps, than Western students of Buddhism commonly recognize. More specifically, it reflects a similar sense of unforced naturalness that is found in the legend of Upagupta at Mathurā. As we shall see, Dharma is in Upagupta's very nature, though he does not know it. He is destined for monkhood even before his birth, and, when his teacher first asks him whether his thoughts are defiled or pure, he does not even know what this distinction means. Later on, he gives his first sermon to the courtesan Vāsavadattā without realizing it is the Dharma that he is preaching, and he attains his first glimpse of the Path when he comes to see the truth of his own words.

Other Previous-Life Stories

Not all texts were willing to accept this sort of simple naiveté in the previous-life tale of one who was to become a great patriarch—a Master of the Law. The *Damamūkanidāna sūtra*, for example, tells a rather different avadāna, claiming that Upagupta was in a previous life a learned Brahmin ascetic, a master who knew everything past, present, and future. Encountering the Buddha's Teaching, he is attracted by it and declares to the Blessed One that if he can be ranked as the equal of Śāriputra in wisdom and debate, he will join the Sangha; otherwise he will not. Śāriputra, however, has been declared by the Buddha to be the foremost of the wise, and this Brahmin, therefore, simply cannot measure up to him. The Buddha tells him so, and he consequently decides not to become a monk at that time. Eventually, however, he is reborn as Upagupta and does join the Sangha, where he attains great wisdom and mastery of the six magical powers (abhijñā).[33] In this new story, what is stressed is Upagupta's learning. He is a man who knows exactly what he knows and what he wants to know. He has mastered the doctrines of all the various philosophical schools and is now turning to Buddhism for more wisdom.

The *Damamūkanidāna sūtra*, however, also recounts the episode of Upagupta's previous life as a monkey, which it pictures as taking place on a peak called Ṛṣi Mountain, located near Benares. The story is basically the same as the one we have already considered, except that it is accompanied now by an additional tale of a still-earlier previous life. The narrator of this tale is not the Buddha on his journey through the Northwest, but Upagupta himself, who is asked by the monks to explain how it is that he happened to have been reborn as a monkey—that is, in a lower animal realm of existence—in a previous lifetime. Upagupta's answer is noteworthy. Ninety-one kalpas (aeons) ago, he declares, at the time of the Buddha Vipaśyi, some bhikṣus lived on Ṛṣi Mountain near Benares. Once upon a time, one of them who had already attained enlightenment was walking up the mountain very briskly. Another, younger monk, seeing him scampering up the hillside, remarked insultingly, "You walk just like a monkey!" Because of this remark, that younger monk had to suffer rebirth as a monkey for five hundred lifetimes. Upagupta then reveals the identity of the young monk: it was none other than himself in one of his previous lives. And he then gives the moral of the tale: all of us in the fourfold community of monks, nuns, laymen and laywomen should be very careful not to speak carelessly and insultingly of others.[34]

It is likely, however, that this tale had more significance than this rather banal lesson would suggest. The figure of ninety-one kalpas was well known in the Sanskrit Buddhist tradition as the amount of time it took Śākyamuni, as a bodhisattva, to realize the thirty-two bodily marks of the Great Man—that is, to attain Buddhahood. In this he was an anomaly, since, generally speaking, Buddhas require one hundred kalpas as bodhisattvas to accomplish this.

A number of texts may be cited in support of this view. The *Mahāvastu*, for example, says, "For one hundred kalpas, the Best of Men strive to attain enlightenment, but the Śākyan Valiant Man [i.e., Gautama] became a perfect Buddha in the ninety-first kalpa."[35] The same notion is found in the *Buddhānusmṛti samādhi sūtra*, where a king is puzzled upon learning from a sage named Asita that a Buddha named Śākyamuni has arrived in his kingdom; according to his diviners, the Buddha Śākyamuni was not supposed to come for another nine kalpas. But then a voice from heaven reassures the king, declaring, "Do not doubt this! The Buddha Śākyamuni, due to his perfection of zeal [vīrya], has moved ahead nine kalpas!"[36]

This mythic theme is especially featured in a story that describes a sort of competition between the future Buddha Śākyamuni and the future Buddha Maitreya.[37] Perhaps the oldest version of this tale, in the *Avadānaśataka*, recounts how long ago, at the time of the Buddha Puṣya, there were two bodhisattvas named, it so happens, Śākyamuni and Maitreya.[38] They differed primarily in that Maitreya was ready for Buddhahood, but Śākyamuni was not. The beings Maitreya was due to convert, however, were not yet ready for him, while the beings that Śākyamuni was due to convert were already ripe. We are not told how this karmic asynchronism between future Buddhas and their future disciples came about,[39] but, determined to resolve it and reasoning that it is easier to modify the fate of one being than that of many,[40] the Buddha

Puṣya climbs a mountain, where he sits down in a cave made of gems and enters into the samādhi of the element of fire (tejodhātu).[41] The bodhisattva Śākyamuni eagerly searches for the Buddha Puṣya everywhere on the mountain[42] and finally finds him in his cave. Seeing him in flames more dazzling than a thousand suns and splendidly adorned with the thirty-two major and eighty minor marks of the Great Man, he falls into an ecstatic devotional trance. For seven days and seven nights he stands on one foot, contemplating the figure of the Buddha Puṣya and repeating over and over again a single stanza in praise of his greatness.[43] Because of the firmness of his mind and the constancy and one-pointedness of his devotion, Śākyamuni is able in this single week to skip over nine kalpas of merit making on his quest for Buddhahood and so move ahead of Maitreya. Maitreya, on the other hand, because he was lacking in such zeal, because he was not in a hurry to get to the top of the mountain ninety-one kalpas ago, has not yet achieved his Buddhahood.

Much the same theme is reflected in a number of other stories featuring comparisons between these two bodhisattvas. For instance, in the *Divyāvadāna* version of a well-known jātaka, King Candraprabha (Śākyamuni in a past life)[44] is temporarily hindered by a well-intentioned but misguided divinity from fulfilling the perfection of generosity by cutting off his head and giving it to a passing Brahmin. He tells the divinity to stand aside; he will not be stayed from his bodhisattva course, he declares—unlike Maitreya, who, at that very spot, was once prevented from giving away his head after having practiced the Path for forty kalpas.[45]

Similarly, in one version of an even more famous jātaka, the future Buddha Maitreya, comes across a mother tigress and her hungry cubs.[46] He goes off in search of food for her, only to find upon his return that his companion, the future Buddha Gautama, had already sacrificed himself by feeding his body to the weakened beast in his fervor and rush to make merit.[47]

A careful analysis of these and other stories reveals an interesting classification of monks in terms of their attitudes towards enlightenment. Simply put, there are two kinds of questers: those who are in a hurry to attain final liberation and those who are not. Śākyamuni is a prime example of the former type and the future Buddha Maitreya of the latter.

Upagupta, from what we have seen of him in this chapter, would clearly seem to belong karmically not to Śākyamuni, but to Maitreya.[48] He is not a monk in a hurry; in fact, as we have seen, in his past life ninety-one kalpas ago, he makes fun of another monk who is. This sets him back by bringing on his rebirth as a monkey, but, more importantly, it also classifies him as one who is willing to wait for Buddhahood.

This delay is merely hinted at here in the *Damamūkanidāna sūtra* story of his past life, but it is an important aspect of his character and may serve to highlight a number of other points about his legend. First of all, it helps explain a fact that we already know: Upagupta never, in either his past or his present lives, meets Śākyamuni face to face. This is one of his great frustrations, but also one of the hallmarks of his career. This feature of the tradition about him now becomes more readily understandable: he is not karmically connected to Śākyamuni. Second, this story sheds new light on Upagupta's designation as a Buddha without the marks. Those thirty-two major and eighty minor bodily signs take time—one hundred kalpas, usually—to acquire. Upagupta, as a monk on a slow track with Maitreya,—with a number of kalpas still to go—has simply not yet developed them. Finally, and most importantly, it also helps explain a feature of Upagupta's legend that will become crucial in Southeast Asia. There, as we know, Upagupta is thought not to die—that is, not to enter parinirvāṇa, but to delay his final enlightenment *until the coming of Maitreya.* In this he is akin not only to bodhisattvas, but to a number of "living arhats," to whom we shall turn in chapter 11. For now, suffice it to say that one of the effects of this feature of Upagupta's legend is to stress his karmic connections with the future Buddha (rather than with Śākyamuni) and with those whom the future Buddha will lead to enlightenment.

CHAPTER THREE

Birth and Lineage, Patriarchs, and the Forest-Monk Tradition

IN VIEW OF what we have seen of his previous life as a monkey, it is not surprising to find that Upagupta was committed to the Sangha even before his birth in Mathurā. Indeed, Upagupta's father, Gupta, a perfume merchant in Mathurā, promised before his son's conception that he would make him a monk. The story is not found in the Gilgit manuscript of the *Mūlasarvāstivāda Vinaya*, but it is told in full in the *Divyāvadāna*, and a reference to it in Kṣemendra's *Avadānakalpalatā* (eleventh century) indicates that it was well known and remained popular for a long time. Kṣemendra begins his versified account of the Upagupta legend with these lines:

> Once, long ago, there lived in Mathurā a perfumer named Gupta.
> He had a son known as glorious Upagupta, who, while yet unborn,
> was made over by his father to the bhikṣu Śānavāsin.
> Promised to him as an attendant [anuyāyin],
> he became attached to him with devotion.[1]

This is rather terse; for the details of the story, we may turn to the *Divyāvadāna*, which was most likely Kṣemendra's source. There we learn that about one hundred years after the parinirvāṇa of the Buddha, the elder Śāṇakavāsin,[2] having founded the Naṭabhaṭika monastery on Mount Urumuṇḍa, began to wonder whether Upagupta had yet been born in Mathurā. He knew that the Buddha had predicted that a great teacher by that name would be born into the family of Gupta, the perfumer, and that it would be up to him, Śāṇakavāsin, to ordain him into the Buddhist Order. Accordingly, he paid a visit to Gupta:

> Now gradually, through his use of skillful means, Śāṇakavāsin managed to make Gupta the perfumer favorably disposed towards the Teaching of the Blessed One. One day, after this had happened, the elder went to the perfumer's house along with many monks; then, on the next day, he went there with only one other monk; and finally, on a third day, he went there all alone.
>
> When Gupta saw that the elder Śāṇakavāsin was by himself, he asked, "How is it that the Noble One has no attendant [paścācchramaṇa]?"
>
> The elder replied, "Why should we who are subject to old age have any attendants? If someone, moved by faith, should be initiated into the monastic life, then he would truly be an attendant and a follower of ours."
>
> "Noble One," said the perfume merchant, "I have always been greedy for the

householder's life and taken delight in sensual pleasures; I can't become a monk! However, when I get a son, I will give him to you as an attendant."

"So be it, my child," said the elder, "but do not forget this firm promise."

Now eventually a son was born to Gupta the perfume merchant, and he was given the name Aśvagupta. And when the boy had grown, the elder Śāṇakavāsin went to Gupta and said, "My child, you promised that when you had a son, you would offer him to me as an attendant. Now this son has been born to you; give me your consent, and I will initiate him into the monastic life."

"Noble One," said the perfumer, "this is my only son. Please exempt him. I will have another, a second son, and I will give him to you as an attendant."

And the elder Śāṇakavāsin, realizing through his meditative powers of concentration that the boy before him was not Upagupta, agreed to this and departed. After some time, a second son was born to Gupta, and he was given the name Dhanagupta. And again, when the boy had grown, the elder said to Gupta, "My child, you promised me that when you had a second son, you would offer him as an attendant. Now this boy has been born to you; give your consent, and I will initiate him into the monastic life."

"Noble One," said the perfumer, "please exempt him. My eldest son will go gathering goods abroad; this second one will have to stay and assure the protection of my home. However, when I have a third son, I will give him to you."

And the elder Śāṇakavāsin, realizing through his meditative powers of concentration that this second son was not Upagupta, again consented to this.

Finally, Gupta the perfumer had a third son. He was pleasing, handsome, amiable, surpassing men in appearance, and almost resembling a divinity. And when his full birth ceremonies had been carried out, he was given the name Upagupta. When he too had grown, the elder Śāṇakavāsin went to the perfumer and said, "My child, you promised that when you had a third son, you would offer him to me as an attendant. This son has now been born; give your consent, and I will initiate him into the monastic life."

"Noble One," replied Gupta, "it is agreed. When [as they say] 'there will be neither profit nor loss,' then I will grant him leave."[3]

It was the custom in India, and still is in some Theravāda countries, for ordained monks going on their alms rounds to take along with them a boy attendant who would walk behind them, carry their food back to the monastery, and assist them in other ways. Such a boy is called a paścācchramaṇa (Pali: pacchāsamaṇa), literally, "a monk [śramaṇa] who goes behind."

The duties and characteristics of a paścācchramaṇa are spelled out most clearly in a short sutta in the *Anguttara Nikāya*. He is to walk neither too far behind nor too close to his master; he is to carry his alms-laden bowl; he is generally not to interrupt his master, but should do so in order to restrain him from committing an infraction of the Vinaya rules; and finally, he should be neither dull-witted nor stupid.[4]

In our story, Gupta is quite surprised to see Śāṇakavāsin without a paścācchramaṇa, and the elder is quick to capitalize on this. If, he hints, a young boy were to enter the monastic order, then he (Śāṇakavāsin) might well have a personal attendant! Gupta is not slow to grasp what is being asked of him, and he promises that when he has a son, he will give him to Śāṇakavāsin as a servant.

This method of recruitment, involving the promise of an unborn son to the Sangha, seems to have been a fairly common one in the Sanskrit Buddhist tradition. Upagupta uses it himself in recruiting his own chief disciple, Dhītika, who is destined to succeed him in his lineage.[5] Exactly the same technique is used by Aniruddha in an avadāna in the *Karmaśataka*,[6] and by Śāriputra in the *Sangharakṣitāvadāna*.[7]

In some of these stories, we are led to believe that the woman in the household is already pregnant with the child who is to become the paścācchramaṇa. In others, however, the family is as yet childless or, significantly, has just suffered several miscarriages. In one tale, for instance, the distraught parents of three stillborn children turn to the Buddha's disciple Aniruddha for help. He convinces them to offer their next son as a paścācchramaṇa, and this time the boy survives. He becomes a monk and eventually attains arhatship.[8] It is clear, then, that this tradition of promising an unborn child to the Sangha was involved, to some extent, with magical practices aimed at insuring the survival and well-being of a baby. Parents could give birth to a live son, ironically, only by giving him up to the Sangha and thereby tapping the powers of the monks, and through them the powers of benevolent deities.[9]

Gupta, however, reneges twice on his promise and fails to deliver either of his first two sons to the Sangha. Śāṇakavāsin, realizing that neither Aśvagupta nor Dhanagupta is the disciple he wants, bides his time. In this cat-and-mouse game between layman and elder, we have what would appear to be a fairly realistic reflection of one reaction to the Buddhist recruitment of new monks in ancient India. Although some families voluntarily and gladly gave up their sons to the Sangha, others were much more reluctant to do so. In some areas, in fact, Buddhist monks had a bad reputation as family-destroyers who ravaged homes by taking their male offspring.[10] Here we have a less extreme case; Gupta is not unwilling to support the Sangha, but he is also concerned about his business and so keeps making up excuses. Nonetheless, he makes the commitment—even though conditional—that eventually will lead to Upagupta's ordination and full membership in the Sangha.

The little charade about Upagupta's identity that the text puts us through is intriguing; later, in Southeast Asia, we shall encounter a ritual form of much the same thing. In certain parts of Laos and Northern Thailand, when the rocks that are to symbolize Upagupta at festivals are fetched from the swamp or river bottom, the person performing the ritual first finds a stone and, respectfully addressing it, he invites Upagupta to come to the monastery. A second man who has accompanied the first declares, "I am not Upagupta, but merely his pupil. . . . Upagupta is farther inside the swamp." The same exchange takes place at a second stone. It is only at the third stone that "Upagupta" replies that he would be pleased to come to the monastery's festival and prevent Māra from disrupting the celebrations.[11] There is no hint in this tradition that these first rocks represent Upagupta's elder brothers, and we shall, in due time, give other interpretations of this ritual; but it is interesting to note here that it, too, reflects a kind of initial uncertainty—if only in pretense—about Upagupta's identity.

Upagupta and the Lineage of Dharma Masters

One thing, however, is certain in the story of Upagupta's birth: Śāṇakavāsin is not looking for just any boy to be his paścācchramaṇa, he is searching specifically for Upagupta. Indeed, he wants much more than an attendant; he is looking for the man to whom he is to pass on the mastery of the Dharma.

The Buddha's apparent refusal to appoint a human successor to himself and his well-known statement at the time of his parinirvāṇa that henceforth his Doctrine—his Dharma (or, alternatively, his Dharma and Vinaya)—would replace him as teacher and refuge[12] have sometimes led students into believing that Buddhism never had a patriarchate. In fact, both the Pali and the Sanskrit traditions eventually developed lists of masters through whom the Teaching was transmitted from generation to generation.

The Theravāda school focussed on the series of Chiefs of the Vinaya (Vinayapāmokkha), according to which the Buddha passed his Teaching—in particular the Vinaya—on to his disciple Upāli, who was well known as the reciter of the Vinaya at the First Buddhist Council. Upāli then transmitted his authority and position to Dāsaka (born in Vaiśālī four years after the Buddha's parinirvāṇa); Dāsaka passed it on to Soṇaka (born in Benares forty-five years after the parinirvāṇa); Soṇaka, in turn, was the master of Siggava (born in Pāṭaliputra eighty-two years after the parinirvāṇa); and Siggava transmitted the responsibility to Moggaliputta Tissa, a famous contemporary of King Aśoka.[13]

The Sanskrit tradition, on the other hand, and in particular the Sarvāstivādins, focussed on the series of Masters of the Law (dharmācārya). According to this tradition, the line of succession went from the Buddha to his disciple Mahākāśyapa (the president of the First Council) and then to Ānanda (the Buddha's own paścācchramaṇa). Ānanda then passed the Dharma on to two of his own followers: Madhyāntika (the converter of Kashmir) and Śāṇakavāsin (Upagupta's teacher in Mathurā).[14]

After Upagupta, the various lists of masters in this line began to differ from each other and obviously were the subject of much sectarian dispute.[15] But up to him, the tradition of the five Dharma masters (Mahākāśyapa, Ānanda, Madhyāntika, Śāṇakavāsin, and Upagupta) was generally accepted, and, in fact, with some minor variations, it came to head many of the later, much longer lists of patriarchs in Chinese Buddhism, especially in the Ch'an (Zen) school.[16] More importantly for our purposes, the legends of the first four of these Dharma masters form a sort of preface to the legend of Upagupta himself, and we shall, accordingly, consider each one of them in turn.

The Story of Mahākāśyapa

In the *Aśokarājāvadāna* and the *Aśokarājasūtra*,[17] the Buddha, right after his journey to Northwest India and the prediction he makes concerning Upagupta, heads for Kuśinagarī, where he knows he will enter parinirvāṇa. On the way, he formally charges his disciple Mahākāśyapa with the responsibility of preserving the Dharma after he is gone. At the same time, he also entrusts Indra and the guardians of the four quarters[18] with the protection of the Dharma. Satisfied now that his Teaching is in good hands, he goes on to Kuśinagarī, where he passes into parinirvāṇa.[19]

The gamut of reactions in the Buddhist tradition to the event of the Buddha's death and parinirvāṇa is a subject worthy of a full-length study in its own right. Some disciples apparently were overcome with grief. Others, such as Upananda, rejoiced, proclaiming they were free at last from the rules and regulations of the Master.[20] In the sources we are dealing with here, however, the reaction that is most emphasized is that of the thousands of arhats who decide to follow the Buddha into parinirvāṇa. Proclaiming that life is not worth living anymore, that the world without the Buddha is like a desert, they all, each in his own place, abandon their bodies and enter into extinction.[21]

The sentiment that without the Buddha there is no reason to go on living is epitomized in the figure of the arhat Gavāṃpati, a disciple of the Buddha who was residing at the time of the parinirvāṇa in Śiriṣa (Pali: Serīsaka)—one of the heavens of the Cāturmahārājika world. Upon learning of the Buddha's death from the monk Pūrṇa, who has come to urge him to return to earth, he refuses and cries out:

> The whole world is empty!
> It is no longer a pleasant place!
> Who cares about Jambudvīpa when it is devoid of the Law preached by the Tathāgata?
> I want to stay here and enter Nirvāṇa![22]

Obviously, such a preference on the part of Gavāṃpati and the other arhats can only precipitate a crisis in the community, for how can the Blessed One's Teaching be carried on if the arhats refuse to stay around and propagate it? Indra and the four lokapālas, in fact, become so worried about this that they go to Mahākāśyapa and tell him that something has to be done quickly or else the Buddha's Dharma—which they are charged to protect—will vanish forever.

Mahākāśyapa's reaction is twofold. On the one hand, he convenes the First Buddhist Council at Rājagṛha so that the Buddha's Teaching can be recited and preserved. On the other hand, he issues an injunction forbidding arhats from entering parinirvāṇa until that task is completed. Indeed, the *Aśokarājāvadāna* has him proclaim:

> From this day forth,
> On which the Sangha is assembled,
> Let no one enter Nirvāṇa
> Until the baskets of the Law have been compiled![23]

The *Mahāprajñāpāramitā śāstra* is even more dramatic. There, Mahākāśyapa beats a great gong and pronounces in a voice that can be heard throughout the Trichiliomegachiliocosm:

> Disciples of the Buddha,
> Let us remember the Blessed One
> and recollect his beneficence;
> Do not enter into Nirvāṇa![24]

These rather striking proclamations have not received the attention they are due in Buddhist studies. The personal attainment of Nirvāṇa, after all, is the soteriological goal of at least Hīnayāna Buddhism; the *Aśokarājāvadāna* is a Hīnayānist text, and Mahākāśyapa, even in the *Mahāprajñāpāramitā śāstra*, is a representative of Hīnayānist doctrine. Yet in this suggestion that the attainment of final Nirvāṇa should somehow be postponed, we have a sentiment that could be seen to be at the root of the bodhisattva ideal.[25]

In our sources, Mahākāśyapa is successful in preventing the early mass exodus of the arhats into parinirvāṇa, and he is able to convene and preside over the First Buddhist Council at Rājagṛha. Ānanda is asked to recite the Sūtra piṭaka, Upāli is asked to recite the Vinaya, and Mahākāśyapa himself recites the Mātṛka, the scholastic summaries that are the predecessors of the Abhidharma.[26] There is no point in going into the details of these events here; they have been much studied elsewhere and are not of immediate concern.[27]

In our texts, as soon as the Council is over, the narrative shifts to the death of Mahākāśyapa. Feeling that he has essentially accomplished his mission of preserving the Buddha's Teaching, Mahākāśyapa goes to Ānanda and formally passes the Dharma on to him. "Ānanda," he declares, "the Buddha transmitted to me the baskets of the Law. Now I wish to enter parinirvāṇa; therefore, in turn, I am committing the Dharma to your good keeping."[28]

Mahākāśyapa is now ready to "die." After paying his last respects to the relics of the Buddha and sending word to King Ajātaśatru of his impending parinirvāṇa,[29] he ascends Mount Kukkuṭapāda[30] near Rājagṛha and sits himself down between the three summits of that peak. There he makes a firm resolve that his body, his bowl, and his monastic robe (which had been given to him by the Buddha)[31] should not decay after his parinirvāṇa, but should remain perfectly preserved inside Mount Kukkuṭapāda until the advent of the future Buddha Maitreya.[32] Then he enters into the trance of cessation; the mountain-top opens up to receive him and miraculously encloses his body.

Unlike other Buddhist saints, then, Mahākāśyapa does not auto-incinerate his own body; nor is he to be cremated by others. Indeed, when King Ajātaśatru begins to gather firewood for a grand funeral, Ānanda stops him. "The Venerable Mahākāśyapa is not to be cremated!" he declares. "His body preserved in an ecstatic trance, he will await the arrival of Maitreya." And Ānanda describes how, in the distant future, the mountain will open up again and how Maitreya will show Mahākāśyapa's body to his disciples and receive (or take) from him the Buddha Śākyamuni's robe. In this way, Mahākāśyapa (or at least his body) is to act as a sort of link between two Buddhas—the last one and the next one—and so as a kind of guarantee of the continuity of the Dharma.[33]

What is not clear in this tradition is just when Mahākāśyapa is thought to attain parinirvāṇa. Is he alive inside the mountain in a deep meditative trance, from which he will emerge at the time of Maitreya? Or is he dead and only a sort of preserved mummy on which hangs the Buddha's robe?[34]

Some texts seem to indicate the latter. Mahākāśyapa, they claim, attains parinirvāṇa before the mountain closes in on him. His body will remain preserved until the coming of Maitreya, but he will not then revive. Thus, in the *Mūlasarvāstivāda Vinaya*, Maitreya shows Mahākāśyapa's corpse to his disciples and displays to them the Buddha's robe, and they are filled with awe.[35] Similarly, the "Maitreyāvadāna" (*Divyāvadāna*, chapter 3) speaks of Mahākāśyapa's "skeleton" (asthisamghāta) and describes how Maitreya will take it up "in his right hand, set it in his left, and teach the Dharma to his disciples."[36]

Other texts, however, appear to indicate that Mahākāśyapa does remain alive in his mountain, in a meditative state of suspended animation. Hsüan-tsang, who visited the mountain in the seventh century, claims that, with Maitreya's arrival, Mahākāśyapa will emerge from his trance, perform his miracles, and only then pass into parinirvāṇa.[37] The *Mi le ta ch'eng fo ching* adds some details to this scenario. It tells how Maitreya will first knock on the summit of Mahākāśyapa's peak and then open it "the way a cakravartin opens a city gate." The god Brahmā will then anoint Mahākāśyapa's head with divine oil, strike a gong, and blow the conch shell of the Dharma. This royal consecration will awaken the saint from his trance; he will get up, kneel down in front of Maitreya, and offer him the robe that the Buddha had confided to him. Only then will he enter parinirvāṇa, his body ablaze with flames.[38] Another Maitreyist text, the Khotanese *Maitreya samiti*, describes a somewhat similar scene. Mahākāśyapa, coming out of his trance, expresses his good fortune at having been able to meet *two* Buddhas personally, and then he launches into a long sermon explaining how the "leftover disciples," initiated but not brought to final Nirvāṇa by one Buddha, are usually saved by the next. He then displays his magical powers and enters parinirvāṇa.[39]

Obviously, this notion of a disciple of the Buddha not entering parinirvāṇa until the time of the future Buddha Maitreya may be seen as an extension of the injunction issued by Mahākāśyapa himself against arhats entering parinirvāṇa at the time of the First Council. At the same time, such stories of disciples who remain behind and protect the Dharma until the advent of Maitreya lie at the basis of the well-established Hīnayāna tradition of the sixteen or eighteen arhats (Chinese: lo-han), which became very popular in East Asian Buddhism. Spread out in the various directions of the compass, these protectors of the Dharma use their supernatural powers to extend their life spans and occasionally appear mysteriously in this world to promote the Buddha's religion.[40]

Whatever the historical development of these various traditions, it is possible to find in them an interesting typology of differing attitudes towards the attainment of parinirvāṇa, a typology which reflects the notion of "fast" and "slow" questers that we encountered in the stories of the bodhisattvas Śākyamuni and Maitreya. At one end of the spectrum, we have Gavāṃpati and the other arhats who, learning of the demise of the Buddha, immediately resolve to abandon their bodies and enter parinirvāṇa themselves. Then there are those arhats, members of the First Buddhist Council, who heed Mahākāśyapa's call to delay entering parinirvāṇa at least until the preservation and continuation of the Buddha's Teaching are assured. A third type consists of those arhats who, like Mahākāśyapa (in some texts, at least) and like the sixteen lo-han, will not enter parinirvāṇa until the coming of the future Buddha Maitreya. In this way, they can protect and preserve the Dharma during the gap that occurs between two Buddhas. Finally, there is the type of the full-blown bodhisattva, who resolves not to enter parinirvāṇa until all sentient beings are enlightened and can join him in that final attainment.

Upagupta, though he is born too late to be an arhat at the First Council, starts out (in some traditions) as a quester of the second type. As his legend develops, however, he tends more and more to belong to the third type—until (as we shall see when we consider the Southeast Asian traditions about him) his ongoing presence in this world until the time of Maitreya is fully recognized.

The Story of Ānanda

Mahākāśyapa, in all of our texts, passes the Dharma on to Ānanda, a figure well known as one of the Buddha's principal and closest disciples. The traditions about Ānanda are so multifarious that we cannot possibly examine them all here; all that we can look at now is his role as a Master of the Dharma. In the *Aśokarājāvadāna*, when Mahākāśyapa transmits the Dharma to Ānanda, he also tells him that, in the future, a young man named Śāṇakavāsin will live in Mathurā. There he will become a merchant and set off to sea. Upon returning, having made a great fortune, he will honor the Sangha by celebrating a great quinquennial festival (pañcavārṣika). At that time, Ānanda is to ordain him as a monk and transmit to him the Dharma.[41]

The scene is thus already set for Ānanda's role as transmitter of the Teaching. Indeed, in all our texts, when Śāṇakavāsin does return from his sea voyage, Ānanda begins the process that will eventually make him the next Master of the Dharma. As soon as Śāṇakavāsin has finished holding his quinquennial festival, the elder approaches him and commends him for having accomplished a great gift of material goods; but, he adds, he must now make an even greater gift—a gift of Dharma. Śāṇakavāsin is perplexed; he does not know what this "gift of Dharma" is. Ānanda then explains that it means to become a Buddhist monk.[42] Accordingly, Śāṇakavāsin agrees to wander forth, and, under Ānanda's tutelage, he quickly masters the entire Teaching and becomes an arhat.[43]

Some time passes, and Ānanda gets to be an old man. Then one day, in the Venuvana monastery, he overhears a young monk reciting—wrongly—some verses from the *Dharmapada*: "It would be better," intones the novice, "to live a single day and see a marsh fowl [shui hu kuan] than to live a hundred years and not see a marsh fowl." Ānanda takes it upon himself to correct this recitation. "The Buddha did not say that," he exclaims. "He said, 'It would be better to live a single day and see the harsh and foul nature of saṃsāra [sheng mieh fa] than to live a hundred years and not see the harsh and foul nature of saṃsāra.' "[44]

The young monk is now confused; this was not the way he was taught the verse, so he takes up the matter with his preceptor. The latter tells him he should continue reciting the way he had been taught; Ānanda, he explains, is getting senile and can no longer remember the Teaching correctly. The novice returns to his recitation, and Ānanda, hearing him still doing it incorrectly, interrupts him again. "Didn't I tell you the Buddha never said that?" he asks. "Yes," replies the monk, "but my teacher said you were old and decrepit and could no longer recall the Dharma."[45]

There could hardly be a more poignant tale of the decline of the Dharma in the context of its oral recitation. Ānanda is the last of the Buddha's major disciples. Śāriputra, Maudgalyāyana, and Mahākāśyapa have all entered parinirvāṇa, and there is no one left in authority to back Ānanda up. Sad, isolated, and alone, he decides it is time for him to enter parinirvāṇa as well.

Accordingly, he summons Śāṇakavāsin and declares, "The Buddha transmitted the Dharma to Mahākāśyapa; Mahākāśyapa transmitted it to me. Now I wish to enter Nirvāṇa; thus, henceforth, you will uphold the Buddha's Teaching."[46] Then, sending word to King Ajātaśatru that he is about to pass away, he heads for the Ganges, always an auspicious place to die in India. He has resolved to enter parinirvāṇa there, in a boat in midstream so as to prevent a dispute over his relics from breaking out between the people of Vaiśālī to the north of the river and those of Rājagṛha to the south. His work, however, is not yet done; at the last moment, five hundred Brahmanical ascetics (ṛṣis) arrive and request admittance into the Buddhist Order. Ānanda agrees to this and ordains them on a golden island which he magically creates in the midst of the Ganges. They all immediately attain arhatship, and their leader, because he was ordained in the middle (madhya) of the river at midday, comes to be known as Madhyāntika. He is also destined to be one of the Masters of the Law, and Ānanda promptly transmits the Dharma to him, even though he has already passed it on to Śāṇakavāsin.

Finally, the time for Ānanda is at hand; rising up into midair, he passes into parinirvāṇa, his body manifesting all sorts of extraordinary displays. His relics, as planned, fall into four shares: one for the people of Rājagṛha on the southern bank of the river, one for the people of Vaiśālī to the north, one for the gods in Indra's heaven, and one for the nāgas under the water.[47]

As is evident from this account, there is a bifurcation in the patriarchal tradition after Ānanda. Śāṇakavāsin, Ānanda's first-named successor, is to go to Mathurā and ordain Upagupta, but Madhyāntika is sent off to convert the land of Kashmir. This accords with a prediction that the Buddha is said to have made during his own journey to the Northwest, and indeed the subsequent account of Madhyāntika's conquest of the dragon of Kashmir is reminiscent of the Buddha's own missionary battles in the region, which we considered in chapter 1.[48]

The Story of Śāṇakavāsin

We shall not follow the career of Madhyāntika further here but shall focus instead on that of Upagupta's preceptor, Śāṇakavāsin.[49] In passing the Dharma on to him, Ānanda also instructed Śāṇakavāsin to go to the land of Mathurā and there to build a monastery on Mount Urumuṇḍa and await the birth of Upagupta. Accordingly, right after Ānanda's demise, Śāṇakavāsin sets out for Mathurā. On his way, he has an experience somewhat similar to that of his master overhearing a novice misreciting a scripture. Stopping for the night at a monastery, he comes across two mahalla monks[50] misquoting not a sūtra of the Buddha, but something that he, Śāṇakavāsin, had said long before. The episode is revealing; clearly, we have moved even further away from the Buddha's time to a situation where not only his teachings are being forgotten, but so, too, are the words of a second generation of his disciples!

Śāṇakavāsin sets the mahalla monks straight and reveals to them his identity.

He then goes on to Mount Urumuṇḍa, where he is destined to found the Naṭabhaṭika monastery. He must first, however, wrest the mountain from the possession of two nāgas who dwell there. Provoking the nāgas to battle, he quickly tames them with his samādhi of loving-kindness and tells them that the Buddha has foretold that a monastery is to be built on this spot. This, apparently, is enough to convince them to acquiesce to the project. Śāṇakavāsin then uses the same technique (recounting a prediction of the Buddha) to convince the brothers Naṭa and Bhaṭa to finance the construction of the monastery that comes to bear their names.[51]

Everything is ready, then, for the recruitment of Upagupta, and there follows the episode with which we opened this chapter: Śāṇakavāsin visits the house of Gupta, the perfumer, and gets him to agree to give up his son to the Sangha as a paścācchramaṇa. He then remains at the Naṭabhaṭika long enough to ordain Upagupta as a monk. It is not altogether clear what happens to Śāṇakavāsin after this. According to the *Aśokarājāvadāna*, he retires to the mountains of Kashmir, since he has heard that that is a good place for meditation. He does eventually return to Mathurā, however, in order to transmit the Dharma formally to Upagupta and to tell him that, in due time, he will in turn have to pass the patriarchate on to Dhītika, whom he will also find in Mathurā.[52]

The Loss and Preservation of the Dharma

Shortly before Śāṇakavāsin actually transmits the Dharma to Upagupta, a curious scene is said to take place. Raising his hand in the air, Śāṇakavāsin opens it to reveal that it is full of milk. "Of what samādhi is this the sign?" he asks, but Upagupta is at a loss to answer.[53] Jean Przyluski, commenting on this story, thinks that its intention is to humiliate Upagupta, and he sees it consequently as an interpolation by a late Kashmiri editor of the text who is seeking to glorify the figure of Śāṇakavāsin.[54] The rest of the passage, however, makes it clear that what we have here is another illustration of the decline of the Dharma. Indeed, his trick over, Śāṇakavāsin tells Upagupta, "The samādhis of the Buddha are not known by pratyekabuddhas; the pratyekabuddhas' samādhis are not known by śrāvakas; the samādhis of Śāriputra and Maudgalyāyana were not known by other śrāvakas; I do not know the samādhis of my teacher, Ānanda; and you, Upagupta, do not know my samādhis! When I enter parinirvāṇa, all my samādhis will be lost."[55]

The same theme of decline may be detected in another story, a tale about Upagupta's encounter with an old nun. One day, we are told, Upagupta, "the mahānāyaka of Jambudvīpa," visited a 120-year-old nun who had seen the Buddha in her youth. He wanted to ask her about the Blessed One's demeanor. The nun, knowing that Upagupta was coming, placed a bowl brimful of oil by her door. In coming into the room, Upagupta disturbed it, and some of the oil spilled. The nun then reprimanded him, saying that the Buddha's demeanor was not at all like that; in fact, during the time of the Buddha, even the worst of the bhikṣus had never spilled her oil.[56]

There is in these and in other stories about the Masters of the Dharma an underlying tension between the feeling that the Buddha's Doctrine is being lost and the feeling that it is being preserved. This tension, which we have found in a number of contexts, seems to play at least two roles. On the one hand, it ironically confirms the Buddha's doctrine of impermanence—that all things, including the Dharma, are subject to decay. On the other hand, it serves the crucial function of contrasting the present with the time of the Buddha, which is thereby glorified. This glorious time of the Buddha, however, may be found both in the past and the future. In the past, it is the golden age of Śākyamuni, when enlightenment was relatively easy and the Dharma was intact. In the future, it is the eschaton, the time of the next Buddha Maitreya, who will come down to earth, restore the Dharma, and make enlightenment possible once again. In this context, it is not surprising that the legends of the Masters of the Dharma have been caught up in the paradox of looking both ways. As preservers of Śākyamuni's Dharma, the patriarchs, including Upagupta, look back to a golden age they know they have lost, yet which paradoxically they try to keep until the time of Maitreya, when, fully lost, it will be completely renewed.

Forest Monks, Ascetics, and Long-haired Meditators

There are other conclusions to be drawn from the legends of these Masters of the Dharma, whose hagiographies collectively form a sort of legendary pedigree for the figure of Upagupta. In particular, it is interesting to find in these legends the conjunction of a number of points featuring Buddhist ascetic and meditative practices, points which will help us better understand the context of the cult of Upagupta in Southeast Asia.

Mention has been made of Śāṇakavāsin's association with two mahalla monks. This curious epithet, sometimes used interchangeably with *mahallaka*, has had a bewildering variety of applications in Buddhist literature. Hubert Durt, in a study of the subject, has concluded that the designation *mahalla* generally refers to a particular kind of monk whose chief characteristics are that he is old, was ordained late in life, and is generally stupid.[57] It is often used as a pejorative term. In the "Mākandikāvadāna," for example, it designates a ridiculous, lascivious old monk who tries to convince the Buddha to accept in marriage a beautiful girl and then pass her on to him (the mahalla); the Buddha refuses.[58] In the *Mūlasarvāstivāda Vinaya*, it is applied to an old monk who kicks a bowl of food belatedly offered by King Agnidatta, thus occasioning a rule by the Buddha against touching food with one's feet.[59]

In other cases, however, the term *mahalla* turns out to be one of those insults that reflect more on the utterer than on the one about whom the insult is uttered. Thus, in the *Sangharakṣitāvadāna*, it is used pejoratively, but by the low-minded ṣaḍvārgika bhikṣus.[60] In the Sanskrit *Mahāparinirvāṇa sūtra*, the Buddha himself is called a kaukṛtika mahalla, an "overscrupulous old man," but by the monk (himself here called a mahallaka) who rejoiced at the Blessed One's parinirvāṇa, saying that now they would no longer be plagued by him always telling them what to do.[61]

The same theme may be found in our own legend. Some of Upagupta's yet-unenlightened disciples are scornful of their master for associating with mahalla monks and upset with him for spurning a Tripiṭaka master from South India. (In actuality, this Tripiṭaka master, though a great scholar, had impregnated a girl and killed his mother prior to becoming ordained, and Upagupta for these reasons refuses to have anything to do with him—but his disciples are unaware of this karmic history.) Matters are about to come to a head when Upagupta decides to invite his own long-gone teacher, Śāṇakavāsin, who has been meditating in Kashmir. The latter soon arrives by means of his supernatural powers. He is wearing his hempen robes and is generally dishevelled; his hair is long, he is sporting a beard, and he enters directly into Upagupta's chamber, where he sits down on Upagupta's seat to wait for him. Upagupta's disciples, not knowing the identity of this man, are scandalized. They rush to find their master and tell him that a mahalla monk has had the audacity to sit down in his place. "Only my preceptor may sit on my seat," declares Upagupta, and he hurries to the room. But there he sees that the monk seated in his chair *is* his preceptor, and he bows down before him. He then reassures his distraught disciples by explaining to them who this man is.[62]

In this tale, we are not told that Śāṇakavāsin actually is a mahalla monk, but it is clear that, in the eyes of Upagupta's disciples, he looks like one. Mahalla monks, like Śāṇakavāsin, have long, unkempt hair and wear coarse, probably dirty robes. The feature of long hair is obviously interesting because Buddhist monks traditionally shave their heads. Indeed, this is one of their chief characteristics, distinguishing them from Hindu and other ascetics. Yet, in the literature with which we are dealing, there are a number of references to unkempt, long-haired, bearded bhikṣus. In the *Divyāvadāna*, for instance, King Aśoka's younger brother Vītaśoka, who becomes a monk and is inclined to ascetic practices and meditation, lets his nails, hair, and beard grow long and his clothes become tattered. Mistaken for a Jain, he is killed in one of the pogroms ordered by Aśoka, much to the latter's remorse.[63] In the *Aśokarājāvadāna*, when the Venerable Aṣālḥa is reprimanded by a nun for his improper bearing, he thinks she is referring to his long hair and his dirty robes. He therefore shaves his head, takes a bath, and does his laundry, only to find out that this was not what concerned her at all—but rather his lack of striving for enlightenment.[64] Finally, in an interesting story in the *Mūlasarvāstivāda Vinaya*, the elder Mahākāśyapa, who elsewhere is actually called a mahallaka,[65] is said to have long hair, a beard, and coarse clothes. He is refused admittance to a meal that the rich layman Anāthapiṇḍada is about to serve to the Buddha and the assembled Sangha.[66]

All of these references may take on additional importance in light of some of the Southeast Asian materials that we will be examining. For instance, in Burma and Thailand, it is commonly maintained that Upagupta is a rather ugly, dark-skinned monk, often dressed in tattered robes, who does not belong to any monastery. He is not the sort of bhikṣu one would want to give alms to. In one place, I was even told that he had long hair—down to his knees.[67]

It might also be pointed out that in Burma, historically, there was a sect of long-haired monks known as the Ari, who for various reasons were held in disrepute by Theravādin orthodoxy.[68] Little is known for certain about the Ari, as most of our sources of information about them are highly prejudiced. They were (perhaps) tantrically inclined, wore dark robes, had long hair, advocated the worship of nāgas, and, according to their detractors, claimed the *ius primae noctis*, the right of deflowering newlywed village girls.[69] Interestingly, the leader and patron saint of the Ari was a monk named Mahākassapa, who, as his name indicates, was felt to be a reincarnation of the Buddha's disciple Mahākāśyapa and who was thought to have taken a vow for future Buddhahood under Gautama.[70]

The precise meaning of the word *Ari* has long been the subject of debate, but basically two schools of thought have emerged. On the one hand are those who see its origin in the word *ariya* ("noble one"), denoting in Buddhism one who is enlightened.[71] On the other hand are those who accept the derivation of *Ari* from *āraññaka* (Sanskrit *āraṇyaka*), meaning "forest-dwelling [monk]".[72] In fact, Than Tun sees the word as equivalent to the Burmese term *taw kloṅ*, indicating monks of the "forest monasteries."[73]

This connection makes good sense in light of the stories we have been considering about Mahākāśyapa, Śāṇakavāsin, and other long-haired monks. The reason for their long hair and unkempt appearance is not only that they are inclined towards asceticism (which the Ari were not), but that they are forest-dwelling monks recently back from a hermitage, where, either for want of any companions to shave their heads or through total preoccupation with their meditative endeavors, they have let their hair and beards grow long. Śāṇakavāsin, when he is maligned by Upagupta's disciples as a mahalla, has just arrived from Kashmir, where he has been meditating in solitude;[74] Vītaśoka lets his hair and beard grow and his laundry go when he is alone and sick in a forest hermitage in the borderlands;[75] Mahākāśyapa arrives in Śrāvastī after dwelling in the forest (āraṇyaka) in a hermitage where the seats and beds are conducive to meditation.[76]

It is well known that the Buddhist Sangha in South and Southeast Asia comprised monks of two distinct types, who were known in Pali as gāmavāsin (town, or village, dwellers) and araññavāsin (forest dwellers). The former were associated with the vocation of scholarship (ganthadhura, literally the "burden of books") and often devoted themselves to preaching and pastoral cares in the communities to which their monasteries were attached. The latter practiced the vocation of meditation (vipassanādhura) and often inclined towards wandering, reclusive, and ascetic life-styles.[77]

Not enough attention has been given to the fact that the Masters of the Dharma, at least in the legends that we have been looking at, fall quite clearly into this forest-dwelling, ascetically inclined tradition of meditators.[78] Śāṇakavāsin, for example, when he is in Kashmir, rejoices at the contemplative life and sings of his meditations on rocky peaks and in deep ravines which keep him warm despite his wearing but a single garment of hemp.[79] When he returns to Mathurā and is taken for a mahalla monk, the text contrasts him to the Tripiṭaka master from South India, who has memorized the whole of the Buddhist canon but knows nothing about meditation. The two vocations are thus laid out clearly here, and quite prejudicially. The Tripiṭaka master belongs to the vocation of books; he looks very learned and saintly, but Upagupta knows he is a matricidal fornicator and will have nothing to do with him. Śāṇakavāsin, on the other hand, follows the vocation of meditation; he may look grubby, have long hair, and appear to be a mahalla; but he is actually enlightened, and he is Upagupta's master.

Upagupta himself, it should be remembered, was the head of the Naṭabhaṭika monastery on Mount Urumuṇḍa, which Śāṇakavāsin founded. Not enough has been made yet of the fact that this monastery, in our texts, is repeatedly called "the foremost of all the Buddha's forest-haunts [araṇyāyatana], where the lodgings [seats-beds] are conducive to meditation [śamatha]."[80] At the Naṭabhaṭika, as we shall see, Upagupta related to political powers (in particular King Aśoka) in ways that were and are typical of forest saints. And there, too, he instructed monks from all over India who came to seek him out as a meditation master.[81] In fact, at one point, the *Aśokarājāvadāna* even declares that the Buddha predicted that Upagupta would be "the foremost of all those who are instructors of meditation."[82]

Mahākāśyapa, too, dwelt in forest hermitages,[83] and he was renowned as the foremost of the Buddha's disciples who maintained the ascetic practices (dhūtaguṇa or dhutānga).[84] This helps account for his wearing coarse "ragheap" robes (pāṃśukūla), which are commonly featured as the first of the ascetic practices. His robes, like Śāṇakavāsin's seem to have been made of rags of hemp (sāṇāni paṃsukūlāni). Indeed, there are some indications that the robe which the Buddha gave Mahākāśyapa to wear and pass on to Maitreya was just such a hempen robe.[85]

Too often, the ascetic practices in general and the pāṃśukūlika practices in particular have been studied from the perspective of the town-dwelling monks, who tolerated but did not follow them, rather than from the perspective of the forest-dwelling monks, who advocated and maintained them. This is understandable, since most of our sources (canonical and commentarial) have, in fact, emerged from the town-monk tradition which followed the "vocation of books." But the perspective brought by this tradition has left the impression that the ascetic practices in Buddhism were optional excesses and that the monks who chose to follow them were somehow deviants from, rather than upholders of, a norm.[86] It is interesting, therefore, to look at the practice of the first of the dhūtaguṇa—the wearing of ragheap robes—from the perspective of a text that is self-avowedly of that ascetic tradition.

The *Paṃsukūlānisaṃsaṃ* is such a text. It is a Pali work of the ānisaṃsa genre (telling the "advantage" of doing good deeds) and has found popularity in Thailand, Cambodia, and Laos.[87] It tells the story of the very first paṃsukūla: A rich merchant of Uruvelā had a daughter who died giving birth to her first child, who was stillborn. The merchant then decided to offer some robe material to the Buddha; he took an expensive piece of cloth, wrapped it around the dead foetus and the afterbirth of his daughter, and kept it for seven days. Then he deposited it on the road where he knew the Buddha was due to pass.[88] The Buddha, seeing it, thought, "This is the first paṃsukūla. . . . The Buddhas of the past wore paṃsukūla; I, therefore, will wear one, too." He picked it up; the decaying foetus and afterbirth fell on the ground, which then shook and trembled to mark what for this tradition was a momentous occasion.[89]

There follows an account of the washing, drying, and dyeing of the paṃsukūla by the Buddha with the divine help of the god Indra; and then, as the text puts it, "the Buddha's old robe disappeared, and he became a paṃsukūlika."[90] Later, the Buddha exalts the wearing of ragheap robes in no uncertain terms: "The paṃsukūla robe," he declares, "is the best. It is while wearing it that the Buddhas have liberated all creatures. . . . O monks, I wear the paṃsukūla robe; you should do likewise."[91]

The real hero of this text, however, is not the Buddha but his disciple, the elder [Mahā]kassapa, whom the story goes on to present as a sort of patron saint of the paṃsukūlikas.[92] The tale passes very quickly over his ordination and then features a noteworthy conversation between him and the Buddha. Mahākassapa asks the Buddha how many "vocations" (dhura) there are open for Buddhist monks. The Buddha replies, "There are two: the vocation of books and the vocation of meditation." The elder then wants to know what is meant by these. "In the vocation of books," replies the Buddha, "a monk memorizes one nikāya, two nikāyas, or all the texts of the canon. In the vocation of meditation, a monk practices awareness of the perishable nature of existence until he reaches arhatship." The Buddha goes on to describe the thirteen ascetic practices and in particular the wearing of paṃsukūla (of which he lists twenty-three different kinds).[93] Kassapa decides to choose the vocation of meditation, but he does so for a noteworthy reason: "I wandered forth," he declares, "to become a monk when I was an old mahallaka; I cannot follow the vocation of books! I will therefore follow the vocation of meditation."[94]

The notion that the vocation of meditation (that is, the way of asceticism and of the forest dwellers) was particularly appropriate for monks who had entered the Sangha late in life (that is, mahallas) has important repercussions and may go far in helping to explain the town-and-book monks' attitudes towards long-haired ascetics and forest meditators. As the Buddhist Sangha evolved, it became clear that the establishment liked to recruit new members when they were young. Not only did this allow for more control in maintaining the status quo, but it had the practical effect of giving more time to young monks for memorizing sūtras when their minds were still supple and not yet preoccupied with pastoral cares and other duties. Monks ordained late in life not only found it more difficult to learn great numbers of texts by heart, but they brought with them habits from lay life that they sometimes found hard to shake and which caused them to be viewed with suspicion.

More importantly, becoming a forest monk late in life seemed to follow a well-established Brahmanical pattern of spiritual development, rather than a typically Buddhist one. According to the doctrine of the four āśramas, or stages of life, after being a student (brahmacārin) and then a householder (gṛhastha), a twice-born Hindu could become a "forest-abiding" hermit (vānaprastha) "when he had seen the birth of his sons' sons and white hairs began to appear on his head." In India, then, forest meditation was classically the prerogative of men who turned to spiritual practice in their old age. Youth, the brahmacārin stage, was the time for the memorization of texts and for celibacy.

In this light, the division of the Buddhist Sangha into two vocations, may be seen from a different perspective. The ganthadhura monks, wandering forth in their youth, engaging in book learning, and living in towns or villages within a clear monastic hierarchy, may be seen as following a brahmacārin model. The vipassanādhura, on the other hand, who wandered forth in old age to practice meditation in the forest, removed from institutional constraints, reflect the model of the vānaprastha.

In a monastery not far from Bāmiān, in present-day Afghanistan, Hsüan-tsang reports having seen the famous hempen robe of Śāṇakavāsin. It was quite small, for, according to local legend, it would endure as long as the Buddha Śākyamuni's religion, but would diminish in size with the decline of the Dharma. But it had not vanished yet, and its presence helped reinforce the faith of pilgrims.[95]

We noted earlier in this chapter a certain tension in the legends of the Masters of the Dharma. Caught up in the dilemmas of preserving a declining Dharma, they sometimes looked backwards to the golden age of the Buddha and his Dharma and other times looked forwards to the coming of the Buddha Maitreya, stressing the millennial age of the future.

This same sort of tension may be found between the two vocations of forest-

and town-dwelling monks. The town dwellers, as we have noted, emphasize the memorization and preservation of texts of the Buddha Gautama's Teaching. Quite understandably, they look backwards, trying to hold on to what was. The forest dwellers, on the other hand, as Stanley Tambiah has shown, are more or less explicitly linked to the Buddhist millenarian tradition and to the figure of Maitreya.[96] The story of Mahākāśyapa is instructive in this regard, for it shows that, in the traditions we are dealing with, the way to await Maitreya is to go into a meditative trance in a remote place! To be sure, in the case of Mahākāśyapa, there is still a certain amount of ambiguity, since it is not clear whether he is dead or alive as he waits for Maitreya. The case of Upagupta, as we shall see it develop in Southeast Asia, is much clearer on this issue; Upagupta too sits in meditation, at the bottom of the ocean, waiting for Maitreya, but he is clearly alive.

But all the Masters of the Dharma are, it seems to me, intractably caught up in this tension. As transmitters of the Buddha's Doctrine, they are intimately involved in both its loss and its preservation. As forest saints and meditators, they are witnesses to both the present possibility of enlightenment and to its postponement until the time of Maitreya.

CHAPTER FOUR

Lay Life, Ordination, and Arhatship

THE STORY of Upagupta's birth in Mathurā makes it clear that his destiny is to be a monk—indeed, a Master of the Dharma. That destiny, however, takes some time to unfold. Though conditionally committed by his father to become Śāṇakavāsin's paścācchramaṇa, Upagupta at first remains at home and helps out in his family's perfume shop. There he leads the ordinary life of a layman, and it is as a layman that he starts his meditative endeavors, preaches his first sermon, makes his first convert, and attains his initial realization of enlightenment. This is significant, for, although Upagupta's fame is to be as a member of the Sangha, his life story also reveals certain possibilities for spiritual attainment that are open to the laity.

Business in the perfume shop is good. According to the *Divyāvadāna*, this is because Māra has filled the whole city with such a horrible stench that its inhabitants are prompted to purchase many perfumes.[1] Māra, as we shall see, plays a crucial and somewhat ambiguous role in Upagupta's career, but his actions here need to be seen in the context of Upagupta's father's agreement with Śāṇakavāsin. Gupta, it will be remembered, had promised he would let his son enter the Sangha when his trade made "neither profit nor loss." Māra, by making sure that his business thrives, is trying to put off the start of Upagupta's monastic career.

Māra's interference, however, does not prevent Śāṇakavāsin, Upagupta's future preceptor, from beginning his spiritual training. Indeed, Śāṇakavāsin visits Upagupta in his family's shop and asks him whether in doing business his mental states (cittacaitāsika) are defiled (kliṣṭa) or undefiled (akliṣṭa).[2] This is a fairly technical question for a young layman, and Upagupta answers frankly that he does not know what is meant by "defiled and undefiled mental states." Śāṇakavāsin defines them for him in straightforward terms: defiled mental states are when humans feel desire, passion, and anger towards others; undefiled mental states are the absence of these emotions.[3] He then teaches Upagupta a simple technique for keeping track of the states of his thoughts: he gives him some black and white "strips" of cloth or of wood[4] and tells him to put aside one black strip every time a defiled thought arises and one white strip every time an undefiled thought arises.[5]

This curious meditative technique is obviously related to the practice of mindfulness (smṛti; Pali: sati), in which meditators endeavor to note and eventually to control mental phenomena as they occur;[6] but, by its use of physical mnemonic devices, it makes that technique very concrete and gives it a specifically moralistic focus.

The colors white and black are in Buddhism, as in many traditions, symbolic of purity and impurity, merits and demerits, good and evil. Indeed, one of the constant refrains of the Sanskrit avadānas is that "the karmic fruit of completely black deeds is completely black; that of completely white deeds completely white; and that of mixed deeds mixed," a statement that is always followed by an exhortation to "shun completely black and mixed deeds and abound in completely white ones."[7] Śāṇakavāsin, it seems, is here showing Upagupta a very practical way of doing just this, and one which encourages him to develop more and more positive mental states, in the midst of his day-to-day activities in the perfume shop. Thus, Upagupta at first finds he is putting aside two black strips for every white one; but he soon comes to put aside equal numbers of black and white strips, then two white ones for every black one, and finally white strips alone.[8]

Appropriately, the result of this meditative endeavor is not a trancelike absorption or a one-pointed focus of the mind; it is, rather, described in terms that reveal its effects on his lay-life situation. When Upagupta finds that he is putting aside nothing but white strips, we are told that "all his decisions were then in accord with the Buddha's Teaching and none of them opposed to it";[9] or, as the *Divyāvadāna* puts it, he came "to do business according to Dharma."[10] The net result of his practice, then, is that by being aware of the quality of his thoughts while carrying on his trade, he becomes an honest merchant with no thought of maligning or cheating his customers. This is dharmic realization in the midst of lay life.

The Story of Vāsavadattā

This tale of Upagupta's dharmic uprightness is but a prelude to the important episode of his encounter with Vāsavadattā, the most famous courtesan of Mathurā. The story is told in several of our texts,[11] but its most concise and poetic version may be found in Kṣemendra's *Avadānakalpalatā*. There the tale begins with Upagupta in the perfume bazaar "selling yellow sandal, musk, camphor, and aloe, and doing business with the praise of his father." Vāsavadattā, desiring to buy some perfumes, sends her servant girl to Upagupta's shop. When the girl goes back and tells her mistress how handsome and kind he is, the courtesan's "passion and excitement" are aroused, and she becomes "intent on [sexual] union with him."[12]

We thus have set up here one of the classic scenarios of Indian literature: the encounter of the ascetic and the harlot, with all the opposition that this implies between dharma on the one hand and kāma on the other. Vāsavadattā sends her maid back to Upagupta with a message making known her sentiments and inviting him to come and "pursue pleasure" with her, but he gently turns down the offer with a smile, saying that this is not yet the time for them to meet. Vāsavadattā is upset by this news, for, as Kṣemendra adds in an aside, "neither in love nor in indifference lies the fate of prostitutes."[13]

The *Divyāvadāna* version of the story provides a few extra details to this scenario. In it, Vāsavadattā's attention is caught not only by her maid's account of Upagupta's physical charms, but also because she has brought back so many perfumes. "You must have robbed that merchant," she exclaims, and is intrigued when her servant reports that she has not, it is just that Upagupta does business "according to Dharma".[14] Vāsavadattā then assumes that Upagupta, being honest, must also be poor, and that he must have turned her down because he could not afford to pay her usual price of five hundred pieces of gold.[15] She therefore invites him again, offering herself free of charge; but upright Upagupta refuses her once more, saying it is not yet time for them to meet.[16]

There follows an account of Vāsavadattā's increasing misfortune. A handsome young caravaneer from the North Country arrives in Mathurā with five hundred horses for sale.[17] He turns a neat profit and wants to celebrate by having a good time. "Which courtesan is the best of all?" he inquires, and, upon being told that it is Vāsavadattā, he is determined to have her. Vāsavadattā, seeking a new source of income, is eager for the match; but she already has a live-in lover, the son of a local guildmaster, who is unwilling to be jilted. She arranges, therefore, to have him killed and his body flung out onto the dungheap. She is then free to pursue her pleasure with the caravaneer.[18]

The murdered lover's relatives, however, turn out to be an influential lot. They go to the king and file charges against Vāsavadattā. She is deemed guilty, and justice is swift: her hands, feet, nose, and ears are cut off, and she is thrown onto the cremation ground. There, in terrible pain, she sits down "in the mud and her own blood with one servant girl to ward off the beasts of prey."[19]

It is then that Upagupta decides to visit her. Accompanied by a servant carrying a parasol, he goes to the cremation ground. Vāsavadattā's maid (perhaps with the blinders of one who has served too long in a house of prostitution and seen too many skewed forms of sexuality) thinks that Upagupta has come there for sex, "impelled by passion and desire."[20] Kṣemendra, too, suggests this possibility. "Who penetrates an inner sanctum," he asks in one of his editorial double entendres, "simply because of its outer ornamentation? Under no condition does the passion of men leave them."[21]

We should not be surprised at these suggestions. The Buddhist *Vinaya* mentions among the offenses involving expulsion from the order (pārājika) sexual intercourse with all sorts of women, alive, half-alive, and dead;[22] and its commentary lists more forms of sexual acts performed by monks on detached parts of dismembered bodies in various states of decomposition than most of us could have ever imagined.[23] The *Visuddhimagga*, too, in its description of the cemetery meditations, warns against possible sexual temptations to be found on the cremation ground.[24]

Upagupta, however, has clearly not come for sexual favors, and Vāsavadattā turns out to be more bashful than her servant girl. She asks her maid to make her a loincloth out of a rag to hide her nudity, and, folding the stumps of her arms over her chest, she says with downcast face, "Even when I invited you with great perseverance, you did not come; why have you come now to see one whom fate has struck down? When I was exciting, luxurious, beautiful, you said, 'This is not the time to see her.' Now my limbs are cut off, and, smeared with blood, I have fallen into the house of defilement. Why is this the time to see me, O Lotus-Leaf-eyed One?"[25]

The question is well taken and the answer not as simple as one might expect. On the one hand, of course, Upagupta has come out of compassion for Vāsavadattā in her suffering. He is full of commiseration and encourages her to take refuge in the Buddha, who alone can give her relief. At the same time, however, Upagupta has come for personal reasons—to further his own spiritual development. In the *Divyāvadāna*, he makes this quite clear: "Sister," he declares, "I have not come to you impelled by desire, but have come to see the intrinsic nature of desires and impurities."[26] He then launches into a diatribe on the impermanence and generally repulsive nature of the body: "How could anyone feel attracted to this body that is held together with skin, encircled by blood, covered with hide, plastered with lumps of flesh, and surrounded on all sides by a thousand muscles and veins?"[27]

In the *Avadānakalpalatā*, he is even more graphic: "Woe! Woe! They are destroyed, those who enjoy this corpselike frame stuck together with bones, covered with hair, and constantly cooked by digestive juices. They are destroyed, those who take pleasure in this burning ground called the body, which is a pile of repulsion, a storehouse of vices. Oh! Out of delusion do beings have affection for their bodies, even though they are oozing and stinking, mutilated and filled with holes."[28]

This sermonic diatribe (which in the Buddhist literature we are considering is more or less common fare) has a double effect. First, it brings about Vāsavadattā's salvation, for, listening to Upagupta's words, she comes to realize the Truth of the Buddha's Teaching (that life is suffering); and, turning away from saṃsāra, she quickly attains the fruit of entering the stream (she becomes a srotāpanna). Second, it has a soteriological effect on Upagupta, for, "coming to an understanding of the inherent nature of Vāsavadattā's body, he himself became disgusted with the realm of desire, and, from this clear understanding of the Truth that came with his own preaching of the Dharma, he attained the fruit of a nonreturner [anāgamin]."[29]

The story of Upagupta's soteriological progress does not end here, however; there follows an account of his ordination as a monk and of his arhatship. Upon leaving the cremation ground, Upagupta returns home; there, Śāṇakavāsin approaches his father and asks him once more to allow Upagupta to be initiated into the monastic life.[30] Gupta apparently is still reticent (for his son is good for his perfume business); but Śāṇakavāsin, with the help of his supernatural power, manages to arrange it so that there is "neither profit nor loss," and the rest follows as a matter of course: Śāṇakavāsin takes Upagupta to the Naṭabhaṭika forest hermitage, and, carrying out the formal ordination ceremony, he makes him a monk. And Upagupta, "ridding himself of all the defilements, experiences arhatship."[31]

In analyzing the full story of Upagupta's enlightenment, it is possible to distinguish at least three important events: his initial enlightenment as a nonreturner (anāgamin), his ordination as a monk, and his arhatship. As we shall see, this pattern is not at all atypical in the literature with which we are dealing, but it does raise a number of questions.

In a recent work, Peter Masefield[32] has reminded us that the basic division in early Buddhism was not between laypersons and monks, or between nonarhats and arhats, or even between humans and gods, but between those who are not on the Path (pṛthagjana)[33] and those who are already on it: stream-winners (srotāpanna), once-returners (sakṛdāgāmin), nonreturners (anāgāmin), and arhats.[34]

The developed Theravāda tradition has seen in these four realizations four successive stages on a single Path culminating in arhatship. According to this view, one starts off on the Path as a stream-winner and then gradually progresses through the other stages, eliminating at each step more and more of the fetters that keep one from complete realization.[35] A number of difficulties arise, however, from such a progressivist view.[36] As Masefield has shown, the distinction between stream-winner, once-returner, nonreturner, and arhat should not be seen as a matter of degree of enlightenment. The arhat is not somehow more enlightened than the others on the Path, for they are all āryas—noble disciples (āryasāvaka). They have all experienced the liberating sight and sound of the True Dharma; they have all had their Dharma-eyes opened, all had a vision of reality as it is, all put behind them the possibility of rebirth in one of the lower realms, all ceased producing new karma; and for all of them, parinirvāṇa (final liberation) is a certainty.[37]

The difference between them thus lies not in the quality of their enlightenment, but in the amount of karmic residue left over from their previous lives that still needs to be worked out. For the srotāpanna, this process will take seven more lifetimes; for the sakṛdāgāmin, it will take only one; for the anāgāmin, it will be accomplished after death but prior to what would have been the next rebirth, either in a sort of intermediate state or in one of the Pure Abodes of the realm of form; for the arhat, it will be done in this very life span.[38] Thus, strictly speaking, there is nothing more for any of these persons to accomplish with regard to enlightenment except to await the exhaustion of their past karma.[39]

It is convenient, then, to think of this Buddhist scheme of liberation as involving not four progressive stages, but two events: initial enlightenment (bodhi), which is a realization of Dharma that gives one a vision of reality as it is, by which one embarks on the Path and ceases to produce new karma; and final emancipation (parinirvāṇa), which is primarily rupalogical—involving a change of form—and which marks the end of the Path, the exhaustion of all karmic residue, and the cessation of death and rebirth as we know it.[40]

The Path which connects these two events may itself be thought of as consisting of four tracks, all leading to the same end, but taking different amounts of time to reach it. The srotāpanna track is the slowest (seven lifetimes); the arhat track is the fastest (this lifetime); and in between are the sakṛdāgāmin and anāgāmin tracks. Once again, which track one is engaged upon following initial enlightenment depends not on the degree of insight one has achieved—since for all āryas this is the same—but simply on the amount of one's karmic residue that still needs to be worked out.[41] In Buddhism, it is not enlightenment that takes time, but karma.

According to Masefield, once one is engaged upon one of these tracks, it is not possible to switch to another. Thus, a srotāpanna, for example, cannot suddenly become an arhat but has to wait a full seven lives for parinirvāṇa. This is the conclusion he reaches on the basis of the Pali materials. In the Sanskrit avadānas, however, we can observe that it *is* possible to switch from one track to another (always from a slower one to a faster one); for Upagupta, as we have seen, first enters the anāgāmin track and then shortly thereafter, following his ordination, embarks on the arhat track. This does not augment his enlightenment, but it does speed up his final liberation.

Furthermore, according to Masefield, both one's initial enlightenment and one's final liberation are entirely occasioned by the oral teaching of the Dharma by the Buddha in person. It is thus only the Buddha's grace that makes liberation possible, for "the Buddha alone can establish persons on the supermundane path."[42] Though this scenario may fit the view of early Pali texts, the Upagupta story, as we have seen, deals explicitly with a time when the Buddha is no longer present. Upagupta himself has never met the Buddha (not even in a previous life), yet for him enlightenment *and* final liberation are still possible.

With all of this in mind, we may now set the agenda for the rest of this chapter. First, we need to look more carefully at Upagupta's initial enlightenment, his becoming a nonreturner (anāgāmin). In particular, we need to consider in more detail two facts about this event: that it is Upagupta's own act of preaching (and not the Buddha's) that occasions it, and that both his preaching and his enlightenment have to do with the contemplation of the impurity of Vāsavadattā's body on the cremation ground and with the realization of its corpselike nature. Second, we need to consider Upagupta's switch from the nonreturner to the arhat track, and, in particular, to investigate the role that his ordination as a monk plays in this event.

Awakening through Preaching

Masefield is quite insistent on the fact that it is the Tathāgata alone, in his personal presence, who can bring individuals to an initial realization of the Truth of the Dharma.[43] It would seem, however, that if this view is to be maintained, the notion of "Buddha" needs to be extended. More specifically, the power of the *Dharma* as the living embodiment of the Tathāgata—as his Dharmakāya—should not be underestimated. Even in the Pali tradition, the Buddha appointed the Dharma as his successor, and the dictum "he who sees [hears] the Dharma sees [hears] the Buddha" *should* be taken at face value.[44] We shall see in chapter 5 that Upagupta interprets his own enlightenment as a vision of the Buddha's Dharmakāya and that, thanks to the good offices of Māra, it is even possible for him to have a vision of the Buddha's rūpakāya, his physical body. Thus, in the tradition with which we are dealing, the fact that the Buddha has passed away does not necessarily imply an end to his personal soteriological effectiveness. Given the right conditions, it may be possible for the Buddha, embodied in his successor or in his Dharma, to occasion a person's enlightenment.

In this light, it becomes easier to understand the *Divyāvadāna*'s assertion that the immediate cause of Upagupta's attaining the state of nonreturner was his own preaching of the Dharma to Vāsavadattā. The text is quite explicit about this, and the passage in question bears repeating: "Then, coming to an understanding of the inherent nature of Vāsavadattā's body, he himself became disgusted with the realm of desire [kāmadhātu], and, from this clear understanding of the Truth that came with his own preaching of the Dharma [ātmīyayā dharmadeśanayā saha], he attained the fruit of a nonreturner."[45]

Upagupta is not the only person in the Buddhist tradition to achieve an awakening in this way. As we shall see, one of his own disciples—the first monk, in fact, whom he is said to have led to arhatship—is also reputed to have attained enlightenment while preaching the Dharma.[46] A more prominent example may be found in the case of the elder Nāgasena, whose dialogues with the Indo-Greek king Milinda (Menander) are well known in Buddhist studies. In the *Milindapañha*, Nāgasena, while still a young monk, preaches a sermon to a laywoman, who thereby reaches the track of stream-winner. At the same time, however, he, too, reaches that goal, "having felt the force of the truths he himself had preached."[47]

It is not too difficult to imagine what is going on here. Buddhist monks, constantly called upon to give the gift of Dharma, must easily have fallen into the pattern of merely mouthing the teachings of the tradition. Then suddenly, one day, they realize in an experiential way that what they are saying is not just traditional but true, in a fundamental, liberating sense. But there is something else that is noteworthy here as well. In both these cases, realization does not occur until the soteriological effectiveness of the sermon has been made manifest in the person to whom it is being preached. Upagupta and Nāgasena do not realize the truth of what they are saying until its transformative effect is made visible in the attainment of enlightenment by Vāsavadattā and the laywoman. Put simplistically, it is only when Upagupta sees that his sermon "works" on others that it "works" for himself, that he himself realizes it is true in a liberating sense. It need hardly be added that we are on the threshold here of an idea that was to see its fullest development in the Mahāyāna—namely, that one's own enlightenment is inseparable from one's actions in enlightening others.

Cemetery Meditations

The specific subject of Upagupta's sermon and the setting in which he delivers it are also not without importance in understanding his realization. For the scene suggests that, though a layman, Upagupta has gone to the cremation ground for the very reason that Buddhist monks usually go there: to carry on a cemetery meditation on the transience of the body and the impurities of the decaying corpse. Upagupta's language implies this; contemplating Vāsavadattā's situation, he refers several times to corpses and "foul, impure skeletons" and, in fact, describes her body in terms that emerge directly from the cemetery-meditation tradition.[48] This setting puts his realization of the Truth of the Dharma into a very specific context.

The practice of aśubhabhāvanā (Pali: asubhabhāvanā), the contemplation of the impurities (of the corpse), was and is a well-known meditation in the Buddhist world. In canonical sources, monks who feel so inclined are urged to frequent charnel grounds or other places where human corpses might be seen, to contemplate various stages in the decomposition of the body and hence the notions of impermanence and non-self. Buddhaghosa includes ten states of decomposition of a corpse among his forty subjects of meditation (kasiṇa),[49] but the Sanskrit tradition generally agreed on a list of nine: bloated (vyādhmātaka), fissured (vidhūtaka), bloody (vilohitaka), festering (vipūyaka), bluish (vinīlaka), chewed up (vihāditaka), scattered about (vikṣiptaka), reduced to bone (asthi), and burnt (vidagdhaka).[50]

The object of contemplating the body in these ways is, of course, to achieve a realization of one's own impermanence and non-self, to see through external appearances and come to understand that one will also soon be—or, in fact, already is—like the bodies one is viewing. This realization cannot be achieved in ordinary circumstances because the true condition of the body is usually obscured by outer trappings—ornaments, fine clothes, perfumes, jewelry, and, by extension, skin and flesh. Buddhaghosa makes this point well: "A living body," he declares, "is just as foul as a dead one, only the characteristic of foulness is not evident[,] . . . being hidden by adventitious embellishments."[51] Upagupta would heartily agree; he tells Vāsavadattā, "When you were covered with clothes, ornaments, and all the other variegated externals conducive to passion, those who looked at you could not see you as you truly are, even when they made the effort. But now, free from outer trappings, your form may be seen in its intrinsic nature."[52]

The process of realizing the true nature of the body thus involves, preliminarily, a divestment of the self—the physical form—of its ornamentation and external coverings. Such a metaphor obviously is not without its repercussions in the Buddhist world. It highlights, for example, the importance of the precept against the wearing of jewelry, perfume, and bodily ornaments—an injunction incumbent upon all Buddhist monks and novices, but also observed by laymen and laywomen on ritual occasions when they visit monasteries on upoṣadha days and take on the so-called eight precepts (aṣṭānga-śīla). More specifically, in the context of the sacred biography of the Buddha, it recalls the paradigmatic event of the Great Departure: Gautama's own getting rid of the ornaments and jewels of royalty (as well as his hair) upon wandering forth from Kapilavastu. The same symbolism is consciously recalled in the ordination ceremony of Buddhist monks when, just prior to entering the order, the candidate for monkhood dresses up in his finest clothes and jewelry, only to shed these for the monastic garb.

The act of divestment—the getting rid of ornamentation—would thus seem to be a Buddhist rite of passage in many contexts. It symbolizes the abandonment of the householder's life (if only temporarily, as in the case of laypersons staying in temples on upoṣadha days), and it connotes the embarking on a quest on which the individual, free from external trappings, has a better chance of perceiving the self as it really is.

Seeing the Body as a Corpse

As the Vāsavadattā story suggests, however, divestment of bodily ornaments may only be symbolic of, or a prelude to, a more thoroughgoing divestment—one which looks through one's very skin and flesh and perceives the body even more directly for what it is: a temporarily animated corpse. Indeed, seeing the body as bones is not only the aim of the cemetery meditations, it is also the subject of many stories in the Buddhist tradition. Two of these in particular are worth recounting here, as they shed new light on the Vāsavadattā episode.[53]

The first is the tale of one of Upagupta's disciples who, having learned how to practice cemetery meditation, thinks he has attained enlightenment and so stops striving. One day, on his alms round, he visits the house of a beautiful woman who, coming out to offer him some food, smiles at him. He suddenly feels desire well up within him, loses his demeanor, and, befuddled, accepts her food in the sling of his bowl. Perceiving his excitement and now feeling desire herself, she marvels aloud that he has become so excited without even touching her hand or hearing her voice. The monk, ashamed, strives for control by practicing his cemetery meditation on her; taking the sight of her teeth as his focus, he realizes that they are bone, and, extending his visualization, he contemplatively transforms her entire body into the dry bones of a skeleton. He then attains arhatship.[54]

The second story is contained in the *Kalpanāmaṇḍitikā*. It is the tale of a courtesan and a Master of the Dharma who is left unnamed but who might well be a clone of Upagupta. Famous for his preaching skills, the master is so popular among the inhabitants of a certain town (also unnamed) that they all cease frequenting the local houses of prostitution and instead go to the monastery to hear his sermons.

The courtesans become very depressed at this, since they can no longer earn a livelihood. "Everyone in this town is going to listen to the Dharma," they complain, "and no one is coming to us." One young courtesan decides to rectify this situation. Accompanied by a bevy of maidservants and dancers, she sets out for the monastery. There a crowd has assembled to listen to the master, who has mounted a high seat to preach. Decked out like a goddess and proficient in all the sensuous arts, the courtesan positions herself right beneath his podium, where, visible to all but the preacher, she proceeds to seduce the crowd with her dancing. The men, gawking at her, poking each other in the ribs and pointing her out, increasingly give in to feelings of lust and lose all interest in the sermon.

The Master of the Dharma, unable to understand what is going on, finally looks down and sees the courtesan there. Then, rebuking her in no uncertain terms, he uses his magical powers to transform her into a sort of living skeleton—only bones devoid of all flesh and skin. "Formerly," he says to her, "you were a marvel of beauty, the focus of everyone's eyes. Now your skin and flesh are gone, you are nothing but bones. Formerly, you excited simple men, but now they have begun to see the Truth." The courtesan, humiliated, repents of her evil ways and takes refuge in the Buddha. The Master of the Dharma then magically restores her to her former self and preaches a sermon on the impermanence and impurity of the body and on the evils of desire and attachment. And among the crowd, some become stream-winners, and others become nonreturners, and still others—after renouncing the world and becoming monks—attain arhatship.[55]

In both of these stories, as well as in the tale of Upagupta and Vāsavadattā, the same basic structure can be detected. An unenlightened person (a pṛthagjana) in some way penetrates through superficial appearances (ornaments, clothes, skin, flesh) and comes to see the human body (their own or that of another) as though it were a living corpse or skeleton. He or she thereby attains enlightenment and enters one of the tracks of the Path. This vision is enlightening because it graphically sums up the three marks of reality as it is—suffering (duḥkha), impermanence (anitya), and non-self (anātman).

It should be noted, however, that this is not a vision of one's body as being dead, for in all of these stories, strikingly, the corpse or skeleton seen or imagined is not dead but alive. The vision is thus one which overcomes the dichotomy of life and death; in this sense, too, it may be thought of as liberating.

Arhatship and the Laity

We shall come back to this theme later, but first we need to return to the story of Upagupta and address the question of his ordination as a monk. As we have noted, an important feature of Upagupta's enlightenment is that, after becoming a nonreturner (anāgāmin), he switches tracks and becomes an arhat—with his ordination as a bhikṣu intervening between these two events.

Though Peter Masefield discounts such instances of track switching, this pattern should not surprise us. It is exactly the sequence found in many Sanskrit avadānas, in which becoming a monk or nun normally occurs just prior to arhatship.[56] The question must be asked, therefore, What is there about ordination that makes it possible for a stream-winner or once-returner or nonreturner like Upagupta to switch to the arhat track and thereby reduce the amount of time needed to exhaust his karmic residue?

The Pali nikāyas, in their systematization of these four tracks and treatment of them as four stages, have little to say about the relationship of ordination to the goal of arhatship. There seems, however, to be a tacit assumption that arhatship is not possible for the layperson, for, in these texts, "no evidence has been found of there having been lay arahants."[57]

This position—that arhatship was not possible for laypersons—did not, of course, go unchallenged. For instance, a sect known as the Uttarāpathakas ("those of [the region of] the Northern road") held as their first proposition that arhatship *was* possible for the layperson, a viewpoint which André Bareau considers to be proto-Mahāyānist.[58] Moreover, a number of important texts which may reflect similar Northwest Indian traditions also raise this possibility. For example, both the *Sūtra of the Bhikṣu Nāgasena* and the *Milindapañha* recount the story of King Milinda's interview with an elder named Āyupāla. The dialogue goes something like this: Milinda asks Āyupāla why he became a monk. "In order to lead a spiritual life and seek enlightenment," is his answer. "Is such a thing possible for one who has not shaved his head and abandoned the householder's life?" Milinda wants to know. "Yes, indeed," answers Āyupāla, who is perhaps acutely conscious of the lay status of the king in front of him. "Well then," replies Milinda, turning the tables on the monk, "your renunciation is of no use." He goes on to speculate that the relatively hard life-style Buddhist bhikṣus follow must be a karmic punishment for some evil deed they did in a past life. To this Āyupāla can give no answer.[59]

A solution to this problem is provided, however, in another version of this story contained in the *Tsa pao tsang ching*, a Sanskrit collection of Buddhist tales translated into Chinese in the fifth century.[60] There Milinda also reduces Āyupāla[61] to silence, but then he turns to ask the same question of Nāgasena: "Why bother becoming a monk, if one can obtain wisdom by remaining a layperson?" This time, an answer is given. The monk, explains Nāgasena, is like a young man sent on a thousand-mile journey and given a fast horse and the provisions and weapons he will need; he stands a good chance of promptly arriving at his goal. The layperson, on the other hand, is like an old man sent on the same trip, but on an old nag and with no supplies or arms; he may get there, but it will be more difficult and take him a lot longer.[62]

Nāgasena's response is noteworthy, for it implies that the whole question about ordination is perhaps wrong in the first place. It is not so much a question of whether ordination is necessary for arhatship as one of what part ordination plays in the quest for final liberation. And Nāgasena's answer to this is unequivocal: it speeds things up. Upagupta, as a lay anāgāmin, *could* wait for his final liberation after death in the rūpadhātu, but ordination makes possible his final liberation in this lifetime—something that comes only with entry onto the arhat track.

The question remains, however, How does it do this? What is there about ordination that accelerates the process of final liberation, especially for someone like Upagupta who has already entered the Path and had the basic Buddhist soteriological insight into the nature of reality?

It might be argued, of course, that becoming a monk affords one increased opportunities for meditation and meritorious pursuits and hence makes arhatship more readily attainable, but this is belied by the examples we are looking at here. Upagupta enters the arhat track *very shortly* after ordination. So do all the arhats of the *Avadānaśataka*, and even the Pali canon contains examples of monks who become arhats immediately upon ordination—as soon, in fact, as the hair is shaven from their heads.[63] It would seem, therefore, that it is not monastic life, but the ordination ritual itself that is somehow soteriologically efficacious.

Ordination and Arhatship

There are many ways of analyzing the Buddhist ritual of higher ordination (upasampadā), and scholars have approached it from a variety of perspectives.[64] Few, however, have paid sufficient attention to the continuities of theme that make ordination as a monk the culmination—rather than the beginning—of a process of spiritual development on the Buddhist Path. It is my intention, therefore, to view the ordination ceremony within a greater soteriological context and to examine it as a ritualization of the same pattern we have found so far in the stories of enlightenment that comes as a result of divestment and visionary ossification.

One of the mythological models for Buddhist ordination, at least as it is presently practiced in Theravāda countries, is the story of the Buddha's own Great Departure from his home in Kapilavastu. His divestment of his royal robes and ornaments, his cutting of his hair, and his giving up of his horse and companion are ritually reenacted in Buddhist ordination ceremonies to this day. It is important, however, to see that, in the biography of the Buddha, this divestment does not end with the Great Departure and is not limited to the Buddha's robes and ornaments. The theme is continued in the episode of the Buddha's extreme asceticism in which he divests himself further of his flesh and transforms himself graphically into a "living skeleton."[65]

The inclusion of this episode in the life story of the Buddha has generally been interpreted by scholars either as a piece of Buddhist propagandistic one-upsmanship designed to show ascetically inclined non-Buddhists that the Buddha could outdo them at their own penance, or as a way of making graphic the extreme of asceticism which the Buddha later rejects in advocating the Middle Way.[66] But if the Buddha's Great Departure is the hagiographical equivalent of his ordination, then it is curious to find him, after this "ordination," engaging in a "mistaken" path. The episode, moreover, has had a tenacious iconographic popularity, and it is probably more significant than these explanations indicate.

What is emphasized in the accounts of the Buddha's asceticism is not his hunger and suffering so much as his body's thinness—which, in fact, is described in terms that recollect cemetery-meditation traditions.[67] Indeed, in the Buddha biography preserved in the *Mūlasarvāstivāda Vinaya*, the culmination of his asceticism comes when, just prior to resuming eating, he goes to a cremation ground and lies down next to a corpse.[68] Within this context, the Buddha's asceticism is not so much an extreme practice to be discarded as it is a part of a myth, a graphic statement of his realization of the true nature of the body—in this case, his own. Seeing his body as a living skeleton enables him to realize its inherent involvement in suffering, impermanence, and non-self, and it leads logically to the next episode of his life: his enlightenment at Bodhgaya.

A curious detail in the *Majjhima Nikāya*'s account of the Buddha's asceticism supports this interpretation. There, his fasting is coupled with the practice of breath retention, and when he collapses in a faint, some deities see him and conclude "the recluse Gotama is dead." Others claim he is not dead yet but dying.[69] Still others, however, seeing the situation rightly, declare, "He is not dead, nor is he dying, *but he is an arhat, for the comportment of an arhat is just like this*."[70] I. B. Horner, puzzled by this last statement, speculated that either these deities were mistaken or they were using the word *arhat* in a pre-Buddhist sense.[71] It is nonetheless interesting to take their statement at face value: an arhat, think the deities, is someone who paradoxically looks both dead and alive at the same time.

This view is relevant to our study of the upasampadā rite, for, as we shall see presently, not only does this rite (like the Buddha's Great Departure) involve the divestment of royal robes and ornaments, but it also hints (like the Buddha's asceticism) at a cemetery meditation followed by arhatship.

One important part of the full ordination ritual, at least as it is presently practiced, is the ceremony in which a candidate is formally given by his preceptor (upādhyāya) the yellow robes he is to wear as a monk. This event is marked ritually by a teaching that the preceptor imparts to the candidate in the form of a mantra. As he gives the candidate the bundle of robes and ties the belt that goes with them around the candidate's neck, he repeats the Pali words: "Kesā, lomā, nakhā, dantā, taco; taco, dantā, nakhā, lomā, kesā" (hair, body hairs, nails, teeth, skin; skin, teeth, nails, body hairs, hair).[72] This is the tacapañcaka, the fivefold "formula of meditation on the perishable nature of the human body."[73] The bodily features listed here are, in fact, the first five in the more developed list of thirty-two parts of the body which is connected to the practice of aśubhabhāvanā—mindfulness of the impurity and non-self of the body. Those who, for one reason or another, are unable to recite the entire listing of thirty-two at the time of their ordination may substitute the fivefold formula for the whole.[74] In this sense, the tacapañcaka is really a cemetery meditation in a ritually encapsulated form, and its net effect is to engender in the ordinand a vision of reality as it is.

This message is reinforced by other aspects of the upasampadā rite. For example, the hair of the head, as the first item of the tacapañcaka formula, may be thought to stand for the body as a whole; with the hair's removal in the rite of tonsure, its perishable nature becomes particularly obvious.[75] Hair and its cutting have, of course, long been seen as important symbols by anthropologists, psychologists, and others.[76] From a psychological perspective, tonsure has been interpreted as castration and, by extension, chastity and renunciation.[77] Within the context we are dealing with here, however, it should perhaps equally be seen as symbolic of the corpse. Indeed, shaving the hair (and cutting the nails—another ritual performed at ordinations) was in India an important part of the preparation of the dead body for a funeral.[78] Thus, whatever psychosexual significance the tonsure of the Buddhist monk may hold, it may also symbolically associate him with the dead.

The monastic robes, too, can be thought of as cremation-ground rags by origin, scraps of shrouds taken from dead bodies;[79] and the monastic belt which is sometimes used in the ceremony to bind the candidate's hands or to bind his robes to his neck may (as we shall see in the next chapter) be homologized to the garland of corpses with which Upagupta binds Māra and by which he transforms him into a sort of living cemetery. The robes and belt are thus powerful symbols of death and impurity (especially in contrast to the ornaments and fine garb that have just been shed). By dressing up in them, the ordinand himself ritually becomes a "living corpse." He is thenceforth fed alms called piṇḍa, traditionally the term reserved for lumps of rice offered to the dead.[80]

The ritual of ordination as a whole, then, fits into the larger process of divestment of bodily ornamentation and gradual realization of the impure and corpselike nature of the body. Whatever else it entails, it is a sort of ritualized cemetery meditation that helps the candidate reflect on impurity, impermanence, and non-self, and thereby realize enlightenment.

Historians of religions looking at the upasampadā have tended to see it as a rite of passage or an initiation. Following Arnold Van Gennep, they have viewed it as a transition ritual involving separation from one state and incorporation into another.[81] Or, following Mircea Eliade, they have seen it as an initiatory scenario caught up in death and rebirth symbolism—death to the old ignorant mode of being and rebirth into a new state of spiritual knowledge.[82] Though such theoretical frameworks may be helpful within certain contexts, they can also be misleading when Buddhist ordination is viewed from the perspective of Buddhist soteriology. In this light, the upasampadā is not ritualized death and rebirth, for it is precisely death and rebirth that it seeks to put an end to.

I would suggest, rather, that the upasampadā be seen as the ritualization of arhatship, that is, the ritualization of the end of death and rebirth. This "end" is ritually difficult to symbolize, for it transcends the polar oppositions of ordinary discourse. For example, it would *not* do, as in certain other rites of passage (e.g., Christian baptism), to have the candidate for ordination symbolically "die" and then "revive" again. That would merely keep him in saṃsāra. Rather, he needs to remain dead, while paradoxically being alive at the same time.

The rite's solution to this symbolization problem is akin to that of the stories of the living skeletons, for, despite all the corpse and funereal symbolism involved in ordination, it is clear that the newly ordained monk is nonetheless alive. Though dressed in shrouds, though shaven (like a corpse), though the recipient and consumer of piṇḍa (like a dead spirit), he is at the same time a living human being. The net result is that the candidate for ordination becomes one who is *both* dead and alive, as the deities saw the Buddha during his extreme ascetic exercises. In the Buddhist context of saṃsāra, this state has definite soteriological implications: being dead, one cannot die again; and, being alive, one cannot be reborn. One thus puts to an end death and rebirth.

It is now perhaps understandable why ordination, if it is successful as a ritual,[83] should enable a stream-winner or a once-returner or a nonreturner to switch tracks and become an arhat: it short-circuits the process of death and rebirth yet to be undergone on the path to final liberation. The stream-winner and once-returner tracks, as we know, still lead one to death and rebirth—seven times for the former, once for the latter. The nonreturner track leads to death one more time. The arhat track alone leads neither to death nor to rebirth. Thus ordination, by enacting the end to *both* death and rebirth, eliminates the possibility of their occurring again and so places one squarely on the arhat track.

It is important not to fall back into the habit of thinking that arhatship is somehow a superior enlightenment experience. We have seen in this chapter that, for Upagupta, arhatship is not so much a dharmic as a karmic achievement. Ordination, too, is a karman (ritual act), and it makes arhatship possible by reducing the karmic residue yet to be expiated—residue which is defined in terms of deaths and rebirths still to be undergone.

Paths to Parinirvāṇa

Though Upagupta's ordination speeds up his final liberation by placing him on the arhat track, his arhatship as a monk should not make us discount his anāgāminship as a layman. Ordination and arhatship may be a path for those hurrying to attain parinirvāṇa, but we have seen enough (e.g., the First Council) to know that Buddhists in India had very mixed feelings about the desirability of quickly doing this. Slower tracks to that goal—slower but just as certain—were also valued, as was to become more and more evident with the rise of the Mahāyāna and the bodhisattva ideal.

Indeed, in our study of Upagupta's previous lives in chapter 2, we saw that Upagupta was associated with this slower path (whose paradigm was the bodhisattva Maitreya) and not with the fast path exemplified in the career of Śākyamuni. The same point was emphasized in some aspects of Upagupta's association with such slow-path masters as Mahākāśyapa and with long-haired mahallaka monks ordained late in life.

The story of Upagupta's ordination and arhatship corrects—or rather completes—this picture by showing him to be associated not only with this slow path, but with the faster one as well. Indeed, we shall find him later, in his dealings with his own monastic disciples at Mount Urumuṇḍa, urging them on to arhatship, something he does not do—at least not in the same way—when he preaches to the laity of Mathurā.[84]

Along with this difference in speed of final liberation goes another. Simply put, while the slower tracks tend to be oriented to the future, the quick one tends towards the past. It might seem strange to assert that those who move faster go backwards in time, but it makes sense in the context with which we are dealing. By accelerating their attainment of final liberation, those on the fast track (like the arhat Gavāṃpati) seek to catch up with Śākyamuni, whose parinirvāṇa is now in the past. On the other hand, the delay of parinirvāṇa, for whatever reasons, suggests (as in the example of Mahākāśyapa) a willingness or need to wait for Maitreya or for some other future time.

On the whole, Buddhists in the present find themselves caught between two Buddhas. Has the Dharma been saved or lost? Should one look backwards or forwards? Should one move quickly and join Gautama by following his example? Or should one stay in this world until final attainment under Maitreya at some future time? The answers depend on one's karmic situation as much as on anything else; but the questions bear asking, for they came to reflect real ideological divisions in the Buddhist community. These divisions were expressed symbolically in a variety of ways. For example, as we have seen, ornaments, hair, and flesh—all of which may be thought of as concealing the not-yet-developed bodily marks (lakṣaṇa) of a Buddha—may be associated with the orientation towards the future and towards the bodhisattva Maitreya, who himself is generally represented as crowned and bejewelled (like Gautama prior to his Great Departure).[85] On the other hand, the manifestation of the bodily marks, the absence of ornaments, a shaved head, and the visionary ossification that sees the body as bone may be associated with ordained arhats and the Buddha and with their attainment in the past. These polarities, among others, are presented in table 1.

Though this table is intended to help us muse some more about the legend of Upagupta and its broader relationship to its Indian Buddhist context, these polarities should not be extrapolated upon too liberally. For instance, though

Table 1
Paths to Final Liberation

	Slow Path to Parinirvāṇa	*Fast Path to Parinirvāṇa*
Orientation	Future	Past
Models	Maitreya Mahākāśyapa Bodhisattvas	Gautama Gavāṃpati Buddhas
Tracks	Anāgāmin Sakṛdāgāmin Srotāpanna	Arhat
Parinirvāṇa	In another time and place	In this lifetime and place
Bodily marks	Not visible (hidden)	Visible (achieved)
Physical traits	Ornaments Hair Flesh (rebirth)	No ornaments Shaved head Bone (relic)

ordination as a monk may be one of the things that can move a person from the slow path to the fast path, this does not mean that we can equate these two paths with a more general division between laypersons and monks. Ordination may make an enlightened person (that is, an anāgāmin, sakṛdāgāmin, or srotāpanna) into an arhat, but obviously not all laypersons are enlightened.

On the other hand, these polarities should probably not be viewed in too hard-set a manner. Indeed, one can see, looking at this table, that there is a variety of symbolic possibilities open to persons who may, in fact, bridge these two poles: Buddhas who wear ornaments, arhats who do not enter parinirvāṇa, monks who do not shave, etc. Part of the richness and appeal of the Upagupta legend is that it suggests that both these orientations are legitimate and perhaps ultimately complementary. Though associated with Maitreya's lineage, Upagupta as a monk becomes a Śākyaputra, a "son of Śākyamuni," and so is connected with Gautama as well. This does not negate his other loyalty; it completes it, for, in the total analysis, Upagupta's legend incorporates both paths. He highlights both the anāgāmin and arhat careers. Like all present-day Buddhists, caught betwixt and between Śākyamuni and Maitreya, he is oriented towards both the past and the future.

CHAPTER FIVE

Upagupta and Māra: Bhakti and the Buddha Body

UPAGUPTA'S ordination and arhatship set the stage for the story of his victory over Māra, the "Evil One" of the Buddhist tradition. "Upaguttena badho Māro" (by Upagutta Māra was bound): this, as we have seen, became one of the standard paradigms for the illustration of the instrumental case in the Pali grammars, and the legend it refers to—a miniature drama in its own right—was clearly the best-known episode of the Mathuran cycle of Upagupta's hagiography. In Southeast Asia, even to the present day, it is to protect against Māra that Upagupta is ritually invited to attend Buddhist festivities.

The traditions about Māra in Buddhism are multifarious. However, students of both Sanskrit and Pali sources generally agree that, in his mythology, Māra symbolizes the notion of Death in its broadest metaphorical sense. Thus, everything likely to keep one under the sway of death and rebirth, that is, in saṃsāra, is attributed to him. In this guise, Māra also symbolizes the figure of Lust (Kāma), and as such can take on the role of sexual tempter, seeking to lead astray celibate monks and nuns. As both Lust and Death, he is often said to be the lord of the realm of desire (kāmadhātu), reigning over the worlds of hellbeings, animals, hungry ghosts, humans, and lower gods from his residence in the Parinirmitavaśavartin Heaven.[1]

The dramatic legend of Upagupta's encounter with Māra was well known in the Sanskrit Buddhist world, and variants of it may be found in numerous sources.[2] In its fullest forms, it is divisible into five episodes: (1) A prologue in which the reasons for Upagupta's action against Māra are set forth; (2) a dramatic encounter in which Upagupta tricks Māra and binds him with a garland made of corpses; Māra, unable to free himself from these fetters, ends up having to return to Upagupta and recognize the superiority of the Buddha; (3) an agreement that Upagupta will free Māra from his fetters if Māra will display for him, here and now, the physical form of the Blessed One (rūpakāya); (4) a caveat that this may involve certain dangers; and finally (5) a climax in which Māra fashions for Upagupta the form of the Buddha, to which the elder, carried away by devotion, bows down and pays homage. We shall present and discuss each of these episodes in turn.

PROLOGUE: MĀRA'S PROVOCATION OF UPAGUPTA

Soon after [his ordination and arhatship] Upagupta was asked to preach at a Dharma meeting in Mathurā; and the word spread throughout the city that, on that day, a

Buddha without the marks named Upagupta would expose the Dharma. And hearing this, several hundred thousand persons set out [to hear him.] . . .

[Recalling] that the Buddha used to make an exposition of the Truth [of the Doctrine] only after first telling a preliminary tale [pūrvakālakaraṇīyā kathā], Upagupta too began by preaching a preliminary tale. However, just as he was going to expose the Dharma *per se*, a shower of strings of pearls rained down on the assembly, and the minds of those who were about to be converted were agitated [by greed], and not one of them came to see the Truth. The elder Upagupta carefully considered the matter of who was causing this disturbance, and he perceived that it was Māra.

Then, on the next day, a very large number of people arrived in Mathurā, thinking "Upagupta preaches the Dharma and strings of pearls come down in a shower!" And again, just when Upagupta had finished the preliminary discourse and was beginning to expose the Truth, Māra caused a shower of gold to rain down on the assembly; the minds of those who were about to be converted were agitated and not one of them came to see the Truth. Once more, the elder Upagupta considered the matter of who was causing this disturbance, and he perceived that it was Māra being even more wicked.

Then, on the third day, an even larger number of people came out, thinking "Upagupta preaches the Dharma and showers of pearls or gold fall down!" And again, on that day, he had finished the preliminary discourse and was just starting to expose the Truths, when, not very far off, Māra began a theatrical performance; heavenly instruments were played and divine apsāras started to dance, and the once dispassionate crowd, seeing the divine forms and hearing the heavenly sounds, were drawn away by Māra.

Māra was so pleased that he had attracted Upagupta's assembly to himself that he hung a garland around the elder's neck. . . . Then Upagupta reflected: "This Māra causes a lot of disturbance to the Teaching of the Blessed One; why was he not converted by the Buddha?" And he realized: "He is to be converted by me; it was with reference to his conversion, and as a favor to all beings, that the Blessed One predicted that I should become a Buddha without the marks!"[3]

In the prediction the Buddha makes about Upagupta during his journey to Northwest India (see chapter 1), as well as in the story of Upagupta's past life (see chapter 2), many things were foretold about the elder; he would become a Buddha without the marks and a prominent preacher, and he would live one hundred years after the Buddha's parinirvāṇa—but no mention at all was made of his future role as the converter and subduer of Māra. Curiously, this aspect of his career, central as it was to become, is missing from the Buddha's prediction, which otherwise functions as a sort of hagiographical blueprint for the whole of Upagupta's career.

In this passage, however, we see that an effort has been made to rectify this situation: Upagupta himself, wondering why the Buddha did not long ago convert Māra, is now said to realize that the Blessed One had reserved that task for him, even though he had not explicitly stated the fact. Much the same point is made in the *Lokapaññatti*; there we are told of a time when Māra prevented some villagers from giving any food to the Buddha on his begging rounds, so that, in the end, the Blessed One and his disciples had to resort to divine aid to nourish themselves. Astonished by their master's apparent unwillingness or inability to deal more directly with Māra, the Buddha's disciples questioned him about it. The Buddha replied that he was doing nothing in this case not because of a lack of power, but because the task of subduing Māra was not his—it had been "reserved" for the elder Upagupta in the future.[4]

Of course, the Blessed One several times during his lifetime outwitted and defeated Māra—most notably at Bodhgaya, where he routed him and his cohorts by reaching down a finger to touch the earth and call it to witness his merits. But this did little more to Māra than to chase him away. The notion that is assumed in the Upagupta legend—that Māra himself could actually be converted to Buddhism—does not seem to have occurred to the formulators of the Buddha's biography. Gradually, however, the developing doctrine of the potential salvation of *all* beings left its mark on Buddhist legend, and even Māra came to be thought of as having within him the possibility of enlightenment, like any other sentient being.[5]

In the *Divyāvadāna*, the immediate occasion for Upagupta's taming of Māra is set by the latter's systematic interruption of Upagupta's sermons. Interestingly, the Evil One's focus in this is not on the preacher (Upagupta), but on his audience (the people of Mathurā), whom he draws away, day after day, with magically fashioned distractions that prove to be more attractive to the Mathurans than the less-glamorous preaching of the Dharma. The same scenario is developed even more spectacularly in a number of other texts.[6]

How are we to interpret such dramatic interruptions? The *Divyāvadāna* (as well as the *Aśokarājāvadāna* and the *Aśokarājasūtra*) are very precise in specifying that Māra's interruptions take place just as Upagupta has finished the preliminary tales (pūrvakālakaraṇīyā kathā) and is about to embark on the exposition of the Truth of the Dharma (satyasamprakāśana).

It is generally agreed that these preliminary tales correspond to the first three sections of the so-called graduated discourse (anupūrvikathā; Pali: anupubbikathā), which is often mentioned in canonical sources and which was used by the Buddha (and by previous Buddhas), especially when preaching to non-Buddhists.[7] In its simplest form, the anupūrvikathā consisted of three discourses on giving (dāna), morality (śīla), and heaven (svarga). These were intended to promote in the minds of listeners a sense of the vanity of worldly existence and the necessity of self-sacrifice and so prepare them for the succinct exposition of the Dharma proper that followed.[8]

It is sometimes claimed that these preliminary edifying tales were all that was ever preached to the laity, while the Dharma proper was reserved for monks. This, however, is simply not the case, there being many instances in which laypersons were taught both.[9] Nonetheless, it is true that occasionally Buddhist preachers would decide not to expound immediately upon the Dharma proper, but to limit themselves to the preliminaries and wait until their listeners had demonstrated their readiness for further instruction. Thus, in the *Milindapañha*, the distinguished laywoman to whom Nāgasena preaches his first sermon has to ask him explicitly for a discourse not just "on matters of mere ordinary morality," but also on those things relating to arhatship.[10] Similarly, in the *Kalpanāmaṇḍitikā*, we find the tale of a monk who is asked to preach to King Aśoka's concubines, who are sitting behind a curtain. The monk, thinking that the women of the harem must surely be attached to worldly pleasures, decides to limit himself to a discourse on giving and other good works. After the discourse, one of the concubines comes out from behind the screen and asks him whether there is not more to the Buddha's Dharma than this! The monk, delighted but somewhat taken aback, replies that he had not realized he was being heard by a person of insight, and he then preaches to her the Four Noble Truths. She immediately attains the fruit of stream-winner.[11]

This pause or hesitation between the preliminary discourses and the exposition of the Dharma per se is significant; it marks a crucial transitional moment in a sermon, the moment in which the intimate connection between the pursuit of merit and the pursuit of enlightenment is revealed. It is no wonder, then, that Māra chooses to intervene at this crucial time, for it is precisely this connection that he wishes to obscure.

Like some buddhologists, Māra wants to disconnect the "kammatic" from the "nibbanic" aspects of Buddhist soteriology.[12] Indeed, in many ways, the magical displays of wealth and sensuality that he puts on—the pearls, the gold, the divine maidens—could be thought of as graphic depictions of the heavenly karmic rewards awaiting devotees who carry out the moral and meritorious practices described in Upagupta's preliminary tales. In this sense, Māra here is not only conceding but actually encouraging the practice of "kammatic" Buddhism, confident that he can obscure the relationship between it and the quest for liberation. This he does by interrupting the preaching of the Dharma per se, which alone can make that relationship clear and show Māra and his illusions to be what they truly are: death and defilement in disguise.

Not all versions of this story, however, focus on Māra's dramatic interruptions of Upagupta's sermons. Some texts, in fact, omit altogether the scene of Upagupta's preaching to the crowd and feature instead a detail that is mentioned only in passing in the *Divyāvadāna*: his being garlanded by Māra with flowers. In the *Kalpanāmaṇḍitikā*, for example, this is presented as the deed that first provokes Upagupta into counteraction:

Once, when the Venerable Upagupta was seated in a forest absorbed in meditation, Māra, the Evil One, crowned him with some garlands of flowers. When the elder came out of his trance, he saw the garlands around his neck, and, through his powers of discernment, realized that Māra had placed them there.[13]

A feature of the realm of desire, garlands of flowers are inappropriate adornments for monks and are, in fact, among those things forbidden in the Vinaya to all novices and bhikkhus.[14] By garlanding Upagupta with flowers, Māra is seeking to make him a perfumer once again, to negate his ordination, and to besmirch his reputation as a great meditator and monastic leader.[15] In one version of the story, Māra actually mocks Upagupta after he has garlanded him, summoning monks, nuns, laymen, and laywomen to come and look at him while he is still in a meditative trance, calling attention to his flowery ornaments and declaring, "Is this the one you call pure and virtuous?"[16]

Perhaps, however, there is an unstated ambiguity in this garlanding of Upagupta by Māra. It is one of the ironies of Buddhist practice that, although flowers are inappropriate for one who is a monk, they are perfectly acceptable for one who is a Buddha. Indeed, the Buddha's own monastic cell—his perfumed chamber (gandhakuṭī)—owes its name to the masses of flower offerings that were made to him there,[17] while in Sri Lanka and Southeast Asia today, flowers form a virtually obligatory part of any Buddha pūjā, their arrangement and display in front of the Buddha image, or Bodhi tree, or stūpa, or relic being a prominent feature of that ceremony.

The importance of these flowers lies not only in their beauty as offerings, but also in their ephemeral nature—in the fact that they fade. Thus, when making such flower offerings, a devotee typically repeats a formula which, in a classic Buddhist manner, emphasizes first the glory and then the impermanence of the blossoms:

> These beautiful, sweet-smelling, fresh-hued flowers
> I offer at the sacred Feet of the Noble Sage.
> With them the Buddha I adore, and
> through this merit may I attain liberation.
> Even as these flowers must fade; so does
> my body reach a state of destruction.[18]

Māra's offering of flowers to Upagupta is consequently fraught with ambivalence. On the one hand, they make him an unenlightened layman, for flowers are forbidden to monks. On the other hand, they have this effect only if Upagupta fails to see their impermanent nature; if he does realize their nature, the flowers become a different kind of offering, one which proclaims him a Buddha (image).[19] The story quickly makes clear which of these interpretations is indicated, for Upagupta immediately demonstrates that the garlands of flowers around his neck are really akin to decaying corpses, that is, objects of impurity and impermanence.

The Binding of Māra

In Kumārajīva's version of this story, Upagupta takes the garland of flowers which Māra has just placed around his neck and, in a feigned gesture of friendship and respect, offers it back to Māra, garlanding him in return. Upagupta then uses his magical powers to transform the flowers into the stinking corpse of a dead dog, which Māra, in horror, finds he cannot remove.[20] Thus bedecked with a corpse, Māra becomes a sort of walking cemetery, akin to the living skeletons we encountered in the previous chapter.

The same transformation is implicit or explicit in all other versions of the tale, sometimes with greater elaboration. The *Divyāvadāna*, for instance, recounts the episode as follows:

> Perceiving that the time for Māra's conversion had arrived, Upagupta took three carcasses—a dead snake, a dead dog, and a dead human being[21]—and, by means of his magical powers, he transformed them into a garland of flowers and went up to Māra. When Māra saw him [and the flowers], he was delighted and thought that he had won over even Upagupta. He resumed, therefore, his own bodily form, so that he could be garlanded in person. Then the elder crowned him with the snake carcass, and hung the dead dog around his neck, and the human corpse over his ears, and taking hold of them, he said:
>
> Just as you, sir, have bedecked me with a garland [of flowers]
> which is inappropriate for a man who is a monk,
> so I have bound around you these carcasses,
> which are unfit for a man of desires.
> Show whatever powers you have,
> but today you have encountered a son of the Buddha.[22]

This is not the first time that Māra is portrayed as being fettered with corpses in Buddhist literature. In their accounts of this episode, both Kumārajīva and the *Damamūkanidāna sūtra* tell a story of long ago when Upagupta and some other monks were meditating in a forest monastery. Seeing a starving dog, they fed it; but its stomach became bloated, and it soon died. As the dog lay dying, they recited the Dharma to it, and as a result the dog was immediately reborn in Māra's realm, the Parinirmitavaśavartin Heaven. In the process, however, it did not quite lose its foul odor, and Māra, noticing the stench, wondered who had caused this "stinking canine" to attain rebirth in his abode. Through his divine powers of perception, he realized that it was Upagupta and thereafter sought to get even with him.[23]

In other tales, it is not Upagupta but some other Buddhist saint who is responsible for plaguing Māra with foul-smelling bodies. Thus, in one text, the Buddha's disciples Mahākāśyapa and Ānanda, in order to combat Māra's attacks on the monks immediately before the First Council, grab him and bind three cadavers around his neck: that of a human, that of a dog, and that of a snake. Only when he agrees not to disrupt the Sangha's activities, so that the Council can do its work in compiling the Buddha's Teaching, do they free him from his fetters.[24]

Māra is not always bound with corpses. In the *Mahāsamnipāta ratnaketu dhāraṇī sūtra*, which contains in its first three chapters a sort of mini Māra epic, the Buddha himself, after converting most of Māra's followers, binds him around the neck with a "fivefold fetter" (pañcabandhana).[25] It is not altogether clear what is meant by this term. In the *Upāyakauśalya sūtra*, the pañcabandhana is a punishment imposed by a king on a prisoner; it can be burst by a magical charm, but it is not evident exactly what it is.[26] In the *Śūraṃgamasamādhi sūtra*, an early Mahāyāna text that also gives an account of the binding of Māra, the "five fetters" are described as attached to the two arms, two legs, and neck of Māra; these are held fast by the magical force of the sūtra itself, every time it is recited.[27] In the Pali canon and the *Divyāvadāna*, the same word is used to describe the torture of the five fetters in hell, a sort of crucifixion which consists of being pinned down by five iron stakes driven through the two hands, the two feet, and the heart.[28] This hardly seems to be what is implied in the other texts, however, even though the connotation that by using the fivefold fetter Upagupta is transforming Māra's world into a sort of hell should be noted.

It may also be that we have here a confusion between the terms *pañcabandhana* and *kāyabandhana*, a word which designates a monastic belt. Indeed, in the *Lokapaññatti*, we find that, after temporarily fettering Māra with the corpse of a dog, Upagupta then binds him with the belt of his monastic robe, his kāyabandhana. This he fastens around Māra's waist and then magically stretches it out so that he can tie it around a mountaintop. There Māra remains bound for seven years, while Aśoka carries out his festival of merit making.[29]

This particular rendition of the episode became well known in Southeast Asia, where, in fact, it passed into the iconography. For example, the large image of Upagupta at Wat Uppakhut in Chiang Mai (Northern Thailand) shows the elder holding the end of his monastic belt, ready to bind Māra (who is not represented); a mural representing the legend of Upagupta at Wat Bunnyavat in Lampang (Northern Thailand) depicts Māra with a dead dog around his neck actually tied to a rock by a monastic belt (see fig. 2); and a popular illustration of the Upagupta chapter of the *Phra Paṭhamasambodhikathā* shows Māra with Upagupta's belt tightly fastened around not his waist but his neck—exactly where the corpse of the dog had been tied.[30]

We have seen enough of the cadaverous connotations of the Buddhist mo-

Fig. 2. The Binding of Māra. Detail from a Mural at Wat Bunnyavat, Lampang, Thailand

nastic garb to be not surprised by this association of the monk's belt with corpses; but, in order to understand more specifically the symbolism of what is going on here, we need to turn once again to the study of the Buddhist ordination ceremony.

In his analysis of ordination rites in Laos, Cambodia, and Thailand, Paul Lévy has highlighted one particular ritual detail which occurs at the beginning of the ordination ritual when the candidate formally receives from his preceptor the robes he is to don later. This is the "ritual fettering" of the candidate with the belt of his monastic robe, which is ceremonially bound around his neck and/or around his outstretched clasped hands.[31] Alternatively, this binding may take place when the candidate is still in his home and his sponsor gives him his robes to take to the monastery.[32] In either case, the binding with the belt occurs right after the candidate has given up the fine clothes and ornaments and garlands that epitomize lay life.

In light of our earlier discussion of ordination and of its cemetery-meditation affinities, Upagupta's act of binding Māra, whether it be with a corpse or with a monastic belt, should thus be thought of as signifying not only Māra's imprisonment, his capture, or his physical restraint, but also his "ordination," his soteriological transformation, his introduction to the Buddhist Path. It comes as no surprise, then, to find in the *Mahāsamnipāta ratnaketu dhāraṇī sūtra* that the binding of Māra leads to his formally taking refuge in the Triple Gem.[33] Even more dramatically, in the *Lokapaññatti*, Māra actually makes a vow—a praṇidhāna—to attain Buddhahood himself in some future lifetime. Tied by Upagupta's belt to a mountaintop for seven years, Māra has time to reflect and ends up declaring: "If I have in me any roots of merit, . . . may I sometime in the future become a Buddha full of compassion, focussed entirely on the well-being of all creatures." Hearing this, Upagupta frees Māra and assures him that the Blessed One himself once predicted that Māra would certainly become a Buddha.[34]

In the *Divyāvadāna*, however, things do not happen so quickly. As king of the realm of desire, Māra is not immediately willing to renounce his old ways and convert to the faith he has so long opposed. The story of his binding is thus followed not by his immediate submission to Upagupta and Buddhism, but by an interlude recalling his attempts to free himself from his fetters: unable to remove the carcasses from his person, Māra seeks the assistance of various other gods—Mahendra, Rudra, Upendra, Draviṇeśvara, Yama, Varuṇa, Kubera, Vasāva, and finally Lord Brahmā himself—but all to no avail; not one of them is able to undo what has been done by a disciple of the Buddha.[35]

For Māra, then, the whole cosmos, from the deepest hells to the highest heavens, has become a cemetery, a place of intolerable suffering, as it was for the nāgas whom the Buddha burnt into submission during his conquest of the Northwest. This is an important aspect of Buddhist enlightenment—the awakening to the truly cosmic dimensions of suffering, the realization that there is no place in this world that one can go to escape it—except the refuge of the Buddhist Path. Thus, just like those nāgas who, in the end, had to seek shelter in the Buddha's shadow, Māra has to return to Upagupta, still suffering but subdued, and imploring Upagupta to release him.

Interestingly, in doing this, Māra focusses not on the glory and power of Upagupta, but on the greatness and compassion of the Buddha; and, remembering the many times when he had personally harassed the Blessed One, Māra is thankful that the Buddha never did anything unkind to him. In contrast, Upagupta's actions in binding him now appear to Māra as crude and cruel, and (none too contritely) he accuses the elder of having abandoned the compassion he should have inherited from the Buddha: "It is true I caused injuries with all my power to Gautama . . . yet he remained undisturbed in his meditation on compassion. But in spite of being a follower of Gautama, you are violent and aggressive. You, ārya, have put me under fetters as soon as I tried the slightest joke."[36]

Rather than take offense at these accusations, Upagupta merely encourages Māra in his newly found respect for the Buddha, seeking to foster in him even greater feelings of faith and devotion. "Yes," he tells him, "you were guilty of many offenses against the Blessed One, [but] by never saying anything unkind to you, . . . he engendered devotion in your heart." This, Upagupta adds, is crucial, for "even a little devotion towards [the Buddha] gives the fruit of Nirvāṇa to the wise."[37]

Māra needs no further encouragement. Continuing his reflection on the glory and benevolence of the Buddha, he gets carried away, and, "his hairs quivering like the buds of a kadamba tree . . . and with a mind filled with faith in the Blessed One, he prostrates himself fully [in front of Upagupta], recollecting the virtues of the Tathāgata."[38]

The contrasts that Māra draws in these passages between the Buddha and Upagupta are revealing; in effect, Upagupta is here being maligned by Māra as a Hīnayānist disciple (śrāvaka), as one who does not have the virtues and especially the patience and great compassion (mahākaruṇā) of a Mahāyānist bodhisattva or Buddha.[39] A number of versions of the story make this connection quite explicit. One text, for example, has Māra declaring, "The Buddha was endowed with great virtue and great compassion, but you śrāvakas are terrible people."[40] In another, we find Upagupta himself stating, "The Buddha is greatly compassionate . . . but I am a man of the Lesser Vehicle [Hīnayāna]; I cannot do as he does."[41] And in the *Lokapaññatti*, where Māra actually makes a vow to become a Buddha, he explains his decision by saying to Upagupta, "Disciples such as you are compassionateless [akāruṇika]; if I were to become such a disciple, I, too, would be compassionateless."[42]

There is, of course, a wonderful irony in this: Māra has just been bested by Upagupta's superior powers and forced to submit to him; yet, in his very submission, he criticizes him and opts for a way out that will enable him eventually to become "better" than Upagupta—that is, to become a Buddha rather than a śrāvaka.

The notion that Māra, archfoe and consistent opponent of the Buddha, could be converted into a devout Buddhist and that he could, in fact, aspire to full Buddhahood also reflects an important shift in Buddhist notions of evil and soteriology. It is sometimes maintained that the problem of evil, especially as it came to be formulated in monotheistic contexts, simply did not exist in India. Mircea Eliade, for example, even went so far as to declare that "in India not only is there no conflict between Good and Evil; there is even a confusion between them."[43] Such statements may make sense from the perspective of Vedantic philosophy, in which all distinctions are ultimately a product of illusion, but this does not mean that the problem of evil was not reflected upon or talked about.

Wendy Doniger has pointed out that "scholars have overlooked the problem of evil in Indian thought because they have sought it in philosophy rather than in mythology."[44] Focussing on Puranic materials, she goes on to present a rich body of Hindu myths and legends that obviously wrestle with the question.

Two points that she raises may help us here in our consideration of the myth of Upagupta and Māra. First, one of the basic frameworks for the problem of evil in India is the potential conflict between duty to one's station in life (svadharma) and one's more general, eternal (sanātana) dharma. For example, it is the duty (svadharma) of demons to be demonic, to fight the gods, rape, loot, pillage, and kill. It is their eternal duty (sanātana dharma) not to do these things.[45] This conflict, however, was not always resolved or felt in the same ways throughout the history of Hinduism; more specifically, a change in its perceived nature came about with the rise of bhakti. As Doniger points out, "In early myths, svadharma usually prevails when any conflict arises, and demons are expected to behave demonically, but in many of the later bhakti texts, 'good' demons are allowed to abandon their svadharma."[46]

This change points to a second context that is of importance in understanding the problem of evil in India: mythological beings are not eternally defined as being solely good or solely evil. Hence we find, in Hindu myths, the paradoxes of "good demons" and "evil gods."[47] In part this is due to the possibilities offered by multiple rebirth; in part it is due to the coalescence in Indian mythology of conversion and conquest, so that one accepts the worth of one's conqueror. For example, the demon king Prahlāda, in one version of his myth, becomes a devout worshipper of his archfoe, Viṣṇu, and recognizes him as supreme god when he is unable to vanquish him. "Prahlāda is 'enlightened' by being conquered by Viṣṇu in battle."[48]

All of this, when translated into Buddhist terms, may be useful in understanding the case of Māra. Though technically Māra is a god, he also "appears as a demon and is even given the name of a demon."[49] And although no mention is made in the Buddhist context of his svadharma, it is in his nature to behave demonically, to represent Lust and Death and to attempt to counter at every turn the spread of the Buddha's Doctrine. Māra is thus, at least in early Buddhist texts, a demon by definition, and there is no hint that his nature might be changed by an act of conversion. The Buddha does not convert him, but merely chases him away.

By the time the story of Upagupta is formulated, however, new possibilities for Māra's transformation do occur. In part, as we have seen, this reflects the growth of Mahāyānist notions such as the developing doctrine of the potential Buddhahood of all beings, including the Evil One. But more specifically, this transformation, as in Hinduism, reflects the growth of bhakti. What finally awakens Māra is not just his conquest by Upagupta, but his devotion to the Buddha, his realization of the power and glory and venerability of the Blessed One.

The question sometimes arises whether Māra's submission to Upagupta and the Buddha in this story is genuine or whether it is just more of his trickery. Has he really been converted, or is he just pretending to feel veneration for the Buddha in order to get Upagupta to free him from his fetters? Is he genuinely praising the Blessed One, or is this just another ploy? Such suspicions are understandable,[50] but they are belied by the apparent seriousness with which some texts seem to have taken Māra's change of heart. In the *Divyāvadāna*, Upagupta does not simply convert Māra, he also extracts from him a promise that he will *never again* harass any Buddhist monks.[51] Logically, this should imply that, in Buddhism, Māra will no longer be a problem, that he has been permanently conquered, converted, and eclipsed as the Evil One. That, in fact, is the assumption in a number of sources which present the whole story of Upagupta's taming of Māra as an explanation of why it is that Māra does not come anymore, as he used to in canonical times. As Kumārajīva, for example, put it: "If people ask you this question: 'In days of yore, Māra used to come to pester and confuse men of learning; why does he not come anymore?' the answer is, 'It is thanks to Upagupta.'"[52]

This does not mean that all Buddhists thought that Māra's eclipse was a total one. For many, though his transformation was genuine, he still symbolized the forces of saṃsāra. Thus, in the "Acintyabuddhaviṣayānirdeśa sūtra," where Māra also vows never to interfere again with the preaching of the Dharma, the point is made that, though Māra may have been converted, his cohorts have not been; untamed, they remain behind, determined to distract the minds of devotees.[53] Similarly, in Southeast Asia (as we shall see), despite his *Lokapaññatti* vow for future Buddhahood, Māra continues to be a disrupting force and a threat to Buddhist festivals.

The Request to Display the Rūpakāya

The story of Upagupta and Māra might have ended with the episode of the latter's change of heart, but it does not. Instead, in all versions, that episode gives way to the even more famous tale of Māra's taking on the form of the Buddha and Upagupta's worshipping that form. For, after subduing Māra, witnessing his conversion, and agreeing to release him from his fetters, Upagupta imposes on him a number of conditions. In most versions of the story, these are said to be two. The first has already been mentioned: Māra must promise to stop harassing Buddhist monks, "for as long as the Dharma shall last."[54] To this Māra agrees, but then Upagupta puts forward a second condition and demands of him a more personal favor. In Kṣemendra's words:

> And for me . . . you will do this favor:
> you will display the form of the Sugata
> who is gone beyond.
> I have seen your skills as an actor;
> you can imitate everything,
> and I greatly long for
> a display of the Blessed One.[55]

The *Divyāvadāna* develops this episode more fully:

> Upagupta said: "[Māra], you yourself know that I was initiated into the monastic life one hundred years after the Blessed One entered parinirvāṇa, therefore:
>
> Although I have seen the Dharma-body [Dharmakāya],
> I have not seen the physical body [rūpakāya][56]
> of the Lord of the Triple World
> who resembles a mountain of gold.
> Thus, in return for this 'very greatest favor'
> [of introducing you to the venerability of the Buddha
> I want you] to make manifest here
> the physical form of the Buddha.
> Truly, nothing would be more pleasing to me
> than this, for I am eager [to see]
> the body of the Daśabala."[57]

This request makes good sense in terms of our story. First, Upagupta was born too late to have been able to meet the Buddha in person, so he takes this opportunity to rectify that situation and view his form.[58] Second, Māra has just been shown to have the potentiality for Buddhahood; it is only mythological that this should be confirmed by his "becoming" the Buddha, if only temporarily. Māra is able to do this not only because of his powers of magical self-transformation, but also because he, being a long-lived god, *has* seen the Buddha, at Bodhgaya and elsewhere, and so knows what he looks like. The theme of exchange also should not go unnoticed here. Upagupta has, through his teaching, shown Māra the Buddha's Doctrine—his Dharmakāya; now it is time for Māra, in return, to show Upagupta the Buddha's physical form—his rūpakāya.

It is important to be clear about the distinctions between these two forms. Clearly, our story assumes the early two-body theory of the Buddha, according to which the Blessed One's actual physical form with which he was born at Lumbinī (his rūpakāya) was contrasted to the body of his Doctrine (his

Dharmakāya). The latter initially did not have the transcendent and eternalist connotations it was to acquire in the Mahāyāna, for it meant nothing more (and nothing less) than the corpus of the Buddha's teachings, his Doctrine.[59]

Both of these "bodies" of the Buddha were thought of as being in some sense visible. The rūpakāya could be seen with the ordinary eye of flesh (maṃsacakṣu), while anyone who understood the Truth of the Buddha's Doctrine, who had experienced initial enlightenment and entered the Buddhist Path, could be said to have seen the Dharmakāya. This was done with the Dharma-eye (dharmacakṣu) or the eye of wisdom (prajñācakṣu).[60]

As long as the Buddha was alive, obtaining this double vision of him presented no major problems. After all, he was physically present in the world, and, thanks to his preaching, enlightenment (the seeing of the Dharma) was then relatively easy. A story preserved in the *Divyāvadāna* is noteworthy in this regard. It tells of the monk Śroṇa Koṭikarṇa, who, under his teacher Mahākātyāyana, had studied Buddhist doctrine, abandoned the defilements, and attained arhatship. Nonetheless, he had never actually seen the Buddha, even though the latter was still living. He therefore asked his teacher for permission to go and visit him. "Master," he declared, in terms closely reminiscent of Upagupta's, "thanks to you I have seen the Blessed One in his Dharmakāya, but I have not yet seen him in his rūpakāya. I want to go see the Blessed One also in his rūpakāya." And, upon receiving his teacher's permission, he voyaged to where the Buddha was.[61]

With the death and parinirvāṇa of the Buddha, however, seeing the Buddha's physical form demanded more than a simple journey, and generations of Buddhists were born who, like Upagupta, had never actually laid eyes on the departed Master. Some Buddhists were content to resign themselves to this absence of the Buddha's physical body, or, in the face of it, to advocate the superiority of seeing his Dharmakāya.[62] Others accepted instead a bifurcation of the Buddhist community along Buddha-body lines, the Dharma being reserved for the monks and the relics (what was left of the rūpa) for the laity.[63]

The Sarvāstivādin tradition, however, seems to have retained a fascination for *both* the dharmalogical and the rupalogical dimensions, hence Upagupta's desire for a view of the Buddha's physical form, even after he has already seen his Dharmakāya. Indeed, Upagupta's chief epithet—that he is a Buddha without the marks—would appear to reflect this longing, for it might alternatively be said that he is one "for whom the Buddha has no marks," that is, one who has never been able to see the Buddha's physical body. Upagupta thus may be thought of as suffering from a rupalogical deficiency, which he seeks to make up by his request to Māra. More specifically, as an alakṣaṇaka-Buddha, what Upagupta is lacking are the thirty-two rupalogical marks of the Great Man. These marks of the Mahāpuruṣa take time and a lot of merit making to develop—"innumerable koṭis of thousands of aeons."[64] Hence this mark-adorned body of a Buddha is so difficult to meet, for "Buddhas are as rare as the blossoms of the uḍumbara tree."[65]

Thus, in seeking to contemplate the rūpakāya of the Blessed One, in seeking to meet the Buddha, Upagupta is trying to leapfrog ahead karmically and speed up his own rupalogical development. In this, he is doing much the same thing that Śākyamuni did ninety-one kalpas ago, when he sped ahead of Maitreya and skipped over nine kalpas of merit making by ecstatically contemplating for a week the mark-adorned body of the Buddha Puṣya.

Upagupta's endeavor to speed things up suggests that the vision he obtains from Māra of the Buddha's body is, in its effect, homologous to his ordination as a monk. In chapter 4, we saw that Upagupta's ordination resulted in his moving to the faster track of arhatship, a move that we interpreted as a karmic one involving putting an end to the possibility of further death and rebirth. Here, it would seem, we have a repetition and further development of the same theme. As a Buddha without the marks, Upagupta is still on the slow track; he has never met the Buddha and is still associated with Maitreya, who likewise does not yet have the marks (or rather whose marks are not yet manifest, being still hidden by his ornaments). When Māra shows Upagupta the rūpakāya, the faith and devotion he develops towards it help him to realize this faster rupalogical track. For, as we shall see, bhakti, like ordination, can accelerate the process of final liberation.

The Dangers of Idolatry

Upagupta's vision and the bhakti it elicits, however, are not without their potential pitfalls, and Māra, before agreeing to take on for Upagupta the form of the Buddha, imposes certain conditions. As he puts it in the *Lokapaññatti*: "I will create for you [the body of the Buddha], but you must not revere me!"[66] The *Avadānakalpalatā* is equally telegraphic: "You," says Māra, "must not bow down before me when I have taken the form of the Sugata."[67] The *Divyāvadāna* once again provides a fuller version of the episode:

> "When," [Māra declares] "all at once you look upon me wearing the costume of the Buddha, do not prostrate yourself [before me] out of respect for the qualities of the Omniscient One. If, your mind tender from your recollection of the Blessed One, you should happen to bow down, I will be consumed by fire, O mighty one. Do I have the power to endure the prostration of one whose passions are gone? I am like the sprouts of the eranda tree that cannot bear the weight of an elephant's trunk."
>
> "So be it," said the elder, "I will not bow down before you."
>
> "Then wait a bit," said Māra, "while I enter the forest. Previously, determined to deceive Śūra, I created . . . a Buddha body that had the lustre of fired gold. I will now create that same body that brings joy to the eyes of men . . ."
>
> Upagupta, agreeing to this, then removed the carcasses [from around Māra's neck] and stood by, anxiously awaiting the sight of the form of the Tathāgata.[68]

It is apparent from this passage that there are two dangers involved in the display of the rūpakāya that Māra proposes to undertake: a danger to himself and a danger to Upagupta. The danger to himself he states explicitly: if Upagupta forgets that what he is seeing is an illusion—a magically fashioned image of the Buddha—and bows down to it, Māra will be destroyed, "consumed by fire."

This is not mere melodrama on Māra's part. It was a well-established tradition in the Sanskrit Buddhist world that nonenlightened persons were not able to endure the prostrations of enlightened ones. Thus, when the Buddha was taken as an infant to the temple of the Śākya tribe to pay obeisance to the goddess Abhayā, he did not bow down to her, because, had he done so, her head would have immediately split into seven pieces.[69] Later, he likewise refrained from prostrating himself in front of his parents, not wishing to do them harm.[70] Māra is thus worried, with good cause, that he will simply not be able to withstand the obeisance of Upagupta, an enlightened master who is like the Buddha.

The situation is also fraught with potential danger for Upagupta. No mention is made of any dire consequences that might befall him were he to commit idolatry, but it should be remembered that, despite his recent conversion, it is Māra whom he is requesting to take on the form of the Buddha—and Māra, in the past, has done this only in order to trick or test certain individuals. Indeed, as Māra himself points out, he will take on the appearance of the Tathāgata *just as he did once in order to deceive Śūra*, one of the chief lay disciples of the Buddha.[71]

Śūra is mentioned in the *Anguttara Nikāya* as foremost among those male lay followers who are of unwavering loyalty.[72] For his story, however, we must turn to the *Kalpanāmaṇḍitikā*[73] or to Buddhaghosa's commentary on the *Anguttara Nikāya*.[74] Śūra (Pali: Sūra or Sūra Ambaṭṭha) was a rich and avaricious merchant from Śrāvastī who supported the heretics until, one day, the Buddha came to his door. Impressed by the Buddha's demeanor, Śūra invited him in and served him a meal. After eating, the Buddha preached a sermon; this further impressed Śūra, who quickly converted to Buddhism and attained the stage of stream-winner. The Buddha then went away. Some time later, however, Māra decided to test Śūra's newfound faith. Able to transform himself into any shape, Māra took on the form of the Buddha, complete with the thirty-two marks of the Mahāpuruṣa; and, with robes and bowl, he went to Śūra's house.

Śūra was surprised to see him. "Bhante," he exclaimed, "just a while ago you finished your meal in this house and departed; why have you returned?" "Ambaṭṭha," came the reply, "when I taught you the Dharma, there was one thing I taught without properly thinking about it. I said all five skandhas are impermanent, marked by suffering, and without self. But this is not true of all of them; some of them are actually permanent, stable and eternal." Śūra reflected on this and then decided that, since Buddhas do not teach anything without thinking about it first, this must not be the Buddha in front of him. "You are Māra," he declared, and then, proclaiming *all* karmic constructions to be impermanent (sabbe saṃkhārā aniccā), he chased Māra away from his door.[75]

Edmund Hardy has claimed that there is no real connection between this tale of Śūra and that of Upagupta and Māra, and he goes on to talk about parallels with the story of the Christian saint Palladius, a fifth-century desert father who was tempted by Satan appearing to him in the form of Christ.[76] A number of features of the Śūra story, however, *are* relevant to an understanding of our text. First, it shows clearly that one of the principal dangers with Māra lies in not seeing the impermanence of things, in falling into the illusion that certain things (the body of the Buddha among them) are stable and eternal. It is no accident that Māra tries to trick Śūra into falsely believing in the permanence of the skandhas, and, significantly, Śūra, in chasing Māra away, uses almost as a mantra the doctrinal proclamation "sabbe saṃkhārā aniccā"—all conditioned things are impermanent. Similarly, Upagupta will have to struggle to reconcile his sight of the Buddha with his knowledge that the Buddha's body has gone to destruction.

Second, the Śūra story raises again the important theme of the necessity of seeing through outward physical appearances, applying it this time not to courtesans or beautiful women, but to the physical form of the Buddha himself. Śūra does not trust his vision of the Buddha's rūpa; instead, he trusts his knowledge of the Buddha's Dharma. As he puts it in the *Kalpanāmaṇḍitikā*: "You can mislead the eye of flesh, but you cannot mislead the eye of Dharma."[77] There is a certain irony, then, in Upagupta's craving for this vision of the rūpakāya, especially in light of the stories we examined in chapter 4 in which beautiful bodies were consistently denigrated and a vision of a person as a skeleton was shown to be a glimpse of the body as it truly is—in all its impermanence. In this context, the glorification of the Buddha's physical form—his flesh—is potentially problematic, for the Buddha's body as it truly is (in all of its impermanence) would best be represented not by the glorious marks of the Great Man, but by the Buddha's relics, his body as bones. For the relics, quite apart from what they say about the ongoing presence of the *Buddha*, do convey a very clear message about the *Buddha's body*—the message that it is no more.

The Worship of the Buddha Image

With all of this in mind, we are now in a position to focus on Upagupta's reactions to his sight of the rūpakāya. It is no mean show that Māra stages,[78] for he displays not only the form of the Blessed One, but a veritable maṇḍala of beings:

> Then Māra, after he had gone far into the forest and magically taken on the form of the Buddha, emerged again from that wood like an actor wearing a bright costume. . . . He fashioned the form of the Blessed One with a pure fathom-wide nim-

bus, and the forms of the elder Śāriputra on the Buddha's right, and the elder Mahāmaudgalyāyana on his left, and the Venerable Ānanda behind him, his hands occupied with the Buddha's bowl. And he also created the forms of the other great disciples, starting with the elders Mahākāśyapa, Aniruddha, and Subhūti; and he made manifest the figures of 1,350 monks gathered in a half moon around the Buddha. Then Māra approached the elder Upagupta, and Upagupta rejoiced, thinking "this is what the form of the Buddha looked like!" With a joyful heart, he rose from his seat and exclaimed:

"Woe! Woe! to that pitiless impermanence
that cuts off forms with qualities such as these!
For the Great Sage's body which is like this
has been touched by impermanence
and has suffered destruction."

Then, with his mind so intent on the contemplation of the Buddha that he came to think that he *was* seeing the Blessed One, Upagupta drew near to that appearance; he clasped his hands together and exclaimed: "Ah! The splendid form of the Blessed One! . . .

His face surpasses the red lotus in beauty,
his eyes the blue lotus,
his splendor a forest of flowers,
the pleasantness of his mind
the moon in its full brilliance.
He is deeper than the great ocean,
more stable than Mount Meru,
and brighter than the sun."

. . . .

Then Upagupta, because of his affection for the Wholly Enlightened One, forgot his agreement [with Māra], and, thinking that this image *was* the Buddha, he fell at Māra's feet with his whole body, like a tree cut off at the root.

This worried Māra who said: "Please, Reverend Sir, please! Do not transgress our agreement!"

"What agreement?" said the elder.

"Did your reverence not promise," asked Māra, "that he would not bow down before me?"

Then the elder Upagupta got up off the ground, and said with a stammering voice:

"Of course, I know that the Best of Speakers
has gone altogether to extinction,
like a fire swamped by water.
Even so, when I see his figure,
which is pleasing to the eye,
I bow down before that Sage.
But I do not revere you!"

"How is it," replied Māra, "that I am not revered when you thus bow down before me?"

"I shall tell you," said the elder. . . .

> "Just as men bow down
> to clay images of the gods,
> knowing that what they worship
> is the god and not the clay,
> so I, seeing you here,
> wearing the form of the Lord of the World,
> bowed down to you,
> conscious of the Sugata,
> but not conscious of Māra."[79]

It is clear here that Upagupta, starting off with a fairly firm notion that what he is seeing is *not* the Buddha, gradually gets carried away by his devotion and comes to think that it is. Forgetting his agreement with Māra, he prostrates himself in front of him.[80] What is noteworthy is that Upagupta then insists that he has not really bowed down to Māra, and, to explain himself, he uses the analogy of image worship: Māra is to the Buddha what a clay image is to a deity. It is not the clay (Māra) that one worships, but the deity (Buddha). This analogy raises the whole question of the worship of the Buddha image, a question that needs some elucidation here.

Art historians have often noted that the passage we are discussing may, in fact, be one of the earliest references to image worship in Buddhist literature.[81] For centuries, Buddhists chose not to represent anthropomorphically the figure of their Master. Instead, as we saw in chapter 1, they used certain symbols—empty thrones, trees, wheels, etc.—to indicate his absence. Actual Buddha images, it is commonly asserted, were first made in Northwest India, probably in the Mathurā region, in the first century C.E.[82]

The question of Buddhist attitudes towards images of the Buddha has long been a matter of debate among scholars. It has often been observed that Buddhists commonly act towards the Buddha image in ritual ways, making offerings, prayers, and prostrations that could easily be understood as worship and as assuming some sort of presence of the Buddha or some kind of communication with him in the statue. Yet Buddhists just as commonly deny that this is the case; the Buddha in parinirvāṇa, goes the argument, is no longer of this world and so cannot be expected to be in or connected to this image, or to hear or respond to the petitions of his devotees.[83]

Various people have tried in various ways to explain this paradox. Many assert that these are not really acts of worship but acts of remembrance, expressions of gratitude to a dead master for his teaching of the Dharma. Richard Gombrich has suggested that we must take the schizophrenia involved here more seriously; while Buddhists *cognitively* know that the Buddha in Nirvāṇa is not in the Buddha image—and they will often mouth that viewpoint when asked—they nonetheless *affectively* feel his presence there and express that in the ritual context.[84] Stanley Tambiah, critical of Gombrich, has taken a somewhat different tack which has the advantage of deontologizing the whole question. He proposes to see the Buddha image as an "indexical symbol" with a double role: relating back to the Buddha by a conventional semantic rule and, at the same time, relating pragmatically, or existentially, to the image's immediate context—that is, to the devotees in front of it.[85]

All of these solutions, however, take as their object the problem as it exists in Theravāda countries. In the Sarvāstivādin context, with its particular notion of time, the situation is somewhat different. There, though the Buddha cannot be said to be "present" (i.e., to be active) in the image, he can be said to be "knowable" (i.e., to exist) in the "past." Images do not make present something that is absent; rather, they enable the worshipper, at least in his or her mind, to overcome the barriers of time and to directly cognize the Buddha as he was. They make possible a religious experience, not of the Buddha's presence, but of his pastness—his impermanence, his nonactivity in the here and now. For, from the Sarvāstivādin perspective, the Buddha may be said to exist (i.e., to be cognizable) after his parinirvāṇa, but entirely in the past.[86] Were he to be in any sense "present," he would have not only to exist, but to be active as well, which he is not. In this, he differs radically from beings still in saṃsāra, who are subject to existence in all three times.

In this context, Buddha bhakti as a process involves a double realization: that the Buddha's body, his rūpakāya, is impermanent in its activity (since it is no longer present); and that, paradoxically, it still exists (since it is in the past, where it can be re-cognized). This paradoxical (though precise) affirmation is strikingly different from the standard Theravāda or Mahāyāna views, in which the Buddha's rūpakāya is seen either as gone entirely to destruction or as never having truly existed in the first place.

The question remains, however, how it is that Buddha bhakti helps engender this sort of double realization. In addressing this issue, we may find it helpful to introduce first a somewhat different account of Māra's taking on the form of the Buddha. It is preserved in the story of Phussadeva, a monk whose legend is found in its fullest version in the *Sīhaḷavatthuppakaraṇa*, an important and often-neglected Pali collection of tales dating from perhaps the fourth century.[87]

The elder Phussadeva was a Sri Lankan monk who resided at the Kāḷakandara monastery. One day, when he had finished sweeping the courtyard of the Bodhi tree and was contemplating the tree, recollecting the qualities of the Buddha, Māra arrived and created a sudden gust of wind. The dust raised made the elder close his eyes, and, in that moment of blindness, Māra threw some trash into the Bodhi-tree enclosure and went away. The elder had to sweep it again.

"Then once more," the text goes on, "the elder recollected the qualities of the Buddha, but Māra came again, as a monkey; he grabbed this and that branch [of the Bodhi tree] and made a mess. Again the elder swept and recollected the qualities of the Buddha. Then Māra became an old ox, and, walking back and forth, he trampled the courtyard of the Bodhi tree."[88]

At this point, Phussadeva wonders who is causing all of these disturbances, and, realizing it is Māra, he denounces him. Māra, knowing he has been found out, shows himself in his true form. Then, Phussadeva declares:

> "You are able to fashion magically and manifest the form [rūpa] of the Buddha. I wish to see that form, Evil One, and I ask you to show it."
>
> "Very well," Māra consented, and he made clearly manifest the figure of the Great Sage, in the [seated] posture of a Buddha [under a Bodhi tree] and bearing the thirty-two excellent bodily marks. The elder Phussadeva, seeing the form of the Buddha, profferred an añjali, and, . . . tears in his eyes, with great faith, pondering the conduct of the bodhisattva from the time of the wholly enlightened Dīpankara, he recollected the qualities of the Buddha.[89]

There follows a long, ecstatic description of the Buddha's body, starting at his feet and working up to the top of his head, touching on each of the thirty-two marks of the Great Man. Clearly, Phussadeva, like Upagupta, is getting carried away by his devotion and vision. Just at that point, however, where one would expect him to prostrate himself on the ground in front of Māra, he abruptly switches gears and declares the truth of impermanence: "Such is the wholly enlightened Jina, the best of all beings," he announces, "but he has succumbed to impermanence, gone to destruction. One cannot see him."[90]

He then resumes his description of the Buddha body that Māra has fashioned for him, this time from the head to the toes and with an interesting twist:

> "Your shining black hair with its curls turning to the right, . . . and your uṣṇīṣa; they are *gone to destruction and cannot be seen.*
>
> "Your ūrṇā with the color and brilliance of the full moon, like the froth of cow's milk, illuminating a thousand worlds, today has *gone to destruction; it is not seen.*
>
> "Your eyes, long, wide, black, pure, and bright, have *gone to destruction and are no longer seen.*
>
> "Your large tongue, red lips, and beautiful lion's jaw, the mouth and resplendent nose, are *gone to destruction and cannot be seen.*"[91]

In this way, all the marks of the Great Man, which have just been glorified, are realized to be impermanent—and, in fact, no longer existing. Thus, "the elder had insight into the form created by Māra, and, developing that insight, he attained arhatship." Māra, realizing that Phussadeva had attained the goal, thought, "'I have been tricked by the elder'; and, defeated and distressed, he disappeared."[92]

There is much to be learned from this story that is relevant to an understanding of the tale of Upagupta and Māra, as well as of the nature of Buddhist image worship in general. Phussadeva illustrates a model of image worship in which bhakti is used as a means for heightening one's awareness not only of the glory of the Buddha, but *also* of his impermanence. Phussadeva, looking at Māra in disguise, reaches a peak of devotion, thinking that the Buddha is there in front of him. But this merely sets up his realization of impermanence, for only such a vivid appreciation of the Buddha can engender a perception, in the fullest sense, of the truth of his impermanence. The Buddha's body both is glorious and is no more.

Phussadeva's image worship, then, might be thought of as a pilgrimage into the past (to a time when the Buddha's rūpakāya exists) and back to the present (when its impermanence is realized). This, I would suggest, is what is going on in the Upagupta episode, with the difference, of course, that what Phussadeva does on his own (that is, realizes the impermanence of his vision), Māra does for Upagupta.

At this point, it may be useful to reintroduce a curious feature of Māra's agreement with Upagupta which we touched on briefly—namely, his statement that he will be burnt up if Upagupta starts to worship him and not the Buddha. In other words, Māra will be destroyed the moment Upagupta loses sight of the rūpakāya's pastness (that is, of its impermanence) and pretends the Buddha is actually present.

This, in fact, seems to be what happens in Tāranātha's abbreviated version of the episode; unable to bear Upagupta's idolatry, Māra falls down unconscious and then simply disappears.[93] Ironically, then, we have in Māra an ideal Buddhist object of worship: a Buddha image that will self-destruct as soon as its worshipper loses sight of its impermanence. With such a figure, no idolatry is possible.

We have already encountered an example of a similar object of worship in the story of the cave of the Buddha's shadow. There, too, the image of the Buddha was such that, as soon as one wanted to make it too real, too *present*, by going up close to see it, it disappeared. There are other parallels as well; the same pattern helps, for example, to understand the early aniconic tradition of Buddhist art. We have already seen that the "blanks" on the friezes of Bhārhut and Sāñcī—the empty thrones, the footsteps, the spaces at the foot of trees—may best be understood as symbolizing the Buddha's absence, his *present absence*. Paul Mus, however, has suggested that these aniconic gaps were meant to be filled in by the Buddhist devotees themselves, who, recollecting the glories of the Buddha, could visualize in the gaps the form of the Buddha's body.[94] Once the devotee's visualization was over, the frieze itself, with its empty spaces, would serve to return the devotee to a realization of the Buddha's present absence, his impermanence. Much the same pattern, it might be added, has been preserved in Buddhist tantric meditations, in which adepts, visualizing the forms of a Buddha or a bodhisattva, always make sure to "deconstruct" their visualizations and return the forms they have created to emptiness at the end of their meditations.[95]

With the advent of permanent anthropomorphic Buddha images, the danger was that this return to the realization of impermanence would be threatened; instead of a blank space at the end of worship, one would find a very real depiction of the Buddha's body. Worse, that very iconographic presence of the Buddha might make it unnecessary to recapture his pastness in the first place. Not only would there be no return to the present, there would be no departure for the past to begin with.

One might speculate that the first Buddhist images were (as the *Divyāvadāna* hints) made out of perishable materials (clay) and that they were not intended to last but to be destroyed at the end of the ritual, in much the same way, perhaps, that the Brahmanical sacrificial altar—also a representation of a great Puruṣa—was destroyed once its ritual purpose was served. But that does not resolve the problem of the later worship of permanent icons.

A different sort of safeguard was needed, and several were found. At Nāgārjunakoṇḍa, for example, there were "double shrines" side by side, one containing an aniconic stūpa and the other a Buddha image. Dutt has suggested that in these the worshipper was free "to offer worship according to his inclination,"[96] but one might also suppose that the two had a combined significance, the image recollecting the former glory of the Buddha and the stūpa acting as a reminder of his impermanence. Similarly, one might speculate about several sculptures in Mathurā that represent the Buddha *both* in symbols and in human form,[97] as well as about the famous shrines in the caves at Ajanta, Ellora, and elsewhere where an image of the Buddha has been sculpted inset into the stūpa.[98] Regarding these, Dutt suggests there may have been a combined worship of both symbol and image;[99] but the stories of Phussadeva and of Upagupta and Māra hint at something more complex, for in both these stories and in all these iconographic examples there is a curious conjunction of a glorification of the Buddha's body (the image of his rūpakāya) together with a reminder of that body's impermanence (its presence as bones, as relics)[100]—a reminder that is driven home in the corpus of the Buddha's Teaching (his Dharmakāya).

I would suggest, however, that one of the strongest safeguards against idolatry is to be found not in the iconography, but in the firm doctrinal assertions that the Buddha in Nirvāṇa is no more—the cognitive assertions of Sri Lankan and other Buddhists that the Blessed One is, in fact, absent from the images they worship. For Richard Gombrich is right that Theravādins affectively feel that the Buddha is present and cognitively know that he is absent. What Gombrich fails to spell out, however, is that such cognitive statements do not contradict the ritual; they are part of it, ritual formulae that remind the devotee of the Buddha's impermanence. Such doctrinal cognition completes the pilgrimage of the devotee who has just had a vision of the past glory of the

Buddha and who now, like Phussadeva and like Upagupta, returns to a present realization of his absence.

At the same time, this devotional pattern serves to reenact the career of the Buddha. In imagining the form of the Buddha, devotees like Phussadeva recall the countless previous lives of the Blessed One, during which he worked at building his body and acquiring the thirty-two marks of the Great Man; devotees then proceed through his life as Gautama to his demise and parinirvāṇa, back to his present existence as relics, bones, symbols of impermanence. The worship of the Buddha image, then, is experientially akin to the circumambulations made by pilgrims around early Buddhist stūpas, where, with the aid of friezes and other symbolic devices, they retraced the life of the Buddha from its beginning to its present end. Both acts should be seen as pilgrimages and as venerations not so much of the Buddha as of his life, his career, his coming and his going (Tathāgata).

Buddha Bhakti

By way of ending this chapter, it may be useful to make a few more observations about the development of devotion (bhakti) in India as it is reflected in the legends we have been studying. The growth of Buddha bhakti was one of the significant features of the whole Sanskrit Buddhist tradition, and specifically of avadāna literature.[101]

Etienne Lamotte has highlighted the simultaneous rise in Northern India of Buddhist and Vaishnavite devotion, both of which had as one of their foci Mathurā, Upagupta's native city.[102] It is no surprise, then, to see in our legends the Buddha becoming, like many of his more frankly divine Hindu counterparts, the object of considerable devotion and faith.

In general, scholars have tended to see devotion in Buddhism as something more characteristic of the Mahāyāna than the Hīnayāna;[103] as a concession to those who are not capable of meditation;[104] as belonging first to the laity rather than to the monks;[105] or as aiming at rebirth in heaven rather than enlightenment.[106] More specifically, in the case of Hīnayāna Buddhism, scholars have been reluctant to see the genuine soteriological dimensions of bhakti so clearly stated in a text such as the *Bhagavad Gītā*, where those who are devoted to Kṛṣṇa are told they will thereby attain liberation from saṃsāra.[107]

In this chapter, however, we have seen how bhakti, engendered in Māra by Upagupta, is responsible for his conversion experience, and we suggested further that bhakti is capable of speeding up the process of final liberation. The aim of bhakti, far from being that of rebirth in heaven, is unambiguously soteriological. As Upagupta put it, it is something which can bring about Nirvāṇa for the wise, that is, for those who realize the impermanence, the nonpresence of the object of worship.

In this regard, it is important to note that Māra's newfound devotion to the Buddha is based entirely on the *recollected* glory and kindness of the Master. He remembers the Buddha's compassion towards him, the fact that the Buddha did not even so much as reprimand him all those times that he, Māra, plagued him in the past; but there is no question here of Māra's focussing on a Buddha who is still alive. This is important, for the model of bhakti that scholars generally have in mind when they discuss the question of devotion in Buddhism is the Hindu one, in which the grace of the deity (always important in any system of bhakti) is a live one and in which the deity can therefore interact with and respond to the devotee in the present. The Buddha, in our story, is not devoid of grace, but his grace is in the past. Māra's chief lament at the time of his conversion is that he did not recognize that grace when he experienced it long ago.

Buddhist bhakti, then, is first and foremost a "recollection of the Buddha" (Buddhānusmṛti), something that involves a journey into the past, to a time when the glory and grace of the Blessed One can be realized.[108] Māra, who can take on the form of the Buddha not just because of his powers of transformation, but also because he *remembers* what the Buddha looked like, makes this pilgrimage possible for Upagupta. But other means are available, foremost among them the Buddha image and the stūpa.[109] In all cases, however, this experience also involves a return to the present. This is not incidental. Where some traditions might see this return as simply a coming down from a peak mystical experience, in the Buddhist context we are dealing with, it is part of the experience itself: a realization of the truth of impermanence.

Sukumar Dutt has called Upagupta "an apostle of bhakti."[110] But it is important to realize that bhakti may have meant different things to Buddhists at different times. As Etienne Lamotte has suggested, the bhakti found in the great Mahāyāna sūtras, such as the *Lotus* and the Pure Land texts, is rather different than that assumed in the devotional petitions recorded in the inscriptions of Northwest India. He associates the former primarily with Vaishnavite influences, while he connects the latter to Greek traditions of prayer.[111] Some, no doubt, would dispute this view, but few would question the recognition of diversity it implies. In these Mahāyāna sūtras, the Buddha is an eternal savior resident on the summit of Vulture's Peak or in a Pure Land, and a vision of him thus involves the devotee in a journey out of time and/or through space. In the Sarvāstivādin tradition, however, the Buddha is a *past* savior, incapable of intervening in the present, but still able to be experienced in a journey through time.

CHAPTER SIX

Master-Disciple Relations

WHATEVER its long-range implications, the immediate effect of Upagupta's taming of Māra was to increase the elder's fame and prestige in the land of Mathurā. Indeed, we are told that Māra himself, after shedding the form of the Buddha, proclaimed the elder's virtues to the people of the city, ringing a bell and announcing that "whoever desires the bliss of heaven and release" should come and listen to Upagupta preach the Dharma.[1] As a result, many humans, as well as other beings, sought Upagupta out as a soteriologically effective preacher, a Buddha for a Buddhaless age. As the *Divyāvadāna* put it: "Gods, humans, serpents, asuras, garuḍas, yakṣas, gandharvas, and vidyādharas all prostrated themselves before him; and the rainwaters of the true Dharma fell on hundreds of thousands of beings who had previously sown seeds of merit in most excellent Buddha fields, and the sprouts of liberation grew in them, there on Mount Urumuṇḍa."[2]

Within this multitude, of course, there were those who decided to enter into a more formal relationship with Upagupta and to seek ordination under him. Indeed, we are told that no fewer than eighteen thousand persons became direct disciples of the elder. In their cases, it is clear that the "sprouts of liberation" not only took root, but came to full fruition, for, "disciplining themselves, they soon attained arhatship."[3]

Their arhatship, as we have seen, was marked by their throwing into Upagupta's cave or chamber on Mount Urumuṇḍa a tally stick (śalākā) four inches in length. We shall deal later with the symbolism of this curious act and the nascent cult of Upagupta that it reflects. First, however, we need to turn to the more detailed accounts of these disciples' attainments. Although the *Divyāvadāna* is silent on this score, other texts did not refrain from providing tale after tale relating the spiritual endeavors and enlightenment of these individuals.[4] These stories are particularly interesting, for, in them, a new dimension of Upagupta's character and career is revealed: his life as a meditation teacher, as a master engaged in the specific problems of training particular disciples.

The importance of the teacher (guru) in the Buddhist tradition need hardly be emphasized here. Not only in India, but throughout the whole of Asia, the succession of pupil to teacher became one of the sociological and soteriological hallmarks of Buddhist monasticism. In China and Japan, especially in Ch'an (Zen) contexts, countless stories were told of the effectiveness of particular teachers and of their sometimes-eccentric techniques in bringing their disciples to enlightenment. In Tibet, where biographies of great masters abound, the formal worship of one's teacher(s) became an established part of spiritual practice; and, more generally, the Teacher (bLama) came to be included as a "fourth refuge" of the tradition, to be added formulaically to the Buddha, the Dharma, and the Sangha.[5] Great teachers were thought to be great masters of upāya (effective means), and if this sometimes led to eccentric techniques and unorthodox behavior, it nonetheless reflected their compassion for their disciples and their hope for their enlightenment.

Upagupta, of course, is neither a Zen master nor a Tibetan guru, but, as we shall see in the stories of those disciples whom he brings to enlightenment, he sometimes appears to prefigure both. For the most part, his disciples remain anonymous. Some of them are still laymen when they first meet with him, others are monks who have come from afar to seek him out; but in almost all cases, the stress is not so much on them as individuals as on the skill of their master, Upagupta, and on the various ways in which he leads them to arhatship. It is on these techniques of Upagupta as a teacher that we shall focus here.

The Power of the Dharma

We will begin with stories that rather straightforwardly emphasize the importance of sermons and the soteriological effectiveness of the Dharma. For this there is no better example than the very first of the legends of Upagupta's disciples in the *Aśokarājāvadāna*, which may be summarized as follows:

> (1) A young man from the North Country wandered forth and became a monk. He was skilled as a preacher, but eventually he got tired of reciting sūtras and giving sermons, and he wanted to practice meditation. He had heard that in Mathurā there was a famous elder named Upagupta who, although he did not possess the thirty-two signs of the Great Man, was the foremost of those monks who taught dhyāna. The young man begged Upagupta to agree to become his meditation master. Upagupta, contemplating the dispositions of this disciple, realized that he was a person who would attain arhatship by preaching the Dharma to others. He therefore told him he would teach him how to meditate, but only on condition that he, as a disciple, do everything he was told. To this the monk agreed, only to find that the first thing Upagupta instructed him to do was to go and preach a sermon! As soon as he had done so, the monk realized the truth of what he was saying in his sermon and attained arhatship. He was the first to throw a śalākā into the cave.[6]

We already noted in our discussion of the Vāsavadattā story the phenomenon of the monk who attains arhatship by virtue of one of his own sermons. Much the same thing happens here. Upagupta masterfully sets up his disciple's enlightenment, but, in the end, he simply lets the Dharma have its own soteriological effect. His disciple is a skilled preacher and reciter of texts, a follower of the vocation of books (ganthadhura). But he tires of this and seeks out Upagupta, who is here described as very much a saint of the forest—a famous meditation master, a great teacher of dhyāna. Nonetheless, Upagupta chooses not to instruct his disciple in the classical forms of the forest monk's vocation, but tells him to continue his practice of preaching, that is, to go on doing the very thing he has become weary of doing. This is effective; Upagupta's didactic technique puts his disciple in a new situation and enables him to see the truth of his own sermons afresh, in a new, meditative way. In Upagupta's hands, then, the Dharma is a powerful soteriological force which can suffice to make a person realize arhatship.

Another tale of Upagupta's disciples, perhaps the shortest and most straightforward of the lot, makes much the same point:

> (2) Once upon a time, the Venerable Upagupta came across five hundred oxherders. They venerated him, and he preached to them the Dharma. They all became stream-winners. They took their oxen back to their owners and then wandered forth and were ordained. Without exception, they all attained arhatship and threw śalākās into the cave.[7]

Here, perhaps, we find the conversion-ordination-enlightenment process at its simplest, where the mere preaching of the Dharma is sufficient to convince not one but five hundred persons of the truth of the Buddha's message. No long meditative enterprise is required, no charismatic or magical displays are needed. The oxherders are simply ready for their experience, and Upagupta catalyzes it for them.

Merit Making and Arhatship

It should be remembered that the act of preaching is also an act of merit. When Upagupta tells his first disciple to keep preaching, he is not only asking him to reflect some more on the Truth of the Dharma in his sermons, he is also telling him to make some more merit. As we shall see, part of Upagupta's concern in dealing with his disciples is that they be "ripe" enough—in terms of merit—for the breakthrough of arhatship to occur. This is made clear in the following two stories:

> (3) Once upon a time, in a kingdom in the east, there was a young man who became a monk. Being a very efficient and responsible person, he was constantly being asked to run the affairs of the monasteries where he resided. Eventually, however, he grew tired of being an overworked administrator, and he longed to devote himself to the practice of meditation. Hearing that Upagupta was the foremost of meditation

teachers, he went to the Naṭabhaṭika hermitage and asked him to be his master. Upagupta realized that this monk was not yet ripe for arhatship and that he needed to make some more merit. He therefore told him that the first thing he had to do was to busy himself with the raising of offerings among laypersons. The monk protested that this was precisely what he had wanted to stop doing; besides, he was new to the region and did not know who the local faithful were. But Upagupta ordered him to proceed with his task. He therefore took his bowl and entered the city of Mathurā. There he happened across a rich layman, who soon volunteered to provide the Sangha with whatever it required. The next day the layman made his offerings to the monk, who, in turn, presented them to Upagupta and the Sangha. They then transferred the merit accrued back to the monk, and he became an arhat. Upagupta told him to take a śalākā and throw it in the cave.[8]

(4) Once upon a time, in the south of India, there was a young man who became a monk. He was an expert at building stūpas and vihāras, and everywhere he went, his fellow bhikṣus would ask him to undertake construction projects. Eventually, he grew tired of this; he wanted to meditate, so he went to Upagupta and asked him to instruct him in dhyāna and samādhi. Upagupta, however, realized that this monk had not yet acquired sufficient merit to attain arhatship; the first thing he asked him to do, therefore, was to go and build some more stūpas and vihāras. The monk protested, saying he was new to the area and did not know who the laypersons were who would assist him in such projects. Upagupta told him to go nonetheless. The next day, the monk went questing for support and happened to enter into conversation with a rich householder. He explained his predicament, and the householder agreed to provide the land and wherewithal for building a new monastery and a stūpa. The monk then went with him to measure out the land, and before the measuring line was fully extended, the monk attained arhatship. Even so, he completed the construction project. Upagupta had him throw a śalākā into the cave.[9]

The pattern here is clear: accepting these monks for instruction in "meditation," Upagupta asks them first to continue doing the good works they have been doing. This is not only psychologically astute (revealing to these searchers that their quest need not be separated from their regular routines), it is also the most effective way for them to earn the merit they still need in order to achieve enlightenment. One more quest for alms, one more building enterprise, or, as in story 1, one more sermon may be all that is needed for the necessary amount of merit to be accrued.

In all of these stories, it is assumed that merit making is a basic way to enlightenment. Although he is qualified as a master of dhyāna—and that is what attracts these disciples to him—Upagupta is never actually portrayed, in these stories, as teaching them what are ordinarily considered meditation techniques. He does not instruct them in mindfulness and strategies of concentration or lead them through various trance levels. Instead, he encourages them to make more merit; and, when they have done so, arhatship occurs, almost effortlessly, in the midst of things, like a ripe mango dropping from a tree.

There is a certain Zen-like quality about the suddenness and circumstances of these disciples' enlightenment. The monk who attains arhatship before the measuring line is fully extended is not a distant kin to later Ch'an masters who have enlightenment experiences in the midst of daily activities. The experience also recalls, however, one closer at hand—that of the Buddha's disciple Ānanda (Upagupta's own teacher's teacher), who attains enlightenment when he is going to bed, just before his head touches the pillow.[10]

Monks can thus effortlessly attain enlightenment because of Upagupta's crucial ability as a master to estimate the readiness of his potential disciples with respect to accumulated merit. He undertakes to "instruct" monks only when he sees they are ripe. If he sees no chance of their accruing enough merit for an arhatship breakthrough to occur, then he refuses to take them on as disciples, as in the following story:

> (5) Once upon a time, in the south of India, there was a young man who fell in love with a girl and had premarital sexual relations with her. His mother reprimanded him, telling him that lust and fornication could only lead to unfortunate consequences. In anger and frustration, he then killed his mother and went to the girl's family to ask for her hand in marriage. He was refused. Depressed, he decided to become a Buddhist monk. As he was very bright, he quickly memorized the entire Tripiṭaka and acquired many pupils. One day, along with his disciples, he went to see Upagupta to ask for instruction in meditation, but Upagupta, divining his criminal past, refused even to talk with him. "A person guilty of such acts [fornication and matricide]," he reasoned, "would be incapable of attaining the fruit of the Path."[11]

Upagupta, then, is careful to assess the karmic state of those who come to him before taking them on as disciples.

Magic and Enlightenment

Merit making is not the only way to enlightenment advocated by Upagupta. As a master teacher, he sometimes deems it appropriate to help his disciples along the Path by using his supernatural powers and performing a magical trick to shock or scare them into a realization of the Truth. Two examples may be cited here:

> (6) Once upon a time, in the kingdom of Mathurā, there was a young man who became a monk. He suffered, however, from a tendency to fall asleep, especially whenever he heard someone preach the Dharma. Upagupta, deciding to cure him of

this habit, told him to go off and sleep under a tree. Then, using his magical powers, he fashioned a very deep crevasse all around the spot where the monk was resting. When the young monk woke up, he became very frightened, but Upagupta magically fashioned for him a narrow bridge across the crevasse and the monk was able to pass over it and rejoin his master. Gratefully, he acknowledged that Upagupta had saved him from falling. The latter, however, replied, "This crevasse is not very deep. The pit of birth, old age, sickness, death, and rebirth in the lower realms is much deeper. If you do not perceive the Noble Truths, you will surely fall into it." With this in mind, the monk thereafter ceased sleeping. He soon became an arhat, and Upagupta had him take a śalākā and throw it into the cave.[12]

(7) Once upon a time, in the kingdom of Mathurā, there was a young man who became a monk under Upagupta. He tended to doze off, however, and because of this he was unable to attain enlightenment. Upagupta had him go and practice meditation in the forest, and he promptly fell asleep. Using his magical powers, Upagupta then created a seven headed ogre (piśāca) suspended upside down in midair directly in front of the monk. The monk awoke, was terrified, and ran to find his master. "What is the matter?" Upagupta asked. "There is a seven-headed piśāca in that forest," came the reply. "Go back there and meditate," said Upagupta. "I can't," said the monk, "I'm scared." Thereupon Upagupta said, "I do not see why you are afraid of a piśāca, since you are not afraid of much more frightening things, such as saṃsāra. You should fear sleep much more than a piśāca! A piśāca can give you trouble only in a single life; sleep can give you trouble in innumerable lives. Go back and meditate." From then on, the monk did not dare fall asleep for fear of the piśāca. Instead, he reflected upon the nature of the Dharma and became an arhat. He took a śalākā and threw it into the cave.[13]

Structurally, these two stories are quite similar. Initially, we are told, two unnamed monks have the same problem: drowsiness. While the one cannot listen to the Dharma (that is, cannot pursue the vocation of books) without dozing off, the other cannot meditate, (that is, cannot follow the vocation of a forest monk). In both cases, Upagupta's solution is the same: to use his magical powers of transformation to jolt the disciples into alertness. The fabrications of the deep crevasse and of the flesh-eating piśāca are quite effective in eradicating all sleepiness and in being metaphors for the even greater terrors of saṃsāra.

Overcoming Attachments

Sleepiness, however, is only one of many problems encountered by meditators. In other stories, Upagupta's disciples suffer from a whole gamut of attachments, which he, in a variety of ways, helps them to overcome. For the most part, these attachments are not only potential barriers to the disciples' spiritual progress, but ties that bind them to their former lives as laymen in a world of desire and indulgence. In what follows, we shall examine four of these ties.

Fondness for Food

In a community of monks who begged for their meals, it is understandable that some of its members should develop a preoccupation with eating. Indeed, the minute monastic rules regulating both the begging round and mealtime etiquette, as well as the general Buddhist advocacy of the ideal of indifference to what one consumes, clearly reflect the fact that some monks, at least, were highly interested in food and that this remained for them an obstacle in their spiritual development. Upagupta is alert to this problem among his disciples:

> (8) Once upon a time, in Mathurā, there was a young man who wandered forth and became a monk under Upagupta. He remained, however, very fond of food and drink, so much so that it kept him from attaining the Path. Then one day, the master told him that he would provide his meal for him. Upagupta filled the monk's bowl with a millet-and-milk gruel and told him to wait until it cooled down before he ate it. The monk waited and waited, blowing on the gruel to hasten its cooling, and at last, when it was cold, he consumed it in one gulp. Upagupta said, "My son, even though the gruel became cold, the fire of desire in your heart was hot. This you must extinguish by the contemplation of impurity." He then placed the empty bowl in front of the monk and told him to vomit into it. The monk did so. Then he told him to eat what he had vomited, but the monk refused; it was disgusting, he declared. Upagupta replied, "Whatever one eats or drinks is no different from this vomit. Meditate on this and contemplate the impurity of food." The monk soon attained arhatship and threw a śalākā into the cave.[14]

This lesson—effective, though somewhat severe—is obviously governed by the well-established Buddhist tradition of meditation on the repulsiveness of food.[15] At other times, however, Upagupta uses gentler techniques—as in the following story, in which he gradually weans a disciple away from his attachment by showing him the advantages of sharing his food with others:

> (9) Once upon a time, in the kingdom of Mathurā, there was a young man who became a monk under the elder Upagupta. He was, however, very greedy, and this prevented him from attaining enlightenment. Upagupta therefore told him to make merit by practicing dāna. "But," replied the monk, "I do not own anything; what should I give?" Upagupta told him to share with other members of the community the surplus food and clothing he received from the laity. The next day, however, he did not share anything, so Upagupta asked two of his enlightened disciples to sit next to the monk. From their ears there issued forth rays of light, and the monk, impressed and awed by this, took a little bit of his food and offered it to them. The following

day, a lay donor brought him much good food; he rejoiced, thinking, "I gave a little yesterday, so today I have received a lot." Thereafter he shared increasingly larger amounts of his food with his fellow monks, and gradually his avarice was corrected. Upagupta then preached the Dharma to him; he attained arhatship and threw a śalākā into the cave.[16]

Fondness for food was only one potential problem on the alimentary spectrum. At the other end stood another hindrance: anorexic infatuation with a life of ascetic self-denial. Buddhism, as a Middle Way, rejected both of these extremes, and Upagupta, though perhaps less harsh with his ascetically inclined disciples, is equally concerned about them:

(10) Once upon a time, in the south of India, there was a young man who had few desires and was content with little. He did not take care of his body, did not wash with warm water, never ate milk products, and became very thin and weak. Tired of saṃsāra, he sought out Upagupta as a meditation master. Upagupta, however, realized that, because the monk was so weak, he would not be able to attain arhatship. He agreed to instruct him, therefore, on condition he follow his orders. He then prepared a warm bath for the monk, had a young novice massage his body with oil and fermented milk, and fed him well with plentiful, good food. Then Upagupta preached the Dharma to him, and he soon attained arhatship; he tossed a śalākā into the cave.[17]

Hoarding of Wealth

Fondness for food (or fasting), though perhaps a common problem potentially recurring day after day at mealtime, was not, however, an avarice for permanent possessions. Uneaten food would soon go bad and so no longer be desired. A more extreme attachment came with the hoarding of more durable goods, such as gold. This, of course, was against the rules of the monastic community. Not only were monks not supposed to touch gold, but, apart from a few personal belongings, such as a bowl, robes, a razor, etc., all possessions were supposed to belong to the Sangha as a whole. Nonetheless, in the following story, a monk, on entering the Sangha, surreptitiously saved some gold coins of his own, "for a rainy day." In reprimanding him, Upagupta does not invoke the Vinaya rules at all. Instead, he again turns to his magical powers to demonstrate graphically to the monk the futility of squirrelling away personal cash:

(11) Once upon a time, in the kingdom of Mathurā, there was a rich layman. Somehow, however, his wealth was lost, and he was left with only five hundred pieces of gold. He decided to wander forth and become a monk under Upagupta. He did so, but he kept his money, hiding it from the other monks, as a provision with which to buy medicines for himself should he need them. Upagupta confronted him, saying

that wandering forth meant leaving behind all personal attachments and that he should offer his five hundred pieces of gold to the Sangha. "But, elder," exclaimed the monk, "that gold is for medicine!" Upagupta therefore used his magical powers and fashioned one thousand pieces of gold. "This gold will buy you medicine," he declared, "give yours to the Sangha." When the monk had done so, Upagupta preached the Dharma to him, and, no longer attached to his gold, he soon attained arhatship. He took a śalākā and threw it into the cave.[18]

Longing for Former Wife and Family Life

In addition to attachment to food and wealth, sexual desire was also one of the hurdles to be overcome on the way to arhatship. More specifically, a number of Upagupta's disciples who had previously been married when they were laymen were tormented by longing for their former wives and family situations.

The theme of a bhikṣu's relationship with the woman he left behind is one which crops up often in popular Buddhist literature. For some monks, this was not a problem; they were easily able to overcome the temptations and enticements of their former wives, who are often portrayed as trying to seduce them and lure them back. The classic example of such steadfastness, of course, is the Buddha himself, who, upon his return to his native city of Kapilavastu, easily resists his wife Yaśodharā's attempt to win him back by means of a potent aphrodisiac.[19] The very real longing, however, that can exist in less-enlightened beings for a former wife is well illustrated in the story of the Buddha's half-brother Sundarananda. This young man, whom the Buddha more or less shanghais into the monkhood, constantly pines for his bride until the Blessed One finally convinces him of her ultimate loathsomeness and impermanence.[20]

Upagupta makes much the same point to one of his disciples in the following story:

> (12) Once upon a time, in Mathurā, there was a young man who had recently gotten married and who expressed a desire to wander forth and become a monk. He asked leave of his parents, but they refused to grant him permission, since he was their only son. He therefore undertook a fast, declaring that he would not eat anything until they gave him leave to be ordained. After six days, they feared he might die and so capitulated. They made him promise, however, to come back and see them. After his ordination, he told Upagupta about this agreement and was granted permission to go back and visit his family. There he saw his former wife, who declared that if he did not return and live with her she would die. At this, the monk had second thoughts about his monastic career and decided to go back to Upagupta and tell him he wanted to return to lay life. Upagupta responded by asking him to wait at least until the following day.

That night, Upagupta caused the monk to dream that he had arrived back home and found his wife dead. His parents were already taking her body to the cemetery, and there he saw it beginning to decompose and exuding a foul odor. He then woke up and reported what he had dreamt to Upagupta, who merely told him to go and see what the reality of the situation was. When he reached his former home, he saw that indeed his wife was dead and that his parents were taking her decomposing corpse to the cemetery. He reflected on impermanence and the foulness of rebirth and quickly attained arhatship. When he got back to Mathurā, Upagupta asked him whether he had seen his wife. "I saw her in her true aspect," he replied, and threw a śalākā in the cave.[21]

In this tale, the tension becomes apparent when the monk returns home for a visit. In the next, Upagupta has first to convince his disciple that his problem lies in not realizing that he is, in fact, constantly pining for his wife:

(13) Once upon a time, in the kingdom of Mathurā, there was a young man who had just gotten married when he decided to become a monk. He went to Upagupta, was ordained by him, and then was instructed in meditation. As he was sitting in dhyāna, however, he kept remembering his wife. Upagupta, therefore, used his magical powers, took on the aspect of his wife, and stood before him. "Why have you come?" he asked. "I have come," she replied, "because you called me." The monk said, "I have been sitting here, cross-legged, without saying a word. When did I call you?" "Though you did not call me with your mouth, you called me with your mind," she answered. The monk thereby realized that he still had desire for his wife. Upagupta, resuming his normal appearance, then preached the Dharma to him and helped him overcome this attachment. He soon became an arhat and threw a śalākā into the cave.[22]

Attachment to the Body and the Self

A monk's longing for his former wife is essentially a matter of sexual desire and craving for the householder state. A number of Upagupta's disciples, however, are portrayed as infatuated with their own bodies. This, too, is an obstacle on their way to arhatship; for, until they realize the fundamental impermanence of their physical frames, they will continue to be preoccupied by false notions of an ego and so fail to attain enlightenment. Upagupta, again making free use of his magical powers, convinces them of the ultimate unimportance of the body and of the self:

(14) Once upon a time, in the south of India, there was a young man who became a monk. He remained, however, infatuated with his body, bathed often, rubbed his skin with oil and fermented milk, and ate only good foods. He sought out the Venerable Upagupta and asked him to instruct him. Upagupta realized that this monk, fat and attached to his body as he was, was not yet ready for arhatship, but he agreed

nonetheless to teach him. By means of his magical powers, he made a tall tree appear and asked the monk to climb it. The monk did so. Upagupta then shouted up to him, "Let go with your right hand!" The monk did so. Then he shouted, "Let go with your left leg!" The monk did so. Next he called, "Let go with your right leg!" and then, finally, to the monk who was now hanging by one arm, "Let go altogether!" The monk, giving himself up as lost, did so and immediately found himself standing safely back on the ground, the tree having completely disappeared. Upagupta then preached the Dharma to him. He attained arhatship and threw a śalākā into the cave.[23]

Though requiring magical powers and demanding total obedience on the part of the disciple, this is actually a rather simple technique. Step by step, limb by limb, it teaches the gradual abandonment of the body and the self. The same approach is made more explicit in the following ghoulish story of a disciple of Upagupta who gets dismembered and eaten by two magically fashioned yakṣas:

(15) Once upon a time, a young man from Mathurā became a monk under the Venerable Upagupta. He remained, however, very attached to his body and wished to return to his family and the householder's life. He asked leave of Upagupta, and he left the next day. Halfway home, however, he began to reflect that his demeritorious action of giving up his monastic career might result in bad karma for his parents. He decided, therefore, not to go home, but to spend the night in a nearby deva temple and return to the monastery the following morning.

Late that night, by means of his magical powers, Upagupta caused the figure of a yakṣa to appear in the temple, carrying a corpse. Then another yakṣa appeared, empty-handed. The two demons began quarrelling, the one saying that the corpse belonged to him, the other denying it. They were about to come to blows when they noticed the monk huddled in a corner, trying to remain unseen, and they decided to ask him to settle their dispute. The monk, thinking that he might as well tell the truth, since his death at the hands of one demon or the other was certain, declared that the corpse belonged to the first yakṣa. At that, the other demon flew into a fury and tore off one of the monk's arms. The first demon, however, quickly replaced it with an arm from the corpse he had brought. The second demon then ripped off the monk's other arm, but again the first demon replaced it with an arm from the dead man. This went on until every part of the monk—his feet, legs, head, and trunk—was torn off and replaced by the corresponding parts of the corpse. Then the two yakṣas, ceasing their quarrel as suddenly as they had begun it, sat down together, ate the fresh limbs that had been ripped off the monk's body, and went on their way.

The monk (if, in fact, it was still he) somehow survived all of this and, contemplating what had happened to him, wondered whether he now had a body or did not have a body. He returned to Upagupta, who told him that this was a good opportunity for him to realize the truth of anātman, for, in fact, his body had always been the way

> it now clearly was: impermanent and not belonging to any self. This caused him to attain arhatship, and he threw a śalākā into the cave.[24]

This tale was retold repeatedly in Buddhist circles to correct disciples' attachment to their bodies—to their lives. Occasionally, however, masters such as Upagupta would encounter non-Buddhists who had sublimated this attachment into a doctrinal assertion of the existence of a self, an Ātman. This must have been a very natural encounter in the India of his time, where the Buddhist-Brahmanical debate over the existence of the ego was a continuing one. Indeed, in the *Mahāprajñāpāramitā śāstra*, the story just recounted is given as part of an argument refuting the tenets of a personalist opponent who advocates the notion of Ātman. But less-spectacular encounters also took place, as in the following:

> (16) Once upon a time, in the kingdom of Mathurā, there was a Brahmin who was very attached to the ātman doctrine. One day, discussing his views with a Buddhist layman (upāsaka), he asked, "Who could ever maintain a doctrine in which there is no notion of self?" The lay disciple answered, "The Venerable Upagupta maintains the doctrine of anātman." The Brahmin, therefore, went to the Naṭabhaṭika hermitage, and there he heard Upagupta expound upon the absence of an ego, of a puruṣa, and on the fact that all the skandhas constituting one's personality are but impermanent dharmas that are subject to suffering and emptiness. The Brahmin, hearing all this, was impressed; he gave up his false view of the self and became a stream-winner. He then became a monk and attained arhatship. Upagupta told him to take a śalākā and toss it in the cave.[25]

Amidst all the stories of Upagupta's use of magical powers and clever didactic devices, it is well to remember that sometimes a purely doctrinal approach could also be effective. In this story, as in story 2, Upagupta has recourse not to the magic of illusory fabrication, but only to sermons and straightforward argumentation based on the Dharma. And, here, too he meets with success.

False Pride in Accomplishment

Attachments to material things—food, wealth, sex, the body—were all serious and turbulent eddies that monks could get caught in on their way to enlightenment, but they were not the only dangers; there were also quiet pools where, becalmed, questers could suddenly find their progress stopped. Some monks apparently thought that, once they had reached a particular stage of the Path, there was no reason for them to strive any further. Hence the following story of one of Upagupta's disciples who was satisfied with becoming a stream-winner and did not see why he should try to become an arhat. The tale is noteworthy because it raises again the whole question of fast and slow tracks to final liberation; it shows that not all monks found embarcation on the arhat track as automatic as their ordinations ideally implied; and it addresses directly an implicit question that must always have been present in the minds of some: since one who has entered the stream is no longer subject to rebirth in hell, or as an animal, or a preta, or an asura; and since he or she will, in no more than seven lifetimes, attain parinirvāṇa, then why bother trying to accelerate this process by switching tracks? Is not the final goal more or less at hand, and should one not just patiently wait for it? Upagupta's response is explicit and reflects his advocacy of the more rapid route of arhatship, at least for his own ordained disciples:

> (17) Once upon a time, in Mathurā, there was a young man who became a monk under the Venerable Upagupta. Upagupta preached the Dharma to him, and he obtained the fruit of stream-winner. The elder then exhorted him to go on and become an arhat, but the monk reflected, "I have escaped from rebirth in the lower realms of existence; why should I strive to attain the fruit of arhatship? The worst that can happen to me is to be reborn seven more times as a human or a deva." The next day, Upagupta accompanied the monk on his begging round. At the house of an outcaste, they saw a child whose body was covered with verminous ulcers. Upagupta said to the monk, "Do you see that child? That child is a stream-winner." And he went on to tell how, in a previous life, that child had insulted an arhat for scratching himself in the meditation hall. Later, he had apologized and become a stream-winner, but he did not then strive to reach arhatship and so was reborn with an itchy, ulcerous body. Hearing this, the monk applied himself with diligence and soon became an arhat. He took a śalākā and threw it into the cave.[26]

Another trap on the way to enlightenment, more dangerous perhaps than giving up striving, was the false thought that one had attained full arhatship when, in fact, one had not. Indeed, no fewer than five of Upagupta's disciples are said to have believed themselves to be arhats when they had reached only the fourth level of meditative trance (dhyāna).[27] This is perhaps understandable, since the fourth dhyāna represents the peak of attainment within the realm of form (rūpadhātu); it is the stage at which supernatural powers are developed and at which one attains equanimity.[28]

Making false claims to any kind of enlightenment or spiritual attainment is, in the Vinaya, considered a very serious offense, involving defeat (pārājika), that is, expulsion from the order. In this, it is akin to the offenses of sexual intercourse, stealing, and the taking of life.[29] Upagupta, however, seems less concerned with the possible Vinaya violations of his disciples than with their spiritual progress. He realizes their false claims to enlightenment are not malicious, but simply mistaken; he does not take disciplinary action against them, but seeks rather to make them perceive their errors.

Once again, he employs various techniques to bring this about. In some cases, he uses his magical powers to create the figure of another monk who can give a fresh perspective to the disciple in question. In doing this, Upagupta seems to realize that, in his own persona, he has reached a point in his relationship with his disciple where he can no longer be effective as a master. Convinced of his own enlightenment, the disciple will simply no longer listen to a master whom he thinks he no longer needs and who appears not to understand his accomplishment. The following story illustrates the point well:

(18) Once upon a time, in the kingdom of Mathurā, a young man became a monk under Upagupta and was instructed in meditation. He soon attained the various levels of dhyāna and mistakenly believed that, with the fourth trance state, he had reached the fruit of arhatship. Upagupta tried to exhort him to continue his practice, but the monk was convinced he had attained the goal. The elder, therefore, resorted to his magical powers and created the figure of a monk who proceeded to question the bhikṣu. "Under whom did you wander forth?" he asked. "Under the Venerable Upagupta," was the reply. "You have much merit; your master is a Buddha without the marks. What texts do you recite?" "I recite," answered the disciple, "the Sūtra, the Vinaya, and the Abhidharma." The monk then asked, "Have you reached the highest degree of attainment?" "I have," replied the disciple, "I have become an arhat." "By what practice did you do that?" asked the monk. "By the practice of the first four trance levels." "If that is the case," retorted the monk, "then you have not yet attained to the Path. You are still a common, ordinary person." The disciple then realized that this was indeed the case, and, going back to Upagupta, he confessed that he was not yet enlightened and begged to be instructed further. Upagupta did so, and, exerting himself, the bhikṣu attained arhatship and threw a śalākā into the cave.[30]

In other cases, the scenario is more complicated, and another "monk's" perspective is not enough; the disciple in question needs more graphic proof of his lack of enlightenment. One story in this genre we have already mentioned in chapter 4: the tale of the disciple who was sexually aroused by a beautiful woman whom he met on his alms round and whose teeth he then took as a focus for a cemetery meditation. In fact, until this encounter, this disciple had mistakenly thought he was an arhat; his meeting with the woman was set up by Upagupta, and his sexual arousal made him realize that he must not yet be enlightened, since arhats, by definition, are beyond such lust. Another tale in this vein is the following one, which enjoyed considerable popularity in the Mahāyāna tradition in China and Japan:[31]

(19) Once upon a time, in Mathurā, there was a young man who wandered forth and became a monk under the Venerable Upagupta. Upagupta instructed him in meditation, and he soon attained the first four degrees of dhyāna. He believed, however, when he had reached the first level of dhyāna, that he had become a stream-winner;

when he had reached the second level, that he had become a once-returner; when he had reached the third level, that he had become a nonreturner; and, upon reaching the fourth level, he believed that he had achieved arhatship. He therefore stopped exerting himself. Upagupta tried to get him to continue his practice, but he was convinced he had attained the goal. Upagupta, therefore, told him to go out, travel through the countryside, and preach to villagers.

Using his magical powers, Upagupta quickly created on the highway the forms of five hundred merchants. Then he also fashioned five hundred brigands who attacked the merchants, killing them all with knives and axes. The monk, stricken with terror, realized that he must not have attained arhatship after all, since true arhats feel no fear. Nevertheless, he still maintained that, though not an arhat, he was at least a nonreturner.

Soon thereafter, on his begging round, he met a woman who said to him, "Master, please take me with you!" "The Buddha," he replied, "does not permit a monk to travel alone with a woman." "I will follow you from a distance," declared the woman; and, taking pity on her, the monk consented to that. Upagupta, knowing through his magical powers what was going on, caused a big river to appear in front of the couple, who were walking apart but in sight of each other. The monk crossed first, but the woman slipped and fell. "Save me," she cried.

Reflecting that the Buddha *did* allow bhikṣus to touch women in order to pull them out of a river when they were drowning, the monk grabbed her. As he held on to her, however, he experienced a moment of desire, and, once they were safely back on shore, this grew into a longing for fornication. Taking her to an isolated spot, the monk was about to satisfy his lustful intentions when he realized that the woman was none other than Upagupta! "Why do you act in this manner if you are enlightened?" Upagupta asked; and, taking him back to the monastery, he had him confess his transgression to the community. He then preached the Dharma to him, and this time the monk truly attained arhatship. He threw a śalākā into the cave.[32]

The experience of fear or of sexual desire is not always the indication that a disciple has failed to reach full enlightenment. In the next two stories, that realization comes about through the experience of pride—pride in one's status and prestige in the eyes of the laity, and pride in one's attainment of magical powers. The point—that these are inappropriate emotions for one who is supposed to be enlightened—is the same in both cases:

(20) Once upon a time, there was a young man who became a monk under the elder Upagupta and was instructed by him in the practice of meditation. When he attained the fourth level of dhyāna, he thought he had reached arhatship. Upagupta, knowing that he had not, ordered him to make offerings to the Sangha for six days. The monk, therefore, went questing for alms among the laity of Mathurā. When the laypersons heard the rumor that he was an arhat, they were greatly impressed, and they vied for the privilege of making offerings to him. At this, the monk felt a great amount of pride, and then immediately realized that he must not be an arhat, since arhats are

free from pride. He went back to Upagupta, confessed that he had not yet attained enlightenment, and requested further instruction. Upagupta complied, and soon he became a genuine arhat and threw a śalākā into the cave.[33]

(21) Once upon a time, in Kashmir, there was a monk named Sudarśana who had reached the fourth level of dhyāna and who was endowed with supernatural powers. Whenever there was a drought, he could always make it rain, and he was very proud of this. He also believed he had attained arhatship. Upagupta, intending to save him, used his magical powers to cause a drought lasting twelve years. People came to ask Upagupta to make it rain, but he answered, "I cannot make it rain. In Kashmir, however, there is a monk named Sudarśana; why don't you go and ask him?"[34]

Thereupon the citizens of Mathurā asked Sudarśana to make it rain. He agreed to do so, and a great rain promptly fell on the whole of Jambudvīpa. The people were very happy and made great offerings to Sudarśana. Seeing that the offerings he received were much better than those given to Upagupta, he felt great pride, but then he immediately realized that he must not be an arhat after all, for arhats do not feel pride. Ashamed, he went to Upagupta and asked for further instruction. Upagupta agreed, and he soon caused Sudarśana to attain arhatship. He took a śalākā and threw it into the cave.[35]

Miscellaneous Stories

Thus far, we have looked at tales of Upagupta's disciples which have all more or less come under one category or another. There are, however, a few stories that are more difficult to classify, although they touch on various themes that have already come up in our discussions. The first of these, for instance, further illustrates the importance both of Upagupta's use of magical power and of the preaching of the Dharma:

(22) Once upon a time, in the kingdom of Mathurā, a child was born in the family of a prominent householder. It died when it was one year old and was reborn in another family. There, it died again when it was one and was reborn once more. This happened six times in a row, until at last the child survived infancy in a seventh household. But then it was kidnapped by brigands when it reached the age of seven. Upagupta, realizing that this child could attain enlightenment in this lifetime, resolved to save it from the brigands. He went to their hideout and, using his magical powers, he created the figures of many armed soldiers come to arrest them. The brigands, filled with fear, prostrated themselves in front of the master. He preached the Dharma to them, and they became stream-winners. After that, they willingly turned over the kidnapped boy. Upagupta ordained him (as well as all the brigands); they all attained arhatship, and each threw a śalākā into the cave.[36]

The second story is more eclectic in nature but recalls the tradition of recruiting novices which we considered in chapter 3:

(23) Once upon a time, on Mount Urumuṇḍa, a starving tigress died after giving birth to two cubs. Upagupta found the cubs and tried to feed them, but, realizing that they would not survive long, he recited to them the following stanza: "All composite things are impermanent and subject to the law of birth and destruction. Once birth and destruction are overcome, extinction is happiness."[37] The tiger cubs soon died and were reborn in the womb of a Brahmin woman in Mathurā. Then Upagupta, along with several bhikṣus, went to her house on his begging round. Day by day, he reduced the number of followers going with him until finally he went there all alone. The woman's husband asked him why he was all by himself. "I do not have any attendant," he answered. The Brahmin then declared that his wife was pregnant and that if she had a boy, he would give him to Upagupta. Soon his wife gave birth to twin boys. When they were eight years old, the Brahmin gave one of them to Upagupta, but the other declared he wanted to be ordained as well. The father was reluctant to part with both of his sons, but, when Upagupta said that they were both destined for enlightenment, he let them go. Upagupta ordained the twins as novices, and they promptly attained arhatship.

Some time thereafter, he asked them to go and pick some flowers from a jambu tree. The novices replied, "But that tree is too high; we cannot reach them!" Upagupta reminded them that they had magical powers, and so they flew into the air and picked the flowers. The disciples marvelled at this, and Upagupta told them that these twins were the tiger cubs of yore.[38]

The third story to be considered here actually comprises two tales, which we shall number 24a and 24b. These recount the adventures of two karmic companions—a layman named Devarakṣita and a monk named Aṣālha. The tales are too long and complex to be summarized here; suffice it to say that Devarakṣita, thanks to his extraordinary merit making, eventually is ordained and attains arhatship, while Aṣālha, goaded by an old bhikṣuṇī and awed by Upagupta's magical power, is encouraged to practice meditation and achieves the same result.[39]

Dhītika: The Last Disciple and Successor

Finally, we come to the last of the stories of Upagupta's disciples. It differs from the others in that it concerns not an ordinary pupil of his, but Dhītika, the monk who, in the Sarvāstivādin patriarchal tradition, was to become the next Master of the Law. As a conversion story, however, his tale is not at all unusual and, in fact, resembles several others that we have considered.

(25) One day, the elder Upagupta asked himself whether or not his chief disciple and successor, Dhītika, had yet been born, and he realized that he had not. So, accompanied by a large retinue of monks, he went to the house of the future parents of Dhītika on his begging round. Then, gradually, he reduced the number of monks accompa-

nying him, until finally he went to their house all alone. "Master," they asked, "why are you all by yourself?" "I have no disciple," Upagupta answered, "that is why I am alone. May those who wish to serve me come and serve me." The lay householder replied, "Master, I wish to remain a layman and cannot serve you myself, but if I have a son, he will serve you." In time, the lay householder had several children, but all of them died. Finally, he had a son named Dhītika. When he had grown up, his parents sent him, as promised, to Upagupta, who ordained him as a novice and instructed him in the Dharma. Then, when he was twenty years old, it was time for his ordination as a monk. At the start of the ceremony, he became a stream-winner, and by its end, he had attained arhatship.

Some time later, when he was old, Upagupta declared, "I have accomplished the conversions I was supposed to accomplish. . . . I have made my fellow monks prosper, as well as the lay givers. In this manner, I have assured the uninterrupted transmission of the True Dharma." . . . And he said to Dhītika, "My son, the Buddha transmitted the Dharma to Kāśyapa. Kāśyapa transmitted it to Ānanda, Ānanda transmitted it to my master Śāṇakavāsin, and my master transmitted it to me. Now I am transmitting it to you. Seven days hence, I will enter parinirvāṇa."[40]

Thus end in both the *Aśokarājāvadāna* and the *Aśokarājasūtra* the avadānas of Upagupta's disciples.

Upagupta's Upāya

The use of skillful means (upāya) for effectuating conversions or bringing disciples to enlightenment has always been a hallmark of Buddhist teachers. In the stories that we have been considering in this chapter, we have seen numerous examples of Upagupta's upāya. Like many good meditation masters, he was extremely flexible, employing a wide variety of teacherly techniques depending on the situation and the psyche of his disciple. It may be useful to tabulate some of these techniques, which may be thought of as falling into five types of situations:

(a) Upagupta's preaching of the Dharma is specifically mentioned and appears to be a crucial part of, or at least an accessory step in, the soteriological process.

(b) Upagupta resorts to the use of his magical powers of transformation and illusion to stimulate or correct a disciple's progress.

(c) The practice of some form of merit making appears to play a central role in the monk's final attainment of arhatship.[41]

(d) The practice of meditation is clearly an important part of a disciple's striving for enlightenment.

(e) Finally, lest it be forgotten, ordination takes place. For virtually every one of Upagupta's disciples, it appears to have been a prerequisite for arhatship.

TABLE 2
Upagupta's Disciples' Ways to Arhatship

Story No.	Upagupta Preaches Dharma	Upagupta Uses Magic	Disciple Makes Merit	Disciple Practices Meditation	Disciple Is Ordained
1	yes		yes		yes
2	yes				yes
3			yes		yes
4			yes		yes
6	yes	yes			yes
7		yes		yes	yes
8				yes	yes
9	yes	yes	yes		yes
10	yes				not clear
11	yes	yes			yes
12		yes		yes	yes
13	yes	yes		yes	yes
14	yes	yes			yes
15	yes	yes			yes
16	yes				yes
17	yes				yes
18		yes		yes	yes
19	yes	yes		yes	yes
20				yes	yes
21		yes		yes	yes
22	yes	yes			yes
23	yes				as novices
24a			yes		yes
24b		yes		yes	yes
25	yes				yes

Table 2 summarizes our findings.[42] One technique Upagupta uses frequently to help his disciples on the Path (employed in fully half of the stories recounted) is to resort to some kind of magical power to make graphic the lesson he wants to impart. Such power is a by-product of the mastery of the meditational trance, but its use by monks was also something which in Buddhism elicited feelings of great ambiguity. On the one hand, supernatural power popularly figured in countless tales of the achievements of members of the Sangha and, in certain contexts, was thought to be a soteriologically effective tool; on the other hand, in some circles, it was denigrated as dangerous and ineffective in developing faith among unbelievers. Thus, the various Vinayas all contain rules forbidding the gratuitous display of magical powers in front of the laity (although this did not stop even the Buddha from using them with heretics).[43]

It should be noted, however, that Upagupta's use of magical powers never occurs in isolation; it is never the sole means of bringing a disciple to enlightenment, but is always used in combination with some other technique—either the teaching of the Dharma or the promotion of meditation. These two techniques, in fact, are also often employed by Upagupta. This should not surprise us, in view of two of the epithets that we have seen applied to him: he was the "foremost of the Buddha's disciples who were preachers"; and he was the "foremost of those monks who taught dhyāna."

Some disciples (for example, in stories 13 and 19) benefited from both Upagupta's sermons and his teaching of meditation, but a remarkable number of them appear to have attained arhatship by the sole practice of either one or the other of these methods. Thus, in stories 1–2, 6, 9–11, 14–17, 22–23, and 25, it is the Dharma alone (sometimes in conjunction with the use of magic) that leads to the disciple's enlightenment, while in stories 7–8, 12, 18, 20–21, and 24b, it is meditation alone (again sometimes in conjunction with magic) that is effective.

This division could reflect a bifurcation between disciples pursuing the vocation of study and disciples following the vocation of meditation, but there is no clear statement of that in our texts. Moreover, although this distinction between these two vocations in Buddhism is a sociologically useful one, it might make more sense from a soteriological standpoint to speak of two distinct endeavors which Paul Griffiths has called *analytic* and *enstatic*.[44]

The first endeavor is associated with the cultivation of insight (vipāśyanā) and the second with the cultivation of tranquillity (śamatha), two well-known meditational practices which various systematizers of the Theravāda tradition have tried awkwardly to harmonize. More broadly, as Griffiths points out, this dichotomy is related to the polarity "visible throughout the history of Indian thought" between the identification of salvation with ecstatic knowledge (as seen in some Upaniṣads) and its association with the pursuit of enstatic withdrawal from the world (as seen in the practice of Yoga).[45]

These distinctions may be useful here when translated into a Buddhist context. The Upaniṣadic path of knowledge (jñāna) involved not so much the scholarly study of books or of texts as the achievement of insight (vipāśyanā) into the nature of reality, the realization of Brahman, which is imparted to a disciple through teaching by a master. Paul Mus and others have stressed the connection and continuity between certain aspects of the Buddhist notion of Dharma and the Upaniṣadic concept of Brahman, and in many texts the notion of Dharma appears to be more "mystical" than many buddhologists would like to admit.[46] Thus, when, in story 2, Upagupta leads five hundred oxherders to arhatship by imparting to them the Dharma, it is clear that something more fundamental is going on than an intellectual discourse on Buddhist doctrine. The liberating Teaching is being not so much taught as transmitted by Upagupta, and not so much learned as realized by his disciples. In this, there are real parallels with other teacher-pupil scenarios in the path of knowledge.

The path of yogic enstasy, on the other hand, though it may require a teacher for guidance, is not one in which anything formal is transmitted. Realization (if that is the correct term) comes in solitude and withdrawal from the world, both physically and mentally. This path is epitomized in the Buddhist tradition in the cultivation of tranquillity (śamatha), which involves progress through various trance states (dhyāna) up to the attainment of cessation.[47] Interestingly, as we have seen, when Upagupta's disciples are said to meditate, they often appear to be engaging in śamatha practices, rather than in the more analytical enterprise of vipāśyanā. Thus, in stories 18–20, we had cases of monks who got stuck at the fourth trance level, a particularly tricky level in the cultivation of śamatha.

But knowledge and enstasy are not the only ways followed by Upagupta's disciples. In a few cases (stories 1, 3–4, 9, and 24a), merit making, either by itself or in conjunction with other practices, is shown to play a crucial role in the soteriological process.[48] The path of merit making does not seem to be as prevalent as that of hearing the Dharma or pursuing tranquillity; but, if the Hindu example of a variety of ways (mārga) to liberation is applicable, we might think of merit making as a Buddhist version of the path of works (karma), which the *Bhagavad Gītā*, for instance, recognizes as legitimate, even though it does not advocate it. The overall picture that emerges from this study of the stories of Upagupta's disciples, then, is one of a multiplicity of paths to arhatship, each monk practicing one or more of them.

Glaringly absent from this scheme, however, is any reference to the importance of bhakti as a path to enlightenment. Upagupta does not do for his disciples what Māra did for him (that is, make manifest the form of the Blessed One). There is no stress in this context on the glories of the Buddha, absent or present, past or future; and no apparent visionary dimension to the disciples' experiences. Nor, for that matter, does Upagupta himself appear to become the object of intense devotion on the part of those whom he guides to arhatship. Unlike the crowds of Mathurans (who, we can suppose, looked upon Upagupta as a Buddha in a Buddhaless age) and unlike Aśoka (who, as we shall see, did the same), Upagupta's own monastic disciples appear to have shown respect and obedience to him, but hardly blind devotion. They express their arhatship and their discipleship to him not by effusive praise or the glorification of the Buddha, but by the simple act of tossing a śalākā into a cave. Nonetheless, these śalākās, which accumulated at the Naṭabhaṭika in great numbers, came to figure significantly in the story of Upagupta's parinirvāṇa and cremation, and they also came to play an important role in the cult which focussed on him after his death.

The Death of Upagupta and His Cult at Mathurā

After reflecting that he had accomplished all the conversions he was supposed to accomplish, and after passing on the Dharma to Dhītika and so ensuring the continuation of the patriarchate, Upagupta, like his predecessors Śāṇakavāsin, Ānanda, and Mahākāśyapa, turned his mind towards death and parinirvāṇa, an event which is quickly recounted:

> Then [Upagupta] reflected, "There is a cave here thirty-six feet long and twenty-four feet wide. It is filled with the śalākās of my disciples who have become arhats. Now is the time for my parinirvāṇa." . . . Then one hundred thousand arhats assembled, and an incalculable number of those still on the path and those observing the precepts, and innumerable myriads of laypersons. The elder rose up into the air and made manifest the eighteen supernatural transformations, bringing great joy to the minds of all those assembled. Then he entered the state of Nirvāṇa without remainder. His body was cremated with the śalākās contained in the cave. . . . The gods brought all sorts of offerings, and a stūpa was built.[49]

Much the same tradition is found in the Sanskrit text of the *Mūlasarvāstivāda Vinaya*, where the Buddha, predicting the future Nirvāṇa of Upagupta, states:

> In a grove of trees there will be a cave measuring eighteen cubits in length, twelve cubits in width, and seven cubits in height. All those who realize arhatship through Upagupta's preaching will throw a stick [kaṭika] four inches long into that cave. And when the cave becomes filled with arhat sticks, Upagupta will enter parinirvāṇa; and when that happens, they will gather all the arhat sticks together and use them to cremate him.[50]

In this way, then, the story of Upagupta's career as a teacher and a Master of the Law at Mathurā comes to an end. He was not, however, soon forgotten, either by his own disciples or by the people of Mathurā; indeed, his memory lived on at the Naṭabhaṭika, which became both a center of pilgrimage and the site of a nascent cult.

Especially interesting in this regard is the account of Hsüan-tsang, who visited Mathurā on his pilgrimage to India in the seventh century. According to him, the Naṭabhaṭika hermitage actually possessed a fingernail relic of the Buddha, but it was most famous for its Upagupta cave—the cell which contained the śalākās. Access to this room (which Hsüan-tsang says was twenty feet high and thirty feet wide)[51] was apparently through the north wall of the monastery itself,[52] and its existence may have earned the Naṭabhaṭika the appellation Guhāvihāra (Monastery of the Cave).[53]

Hsüan-tsang's account of his visit to Upagupta's cave is noteworthy, for a number of reasons. First of all, despite the tradition that Upagupta was cremated with the tally sticks of his disciples, the Chinese pilgrim claims that those sticks were still piled high in the cave when he visited it. One wonders how this could be if they were all removed and burned at the elder's funeral centuries earlier. Clearly, here we have evidence of a cult of Upagupta that continued long after his time at the Naṭabhaṭika. Whether or not he was cremated with the original tally sticks of his disciples, the practice of tossing these sticks into his cave must have been kept up by subsequent generations, who did this in the course of their pilgrimages as a gesture of respect and devotion to him.

In this regard, two questions arise: what was the meaning of this ritual act, and what kinds of persons engaged in it? The answer to the latter question comes, in part, through a consideration of a second curious detail about Hsüan-tsang's description of his visit to the Naṭabhaṭika—the fact that he was told that the śalākās there were those only of *married couples* whom Upagupta had led to arhatship; in the case of single persons, "although they became arhats, no record . . . was kept."[54]

Scholars have generally dismissed this statement as simply intended to magnify Upagupta's greatness as a preacher: despite its largish dimensions, Upagupta's cave could not contain the tally sticks of *all* of his converts—they were so numerous. This great pile of sticks belonged, rather, only to those married couples who had attained arhatship!

Thomas Watters, discussing this tradition, thought that it was "very silly."[55] If it is, it is nonetheless the kind of "silliness" which lends itself to various lines of speculation. In the context we are dealing with here, married couples are by definition laypersons, and though they may decide to enter the Sangha together, in doing so they opt for ending their marital relationship. However, it is hardly likely that distinctions between arhats would be made on the basis of whether or not they had previously been married. Are we to assume, then, that Upagupta led many *laypersons* to arhatship? This, too, seems hardly likely in view of the constant assertion in this tradition that ordination as a monk or nun normally precedes that attainment. Could it be, then, that, as time went on, the significance of tossing a tally stick broadened and no longer literally meant the attainment of arhatship, but more generally came to symbolize a commitment (in the form of a vow) to future arhatship, or to the postponement of arhatship until the coming of Maitreya,[56] or, perhaps, in a Mahāyānist context, to the bodhisattva path?[57] This interpretation, of course, does not resolve the question of why these devotees are specifically said to be married. Did Upagupta's cave, like a number of other Buddhist shrines throughout Asia, become the site of a cult for couples who, seeking offspring perhaps, would deposit a śalākā there as a sort of votive prayer stick? Unfortunately, Hsüan-tsang's testimony is simply insufficient to allow us to resolve any of these questions.

THE USE AND MEANING OF THE TALLY STICK

Before engaging in further speculations, however, we need to say something more about the śalākā itself. The tally stick was a little piece of wood or bamboo[58] meant, in theory, to be anywhere from five to twenty-four finger-breadths in length, although, as we have seen in our text, it was a little shorter than this. As Hubert Durt has shown in his pioneering study of the subject, these sticks had a bewildering variety of uses in the Buddhist monastic tradition. Their primary purpose appears to have been a computational one. Śalākās were used as voting tallies in ascertaining the majority opinion in a dispute; they were distributed to members of the community to determine the number of monks present in an assembly, or as meal tokens to ensure the distribution of food to a set number of monks, or as lots in determining who should receive certain items.[59] Thus, in a real sense, possession of a śalākā meant being a participant in the community—a voting, eating, attending member.

Beyond this, however, the śalākā also came to have a qualitative or symbolic significance. As we have seen in our texts, it was used to signal the arhatship attained by Upagupta's disciples. It comes as no surprise, then, to find in the works of the Chinese masters of the Vinaya school, where the rules of usage for the śalākā are fully spelled out, that the sticks are said to symbolize wisdom, the vajra-like Dharmakāya of the Buddha, and liberation. Possession of a śalākā meant realization of all these things.[60]

At a more popular level, emphasis was put on one particular aspect of arhatship, and the śalākā became more specifically a symbol of the possession of magical powers. Thus, in a number of avadānas, we find that the sticks are still distributed as tokens for meals, but meals that will be served to the Sangha in a city so far away that it can be reached only by magical flight. Receipt of a śalākā, then, signifies the magical ability to make the journey. This is the case, for instance, in the many stories of the monk Pūrṇa Kuṇḍopadhānīyaka, whom the *Anguttara Nikāya* lists as "foremost of those who receive a tally stick"[61] and who obtains magical powers just when he seizes a śalākā as they are being distributed.[62]

Much the same scenario may be found in the *Svāgatāvadāna*, except that instead of emphasizing arhatship in general or the attainment of magical powers in particular, it places the stress more specifically on the willingness and ability to combat a nāga king.[63] Thus, in one version of this avadāna, we are told that the nāga Aśvatīrthika was oppressing the people of Śuśumāragiri, who asked the Buddha for help. The Buddha, instead of responding personally, decided to send a volunteer. He therefore returned to the monastery and instructed Ānanda to distribute the śalākās to the community, saying "Let the one among you who is capable of subduing the nāga Aśvatīrthika take a śalākā." When none of the senior monks took a stick, the relatively junior Svāgata realized that the Buddha intended him to prove his powers. He promptly took a stick and was then able to conquer the monster.[64]

But if the possession of a śalākā implies arhatship and the magical powers needed to combat nāgas and other demonic forces, the dispossession of the tally stick—specifically, its being tossed on the ground—involves a rather different set of connotations. In the *Mūlasarvāstivāda Vinaya*, for example, when the monk Vaḍḍha is excommunicated, one of the acts that is done, in addition to the overturning of his begging bowl, is the throwing of his tally stick on the ground.[65] Similarly, in the story of the so-called trial of Ānanda at the Council of Rājagṛha, when Ānanda is accused of a series of misdeeds, the elder Mahākāśyapa punctuates each accusation by throwing a śalākā on the ground.[66] Much the same scene is reported at the Second Council at Vaiśālī, where the elder Revata (or, alternatively, his associate Samboka) throws down a śalākā in denouncing each of the ten heterodox points of the Vṛjiputraka monks;[67] and, in a Tun-huang transformation text, any victory of the demonic heretical masters in their contest of magical powers with the elder Śāriputra is likewise said to be marked by the laying down of a golden śalākā.[68]

From all of this, it would appear that the act of throwing a śalākā was itself a ritual which carried certain magical and negative connotations, often implying the presence of heresy.[69] For this reason, perhaps, the Vinaya of the Mahīśāsaka school had a rule specifically against the throwing of tally sticks,[70] while in the Theravāda Vinaya, the Buddha is said to allow for a śalākā box in which to keep the tally sticks so that they will not fall on the ground.[71] Finally, and most interestingly, we are told by the Chinese Vinaya master Tao-hsüan (seventh century) that the noise or rattling of tally sticks upsets evil spirits and that their falling on the ground marks the coming of Māra with intentions of harassing and disturbing the monks.[72]

Clearly, then, the act of tossing a śalākā is fraught with considerable ambiguity. Nonetheless, it is not impossible to find some way through this bewildering array of significances. As we have seen, the śalākā, quite apart from its computational value, implies the attainment of enlightenment. At the same time, it denotes and exposes the presence of heretical or malevolent forces, especially when it falls or is thrown onto the ground. But these two events are not unrelated, the attainment of enlightenment and the magical powers that go with it being precisely that which enables one to see clearly what is heretical or malevolent and what is not.

In this light, the rite of tossing a śalākā into Upagupta's cave, whether it be done by his own direct disciples or by subsequent pilgrims to the Naṭabhaṭika hermitage, makes good sense. As an act, it does indeed symbolize the attainment of enlightenment, but in a particular context: it is enlightenment as a victory over a recognized evil, Māra, who seeks to entrap one in the cycle of saṃsāra. Simply put, it is a statement: "Here is Māra, king of saṃsāra; we have recognized him for what he is, and, by recognizing him, we have overcome him and his realm." As such, the act is also an appropriate declaration of discipleship to Upagupta, for, in tossing their śalākās into his cave, his followers not only attest to their own achievement, they honor and reenact their master's conquest of the Evil One as well.

The Cult of Upagupta in India

We have suggested in this chapter not only that Upagupta attracted to himself a large number of disciples and led them to arhatship in a wide variety of ways, but also that we can find, incipient in the respect those disciples showed to him, a cult of Upagupta which persisted at Mathurā after his death.

In his memoirs of his travels to India, Hsüan-tsang prefaces his account of the Naṭabhaṭika cave and its śalākās with a more general description of the cultic life of Buddhists in the Mathurā region. In that country, he points out, there were stūpas honoring the past Buddhas, stūpas for the relics of Śākyamuni, and various stūpas for major bodhisattvas, such as Mañjuśrī, and for important disciples of the Buddha, such as Śāriputra, Maudgalyāyana, Pūrṇa Maitrāyaṇīputra, Upāli, Ānanda, Rāhula, etc. In particular, it was the stūpas of these disciples that were the object of a cult that Hsüan-tsang then describes:

> In the "Three Longs" of every year, and on the six Fastdays of every month, the Brethren with mutual rivalry make up parties, and taking materials of worship with many valuables, repair to the images of their special patrons. The Abhidharma Brethren offer worship to Sāriputra, the Samādhists to Mudgalaputra [Maudgalyāyana], the Sūtraists to Pūrnamaitriyāniputra, the Vinayists to Upāli, the bhikshunis to Ānanda, and the śrāmaṇeras to Rāhula; and the Mahayanists to the various P'usas [bodhisattvas]. On these days the topes [stūpas] vie with each other in worship: banners and sunshades are displayed, the incense makes clouds and the flowers are scattered in showers, sun and moon are obscured and . . . the king and his statesmen devote themselves to good works.[73]

Much the same situation was described by Fa-hsien during his visit to the region over two centuries earlier. He makes it clear that these festivities were held in conjunction with the annual ceremonial distribution of new robes (kaṭhina), which traditionally took place after the end of the rains.[74]

The interesting element that emerges here, however, is the ritual specialization that took place within Buddhist worship. Not everyone made offerings to all foci of worship, but certain specific groups within the Buddhist community came to focus their devotion on certain great disciples of the Buddha who were well known for particular attributes.

To some extent, this specialization reflects the tradition, embodied most visibly in a well-known list of the *Anguttara Nikāya*, which attributes to each chief disciple of the Buddha certain qualities in which he or she was thought to be "foremost." Thus, for example, it makes sense for Vinaya specialists to pay special honors to Upāli, since he was "chief among those disciples who knew by heart the rules of the Discipline."[75] More generally, however, this specialization reflects the overall legendary traditions that developed around the various disciples. Thus, Ānanda is here especially worshipped by nuns not because of any personal achievements, but because of the legends which consistently depict him as looking out for the interests of the bhikṣuṇīs.[76]

There is another aspect of this system of patron saints which needs to be highlighted here. Devotees of these various disciples of the Buddha did not honor them simply out of respect for their memory; they also worshipped them in order to obtain the qualities and benefits they embodied. This is not clearly brought out by Hsüan-tsang or Fa-hsien in their accounts of the situation at Mathurā, but it is evident in the contemporary Burmese practice of making votive offerings to images of the Buddha's disciples, a practice which would appear to be closely connected to the type of specialization we have been talking about. A single example will have to suffice here. At the Sule pagoda in Rangoon, there is a series of shrines containing images of various disciples of the Buddha, with, for the benefit of devotees, signs announcing what each saint is good for. Thus, if you want wisdom, you should make offerings to Shin Sāriputta; if you want magical powers, Shin Moggallāna; if you want wealth, Shin Sīvalī; if you want to be free from disease, Shin Bakkula, etc.[77] No shrine is here erected for Shin Upago (Upagupta), but there is one nearby with a similar sign saying he is good for protection from Māra—and this, as we shall see, is the constant reason given in Southeast Asia for why one should worship him.

At this point, we are in a position to come to a more specific conclusion about the cult of Upagupta in Mathurā. First, the context there was one of cultic specialization focussing on certain immediate disciples of the Buddha. Although Hsüan-tsang does not specifically include Upagupta in this group, his description of the shrine at the Naṭabhaṭika immediately follows his account of these worship practices in Mathurā. Second, the only known feature of the cult at the Naṭabhaṭika—the tossing of a śalākā into Upagupta's cave—was associated both with the attainment of arhatship and with the overcoming of Māra. It seems logical, therefore, to conclude that in this peculiar act, carried out by all of Upagupta's direct disciples and apparently by devotees of his after his death, we have a votive ritual that was specifically aimed at Upagupta and that sought to capitalize on the powers for which he was especially famous. As a preacher and meditation teacher, Upagupta could lead his followers to arhatship, but, even more specifically, as the subduer of Māra, he could help his devotees—monks and laypersons alike, married and unmarried—to conquer the Evil One.

CHAPTER SEVEN

Upagupta and Aśoka

THE MATHURAN cycle of stories with which we have thus far been concerned represents one of the basic Indian recensions of Upagupta's hagiography. But the legend of the elder was not limited to it. There exists a second Indian cycle of stories about Upagupta which feature his association with the great Mauryan ruler of the third century B.C.E., King Aśoka.

Aśoka is best known today for the edicts and rock inscriptions that he had engraved all over his empire.[1] In these, he set forth his polity of rule by Dharma, which has been much discussed and widely admired.[2] On the basis of the edicts, the question of whether or not Aśoka himself actually became a Buddhist has long been debated.[3] Traditionally, however, in Buddhist circles, Aśoka was known not on the basis of his edicts, but through the legends that were told about him; and these, regardless of their historical accuracy, portray him clearly as a convert to the Buddhist faith and as a strong supporter of the Buddhist Sangha.[4]

Jean Przyluski has argued that the legendary association of Upagupta with Aśoka was essentially an invention of Mathuran authors who were anxious to glorify their own community's abbot by connecting him with the great Mauryan monarch.[5] But it is important to realize that the association of Upagupta with Mathurā is not nearly as universal as Przyluski would have us believe. In a wide variety of sources—some of them quite old—the elder is not associated with Mathurā at all. Thus, in the *Avadānaśataka*, he is portrayed as residing at the Kukkuṭārāma monastery in Pāṭaliputra, and it is there that he meets Aśoka.[6] The same assumption, as we shall see, is found in a number of avadānamālās. In any case, by the tenth century, Chinese pilgrims were visiting Upagupta's hermitage in Magadha,[7] and L. A. Waddell even claims to have identified the "little mountain" near Pāṭaliputra—on which Upagupta is supposed to have lived—with a hill south of present-day Patna.[8] More bewilderingly, Hsüan-tsang reports that the saint resided for some time in the land of Sindh, although elsewhere he also seems to assume that Upagupta dwelt at Pāṭaliputra—where, he asserts, he actually converted Aśoka and helped him with the construction of the eighty-four thousand stūpas.[9] The *Damamūkanidāna sūtra*, on the other hand, has Upagupta as a native of Benares and disciple of the arhat Yaśas,[10] while Tāranātha claims he once resided in Videha in a monastery built for him by a layman named Vasusāra.[11]

Suffice it to say, then, that the traditions about Upagupta's domicile are mixed and do not necessarily all belong to the Mathuran cycle. By considering together these non-Mathuran traditions, as well as the parts of the *Divyāvadāna* and related texts that feature Upagupta's association with the Mauryan king, it is possible to identify a distinct Aśokan cycle of Upagupta legends that may be said to include the following events: (1) the meeting of the elder and the king at Pāṭaliputra; (2) the celebration there of Aśoka's great stūpa festival; (3) the conversations of Aśoka and Upagupta preserved in a whole series of late avadāna works; and (4) the pilgrimage the king and the elder make together to sites marking events in the Buddha's life. In this chapter, we shall examine each of these episodes in turn and see how, in a variety of ways, they not only develop further the Mathuran stories we have looked at, but also prefigure many of the Southeast Asian cultic and legendary traditions we shall encounter in Part 2.

The Meeting of Upagupta and Aśoka

In the *Divyāvadāna*, the episode of Upagupta's meeting with Aśoka is introduced somewhat abruptly. The king, residing in the capital city of Pāṭaliputra, is talking to Yaśas, the abbot of the nearby Kukkuṭārāma monastery. From him he learns that, just as the Buddha long ago made a prediction about him—Aśoka—at the time of his gift of dirt, so, too, he foretold the coming of a great elder named Upagupta.[12] There is no real connection between the two predictions, except that in both of them the Buddha foretells events that will happen one hundred years after his parinirvāṇa. This, however, is enough for Aśoka. When he learns that Upagupta even now is residing on Mount Urumuṇḍa at the head of a circle of arhats, he is instilled with a great desire to meet the elder and orders his ministers to "equip an escort of [men], elephants, chariots and horses, so that he can go himself to Mount Urumuṇḍa.[13]

This desire raises, however, the whole question of protocol which perforce surrounds such meetings. Aśoka's ministers, hearing their sovereign's wish, quickly tell him that it would be inappropriate for him—the king—to go all that way to Urumuṇḍa; he should rather send a messenger and ask Upagupta to come to the capital. Aśoka replies that Upagupta is a great elder, a meditation master; he is not someone who should have to come to the king, but rather someone to whom the king should have to go. Besides, he adds, hinting at the possibility of an even worse loss of royal face, Upagupta is a man whose "body is made of vajra [adamant]" and who could well refuse an order.[14] He therefore declares a second time his intention of going to Mount Urumuṇḍa, and he sends a messenger to tell Upagupta that he is planning to come. This plan, however, is again countermanded, this time by Upagupta himself; thinking that the large number of men in the king's escort would result in injury to many people and to the country, the elder announces that he will go to Pāṭaliputra after all. Aśoka then arranges for his passage to the capital by boat, and

Upagupta, boarding the ferry along with his eighteen thousand arhat-disciples, soon reaches the city. Aśoka goes down to the river to meet him, and there, "standing with one foot on the shore and the other on board the boat, he clasped the elder in his arms and lifted him from the ship on to the dry land."[15]

It is not possible to study this story without noting the clear resemblances it bears to the Pali accounts of the meeting of Aśoka and the elder Moggaliputta Tissa. In short, in the Pali tradition, Moggaliputta Tissa takes the place of Upagupta. He is said to be residing on Mount Ahogangā, "up the Ganges," when Aśoka, in Pāṭaliputra, wants to see him. The king sends envoys, repeatedly inviting him to come to the capital; but the elder declines twice, accepting only on the third occasion, when he is asked to come for the sake of Buddhism. He then proceeds to the capital by boat and is met by King Aśoka, who, coming down to the river's edge to welcome him, physically helps him ashore.[16]

These and other parallels are sufficiently striking to have caused some scholars to conclude that Upagupta and Moggaliputta Tissa were one and the same person. Waddell, for example, suggested long ago that the name Moggaliputta Tissa was merely a title of Upagupta's "formed possibly by the fusing of the names of the two chief disciples of the Buddha, Maudgalyī-putra and Upatiṣya (or Śāriputra)."[17] Vincent Smith agreed: "Waddell has proved conclusively . . . that the Tissa of the Ceylonese is the Upagupta of Indian tradition."[18] And, more recently, Alex Wayman has added some new dimensions to this assertion, presenting evidence for the connection of Moggaliputta Tissa with Mathurā and arguing that Upagupta (like Tissa) may have been involved in the religious upbringing of Aśoka's children.[19]

In his contribution to this question, Waddell tried to list systematically all of the Upagupta-Moggaliputta Tissa parallels.[20] Some of these seem farfetched and others do not concern the story of the meeting of Aśoka and the elder, but four of them will detain us here: (a) both Upagupta and Tissa are said to reside in a meditation hermitage on the upper reaches of the Ganges; (b) both are invited to come to Pāṭaliputra by King Aśoka and agree to do so only after some hesitation; (c) both journey to the capital by boat; and (d) both are personally welcomed ashore by the king.

Urumuṇḍa and Ahogangā

There can be little doubt that Tissa's residence in the Pali sources, Ahogangā, may be equated with the place known in Sanskrit as Urumuṇḍa. Both names refer to famed mountain monasteries located in the region of Mathurā; both were originally associated with the elder Śāṇakavāsin (Pali: Sambhūta Sāṇavāsī); both were centers for meditatively inclined forest monks.[21] More important than these particular identifications, however, is the common tradition they point to of a famous mountain meditation hermitage, remote from but renowned in the capital of Pāṭaliputra.

Stanley Tambiah has studied such "peripheral centers" of prestige and charisma in his work on Buddhist saints of the forest in modern-day Thailand. In his description of one such monastery, Wat Phūthok, the Barren Mountain retreat of the forest saint Acharn Cūan, he emphasizes two points (besides the obvious one of its being a place for the practice of meditation under a charismatic teacher). The first is that this retreat in a distant border region of Northeast Thailand has close contacts with worldly lay sponsors hundreds of miles away in the capital city of Bangkok, sponsors who enjoy close relations with Thai royalty and government. There is, then, a strong and complex center-periphery relationship here, which is channelled through Acharn Cūan's charisma and expressed and enhanced by the making and selling of amulets bearing his image.[22] Second, Wat Phūthok is a place whose location and layout are of cosmological significance. The mountain itself is thought to be a peak like unto heaven where contact with deities and various supernatural beings is possible, and the ascent to its summit may be homologized to a journey through various levels of meditation.[23]

Much the same point could be made about Urumuṇḍa/Ahogaṅgā. There, Upagupta enjoys relations not only with humans, but with devas, yakṣas, and nāgas.[24] Moreover, Upagupta's forest hermitage was well known in the capital of Pāṭaliputra and was a focus of interest and sponsorship for Aśoka, as Wat Phūthok is today for sponsors in Bangkok. Though the *Divyāvadāna* pretends that Aśoka has never heard of the place, the *Aśokarājasūtra* has preserved a story recalling that Aśoka, at Upagupta's instigation, issued a special edict (which he wrote himself and sealed with his own teeth) ordering the enfeoffment of one kingdom to the Naṭabhaṭika and thereby assigning its revenue to it.[25]

Aśoka's Invitation

Whatever the connections of Urumuṇḍa and Ahogaṅgā, Aśoka would clearly like to go to Upagupta's hermitage to meet with him. In the *Divyāvadāna*, as we have seen, he twice declares his intention to do so; he is countered first by his ministers and second by Upagupta, but then finally the problem is resolved by the elder's decision to come to the capital himself.

This "two-plus-one" pattern is even more evident in the Pali story of Aśoka's invitation of Moggaliputta Tissa: Aśoka sends four elders and four ministers to Ahogaṅgā, charging them to invite Tissa and return with him; but he declines to come. Aśoka therefore sends eight elders and eight ministers to the mountain, but again with the same lack of success. Finally, he asks the monks how the elder can be persuaded, and they reply that, if the messengers ask him to come for the sake of the religion, then he will surely consent. So again Aśoka tries: he sends sixteen elders and sixteen ministers, and this time Tissa agrees to come as soon as he hears their message.[26]

It is interesting to see in these two accounts a prefiguration of a number of later Southeast Asian traditions. Both the story of Aśoka's invitation of Tissa and that of his invitation of Upagupta make it clear that the elder will come only for the sake of assisting and preserving the Buddhist Order (and not to seek greater glory and prestige or to curry favor with the king). Otherwise, he would prefer to remain in the seclusion of his meditative mountain retreat. Much the same could be said of modern-day saints of the forest in Thailand[27] and of the *Lokapaññatti*, where, as we shall see, it is likewise for the sake of the Sāsana—in order to protect it from the incursions of Māra—that Upagupta agrees to come to this world.

The threefold nature of Aśoka's invitation is also interesting in light of the Southeast Asian ritual tradition of having to invite Upagupta three times. As we have seen, in certain parts of Laos and Northern Thailand, when villagers go to fetch the rocks that symbolize Upagupta's presence from the bottom of a river or a swamp, it is only the third rock that is declared to be the saint and carried back to the monastery in procession. In chapter 3, we cited this ethnographic fact in the context of Upagupta's birth: the story of Śāṇakavāsin realizing that Gupta's first two sons—Aśvagupta and Dhanagupta—were not Upagupta, who came only third. Here an analogue may be found in the tradition of Aśoka's invitation of the elder—twice refused but accepted the third time.

The Journey by Boat

Once they have accepted Aśoka's invitation, both Upagupta and Moggaliputta Tissa decide to proceed to Pāṭaliputra by boat. Once again, the Pali tradition explains this in a straightforward manner. It points out that Tissa is very aged (a mahallaka!), so that presumably he cannot walk far; and that, being a monk, he cannot ride in a carriage or a palanquin. Aśoka thus provides a ship to bring him down the Ganges.[28] The Sanskrit version is likewise straightforward—stating simply that the king, assuming Upagupta will come by boat, decides to arrange for his passage (although there is some confusion about the curious term *nausaṃkrama* that is used here to designate the type of boat Aśoka provides[29]).

Geographically, this trip by boat makes good sense; Mathurā is located on the Jumna (Yamunā), a major tributary of the Ganges, near the shore of which, far downstream, was the ancient city of Pāṭaliputra. But the journey also has other, more symbolic repercussions. It is noteworthy that Upagupta does not simply employ his magical powers and fly through the air to the capital; it is important that he proceed by boat. This may simply have been a way for him to give Aśoka a chance of making more merit (by providing the means of transportation), but the specifics here are interesting as an early sign of what was to become in Southeast Asia an important ritual tradition associated with Upagupta.

We have already mentioned Upagupta's association with rivers in the threefold ritual invitations that are made to him in Thailand and Laos. We shall see in chapter 9 how this connection is reinforced by Upagupta's association in those countries with the festival of lights (Loi Krathong), during which hundreds of little rafts are set afloat on the river, each with a small oil lamp burning on it. In Burma, moreover, it is common for images of Upagupta at temples to be enthroned on small rafts that are kept afloat in a tank of water. Even more relevant is the Burmese tradition of constructing a real raft or boat, placing on it an image of Upagupta, and floating it downriver.[30] This act, which virtually repeats what Aśoka does for Upagupta in the legend, is said to be for the purpose of returning the saint to his brazen pavilion in the midst of the waters of the ocean. All rivers are the Ganges, not only in India but in Southeast Asia as well,[31] and it seems clear that in these Burmese traditions of building a raft and floating Upagupta downstream on it, we have an echo of the legend of Upagupta's coming to Aśoka's capital on a boat.

A number of scholars have chosen to emphasize the symbolic importance of this journey by water. One line of interpretation has it that Upagupta's trip symbolizes the crossing of the stream of saṃsāra, the attainment of final liberation.[32] It is true that the metaphor of the Buddha's Teaching as a raft that enables one to traverse a sea of suffering is a common one, but there are two reasons why it seems inapplicable here. First of all, as we shall see in full detail in chapter 11, although Upagupta is an arhat, he is an arhat who chooses to remain in saṃsāra. He refrains from crossing the "stream" completely; having reached the other shore, he stays on the raft. Second, and more immediately, the emphasis in this story is not on a journey *across* a stream, but on a journey *down* a stream, from Mathurā to Pāṭaliputra. This is a descent and not a fording, and, as such, it carries a rather different set of connotations.[33]

A more fruitful line of interpretation emerges from remembering that this is the Ganges that Upagupta is descending. In Indian lore, the Ganges, of course, is a channel of great sacrality, but one of its chief mythical roles is that of acting as a link, a conduit, between heaven (the realm of the gods) and this world (the realm of humans).[34] Indeed, the theme of the Descent of the Heavenly Ganges crashing to earth through Śiva's matted locks, so well loved in Indian art and myth, serves to emphasize this notion: the Ganges is one way to get from heaven to earth and eventually back again.[35]

In Buddhism, however, "descent" from heaven to earth is not generally associated with the Ganges or with rivers. It is, rather, connected with the example of the Buddha himself. In the Buddha's biography, there are several famous "descents," but one of them in particular is worth recalling here: the Buddha's own return to earth from the Trāyastriṃśa Heaven after he had spent a rains retreat there preaching to his mother.[36] The story is well known and may perhaps best be recalled in Alfred Foucher's words:

> [I]t was during the sixteenth year after Enlightenment that the Buddha decided to go up to the Heaven of the Thirty-three Gods, where his mother Māyā had been reborn, and teach her the Good Law. So he mysteriously disappeared from the earth and came back only three months later, on the day of the full moon in October, near the town of Sānkāśya. His ascension, which was considered rather commonplace and within the power of others, was barely noticed. The Descent, however, was quite another matter. It became an occasion of great pomp and took place on a triple stairway made of precious materials and specially built by the gods. The Buddha descended between Brahmā on his right and Indra on his left against a sky entirely peopled with divinities singing his praises and showering down flowers. At the bottom of the steps his principal disciples and a crowd of his faithful were waiting for him.[37]

A number of comments about this legend need to be made here. First of all, Sāṃkāśya, where this descent of the Buddha took place, was located—perhaps not insignificantly—on the upper reaches of the Ganges.

Second, though not mentioned here by Foucher, one of the persons in this legend who figures prominently among those welcoming the Buddha back to earth is the nun Utpalavarṇā. She, in order to be the first to greet the Buddha, uses her magical powers to take on the form of a great cakravartin king, and others consequently make way for her. Here, then, as in the case of Upagupta's descent of the Ganges to be welcomed by Aśoka, we have an instance of a great monk coming down from a heavenly abode to be honored and welcomed by royalty.[38]

Third, it is important to note in what sense the Trāyastriṃśa is here viewed as a heaven. Though physically (that is, rupalogically) it is the abode of the thirty-three classes of gods led by Indra, the Buddha's presence there transforms it into a sort of supernatural monastery—a "dharmalogical heaven." Indeed, what is emphasized in this story is the preaching of the Dharma—more specifically the Abhidharma—which the Buddha expounds nonstop to his mother (and the assembled deities) for the entire three months of the rainy season.[39]

Fourth, intriguingly, the Buddha's descent from the Trāyastriṃśa Heaven, once his sermon there is over, is generally called not a Buddhāvatāra (descent of the Buddha) but a devāvatāra or a devorohana (descent of the deities).[40] This points to an important feature of this descent: it is a time not only when the Buddha comes down from heaven, but when the gods—in particular Indra and Brahmā, who accompany him on ladders of their own—become visible to humans. Apparently, there is a breakdown of the usual barriers that separate these beings from one another. Indeed, as one account of the legend puts it:

"When the Buddha descended from the Trāyastriṃśa Heaven . . . the gods saw the humans and the humans saw the gods. On the dais were the Buddha, a noble cakravartin king, and the great assembly of the gods; the meeting was more adorned than it had ever been before."[41] In this regard, it makes sense that the festival for welcoming the Buddha on this occasion is, at least in one source, described as a devamanuṣyasaṃpadā (a concord of men and deities).[42]

Fifth, the departure of the Buddha to the Trāyastriṃśa Heaven is, at least in some texts, treated very much as though it were his permanent extinction in parinirvāṇa. He does not announce where he is going, but simply disappears, and the multitude, at least initially, fears he is gone forever. Thus, in the *Dhammapadaṭṭhakathā*, the assembled faithful loudly lament and exclaim, "He that delights in solitude, he that is steadfast will not come back again to this world. We may not see the Supremely Exalted, the Prince of the World, the mightiest of men."[43] This reaction is significant, for it means that the eventual return of the Buddha from the Trāyastriṃśa Heaven is not only a miracle which is fraught with marvels, but it is a sort of mythological dry run for the Buddha's disappearance at parinirvāṇa and his reappearances thereafter. The return is something which overcomes extinction and hints at one way in which the physical form (rūpa) of the Buddha can be recaptured, despite its absence.

Finally, the timing of the Buddha's descent at Sāṃkāśya is noteworthy. It is made to coincide with the end of the rainy season, a very important ritual occasion in the Buddhist tradition. Not only is this a special season of offerings made by laypersons to Buddhist monks, but even today, in Thailand and elsewhere, the festival closing the "Lenten" rains retreat (Org Phansa) is marked by ritual reenactments of the Sāṃkāśya story. In Chiang Mai, for instance, a citywide festival is held in October each year in which an image of the Buddha is slowly brought in procession down from a monastery on a hilltop (symbolically associated with the Trāyastriṃśa Heaven) to the campus of Chiang Mai University. There it is welcomed by crowds of laypersons, who take this occasion to make major offerings to the monks as well.[44] Elsewhere in Northern Thailand at Org Phansa, highly elaborate bamboo and paper pavilions are made for the Buddha, both to symbolize the Trāyastriṃśa Heaven which he is leaving and to welcome him back to earth with royal splendor.

The use of these pavilions is especially relevant to our study, because, in far Northwestern Thailand, along the Burmese border, the custom has persisted of making such paper pavilions for *Upagupta* at the close of the rainy season. At one wat, six kilometers north of Mae Hong Son, for instance, pavilions are prepared at Org Phansa for both the Buddha and Upagupta. In the latter, small offerings are placed, as well as a painted picture of the saint. The same custom exists elsewhere in the region and is locally said to have once been very common in the Shan States in Burma.[45]

This conjunction of traditions reinforces, then, the parallelism we have been tracing between the descent of the Buddha at Sāṃkāśya and Upagupta's descent of the Ganges to Pāṭaliputra. Both involve a "coming down" from a heavenly abode; both involve the welcome of a great saint by a great king; and both involve, as we shall see presently, the possibility of a particular kind of contact between gods and humans.

Upagupta's Royal Welcome

Upagupta's arrival at Pāṭaliputra is described in the texts in rather meticulous detail. Aśoka has the city decorated in anticipation of his coming, and, together with his retinue and all the citizens of the capital, he proceeds to the river to welcome the elder personally with garlands, perfumes, music, and blossoms. When the elder's boat arrives, Aśoka alights from his elephant and goes down to the riverbank on foot. There, clasping Upagupta in his arms, he physically lifts him onto shore and declares:

> When I cut down the enemy hosts and placed
> the earth and its mountains ringed by the sea
> under a single umbrella of sovereignty,
> my joy was not then what it is now
> that I have seen you, O elder.
> The sight of you has doubled my faith
> in this most excellent order.
> Looking at you today I see in you
> the incomparable Self-Existent Pure One
> even though he is gone beyond.[46]

This is, of course, not the only time that Aśoka is thus reminded of the Buddha;[47] moreover, we have already seen and shall encounter again a number of other instances of this kind of vivid recall of the Buddha in the mind of a devotee.

The Pali tradition, however, in its depiction of Aśoka's welcome of Moggaliputta Tissa, seems to want to stress the *physical* contact that occurs here between king and elder. The *Mahāvaṃsa*'s account of the episode is as follows: "Going down even knee-deep into the water, the king respectfully gave his right hand to the thera, as he came down from the ship. The venerable thera took the king's right hand from compassion toward him, and came down from the ship."[48] Buddhaghosa and the *Extended Mahāvaṃsa* that was compiled in Cambodia make it clear that this physical contact needs to be interpreted in the context of a society in which the king's person was generally thought to be inviolate and could not be touched by commoners. Indeed, in these texts, we are told that, when the elder Moggaliputta Tissa actually touched the king's hand, the royal bodyguard drew their swords, intending to cut off the elder's head on the spot for violating the taboo on physical contact with the king. Aśoka, however, stops them, explaining that he is already sad about the wrongs done to members of the Sangha and that no harm should be done to the elder.[49]

A taboo on touching the king was, of course, a very widespread phenomenon in the ancient world. In India, one of the reasons for its occurrence was that the king's person was considered to be in some way divine. The word *deva* was commonly applied not only to gods, but to monarchs as well; and, as Jean Filliozat has pointed out, it is in this light that we should interpret the story just recounted.[50] In allowing Aśoka to come into bodily contact with the elder, and, indeed, in emphasizing that fact, the legend is once again asserting the breakdown of the usual barriers that separate humans from devas.[51] Much the same thing, as we have seen, occurred at the time of the welcoming of the Buddha upon his descent from the Trāyastriṃśa Heaven. There the devas were actual deities rather than kings, but the point is in both cases the same: as a result of these descents (avatāras), not only is there to be dharmalogical contact with divinity, but rupalogical contact as well.

Upagupta and the Great Stūpa Festival

The same point is made, perhaps, in the next episode of the Aśokan cycle: the legend of Upagupta's involvement in the Mauryan emperor's most famous meritorious act, his construction and dedication of eighty-four thousand stūpas over the relics of the Buddha. The story of Aśoka's gathering of the relics from the eight stūpas where they had originally been enshrined and of his redistribution of them into the newly built stūpas all over his empire need not detain us here.[52] It became Aśoka's most famous legendary act and, for centuries thereafter, Buddhist pilgrims in India and beyond habitually thought of any ancient stūpas they came across as being ones that Aśoka had built.[53] The construction of these stūpas may be interpreted as the symbolic spread and establishment throughout the whole of Jambudvīpa of the Buddha's physical body (his rūpakāya), but in such a way as to make concrete at the same time the Buddha's Doctrine—his Dharmakāya.[54]

What we need to focus on here, however, is not just the symbolic significance of the gathering and enshrinement of the relics, but also the role that Upagupta plays in this enterprise, for, in one version of the tale at least, it is he who makes the final and crucial dedication ceremony possible.

Hsüan-tsang recounts in his memoirs the tale of how, following his conversion, Aśoka tells Upagupta of his desire to build many stūpas in honor of the Buddha's relics. The elder responds approvingly and suggests that the king employ the services of local divinities to carry out the project. Accordingly, these godlings prepare stūpas—eighty-four thousand of them—in population centers all over Jambudvīpa, each one intended to enshrine a share of the relics. Aśoka would like to have all of the Buddha relics deposited in the stūpas simultaneously, and again he asks Upagupta to help make this possible.

Upagupta responds by stretching out his hand and covering the face of the sun at midday; the gods, seeing this signal throughout the kingdom, know that the right time for enshrinement has arrived, and, all together, they deposit the relics in the stūpas.[55]

It should immediately be pointed out that, in the *Divyāvadāna* and other Sanskrit texts, it is not Upagupta but Yaśas, the abbot of the Kukkuṭārāma, who signals the moment of the enshrinement of the relics by hiding the orb of the sun with his hand.[56] Moreover, in the *Mahāvaṃsa* and the Theravāda tradition, there is no mention of this "eclipse" at all; instead, the simultaneous completion of the eighty-four thousand vihāras is made possible by an elder named Indagutta.[57]

It is Hsüan-tsang alone, then, who highlights the role of Upagupta here, and, as a result, some may be inclined to dismiss his version of the story as an aberration. Nonetheless, his account is significant. It reflects, perhaps, a tradition that was current in India in the seventh century; moreover, in the *Lokapaññatti* and in Southeast Asian legend, it is to this same ceremony enshrining the relics in the eighty-four thousand stūpas that Aśoka invites Upagupta so that he can use his supernatural powers to ward off any potential interference from Māra.

Scholars studying the story of Upagupta/Yaśas stretching out his hand to cover the face of the sun have generally seen in it a reference to an actual solar eclipse that occurred in India during the time of the historical Aśoka, and some have thereby sought to establish an absolute chronology for events in Aśoka's reign.[58] It should be remembered, however, that the ability to touch the sun (or the moon) was one of the standard magical powers (ṛddhi; Pali: iddhi) achieved by Buddhist meditators, along with such things as walking on water, flying through the air, becoming invisible, passing through walls, penetrating the earth, creating doubles of oneself, and emitting fire from one's body. Though less commonly described than some of these other feats, it is nonetheless always included with them in the usual listings of such things.[59]

Buddhaghosa, in fact, distinguishes three types of touching the sun and moon. The adept can, if he wants to, travel to the sun and moon and touch them; or, while sitting down here on earth, he can resolve that the sun and moon come down into his hands; or, finally, he can make his hand grow, stretching it out until it reaches up to the sun and moon.[60] Clearly, Upagupta's feat is an example of the latter type. By virtue of the magical powers he has gained through his accomplishments in meditation, he extends his arm in order to bring about a concrete and positive event: a solar "eclipse" that can be seen throughout Jambudvīpa and that can therefore signal the simultaneous enshrinement of the relics of the Buddha.

Generally speaking, however, in Buddhism, as in the Indian tradition as a whole, eclipses are not thought of in positive terms. They are attributed to the demon (asura) Rāhu and are times of panic among the gods. Usually, Rāhu is said to swallow the sun or the moon, causing the sun-god or the moon-god to flee their abodes in terror. A well-known story preserved in a short paritta text, the so-called Candrasūtra (Pali: Candimasutta), tells of the time the moon-god Candima, about to be swallowed by Rāhu, seeks refuge in the Buddha. The Blessed One then rather severely reprimands Rāhu and orders him to release the moon, which Rāhu does because he realizes that otherwise his head will split into pieces.[61]

In some Pali sources, Rāhu is said not to swallow the sun and moon, but merely to caress them with his hand.[62] This is also the case in certain Southeast Asian traditions; in a number of Northern Thai stories, for example, Rāhu is portrayed as a frog who hides the sun or moon with his thumb.[63] In Shan versions of this tale, it is said that Rāhu uses his hand to hide the heavenly orbs because the Buddha (or, alternatively, Phra In, that is, Indra) will no longer allow him to swallow them.[64]

Rāhu is not famous only for causing eclipses. He is also known as chief among those beings possessing personality (attabhāva), which is taken to mean that he has a huge body (forty-eight hundred leagues high) and an imposing presence.[65] Elsewhere, he is said to be one of the five causes of drought, for he sometimes gathers rainwater in the sky and causes it to fall not on land but in the ocean.[66]

It is tempting to see in Upagupta a sort of positive counterpart to Rāhu. Like Rāhu, he can cause an eclipse, but he does so for beneficial rather than detrimental purposes; his act does not cause general panic, but signals the enshrinement of the Buddha's relics. Also, like Rāhu, Upagupta can keep the rain from falling; he never does so to cause a drought, but rather to ensure the success of a merit-making festival.[67] Even more intriguing is the Southeast Asian tradition of worshipping Upagupta especially on full-moon nights that fall on Wednesdays. Wednesday afternoon and night, in a common Southeast Asian astrological assignment of the days of the week to various planetary deities, is the intercalary day that belongs to Rāhu. It makes sense, therefore, for Upagupta to be especially called on at this time of high risk to counter any possible action by him.[68] Finally, as we shall see, in Burma and Thailand, Upagupta's iconography generally portrays him as particularly focussed on the sun. The usual representation of him in statues and paintings is that of a monk, his hand in his begging bowl, gazing up over his shoulder at the sun in order to see whether or not it has passed the meridian so as to determine whether or not he can eat his meal. Alternatively, it is said that he is using his magical powers to stay the sun in its course, in order to be able to eat after noon.[69] In either case, it is worth remembering that, according to Hsüan-tsang, it was right at midday that Upagupta reached up to touch the solar disk with his hand. This act, then, was perhaps designed not simply to signal a festival occasion, but rather to halt the process of time so that the stūpa celebrations (also involving the feeding of monks) could take place without being interrupted.[70] In these various ways, then, Upagupta, like his counterpart Yaśas, may be seen as a facilitator of Aśoka's festival.

Upagupta and Indagutta

The Theravāda tradition, however, assigns this role of facilitator to another monk, the arhat Indagutta. Though the -gutta (Sanskrit: -gupta) ending of their names is perhaps what first led scholars to see (and the tradition to develop) parallels between them, the similarities between Upagupta and Indagutta go beyond this nominal coincidence.

The *Mahāvaṃsa*, in its description of the building of the eighty-four thousand vihāras, states that the Great Monastery in the capital, known as the Asokārāma, was quickly completed thanks to the elder Indagutta, who acted as the "superintendent of work" (kammādhiṭṭhāyaka) for that construction.[71] Buddhaghosa goes further than this and suggests that Indagutta was responsible for the completion of all eighty-four thousand vihāras, for he used his psychic and supernatural abilities to finish on time whatever work had not yet been completed.[72] The *Sahassavatthu*, a pre-ninth-century collection of legends, adds that this great thera Indagutta, who was fully endowed with the various magical powers, was invited by Aśoka to come to the capital, where he was welcomed with great ceremony. On his way to Pāṭaliputra from his monastery in a city called Devaputtanagara, he and his sixty thousand disciples had to cross a river. To assist them in this crossing, Aśoka arranged for some yakkhas to build a bridge (just as he arranged for Upagupta's journey by boat to the capital). C. Witanachchi, who has studied these stories, rightly recognizes in them some potentially striking parallels to our legend.[73]

The Theravāda tradition, however, knows of another Indagutta (whom Witanachchi calls Indagutta II) who lived at the time of King Duṭṭhagāmaṇī of Sri Lanka. His legend is similar enough to that of Indagutta I that it is hard to believe it was not patterned after it. Like Indagutta I, Indagutta II was a "superintendent of work" directing the construction of a great stūpa (not Aśoka's, but Duṭṭhagāmaṇī's) and supervising the enshrinement of Buddha relics (not in Pāṭaliputra, but in Anurādhapura). Like Indagutta I, Indagutta II was endowed with supernatural powers and was invited by the king to come to the capital for the occasion (not from Devaputtanagara, but from the region of Rājagṛha, whence he journeyed together with eighty thousand bhikṣu-disciples).[74]

But the *Mahāvaṃsa* adds one interesting detail about Indagutta II which is not found in the legend of Indagutta I. Duṭṭhagāmaṇī's ceremony for the enshrinement of the relics is said to be a possible target for Māra. Indagutta II, in order to ward off the Evil One, uses his magical powers to make a huge brazen umbrella (lohacchatta) with which he covers the entire world (cakkavāḷa).[75] This supernatural feat is noteworthy for the connections it suggests. The theme of a protective umbrella raised to ward off the incursions of a threatening deity first calls to mind the Mathuran story of Kṛṣṇa sheltering the inhabitants of Vṛndāvana from the storm unleashed upon them by the god Indra by lifting up over them, as one giant umbrella, the whole of Mount Govardhana.[76] Such an "umbrella" is obviously symbolic of sovereignty and of the protection that comes with it, but, more concretely and specifically, it serves also to ward off the rain. We have already seen that one of the functions and powers of Upagupta in Southeast Asia is to protect Buddhist festivals from rain, and this theme will become more significant as we go along.

All these stories of Upagupta-Yaśas-Indagutta point to a well-established tradition of an elder endowed with supernatural powers who is involved in ensuring the success of Aśoka's ceremonial dedication of relics, and, by extension, the success of any great festival occasion in honor of the Buddha.

The Conversations of Upagupta and Aśoka

This dedication is not the only enterprise in which the elder and the king are involved at Pāṭaliputra. According to a rather different Indian Buddhist tradition, Upagupta is also featured as the narrator of avadānas, which he recounts at the request of the Mauryan monarch and for his edification.[77] These "conversations of Aśoka and Upagupta" (Aśokopaguptasambhāṣana)[78] form an aspect of the elder's legend and cult that we have not yet touched upon, but one which is not unrelated to the materials that we have been considering.

Conversations between kings and Buddhist monks—whatever their historical basis—were not unknown in Buddhist literature. The *Milindapañha* is perhaps the most famous example of this genre, but the pattern may be found in other Pali texts—for instance, in the series of dialogues between the Buddha and King Pasenadi recorded in the *Samyutta Nikāya*.[79] Even more relevant, perhaps, is the conversation at the Kukkuṭārāma in Pāṭaliputra between the elder Nārada (like Upagupta, a master of śamatha meditation) and the Magadhan king Muṇḍa (an ancestor of Aśoka).[80]

The dialogues between Upagupta and Aśoka are somewhat different in that they are not limited to a single work but extend over a whole series of texts—several anthologies of avadānas—compiled over a number of centuries. The pattern may first be detected in the very last tale of the *Avadānaśataka*. This collection, which has been dated as belonging to the first century C.E.,[81] consists of one hundred tales organized into ten chapters of ten tales each; it recounts the karmic fortunes of various individuals. For the most part, the stories are very stereotyped and intended primarily to illustrate meritorious acts of devotion that result in their perpetrators variously becoming, in the future, Buddhas, pratyekabuddhas, arhats, arhatīs, devas, and pretas.[82]

The last story, however, differs from all the others in the anthology. Long ago it caught the attention of scholars because it contains a brief and seemingly ancient account of the Buddha's parinirvāṇa,[83] but it is the unusual sequel to this event that interests us here—for in it Upagupta is introduced for the first time as the narrator of an avadāna story. Indeed, following the account of the Buddha's demise, the time and place of the narrative shift suddenly, and we are told that, one hundred years later, King Aśoka ruled in Pāṭaliputra and had a son named Kuṇāla.[84] Kuṇāla was a remarkably handsome lad, and one day, boasting of his beauty, Aśoka asked some visiting merchants from Gandhāra whether they had ever seen a boy like him. Somewhat to the king's surprise, they declared that in fact there was, in their home country, a young man named Sundara ("Handsome") whose appearance was finer than that of any human and almost equal to that of the gods. At his birth, a beautiful tank and flowery park had appeared, and they continued to manifest themselves magically wherever he went.

Upon learning this, Aśoka desires to meet this marvellous Sundara and summons him to the capital. He soon arrives, park and all; and Aśoka, wishing to show this marvel to Upagupta, takes Sundara to the Kukkuṭārāma monastery, where he introduces him to the elder. Upagupta, noting the lad's extraordinary qualities, undertakes a marvel of his own: he preaches a sermon which moves Sundara to wander forth and instantly brings him to arhatship. Aśoka then asks Upagupta to explain the karmic causes of these various phenomena, and this the elder does by relating the avadāna of Sundara—the story of the lad's previous life, at the time of the First Council, when he offered a perfumed bath to the elder Mahākāśyapa (whence the tank and his own beauty) and took a vow to be initiated into the teachings of Śākyamuni and to attain enlightenment (whence his arhatship).[85]

This pattern is a perfectly commonplace one in Buddhist literature; the *Avadānaśataka* itself is full of stories of marvellous and extraordinary happenings that are said to give rise to doubts or result in the astonishment of monks who then question the Buddha about them, asking him to explain how they came about. What is unusual here is that it is not the Buddha but Upagupta who is resolving these doubts, and not the monks but King Aśoka who is having them.

Given this situation, it is noteworthy that in the *Chuan chi po yüan ching*, a Chinese translation of the *Avadānaśataka* which is widely thought to be older than the present Sanskrit recension of the text, Upagupta does not appear at all in the final chapter.[86] Instead, Kunāla is said to be the son not of Aśoka but of King Prasenajit, and the story of Sundara's previous life is told not by Upagupta but by Śākyamuni himself.[87]

Taken together, these two versions hint at one important aspect of Upagupta's role as narrator of avadānas: he may replace the Buddha in post-parinirvāṇa times as the person who can remove doubts about the karmic history of a particular event. As a "Buddha without the marks" who will do the work of a Buddha, he takes over this function of the Blessed One and becomes the authoritative narrator of the past deeds of individuals.

This role of Upagupta was to be much emphasized in subsequent developments in the avadāna genre. It is found, for instance, in the series of "garlands of avadānas" (avadānamālās) that sought to retell in verse tales systematically selected from the *Avadānaśataka*. The overall scheme of this selection process has long intrigued scholars and need not be described here.[88] Suffice it to say that it involves a number of different anthologies that all exhibit the same method in their reworking of stories chosen systematically from the various chapters of the *Avadānaśataka*. The pattern can first be detected in the *Kalpadrumāvadānamālā*,[89] and it continues in the *Ratnāvadānamālā*,[90] the *Ratnamālāvadāna*,[91] the *Aśokāvadānamālā*,[92] and, to a lesser extent, the *Dvāviṃśatyavadāna*.[93]

In all of these anthologies, the individual avadānas are presented as being recounted by Upagupta to King Aśoka at the latter's request. Each recitation, then, is set in the framework of a short and generally stereotyped dialogue between the elder and the king. For instance, in one of the published chapters of the *Kalpadrumāvadānamālā*, we can read the following (the setting for the tale is the Kukkuṭārāma at Pāṭaliputra):

> Now Aśoka, the great king who had dispelled all sorrow, bowed down in front of the guru Upagupta and, his hands cupped in devotion, said, "Bhadanta, I wish to hear yet another fine tale. You can tell me what was said by the Lion of the Śākyas." Thus being asked by the king and beholding the assembly, the best of yatis Upagupta related this fine tale: "Listen, mighty king, for the benefit of the whole world, I will recite the avadāna of Subhūti."[94]

Upagupta then proceeds to narrate the legend of the Buddha's disciple Subhūti, at the end of which Aśoka thanks him, praises him, and then requests to hear yet another tale. Upagupta complies and proceeds with the story of Yaśomatī. This tale finished, Aśoka requests another one, and then another, and another, and so on.

The other avadānamālās in the cycle follow this same pattern, sometimes reducing the dialogue to almost nothing, sometimes embellishing it. For example, one version of the *Ratnamālāvadāna* begins with Upagupta awakening from samādhi and mounting the lion's throne in order to preach to Aśoka, who is now accompanied by all the townspeople of Pāṭaliputra.[95] There then follows the entire anthology of the *Ratnamālāvadāna*, each story being introduced by a renewed request on Aśoka's part to hear "yet another fine tale."[96]

The *Aśokāvadānamālā* sets an even more elaborate scene. It begins by recounting the entire legend of King Aśoka in terms that more or less follow the *Divyāvadāna*. The initial stories are put in the mouth of an elder named Jayaśrī, who resides at the Kukkuṭārāma in Pāṭaliputra. Aśoka's genealogy is recounted, as well as his accession to the throne and his early career as a cruel and impetuous monarch. Then comes his conversion to Buddhism by the novice Samudra and his erection of thousands of stūpas over the relics of the Buddha. There follow the tales of his further sponsorship of Buddhism—his proclamation of it as the religion of the country and his holding of a great quinquennial festival under the leadership of the arhat Piṇḍola. Soon, however, the story turns to a number of tragic episodes: the jealousy of Aśoka's queen Tiṣyarakṣitā and her attempt to destroy the Bodhi tree, the blinding of Aśoka's son Kunāla, and the beheading of his brother, who was mistakenly taken for a Jain.[97] It is this last story that sets up the second part of the text: Aśoka turns in his grief to Upagupta, whom he has invited down from Mathurā; and the elder then narrates, purportedly in order to console and further edify the king, no fewer than nineteen separate avadānas, which make up the rest of the anthology. A few of these have been edited, and in them Upagupta's appearance and his dialogues with the king are just as stereotyped as in the other avadānamālās.[98]

The avadānamālās in this cycle of texts are not the only ones to feature conversations between Upagupta and Aśoka. Other anthologies having little to do with the *Avadānaśataka* exhibit this scheme as well.[99] More intriguing for our purposes, however, are a number of late Mahāyānist or Vajrayānist works which, like the *Aśokāvadānamālā*, introduce the figure of the elder Jayaśrī—from whom a king named Jinaśrī now requests to hear the tales. Jayaśrī always consents, but in so doing, he makes a reference to the fact that he will tell the story the way Upagupta told it to Aśoka in days of yore. This is the case, for example, in the *Vrātāvadānamālā*:[100]

> The eminent monk Jayaśrī said to Jinaśrī: "Please listen, and I will describe the great observance [vrata] relating to hundred thousand Caityas." He [Aśoka] asked Upagupta who was residing at the Kukkuṭa Monastery, "Tell the story of the observance relating to Caityas [Caityavratakathā] and likewise the story of the Śṛngabherī." The son of Gupta [Upagupta] then announced: "Listen, O son of Bindusāra [Aśoka] [and I will tell it to you] as taught by the preceptor of Śāṇavāsi [Ānanda] desirous of the welfare [of others]."[101]

The same pattern may be found in the *Bhadrakalpāvadāna*, a work which presents itself as a sort of poetical continuation of the *Lalitavistara*;[102] as well as in the *Svayambhūpurāṇa*, a late Buddhist work in which Jinaśrī asks Jayaśrī (who is here presented as a bodhisattva in Bodhgaya) to recount what he heard Upagupta tell Aśoka about the different holy places associated with the Svayambhūnātha temple in Nepal.[103]

Perhaps the most elaborate version of this pattern, however, is found in the *Mahajjātakamālā*.[104] The first chapter of this text is entitled "The Extensive Qualities of the Triple Gem as Related by Upagupta upon Aśoka's Request." It begins with the bodhisattva Jayaśrī agreeing, in conversation with another bodhisattva named Jinamuni, to recite the story of the Buddha's life, just as he heard it from his teacher. He starts his narration, however, by recalling how Aśoka one day went to the Kukkuṭārāma monastery, where he met the arhat Yaśas. Yaśas asked the king what he wanted, but, when he found out it was an account of the life and teachings of the Buddha, he deferred to Upagupta, who then agreed to instruct Aśoka on the following day. Accordingly, the next morning, Upagupta set out to the king's palace. There he was received and welcomed by Aśoka; and the rest of the chapter consists primarily of a quotation of his sermon. It begins with a lengthy praise of the Buddha, the Dharma, and the Sangha; taking refuge in this Triple Gem brings salvation, the elder tells the king, while turning away from it leads to continued damnation. His speech finished, Upagupta then goes back to the Kukkuṭārāma, and the chapter ends.[105]

The complexity of this scenario is interesting. There is nothing particularly unusual about the contents of Upagupta's sermon; the arhat Yaśas, or even Jayaśrī, both of whom are endowed with a certain charisma of their own, would have been perfectly capable of delivering it. Yet the text sets up the situation in such a way that Upagupta's personal presence and preaching are crucial. Indeed, in the second chapter, when Aśoka, in the absence of Upagupta, wishes to hear more about the Triple Gem, the elder once again has to make an appearance; divining the king's thoughts from afar, he arrives (flying through the air), takes his seat, and resumes his sermon.[106] Clearly, no other preacher would do.

It is apparent in all of these texts that Upagupta has become something more than just a narrator of avadāna stories and an allayer of doubts. He has, in fact, become the authenticator of a whole tradition, lending authority to the works and acting as a sort of guarantee that what is being said is genuinely the Buddha Dharma. Late sūtras, in order to overcome doubts that they were attributable to the Buddha, were commonly prefaced with the words of Ānanda "Evam mayā śrutam" ("Thus have I heard"). Similarly, avadānas claimed that their contents had been handed down from one teacher to another, something that is reflected in the words "Evam anuśrūyate" ("Thus it has been repeated") with which some of them begin.[107] In this chain of legitimation of avadānas, Upagupta came to be seen as a crucial link, and his appearance as narrator thus became a telltale sign of the genre just as surely as the "Thus have I heard" was the introductory mark of a sūtra. The question remains, however, Why was Upagupta in particular "chosen" for this role?

Upagupta and the Legitimation of the Quasi-Canonical

Some time ago, on the basis of certain references in the *Kalpadrumāvadānamālā*, I suggested that Upagupta might have been the patron saint of a whole class of monks (called avadānikas or avadānārthakovidas) specializing in avadāna recitations, in much the same way that the Buddha's disciple Upāli was the patron saint of specialists in Vinaya literature and Śāriputra that of specialists in Abhidharma literature.[108] This conclusion, however, is not entirely supported by the evidence of the cult of Upagupta in Southeast Asia, where the saint is invoked not by specialists in storytelling, but to help preserve festivals from the incursions of Māra. It now seems to me that there are other, more specific reasons for Upagupta's selection as narrator of avadānas, reasons that have to do both with his cult and with the nature of the avadāna genre.

To begin with, it must be remembered that the canonical status of the avadānas as a genre was fraught with ambiguity. In the Pali Tipiṭaka, it is true, the Khuddaka Nikāya came to include a collection of avadānas known as the *Apadāna*, a fact that would seem to indicate an acceptance of the genre's canonicity. Not all Theravādin groups, however, agreed to the *Apadāna*'s insertion there;[109] and the Theravāda tradition as a whole, in its classification of the Buddha's Word into nine generic categories (navānga), omitted the apadāna altogether.[110]

The Sanskrit tradition, on the other hand, *did* include the avadānas in its generic classification of the Buddha Dharma into twelve types (the dvādaśānga Buddhavacana),[111] although among Sarvāstivādin and other schools there were disagreements about this issue. According to some accounts, the avadānas were eventually excised from canonical works such as the *Vinaya* because they were not thought to be essential.[112]

In both the Sanskrit and Pali schools, then, there appear to have been rather mixed feelings about whether or not the avadānas were to be considered as part of the Buddha's Word. These uncertainties, I would suggest, underlay the need for some sort of further legitimation—or legitimizer—of the genre as a whole. Merely stating that the stories were the Buddha's Word or were passed down from him was not enough in the post-parinirvāṇa period, when people were easily misled and when, moreover, it was not always clear just who or where the Buddha was.

As we have seen, one of the thrusts of the story of Upagupta and Māra was that Māra was able to take on the form of the Buddha and, in this guise, trick people into thinking that he was the Buddha. Not only that, but he could, as the Buddha, preach false doctrines and attempt to convince the unenlightened that they were true (as in the story of Śūra recounted in chapter 5). Buddhist texts are full of stories of Māra trying to lead monks and nuns astray, often with transparent temptations. Here, however, we come to a more basic and underlying worry that the Buddha might in fact not be the Buddha at all and that what was being proclaimed, by some at least, as the Doctrine of the Blessed One might actually be the teaching of the great misleader, Māra.

This fear—which was perhaps more common in Buddhism than has been recognized—needs to be seen in the context of a religion that was periodically given to schisms and to the need for councils to reassert "what the Buddha said." Māra not only was deemed responsible for various temptations of the flesh, he was also seen as the cause and supporter of heretical views. For instance, in Upagupta's long and strikingly original sermon to Aśoka on the ups and downs of the Dharma, in the third chapter of the *Mahajjātakamālā*, Māra plays a constant role in supporting schisms in the Sangha.[113]

An intriguing passage in the *Lotus Sūtra* is even more relevant in this regard. There, we are told that the Buddha's disciple Śāriputra, when he first heard the Buddha preach the *Lotus* and make some of its new Mahāyānist doctrinal revelations, had real doubts about their authenticity; he, too, was worried about Māra. "When first I heard the Buddha's preaching," Śāriputra confesses, "In my heart I was greatly alarmed: / 'Surely Māra is playing Buddha, / Confusing my thoughts!'" But then he realizes "that this is no Māra playing Buddha / But that I, through having fallen into a net of doubt, / Thought this was the work of Māra."[114] Or, as the Sanskrit text puts it: "This is not Māra; it is the Lord of the World, who has shown the true course; no Māras can here abide."[115] The tradition that "the Mahāyāna is the word of Māra" is found (and denied) in other texts as well,[116] but the point here is a broader one: that doubt about the orthodoxy or canonical status of certain texts was related to worries about the workings of the Evil One.

With this in mind, we may now turn to the specifics of Upagupta's role as narrator of avadāna texts. According to the Mathuran legend about him, Upagupta by reputation (one might almost say by definition) was—simply put—the tamer of Māra. With him as narrator, therefore, there is no worry about authenticity. His very presence *in the text* is a guarantee that what is being said is not, in fact, the trickery of the Evil One, because Upagupta has shown himself to be one who can see through the Evil One's disguises. Argument and logic and reason have been bypassed: where Upagupta is narrator, no Māras can abide.

Upagupta thus serves to "frame" an avadāna text in much the same way that he "facilitates" Aśoka's stūpa festival. In both cases, he makes sure that the event (recitation, ritual) does not go wrong—that it is not marred by the incursions of the Evil One, but in fact represents genuine Buddha Dharma and not heterodoxy.

Pilgrimage

There is one final event in the interaction of Aśoka and Upagupta that needs to be considered here. Soon after their meeting in Pāṭaliputra, Aśoka expresses to Upagupta his desire to go on a pilgrimage—to visit all of the places that are associated with the life of the Buddha and to mark them with "signs" (cihna) for the benefit of future devotees.[117] In this, Upagupta is to act as his guide, pointing out where the Buddha was born, where he grew up, attained enlightenment, preached, and undertook a host of other activities. Together, then, they visit no less than thirty-two sites in such places as Lumbinī, Kapilavastu, Bodhgaya, Sārnāth, Rājagṛha, Sāṃkāśya, Śrāvastī, and Kuśinagarī.[118]

It is clear that this narration forms a sort of minibiography of the Buddha, and it has often been used as such by scholars studying his life story.[119] At the same time, Upagupta and Aśoka's tour may be seen as a deliberate attempt to establish a pilgrimage tradition, in such a manner as to make concrete, to make "relivable," the life and person of the Buddha.

In this connection, two of the sites that they visit are perhaps of greatest importance. At Lumbinī and then again on the road to Bodhgaya, Upagupta, in order to enhance Aśoka's faith, summons indigenous divinities (the female sylvan spirit still resident in the tree under which the Buddha was born, and the nāga king Kālika) to act as witnesses to the events of the Blessed One's life. These deities recall for the sake of the king the times they saw the Buddha, and they describe in vivid detail the glories of his physical appearance—the golden hue of his skin, the marvels of his Mahāpuruṣa marks, the words that he spoke.[120]

In this manner, they make the Buddha come alive in a special way, for, in the Sarvāstivādin context, such testimonials amount to more than mere remembrances. They are recalls of realities that "exist," projections to an aoristic past. As a result, they overcome the Buddha's absence and give him a vividness which is not without its effects on Aśoka. Indeed, the Lumbinī tree spirit's stated intention of "further increasing the faith of the king" is successful, for Aśoka, tremendously moved by her portrayal of the Blessed One, has a caitya built on the spot and makes to it an offering of one hundred thousand pieces of gold.[121]

Ultimately, however, what is emphasized in this pilgrimage is the impermanence of that Buddha. For Aśoka's greatest emotion is reserved for the Bodhi tree at Bodhgaya, where the Buddha first realized the truth of anitya, and for the sal grove at Kuśinagarī, where he passed completely away into parinirvāṇa. To the former place Aśoka will return repeatedly as king,[122] while at the latter he falls on the ground in a swoon of devotion and makes his offerings only after regaining consciousness.[123]

In this way, then, the story of Upagupta's and Aśoka's pilgrimage, like the sacred biography of the Buddha, participates in the same basic Buddhist dynamic that we saw operative in the worship of the Buddha image. By tracing the life of the Blessed One, from birth to final extinction, it seeks first to recapture his presence through glorification and praise and then to return the devotee/pilgrim to the fact of his absence in these post-parinirvāṇa times.

This absence, as we have seen, does not contradict the recall of the Buddha's presence; rather, it completes it and so reinforces the emotion of bhakti. In this context, it is perhaps well to remember that "separation" (viraha) is one of the primary modes of experiencing the divine in India.[124] As David Shulman reminds us: "The very presence of the deity, his revelation before our eyes, evokes in us the unbearable sense of his absence—of our finitude, our inability to hold the god here, our frustration at the awareness of his total transcendence."[125] To be sure, the mythologies of Buddhism and Hinduism are radically different, and emotions of Buddha bhakti, at least as they are expressed in our texts, are not as intense as those of some forms of Śaivite or Kṛṣṇaite devotionalism. Nevertheless, the basic emotional patterns found in such things as the biographies of the Buddha and the practice of Buddhist pilgrimage may well overlap with some of those set by Hindu bhakti.

The Stūpas of the Buddha's Disciples

Aśoka's pilgrimage does not stop with the Buddha's parinirvāṇa, at Kuśinagarī. Indeed, as soon as he has made his offering of one hundred thousand pieces of gold and built a caitya there, he turns to Upagupta and requests that he now be able to pay homage to the bodily relics of the disciples whom the Buddha declared to be foremost in one category or another.[126]

The reference is to the tradition preserved in the *Anguttara Nikāya*, where no less than forty-one monks, thirteen nuns, ten laymen, and ten laywomen are each described as being preeminent among the Buddha's followers in possessing one quality or another. This is far too great a number of saints for even Upagupta and Aśoka to honor, so in fact they pay their respects to only five of these "preeminent ones": Sāriputta (chief among those of great wisdom), Mahāmoggallāna (champion in supernatural powers), Mahākassapa (foremost of those who meticulously observe forms), Bakkula (chief of those of good health), and Ānanda (best of personal attendants and best of those of wide knowledge, retentive memory, good behavior, and resoluteness).[127]

The stūpas of these five are said in the *Divyāvadāna* to be all located in the Jetavana monastery in Śrāvastī. Such a claim is placed in serious doubt by other traditions, if by *stūpas* is meant monuments actually containing bodily relics of these great disciples; for, as we have seen, Mahākāśyapa's body was thought to be still intact in its mountain chamber, awaiting the coming of Maitreya, and Ānanda's relics were supposed to have been divided between Rājagṛha, Vaiśālī, Indra's heaven, and the nāga kingdom.

It is more likely, then, that we should think of these "stūpas" of the Buddha's disciples at the Jetavana not so much as reliquaries or funeral mounds, but more as shrines erected in memory and honor of the different disciples, where devotees could come to pay their respects and to vow or hope to achieve the qualities symbolized by each of the individuals enshrined. We have already seen this same tradition described in Hsüan-tsang's memoirs, and much the same sort of thing may be found in parts of Southeast Asia today.

In this account of the visit to the saints' stūpas, then, we may find the beginnings of an Indian cult of arhats that was to develop and flourish spectacularly and much influence the cult of saints in Southeast Asia. At this point, the arhats venerated by Aśoka in their stūpas are all, like the Buddha, beings who have gone beyond. They are reminders of the truth of impermanence. But it was not long before buddhology and "arhatology," developing in tandem, came to assert the possibility of their ongoing involvement in the world. Indeed, the accounts of Fa-Hsien, Hsüan-tsang, and other pilgrims are filled with stories of miracles wrought by arhats, of mysterious lights shining from their stūpas, even of their appearances.

We shall trace this development later, in chapter 11, when we consider the arhat cults that were established in Burma—the cult of Upagupta among them. For now, however, Aśoka is more interested in his own enterprise of merit-making, for, after honoring the stūpas of all the elders, he prostrates himself one final time before Upagupta and declares:

> I have profited from the human condition . . .
> by making hundreds of offerings. . . .
> I have ornamented this world with hundreds of caityas
> resplendent as cumulus clouds.
> In fulfilling today the Teaching of the peerless Master
> have I not done the difficult to do?[128]

We are not told in the *Divyāvadāna* what the elder's answer to the king was. Instead, the two of them, their pilgrimage over, part company. Aśoka goes back to his palace and then to Bodhgaya, where he becomes particularly devoted to the Bodhi tree; and Upagupta, presumably (although this is not certain), returns to Urumuṇḍa, never to see the king again.

PART TWO

Upagupta in Southeast Asia

CHAPTER EIGHT

The Southeast Asian Context: Upagupta and Theravāda Orthodoxy

THE LEGENDS concerning Upagupta at Mathurā and those featuring his relations with King Aśoka at Pāṭaliputra were part and parcel of Buddhism in India until the religion's eventual demise there. Today these traditions are no longer living on the subcontinent, but they have survived in a different milieu, in parts of Southeast Asia. The area where the cult of Upagupta can still be found may be fairly easily described: it consists of Lower Burma and a broad region to the east and north that cuts across the frontiers of several modern nations. Even so, that region may be viewed as a single internally diverse ethnolinguistic conglomerate: the Shan States, Northern and Northeastern Thailand, Laos, and parts of Yünnan. Outside of this area—which, for want of a better term, I shall call northern Southeast Asia—Upagupta is hardly known. In Central and Southern Thailand, most people have never heard of him, and there is little evidence of his cult ever having existed in Cambodia or Vietnam.[1] In Sri Lanka, he does not appear to have ever figured at all.

The history of religions in northern Southeast Asia is a subject that is fraught with difficulties. Without question, Burma, Thailand, and Laos may today be defined as Theravādin countries; yet the study of their Buddhism has too often suffered from the blinders that have come with this definition, particularly when it has been understood from the perspective of a certain brand of orthodoxy. The persistence in these countries of the legend and cult of Upagupta offers, therefore, a rare opportunity to study the survival and transformation of a Northwest Indian Sanskrit tradition within the context of Theravādin hegemony.

Today, it is possible to distinguish between two subcults of Upagupta in northern Southeast Asia: an iconic one centered in Burma in the valleys of the Irrawaddy and the Salween, and an aniconic one situated in Thailand and Laos in the basins of the Menam and Mekong.

The iconic cult focusses on statues of Upagupta depicting him as a monk, seated cross-legged with his right hand in his bowl on his lap and gazing upwards over his shoulder at the sky. Such images may often be found in small shrines at major pagodas (sometimes set on a raft in a tank) or in people's homes, where they are venerated to bring protection, good weather, and other boons. One of the perennial features of the cult of these images is their being set adrift on a raft on a river, a symbolic act which, as we shall see in chapter 10, has the intention of returning the saint to his home in the ocean.

The aniconic cult, found principally in Thailand and Laos, knows no such images. Instead, as we have mentioned, Upagupta is represented in the form of stones taken from a riverbed or a swamp and temporarily installed in a makeshift shrine for the duration of a festival. Here the cultic emphasis is not on sending the saint away back to his home, but on inviting him to come to one's own place. We shall fully examine such invitations in chapter 12.

These general distinctions between iconic and aniconic cults, however, should not be seen as absolute. For one thing, both traditions draw on the same basic legend of Upagupta, first formulated in Southeast Asia in the *Lokapaññatti* (see chapter 9) and subsequently developed there in a variety of ways (see chapters 10 and 11). Moreover, the dividing line between iconic and aniconic is not always clear-cut; in certain parts of Thailand, in addition to his cult in the form of stones, Upagupta also came to be venerated in a number of other guises, some anthropomorphic, some not (see chapter 13).

Before turning to these various matters, however, it is necessary to make some introductory comments on the history and present situation of the legend and cult of Upagupta in Southeast Asia and on the religious milieu in which it finds itself. Generally speaking, three polarities have informed the study of religion in Theravādin contexts: (1) that between monks and laypersons, (2) that between Buddhism and animism, and (3) that between orthodoxy and heterodoxy.

In its most extreme form, the first of these polarities actually posits two kinds of religion: the "Buddhism of the monks," who engage in the practice of meditation and doctrinal study and aim at achieving Nirvāṇa; and the "Buddhism of the laypeople," who aim at a better rebirth in this world or in heaven through acts of devotion and merit making. We have already suggested that there are real difficulties with such a view—that all Buddhists, in fact, are concerned with merit making; that all likewise share the same goal of final enlightenment; and that differences between monks and laypersons lie more in their karmic situations (which may determine the speed of their liberation) than in their soteriological aims. We have also seen how, in India, Upagupta himself tends to bridge the distinction between layperson and monk in his own career and preaching.

The same continues to be true of Upagupta in Southeast Asia. Unlike a number of protective deities and spirits, Upagupta is a monk (at times a virtual symbol of the Sangha), and to that status he owes his prestige and powers. His cult, however, is primarily the affair of laypersons; in both Burma and Thailand, it is the lay leaders of the community and not the bhikṣus who take on the leading ritual roles in his invitation and propitiation. Moreover, as we shall see, there are some real ambiguities in Upagupta's own monasticism. Offerings made to him and legends told about him tend to present him as a "supermonk," devoted to meditation and strict in his adherence to discipline. Yet, at the same time, other traditions show him to be more lax in this regard; for example, he does not live with the rest of the community, and he violates certain monastic rules. This is not the place to embark on a full discussion of lay and monastic paradigms in the Buddhist tradition, but only to signal that we shall encounter both of them again in the Southeast Asian cultic traditions that we will be examining.

A second polarity that has governed the study of Theravādin cultures is that which characterizes them as comprising two coexistent complexes: "Buddhism," on the one hand and "supernaturalism" or "spirit cults" on the other.[2] By "Buddhism" is usually meant the *Theravādin* set of beliefs and practices centering around one or several of the Three Refuges. By "spirit cults" is meant a whole gamut of folk rites and beliefs—some indigenous, some not—involving a great "parade of supernaturals"[3]—ghosts, nāgas, tutelary spirits, demons, and others—but usually featuring the worship of those beings known as nats in Burma and phī in Thailand and Laos.

Scholars have described the relationship between Buddhism and the spirit cults in a variety of ways which cannot be examined in detail here. In shorthand fashion, their views might be summarized as falling under one or more of the following formulae: Buddhism vs. animism,[4] Buddhism = animism,[5] Buddhism + animism,[6] Buddhism – animism,[7] and Buddhism > animism.[8] But, however this relationship is described, if it is presented in too simplistic or clear-cut a manner, there is a danger that certain elements of the tradition may get ignored because they will fall into the interstices between categories.[9] Thus, when "Buddhism" is understood as the Theravāda tradition according to the Pali canon and commentaries and "spirit cults" is understood as the worship of nats, a figure such as Upagupta—who does not appear in the Pali canon and commentaries and who does not belong to the nat cultus either—will probably be overlooked.

One example of this possibility will have to suffice here. Melford Spiro, in the course of two important books on Burmese religion—one on Buddhism, the other on supernaturalism—refers to Upagupta but once, in a footnote. There, as an afterthought to his discussion of deities, he mentions a 1923 report referring to shrines and images in honor of Shin Upagok (Upagupta), one of "four Burmese Buddhist saints whose favors . . . can be solicited by means of spells." But, he adds, he himself has never seen any such shrines or images.[10]

This is a remarkable statement by one as observant as Spiro. It may be, of course, that in the pseudonymous village of "Yeigyi," where he did much of his fieldwork, the cult of Upagupta was unknown; for, as we shall see, belief in or even knowledge about Upagupta is by no means universal in these regions. But it is hard to see how he could have missed the Upagupta shrines at such places as the Mahāmuni temple in nearby Mandalay or in the shadow of the Shwe Dagon in Rangoon, *had he been looking for them.*[11] That he was not can only be attributed to his focus on other things—namely, the relationship and distinction between Buddhism (defined in terms of the Theravāda) and the cult of the nats. In what follows, therefore, we will need, if not to make new categories, at least to break down some old ones if we are not to find Upagupta effaced from our field of vision.

Implicit in this problem is a third polarity which has also characterized the study of religion in Theravāda countries: that which sees the history of Buddhism in these lands as a cyclical series of reforms and corruptions and which consequently distinguishes an official, pure, orthodox Theravāda Buddhism (often associated in Southeast Asia with the Mahavihāra school of Sri Lanka) from a more heterodox Indo-indigenous Buddhism which tends to be more syncretistic and willing to incorporate not only animistic notions, but also a variety of other *Buddhist* traditions in its beliefs and practices.[12]

Again, it is not my purpose here to trace the history and the fluctuations of this polarity, but only to suggest that we not take it too simplistically. Reform in Southeast Asian Buddhism has rarely meant eradication; rather, it has involved the reformulation of relationships in such a way that orthodoxy is clearly defined, for a while, and everything else is (at least officially) subordinated to it. For Burma at least, "even under the strongest purifying kings, Burmese Buddhism has tolerated an amazing degree of doctrinal variance, incorporating a number of Mahayanist, Sanskrit Hinayana, and Tantric beliefs. Rather than exclude, Burmese Buddhism absorbs competing ideas . . . and places [them] into a hierarchy with Pali Theravāda beliefs considered the highest insights."[13]

Official Buddhism and the Sanskrit Tradition

Historians, of course, have long been aware of the presence and influence in Southeast Asia (as well as Sri Lanka) of a number of forms of Buddhism other than Theravādin, and they have typically found in the religious life of this area a rich mixture of many traditions.[14] Let us consider again, for example, the case of Burma, where the Southeast Asian cult of Upagupta first took root. There, early on, the Pyus, whose urbanized culture at Śrī Kṣetra and elsewhere dominated the Irrawaddy Valley from 200 B.C.E. to the ninth century, had a belief system that "included Sarvāstivādin Buddhism[,] . . . elements of Hinduism[,] . . . and a rather widespread Southeast Asian practice of urn burial."[15] At the same time, however, it is at Pyu sites that archaeologists have uncovered early fragments of Pali canonical texts.[16]

Likewise, the Mons of Lower Burma, who speak a language akin to Khmer and played a crucial role in the development of culture not only in Pagan but throughout northern Southeast Asia, also appear to have mixed a variety of Buddhist, Indian, and indigenous elements. In their settlements in sixth- and seventh-century Dvāravati (in what is now Central Thailand), the Mons used Pali and seem to have been "strongly Theravādin,"[17] but researchers into their culture in Lower Burma have more recently stressed their Sarvāstivādin and other Sanskritic affinities.[18] This is important, for it was most likely at Thaton, the ancient Mon capital in Lower Burma, that traditions about Upagupta became established in Southeast Asia. The Upagupta story in Burma, in fact, bears certain close resemblances to the myth of the patron saint of the Mons, the arhat Gavāṃpati; and it was at Thaton that the *Lokapaññatti* was written, a text in which we may again find a syncretic base of Sanskrit traditions mixed with an overlay of Theravādin doctrines. The same mixture may be found among the Mons today. As R. Halliday has pointed out, "In mere personal everyday contact [with Mon people] one gets the impression that their religion . . . has come through Pali and Southern Buddhism. However, a look into their language and literature shows that some of the commonest religious and other terms have come to them through Sanskrit and other Northern influences."[19]

Similarly, the people of Nanchao in Yünnan (cultural cousins to at least some of the Burmese) appear to have had a syncretic mix of traditions.[20] Though practicing Mahāyānists, they traced their Buddhism (and the ancestry of their kings) to the Emperor Aśoka, who was said (apocryphally) to have visited Nanchao, flying through the air with his seven sons and in the company of hundreds of arhats.[21] Nanchao armies periodically made their presence felt in Burma, sacking Pyu and Mon cities in the ninth century and having to be contained by King Aniruddha in the eleventh.[22] Moreover, as Paul Pelliot has pointed out, Yünnan in general and Nanchao in particular became identified in the minds of the Burmese and other Indo-Chinese with parts of North India, specifically Gandhāra. This resulted from the tendency among Indianized Southeast Asians to create in their own country a "new India" and transfer to the places around them Indian geographical names. Thus "Yünnan, being to the north of Indochina, was akin to Gandhāra which was to the north of India. . . . so Yünnan became Gandhāra."[23]

This notion was reinforced by the claim that one could find in Nanchao many of the pilgrimage sites usually thought to be in India. Thus, by at least the tenth century, one could visit in Yünnan the Bodhi tree, Vulture's Peak, the Pippala cave (where the First Council was held), Mount Kukkuṭapāda (under which Mahākāśyapa waits[24]), a stūpa which held the relics of half of Ānanda's body, and—significantly, for our purposes—the stone house (cave) of Upagupta.[25] Clearly, then, Nanchao shared in at least some of the traditions that interest us, and we shall explore these further when we examine new developments in the legend of Upagupta in Southeast Asia.

Pagan and After

With the establishment of the Pagan dynasty (ninth to thirteenth centuries), the Burmese religious situation was transformed by the official endorsement of the Theravāda tradition along Sri Lankan Pali lines. The introduction of Sinhalese-style Buddhism to Pagan in the eleventh and twelfth centuries is a complex issue and one which is much caught up in myth. Part of the complexity is due to the fact that, although the dynasty turned to Sri Lanka for its official *Dharma*—its doctrine—it continued to find its first refuge, the *Buddha*, in North India. This was especially true iconographically,[26] but it may also have been the case ritually and devotionally. Thus, though Pagan Buddhism was officially Theravādin from the twelfth century on, to describe it as such "oversimplifies the religious milieu,"[27] which was in actuality "widely syncretistic" and "far from pure . . . whatever the Chronicles may say."[28]

This remained true even after the end of the Pagan period. Scholars interested in the persistence of this "far from pure" Buddhism have tended to focus on the so-called Ari sect of Buddhist monks, who have been labeled variously as Tantric, Mahāyānist, Sarvāstivādin, and even Vaishnavite.[29] According to Burmese orthodoxy, King Aniruddha of Pagan put an end to their "heresy" in the eleventh century; but—as we shall see presently—if they in fact already existed in his day, they survived underground for long thereafter.

The *Glass Palace Chronicle* is explicit in accusing the Aris of a host of heterodox practices: they worshipped nāgas; they made morning and evening offerings of rice, curry, and fermented drinks to idols "that were neither spirit-images nor images of the Lord"; they rejected the Dharma as preached by the Buddha and wrote books expressing their own views; they advocated the use of mantras to counter the course of karma; and they claimed the right of *ius primae noctis* on all village girls on the eve of their weddings.[30]

Understandably, whatever the truth of these allegations, it is the latter one—the sexual initiation of girls by Buddhist monks—that has most intrigued and excited scholars. Long ago, parallels were pointed out between this reputed Ari practice and the reports of female puberty rites recounted by Chinese travellers to thirteenth-century Cambodia and fifteenth-century Thailand.[31] For instance, Chou Ta-kuan, in his narration of his visit to Angkor in 1297, recalls the annual ceremony for seven- to nine-year-old girls known as ch'en-t'an. For this grand merit making occasion, parents would invite a monk to their home, escorting him with great fanfare from his monastery. Altars with various images on them would be set up outside the house and two pavilions erected—one for the bhikkhu and one for the girl. Great sums were spent on dāna, as well as on the all-night entertainment of family and friends. The sound of the music was deafening, and when the time for the actual ritual came, the monk would enter into the young girl's apartment. The rest is best told by Chou himself:

> I have heard it said that he then deflowers her with his fingers and dips his hand in wine. Father and mother, relatives and neighbors then rub the wine on their foreheads; some say they even drink it. I have also been told that the monk actually has sexual intercourse with the girl, though others deny that this is the case. It is hard for a Chinese to be sure about such matters. In any event, at the break of day, the monk is accompanied back to his monastery with palanquins, parasols, and music. The girl

must then be ransomed with presents of cloth and other things; otherwise, she will remain the "property" of the monk and will never be able to get married.[32]

A similar ritual is described by Ma Huan, who accompanied the famous Chinese admiral Cheng Ho on his South Asian expedition in 1413. He reports that in Thailand, as a preliminary to the marriage ceremony, a monk deflowered the young bride and then marked with red the forehead of the groom.[33] In fact, possibly related practices have been traced right up into the modern period. Thus, Charles Duroiselle calls attention to the so-called "breast-offering" ceremony among the Shan, in which, at the end of the rains retreat, a Buddhist monk passes in review the assembled girls of the village and chooses one of them to come and serve him in his monastery until the beginning of the next year's rains retreat.[34] And W.A.R. Wood reports the presence of specialists among the Akha whose function is to "prepare all the virgins for marriage by deflowering them at certain ceremonies each year."[35]

As might be expected, debates have raged over these reports, some seeing in them proof of the ultimate Tantric depravity, others claiming that they must be discarded as total fabrications by the maligners of Buddhism or, at least, not interpreted literally. Actually, as François Bizot has recently argued, there is plenty of evidence—textual and ethnographic—for the ritual initiation of girls by Buddhist monks in Southeast Asia, but it should hardly be seen in orgiastic terms; as practiced in rural Cambodia, for example, it was and is a solemn rite of passage, part of a complex of puberty rituals aimed at preparing a girl not only for marriage and motherhood, but also for certain mystical realizations and corresponding most closely, perhaps, to a boy's temporary ordination as a monk.[36]

In chapter 3, we noted various etymologies of the word *Ari* and suggested that the adherents of this sect might perhaps better be viewed as saints of the forest (āraṇyaka) than as degenerate deflowerers of village virgins. In fact, this is the argument of Than Tun, who has presented a lively picture of a sect of forest monks whom he identifies with the Ari and who thrived in Burma from the end of the Pagan period well into the sixteenth century. This sect, which was well endowed with monastic lands and whose numbers included nuns (bhikṣuṇī), apparently engaged in a number of practices that would not today be considered orthodox. They regularly partook of an evening meal; they participated in festivals and celebrations at which they joined laypersons in the slaughtering of meat and the consumption of alcohol; and they helped in clearing jungle land and bringing it under cultivation.[37]

The charismatic patron saint of the sect was the elder Mahākassapa, who is said to have been born in 1169. He is credited with the establishment of many forest hermitages, was thought to have possessed magical powers, and was asked repeatedly to go to Pagan to cure the king. He also seems to have spent considerable energies vying for royal patronage for his sect over against those monks who were encouraging Sinhalese-style orthodoxy.[38] Mahākassapa is said to have met the Buddha in a previous life and received from him the prediction of future Buddhahood; he is therefore technically a bodhisattva. In legend, however, he is connected to his namesake, the Buddha's disciple Mahākāśyapa, and, like him, is thought to be buried in a trance under a mountain someplace in Northern Burma.[39]

It is quite possible that in figures such as Mahākassapa and the Ari we should see the predecessors of the weikza (see chapter 11) and/or of the yathes (hermits), who are today still a part of the less-than-orthodox Burmese Buddhist scene.[40] More interesting for our purposes, however, is the fact that, through Mahākāśyapa—as well as in a variety of other ways—these figures are also connected to the same Sanskritic forest saint tradition as Upagupta. Indeed, as we shall see, Mahākāśyapa is still worshipped in Burma today as one of the four "dead saints" living mysteriously on mountaintops and, in this guise, is paired with Upagupta, who is presented as one of the four "living saints" dwelling in the midst of the oceans.

The Myth of Theravāda Orthodoxy

Despite all of this evidence of a rich and varied tradition (or perhaps because of it), what might be called the myth of Theravāda orthodoxy has largely prevailed in Burma, where it has served to reinterpret history and to stress certain sectarian affiliations.

Like many other Theravādin Buddhists, the Burmese have retained the Pali/Sinhalese chronicles' assertion that, after the Third Council of Pāṭaliputra, the elder Moggaliputta Tissa sent out missionaries to propagandize neighboring countries. These missionaries included not only Aśoka's putative son Mahinda, who went to Sri Lanka, but also the elders Soṇa and Uttara, who were sent to Suvaṇṇabhūmi, the Land of Gold, which is often identified with the region around Thaton or more generally with the homeland of the Mons.[41] The point is thus made: not only was Buddhism early on established in Burma, but the Buddhism that was established there was Theravāda *in a very pure form*, since it had just been purged of all heterodox elements at Aśoka's Third Council.[42]

This myth of orthodoxy does not stop here. Like all such legends, it gets reiterated and reinforced by other stories. This is partly the intention, for instance, of the saga of King Aniruddha (Anawrahta), the great eleventh-century ruler of Pagan who is reputed to have unified all of Burma and (re)purified the faith. The legends of Aniruddha's exploits are many, but the most famous of these recounts his expedition to Thaton. Converted to "true Theravāda" by the Mon monk Shin Arahan (who effected the king's change of heart with the same sermon that the novice Nigrodha used to convert Aśoka[43]), Aniruddha sent to Thaton for a set of Pali scriptures. His request was refused, however; so he mounted a massive expedition, laid siege to the city, and captured what he had asked for, returning to Pagan with the Triple Gem: Buddha relics, Theravādin monks, and thirty-two white elephants bearing the Pali Tipiṭaka.[44]

It is unlikely, of course, that any of these events happened in quite this way. The historicity of Soṇa and Uttara is much debated,[45] and, as Gordon Luce (along with others) has pointed out, "it is probably wrong to regard Aniruddha as a Theravādin," or at least it is clear that he did not bring back the Pali Tipiṭaka from Thaton.[46] Nonetheless, the image of Thaton and of the land of the Mons in Lower Burma as a sort of center for the diffusion of Theravāda orthodoxy persisted.[47]

The Myth of Gavāṃpati

This persistence is particularly interesting, for it is in this same region that we also find an alternative, nonofficial, non-Theravādin myth of the establishment of Buddhism. The Mons of Lower Burma, in fact, paid comparatively little attention to the story of Soṇa and Uttara.[48] Instead, in what may be a fine example of mythic one-upsmanship, they emphasized the mission of their patron saint Gavāṃpati, who is supposed to have introduced Buddhism to Burma during the lifetime of the Buddha himself and to have fully established it there shortly after the Buddha's parinirvāṇa. The basic myth, as preserved in a series of Mon pagoda inscriptions found near Pegu, may be summarized as follows:

> In the eighth year after his enlightenment, the Buddha came to Mithilā along with twenty thousand arhats. At that time, the elder Gavāṃpati reflected on his life in a previous existence in the neighboring country of Suvarṇabhūmi. He went there, therefore, and preached the Dharma to the people of Thaton and to their king, Sirimāsoka, who had been his kinsman in a former life. The latter requested that he might meet the Buddha in person. Gavāṃpati, therefore, quickly flew back to Mithilā and communicated the king's wish to the Blessed One.
>
> Out of compassion for Sirimāsoka and for all the people of Suvarṇabhūmi, the Buddha himself then flew through the air to Thaton. There he was entertained with a great alsmgiving, and there he preached the Dharma for seven days to men and gods. When it was time for him to depart, Sirimāsoka was much saddened and asked for a substitute for the Blessed One through which he might continue to feel his presence and worship him. The Buddha, however, denied his request, explaining that he had already given some hair relics to Trapuṣa and Bhallika for enshrinement in Suvarṇabhūmi; but he promised that, thirty-seven years later, as soon as he had achieved parinirvāṇa, he would send Gavāṃpati with one of his teeth to be worshipped, and it, through the power of his resolution, would become multiplied into thirty-three.
>
> Thirty-seven years later the Buddha died, and Gavāṃpati, remembering his instructions, took the tooth from the still-burning funeral pyre and bore it to Suvarṇabhūmi,

where it miraculously multiplied. King Sirimāsoka built thirty-three stūpas for it and worshipped it the rest of his life, giving alms and observing the precepts.[49]

A number of points need to be made about this story. First of all, it is clear that we are here dealing with a rather different tradition from that studied in chapter 3, which associated Gavāṃpati with the Śairīṣaka (Pali: Serīsaka) palace in the Cāturmahārājika Heaven and asserted that he passed away into parinirvāṇa there, immediately after the Buddha's death, refusing to come even to the First Council.

Second, it is also clear that this tradition presents a rather different picture than that painted by Jean Przyluski, Paul Lévy, and others who sought to attribute to Gavāṃpati a basically bovine nature and to claim that he was the Buddhist embodiment of an ancient bull cult.[50] Przyluski's interpretation is based on a passage of the Chinese commentary on the *Ekottarāgama* in which the name Gavāṃpati is translated as "ox-foot" and in which the author, to justify his translation, adds that Gavāṃpati's feet, in fact, resembled a bovine's hooves and that he ruminated after meals. The Buddha, worried that heretics seeing him ruminate would think he was eating after hours, made him leave this world and take up his residence in heaven.[51] Whatever the validity of Przyluski's view, his application of it to the Burmese—and in particular the Mon—cult of Gavāṃpati has been soundly criticized by H. L. Shorto, who has shown his attempt to be a dubious interpretation based on a too-easy acceptance of Pierre Lefèvre-Pontalis's misreading of Charles Duroiselle's misleading report on the questionable discovery of a Gavāṃpati amulet near Pagan.[52]

Third, despite these caveats, it is still quite possible that the Mon story of Gavāṃpati is picking up on an Indian Sanskrit tradition. Indeed, the Pali listing of missionaries which has Soṇa and Uttara going to Suvaṇṇabhūmi, Mahinda to Sri Lanka, Majjhantika to Kashmir, and so on, has its Sanskrit counterpart in a catalogue of missionaries found in the *Mahākarmavibhanga.* There, we are also told that Mahendra (Mahinda) was sent to Sri Lanka and Madhyāntika (Majjhantika) to Kashmir, but the missionary to Suvarṇabhūmi is listed as Gavāṃpati.[53] The same point, perhaps, is emphasized in the *Mūlasarvāstivāda Vinaya*, where Gavāṃpati is portrayed as having dwelt for some time in the border regions and thereby earned the Buddha's designation as "the foremost of disciples living in frontier lands."[54]

Fourth, it is important to realize that the cult of Gavāṃpati was not limited to Lower Burma. It also became established in Pagan, after Aniruddha's conquest of Thaton, and there it may have undergone some changes. One Pagan inscription describes how Aniruddha himself had an image of Gavāṃpati carved out of a log the height of a man and how he made ritual offerings to it of an elephant, a horse, and a minister's robe before installing it in a "monastery" and endowing it with the revenue from 144 acres.[55] Similarly, at the dedication ceremony for the palace of King Kyanzittha (1084–1112), a shrine was constructed to the east of the great hall, and in it were placed on three thrones a Buddha image, volumes of the Tripiṭaka, and a statue of Gavāṃpati. Here, as Shorto points out, our saint seems to have come to symbolize the whole of the Sangha—the third of the Three Refuges.[56]

Finally, it is noteworthy that, in still other developments of this Mon tradition, what is stressed and elaborated is the theme of Gavāṃpati's karmic connections with Thaton in a past life. This is done in several ways. In the Thaton chronicle, as well as in an eighteenth-century Mon work entitled *Gawampati*, the story is told of the saint's search for his now-reborn mother, whom he finds in a small village near Thaton—a seven-year-old girl whose former relationship to him is revealed when milk starts to flow from her breasts. At the same time, the claim is also made that he was in a former life the twin brother of the present king's father, born, like him, from the eggs that resulted from the union of a wizard (weikza; Pali: vijjādhara) and a serpent princess (nāgī).[57]

Gavāṃpati and Upagupta

There is much that can be learned from all of this that is relevant to our study of the cult of Upagupta. Despite important differences between them (Gavāṃpati became the object of a state cult, Upagupta the protector of Buddhist festivals), the two saints are both figures of the Sanskrit tradition whose basic legends came from India and then developed in parallel ways in Lower Burma, undergoing similar transformations and acquiring analogous accretions.

In India, as we have seen, Gavāṃpati was a prototype of the arhat who instantly passed away into parinirvāṇa after the Buddha's demise; in Thaton, however, he lives on as a protector of the religion. Similarly, in the Mathuran tradition, Upagupta was presented as dying and being cremated at Mount Urumuṇḍa, while in Lower Burma he becomes an arhat who does not die, but lives on in his palace in the midst of the Southern Ocean.

In India, Gavāṃpati was born in Benares as the son of a merchant;[58] in Burma, however, efforts are made to indigenize him. His mother is said to have been from a village near Thaton; or, alternatively, it is claimed that he was of royal blood, the offspring of a nāgī and a sage. Such stories, as we shall see, are common in the foundation myths of Southeast Asian kingdoms (including the Mon cities of Thaton and Pegu). Moreover, they are also told about Upagupta. Though in India he was the son of a perfumer, today, throughout Burma and Thailand, he is believed to have been the progeny of an ascetic and a fish princess—or, in one myth, of the Buddha and a nāgī.[59]

Finally, it may be argued that the cults of Gavāṃpati and Upagupta, despite their differences, suffered similar fates: with the official establishment of Sri Lankan Theravāda orthodoxy, they both ceased to have a recognized place, and so they gradually were transformed and persisted in the interstices of popular practice. As long as Mon influence at Pagan remained strong—during the reigns of Aniruddha and Kyanzittha—the cult of Gavāṃpati enjoyed prestige and recognition. After their reigns, however, with the increasing influence of Sinhalese Buddhism, Gavāṃpati ceases to play a prime role; as Shorto has shown, there continue to be references to him, but he seems more and more to take on the function of an arhat-guardian, a protector of one of the points of the compass. Indeed, as we shall see, it is chiefly in this capacity—as one of the eight arhats associated with the different directions in the paritta rite known as the ceremony of the nine gods—that Gavāṃpati is still venerated in Burma today.

Similarly, in Pagan, Upagupta is referred to only in a Mon context: in 1113, Kyanzittha's son, Rājakumār, had included among the frescoes of the Kubyauk-gyi at Myinkaba (the "last of the Mon temples"[60]) a depiction of Upagupta which, according to the inscription, shows him in conversation with King Aśoka about the spread of the religion.[61] Already here, however, the saint is being subordinated to the Theravādin tradition. He is called Tisapagut ("Tissa-Upagupta"), a name which, as we have seen, is open to several interpretations but which may be meant to confuse him with the arch-advocate of Theravādin orthodoxy, Moggaliputta Tissa.[62] Moreover, this portrayal of him and its inscription, located in a window embrasure off the back corridor of the temple, were hardly put in a prominent spot.[63] Such out-of-the-way depictions at the Kubyauk-gyi, in fact, all deal with miscellaneous subjects that are hardly central to the overall thrust of the temple's art, which is largely given over to a narrative of the past lives of the Buddha and to a glorification of the *Mahāvaṃsa* story of the establishment of Buddhism in Sri Lanka.[64] Indeed, as Gordon Luce has argued, the temple as a whole appears to catch Pagan Buddhism at a moment of transition: it still has images of bodhisattvas attended by their śaktis and still shows signs of syncretism with Mahāyānist and Brahmanical elements, but it is a syncretism that is being subordinated to a new Sinhalese Theravādin ideal.[65]

The Persistence of the Upagupta Tradition and Orthodox Opposition

After the Kubyauk-gyi, there are no further references to Upagupta in the Pagan inscriptions. This does not mean, however, that the traditions about him died out. As we have seen, when Aggavaṃsa wrote his Pali grammar, the *Saddanīti*, in Pagan in 1154, he retained the phrase "By Upagutta Māra was bound."[66] Although we have no idea how much oral tradition, if any, went along with this paradigm, the grammar itself was clearly considered to be an important product of this period, since it was among the gifts that were later taken to Sri Lanka in order to reflect the accomplishments of the Burmese Sangha.[67]

Moreover, the *Lokapaññatti*, as a text, also continued to be known in a widespread area. In 1345, it was used by Phya Lithai of Sukhothai as a source in compiling the *Traibhūmikathā*,[68] and in 1442 it was among the many manuscripts given to the Sangha at Pagan by the governor of Taungdwin (Central Burma) and his wife.[69] In 1714, U Kala used it to retell the tale of Upagupta and Māra in his *Mahāyāzawin-gyi* (Great Chronicle of the Kings of Burma),[70] and in Thailand the same story was incorporated into the *Paṭhamasambodhikathā*.[71]

At the same time, however, the forces of Theravāda orthodoxy continued to look askance both at the legend of Upagupta and at the *Lokapaññatti*. Both the elder and his story were explicitly condemned in the *Glass Palace Chronicle*, written in 1829 by a committee of "learned monks, learned brahmins, and learned ministers." This group was charged with compiling a chronicle "in accordance with all credible records" which would be a standard "for all duties of the king, all affairs of state, all matters of religion, and not a thing full of conflicting and false statements."[72] The first half of this book, which Pe Maung Tin and Gordon Luce unfortunately left untranslated, contains an almost verbatim repeat of the *Lokapaññatti* story of Upagupta's protection of Aśoka's stūpa festival against the incursions of Māra. What is of interest here, however, is the committee's verdict on the story, which they pronounced in an editorial aside:

> The facts above-mentioned are . . . derived from the *Lokapaññatti*, a work which is not accorded recognition by the Buddhist Councils. We must note that these facts are not to be found in the acknowledged Commentaries and sub-commentaries. . . . Only in the *Lokapaññatti* is there told the story of Shin Upagutta subduing Māra at the request of the Sangha, and of his assuming the guises of the tiger, Galon [Garuḍa], etc. . . . We must not lose sight of the fact that . . . exercising magic powers for the purpose of turning oneself into the forms of nāgas, etc., is a faculty condemned by the Buddha and is put down as being contrary to the 227 rules of conduct to be observed by monks. These rules are binding even on ordinary members of the Sangha. Thus Arahats who have totally done away with the "influxes" are certain to adhere strictly to them, even under circumstances that threaten their lives. . . . This being so, what the *Lokapaññatti* says about Shin Upagutta transforming himself into a tiger, Garuḍa, etc., in the course of his fight against Māra goes very much against the spirit of the Vinaya regulations. The story, therefore, must not be taken seriously by thoughtful people.[73]

Here, then, the chief objections to the Upagupta story are that it comes from a text that is not part of Theravāda orthodoxy as defined by an official elite, and that it attributes to its hero actions that violate the Vinaya code and so do not fit into the accepted definitions of arhatship.

It was not long, however, before the legend and cult of Upagupta were to suffer from a different sort of attack and be condemned simply as superstitious or unbelievable. Indeed, in time, the myth of Theravāda orthodoxy found an ally in that elite brand of interpretation that has sought to highlight the "rational" or "scientific" side of the Buddhist tradition and emphasize its divorce from theism, faith, and foolishness, all of which are then relegated either to indigenous beliefs or to the Mahāyāna—or, more generally, to the "populace." Thus, in Thailand, when King Mongkut (1804–68) and his son Prince Patriarch Vajirañāṇa (1860–1921) took seriously the canonical injunction to test their beliefs in the light of reason and demythologized the life story of the Buddha, creating a new version of the *Paṭhamasambodhikathā* by purging the old text of all "miracles," one of the chapters they expunged was that which told the tale of Upagupta.[74]

Much the same attitude can be found in Burma today. In Rangoon, I was repeatedly told by various elite acquaintances that faith in Upagupta was not truly Buddhistic; it was "superstition," adhered to by the masses, perhaps, but clearly not part of the Blessed One's religion. The latter (I was assured by a retired colonel who carried with him a Burmese translation of Walpola Rahula's *What the Buddha Taught*) has to do with the Four Noble Truths, the Five Aggregates, the Twelve Sense Spheres, and the Eighteen Elements; it has no room for Upagupta at all.

The same sort of conclusion may be found in Maung Kin's 1903 article "The Legend of Upagutta": "This," he states, "is rather a belief of the people than of the learned in our Faith; and, long as it has seemingly existed in Burma, there are not wanting able and learned Monks and Laymen, who categorically deny the possibility of the existence of Upagutta, asserting . . . that such belief is altogether opposed to the pure Doctrine of the Master."[75] And, in conclusion, Maung Kin offers his own hope that his countrymen "shall endeavour to make headway against this popular superstition—a superstition unworthy of the followers of the greatest of the world's Religions, a relic of the bye-gone days of darkness and ignorance which were in this land before the advent of the Most Excellent Law."[76]

Official views of this sort, however, represent but one side of the coin. Not only are such condemnations of Upagupta by the orthodox elite simply ignored by many, but, in certain circles, they may actually be counterproductive and become the very reason for an espousal of his worship. Thus, on several occasions in Burma, I was told that Upagupta is a saint who is *particularly effective* precisely because he is *not* one of those "ordinary arhats whom you will find in the Pali canon." In these instances, Upagupta's very lack of canonicity serves not to malign him but to make him special, more esoteric perhaps, and thereby to enhance his prestige and power.

This view, though not very common, is noteworthy, for it reflects the complexity and ambiguity of attitudes found within Burmese Buddhism towards the noncanonical and the heterodox. For too long, students of the Theravāda in Burma and elsewhere have blithely assumed a lack of self-consciousness on the part of "popular Buddhism," which, syncretistic and need-oriented, is seen as retaining all sorts of things without even realizing that they are "corrupt" or "incorrect." It would appear, however, that, at least sometimes, certain beliefs and practices actually owe their popularity and prestige to their ostracism from official orthodoxy. They are, in other words, representations of a counterculture, reflecting another side of Buddhism in Theravāda lands, a complement and antidote to orthodoxy.

In recent years, François Bizot has pointed to the continuing survival in Southeast Asia of a number of such Buddhist countercultures, in particular the seemingly unorthodox practices which he likes to call the "unreformed" or the "ancient Mahānikay tradition." Bizot has devoted himself to elucidating the considerable body of Khmer texts that represent this school—which, he points out, is not confined to Cambodia; it is rather broadly Indo-Chinese, having clear manifestations in Laos, Thailand, and Burma.[77]

Bizot, it should be said, occasionally suffers from an overenthusiasm for the unconventional and sometimes lumps together variegated practices and beliefs simply on the grounds that they are unorthodox. Nevertheless, he has managed to show that, where many had once seen only "corruptions" or "popular aberrations," there may in fact be found a genuine tradition, complete with its own history, ideology, ritual, and soteriological endeavors. He suggests that the roots of this tradition lie as much in Sanskrit as in Pali sources and that one will fail to understand the practice of Southeast Asian Buddhism so long as one does not recognize in it "the presence of two factions: the one orthodox, resulting from the official Buddhism of Sri Lanka, the other heterodox, coming from ancient traditions of India."[78]

CHAPTER NINE

The *Lokapaññatti* Legend

ANY STUDY of the cult of Upagupta in Southeast Asia must begin with the *Lokapaññatti*, whose chapter on the saint became the fountainhead for subsequent Burmese and Thai traditions about him. Written in the eleventh or twelfth century by a monk whom we might as well keep calling Saddhammaghosa,[1] in Pali but based on Sanskrit sources, in Thaton (in Lower Burma)[2] but using Indian traditions, the text exemplifies the complexity and syncretic nature of Burmese Buddhism.

Searching for the sources of the *Lokapaññatti* is somewhat like playing a game with Chinese boxes. As a whole, the text is a treatise on cosmology seeking to give a description of the universe—its creation and destruction, its physical features and anomalies—and the various types of beings who inhabit its many realms. About 65 percent of it is a more or less faithful rendition of materials taken from a Sanskrit source, the *Lokaprajñapti,* which still exists in Chinese translation.[3] Into this, however, another text has been inserted which gives additional descriptions of the various realms of rebirth (gati);[4] and within this, yet another insert has been made, consisting primarily of a legend of King Aśoka but dealing also with stories about Mahissara (Śiva) and Māra. It is, finally, within *this* subtext that we find the tale of Upagupta (Pali: Upagutta) which interests us. In sum, then, the Upagutta story in the *Lokapaññatti* is situated within the framework of a legend of Aśoka which has been included in a description of the six realms of existence, which in turn has been placed into a broader cosmological treatise on the universe as a whole.

The question of sources, however, does not stop here. The *Lokapaññatti*'s account of Upagutta can itself be divided into two halves. The second half—featuring the saint's binding and conversion of Māra—we have already discussed. It has clear affinities with the Mathuran cycle of Sanskrit tales and need not concern us further here. The first half—relating Aśoka's invitation and testing of Upagupta and the saint's several preliminary battles with Māra—contains materials we have not yet examined. In the remainder of this chapter, we will have occasion to speculate on a few of its sources and connections, but it is not impossible that some of it was simply made up by Saddhammaghosa for dramatic purposes.

Indeed, throughout this first section, the *Lokapaññatti* shows occasional signs of remarkable originality. The Upagutta episode, for example, is prefaced by a striking version of the story of Aśoka's gathering of the Buddha relics, which are protected by mechanical robot guardians that are said to have come from Rome (Roma-visaya). Similar relic-guarding devices are mentioned in other sources,[5] but not their provenance; and the *Lokapaññatti* is perhaps unique in relating at length the saga of the Indian engineer who, hoping to steal from the Romans the secret of the manufacture of these robots, vowed on his deathbed to be reborn in Rome. There, in his next life, he managed to marry the daughter of the robots' inventor and to acquire from his father-in-law the sought-after blueprints. Eventually, by means of a clever stratagem, he arranged for his young son to smuggle the secret back to India and to take it to Pāṭaliputra, where he arrived just at the time of the Buddha's parinirvāṇa. King Ajātaśatru, seeking a way to ensure the safety of the Buddha's relics, learned of the son's arrival and promptly had several of the Roman robots made and stationed as guards around the newly dedicated stūpas of the Blessed One. A hundred years later, when King Aśoka uncovered these stūpas in an effort to gather all the Buddha's relics, the robots were still actively on guard, twirling their swords and ready to strike. In order to pass, Aśoka had to find the Roman engineer's son (apparently still living!) and get him to disarm them. Only then was he able to collect the relics and distribute them into the eighty-four thousand stūpas.[6]

It is the occasion of Aśoka's dedication of these stūpas that marks the start of Upagupta's involvement in the *Lokapaññatti* story. This begins with (1) a sort of prologue, in which Aśoka declares his fear that Māra will in one fashion or another thwart his meritorious intentions by interfering with the dedication festival. He thus asks the Sangha to appoint someone to oppose Māra. No one in the Sangha, however, is willing or able to do this, until a young novice (who himself is endowed with magical powers) suggests Upagupta. (2) The novice reveals that Upagupta (here called Kisanāga Upagutta) resides in meditation in a palacelike pavilion in the midst of the Southern Ocean. (3) Two monks are then dispatched to invite Upagupta to come to the assembly, which he does, flying through the air. (4) The question arises of who shall provide food for Upagupta in order to fortify him for his struggle against Māra; various bhikṣus volunteer to do so, but Upagupta rejects their offers and announces he will go on his own quest for alms. (5) Aśoka, however, is not convinced that Upagupta will be capable of subduing Māra and so tests him by having an elephant in rut charge him from behind; Upagupta shows his powers by turning the elephant to stone. (6) Finally, the celebration of the stūpa festival begins, and so does the battle with Māra. Māra seeks to disrupt things by causing a thunderstorm and then by taking on various forms (bull, nāga, yakṣa); but Upagupta counters all of these tactics by preventing the rain from falling and by himself taking on different forms (tiger, garuḍa, bigger yakṣa).

We shall, in the rest of this chapter, consider in some detail each of these six episodes, for they, more than anything else, mark the *Lokapaññatti* as a pivotal text in the legend and cult of Upagupta. They are, in fact, a transition point between the Indian and the Southeast Asian traditions and will force us to look both backwards at Sanskrit materials we have already covered and forwards at ritual traditions of Burma and Thailand.

Prologue

The *Lokapaññatti* begins its tale with a long account of how the Sangha, at the request of King Aśoka, looked for someone capable of subduing Māra:

> Aśoka, intending to go ahead with his plans for a grandiose festival, reflected that, since his merit making would take a long time (seven years, seven months, and seven days), it was quite likely that someone, during that period, would try to disrupt it. He asked the Sangha, therefore, to assist him by assigning a monk the duty of thwarting all attempted interferences with his meritorious actions. To this the Sangha readily agreed.
>
> When the monks got together and thought about this request, however, some of them, more perspicacious than others, realized that opposition to the king's celebration was likely to come from Māra. They went, therefore, to the eldest member of their community and asked him to counter the Evil One. But the dean declined. "Brothers," he declared, "I am too old, and I have many duties, and I am weak; I cannot oppose Māra!" The monks therefore went to the next most senior elder, but he refused as well. And so it was with the third and the fourth, all the way down to the most junior bhikkhu; they all declined, and the community, having agreed to Aśoka's request, was now in a quandary about how to fulfill it.
>
> Just then it happened that a nāga king arrived, intending to venerate the monks. Then a garuḍa king, flying through the air, also arrived, wishing to pay his respects. [Garuḍas and nāgas are traditional enemies,] so when the bird king saw the snake lord, he forgot his devout intentions and plummeted down from the sky, intending to seize him. The nāga king, hearing the sound of the rushing air, was afraid. He sought refuge at the feet of the dean, exclaiming in terror, "Bhante, save my life!"
>
> The dean, however, declared that he was not able, just then, to enter into the requisite meditative trance, and so he asked the next most senior monk, "Brother, you save the nāga king from the garuḍa."
>
> "Me?" replied the second elder. "I'm but the second most senior monk, I can't protect the nāga king." And so he asked the third elder, but the third elder said, "I can't do it!" And so it went, on down the line to the most junior monks, who also declined. There still remained, however, a seven-year-old novice, whose duty was to chase away the crows; and, in desperation, the dean and the whole community asked him to protect the king of the nāgas.
>
> Now, in actuality, this novice was endowed with supernatural powers; smiling, he replied to his elders, "In a bit, brothers, wait until the garuḍa king is but a few feet away; then I will hold him back." As the rush of air got louder and louder, however,

the monks became more and more panic-stricken, and again they pleaded with the novice to do something. "In a bit, brothers," he replied, "in a bit." Finally, at the last possible instant, he entered into the fourth meditative trance, focussed his mind, and made the following resolve: "May the garuḍa not be able to seize the nāga!" All at once the creature's fall was arrested as though he had hit a rock wall, and, frightened, he fluttered off.

The nāga king was ecstatic. "O venerable novice," he exclaimed, "you have saved my life!" And, with renewed faith in the Sangha, he took his leave. The novice's brethren, however, were less pleased. Upset with their young colleague, they rebuked him, saying, "Why didn't you volunteer when the community first asked for someone to protect the nāga king? Why did you say, 'In a bit, brothers, in a bit'?" And they resolved to punish him.

Since he had clearly demonstrated supernatural powers, they decided that his penance would be to stop Māra from hindering Aśoka's merit making activities. "Sirs," he replied, "do not request this of me. I am but a small novice with minimal magical powers. How can I stop Māra? I will, however, recommend to you another monk, more powerful than I; he will be able to do the task."[7]

A number of comments need to be made about this prologue. Though it is sometimes possible to think of Buddhist kings as defenders of the faith, or protectors of the Sangha, it is often misleading to do so. It is noteworthy that here it is not Aśoka who is to defend the monastic community in its celebration of rituals, but the monks who are to protect him in what is essentially a lay or a royal state festival. This is important; as we shall see, much the same mentality pervades the ritual invitations of Upagupta in Northern Thailand and elsewhere: his presence is primarily sought not by the monks, but by the laity; and he is invited not to officiate at a function nor even to be an object of worship, but to stand guard and ensure that devotional celebrations can occur uninterrupted.

In this context, it is clear that the Sangha's primary role is to be a source of protective power. Preservation of the Dharma is not enough; it must also protect the Dharma from harm, symbolized here by the threat of Māra. And, indeed, everything the Sangha does—its chanting of texts, its disciplined lifestyle, its practice of meditation, its housing of the Buddha image—may be interpreted as contributing to this end.

This role requires, of course, that the Sangha have such power, in the form of supernatural endowments. But alas, in this day and age, when the religion is in decline, this is not always the case. In the prologue, a good deal of fun is poked at the regular hierarchy of monks for their false pretensions; they assure the king they will protect his ceremony, but, in fact, not one of them is able to do so. They assure the nāga he will be safe from his enemy, but, in the event, they need to turn to a small novice, who is outside of their regular hierarchy but is the only one endowed with magical powers and with the knowledge of where to find Upagupta.[8] There is much humor in all of this, but behind it lies a recognition of the dissipation of power that has occurred over time in the history of the Sangha. In the face of this, arhats—real arhats—are needed, but they are apparently no longer to be found in the regular community of monks.

Kisanāga Upagutta

Indeed, the novice appears to be alone in knowing about Upagupta and his powers. The other monks are bewildered by his piece of news. "Who is this bhikkhu more powerful than you?" they ask, "and where does he live?" And this gives the śrāmaṇera a chance to describe formally the hero of the episode:

> "Reverend sirs," he replied, "this bhikkhu dwells in the midst of the ocean. Having parted a great mass of water and magically fashioned in it a palace made of all kinds of gems, he stays there, seated on a splendid divan adorned with jewels, wafted by fragrant perfumes, bedecked with myriads of flowers filled with sparkling water. His name is Kisanāga Upagutta. Without eating, he spends his days in meditative trance and does not attend assemblies of monks. But there is no one more qualified than him for taming Māra. He is, in fact, just the person for the task, since long ago the Buddha himself predicted that a monk named Upagutta would admonish Māra and cause him to resolve to attain Buddhahood."[9]

In this brief description of our saint, we can find the *Lokapaññatti*'s first major departure from the Mathuran tradition: Upagupta is no longer portrayed as living in a forest monastery on Mount Urumuṇḍa, but as dwelling in a magic pavilion or palace located under the sea or, alternatively, on a sort of floating island in the midst of the ocean. We will deal in our next chapter with some of the legends that tell how Upagupta came to take up this watery abode. For now, we need to focus on another important element in this passage: the epithet Kisanāga ("thin" or "emaciated" nāga) that is here given to him.

The word *nāga* is best known for denoting the snake, or, in a more mythological context, the serpentlike being who inhabits the underwater or underground domain, who has the power to take on various forms (including human ones), who is often connected with the control of water, and who may or may not be a devotee of the Buddha.[10] Upagupta's epithet, along with certain other features of his legend, has understandably led some scholars to identify him with this mythological figure and to see in his cult another example of Southeast Asian nāga worship. Thus, Eugène Denis states, "Upagutta is a nāga";[11] Stanley Tambiah interprets the invitation of Upagupta to a festival as a ritual that symbolizes "the taming and conversion of the *Naga* or spirit of the water to Buddhism";[12] and Kenneth Wells, noting Upagupta's connection with the festival of lights, even calls him "the Lord of the Nagas."[13]

These conclusions are, perhaps, ultimately justifiable, but it is important to realize that there are several other Buddhist connotations to the word *nāga* which must be taken into consideration. First, besides "serpent," or "serpent-like mythological being," *nāga* also means "elephant." This application may not be immediately apparent, but it is clearly played upon a bit later in the *Lokapaññatti* when King Aśoka, thinking this Upagutta to be a rather "skinny [kisa] nāga," tests his powers by setting on him a very large and ruttish royal elephant (hatthi-nāga). The irony highlighted, then, is that such a thin weakling nāga should be able to defeat such a big strong one.

Second, the word *nāga* also came to be an epithet more generally implying greatness; as such, it was commonly applied to arhats.[14] Since *kisa* was by itself a common designation of ascetics, one interpretation of the name Kisanāga might be simply "great ascetic arhat"—which is, of course, precisely what Upagupta is.

Third, and perhaps most significantly, *nāga* is also the name given to candidates for higher ordination in Buddhism. This curious designation is said to be in memory of an actual nāga (snake) who sought and obtained ordination as a monk by taking on the guise of a human being. His true identity was discovered, however (when, much to the horror of his roommate, he reverted to his serpent body while asleep), and the Buddha promptly excommunicated him, telling him he could not remain a monk because he was a nāga. He should, rather, become a devout layman in order to be reborn as a human being and enter the Sangha in his next life. Ironically, human candidates for ordination were thereafter called nāgas in memory of his unsuccessful bid for monkhood.[15]

In this context, then, we may wish to think of Aśoka's invitation of Upagupta to his festival not just as the fetching of a great elder, but also as the bringing of a candidate for ordination. Indeed, today, as we shall see, the ritual invitations of Upagupta (Phra Uppakhut) in Northern Thailand and elsewhere have clear affinities with the upasampadā rite, and the offerings made to him at that time are "precisely the offerings presented to a man about to be ordained as a monk."[16] Thus, when Upagupta is called Kisanāga, one of the possible intended meanings is that he is an "ascetic ordinand" or a "skinny novice."

It is important to remember, however, that, in many parts of Southeast Asia, monkhood is not so much a lifelong career as a stage on life's way, a period of passage or preparation for full existence as a layman. Thus, the Vinaya legend about the nāga who wanted to become a monk must be paired with the less well known but equally important story of the novice-monk who wanted to become a nāga. In brief, it runs as follows:

> Once upon a time, there was an arhat who used to fly through the air (atop his bed) to go and take his food in the palace of the nāgas, in the midst of a lake. Upon his

return, he would give his empty alms bowl to his novice to wash. One day, there happened to be a few grains of rice left in the bowl, and the novice ate them; they were exquisite. Suspecting that his master might be obtaining his food by some supernatural means, he hid under the bed and then held on to it when the arhat flew off the next morning. Arriving in the underwater palace, he was not exactly welcomed by the nāgas, but, as he had come with his master, they served him some of the "divine" rice anyway.

While eating, he happened to see an extraordinarily beautiful nāgī maiden and became passionately attracted to her. Then and there he resolved to be reborn in the nāga kingdom; and, upon returning home to his monastery, he applied himself to acts of dāna and of morality (śīla), vowing all the time to become a nāga and so to rejoin his beloved. Finally, one day, as he was devoutly circumambulating a caitya, he saw water appear beneath his feet; and he realized his dream was to come true. He therefore went to the shore of a lake; and, covering his head with his monastic robe, he entered the water, died, and was reborn as a nāga.[17]

In this story, we see clearly that the designation "nāga" given to candidates for ordination is an ambiguous epithet, reflecting the liminal nature of the Sangha; in that one word is epitomized a double ideal—that of entering the monkhood and that of returning thereafter to lay life. As we shall see, much the same process may be found in the ritual invitations of Uppakhut in Northern Thailand: he is brought as a nāga—a kisanāga—from the waters to the monastery; but, precisely because he is a nāga, he will be returned to those waters once the ceremonies he guards are over.

Kisanāga, however, is not the only epithet given to Upagupta in Southeast Asia. Indeed, the *Lokapaññatti* would appear to be the only text actually to call him that. In most of the Burmese reworkings of the legend, that designation has been changed, and Aśoka is told that the saint he seeks is named Upagutta *Tissa*nāga.[18] Some may be tempted to see in this "Tissa" a further connection with the figure of Mogalliputta Tissa. It is important to realize, however, that "Tissa" is another set name that is used in the upasampadā ceremony; it is, in fact, the appellation that designates the elder who is acting as the "nāga's" preceptor, his upādhyāya. Thus, the ritual questions put to the ordinand are full of references to both "Tissa" and "Nāga":

> "Your name is Nāga?" "It is so, Lord." "Your superior is the venerable Tissa?" "It is so, Lord." . . . "Listen, Nāga. This is the time for you to speak the truth. . . . Have you any such diseases as these: Leprosy?" "No, Lord." "Boils?" "No, Lord." . . . "Are you a human being?" "Yes, Lord." "Are you a male?" "Yes, Lord." . . . "What is your name?" "Lord, I am called Nāga." "What is the name of your superior?" "Lord, my superior is called the venerable Tissa."[19]

Even outside the ritual itself, conversations at ordination time are permeated with these two words. I once told a Theravādin monk that Upagupta was called Tissanāga and asked him what the name meant to him; he immediately said it reminded him of his ordination, for, as he put it, when elders and ordinands gather for an upasampadā, among them there is constant talk of "your Nāga, my Nāga; your Tissa, my Tissa."[20]

In "Tissanāga," then, we have another reminder of the ordination ritual, but one that is more openly paradoxical, implying that Upagupta is both Nāga and Tissa, pupil and master, ordinand and ordainer. Such ambiguity should not surprise us. Clearly, Upagupta is more than an ordinary candidate for ordination; if, on the one hand, he takes on the role of ordinand expected to return to lay life, he remains on the other an accomplished arhat, a master being invited to guard against Māra's incursions.

This same ambiguity is reflected in another rite of passage for Buddhist monks in which Upagupta and the symbolism of the nāga also play an important role. The upasampadā, which transforms a nāga into a bhikṣu, is not necessarily the last initiation of a Buddhist monk. For fully ordained monks who choose to remain in the Sangha, there exists a whole series of higher grades that they can pass through,[21] and attainment of these grades involves, especially in Laos and parts of Thailand, a peculiar form of initiation (called Bun kong h'ot) which is quite distinct from the upasampadā (Bun kong buat). It includes a fetching of the candidate from his hermitage, a mock struggle among various forces, a sprinkling or aspersion (abhiṣeka) of the candidate by the entire village, and a final return to the monastery. The ritual has been summarized and analyzed by a number of scholars, but its most thorough description is given by Pierre Bernard Lafont and Pierre Bitard.[22] It is of particular interest to us for its different use of the nāga symbol and for its explicit involvement of the figure of Upagupta.

The ceremony starts with a mock search in the forest by the laypeople of the village for the man who is to be ordained. Interestingly, the first two hermitages they come to turn out not to be the right ones, and it is only on their third try that they find their candidate. I would suggest we have here another instance of the pattern found in the threefold attempt at inviting Upagupta which we have already detected in several contexts.[23] On the third try, then, the procession comes to the right candidate's hermitage. It is marked off by sacred white cotton threads and other magical barriers and surrounded by two rows of staffs, which are later also carried back to the monastery. These staffs are surmounted by various symbols said to represent the weapons that Māra used against the Buddha. Having failed to harm him, they then came to assure his protection. Their symbolic intent would appear to be clear: Māra is still a potential threat, but he has effectively been kept at bay. Upagupta's presence is meant also to reinforce this protection.[24]

The right candidate is then honored in his hermitage and asked by the lay leaders to come to the monastery and receive ordination. He is invited to sit in a waiting palanquin, and then, installed in it, he is jostled back and forth for a while by his bearers in a curious sort of tug-of-war. An intriguing explanation of this was given to Lafont and Bitard by the palanquin bearers.[25] They claimed their action signified an attempt to "stop the flow of time," more specifically "to delay the coming of the year 2500 of the Buddhist era."[26] This year, said to mark the halfway point in the duration of Gautama's Dharma, was widely celebrated in Theravāda lands as the Buddha Jayanti in 1956. The ritual observed by Lafont and Bitard in 1955, however, would seem to reflect not an eager anticipation of this halfway point, but a worry about its coming, a worry governed by the widely known legend that, from then on, Buddhism would be marked by increasing decline and decay.[27] At the same time, it must be remembered that this decline and decay will end with the advent of Maitreya, who will restore the Dharma in its purity and full effectiveness. The Buddha Jayanti, then, marks the midpoint between two Buddhas. In the tug-of-war over the palanquin of the candidate for abhiṣeka, we thus can find once again an expression of the tension between orientation towards Śākyamuni (the wish to go back) and orientation towards Maitreya (the wish to go forward).

After this jostling, the candidate for higher ordination is carried to the monastery, where the initiation proper begins. The high point of the ceremony is the aspersion of the candidate in a shower of holy water that is ritually poured over him through a bamboo tube (hang lin) carved in the form of a nāga.[28] The entire village takes part in these repeated showerings, while an old layman, crouching down just outside the shower stall, recites verses that affirm the enactment of the initiation. This man, who in a sense is the facilitator of the rite and ensures its continuity from one aspersion to another, is explicitly said to represent Upagupta.[29] Upagupta is also present inside the wat, where an altar to him has been set directly opposite the porcelain figure of an elephant—an apparent reference to the *Lokapaññatti* story of Aśoka's testing of Upagupta's strength.[30]

We shall return to this ordination ceremony later in our discussion. For now, after this excursus on the use of the term *nāga* as an epithet and on its appearance in ordination rituals, we need to go back to the text of the *Lokapaññatti*.

The Invitation of Upagupta

The *Lokapaññatti* legend, having identified Upagupta as residing in the midst of the ocean and having suggested that he may be able to counter the powers of Māra, then proceeds to recount the tale of his actual invitation to Aśoka's assembly:

> At these words [of the novice], the monks rejoiced, and immediately the community officially dispatched two bhikkhus on a mission to invite Upagutta. Diving into the earth, those bhikkhus came up again in Upagutta's palace in the ocean, where they

uttered [a few lines of scripture]. The elder, aroused from his trance of cessation by the sound of the Dharma, asked the bhikkhus why they had come. "Bhante," they replied, "by order of the Sangha, we are to take you to the assembly of monks."

"Very well," Upagutta agreed, adding, out of respect for the Sangha, "Brothers, you go first, and I will follow."

Thus, the two bhikkhus went off first, but Upagutta, with his quicker magical powers, arrived at the assembly of monks before them. He prostrated himself in front of the elders and sat down on his own seat. When the two messenger monks, who had . . . proceeded by means of their own magical powers, arrived, they were astonished to see the elder already seated.

"Sirs," they exclaimed, "he sent us off first and left later, but we have arrived after him. What a monk of great power he is!"

But the community of monks wished to impose its punishment on the elder Kisanāga Upagutta. "Brother," they declared, "why have you not been coming to the uposatha celebrations or to assemblies? Why do you not take seriously the affairs of the Sangha but only consider your own convenience? You ought to have more respect for the monastic community. You are just like the elder Mahākappina, who was reproached by the Blessed One and who . . . had to do penance. So, like him, you will have to be punished."

The elder Upagutta said, "Sirs, whatever the penance, I will receive it, having performed an ablution, as though it were a garland of blue lotuses."

The dean of the Sangha then said, "Brother Upagutta, King Aśoka, who waits upon the assembly of monks, will soon carry out the dedication ceremony of the eighty-four thousand stūpas and will pay grand pūjā to this Mahāstūpa for seven years, seven months, and seven days. During this time, whenever Māra, the Evil One, comes to thwart the merit making of the king, you must undertake to ward him off, to discipline him."

The elder Upagutta said, "I respectfully accept the order of the Sangha."[31]

In chapter 7, we analyzed in some detail the Sanskrit story of Aśoka's invitation of Upagupta and of his provision of a means for the elder to descend the Ganges by boat and come to the capital of Pāṭaliputra. This *Lokapaññatti* tale is rather different. First of all, it is not Aśoka who is doing the inviting here, but the Sangha, albeit at the king's request.[32] Second, while in the Sanskrit story emphasis was placed on Upagupta's transportation by *natural* means (the boat provided by Aśoka), here the stress is clearly on Upagupta's *supernatural* powers: he outflies the monks who came to invite him, even though they left ahead of him on the return journey. This flight is intended as an initial demonstration to the Sangha of Upagupta's superiority and his abilities to counter Māra.[33] Third, it is noteworthy that the monks ask Upagupta to ward off Māra not as a favor to themselves or to the king, but as a penance for not regularly participating in the Sangha's activities, specifically for not attending the hepdomadary upoṣadha meetings or the bimonthly confession ceremonies (prātimokṣa). In this he is accused of being just like the Buddha's disciple Mahākappina. The comparison is significant; Mahākappina (Sanskrit: Kapphiṇa) was renowned for spending much of his time in a trance, and it was in part for this reason that he once missed the prātimokṣa assembly.[34] So, too, Upagupta is here abiding in a "trance of cessation," from which he has to be aroused. This fact not only justifies the comparison to Mahākappina (as well as to Mahākāśyapa), it also explains why the two monks dispatched to invite him have to recite some verses of scripture before being able to make the invitation. Apparently, the sound of the Dharma is one of those things which can awaken a meditator from samādhi.[35]

The Provision of Food

One of the results of Upagupta's dwelling in a trance in the midst of the ocean is that he has not been eating. He is quite literally kisa (emaciated), and if he is to oppose Māra now that he has arisen from meditative absorption, he needs to find food to sustain himself, he must be fortified. The next episode in the *Lokapaññatti* makes this clear:

> The elder Upagutta said, "I respectfully accept the order of the Sangha. But where am I to get suitable nourishment?"
>
> Hearing this, a certain monk in the midst of the assembly said, "Reverend Upagutta, I will give you as much food as you need."
>
> Upagutta asked, "How did you come by it?"
>
> "Sir," answered the monk, "it has come to me by the ripening of my merit. Early each morning, four bowls filled with foods and curries of various flavors appear in front of me. Of these four bowlfuls of almsfood, take, as you will, two or three, setting aside but one for me."
>
> "Brother," the elder said, "what is the karmic cause of your getting these four bowls of almsfood? I want to know the root of the matter, so tell me."
>
> "Sir, as you know, in a previous life, my parents lived here in Pāṭaliputta, as prosperous and successful merchants, and I was their only son and very dear to them. By and by, I came into contact with good spiritual friends; I wandered forth and abounded in moral practices. Four monks were my close companions, with me in happiness and sorrow. Now because they loved me, my parents always invited me to come and eat at home. I used to take my monk companions along, and my parents, understanding my intention, also fed them. As a result of this act, I now receive four bowls full of alms."
>
> The elder Upagutta said, "If that is the case, the alms you receive are impure—linked to parental love. They are not a gift of faith! They are unsuitable and not for me!"
>
> Then another monk said, "I will give suitable almsfood to the unsatisfied Upagutta."
>
> The elder asked him, "Brother, how have you come by your food?"
>
> "Sir, I obtain it as a result of my past merit."

"By the maturation of what act do you obtain it?"

"Sir, in a former life, right here in Pāṭaliputta, I was a Brahmin well versed in the Vedas, and a great many people would invite me to receive sweetened milk-rice with hardly any water, and various treats cooked with butter, honey, molasses, and oil. One day, after satiating myself, I left the city, wishing to go for a walk in the countryside. I went by way of a tank, and there, by the side of the water, dwelt a miserable bitch with a brood of pups. Her young ones, not getting any food, cried from hunger. At the sound of my footsteps, the hungry bitch came over and held up her front paws and barked, 'Woof! Woof!' Seeing her standing there, I thought, 'This hungry dog wants food; her starving pups are crying. . . . How am I going to give her some?' Then, out of compassion for that dog, I vomited the milk-rice . . . that was in my stomach, and I gave it to her. She also satisfied her pups. Together they ate and drank. And seeing them, I was pleased, thinking, 'Aho! I have made an offering to hungry beings.' In time, I died, contented, and received, as a result of my act, a hundredfold return; every day now, very early, two bowls appear before me, filled with suitable foods and curries of various flavors, mixed with butter, honey, molasses, and oil. I will give your honor one of these two bowls; you need not go on your alms round at all."

At this the elder Upagutta laughed a little and said, "Away with this almsfood which is the result of having vomited! It is not suitable and has not been brought about by faith."

Then the elder Kisanāga Upagutta, having refused the two [offers of] alms, bowed down at the feet of the elder monks and said, "Sirs, I will myself obtain suitable almsfood and keep myself going, and I will carry out the order of the community of monks and tame Māra shortly, by the very act of going on alms rounds. He will not thwart the king's merit making, for the Blessed One predicted that I, Upagutta, would in a future time subjugate Māra."[36]

This semihumorous passage, which one can easily imagine being told with relish as part of the oral tradition, is not difficult to interpret. It stresses Upagupta's need for sustenance in order to combat Māra and yet also shows his concern for the purity of the food he is to receive: his nourishment must be untainted by dubious past attachments.

That Upagupta is concerned with food offerings should come as no surprise. After all, a prominent feature of his iconography is his alms bowl, into which he is usually portrayed as putting his right hand. Some images even show him in the process of raising food to his mouth (see fig. 3). He is, in other words, depicted in the act of eating, and even his tilting his head to look up at the sun reinforces this notion: he wants to make sure he completes his meal before high noon. The full importance of this episode, however, can be appreciated only in light of Southeast Asian ritual traditions about Upagupta and almsfood. This episode is, in fact, the first indication that we have had of the importance of giving food to Upagupta, something that is much emphasized by merit seekers in Thailand and Burma to this day.[37]

Fig. 3. Upagupta Eats While Looking at the Sun. Image from a Private Collection, Chiang Mai, Thailand

The *Lokapaññatti* puts such food offerings to Upagupta in a new light: the saint is fed not just to make merit, but to fortify him in the fight against Māra. This is an interpretation that is not commonly made in Southeast Asia today; villagers, accustomed to thinking of dāna as a meritorious act from which one should reap benefits in this or a future lifetime, do not think of the food offerings they make as protective measures designed to defend themselves against evil. Yet this is clearly the case with offerings to Upagupta. The food given to him is intended to give him strength in his upcoming task and is especially important because, in his weakened condition, he needs it. In this way, the whole community can participate in the fight against Māra, for without their offerings it is possible that Upagupta would fail. For this reason, perhaps, Upagupta's food must be given to him directly by laypersons and not by other monks. As the *Lokapaññatti* makes clear, this saint does his own begging; having rejected as impure the offers of other monks, he goes out himself, bowl in hand.

The Testing of Upagupta

Upagupta begins his begging round at Aśoka's palace, and there the effectiveness of food offerings is immediately put to the test. Aśoka, having met Upagupta for the first time the day before, is worried that he is "very thin"; and, despite the assurances of the Sangha elders, he is uncertain whether or not Upagupta will be able to keep Māra at bay:

> Aśoka stood up, approached the elder, venerated him, and looked him over. He saw that he was very ugly and very thin, and his first thought was, "How much will he have to eat in order to become strong enough [to stop Māra]?" With this in mind, he got up and departed.
>
> The next day, it happened that Upagutta entered the royal house for alms. The king gave him almsfood and dismissed him, but then, just as he was going off, he had the state elephant who was in a state of rut released. The elephant, gone amuck, charged after the elder and was soon close behind him. But the elder saw his shadow and thought, "The king wants to test me and is having me pursued by this elephant." So, without breaking stride, he used his supernatural powers of determination to make a mental wish, and the elephant was turned to stone on the spot and stood still, his trunk still raised in the air. Upagutta went off without even looking back.
>
> Then the king, surrounded by his ministers, went up to the beast, examined it, and was astonished. "Aho!" he exclaimed, "the elder does have great might and supernatural power! How else could he turn such a strong state elephant to stone?" And, very pleased, he reflected that the venerable one would be able to subjugate Māra. As quickly as possible and surrounded by his ministers, he went up to the elder Upagutta and apologized: "Forgive me, Venerable Sir, I did not intend to be hostile towards you; this was only a means of testing you."
>
> "Great king," the elder replied, "I trust you are satisfied. Now may the elephant resume its original form and return to its stable."
>
> And as soon as he had said these words, the great elephant went back to its stable, and the whole world was amazed at this astonishing display of the elder's supernatural powers.[38]

This story of Upagupta and Aśoka's elephant, which is perhaps related to a number of similar legends,[39] remains well known in Northern Thailand today (see fig. 4). Stanley Tambiah, who recounts a slightly different version of the tale,[40] interprets it as posing "the opposition between religious or spiritual power (thin ascetic) and royal power (symbolized in the elephant)" and as showing that Upagupta is "superior to temporal power."[41] Certainly, at one level, this is the case, but the resolution of this opposition by Upagupta's overcoming the elephant is more complex than indicated by Tambiah. As the

Fig. 4. Upagupta Turns Aśoka's Elephant to Stone. Detail from a Mural at Wat Bunnyavat, Lampang, Thailand

Lokapaññatti makes clear, Upagupta turns Aśoka's elephant to stone only after Aśoka has fed Upagupta. In the immediate context of the tale, this may only be intended to indicate the effectiveness of feeding Upagupta: it gives him strength. More generally, however, we can find here, epitomized, the whole of the Sangha-state relationship in all its lopsided symbiosis: Upagupta is superior to temporal power only because of temporal power's material support of him. But, having demonstrated his superiority, he returns sovereignty to the king by restoring the elephant to its original form and sending it back to the stable.[42]

The Battle with Māra

Everything so far in the *Lokapaññatti* account has prepared us for the final episode to be considered here: the series of confrontations between Upagupta and Māra. Upagupta has been identified, invited, and judged capable both by the Sangha and by the king; now is the time for the task for which he was destined:

> Then King Aśoka, wishing to begin the pūjā for the Great Stūpa on the bank of the Ganges, had constructed a stand for oil lamps a short distance from the river. Within the boundaries of the Great Stūpa, the lamps burned brightly, and the people and a great number of monks assembled there in order to worship and pay pūjā.
>
> Soon, however, Māra caused the wind to blow and the rain to fall, hoping to

extinguish the lamps and to thwart the stūpa pūjā. But at that moment, the elder Upagutta, using his supernatural powers of resolution, enveloped all of Māra's disturbing wind and rain and blew it far away. Then Māra caused a shower of sand and gravel and burning coals to fall down; but the elder, by the power of his resolution, caught them all in a large sling and flung them out beyond the limit of the world.

Then Māra, furious, took on the form of a great bull and charged the lamp stands, intending to destroy them; but the elder fashioned the form of a tiger and attacked that bull, which, being weaker, bellowed horribly. The great crowd of people saw it, as well as the king, the community of monks, and all beings.

Then Māra, realizing he was losing [that battle], abandoned the form of the bull and created that of a seven-headed nāga, intent on biting the tiger; but the elder quickly gave up the form of the tiger, fashioned the form of a garuḍa, and, seizing the nāga by the neck, dragged it about.

Finally, Māra, again realizing he was losing and suffering from being tricked and beaten, abandoned the form of the nāga and created that of a yakkha with a huge head and an iron club as big as a palm tree; and, grasping that flaming club, he tried to strike the garuḍa's head with it. But the elder quickly gave up the guise of the garuḍa and created the form of a yakkha that was twice as big as the other one. And he fashioned two flaming, burning iron clubs, and with these he tried to strike Māra on the head.

Māra became frantic with worry. "Whatever form I create," he reflected, "this ascetic creates one with twice the qualities. What am I to do now? I am defeated." He therefore took on the appearance of a handsome gentleman, courteous, eloquent, and adorned with ornaments and perfumes, and he stood in front of the elder.

Seeing him, Upagutta reflected, "I will now work it so that this yakkha becomes sapless." And, fashioning the foul-smelling carcass of a dog, filled with worms, rotting, impure, and utterly loathsome, he fixed it around [Māra's] neck so that no one could free him from it, not even the gods of the Brahma heavens. Then he dismissed him, saying, "Be off, Evil One!"[43]

Such miracle contests between Buddhist and non-Buddhist masters were popular features of the literature with which we are dealing, and this episode can be read for its sheer entertainment value. The succession of attacks by Māra, each countered by Upagupta, makes for good storytelling and perhaps even better theater. Anything Māra tries, Upagupta can do better. Māra's initial storm of wind and rain, Upagupta blows far away; his shower of sand and gravel and coals, he catches in a sling. Then comes a series of transformations: as a bull, Māra is overcome by a tiger; as a nāga, he is overcome by a garuḍa; and as a yakṣa, he is overcome by a bigger yakṣa.[44]

It should be noted that this particular series of oppositions also figures in what was perhaps the best-known story of this genre in the Sanskrit Buddhist world: the duel of supernatural powers between the Buddha's disciple Śāriputra and the six heretical masters (sometimes represented by Raktākṣa). Thus, in the *Damamūkanidāna sūtra* version of the tale, we are treated to a series of six transformations, including the three that interest us here: in rapid succession, the heretic takes on the forms of a nāga, a bull, and a yakṣa, only to be countered and defeated by Śāriputra in the guises of a garuḍa, a lion, and Vaiśravaṇa (the lord of the yakṣas).[45]

The Ritual Context: The Riverine Festival of Lights

The mythic and cultic connotations of these oppositions are worth exploring, and we shall do so in due time; but first it is important to pay some attention to the ritual dimensions of their context. The *Lokapaññatti* makes it clear that the setting for this battle between Upagupta and Māra is Aśoka's stūpa festival. This celebration is a festival in which myriads of oil lamps are lit in honor of the Buddha; it is held by the side of a river—on the banks of the Ganges. Māra's first attack is an attempt to extinguish these lamps with wind and rain, something that Upagupta easily thwarts, thereby establishing his reputation as a "rain-stopper"—for which he is still famed in Burma today. Māra's second attack—a shower of sand and gravel and coals—may also be aimed at destroying the lamps, but it is stopped by Upagupta's catching all of these missiles in a large sling reminiscent of Indagutta's great "umbrella."[46]

The lighting of oil lamps is, of course, a nearly universal feature of Buddhist festivals and devotionalism. Here, their illumination in great numbers and the nearby presence of the river point us in a particular direction: to the riverine festival of lights which is celebrated annually in different parts of Southeast Asia.

Loi Krathong (as this festival is called in Thailand) takes place on the full-moon night of October-November right after the end of the Buddhist rains retreat. It features the floating (loi) of small leaf cups (krathong) or other floats on which are placed candles or lamps. As a festival, it has been related to the Indian Dīvalī, as well as to other Asian celebrations in China and Japan.[47] Travellers have often been deeply moved by the beauties of the celebration:

> I remember once I was going up the river on a festival night by the full moon, and we saw point after point crowned with lights upon the pagodas; and as we came near the great city we saw a new glory; for there was a boat anchored in mid-stream, and from this boat there dropped a stream of fire; myriads of little lamps burned on tiny rafts that drifted down the river in a golden band, . . . until at length they died far away into the night.[48]

H. Fielding Hall, whose account this is, adds that he does not know what all these lights signify, but that he does not really care; Loi Krathong is important as a time of beauty and enjoyment and romance.[49] Nonetheless, many explanations of this ceremony have been given, in Burma, Thailand, and Laos. Some have viewed it as an offering to the manes (souls of the dead) and a symbolic sending back of the visiting manes.[50] Others represent it as a purging of evil and bad luck, the floating lights playing the role of a scapegoat to be gotten rid of.[51] For still others, it is a ritual aimed at appeasing the Mother of the Waters, to prevent deaths by drowning and to ask forgiveness for the pollution of the streams and rivers.[52]

The most immediately relevant interpretation from our perspective, however, is that it is a festival in honor of Upagupta. The offerings of lights (as well as the food that is sometimes placed on the small rafts) eventually sink into the stream and so go down to Upagupta's underwater palace. In fact, the ceremony is directly associated with Aśoka's stūpa festival. As Kenneth Wells put it: "[Once] King Asoka decided to build 84,000 cetiyas but Mara threatened to destroy them. The king appealed to the Lord of the Nagas, Phra Upagota, to help him by capturing Mara. This the Naga Lord did and since then the people have shown their gratitude to [him] by this river festival."[53]

These explanations of Loi Krathong need to be put into the context of yet two other interpretations that will help us explore further the *Lokapaññatti* story. The first of these is that the festival is a ceremony in honor of the footprint that the Buddha left in the bed of the Nammadā River.[54] In brief, this story has it that the Buddha, after visiting his disciple Puṇṇa (Sanskrit: Pūrṇa) in Sunāparanta (Sanskrit: Śroṇāparānta), was entertained by a nāga king who dwelt in the Nammadā River and who asked the Buddha for something to remember him by. The Buddha obliged him by leaving the imprint of his foot in the riverbed, where it remained visible, though it was covered over each year during the rainy season.[55]

The second explanation is that the lamps that are floated on the water at Loi Krathong or lit in and around the pagodas are in honor of a white female crow who, in a previous existence, was the mother of the five Buddhas of the present kalpa.[56] The focus of this association is on the white cotton wicks that are used in the oil lamps. The bases of these wicks are split into three strands to help them stand up, and, after all the oil has burnt away, the strands leave in the lamp cup a black impression that is likened to the shape of a crow's foot. The new wicks, therefore, are called "white crow's feet."[57] This appellation is further justified by a myth of origin that has several different versions in Southeast Asia but that may be summarized as follows:

> Once, long ago, there was a white female crow who had laid five eggs. One day, a storm destroyed her nest and the eggs fell into the water. The crow searched for them in vain, and then died of grief and was reborn in one of the Brahma heavens. Her eggs were found by five different animals: a hen, a nāgī, a turtle, a cow, and a lioness (or tigress). In time the eggs hatched, and five sons were born: a wild rooster, a nāgarāja, a tortoise, a great bull, and a lion. These five were actually bodhisattvas who were destined to become the five Buddhas of the present aeon (Bhadrakalpa): the rooster was to be Kakusandha (Sanskrit: Krakucchanda), the nāga Konāgamana (Kanakamuni), the tortoise Kassapa (Kāśyapa), the bull Gotama (Gautama), and the lion Metteyya (Maitreya).[58] Though brought up separately, the five brothers all be-

came hermits and happened to meet in the forest. They resolved to try to see their mother again, and she, now a deity in heaven, heard their prayer and appeared in their midst. When it came time for her to leave, she took pity on them and left them one of her white feet as a token by which they could remember her. Thus, today, once a year, in honor of her search for them along the riverbank, people light "white-crow's-feet" lamps and let them float down the stream.[59]

These two myths are significant for the emphasis they place on the worship of traces. The footprint of the Buddha and the claw of the mother crow are both remains—relics—of former times when the Buddha (or, in the case of the latter myth, the Buddhas) were present in our world. At the same time, in a dynamic that we have already examined, these traces testify to the Buddhas' present absence. The Buddha's footprint appears and disappears depending on the height of the river water. The white crow loses her eggs when the river floods, and she searches for them in vain; she meets "them" in a later life, only to leave them again. The Loi Krathong festival associated with these stories may thus be seen as a recapture first of the presence of the Blessed One (the lighting of the lamps) followed by his inevitable absence (their floating away and extinction). In this regard, it might be added, it is appropriate that Aśoka's riverine festival of lights in the *Lokapaññatti* should have been a stūpa festival, for the stūpa, like other traces of the Buddha, is a powerful focal point for a double realization—of both his presence and his absence.[60]

The Transformations of Upagupta and Māra

With all of this in mind, we may now turn to a more specific interpretation of the series of oppositions featured in the *Lokapaññatti* story of Māra and Upagupta. It will be recalled that, in the course of their battle, Māra successively takes on the form of a bull, a nāga, and a yakṣa, only to be defeated by Upagupta in the guise of a tiger, a garuḍa, and a bigger yakṣa. We shall not touch on the first of these oppositions here, but only the latter two.[61]

The antagonism between nāga and garuḍa in Indian and Southeast Asian mythology is legendary.[62] The great bird is the traditional enemy of the ophidian, swooping down from the skies to attack it with its talons; and in this story we have another illustration of this opposition. It is curious, however, that Upagupta here takes on the role of garuḍa, since elsewhere he is closely identified with the nāga. Perhaps for this reason, Richard Davis has argued that Upagupta should be seen as a fusion of nāga and garuḍa. In support of this view, he points out that, in parts of Northern Thailand, the word *garuḍa* is pronounced in the same way as the second half of the local pronunciation of *Upagupta* ("Upagrutta"). Thus, though "the garuḍa and the nāga are diametrically opposed in mythology and pseudo-astrological texts, Upagrutta . . . dramatically combines them in a single symbol."[63]

Davis further supports this argument by reference to an anomalous Northern Thai image of Upagupta found at Wat Muang Haam, near Amphur Saa in Nan province. This image is about five feet high, carved from a single log, and placed to one side of the main altar of the wat. A second, identical image stands on the other side. Both show Phra Uppakhut as a figure with a prominent brow, well-delineated eyes, and a nose that apparently terminates in a beard or a beak instead of a mouth. He firmly grasps with both of his hands a nāga, whose head surmounts his own but whose body is draped around his neck and extends down his sides. Lower down, Uppakhut also grasps this nāga with his clawlike feet. That these feet are indeed talons is further suggested by the fact that the statue's lower body is wrapped in a pair of folded wings.[64]

Davis, always on the lookout for psychosexual symbolism, claims that the general shape of this figure is "strikingly reminiscent of an uncircumcised penis . . . ramrod straight."[65] He goes on, however, to discuss it as an example of Upagupta's "enigmatic bivalence," a *coincidentia oppositorum* in which garuḍa and nāga are paradoxically combined, a sort of Northern Thai equivalent of the Chinese symbol for the interpenetration of yin and yang.[66]

Such grandiose exegeses are not very helpful. The *Lokapaññatti* legend suggests rather that what we have here is a depiction of Uppakhut as a garuḍa engaged in battle with a nāga, an interpretation that was, in fact, confirmed by one of the monks at Wat Muang Haam.[67] In what follows, therefore, I would like to offer a much more specific interpretation of this story, one which may help explain why, in this context, Upagupta is closely associated with the nāga's enemy, the garuḍa.

It is important to remember that, in the *Lokapaññatti*, what Māra is seeking to disrupt is Aśoka's enshrinement of the Buddha relics. Nāgas are consistently portrayed in Buddhist legend as great worshippers of the relics of the Buddha. For this they are generally respected and admired, but problems arise due to the fact that their devotion may sometimes lead them to steal relics and jealously keep them in their underwater world. This prevents others—namely, human beings—from worshipping the relics. Under these circumstances, someone is needed who can take the relics back from the nāgas and ensure their proper enshrinement in the human world.

This basic scenario is illustrated by a relics-and-nāga story best preserved, perhaps, in the Pali Chronicle of the Tooth (*Dāṭhāvaṃsa*). According to this text, the Buddha's tooth relic, which was destined for enshrinement in Sri Lanka, was, for a time, kept in Kalinga in the city of Dantapurā ("Toothville"). When that city was in danger of being attacked, the king entrusted the tooth to his daughter Hemmamālā and his son-in-law Dantakumāra ("Tooth Prince") and told them to flee with it to Sri Lanka. On their way south, the couple crossed a river and temporarily hid the relic in the sand of the riverbank. The rays emanating from it attracted a Buddhist arhat who happened to be flying by, and he alighted there to worship it. The rays, however, also attracted a nāga king who lived in the river, and he, wishing to possess the relic, swallowed it, casket and all, and made off with it to his kingdom. The young couple, very distressed, turned to the arhat for help. He promptly transformed himself into a great garuḍa and belabored the nāga king until he gave up the tooth relic. Hemmamālā and Dantakumāra were then able to resume their journey to Sri Lanka, where the tooth remains enshrined to this day.[68]

The parallels with our *Lokapaññatti* story need hardly be pointed out. In both instances, an enlightened Buddhist elder takes on the form of a garuḍa to defeat a nāga king. But here the purpose of the battle in these particular forms is more fully spelled out: the elder stops the nāga from stealing the relics of the Buddha and preventing their enshrinement. Moreover, the tooth relic's burial in the sand of the riverbank recalls the Buddha's footprint left in the bed of the Nammadā. We may thus find expressed once more in this story the tension between the desire for the presence of the Buddha in his relics and the fear of his complete absence should the relics be stolen.

This interpretation is reinforced in the very next episode—that in which Māra takes on the form of a great club-wielding yakṣa, only to be countered by Upagupta as an even greater yakṣa wielding two clubs. Ananda Coomaraswamy and others have studied the importance of yakṣas in the early development of Buddhist legend, cult, and iconography,[69] but here again we must interpret this episode in terms of its own specific context.

In the context of the establishment of the stūpas by Aśoka, the scenario of one yakṣa being defeated by another, bigger yakṣa recalls the tale of the yakṣa Daṃṣṭrānivāsin ("he who dwells by the tooth relic"), who put an end to the persecution of Buddhism by one of Aśoka's descendants, King Puṣyamitra. Specifically, Daṃṣṭrānivāsin took action against a yakṣa bodyguard who always stood right behind Puṣyamitra.[70] This story is relevant here because Puṣyamitra's persecution had as its immediate aim the destruction of Aśoka's eighty-four thousand stūpas and more specifically of the Aśokārāma at Pāṭaliputra—the very same Great Stūpa which Aśoka, in the *Lokapaññatti* legend, is trying to dedicate.

The story of this attempted destruction was well known in Buddhist circles[71] and must have been highly relevant to someone who, like the author of the *Lokapaññatti*, was trying to write the tale of how the worship of the stūpas came to be established in the first place. For the threat to the stūpas by Puṣyamitra and his yakṣas is not so different from that posed by Māra, and its countering by Daṃṣṭrānivāsin and other yakṣas is not unlike the action taken by Upagupta.[72]

Epilogue

With the conclusion of the story of the two yakṣas, the *Lokapaññatti* tale of the transformations of Upagupta and Māra comes to an end, and we return to more familiar episodes: Upagupta, victorious, fastens around Māra's neck the carcass of a dog. Māra is unable to remove it; he goes to all of the gods, seeking their help, but they only tell him they are powerless in this matter. Māra therefore returns to Upagupta to plead for mercy. Upagupta removes the carcass of the dead dog, but, still suspicious, he ties Māra to the mountaintop with his monastic belt and leaves him there for the duration of Aśoka's festival (seven years, seven months, and seven days). At the end of this time, Upagupta returns and overhears a now-subdued Māra reflecting on the qualities of the Buddha and making a vow to attain Buddhahood himself in a future lifetime. At this, Upagupta releases Māra and asks him, as a favor, to display the physical body of the Blessed One, which he has never seen. Māra does this and is venerated by Upagupta, who then justifies his action by referring to the practice of image worship. These events are all part of the Mathuran legendary cycle and need not be reexamined here.

It is important to remember, however, that all of this is presented in the *Lokapaññatti* as occurring in the context of King Aśoka's stūpa dedication, a ceremony that, in many ways, became paradigmatic for Buddhist festivals in general in Southeast Asia. In the *Lokapaññatti*, Upagupta, by warding off Māra, makes possible not just the dedication of the stūpas, but also the dedication or rededication of the king himself to Buddhism. For the climax of Aśoka's festival of lights comes at the very end of the story: Just after Upagupta takes his final leave, Aśoka sets himself on fire in front of the stūpa and burns as a human lamp for seven days and seven nights. Strictly speaking, in the *Lokapaññatti*, this does not form part of the Upagupta legend per se, since the elder is not present on this occasion. Kingkeo Attagara, however, cites an oral version of the story in which it is Upagupta (and not Aśoka) who wraps his body in oil-saturated cloth and burns as a lamp offering at the festival.[73] In any case, the episode merits citing here:

> Then, King Aśoka, wishing to pay [even] great[er] pūjā to the Mahāstūpa, had his own body wrapped in cotton up to his neck and his limbs up to his wrists, and he had himself soaked with five hundred pots of scented oil. Then, standing facing the Great Stūpa, with folded hands, his head anointed with oil, and mindful of the Buddha, he had his body set on fire; and the flames rose up in the air to a height of seven persons.
>
> The king kept repeating a stanza in praise of the Buddha: "Hail to the Blessed One, the arhat, he who is altogether enlightened [namo Bhagavato arahato samasambuddhassa]. . . . For the benefit of many he taught the Dharma. . . . His is the community of disciples which conducts itself uprightly, properly, and correctly."
>
> In this way, he recollected the Triple Gem, and, while he was so meditating, the flames did not burn his body in the slightest, and he remained as cool as though he had been smeared with sandalwood paste. And so it was on the second, third, and up to the seventh day; the king paid pūjā to the Great Stūpa with his entire body ablaze. Then he bathed, and, adorned with all his ornaments and surrounded by his ministers, he worshipped the stūpa, circumambulating it three times. Then he listened to

the preaching of the Dharma for seven days and nights, offered food to the community of monks, worshipped it, and went off together with his entourage.[74]

It is not possible to examine here the various parallels in other texts to which this tale may be related.[75] Suffice it to say that, though the application of this story to Aśoka appears to be an original feature of the *Lokapaññatti*, its thrust is akin to that of similar tales in highlighting the ultimate significance of the festival of lights in honor of the stūpas: the lamps lit there are not simply votive offerings or marks of respect paid to the Buddha. They lead to and finally signify the highest form of devotion: the giving up of the self through offering and the simultaneous realization, through bhakti, of some of the fundamental truths of Buddhism.

CHAPTER TEN

Mythic Elaborations and Ritual Developments

THE *Lokapaññatti* represents a significant transition point in the evolution of the Upagupta legend in Southeast Asia, but the legend's transformation did not stop there. As cultic patterns developed, certain legendary traditions were elaborated, so that a number of stories told about Upagupta today in Burma, Thailand, and Laos go far beyond what is hinted at in Saddhammaghosa's text.

In this chapter and the next, we shall consider two of these legendary elaborations: first, that which stems from the *Lokapaññatti*'s assertion that Upagupta resides in a magically created pavilion in the midst of the ocean; and second, that which rests on the assumption that Upagupta, as an arhat, did not die but chose to extend his life span and remain in this world for the benefit of the Dharma.

In the *Lokapaññatti*, Upagupta's pavilion (which in later tradition is usually said to be brazen or made of copper) is described as "a palace [pāsāda] made of gems," maintained by magical powers in "the midst of the waters of the ocean."[1] It is not altogether clear whether this residence is to be thought of as underwater, at the bottom of the sea, or as simply floating somewhere in the middle of it. Iconographically, both depictions are found. Thus, it is common in Burma to see Upagupta statues set in pavilions on small floats that freely drift about in tanks of water; at one shrine especially dedicated to Upagupta in Rangoon (the Shin Upago Mahāthera Festival Pavilion), his image sits on a "raft" which a hidden mechanism moves back and forth across an artificial papier-mâché ocean (see fig. 5). Elsewhere, popular illustrations may portray the saint as living in an underwater palace in the depths of a pond, river, or ocean.

Legendary accounts likewise vacillate on this point. For instance, the floating-pavilion view may be found in an oft-quoted newspaper account of the mid-1860s which claims that two "celebrated English scientists" once decided to sail south from India to see what they could find. After going further than anyone had ever gone before, they were amazed to see a rocky outcrop, floating in the midst of the ocean, on which they could discern a brazen pavilion. Despite their attempts to reach it, they could never get closer than a gunshot away.[2] The other view is reflected in the following Burmese story:

> In grandfather's village, there were three men who could dive and remain underwater from three to six hours without a mishap. One day, the three held a competition

Fig. 5. Shin Upago Mahāthera Shrine, Rangoon

> to see who could remain under the longest, and several of the villagers gathered at the riverbank to watch. The contest began at 7:00 in the morning, and at 10:00 A.M. one of the three came to the surface. The second man appeared at about noon, but the third stayed under longer. At sunset, he had not yet come up. The ensuing night and day passed with no sign of him either, and it was decided he had met with an unfortunate accident. Accordingly, his relatives prepared for his funeral despite the absence of his body. But on the seventh day, just as the funeral was coming to a close, the mysterious diver appeared in midstream, to the amazement and joy of everyone. When people asked him what had happened to him, this was the tale he told: "When I dived, winning the contest was not my sole aim. I also wanted to find out how deep the river was and what things there were on the bottom. I went down and down for a long time until I stepped on something hard, and I found that it was the roof of a building. I slid down its slope and looked in under the eaves. The interior was well lit, and there inside was an elderly person clad in white saying his prayers before a Buddha image, and next to it an image of Shin Upago that was captivating to behold."[3]

This account goes on to relate how the diver was so awestruck by the image and by his surroundings that he ended up spending a week in trancelike veneration, forgetting all about the contest, his village, and his family. But the main point here is that this is clearly an underwater pavilion, and Upagupta in this context is a saint of the depths. Much the same assertion is found in Thai and Laotian tradition, where Upagupta is not represented anthropomorphically, but is thought to be embodied in a stone taken ritually from the bottom of a river or of a swamp.

The question may be asked, How is it that in Southeast Asia Upagupta came to be thought of as residing on or in water? Groping for an answer to this long ago, L. A. Waddell suggested that his "residence in the sea . . . could be explained by his reputation for supernatural power and his special association with Sindh or 'sea-salt,' his coming to Aśoka by boat, and the connexion of his name with the conquest of nāga-kings."[4] Shway Yoe (James George Scott) and R. Grant Brown, more in touch than Waddell with Burmese traditions on this matter, both report that Upagupta's dwelling in the water was a karmic *punishment* for his having, in a past life, run off with the clothes of another bather; just as his friend, being modest, was forced to remain in the water to hide his nudity, so in this life he, Upagupta, is obliged to stay in the water until the coming of the future Buddha Maitreya.[5] I myself have never heard mention of this story, and Brown suspects it may be very "modern";[6] but what is interesting about these explanations is not so much the theories that they set forth as the point that they fail to make: not a single one of these authors suggests that Upagupta resides in the waters because he is a nāga. He may, it is true, sometimes be called a nāga (although, as we have seen, that is an appellation with many connotations); he may sometimes be thought to dwell amongst the nāgas and even to have the powers of a nāga; but to suggest his residence is in the sea because he is a nāga is to reason in a backwards manner. Rather, he is sometimes thought to be a nāga because of where he resides.

Legendary Traditions

The tradition of Upagupta's dwelling in the midst of the ocean is connected to an important new Southeast Asian development in his legend: the story of his birth from the union of a mother who, by virtue of being the offspring of a fish, is associated with the sea, and of an ascetically inclined father who is portrayed as a hermit, an ṛṣi, or even as the Buddha himself.

In what follows, I shall present and comment on three different versions of this legend. The first is found in a number of contemporary Burmese books on Shin Upago.[7] The second, with a somewhat different emphasis, comes from a pre–World War II Burmese film about the saint. The third represents the legend as it has taken shape in parts of Thailand and Laos. It is much less elaborate than the Burmese stories but is nonetheless worth examining, since it makes the rather striking claim that the Buddha himself was responsible for engendering Upagupta.

Version 1: Macchadevī and Upa

This story begins two hundred years after the death of the Buddha, not far from the city of Rājagṛha, in a village of fishermen. One day, some of the men of the village happen to catch a large golden fish. Once it is dead, they are surprised to see something still moving inside of it. An old man suggests that the fish must have swallowed something still living; so they carefully slit open its stomach and find in it a charming baby—a little girl of golden complexion, alive and well. Everyone thinks it a wonderful find, a miracle. They take the child and show it to the king of Rājagṛha, who is much pleased and moved with affection at the sight of the infant. As he is without children, he decides to adopt her as his own, and he names her Macchadevī (Fish Princess).[8] Well looked after by her nurses, the little girl soon grows up to be a beautiful young woman, wondrous to behold. But despite her peerless beauty, she continually exudes a foul odor, as though she has just bathed in rotten-fish water. The ladies of the court do everything they can to rid her of this smell, but to no avail. The more beautiful she becomes with age, the stronger her stench. This misfortune is due not only to the circumstances of her birth, but also to the fact that, in a previous lifetime, she once, in anger, threw foul water on someone who offended her.

In time, the king, despite his deep paternal affection for her, decides she can no longer remain in the royal palace, and he resolves to have her sent away. She is placed on a raft and set adrift on the river,[9] alone and unattended. The raft touches at several places; at each one, a ruling monarch, captivated by her charm, thinks of making her his queen. But all find her smell unbearable, and on each occasion she is sent on her journey, never being permitted to stay.

Eventually the raft lands at a rocky outcrop where a hermit named Upa leads an ascetic life. Upa sees Macchadevī from the shore, takes her to his hermitage, and looks after her as his own daughter. Surprisingly, as soon as she meets him, her foul smell disappears. She lives with Upa, regarding him as her father. Nevertheless, alone with him in a solitary wood, she sometimes loses control over her untrained mind and harbors amorous longings for him. These thoughts, occasional but recurring, lead to a child being conceived in her womb, though at no time is there any physical contact between them.[10]

When Macchadevī becomes aware of her pregnancy, she tells Upa about it. He assures her that she has no cause to worry and that he will do all that he can to take care of both her and the child. Every day he goes out searching for extra fruit and vegetables, and in due time Macchadevī gives birth to a son, who, because he is "protected" (gutta) by the hermit Upa, is given the name Upagutta.

The boy, however, is of uncouth appearance and has a dark complexion.

He is a savage with rude manners, intractable and always dissatisfied. He likes to go into the jungle and delights in the roars and screechings of the wild animals and birds around him. His frame of mind resembles that of a beast of prey, always cruel and angry; and his features are grim and hostile. He keeps aloof and is sullen and uncommunicative.[11]

The sage Upa, able to divine the future, knows that Macchadevī and her son will have much better fortune if they return to Rājagṛha. Thus, in compliance with his wishes, she makes her way back upstream along the river, taking the boy Upagutta with her. Soon they come to the royal city. When the king hears that his daughter has come back and that she no longer smells bad, he is delighted. But he is even more pleased when he learns that she has a son with her, since he is now getting old and, still with no issue of his own, he does not know how to arrange the matter of his succession.

He consequently welcomes Macchadevī, reinstates her as princess, and makes preparations to place his grandson, Upagutta, on the throne. But Macchadevī knows from Upa the hermit that her son is destined to be an arhat, and so she opposes her father's plan. In her eyes, an arhat is a far greater personage than a king, however powerful he may be. She and her father, therefore, have a heated argument about what Upagutta's future should be—a dispute she stands little chance of winning, except that in the midst of it, something totally unexpected happens.

A deva decides to exercise his celestial powers and hasten Upagutta's becoming what he is in any case destined to be. He comes down from his heaven and flies off with the child up into the sky. Upagutta knows that he is being carried aloft by a deity, but he is not yet sure whether his captor's intentions are good or bad. Fearing the deva might be planning to drop him, he decides, just in case, to prepare himself to die, and he begins to meditate on the impermanence of all phenomena: "Sabbe saṃkhārā aniccā. . . ." (All compounded things are impermanent . . . and are ultimately dissolved . . . and their dissolution is bliss.")[12] Thus he keeps meditating as he is carried higher and higher, and, all of a sudden, this results in his arhatship. Right there in midair he achieves the highest goal, exhausting all of the defilements that until this moment have kept him whirling in saṃsāra. The deva, realizing that Upagutta has attained enlightenment, releases his hold on him. Thanks to the magical powers that come with his arhatship, Upagutta simply stays aloft, to everyone's astonishment.[13]

Some time later, Upagutta decides to come out of his meditative trance; he looks down to find that below him now there is only the broad, watery expanse of the ocean. As he gazes down, however, due to the good deeds he performed in previous lives, a brazen pavilion appears in the midst of the waters. "This brazen pavilion in midocean," he reflects, "has arisen as a result of my past karma. I will spend the rest of my life inside it and, removed from the rest of humanity, dwell there constantly in meditation."[14]

Version 2: The Film Story

A number of themes in this legend need to be investigated, but, before we do so, it may be best to present the significant variants found in the film version of the tale. The film *Shin Upago* was a 1930s production of the Maung Maung Soe Film Company in Rangoon. It is important because, as a popular movie, it has—perhaps more than anything else—informed some of the things that contemporary Burmese know and repeat about the saint's life.

The film contains a more elaborate version of the tale just recounted, developing in particular the relationship between Macchadevī and Upagupta's father, who here is presented not as the hermit Upa, but as a handsome young layman studying in a Buddhist monastery. The love story between these two is, in fact, the main focus of the film, although, at its very close, it does turn to the *Lokapaññatti* tale of Upagupta's struggle with Māra and of his protection of Aśoka's relics festival. This tale is given more or less as an epilogue, however; by far the bulk of the narrative is devoted to the adventures of the saint's mother and father.[15]

The movie starts out in much the same way as the books. A number of fishermen catch an unusually large fish and take it to the king, where Macchadevī is discovered inside it. She grows up to become a beautiful and foul-smelling princess. The king does not set her adrift on the river, however; rather, he is told that he can cure her of her repulsive fish smell by sending presents to the gods of the sea and invoking their aid. This he does by constructing a large raft, loading it with votive offerings placed in a brazen pavilion, and setting it to float downstream so that it will make its way to the abode of the sea gods. The propitiation works; after an interval of several days, during which it is estimated the raft has probably reached its goal, the princess is suddenly and miraculously cured of her problem. The king and the court decide that this is an occasion worth celebrating; and they arrange for a nationwide festival, in which the entire population is to participate and the princess herself is to distribute alms to members of the Sangha.

The scene then shifts to a pagoda outside the city, where a bright young lad—still a layman—is studying at the monastery's school. Hearing of the exceptional charm and beauty of the princess, he resolves to try to see her. Knowing that she will be distributing alms to monks, he dresses up as a bhikkhu, hiding his hair with a corner of his robe. Bowl in hand, he then joins the line of monks, hoping in this way to get a closeup view of the woman of his dreams.

In this (and in more) he succeeds; the princess, about to put alms into his bowl, catches sight of his ill-concealed hair and realizes he must be a layman in disguise. Scrutinizing him more carefully, she looks into his eyes and instantly falls in love with him. Throwing all caution to the wind, she catches hold of his hands and holds them tightly. Our hero, fearful of his ruse being discovered and of the dire consequences that would ensue, breaks free from her grasp with some effort, knocking her over in the process and causing a major melee. He manages to escape from the crowd, but, unbeknownst to him, he is followed back to his monastery by two secret agents of the king.

His brief encounter with the princess, however, is destined to have lasting consequences, for it is soon discovered that she is pregnant, despite the fact that no other physical contact occurred between them. When the king learns of this, he demands that his daughter divulge the name of her lover; but, being innocent of any wrongdoing, she is unable herself to offer any reasonable explanation for her condition. It is not long before suspicion falls on the young man dressed as a monk who had caused so much commotion and whom she had caught hold of with such impetuosity. And a party of soldiers is promptly sent to the monastery to arrest him.

In the course of the ensuing trial, with the king himself acting as judge, both the princess and the young student stoutly maintain their innocence. The king refuses to believe them and declares them guilty of shameless immorality. He condemns the young man to an ignominious death and his daughter to banishment from the kingdom. She is promptly sent off to an uninhabited wilderness, where, all alone, amid the wild beasts, she bemoans her fate. The young man is carted off to the city's dungeon while preparations for his public execution are made.

However, when everything is ready and he is about to be put to death, a friend of his—a monastic schoolmate—daringly runs up and tries to rescue him. But alas, without success; his friend is caught and killed on the spot, and the process of execution resumes. Still, all is not lost; due to this good deed of self-sacrifice in trying to save someone from a cruel and unjust death, his friend is immediately reborn as a deva in one of the heavens. There, he realizes that there is still time for him to intervene and that, as a god, he now has the power to do so! He swoops down from the heavens and, at the last moment, wrests the student from the very hands of the executioners. He carries him off and takes him—where else?—to the forest wilderness where his beloved princess is languishing.

At this point, the film more or less picks up on the book version given above: The student and the princess live happily together in their forest "hermitage," and in due time she gives birth to her son—Upagutta. In the film, however, Upagutta is portrayed as being born from his mother's ear—an unusual event, the veracity of which is today stoutly maintained by some and hotly disputed by others. This curious assertion may be intended to emphasize further Upagupta's purity, already stressed in the tradition of his virgin birth. In the greater South Asian context, passing through the birth canal was deemed especially sullying and was, in fact, something that a number of great saints avoided—such as the Buddha himself, who, it will be recalled, emerged from his mother's side.[16] It may be, however, that we are dealing here simply with a Burmese dramatic convention for representing births on stage.[17]

Be this as it may, in the film, the news of Upagutta's extraordinary birth is soon communicated to the capital, and the king now realizes that he had perhaps been mistaken in his hasty condemnation of his daughter and son-in-law. Resolving to make amends and wishing to see his grandchild, he sets out for the forest to visit them. On his way, he meets the student's former teacher, the monk who was head priest of the monastic school. This monk had always believed in his pupil's innocence, and he is also journeying to the forest to see the happy couple and their wonder child.

Upon reaching the forest, however, the king and the monk start quarrelling; at the sight of the newborn baby in the arms of the princess, each of them claims the child as his own legitimate possession. A vehement argument ensues, the monk saying that the child's father is his pupil, the king declaring that its mother is his daughter; the monk claiming the king forfeited his right to the child by passing harsh and unfair judgment against its parents, the king arguing that he wishes to make amends for his mistake and that, in any case, looking after a child is not the right choice for a monk.

It is clear here that we are dealing with the same dispute which, in version 1 of the story, set the king against the fish princess: is Upagutta to become a monk—an arhat—or is he to inherit the throne and become a great ruler? In version 1, this dilemma was resolved by the intervention of a deus ex machina. The same solution is found in the film story, except it takes a slightly different form. The couple's "guardian angel" (the deva friend who had saved the student from the executioners) shows himself and suggests a way of resolving the dispute. "Nearby in this forest," he declares, "there is a celestial pond. By the power of the gods, any child bathed in it immediately becomes fully grown. We will see what decision the gods have in store for this child. If, after his bath, he grows to be a monk, then we must understand that the priest is his legitimate guardian. If he grows to be a layman, we are to understand that the gods decide in favor of the king."

To this everyone agrees, and they dunk the infant Upagutta into the pond. To their amazement, the baby is immediately transformed into a full-grown monk clad in a shining robe and equipped with all the paraphernalia of his status. Emerging from the water, he rises up into the air, where he remains suspended. In one stroke, then, everything has been resolved: the priest has won, but it is no longer necessary for him to look after the child, since, in an instant, Upagutta has already passed beyond his childhood, his novitiate, and his ordination, and into his arhatship.

One question still remains to be resolved: where is Upagutta to stay now that he has attained enlightenment? The film's solution is, again, very similar to that in version 1: Bidding farewell to his parents, to the king, and to the head priest, Upagutta flies off through the skies across the ocean until he comes to the raft whose launching had rid his mother, long ago, of her foul odor. The raft, floating about on the high seas, is still intact, as is its brazen pavilion. There Upagutta takes up residence, and there he still dwells today.

The film does not stop here, and we shall consider its dénouement later; but, at this point, we need to interrupt the narrative in order to comment on a theme that emerges from the two versions of the story looked at so far. This is the theme of the classic Buddhist dilemma faced by the young Buddha and by all great beings: the twin careers of kingship and Buddhahood, palace and hermitage, home and homelessness, family and forest, sexuality and renunciation. The Buddha resolved this dilemma by choosing the second path in each of these oppositions, but he did so in such a way as to suggest, at the same time, a mediation in the fundamental polarity involved. Thus, for example, he rejected extreme asceticism while renouncing hedonism; he abandoned the householder's state without opting for a solitary existence, choosing instead life within a new family—the Buddhist community; and he established monasteries outside of cities, yet not far off in the forest. There are many expressions of the Middle Way.

In the stories of Upagupta's origin, many of these same polarities are played out, with all of the resulting paradoxes: Upagutta is the sexual product of an asexual union, the son of a virgin, born from his mother's ear; his mother is a princess but not of royal blood; she is human but born in a fish; his father is sexually active but an ascetic, or, alternatively, a layman but dressed as a monk.

Binary oppositions, however, are not the only defining structures here. More broadly, one needs to speak of a whole classificatory system of persons and beings, in which various types of individuals can be distinguished and arranged more or less hierarchically with reference to their proximity to the Buddha. One such system for Burmese Buddhism has been described by Alton Becker, who bases it not only on his knowledge of Burmese culture, but on a linguistic analysis of the Burmese use of classifiers in designating certain types of animate beings. According to this system, all beings may be arranged into four distinct "orbits" centered around the Buddha and around various things associated with the Buddha such as his relics, images of him, and the Dharma. In the first orbit around this center, are beings such as deities, monks, and kings. In the second orbit are persons of status, teachers, and scholars. In the third orbit, are ordinary beings; and in the fourth, outermost orbit are animals, ghosts, dead bodies, and children.[18]

In Burmese, a different numerative classifier is used when referring to beings in each of these different orbits,[19] but obviously such a classification system is interesting for more than strictly linguistic reasons. For instance, as Becker points out, spiritual progress may be viewed as movement from the outer orbit to the center, "from animality to Buddhahood."[20]

Since Upagupta, in India at least, was a monkey in his past life and a Buddha (without the marks) in this one, and since, in Southeast Asia, his parentage includes an aquatic animal, it may be useful to read the stories of his origin in terms of his own progression through this scheme. Clearly, early on, he moves out of the fourth orbit of wild animals, ghosts, etc. This is the realm which his mother leaves behind when she conceives him and loses her fish smell. This is also the realm of the forest, which he himself departs, although not quite so quickly.

The realm of the forest, and indeed the whole of nature, were often seen in South and Southeast Asia as wild, chaotic, threatening places, the very antithesis of civilized order. Michael Rhum, for example, has proposed that "one of the central problematics of classical Pali literature [and Northern Thai] ritual" revolves around the question of the relationship of the untamed forest to civilized settlements, embodied most clearly in the capital city and other towns (muang).[21] Richard Davis has expressed much the same view:

> The word "forest" has negative and often pejorative overtones. Contraband articles like bootleg liquor and unregistered firearms are literally "things of the forest wilderness." Undisciplined or immoral people are designated in the same fashion. To "go to the forest" means, in addition to its literal sense, to defecate or to enter a cemetery. The forest is the domain of wild animals, spirits and uncivilized aboriginal hill peoples. There is no "natural" beauty. All beauty lies in human settlements, and the degree of a settlement's beauty corresponds to its level in the muang hierarchy.[22]

Thus, traditionally at least, a forest-dwelling monk was not primarily someone who was seeking a retreat from the world or peace and quiet in the woods; on the contrary, it was someone who was looking to face and hopefully overcome the full chaos and threat of saṃsāra. There is, in fact, a real ambivalence in Buddhist tradition about the dwelling places of forest monks. Their hermitages may be seen on the one hand as heavenly palaces, the epitome of civilization; but on the other as just the opposite—wild and threatening places. Thus, part of the greatness of the Buddhist Sangha (with its dual tradition of town-dwelling and forest-dwelling monks) is that it has the ability to overcome the plaguing polarity of forest vs. settlement, jungle vs. civilization, nature vs. culture. It does this not only by taming the chaos of the forests in its hermitages, but also by structuring the cosmos of the town in its city monasteries.

In the two stories we are looking at here, Upagupta's relation to the forest would appear to be similarly complex. He himself is a product of the jungle, born and brought up in it. As a boy in his father's hermitage, he is animal-like, wary, wild. In one version of the tale, he is even said to climb trees, a distant echo perhaps of his previous life as a monkey. In one sense, then, he is unaffected by the threat of chaos in the forest. Not knowing civilization, he has no fear of the jungle; he delights in the cries of the wild animals. In another sense, however, as his father Upa correctly discerns, he is falling prey to the forest; he is becoming part of it and needs to leave it in order to overcome it.

Having overcome the forest, Upagupta clearly does not settle for the orbit of ordinary human being—for the life of a householder. And, just as clearly, he does not opt entirely for the next orbit, that of teacher or scholar, which one is tempted here to associate with the career of the head of his father's monastic school, the town-dwelling monk who, in the film story, tries (and fails) to get Upagupta to return with him to the capital.

The focus then falls on the first orbit—that of deities, monks, and royalty—and here again we come face to face with the full ambiguity of Upagupta's status. On the one hand, he may be said to embody aspects of all of these careers. On the other, he rejects them all and goes beyond them. Thus, though he does not become a deity, his interventions in the world, as we shall see, often emphasize his supernatural powers. And though he does not opt for kingship, there are nonetheless elements of royalty within him. His mother is a princess; the legend of his birth significantly resembles Southeast Asian stories that tell of the establishment of kingship as the result of the union of a civilizing hero and a nāga princess;[23] and his residence in the midst of the ocean is a brazen *palace* (pāsāda), a splendidly ornate building made of all kinds of gems, in which he sits enthroned on a "divan adorned with jewels, wafted by fragrant perfumes, bedecked with myriads of flowers."[24] Finally, though he *does* become a monk, he does not do so in regular ways. Questions are raised about his ordination; he emerges fully grown as a bhikkhu without ever having undergone monastic training. Moreover, he does not live as part of a regular monastic community, but alone, spending his time in meditation. He might therefore be thought of as a forest-dwelling monk, an āraṇyaka such as he was in Mathurā, except that he has left the forest—his father's hermitage-home—to reside in the depths of the sea, his mother's original abode.

All of this ambiguity merely serves to bring Upagupta closer to the Buddha at the center of this scheme. For the Buddha, too, has intimate links that connect him in a variety of ways to kingship, to divinity, and to monkhood, but that point at the same time to his transcendence of all of these categories.

Version 3: The Buddha and the Fish Queen

Upagupta's connection to the Buddha becomes even more intimate in the third version of the legend we are considering, a version which is virtually unknown in Burma but is popularly told in Laos and parts of Thailand. It differs from versions 1 and 2 in at least two significant ways. First, it features a fusion of generations so that the piscine or otherwise aquatic being is not here said to give birth to Upagupta's mother, but to give birth to Upagupta himself. Second, and most importantly, Upagupta's father is presented not as a more or less unknown ascetic ṛṣi, but as the Buddha Gautama, who impregnates (indirectly) that aquatic being.

A number of variants on this story have been recorded. Stanley Tambiah, working in Northeastern Thailand, recounts what was told him by "two elderly informants, one of them very learned in ritual matters": "Phra Uppakrut was the son of Buddha and his mother was a mermaid. It is said that once the Buddha forced his semen into the water and a mermaid swallowed it, became pregnant and gave birth to Uppakrut. He was subsequently ordained as a novice (or monk) and lives in the water, for he is a mermaid's son."[25] A similar story was told to Michael Rhum by an aged monk in a village in Northern Thailand: "The Buddha once ejaculated into the Ganges to show a disciple how one must eject all impurities from the body (semen = *nam asuci*, "*impure fluid*"). A *female naga* . . . was impregnated by this semen and later gave birth to Upagutta who was ordained as a novice in his father's religion when he reached the proper age."[26] But the most developed version of this myth remains that recorded by Charles Archaimbault in Southern Laos, which presents Upagupta as the son of the Buddha and of the goddess of fishes, Nang Matsa:

> Once, when the Buddha was preaching the Dharma in Laos,[27] one of his disciples, who was evil-minded, tried to undermine his prestige. "Our teacher's ascetic restraint," he declared to his fellow monks, "does it not seem to you to be unnatural? Perhaps his virtuous conduct is really a cover for some imperfection, some actual impotency. . . ." In this way, the faith of the disciples was shaken. The Buddha, divining their doubts, asked, "Do you really question my virility? Do you actually think my virtues are a reflection of impotence?" And going off a ways, he came back with his hands full of semen. "Here is the proof of my manhood," he declared, and, walking to the nearby bank of the Mekong, he threw his sperm into the water. Now it happened that just then Nang Matsa, the fish goddess, was swimming by. She gulped down the Buddha's sperm and, a few months later, gave birth to Upagutta, who still resides in the depths of the waters, in a rock crystal palace.[28]

Such a story could hardly be welcomed by the orthodox-minded, the deliberate emission of semen being a violation of the Vinaya code.[29] Eugène Denis has suggested that we should look for Śaivite influence here, and he concludes that this story may be seen as a Buddhist reworking of the myth of Śiva and Skanda.[30] A more intriguing parallel may be found, perhaps, in the first part of the Hindu tale of Vyāsa, the legendary author of the Vedas and recounter of the *Mahābhārata*.[31] But whatever the Nang Matsa story's roots and connections,[32] it is important not to overlook something that, from a Buddhist perspective, could only be a major thrust of this version—namely, that Upagupta's father was not some king or nameless ṛṣi, but the Buddha himself.

Tambiah has suggested that this tale be interpreted as the Buddha's taming of the spirit of nature (the nāgī/fish) and its conversion into a Buddhist agent.[33] Structurally, then, the story would not be fundamentally different from the many accounts of the Buddha's conquest of nāgas, yakṣas, and other autochthonous forces. But this view ignores some of the richness that is found in Archaimbault's more-detailed version of the tale. There, the fish is less central: what is being demonstrated first and foremost is the Buddha's masculinity, his humanity, his sexuality. The thrust of the story is to show not the Buddha's overcoming of nature, but his participation in it.

In the Sanskrit tradition, this is, in fact, not the only time that the Buddha decides to prove his manhood. In the *Mūlasarvāstivāda Vinaya*, for example, it is precisely to allay such doubts that he engenders his son Rāhula. He declares, on the night of his Great Departure, that he will now enter his harem "lest others say that the prince Śākyamuni was not a man [apumān, a eunuch] and that he wandered forth without paying any attention to his sixty thousand wives." He then makes love to Yaśodharā, who thereby becomes pregnant.[34]

This is an important tale, for it sets up a whole series of stories about the Buddha and his son Rāhula which intriguingly overlap at a number of points with stories about the Buddha and his other "son" Upagupta. Most of these tales—some of which are jātakas—concern the Buddha's virility, his son's legitimacy, or his wife's faithfulness; but all of them touch on the degree of his involvement in the world, and all of them illuminate points found in the Southeast Asian Upagupta tradition.

The Buddha, Yaśodharā, and Rāhula

In the *Mūlasarvāstivāda Vinaya*, Rāhula is not born but only conceived prior to the Buddha's Great Departure. His birth occurs much later, on the day of his father's enlightenment at Bodhgaya—for, mysteriously and miraculously, his mother Yaśodharā carries him in her womb for six years. Thus, when he is finally born, questions are raised both about the identity of his father and about Yaśodharā's purity and faithfulness to her husband.

In order to prove her own innocence as well as her son's legitimacy, Yaśodharā undertakes several actions. First, she takes the boy and sits him on the bodhisattva's old exercise stone, which she then has thrown into a lotus pond with her son still on it. The rest of the story is as follows:

> Undertaking an act of truth, Yaśodharā then solemnly declared, "If this be the son of the bodhisattva, may he float." Immediately, he floated [on the stone, which also did not sink]. Then she said, "Let him go from this shore to the other shore and back again." He did, and everyone was amazed. Yaśodharā then said, "Sirs, I have demonstrated to you that this is the child of the bodhisattva; I have not gone astray!"[35]

There is nothing particularly extraordinary about this miracle—Buddhist saints can walk on water as a matter of course—but, in the context of the tale of Upagupta and of his association with water, rafts, and stones, it is noteworthy that the sign of being the Buddha's son is here portrayed as the ability to float back and forth on a raftlike rock.

This is not the only way, however, in which the Buddha's paternity to Rāhula is demonstrated. In an immediate sequel to this story, the *Mūla-sarvāstivāda Vinaya* recounts the tale of Rāhula's recognition of the Buddha upon the latter's return to Kapilavastu six years after his enlightenment. The anecdote is complicated by the attempt of Yaśodharā on the same occasion to win back her husband; hoping to bewitch him, she gives Rāhula an aphrodisiac sweetmeat (vaśīkaraṇamodaka) and tells him to take it to the Buddha, knowing he will not refuse something offered to him by his own son. The Buddha knowing the calumnies that Yaśodharā has suffered, turns this into an occasion to clear her name and demonstrate her innocence. Using his magical powers, he creates there in the midst of the hall five hundred identical replicas of himself. A true son always knows his own father, and so young Rāhula, faced with the task of delivering the sweetmeat, is not confused; he quickly passes by the clones and gives the aphrodisiac to the real Buddha, thus proving his sonship. This aphrodisiac backfires, however; the Buddha returns it to Rāhula, who then consumes it himself. As a result, he becomes "enamored" of his father and promptly joins the Sangha as a novice.[36]

The Bodhisattva as Thief and Rapist

By itself, the story of Rāhula's recognition of his father would appear to have little relation to the legend of Upagupta, but it gives rise, in the text, to a jātaka that does. This is the story of the Buddha's past life as a masterful thief (mahācora) who repeatedly tricks a king and eludes the traps that are set for him. The last of these traps is the king's own daughter, who is set on a boat planted with all kinds of vegetation—a sort of floating raft-garden—in the middle of the Ganges. Her father tells her to cry out should anyone try to molest her, and he stations guards hidden on either bank to lie in wait. But once again the thief outwits him. Going upstream, he starts throwing empty pots into the river; the guards, suspicious at first, smash these to pieces when they approach the boat-island. Eventually, however, they tire of breaking these always-empty pots and start ignoring them. This, of course, is the moment the thief has been waiting for. Slipping a pot over his head, he floats downstream and climbs on board the boat, where, threatening to kill the princess if she cries out, he rapes her. By the time she sounds the alarm, he is long gone, and she has been impregnated. Nine months later, she gives birth to a baby boy. This, however, gives the king one last chance to catch the thief. He has an immense assembly hall built—it takes him six years—to which, on a given day, he convokes the entire population of his kingdom. He then gives a garland to his little grandson, telling him to offer it to his father. The boy, despite the fact that he has never seen him before, has no difficulty in picking out his father—the thief—in all the crowd. The latter is immediately arrested; but, instead of having him executed on the spot, the king decides to give him his daughter in marriage, having gradually, over the years, come to admire his cleverness and skill. Thus, they all live happily ever after after all.[37]

Rāhula and Upagupta

This jātaka of the thief purports to explain an occasion in the Buddha's previous life on which his son was able to recognize him. The *Mūlasarvāstivāda Vinaya* then goes on to recount a previous occasion on which Yaśodharā tried to win the Buddha's affection by means of an aphrodisiac cake. This is the well-known tale of the seduction of the bodhisattva as the unicorn hermit Ṛṣyaśṛnga.[38] It need not be recounted here, for we have seen enough to draw some initial conclusions about these stories as a whole.

The tales of the birth and career of the Buddha's son Rāhula, whether in this or in a past life, touch on a particularly sensitive and important aspect of Buddhism—namely, the relationship of a monk (the Buddha) to his family, left behind in lay life. But, in the Sanskrit tradition at least, they also appear to do more than this, for they are connected to a broader mythological scenario of what it means to be a son of the Buddha. When all of these Rāhula tales are considered together, the following points emerge: (1) The Buddha engenders his son in order to prove his manhood and, more generally, his humanity; (2) there is something strange about the birth of the Buddha's son: either he undergoes an extremely long gestation period, or he is portrayed as the accidentally engendered hybrid offspring of a human sage and an animal; (3) one proof of being the Buddha's son is the ability to float, specifically to ride a raft (rock) across a body of water and back again; (4) the mother of the Buddha's son is, at the time of her conceiving, floating alone on a boat in midstream; (5) the hybrid offspring of the sage and the animal has the power to control the weather—specifically, to stop the rain—a power which he loses if he engages in sexual relations;[39] (6) the Buddha's son has never seen his father, though he can recognize him when he does; and (7) the Buddha's proper relationship to his son is defined by the latter's taking on the role of a novice.

All of these points could equally well be made of Upagupta: (1) In version 3 of the story of his birth, he is conceived when the Buddha's manhood is challenged; (2) he is accidentally or virginally engendered and born in an unusual manner; (3) he floats about on a raft or dwells on a rocky island in the midst of the sea; (4) his mother is travelling on a boat in midstream when she encounters his father; (5) he has the power to control the weather and is specifically thought to prevent rain from falling when he is present; (6) he has never seen his father the Buddha, having been born too late for that; and (7) Upagupta, as we shall see, comes to be thought of as a novice in certain ritual contexts.

Przyluski's Parallels

Despite all of these similarities, it would be wrong to think of the Rāhula stories as forming the only backdrop for the Southeast Asian legends of Upagupta's upbringing. The mythological baggage that went along with the assertion of sonship to the Buddha was clearly only one of the factors affecting the elaboration of our story.

Jean Przyluski, in his study of this legend (as related by Maung Kin), was eager to link it to a vast number of other myths from India, Southeast Asia, and China featuring the sexual union of a civilizing hero with an autochthonous nāga princess.[40] Przyluski felt he could connect these myths to the Upagupta tale on the grounds that they all featured heroes whose greatness was due to the fact that their mothers were aquatic beings. This, he argued, showed that this tale type was in origin not Indian or Chinese, but a reflection of an ancient indigenous Austroasiatic maritime culture which associated fertility, abundance, power, and sovereignty with the waters.[41]

There are real problems with Przyluski's lumping together all of these stories. The hero-and-nāgī tales, for example, all emphasize the sexuality of the male founder and of his union with the female snake princess, a feature that makes sense for the story of a founder-ruler-king but that is in marked contrast to the tale of Upagupta's "virgin birth" from parents whose ultimate innocence and purity are much emphasized. Similarly, it may be argued that Upagupta, far from owing his superiority to his aquatic-animal roots, traces it to his overcoming of that origin.

White Water Snail

Be this as it may, it is still profitable to consider here one of the parallels mentioned but not fully explored by Przyluski, the Palaung myth of White Water Snail (Hō-i k'āū).[42] The story is too long to be cited here in its entirety, but the relevant portions of it may be summarized as follows:

> A king and a queen have no children, so they fast and pray. At the end of seven days, the queen has a dream in which the Buddha comes to her and gives her some long golden mangoes to eat. Ten months later, she gives birth to a kind of water snail. People begin to talk. "When you have a water snail for a child," they declare, "the father is a nāga." The royal parents are embarrassed by this. The mother loves and pities the child, but as the king points out, they do not know if it is a boy or a girl or what it does inside its shell. So eventually, they decide to get rid of it. They have a

raft built, place White Water Snail on it in a great golden pot, and let it float away down the river. In order to protect it, they place a letter on the raft declaring, "Wherever White Water Snail arrives, do not play with it, it is the child of a king."

The raft first comes to the land of the nāgas, where the nāga queen wishes to adopt White Water Snail. But her husband tells her that it comes from the world of men, and, if it should happen to smell their nāga breath, it would die. So, reluctantly, she sends it on its way, asking it (by letter) not to forget her when and if it becomes a Buddha.

The raft next arrives in the land of the yakṣas, and there White Water Snail is taken in by a demoness. Cared for in her house, he soon grows up and changes into a human being. He lives there happily for ten years, never knowing his mother's true identity. When he discovers the bones of various animals and humans in the storeroom, he figures out that she must be a demoness, and he flees. She catches up with him only after he has escaped from her territory, on the shore of the ocean; she pleads with him to come back, but he refuses. And sadly she lets him go, asking him not to forget her when and if he becomes a Buddha.

Wandering about the earth, he eventually comes to a country where the king is about to give away his beautiful daughter in marriage. He has placed her in a tower, from where she will toss down a long turban; and whoever it falls on will become her husband. All the young men, including White Water Snail, assemble at the foot of the tower. Because he is still wearing his mother's demoness coat, he smells bad, and everyone moves away in disgust—leaving him alone to catch the princess's turban.

The king is furious. The people are all laughing, saying how bad his son-in-law smells. He allows the marriage to take place but exiles the couple, forcing them to live by themselves in the forest. There they build a hut of leaves, where they live together but do not cohabit. After a while, their supplies run out. They have no food or money, but White Water Snail shows his wife a hidden valley filled with gems, and they soon build for themselves a magnificent dwelling in the forest. He loses his bad smell, they are reconciled with her father, and they live happily ever after in their palace in the woods.[43]

Despite considerable differences, a number of parallels between this story and our Upagupta legends can be drawn. First of all, it should be stated that this tale is particularly relevant, since, as we shall see in chapter 13, Upagupta is identified in parts of Thailand with just such a water snail. Small amuletlike images of him are made, showing a little human figure poking its head out of the inside of its shell.

Second, the story as a whole, somewhat like the Upagupta legends, can be read as an epic search for White Water Snail's true identity. At the beginning, there is the lack of clarity as to his parentage. In the queen's dream, he is shown to be the son of the Buddha; by virtue of his birth and of his mother's feelings for him, he is a human child; in the eyes of the people, he is the son of a nāga; in the message attached to the raft, he is affirmed to be the son of the king; but by virtue of his being adopted, he is also the son of a yakṣa. Clearly, then, we have here an extraordinary hybrid—a creature who is all of the above, and at the same time none of them. As the king puts it, one does not know what he/she/it is doing inside the shell.

As the story unfolds, however, these different possibilities are explored, and gradually White Water Snail's identity is revealed. He first sheds his animal and/or monster nature (something that would correspond to leaving the fourth orbit in the scheme we borrowed from Alton Becker). The raft stops in the land of the nāgas, and it is made clear that, despite the murmurings of the people and despite the claims of Przyluski—who quickly glosses over this episode—White Water Snail is *not* the son of a nāga; he would, in fact, die were he to stay with them. He then arrives among the yakṣas, where he soon sheds his snail-like animal nature and evolves into a human being. There, too, he eventually realizes that his mother must be a yakṣa, something that causes him to leave her behind. Wearing her coat (which endows him with the power of flight), however, he still smells like a yakṣa and so cannot fully enter the society of ordinary humans.[44]

Like Upagupta, he is left, finally, with the option of kingship—and here, once again, the real ambiguity begins. He seems to be destined for royalty: he marries the princess, who, Rapunzel-like, throws down not her hair but a turban to him from a high tower. But is he the handsome prince or the ogre(ss)? He is chased away from the palace to the hermitage in the forest because of his bad smell, and there he leads a celibate life, despite the presence of his wife. Finally, he sheds his foul odor and is reconciled with his father-in-law the king; but he does not appear to inherit the throne. And at the end of the story, ambiguity still remains. He is reigning like a king in a magnificent palace of his own, but not in the capital city.

Part of the uncertainty here lies in the fact that, throughout the story, it is strongly implied that he will go on to become a Buddha. At a number of points, he is actually called an embryo Buddha;[45] the same thing is hinted at by the nāga and yakṣa mothers, who, when he leaves them, ask him to remember them when he achieves Buddhahood; and, in a different, nursery-rhyme version of the legend, the whole tale is presented as a jātaka.[46] But his Buddhahood is still a thing of the future. For now, he will continue to dwell in his hermitage-palace-heaven-pavilion.

Ritual Traditions

We have thus far been considering the legendary traditions associated with Upagupta's origin and residence in the waters. There is, however, also a ritual side to this association, and to this we must now turn. We shall reserve for a later chapter the cultic tradition, most prevalent in Thailand and Laos, of inviting Upagupta to come back from his underwater domicile, and focus here instead on the Burmese custom of setting Upagupta rafts adrift on a river where they can float down to the ocean.

There are two closely related forms of this custom. The first consists of using small rafts to send offerings of food and other necessities to Upagupta, the monk in midocean. This practice is mentioned already by Maung Kin and H. Fielding Hall in the context of their discussions of the festival of lights, which we examined in chapter 9. They point out that sometimes, in the midst of the tiny floats bearing oil lamps or candles in Upagupta's honor, one comes across larger rafts sporting miniature pavilions or small monasteries, in which various offerings to the saint (such as the requisites for a monk) have been placed.[47] This makes good sense in view of the legendary traditions we have looked at in this chapter: Upagupta in the midst of the ocean is, after all, a monk, and it is the meritorious duty of laypersons to provide for his needs. The raft, which bore his mother down the stream, is a logical way of communicating with him. Indeed, exactly this point is made in the end of the film on Shin Upago, which we have not yet considered but which may be summarized as follows:

> Sitting in meditation on his raft, Upagupta realizes that his parents would like to see him and offer him almsfood, so, in time, he goes back to their forest dwelling to visit them. They are overjoyed, give him a warm welcome, and fill his bowl with food. Then they enquire how they can get in touch with him again and offer him more alms. He suggests they employ the same method that was used to propitiate the sea gods in order to get rid of his mother's foul smell: load a raft with offerings and set it adrift. Given the ambivalence in the tradition about Upagupta's residence, this method cannot fail: if the raft sinks, the offerings get to him at the bottom of the river; if it floats out into the ocean, they will reach him there.[48]

The second form of this custom differs from the first in that it features the floating not just of offerings to Upagupta, but of an image of Upagupta himself. As a consequence, the whole symbolism of the ritual is suddenly made more complex. No longer is it a matter of simply communicating with the arhat across the sea, but it involves returning that arhat to his permanent abode. As the ending of the film implies, and as we shall see in greater detail, once he is established in his pavilion in the midst of the waters, Upagupta does not, in fact, remain there constantly. He is able to return to this world and intervene in its affairs. In this respect, he differs significantly from the traditional portrait of arhats, who, having crossed over the ocean of saṃsāra, abandon the raft that has gotten them to the other shore. The Buddha rightly criticizes those monks who, having crossed over, would then carry their raft on their shoulders. But Upagupta is not like that: he stays on his raft, which means that, although he has crossed over, he remains in saṃsāra, he can come back again. We may recall that the sign that showed Rāhula was truly the

Buddha's son—and thus akin to Upagupta—was that he could float, on his stone, across the pond *and back again.* Upagupta's being ritually returned to his own abode by raft recognizes, then, that he has been present, that he has come back again; but it also recognizes that he cannot remain present in this world permanently—that he must go home.

The Floating of Shin Upago

In Burma today, shrines that house Upagupta images rarely keep them permanently. For instance, the Shin Upago Mahāthera Festival Pavilion on the road to the Shwe Dagon pagoda in Rangoon floats its image of the saint every year in May, in what marks its major annual festival. According to one of the laymen in charge of the pavilion,[49] after feeding 250 monks and 25 nuns, the participants in the festival take the statue in a great procession to the river, where it is installed (together with a Buddha image) on a magnificently bedecked pavilion set on a raft and laden with offerings. It is then towed out into midstream and let go to drift and bring luck to wherever it will. Then, in a separate ceremony, a new image of Shin Upago is installed back at the shrine, and the whole ritual is repeated the following year.[50]

Such ceremonies, however, are not always so regular, grandiose, or well organized. In February 1983, I was fortunate enough to be able to observe in one of Rangoon's riverside neighborhoods yet another set of preparations for the floating of an Upagupta image. The ceremony was being sponsored by a youngish, seemingly well-to-do widow. The image to be floated had long been in her home, and she and her late husband had always planned to float it someday from the town of Prome, upriver on the Irrawaddy, where they had family roots. But they had never gotten around to it, and in 1980 he passed away.

Then one day, in late 1982, while she was telling her beads, she heard a voice in her ear saying that Shin Upago wanted to be floated. Not knowing very well how to go about doing such a thing, she sought the help of the neighborhood headman; together they raised money, had a temporary open-air shrine built, installed the image on an altar there, and left it on public display. By the time I arrived, it had been there almost two weeks and was due to be floated two days later. The following account is taken from my field notes of that period.

The altar, a multitiered affair, is covered with a jumble of meritorious offerings. A small statue of the Buddha asserts his authority over the gathering, but the main focus here is clearly the image of Shin Upago (see fig. 6). About eighteen inches high, showing him in the posture of looking up in the air with his hand in his bowl, it is set inside a four-pillared open pavilion with a three-tiered "brazen roof." This pavilion, in turn, has been placed on the back of a great golden papier-mâché mythological bird (thalein) which is also destined to be mounted on the raft, thereby transforming the raft into a royal barge.

Fig. 6. Veneration of Upagupta Image Prior to Floating, Rangoon

Long locks of hair have been attached to the pavilion itself—votive offerings made by women in the hopes of bearing children. I am reminded that Macchadevī did become pregnant at the end of her raft journey. . . .

On the penultimate night, an all-male committee, led by the neighborhood headman, is busy finalizing plans: Should they invite monks to receive food before taking the image to be floated? Yes. How many? Nine. At what time? 5:30 A.M. From different pagodas? Yes, three each from three monasteries. When should they hold the procession to the river? At about 10:00 A.M., but it would have to be kept small since otherwise they would have to apply for a parade permit. Also, someone should go along with the raft to make sure there was no trouble and that it didn't get stuck. How many people? Three; they could see who got the image downstream. What if no one wanted it? Well, then they'd have to accompany it all the way to the ocean. . . . [51]

In this way, preparations are made and remade. In the meantime, devotees keep arriving to make offerings—mostly of fruit and rice and money—to the image of Upagupta enshrined on the altar, and then to gather to chant sūtra passages and paritta under the leadership of various lay devotional groups.

On the last night, a devotee arrives and installs a second Upagupta image on the altar; this, too, is intended to be floated—on the same raft with the other—a sort of poor man's image. It is to replace the gold-encrusted statue of the Buddha that ordinarily might go along with Upagupta but that has apparently been deemed too valuable to be sent off in this way.

Fig. 7. Blessing of Image by Monks, Rangoon

On the day of the raft launching, things begin at about 5:15 A.M. with the arrival of ten monks for breakfast. Only nine were invited, but ten have come. This is not unexpected, it being customary to have an extra monk show up at such affairs, as part of a belief that the additional "unknown" bhikkhu might be Upagupta himself. The monks are served an overabundance of dishes that have been prepared and brought by families in the neighborhood and set out for the monks on low round tables. These dishes consist only of vegetarian food—which is unusual, but done on account of Upagupta.

After the meal, the dishes are quickly cleared, and the images of Shin Upago that are to be floated (and the Buddha image that is not) are taken down from the altar. Laywomen quickly spread their shawls on the table; the images are set on top of these, and the monks then gather around the table to chant paritta texts in order to "bless" and protect the images and imbue them (as well as the women's shawls) with the power that comes with the Dharma (see fig. 7).

After about ten minutes of this, the images are returned to the altar. The monks, sitting now in a semicircle facing the laity, lead them in the chanting of the refuges, the five precepts, etc., giving them an opportunity to pour out water to transfer merit to their deceased relatives. There follows a brief sermon by the most senior monk—which, however, has nothing whatsoever to do with Shin Upago, but consists of a general exhortation to the people to respect the Buddha, follow his teachings, and make merit so as to be reborn

Fig. 8. Procession to the River, Rangoon

in heaven. After this, the monks depart in the trishaws provided for them; and the laypersons dig into the leftover food and have breakfast.

The procession to the river, which is only about a hundred yards away, takes place around midmorning. It is kept extremely simple and consists only of the donor and two other laywomen carrying the three images on their heads (see fig. 8). The images are then placed on a temporary altar set up at quayside, while volunteers less formally transfer the whole of the pavilion and golden bird down to the river and several men busy themselves with preparing the raft (see fig. 9). Offerings continue to be made to the images, but their placement on the raft and its launching will have to await high tide at 4:00 P.M. Then, that evening, the raft will be taken around to nearby places along the shore, where further offerings can be made to it. Finally, on the following day, it will be towed out to midstream by motorboat, where it will be released.[52]

Journey to the Sea

The final destination of all such Shin Upago rafts is supposed to be the ocean, and everything is done to ensure that they get there. But it is also expected that most rafts will stop at several places along the way and will need to be sent on

Fig. 9. Raft in the Making, Rangoon

by persons downstream. The effort to return Upagupta to his abode is therefore not just that of the original sponsor of the floating, but of all the communities along the riverbank.

In this regard, the following addendum to R. Grant Brown's 1908 report to the anthropological journal *Man* is pertinent:

> These notes were written on a house-boat in one of the branches on the Irrawaddy River. I had just addressed them to the editor of MAN when I was told that we had passed a raft containing the image of Shin Upagok. Turning the launch and going alongside I found two pavilions each containing an image of Shin Upagok thickly covered with gold, and numerous offerings, chiefly plates [of food], lamps, and wisps of human hair. There were men on the raft, but they came from the village on the bank, and had just caught it. The raft was believed to have drifted down from Upper Burma. Anyone who feels inclined to do so boards it, makes his offering, and sends it on its way again.[53]

In fact, today, it is perhaps more common for villagers to tow the raft to shore and install the image for a while in their own village before sending it on. The arrival of an image is deemed to be a very fortuitous occasion, and it would be silly to let it pass by too quickly and not to share it with other members of one's community. Thus, the workers at a Rangoon sawmill that I visited felt themselves to be especially blessed since, twice in three years, a Shin Upago raft had floated right into their mill. Such images, they agreed, were most propitious, and they were quite contemptuous of "that place over by the Shwe Dagon" that never *found* its images, but simply floated new ones each year that they bought in a shop.

The statue that had just come to the sawmill workers (in February 1983) and that they had installed in a basin in their assembly hall while waiting to relaunch it was a small image that had gotten stuck between some logs on the river. In 1981, however, a very large raft had arrived. It had been half destroyed by fire, probably from a votive candle burning down. They had installed that image in their community hall as well, but, in order to raise money for its relaunching, they had paraded it in a cart around the streets of the neighborhood, twice a week, so that people could make donations of food and cash. Even though this was during the monsoon season, it never rained on these occasions. With the money raised, they repaired the raft, reinstalled the image on it, loaded it with offerings, and sent it on its way.

Wishing to share their merit with their own kin, however, the mill workers notified their home village down in the delta to be on the lookout for the raft. (There is no reason to leave such things to chance.) Their relatives were consequently out in their sampans and ready when the image floated by. They hooked it and began towing it to their village. But news of such events travels fast, and soon men from another village showed up in four motor launches. They also attached towlines to the raft, and a veritable tug-of-war ensued: outboards vs. sampans. By all logic, the motorboats should have won, but they apparently did not have the favor of the saint: miraculously, their cables snapped, and the sawmill's villagers got the image. They kept it for the better part of a year, worshipping it to bring prosperity to their community, before sending it on its way to the ocean.[54]

Myths and Rituals

How are we to interpret such stories and rituals? It is obvious that the legends recounted in the first part of this chapter and the rites described in the second part are related to one another, but it is equally obvious that there are significant differences between them. In the legends, for instance, though Upagupta ends up floating on the brazen pavilion in midocean, it is never he who travels downstream on the raft, but his mother. And the only time when he (or rather White Water Snail, who is like him) does go on the raft, it is not to end up in the ocean, but in the forest. Clearly, then, there are some discrepancies here between the myths and the rituals, and clearly the one is not the simple expression or coordinated reflection of the other.

This should not surprise us. Anthropologists and historians of religions long ago gave up advocating too-easy relationships between myth and ritual. Indeed, dealing with the Thai context, Stanley Tambiah has proposed that "the relation between myth and associated rite . . . is not a simple parallelism or isomorphism, but an inversion or a statement of the two sides of a paradox" which both myth and ritual may attempt to mediate in alternative ways, though it is ultimately unsolvable.[55] Interestingly, in this attempt to combine insights from both Lévi-Strauss and Malinowski, Tambiah uses as one of his chief examples the case of Upagupta.[56]

Similarly, Richard Davis, concluding his study of Northern Thai myth and ritual (in which the legend and cult of Phra Uppakhut also occupy an important position), claims that, while myth exhibits a high tolerance of ambiguity, ritual reflects a high intolerance of it. Nonetheless, the two work together, the one providing a sort of outlet valve for the strictures imposed by the other.[57]

Both of these views may provide us with some useful perspectives. They hint that myth and ritual together are not only, to use Lévi-Strauss's phrase, "bon à penser" (good to think with), but also (to make a bad pun) "bon à panser" (good to bandage with, or good for applying as a dressing). They thus not only explore options, but they also affirm structures, by healing any bruises or infections due to that exploration.

In looking at the Upagupta myths and rituals we have presented in this chapter, we are dealing not so much with two sides of a paradox that are somehow fused and toyed with from opposite angles as with multiple aspects of a single complex that has both mythic and ritual expressions. We cannot, therefore, expect to end up with a single interpretation without violating the richness of this complex.

Let us take as an example the theme of the journey downriver on the raft. We have seen in some of the legends that this is a way of getting rid of something that is unwanted—for example, an embarrassing hybrid, whether that be a water-snail child or a princess who smells of fish. Clearly, this is an exorcism, a way to carry away a malevolent spirit; and other examples from the culture supporting this view can easily be cited.[58]

But there is also ambiguity here, for the fish princess and White Water Snail are not entirely unwanted—they are also loved. Sending them away on a raft is then an attempt not only to get rid of them, but also to transform them into what one would like them to be. And this is effective, for the exile of the fish princess brings about her shedding of her bad smell and results in the birth of a great saint; likewise, White Water Snail sheds his animal nature and becomes a (future) Buddha. Thus transformed, they can now return, no longer foul-smelling, no longer hybrids. Indeed, in every one of these legends, the theme of return is addressed in one fashion or another. But the return cannot be permanent; relationships have changed and new homes have been established, and Upagupta, the end product of all this, goes off to reside in his pavilion in the midst of the waters.

In ritual, however, he can come back again, and his departure, too, can be repeated. But the Upagupta rituals do not so much reenact the myth itself as they do its overall message. Indeed, it is not the ambiguous, worrisome, hybrid fish mother that is sent off in the ritual, but the saint, Upagupta. And the reason for this is no longer an exorcistic one, but a new, doctrinal one: his sainthood, his very power as an enlightened being, depends on his impermanence, on his absence. Just like the Buddha, who cannot be the Buddha if he is permanently present, Upagupta cannot be Upagupta if he is not sent away. If he were to be permanently sent away, he would, of course, run the risk of becoming otiose, and there the ritual would end. If he were to be completely brought back and permanently made present, ritual worship could continue, but there the myth would end. The solution, then, is akin to that found in the worship of the Buddha: just as the Buddha is best worshipped when it is realized that he is no longer here, so, too, Upagupta is best worshipped when he is sent off on a raft.

CHAPTER ELEVEN

Upagupta and the Arhat Cults

REGARDLESS of the significance of his watery abode, and regardless of his affinities with the figure of the Buddha, Upagupta remains in Southeast Asia what he already was in India: an enlightened Buddhist arhat. That much is clear in the *Lokapaññatti*. Implicit in his continuing cult in Burma and Thailand, however, is another assumption: not only is he an arhat, but he is an arhat who does not die, who does not pass away into parinirvāṇa. In this way, he remains available to his devotees, who can, even centuries after what should have been his normal life span, continue to recall him from across the ocean or from the depths of the water. This assumption, obviously, is in contrast to the Mathuran tradition about the saint, which portrays him as passing away at the Naṭabhaṭika hermitage on Mount Urumuṇḍa. It is also in contradiction to the usual orthodox Theravādin notion of the arhat. Nevertheless, as we shall see, it fits in comfortably with developments in the notion of the arhat found in North Indian Sanskrit Buddhism, developments which came to play an important role in the popular practice of Buddhism in northern Southeast Asia.

The usual Theravāda orthodox understanding of arhatship can be stated fairly simply: arhats are human beings who, thanks to the Buddha, have attained full enlightenment and who, like the Buddha, will no longer be subject to rebirth when they die. In theory, then, there should be no question of venerating or worshipping or seeing arhats after their deaths, for they have "gone beyond"; they are no longer in this or any other world and cannot, in any sense, be in contact with us.

This, however, is only a theory; and just as Buddhism as it developed in India saw radical changes in its buddhology, so, too, it witnessed transformations in its "arhatology." Uneasiness with the doctrine of totally transcendent saints eventually contributed to the rise, in the Mahāyāna, of the ideal of the bodhisattva, a being who refrained from departing from saṃsāra out of compassion for others. Within the Hīnayāna itself, however, there were several analogous developments. Early on, the possibility was raised that arhats could employ their magical powers (mastered on the way to enlightenment) to extend their life spans for the rest of the aeon (kalpa). Indeed, according to the "Mahāparinibbāna Sutta," this option was open to the Buddha himself, who repeatedly reminded Ānanda that he could, if asked, prolong his life and remain in this world. Unfortunately, Ānanda failed to request him to do so.[1]

In the Sanskrit tradition, this option that was denied the Buddha *was* extended to some of his disciples. We have already examined the case of Mahākāśyapa, who did not enter into extinction but remained alive, in a trance, inside his mountain, where he still awaits the coming of Maitreya. According to some sources, not just Mahākāśyapa, but a number of other important disciples—such as Piṇḍola Bhāradvāja, Kuṇḍopadhānīya (Pūrṇa), and the Buddha's own son Rāhula—were asked by the Blessed One prior to his death to prolong their life spans and not to enter parinirvāṇa for as long as his Dharma should last. Only with the coming of Maitreya would they themselves be authorized to pass beyond this world of death and rebirth.[2]

The context for this, of course, is concern for ensuring the preservation of Buddhism against decline in the critical period in between the time of two Buddhas. The assumption is that these arhats, much like Mahāyānist bodhisattvas, will remain actively involved in the affairs of the world (in ways perhaps that Mahākāśyapa does not) and undertake to be protectors of the Dharma. Their motivation, however, is different from that of the bodhisattvas. Unlike their Mahāyāna counterparts, these arhats do not volunteer for this job out of compassion for others. They are, rather, assigned the task by the Buddha, who is concerned for the preservation of his Doctrine. In one tradition, in fact, Piṇḍola's remaining in the world instead of entering Nirvāṇa is presented as a punishment for his violation of the Vinaya code.[3]

In later texts, the number of these disciples/protectors of the Dharma gradually increases. In the introit to one avadāna, for instance, we find preserved a salutation to nine arhats, whom the author invokes "now that the Buddha has entered Nirvāṇa."[4] What is striking about this is that, canonically at least, some of these disciples (e.g., Śāriputra and Maudgalyāyana) were thought to have *predeceased* the Buddha, passing into final extinction before him. Technically, they should be just as dead and gone as the Buddha, yet here they are being summoned. Clearly, then, we may find here a stage of tradition that has accepted the fact of absence in parinirvāṇa for the Buddha but rejected it in the case of his arhat-disciples.

The best-known development of this trend emerged with the doctrine of the sixteen (sometimes eighteen) arhats (Chinese: lo-han), whose cult became well established in Central and East Asia.[5] The lists of their names vary, but almost all of them are headed by Piṇḍola Bhāradvāja, whose cult became popular in China and Japan and whom we shall consider more fully when we encounter him again in a more strictly Burmese context.[6] The traditions concerning the sixteen arhats have been thoroughly examined by Sylvain Lévi and Edouard Chavannes and by others. For our purposes, only three things about their cult need to be recalled. First of all, as protectors of the Dharma, they—or at least the first four of them—were spread out in the cardinal directions, each taking up his station in a particular "continent." Thus, Piṇḍola is said to reside in the west in Aparagodānīya, Kanakaparidhvaja in the east in Pūrvavideha, Subinda in the north in Uttarakuru, and Nakula in the south in Jambudvīpa.[7] In terms of this geographic distribution and in terms of their basic functions, they thus much resemble the lokapālas—the guardian deities of the four quarters—to whose care the Buddha also entrusted his Dharma.[8] Second, from these mythical regions, these arhats can come to our world, appearing mysteriously in person when needed or summoned in times of crisis. They thus are akin to deities and certain bodhisattvas in their capacities to intervene actively in the affairs of humans. Finally, when summoned, these arhats act not only as protectors of the Dharma, but also as potent fields of merit, available to devotees who are interested in reaping the rewards of good actions and offerings to them.[9]

The tradition of the sixteen arhats does not appear to have become very popular in Southeast Asia, though individual saints among them were known there. Several other similar schemes, however, came to be firmly rooted in the region, and, in some of these, we may find Upagupta included for the first time. More specifically, in what follows, we shall consider (1) a maṇḍala pattern in which eight (rather than sixteen) disciples of the Buddha are stationed at the points of the compass and associated with the days of the week; (2) the Burmese cult of the four saints, one of whom is Upagupta (the other three being Sīvalī, Angulimāla, and Piṇḍola); (3) the so-called scheme of the four living and the four dead arhats, dwelling respectively in the four oceans and under the four mountains (one of the four living is Upagupta, while one of the four dead is Mahākāśyapa); and (4) the Burmese tradition of the weikzas (wizards), who even today are renowned for their supernatural powers and presence in the world and whose cult is not devoid of connections to that of Upagupta.

The Eight Disciples

A directional scheme according to which the eight days of the week,[10] the astrologically important planets, and the animals and numbers associated with them are all arranged at the eight points of the compass is of paramount ideological importance in South and Southeast Asia. In this system, Sunday, the sun, and the garuḍa are associated with the northeast; Monday, the moon, and the tiger with the east; Tuesday, Mars, and the lion with the southeast; Wednesday morning, Mercury, and the tusked elephant with the south; Saturday, Saturn, and the nāga with the southwest; Thursday, Jupiter, and the rat with the west; Wednesday afternoon, Rāhu, and the tuskless elephant with the northwest; and Friday, Venus, and the guinea pig with the north.[11]

In Burma, where this scheme is particularly prevalent, the day of the week on which one is born not only sets one's horoscope (and traditionally determines one's name through a system of further correspondences with consonants of the alphabet), but it also governs one's personal worship pattern at a Buddhist pagoda. Thus, generally speaking, there are eight shrines at the eight directional "corners" of a pagoda's spire, each one identified by an image of the animal (the "mount") of the particular planetary deity and day appropriate to that direction. When worshipping at the pagoda, devotees will tend to do so at their own birth day's corner and/or at the corner of the planet under whose astrologically baneful influence they happen to be at that particular time.[12]

Less well known is the inclusion into this astrological scheme of eight disciples of the Buddha, all of them arhats. The eight are Kauṇḍinya (Pali: Koṇḍañña), Revata, Śāriputra (Pali: Sāriputta), Upāli, Ānanda, Gavāṃpati (Pali: Gavampati), Maudgalyāyana (Pali: Moggallāna), and Rāhula. They are respectively associated with the east, southeast, south, southwest, west, northwest, north, and northeast, in a maṇḍala scheme that assumes the presence of the Buddha at the center, in their midst.

Most of these disciples are well known from canonical sources, and many of them, in fact, already figured in the various lists of arhats given above. Two of them, however, appear to represent more specific local interests: Gavāṃpati, whose cult among the Mons we have already dealt with; and Revata, who figures in both Pali and Sanskrit texts but who came to be thought of in Southeast Asia as a patron saint of "magicians, alchemists, hermits, and monks who dwelt in the . . . forest performing austerities."[13]

Whatever the individual characters of these arhats, what is important here is the overall protective scheme into which they fit. This is sometimes expressed physically in the layout of the sīmā (boundary) stones around Buddhist uposatha halls (in which Sangha rites are held). With the Buddha symbolically *inside* the hall, the eight sīmā stones around the outside of the building are placed in the eight directions and identified with the eight disciples. Sometimes, in fact, each of the boundary stones is actually inscribed with the name of the disciple who, according to the above scheme, is posted in that particular direction.[14] As a group, then, they form a magical boundary line for protection against evil not only around the ceremonial hall, but around the Buddha as well.[15]

The same system is found in a Burmese paritta ritual in which images of these same eight arhat-disciples are directionally arranged around the Buddha and placed in a small replica of a Buddhist monastery. This rite, which Maung Htin Aung calls "the ceremony of the nine gods" but which is actually termed "the Offering of Almsfood to the Nine Buddhas,"[16] is designed to ward off or cure sickness in the home. It is conducted by an "expert" (saya), who begins with the construction out of light materials of a nine-chambered miniature vihāra in which images of the Buddha and of the planet Ketu are set up in the center "room." Representations of the eight arhats, along with figures symbolizing the eight planetary deities, are placed in the "rooms" all around (see table 3).[17]

The origin of the paritta ritual that makes use of this scheme is traced to a story in the *Dhammapada Commentary* that recounts the tale of a boy who had only seven days left to live. His parents, greatly distressed, go to the Buddha

TABLE 3
The Eight Arhats, Planetary Deities, and Days of the Week

Northwest	*North*	*Northeast*
Wednesday afternoon	Friday	Sunday
Rāhu	Venus	Sun
Tuskless elephant	Guinea pig	Garuḍa
Gavāṃpati	Maudgalyāyana	Rāhula
West	*Center*	*East*
Thursday		Monday
Jupiter	Ketu	Moon
Rat	Hybrid animal	Tiger
Ānanda	Buddha	Kauṇḍinya
Southwest	*South*	*Southeast*
Saturday	Wednesday morning	Tuesday
Saturn	Mercury	Mars
Nāga	Tusked elephant	Lion
Upāli	Śāriputra	Revata

and ask him if there is any way they can avert their son's fate. The Buddha tells them that if they build a pavilion in front of their house, set a place for him in the middle of it and eight seats round about, and undertake to recite paritta for a week, then he will send his eight disciples to sit on the seats and, on the seventh day, will come himself to take his place in their midst. This will be enough to chase away the evil spirit plaguing the child, and the boy, thus saved, will be assured of a long life.[18]

The ceremony of the nine gods, with its use of a miniature monastery, is clearly a ritualization in post-parinirvāṇa times of this invitation of the Buddha and his disciples to be present for protective purposes. It not only recalls the scheme of the sixteen arhats (lo-han) who were "sent" by the Buddha before his death, but it also looks forward to some of the rituals involving Upagupta in Thailand. As we shall see, in Northern Thailand, when Upagupta is invited to come to protect a ceremony, he is installed in a small pavilion or in a miniature structure sometimes called "the small vihāra" or even "Upagutta's vihāra."[19] There, according to some ritual specialists, nine candles or nine sticks of incense are to be lit for him. The number nine is a generally auspicious figure with many different connotations, but in this case it is explicitly said to represent the Buddha and his eight disciples.[20] Moreover, in one ritual instance in Northeastern Thailand, when Upagupta was invited to come out of his swamp, the eight planetary deities of the eight directions were summoned at the same time.[21]

None of this, of course, means that the paritta ritual of the nine gods is genetically connected to the rite of inviting Upagupta. Upagupta is not one of these eight disciples of the Buddha, just as he is not one of the sixteen arhats; but the ideological contexts here are similar.

The Four Saints

Upagupta is explicitly connected, however, to another tradition involving arhats who are said to come to the aid of their devotees. These are the four elders whom Charles Duroiselle described almost seventy years ago as "especially well known in Burma and worshipped as saints" and whom he listed as Shin Upagok, Shin Thiwali, Shin Angulimāla, and Shin Peindola.[22]

Shin Upagok, of course, is Upagupta, and Duroiselle provides a fine, concise description of his cult in Burma.[23] Shin Thiwali is the elder Sīvalī, a disciple of the Buddha who, because of his excellent karma, was proclaimed to be "foremost of those who receive offerings."[24] What this means, in effect, is that he is perceived as a sort of living cornucopia who can always be counted on for provisions. In Burma today, Sīvalī remains very popular and is propitiated by those seeking material prosperity and general good luck and success. Many people have images of him in their homes; he is always portrayed in the standing position, as a monk holding the requisites of a bhikkhu, such as a fan, and a staff.[25]

Angulimāla, another early disciple of the Buddha, is also the subject of a well-known legend. He owes his name to his pre-Buddhist life as a murderer who cut off the finger bones (anguli) of his victims and hung them around his neck in a garland (mālā). He was one finger bone short of his goal of a thousand, and was about to get his last by murdering his mother, when the Buddha converted him. His example is thus often cited as a case of an extraordinary conversion in which great bad karma was overcome.[26] In Burma, however, he is worshipped by pregnant women in order to ensure a safe and painless delivery. This appears to relate to a later incident in his life, when, after becoming a monk, he met on his alms round a woman who had been in labor seven days; by means of an act of truth, he managed easily to bring about the birth of her child.[27] The people witnessing this miracle established a bedstead on that spot, and thenceforth all women in difficult labor who lay down there were instantly delivered. Those who were too weak to come were washed in water that had been poured over the bed, with the same happy results,[28] while the words that Angulimāla had originally uttered in his act of truth became famous as a special "Angulimāla paritta" to be used to facilitate childbirth.[29] Duroiselle mentions only one image of Angulimāla—at the Shwezigon in Pagan—where he is shown as an ordinary monk. Pregnant women nearing their time would petition him with offerings.[30]

Shin Peindola, finally, is none other than Piṇḍola Bhāradvāja, whom we have already encountered as the leading figure in the group of sixteen arhats. Duroiselle and others are agreed that his cult was not very popular in Burma in their day, although formerly he was propitiated as a great healing saint.[31] This is somewhat of a surprise, since, in the Sanskrit and Pali traditions, Piṇḍola is principally associated not with healing, but with the consumption of almsfood. His chief legendary and iconographic feature is his large begging bowl; this he got illicitly from the top of a high pole by the wrongful use of his magical powers—something that earned him a reputation as a glutton, as well as a reprimand from the Buddha.[32] In China, he becomes a patron saint of monastic refectories, where a place is set for him and he is ritually invited to partake of meals, his mysterious presence being determined by certain signs and taken as proof of the meritoriousness of the donors.[33] In none of this is there any suggestion of his healing powers; but in Japan, where he is known as Binzuru, that was very much a part of his cult. Sick and diseased persons would flock to his images and rub the spot on the statue corresponding to the place of pain on their own body, while praying for a cure.[34] It is possible that this tradition, surfacing here in Japan, knew something analogous in Burma.

Despite the fact that several of these saints are figures well known in the Pali tradition, Duroiselle makes it clear that we are dealing here with a Buddhist counterculture—a relic, he thinks, of early Mahāyānist influence. The worship of these saints, he claims, is carried out "with a view to obtaining worldly advantages and particular favours" and is "regarded as unworthy by the more enlightened among the Burmese," for "such practices are properly not tolerated by the Theravāda system of Buddhism now prevailing in Burma."[35]

Nonetheless, they obviously form an important part of contemporary Buddhist practice and, as we have suggested, most certainly had their analogues in ancient India. Like saints in other traditions, these Burmese arhats are looked upon as potential wish granters and miracle makers; as such, they help clarify the context of the cult of Upagupta.

The Four Living and the Four Dead Arhats

The propitiation of the four saints is not the only arhat cult involving Upagupta in Southeast Asia. According to a different but equally widespread tradition, he is also the chief figure of a quatuor of Buddhist saints known as the four living arhats. And they, as a set, are paired with another group who are called the four dead arhats.

The four living arhats all dwell in palaces in the midst of each of the four oceans. These four oceans, located in the four cardinal directions, appear to be the watery counterparts to the well-known cosmological scheme of the four islands or continents.[36] "Our" ocean, then, is the southern one, since "our" island, Jambudvīpa, is in the south. As a result, Upagupta, who lives in a

Fig. 10. The Four Upaguptas, Wat Daun Chedi, Mae Hong Son, Thailand

brazen pavilion in the Southern Ocean, is properly "our" living arhat. The others in the group are Shin Tharadatta, who lives in a golden pavilion in the Northern Ocean; Shin Thetkawthara, who lives in a golden pavilion in the Eastern Ocean; and Shin Maedara, who lives in a brazen pavilion in the Western Ocean.[37]

Not many persons actually know all of these names, and often this group of arhats is more simply called the four Upaguptas—for, indeed, they are all thought to resemble him in their powers and abilities; and, iconographically, they all are portrayed, like him, as Buddhist monks in the seated position, with their right hands in their begging bowls.

This is the case, for instance, at a Shan monastery in Mae Hong Son in Northern Thailand, where four identical images of Upagupta—in storage when I saw them—are used once a year in a rite called Khao Wong Kot (Mountain-Ring-Jewel) (see fig. 10). This involves proceeding through a large and elaborate labyrinth (made of picket fences) set up surrounding a central platform, on which an image of the Buddha is enthroned. Devotees try to get to the Buddha by finding their way through the maze; when they fail, they must make a donation to the monastery by paying a helper who will assist them on their way. The four Upagupta images are installed on four smaller platforms at the four corners of the labyrinth, where they appear to play a guardian role similar to that of the lokapālas.[38]

Sometimes, however, certain minor iconographic differences between the figures of the four living arhats may be found. Thus, at the Kyakka Mar Sein pagoda in Rangoon—the only place where I have seen images of the group permanently set up—Upagupta and Maedara are portrayed as looking up at the sky over their left shoulders; Tharadatta, on the other hand, looks up over his right shoulder, while Thetkawthara does not look up at all but gazes straight ahead. When asked for an explanation of these discrepancies, the layman who had sponsored the setting up of the images declared that the right-hand side was the side of lokottara (otherworldly) matters, while the left-hand side was that of laukika (this-worldly) ones. Thus, Upagupta and Maedara are concerned with our present world, while Tharadatta is concerned with future worlds. As for Thetkawthara, he does not look up at the sun at all, for he is permanently engaged in meditation and, like Maedara, is concerned with lokottara matters.[39]

Unfortunately, no further details about these individual differences were forthcoming. Elsewhere, however, I was told that only Upagupta was concerned with this world, because he was the only one of the four to bind Māra. It seems safe to conclude that one of the primary preoccupations of the overall scheme here is that of the degree of involvement of an arhat in the affairs of this world.

Much the same concern may be found in the contrast that is drawn between these four living arhats and the second group, known as the four dead arhats.[40] These saints are said to lie on or under four mountains in the four cosmic continents, and their names and places of rest are given as follows: Mahākassapa on Mount Vebtrara; Mahāsubhara on Mount Uttama; Upekkhara on Mount Makula; and Dhammasara on Mount Matrula.[41] Once again, all of these names, except the first—Mahākāśyapa—are quite obscure, and John Ferguson speculates that in former times these lists of living and dead arhats may have included better-known disciples of the Buddha who were subsequently replaced with more or less unknown entities by orthodox forces seeking to defuse the whole concept of arhat worship.[42]

The first patriarch Mahākāśyapa, however, was well known, as was the tradition of his resting inside his mountaintop awaiting the coming of Maitreya. In Burma, as we have seen, he became associated with the previous Buddha Kāśyapa, as well as with the twelfth-century Burmese saint Mahākassapa, who was the charismatic leader of a sect of forest meditators which Than Tun has identified with the Ari.[43] His worship, decried by the forces of orthodoxy, continues to this day.[44]

Since he has thus remained the object of a cult and is petitioned by devotees who ask him to protect them from danger, it is once again hard to know in what sense Mahākāśyapa is "dead." In fact, in certain nineteenth-century tatoo charms where the names of the living and the dead arhats were used to ensure the protection of the tattooed person against firearms and epidemics, Mahākāśyapa appears not in the group of the dead arhats, but among the living.[45]

Nevertheless, it is still possible to discern a basic difference between the dead and the living arhats. Both types, of course, are waiting for Maitreya to come, but they seem to vary in their abilities to emerge, in the meantime, from their meditative trances and make appearances here and now. Upagupta can do this, visiting our world from his underwater pavilion; he is therefore still "alive." Mahākāśyapa, on the other hand, is generally thought not to do this, but to remain on his mountaintop; he is therefore "dead." Simply put, then, it would seem that by "living" is meant continued involvement in this world, and by "dead" is meant retirement from it.

This dual tradition of living and dead arhats is, as far as I know, unknown outside of northern Southeast Asia. It fits, however, into a greater context emerging from some of the concerns of Indian Buddhism. Most strikingly, I would suggest, it reflects the ambivalence with which Burmese Buddhists reacted to the Theravāda arhat ideal. Though not completely canonical, the notion of dead arhats inclines one towards the orthodox realization that arhats, having passed away, are no longer relevant to this world. The notion of living arhats, on the other hand, tends more towards the bodhisattva or the lo-han ideal of continuing relevance and intervention in this world—at least until the coming of Maitreya.

Weikzas

There is one more tradition to be considered here which is not unrelated to the worship of Upagupta. This is the Burmese cult of the weikzas—those charismatic masters who, through alchemical and meditational prowess and through the knowledge of mantras and cabalistic signs, are reputed to have acquired various types of supernatural powers, including the ability to extend their life spans until the advent of the future Buddha Maitreya.[46]

Unlike the four living and the four dead saints, the weikzas are laymen rather than monks. In Burma today, they are perhaps the most spectacular example of a whole series of charismatic figures who, in addition to regular bhikkhus, enliven the religious landscape. These figures include "red-robed masters of the occult" (zawgyi), ascetically inclined hermits (yathe), and various types of "masters" or "experts" (saya) in astrology, medicine, and other fields.[47]

Paradoxically, weikzas are sometimes claimed by their followers to be dead, sometimes affirmed to be alive, sometimes thought to be incarnations of great figures of the past, and sometimes thought to have incarnated themselves in still-living masters, who may then deny that this is the case, yet allow the allegations to thrive. Weikzas are sometimes thought to be living in several places at once and to appear mysteriously in still others, and those who believe in them credit all sorts of marvels to their powers. Weikza devotees—mostly laypersons, but sometimes monks—may be solitary disciples, or they may form associations called gaings, which, in their activities and beliefs and relationship to their master, exhibit many of the features of millenarian movements or crisis cults.[48]

Melford Spiro has stated that "neither [the] weikza [themselves] nor aspiration to weikza are Buddhist in character," and that belief in weikzas becomes Buddhistic only when it intersects with belief in the future Buddha or belief in the coming great cakravartin king.[49] Many strict orthodox monks in Burma today would no doubt agree with this.[50] Such a view, however, comes from a rather narrow definition of Buddhism. The word *weikza*, in fact, is derived from the Pali *vijjā* (Sanskrit: vidyā), meaning "knowledge," especially magical or esoteric knowledge;[51] and the lineage of Buddhist vidyādharas (practitioners of magic) and vidyārājas (spell kings) is a long one, at least in the Sanskrit tradition.[52] Other parallels have been noted with the siddhas of late Indian Buddhism, who became well known in Tibet.[53] Many weikzas, moreover, are specialists in śamatha meditation and attribute their powers to that practice.

It is not possible for us to embark here on a full study of the weikza tradition, but a few remarks about its relationship to the cult of Upagupta are in order. Images and shrines of Upagupta in Burma today are, in fact, often found in conjunction with images and shrines of famous weikzas. Thus, for example, in the courtyard of the Shwe Phone Bwint pagoda in Rangoon, there is a series of small pavilions in a row, and worshippers, going down the line, can venerate, in turn, Ariya Metteyya (the future Buddha), Bo Bo Aung (a famous weikza of the nineteenth century), Bo Min Gaung (a more recent weikza who died in 1953 and is said to be now dwelling on Mount Popa), and Shin Upago (Upagupta).[54] The same sort of connection is stated even more strongly a few blocks away at the Kyakka Mar Sein pagoda, where, as mentioned, one finds arranged in a back courtyard images of the four Upaguptas. When I asked the layman who had sponsored the erection of these shrines why he had done so, he replied that, one day, while he was meditating, his late "godfather/grandfather" had appeared to him and told him to do it. When I asked who his "godfather" was, he pointed to another statue to one side of the courtyard: it was Bo Min Gaung.[55]

Such conjunctions and associations are hardly surprising, for there are a number of points at which the cult of Upagupta intersects with weikza belief. Like the weikzas, Upagupta is associated with the future Buddha Maitreya, and he is thought to be mysteriously still alive and to be able to appear to people in person or in dreams; like weikzas, also, he sometimes becomes the focus of semi-esoteric worship groups.[56] Moreover, both Upagupta and the weikzas are specialists in śamatha meditation, which they practice in remote, palacelike dwellings; and both are thought to be endowed with great amounts of magical power which they can use to benefit their devotees.

Features of the Arhat Cults

When all of these various cults of Burmese and other saints—the sixteen lo-han, the eight disciples, the four saints, the living and dead arhats, and the weikzas—are considered together, a number of characteristics about them emerge. It may be useful to list four of these here, as they will help set the agenda for the chapters that follow.

First, these saints clearly take on the role of protectors or guardians of the Buddhist religion. This function is often expressed cosmologically, with the various arhats set in a maṇḍala pattern to ensure the protection of all points of the compass. In this they resemble various deities such as Indra and the guardians of the four quarters (the lokapālas)[57] or various gods entrusted with the protection of specific lands (e.g., Natha, Viṣṇu, Kataragama, and Pattini in Sri Lanka). But individual arhats can also act as guardians, and they may be invited by devotees to come and protect particular countries, cities, monasteries, homes, or even persons from malignant forces. This is one very important feature of the cult of Upagupta, and we shall, in our next chapter, explore the various ways and levels in which he may be thought to act as a protector.

Second, apart from this guardian function, the arhats also have the task of acting as effective fields of merit who can ensure their devotees the karmic rewards of any offerings that are made to them. The arhats are thus not only cosmological protectors capable of keeping the forces of chaos at bay, but also karmalogical providers bringing palpably positive results to their petitioners. This is true of the sixteen lo-han in general and, in a more specialized context, of such individual saints in Burma as Angulimāla (who brings easy childbirth), Piṇḍola (who brings cure from disease), Sīvalī (who assures the easy procurement of food and goods), Moggallāna (who grants magical powers), and Sāriputta (who gives wisdom). We shall, in our next chapter, see the various ways in which Upagupta, in addition to his role as a protector of Buddhist festivals, acts as a provider of tangible results to devotees who make offerings to him.

Third, many of the arhats we have looked at are contracted to act, both as protectors and as providers, in the interstitial age between the two Buddhas Śākyamuni and Maitreya. The coming of Maitreya, we have seen, is a major preoccupation not only of the cult of weikzas, but also of the cult of Mahākāśyapa, whose career will end with that event. So, too, will those of the sixteen lo-han, whose own entry into Nirvāṇa is, at least in one text, very precisely described: it will occur immediately after they witness the so-called parinirvāṇa of the relics of the Buddha Śākyamuni and immediately prior to the advent of Maitreya.[58] Much the same thing is said about Upagupta in both Thailand and Burma. As one informant (a monk) put it, "Upagupta will remain in this world for a long time, but will 'go off' [to parinirvāṇa] just prior to Maitreya's coming, since Maitreya will have twenty-five hundred brand-new arhats of his own. With him, there will be no Sāriputta, no Moggallāna, no Upagutta."[59] Others, however, were of a different opinion. They recognized that Upagupta would have nothing to do once Maitreya came, but they claimed that, nevertheless, he would not then enter parinirvāṇa; rather, he would return again, after the time of Maitreya, as the sixth or even seventh Buddha of our age.[60]

Fourth, despite this variety of opinions, it is generally agreed that, until Maitreya's advent, Upagupta and the other arhats—at least those who are "living"—can and do remain active and available within saṃsāra. What is more, they are thought to be able to appear on occasion in person. Devotees are thus not limited to focussing on their statues or on other representations of them; they can also hope to see living proof of the saint's activities in the world. This, as we have seen, was the case with Piṇḍola, who was thought sometimes to be mysteriously present in an assembly. It is also very much the case with Upagupta, who is thought to appear at particular times and in particular guises, often as a dark-skinned monk on his begging round, and often very early in the morning on those occasions when the full moon falls on a Wednesday.

Full-Moon Wednesdays

We shall, in chapter 13, consider a number of personal accounts of such sightings of the saint; for now, we shall limit ourselves to the tradition that these occasions are most likely to occur on full-moon Wednesdays, a theme that is connected to Upagupta's character as an arhat.

In Northern Thailand today, it is often asserted that the most propitious time for inviting and actually seeing Phra Uppakhut is on the one or two occasions each year when the full moon falls on a Wednesday. On such days, people believe that Uppakhut goes out on his begging round very early in the morning—at 2:00 or 3:00 A.M. Because he can appear in many guises, people are not sure exactly what he looks like, but they know that he is a monk, and they believe that if they get up and give food at that time, they may be lucky enough to give to Uppakhut. To accommodate them, therefore, the regular bhikkhus also get up and go out begging before dawn.

Today, this custom is by no means observed at every wat, and it would appear to be another old Northern Thai tradition that may be doomed to extinction. When he first came to Chiang Mai from Central Thailand in the early 1950s, the abbot of Wat Uppakhut had never heard of this practice, and he was quite astounded when the laypeople of the temple came and woke him up in his kuṭī at two o'clock in the morning and requested him to go out on piṇḍapatha. He asked them to bring the food for Uppakhut inside the wat, but they would not, claiming that it is only outside that they might meet the saint and, as a result, obtain great merit and become rich. He acquiesced, therefore, and went out on his alms round.[61]

Much the same tradition is known in other parts of Northern Thailand. In Mae Sariang, one lay leader told me that people think that on full-moon Wednesdays the bhikkhus represent Uppakhut. Therefore they get up early (and the monks go out early) and they give, hoping to become rich.[62] So important is this custom that, in at least one ritual in Laos, a pretense was made that it was a full-moon Wednesday when, in fact, it was not: In the higher ordination ceremony described by Pierre Bernard Lafont and Pierre Bitard (which, as we have seen, prominently involved Uppakhut), one of the masters of ceremonies at one point reads from a golden plaque and solemnly declares, "It is the year Kot Yi . . . , the full-moon day of the fourth month, a Wednesday."[63] In fact, the day on which this pronouncement was made (7 February 1955),[64] though indeed the full-moon day of the fourth month of the local Thai-Lü calendar, happens to have been a Monday. Here, then, ritual demands appear to have resulted in a fictional claim.

A number of other points about this curious full-moon Wednesday tradition are striking. First of all, technically speaking, giving food to monks in the middle of the night involves a violation of the Vinaya rules about alms rounds. According to the monastic code, a monk should not go out begging until he can see the lines on his hand, that is, until at least daybreak. For monks to go on piṇḍapatha at two or three o'clock in the morning, therefore, and for laypeople to feed them at such times, is not only unusual but wrong.

Perhaps because of its questionableness, the custom has, at various points, been attacked by reformist forces. For instance, Bhikkhu Pannya Nantha, one of the leaders in the movement to spread a particular brand of Central Thai Theravāda orthodoxy to the provinces, cites it as an example of the many things he campaigned against in the north. Once, he recalls, years ago, he went to Chiang Mai and found that people there got up at 2:00 A.M. to give food to the monks on full-moon Wednesdays. He asked them why; they told him that on that night Phra Uppakhut would come from the deepest sea, and if one could give him food at this time, one would become very rich. He decided he must change this practice, so he started preaching that it was wrong, that monks who accepted food in the middle of the night were committing serious breaches of the discipline. People objected that it was an old Northern Thai tradition, but he explained to them that it was a Burmese custom. Once, he claimed, he went to Rangoon, and when he was sleeping the monks woke him up. He asked them why; they said that it was a full-moon Wednesday and that a rich donor was going to give food to the monks at 2:00

A.M. At the time he did not object; he got up and pretended to eat, but he thought that this practice was not right.[65]

Despite Pannya Nantha's campaign, it is clear that the tradition has not been completely eradicated in the north, even though it may be dying out. Less concerned, perhaps, than some outsiders with the purity of their own practices, at least some villagers and a few monks still persist in this custom. Elsewhere, the ritual may be taking on new forms. In Chiang Mai, for instance, a senior monk at Wat Chedi Luang recalls that "some monks used to do this," but not anymore. Instead, laypeople who have images of Phra Uppakhut in their homes now get up at 3:00 A.M. on full-moon Wednesdays and make special food offerings to the image, but they do not go out to feed the monks.[66]

Whatever form the practice takes, one basic question about it remains to be addressed: what is so special about full-moon Wednesday nights? Why does Uppakhut choose that day to appear among humans? When asked this question, most people could not answer it and just said that it was tradition. Nonetheless, it is a tradition with many reverberations, and a number of these need to be explored here.

Pannya Nantha's assertion that the tradition of feeding monks at night on full-moon Wednesdays comes from Burma is intriguing. No one I spoke to in Burma about Shin Upago had ever heard of this custom; yet the importance of full-moon Wednesdays may be traced far back in history, at least in Lower Burma. Indeed, in its account of the Shwe Dagon pagoda in Rangoon, the Mon Chronicle of Kings specifies that "in the year 1030, the full moon of Phālguna (February-March) fell on a Wednesday. Every year whenever a full moon fell on Wednesday, all the Shans, the Mons, and the Burmese monks and people came to worship and make offerings in great crowds."[67]

Unfortunately, no explanation is given here as to why this would be a particularly festive time. According to Burmese astrology, however, Wednesday night is associated with the planet Rāhu, whose influence is generally malignant and whose chief function is the creation of eclipses. It may be that the conjunction of the full moon (a generally beneficent planet associated with the east) and Rāhu (and the threat of a possible eclipse) served to heighten the tension of the day, tension to be dealt with by a festival in honor of the Buddha (or by calling on the powers of Upagupta).

In Thailand, where the assignment of Wednesday night to Rāhu is also known,[68] a popular tradition further asserts that the Buddha was born on a Wednesday, probably because the Thai word for Wednesday (Wan Phut) resembles the name of the Buddha (Phra Phutachao). This Wednesday would also have been a full-moon day, since the Buddha's birthday (as well as his enlightenment and parinirvāṇa) is supposed to have taken place at the time of the full moon of Visākha (April-May). It may be, in fact, that we should focus not so much on the Buddha's birthday as on his enlightenment at Bodhgaya, for here we find textual backing for an assertion that this event, too, took place on a Wednesday. Indeed, the *Traibhūmikathā*, though silent on the question of the day of the week of the Buddha's birth, specifically states that his enlightenment at Bodhgaya fell on a Wednesday. In this, it differentiates the day of his enlightenment from the day of his parinirvāṇa, which, though also falling on the full moon of Visākha, is said to have taken place on a Tuesday.[69]

None of this fully explains the importance of full-moon Wednesdays in the worship of Upagupta, but it helps set a context for it. Simply put, Upagupta may be said to be present, to be needed, whenever there is an eclipse—actual, potential, or symbolic. We already saw one hint of this in the story in chapter 7 of the eclipse of the sun signalling the start of Aśoka's stūpa festival; mention might be made here of another tradition, dealing with the question of when and how to cast or carve an image of Upagupta. These are the instructions given in a modern Burmese ritual manual:

> At times when there is an eclipse of the sun or the moon, . . . start reciting the following incantation: "Om, I take refuge in the Buddha, the Arhat. May Rāhu, the Dark Planet, release the Sun (or the Moon)." Then carve an image of Shin Upagutta in a seated pose with his legs crossed, holding the bowl in his left hand, and his right hand in the bowl to take his food, and his eyes directed to the sun up in the sky. . . . When the image is ready, make a cavity in its underside. On the surface of a copper or gold sheet, in clear, legible handwriting, inscribe the following verse in Pali: "The Sun shines in the day and the Moon at night. The Warrior shines when he has donned his armor, and the Brahmin shines when he meditates. But the Buddha shines by his power, day and night. May Reverend Upagutta, who lives in constant love and meditation and who subdues Māra, dispel the wind and the rain by his magic power."[70]

It is probable that several interpretations of these instructions could be offered. From our present perspective, however, it is clear that Upagupta here again "appears" (i.e., his image is made) when Rāhu threatens an eclipse. More importantly, he is crucially involved in the defeat of Rāhu, which makes it possible not only for the sun to shine in the daytime and the moon at night, but also for the Buddha to shine by his power both day and night.

At this point, a number of the ramifications of Rāhu's role become apparent. His function here is much akin to that of Māra. He and his eclipses are more broadly symbolic of attacks on world order, specifically Buddhist world order. Without falling into the excesses of nineteenth-century solar mythologists, we may still state that Rāhu's obscuration of the light of the moon or sun is seen as a threat to the power of the Buddha, who is universally associated with light. And it is precisely when such threats occur that Upagupta comes.

An actual eclipse, of course, is a prime symbol of such a threat. But actual eclipses are rare events and so not good for regular rituals. Full-moon Wednesdays, which, as we have suggested, are times of symbolic or potential eclipses, are somewhat better in this regard. They have the advantage of falling on an already-recognized holiday (a full-moon day), and they, too, are marked by Upagupta's presence. But, more generally, what obscures the light of the sun or the moon is not an eclipse or a threatened eclipse, but rain clouds and the darkness of night. And so it makes sense for Upagupta to be a guarantor of fine weather when rain threatens, and to be a saint who comes when it is still dark, before sunrise, and after the moon has set. To feed him at that time may be a violation of the Vinaya, but it also fortifies him for his struggle when he is most needed.

CHAPTER TWELVE

Communal Cults: Upagupta as Protector of Festivals

IN OUR last chapter, we made a distinction between two dimensions of the cults of arhats in Southeast Asia: on the one hand, they are called upon to be cosmological protectors of Buddhism, guardians of order; on the other, they are thought of as karmalogical providers of benefits, potent fields of merit.

Another way of making this distinction might be to focus on two social contexts or levels of ritual activities: on the one hand, there are community-wide cults that call upon the saint's protective powers and aim at the success of activities of the group as a whole; on the other, there are more domestic and personal rites that seek benefits for individuals and their families and that aim at the prosperity and protection of homes and persons. Obviously, there can be a considerable degree of overlap between these categories (individuals may choose to use to their own ends the opportunities provided by communal occasions), but the distinction is nonetheless a useful one, and we shall employ it here. Accordingly, in this chapter we shall focus on those rituals that have as their primary purpose the invitation of Upagupta to protect community festivities, before turning in our next chapter to consider more domestic and personal dimensions of his cult.

Generally speaking, in Burma, quite apart from the ritual floating of Upagupta images, the saint may be asked to be present at certain communal gatherings (such as ordinations or other ceremonies) and called on to exercise his protective powers—especially his ability to prevent rain and wind from marring the occasion. As might be expected, there are a variety of theories as to how best to go about inviting Upagupta. Some believe that the statue of the saint kept in the monastery must first be carried to a body of water and set afloat for a while, and then taken to where the festival is to occur. Others, however, object to this as unnecessary, especially if the image at the pagoda has been kept in a tank of water all along. Similarly, some think that special offerings of fruit, flowers, and almsfood need to be made to the statue, while others, more reformist, claim that these, too, are optional.[1]

All are agreed, however, that—at the very least—Upagupta needs to be verbally invoked and that his aid needs to be sincerely sought. There are many versions of such invocations, which are commonly recited in a mixture of Pali and Burmese. The following is a rather flowery example:

> Noble monk, son of Macchadevī, when you were born there was a great noise in the forest; wild animals barked and howled and growled. These are the signs of a person's greatness. O hermit, practicing jhāna, who is honored by the king of nats, who flies through the air in a trance, who has powers due to the practice of perfections in past lives, who dwells in a brazen pavilion in the Southern Ocean, who has pity, compassion, and love for all living beings, great thera who can blow away all the evil doings of Māra (who is ever trying to defame the Sāsana)—we now respectfully, with joined hands, make obedience to you, Upagutta, and invite you to come to our festival.[2]

In Northern Thailand and Laos, such invocations are also made, but the ritual as a whole takes a rather different form, due, in part, to the general absence of images of the saint. Instead, in those regions, Upagupta—in the form of a stone taken from a swamp or riverbed—is usually invited to come to a village monastery the day *before* a major festival and then returned to his abode the day *after*. Comparatively little attention is paid to him during the festival itself, when villagers have other preoccupations and pastimes; but his presence at the wat is thought to be a protective one throughout, guarding the celebrations from mishaps.

The Invitation of Phra Uppakhut in a Northern Thai Village

To begin our discussion of this Thai and Laotian tradition, I want to present from my own field notes an account of one such ritual I observed in Northern Thailand. The ritual took place in connection with the celebration of Org Phansa—the end of the Buddhist rains retreat—that occurred on 1–2 October 1982 at Ban Huay Cho, a medium-size village of about 150 households some seventy kilometers north of Chiang Mai, on the banks of one of the tributaries of the river Ping. I had visited the village wat (temple) a week earlier and found out about the ceremony from a Mr. Pannya, a sixty-three-year-old Shan who had formerly been a monk in Burma and was now a leading layman (acharn wat) of this Northern Thai community.[3] I travelled to the village in the company of three others: my research assistant, the twenty-four-year-old abbot of the wat, and a friend of his, a twenty-two-year-old monk from Chiang Mai.[4]

October 1. We arrive late in the afternoon to find the shrine for Uppakhut already half built at the foot of the steps on the northeast side of the main assembly hall of the wat. Banana branches and an archway of leaves and flowers have been arranged on what appears to be a permanent wooden platform about one meter square. Uppakhut has not yet been invited from the river, but already on some mats underneath a "royal" parasol are set a monk's bowl, a water pitcher, a spittoon, and some flowers.

We chat some with Acharn Pannya, who is clearly in charge of things and who has already donned his white clothes for the upcoming ceremony. He introduces me to Acharn Mūn, an old lay leader who has brought the tray of offerings to be used in the invitation of Uppakhut and who soon launches into a story about the saint. This story is a garbled version of the basic *Lokapaññatti* legend, but it is interesting as an example of the kind of variants that can arise in the oral tradition. I call it "Mr. Mūn's myth":

> When the Buddha [*sic*] built eighty-four hundred [*sic*] wat [*sic*], he wanted to have a big ceremony to celebrate the occasion during seven years, seven months, and seven days. But he feared the interference of three kinds of Māras: drunken men, youths who don't respect their elders, and people who like fighting. The Buddha did not want any of this, so he hung foul-smelling dead dogs around the necks of these three Māras. He refused to remove these garlands, which the Māras couldn't take off or get anyone else to take off. He only said, 'Go and see Uppakhut, who lives at the bottom of the ocean where the nāgas are.' The three Māras then went to look for Uppakhut, but they failed to find him. They returned to the Buddha and asked him to take them there personally. He did so, and this time they met Uppakhut, whom the Buddha himself asked to remove the dead dogs from the Māras' necks. Uppakhut agreed to do so, but not until the Buddha finished celebrating his seven-year, seven-month, and seven-day ceremony.

Mr. Mūn tells all of this with great animation and is frequently backed by Mr. Kaeo, a genuinely wizened white-robed layman who has joined the group. We are soon interrupted, however, by the news that the procession to the river is ready to start. The acharns take up the offering tray, the royal umbrella, and a monk's fan, the other necessities for the occasion—in particular a set of monastic robes and a monk's begging bowl—being left on the Uppakhut shrine until our return; they are too bulky, it is claimed, to carry to the river. Then a long drum starts to beat, a hand-held gong to clang, and a pair of cymbals to crash; and we start off. Altogether there are about ten laypersons (no monks) and a dozen children, eager for a parade.

It is dark, and a limpid moon, one day short of full, is rising. We make our way down through the mud-spattered alleys of the village, a small procession arousing the barking of dogs. We soon cross a footbridge to the other bank of the river, where there is a small beach and where the music stops.

Having arrived at the river, Acharn Mūn and Acharn Pannya squat down by the water's edge, with everyone else squatting behind them in devout postures, knees up, hands raised (see fig. 11). A minute of chanting by Acharn Pannya in Pali and Northern Thai suffices to invite Phra Uppakhut: "We ask forgiveness for the demerits we have committed, before bringing the great elder Upagutta from the water so that he can put a stop to everything that may go wrong. In former times, Phra Uppakhut made good merit, and he can now share it with everyone—at home, at the wat, or in the forest. Obeisance to

Fig. 11. Riverside Invitation of Upagupta, Ban Huay Cho, Thailand

Phra Uppakhut, who will give merit to the village, who has magical powers, and who can go everywhere. Please give good things to the villagers." Then the candles are lit—two on the edge of the offering tray and four in the sand on the beach. The two on the tray (where there are also three bunches of flowers signifying the three refuges) are said to symbolize the Buddha and the Dharma. No candle is lit for the Sangha, because, as I was told later, "Uppakhut represents the Sangha." The four candles on the ground, I initially assume, are meant to symbolize the four Uppakhuts, but later inquiry reveals that this is not the case. According to Mr. Pannya, they signify totality: the four elements of earth, air, fire, and water. As he put it: "The whole world, in all its aspects, wants Uppakhut to come."

Then a young man is dispatched into the river to find the four stones that represent (the four) Uppakhuts. It being quite dark by now, he quickly vanishes into the stream. A minute passes and nothing happens. Acharn Mūn shouts into the darkness, "Hey, hurry up, will you?" An indistinct cry from far downstream brings general laughter to the group. Apparently, what would be a simple task in daylight—finding four suitable rocks on the river bottom—is actually quite difficult in the dark. Finally, however, the young man reemerges, soaking wet and clutching four stones. They are round and flattish, a bit smaller than a fist. There are shouts of "Phra Uppakhut! Come! Let's go back to the village!" The stones are placed on the tray, the royal umbrella is held over the tray bearer, the band starts playing, and the procession heads back (see fig. 12).

When we arrive at the wat, the abbot, some of the novices, and a few others who had not gone down to the river are waiting. The pavilion where Uppakhut is to be installed has by now been made ready. It has been covered with white cloth, and a monk's seat has been laid for the saint. His begging bowl, his packet of monk's robes, his spittoon, and his water pitcher await him. A huge candle on the ground in front of the shrine has been lit. It is to burn all night, and it provides some light. Mr. Pannya again lights two candles symbolizing the Buddha and the Dharma and places them in front of the seat. The abbot then approaches, lights nine sticks of incense from one of the candles, and places them in a burner. The tray with the flowers and the four rocks on it is then brought forward and reverently placed on the seat, the parasol is set up over it, and the monk's fan is put nearby. The small gathering then kneels down behind the lay acharns and the abbot, who leads them in the chanting of the refuge formula and other standard Pali verses and then adds in Northern Thai, "We all bring Phra Uppakhut from the river Ping to thank him. We want to live happily, with good fortune, and we want everything that is bad to leave. And we all hope for long life, social position, happiness, and increased strength."[5] Uppakhut thus being installed in his pavilion, the gathering breaks up. It is understood that people can come and make offerings of food to him in the morning, starting at four o'clock.

Fig. 12. Procession Back to the Wat, Ban Huay Cho, Thailand

After dinner, we retire to the kuṭī and chat a while with the abbot's friend, the monk from Chiang Mai. When asked to tell us the story of Phra Uppakhut, he responds first that the traditions about this elder are very mixed up—they are like a myth. He himself has never heard of the three or four Uppakhuts, and if we really want to know about him we had better consult some old monks in Chiang Mai rather than these local laymen. He then proceeds to recount, without any relish whatsoever, two stories. The first is the tale of the Buddha ejaculating into a stream and of his sperm being gulped down by a nāga princess. She gets pregnant and gives birth to Uppakhut, who then becomes an arhat. The second story is that of a Chinese merchant who once got up very early in the morning to give food to the monks. He subsequently made a fortune, and he concluded that the reason for this was that one of the monks he had fed was Uppakhut. So he encouraged others to get up early and make food offerings if they wanted to get rich.

October 2. After an almost sleepless night in the mosquito-plagued altar room of the kuṭī, reveille comes at 4:10 A.M., when one of the more enthusiastic novices gets out the wat's loudspeaker equipment, turns the volume up as far as it will go, and puts on a tape. It is still pitch dark, but presumably the villagers appreciate this reminder that today is Org Phansa. The only lights are the candle in front of the Uppakhut shrine and a flickering taper in the wat's latrine. At 4:50, an old man arrives and makes an offering of food to the saint; he is the first, and presumably he will reap the merit thereof.

By daybreak, dāna is in full swing at three centers of operation. At the Uppakhut shrine, villagers come to make food offerings to the saint, offerings sometimes accompanied by prostrations on the ground. As Mr. Pannya pointed out, these are purely vegetarian, consisting mostly of rice, fruit, sweets, pickled tea, incense, and candles. "No meat for Uppakhut," declares one layman, "because he is an arhat!" By no means, however, does everyone stop here. We later figured that only about 20 percent of the villagers actually made offerings to Uppakhut, the others simply proceeding straight to the assembly hall or the abbot's kuṭī.

At the top of the staircase to the main assembly hall, a large number of receptacles—monks' begging bowls and large offering dishes—have been set out on a long table to receive the offerings of the laity, who go down the line and fill them with rice and other foodstuffs. These offerings are destined for the monks and novices but are made in the presence of the Buddha, whose image is just inside the hall. The merit the lay donors make here they quickly transfer to others (such as deceased parents) by pouring out bottles of water into small enamel basins.

Meanwhile, more food offerings—nicely prepared dishes and sweets—are being made to the abbot and to his friend, the monk from Chiang Mai, in the kuṭī. The offerings in bowls are spread out all over the floor in front of the two monks, who dole out blessings and administer the precepts to the prostrate laypersons. Then the dishes are cleared, and a new group bow down and make their presentations.

By 7:30, all of this giving has stopped, and everyone assembles in the hall of the wat. It is filled to capacity with about 250 persons present. They are all waiting for things to begin, when, to the obvious surprise and confusion of most, Acharn Pannya announces that it is now time for a special communal offering to Phra Uppakhut, which will take place outside, down at the saint's shrine. This is clearly not part of the usual course of things, and a number of persons are hesitating, concerned that they will lose the good seats they have managed to capture in the hall.

Nevertheless, a fair number of laypersons file back out of the hall and kneel down in front of the shrine (see fig. 13). A boy appears with a truly mountainous pile of sticky rice in a bowl which he dramatically holds up high in front of him, proffering it to the saint, while Acharn Pannya takes out a piece of paper and chants an offering formula in a language purporting to be Pali

Fig. 13. Morning Communal Worship of Upagupta, Ban Huay Cho, Thailand

mixed with Lanna Thai but taken, he says, from an old Burmese text he read forty years ago. The transcription of what he said verges on the mantraic, and I can offer here only an approximation of his words:

> We now pay obeisance to a person of good morals who is respected everywhere and who wants to help the villagers. We pay obeisance and ask the Buddha and the elder Mahā Upagutta, who has holy magical powers, to help all the villagers and animals. Everyone who comes to this place to give rice and fruits and sweets to the monks who go on their alms rounds wants to have loving-kindness [mettā]. Phra Uppakhut lives a long time, so that we bring offerings to him, desiring good health, prosperity, longevity, and vigor. We want good fortune and to have a long life. Uppakhut will help us, men, women, and old people. Now we bring flowers, candles, incense, puffed rice, rice, fruit, sweets, everything in this place; we wish to have good fortune, and, when we die, we want to go to heaven and attain Nibbāna.

The sticky rice is then placed on the shrine, and everyone proceeds back up to the assembly hall. As he goes by, Mr. Pannya announces to me with a smile that that is all for Uppakhut.

Indeed it is. Thereafter, the celebration of Org Phansa follows its normal course, and little attention is paid to Uppakhut and his shrine. The monks lead the congregation in chanting the refuges and the precepts. The abbot exhorts them at great length to keep contributing to the pet project of his predecessor—the completion of a new kuṭī—which, half finished for several years, now stands as an eyesore and an embarrassment to the whole village. After lunch, some old laypeople (mostly women) gather in the assembly hall for a period of quiet meditation. Later still, the abbot preaches a sermon. The next day, Uppakhut is returned to the river with virtually no ceremony at all by the layman dismantling the pavilion, who simply takes the tray with the stones on it and dumps it.[6]

In this narrative of the invitation of Phra Uppakhut at Ban Huay Cho, I have not tried to gloss over the particularities and eccentricities of the individuals involved or the anomalies brought to the occasion by my presence in the village. In the remainder of this chapter, I would like to move to a more general level and to analyze this rite by taking into account the reports of ethnographers who have witnessed similar rituals elsewhere. In this analysis, we shall focus on three important topics. We shall first reexamine the waterside ritual invitation of the saint, that is, the ways in which Uppakhut is asked to come from the river or pond to the wat. Second, we shall explore the ways in which the particularly Buddhist identity of the saint and of his invitation is emphasized. Finally, we shall look at some of the reasons for which he is invited, a topic which itself may be subdivided into two subjects: the desire to have a trouble-free festival; and the wish to prevent the rain from falling.

The Rites of Invitation

Anthropologists and other students of ritual have commonly distinguished, in one fashion or another, between communal calendrical rites, which occur and recur at prescribed points in the cycle of time, and what some scholars have called critical rituals, which may occur at any time and which try to resolve the quandaries and crises of particular individuals.[7]

Most scholars, of course, are quick to admit that there are often overlaps between these two categories. In the case of Upagupta, these overlaps become particularly apparent, since the rite of inviting him (at least as we have been discussing it so far) is never carried out independently, on its own, but always in conjunction with other ceremonies. Thus, the invitation of Upagupta is a supportive ritual whose purpose is to ensure the successful celebration of other rites. If I were forced to describe it in terms of the above typology, I would say that it is a critical rite that has attached itself to other, mostly calendrical, rituals. In the case of the rite at Ban Huay Cho, the calendrical occasion was Org Phansa—the end of the Buddhist rainy season. But, as the village headman pointed out, Uppakhut is also invited for the opening of Lent, for New Year's, and for Loi Krathong, when they recite the Thet Mahachat (Vessantara Jātaka). In other parts of Thailand and Laos, he may be asked for these ceremonies, as well as for Bun Bang Fai (the rocket festival) and for semicalendrical occasions such as the ordination of new monks, the dedication of new wat buildings, or the consecration of a Buddha image.[8]

Another way of interpreting Upagupta's role is to think of the invitation and dismissal of Upagupta, at the start and the end of a festival, as forming a ritual framework for the occasion as a whole. In this sense, Upagupta's role here is structurally parallel to his role as narrator of avadāna texts which we investigated in chapter 7. At the beginning of each avadāna story in an anthology, King Aśoka asks Upagupta to narrate the text; so, too, at the start of each festival, a chief layman invites him to be present. The saint's agreeing to do so creates a space and time that will be free from disruption by Māra; it "opens the proceedings" by ensuring that they will be a genuine occasion of Dharma. Thereafter, however, his role tends to be effaced. In the avadānas, no mention is made of Upagupta in the text during the course of his narrative; so, too, no further attention is paid to him during the course of a festival, though, in both instances, he remains present all along. Finally, he usually reappears briefly at the end of each avadāna, to be thanked by Aśoka and to go off where he will; so, too, at the end of each festival, he is ritually returned to the river or swamp (see fig. 14). In both cases, this dismissal (which is not always found) is comparatively uneventful, though it serves to mark a closing off of the ritual or narrative space and time.

None of this can happen, however, unless Upagupta is genuinely made present at the start of things—unless his invitation is successful. In many rituals, the moment when a divinity, saint, or supernatural being comes to be thought of as present is a time of uncertainty and tension, regardless of the degree of seriousness with which that presence is taken. In this regard, a number of elements in the ritual invitation are particularly important. We shall examine three of them here: the physical representation, in one form or another, of the saint; the words used by the ritual specialist to invite him; and the environment created by offerings and other things to welcome him and further assert his presence.

The use of small, roundish stones to symbolize the presence of Uppakhut is a noteworthy feature of his cult throughout Northern Thailand and Laos. Though he is sometimes represented in the same region by other, more anthropomorphic forms (as in Burma), rocks found in bodies of water—rivers, swamps, ponds—are the norm for signalling his protective presence at a festival. At Ban Huay Cho, four stones were taken to signify the four Uppakhuts, but there would not appear to be any standards in this matter of number. Thus, in Mae Sariang, a ritual specialist insisted that only one was proper; and elsewhere, in Laos, two or three are sometimes collected.[9]

The veneration of stones in one form or another is a widespread phenomenon in the history of religions. Within the Southeast Asian context, however, it takes on particular significance. Paul Mus, for instance, has highlighted the

Fig. 14. Return of Upagupta to the Swamp, Bassak, Southern Laos

use of stones by indigenous peoples throughout monsoon Asia to represent territorial earth spirits meant to assure the rainfall, fertility, and protection of their own domain.[10] Paul Lévy has sought to associate stone spirits in Laos with the "town posts" (lak muang) still found today in many cities or principalities.[11] And Henri Maspero has described how, among the so-called White Thais and Black Thais, the protective spirit of each village is represented by a stone that is put in a small hut built for it just outside of the settlement area.[12]

It is clear, then, that the use of stones to represent Upagupta may have many ancient reverberations in Southeast Asian animism, although we shall examine later certain ritual ways in which the particularly Buddhist nature of his cult is maintained. At the same time, the choice of river rocks to represent Upagupta is simply common sense. Like him, they "live" at the bottom of the ocean (or pond or river). Like him, they can come out of the water and be returned to it without changing their shape or character. And, though sometimes hard to find (as in the dark at Ban Huay Cho), they are usually readily available.

As important as the physical representation of the saint is the formula used for inviting him. The words of Acharn Pannya at the river in Ban Huay Cho were very simple, but they constituted a crucial part of the ceremony, combining praise of Uppakhut, promises of offerings to him, and expressions of the villagers' need for his help.

Much the same features can be detected in the sometimes more elaborate invitations recorded by other scholars. Richard Davis, for example, has translated a short text containing a standardized "formula for inviting Mahā Upagrutta." It gives ritual instructions for what should be spoken when installing the saint in his pavilion:

> We pay obeisance to Lord Upagrutta Thera, most excellent *arahant* who rests waiting for Nirvana in his three-*yojana*-tall copper palace at the bottom of the sea to the south. We declare ourselves your servants, most excelled *arahant* of awesome *iddhi* powers. The Lord Buddha prophesied that you would defend the religion for 5,000 *vassa* and prevent any dangers from coming to the people in their merit-making. Only you have the power to defeat and scatter Mara's evil host. All of us in the villages and *muang* of Jambu, both monks and simple village folk, follow the customs of making merit as they were set down by the supreme teacher Sakyamuni Gotama when He first established the religion. All of us, the congregations of every temple in the land, remain faithful to the religion. All of us still believe in the power of merit-making to affect our future lives. We therefore call upon you to forbid Mara to infiltrate and disturb us.[13]

Such formulae are most commonly pronounced by male lay ritual leaders, and there is a general understanding that the rite of invitation is their bailiwick and not that of the monks. Indeed, at Ban Huay Cho, no monks went down to the river, the whole ceremony there being handled by the acharn wat. Elsewhere, bhikkhus may accompany the procession; but if they do, they play supporting, rather than leading, roles.[14] Sometimes, however, a Buddhist novice may play an important part in the ceremony. Thus, at one wat in Mae Sariang, it is a śrāmaṇera who goes into the river and says, "I am a novice come to invite you. We are having a big ceremony; please come and protect it from rains, drunks, thieves, and bandits." He then takes one stone from the water and gives it to the acharn wat. This novice is said to recall the seven-year-old novice endowed with magical powers who, in the *Lokapaññatti* legend, was instrumental in finding and inviting Upagupta from the midst of the ocean.[15]

A different interpretation is given to a similar ritual found in parts of Laos, where a very young novice carries Uppakhut's begging bowl and umbrella to the river and is said to represent his monastic servant—his paścācchramaṇa.[16] Finally, some would argue that the novice in these rites is not only the inviter or servant of Uppakhut, but also a living symbolic embodiment of the saint himself. Indeed, Stanley Tambiah reports a tradition asserting that Uppakhut is thought of as a novice, something that may be reinforced by his status as a nāga—a candidate for higher ordination.[17]

Regardless of who is involved in the invitation ritual, a crucial moment of the ceremony is the emergence of Uppakhut from the waters. In Ban Huay Cho, Uppakhut's name was shouted at that time, and a cheer of welcome went up. Elsewhere, guns are fired and drums beaten (to help frighten away Māra), and shouts of "Victory!" are heard.[18]

Words of invitation and the finding of stones, however, are not always enough to draw Uppakhut out of the water. Various other inducements are also used, and the right environment for welcoming him has to be created. Generally, a particular set of articles—called, according to Tambiah, "kryang Phraa Uppakrut" ("Upagupta things")—is thought to be necessary to lure Uppakhut out of his swamp or river and bring him to the wat. These include a monk's bowl, a set of monk's robes, an umbrella, a pair of sandals, flowers, puffed rice, cigarettes, a kettle, and two small images of the Buddha.[19] Similar lists—with variants, of course—may be found in other places.[20] It is possible to distinguish in this prescribed set of items three sorts of things: regular devotional offerings (such as flowers and puffed rice); apparel and other items intended for a monk (robes, bowl, sandals, and umbrella); and Buddha images—which, as we shall soon see, play an important, though somewhat obscure, role.

The devotional offerings are intended to honor but also to attract the saint. Tambiah graphically describes the way the puffed rice is thrown onto the seat prepared for Uppakhut in an effort to induce him to take his place there.[21] At Bassak in Southern Laos, where Upagupta is invited to come from the Mekong River, quids of betel and cigarettes are thrown into the water as an extra enticement.[22] And in Ban Huay Cho, four candles were lit on the sand because, as Mr. Pannya said, the whole world wanted Uppakhut to come.

The monk's apparel is also intended as an offering, but, more specifically, it recalls the occasion of an upasampadā ritual. The nāga Uppakhut is here thought of as a candidate for ordination. Indeed, the whole procession back to the wat, with its royal umbrella and marching band (and, in Tambiah's experience, a sedan chair on which Uppakhut is symbolically carried) recalls the parades that normally accompany candidates to the monastery. The invitation as a whole, then, serves ritually to repeat the transformation of Uppakhut into a fully ordained monk, to reassert his identity as a member of the Buddhist Sangha. In his river or his swamp, he may well be a nāga (ophidian/novice), but, in emerging from the water and coming to the wat, he leaves his nāga nature behind; he sheds his ambiguity and is fully seen to be a Buddhist bhikṣu.[23]

At the same time, the pavilion where he is installed as a stone is transformed into a monastery. In many wats in Northern Thailand, in fact, this pavilion is not a temporary construction of bamboo and banana branches built anew for each festival, but a "wooden structure, usually no more than a foot high . . . resting on a temple wall or on a small truncated pagoda . . . [and] called the 'small vihāra' (*wihaan nauy*) or 'Upagrutta's vihāra' (*wihaan up-pakhut*)."[24] Such "small vihāras" recall the miniature monasteries used by the Burmese in the paritta ceremony of the nine gods. There, it is not Uppakhut who is invited to be present, but the Buddha and his eight disciples (along with Ketu and the eight planetary deities); but the homology may stand nonetheless. At Ban Huay Cho, when Uppakhut is installed in his pavilion, nine sticks of incense are burnt for him—a generally auspicious number with many connotations, but one specifically said to call to mind here the Buddha and his eight disciples.[25]

The ritual invitation of Uppakhut, then, not only transforms him into a monk; it may also serve to make him into a Buddha, or, more precisely, to give him the characteristic marks (lakṣana) of the Blessed One. And here we must turn to the small Buddha images—the third category of items that form part of the "Upagupta things" necessary to invite him from the water. According to Tambiah, in the ceremony he observed in Northeastern Thailand, these small statues were taken along to the pond where the invitation was to take place, and there they were "shown to Uppakhut"—displayed on the cover of the alms bowl—by one of the lay elders. Later, for the procession back to the wat, they were put in the alms bowl itself.[26]

A number of interpretations of this curious ritual have been suggested. Although Tambiah does not comment extensively on the significance of these acts, he seems to indicate that the Buddha images here are used to tame or convert Uppakhut—a spirit of the water—to Buddhism. From this perspective, the Buddha images are needed for their power, for their ability to control a possibly threatening force. The Buddha alone is strong enough to do this.

Eugène Denis, reading Tambiah's account in the light of the *Lokapaññatti*, proposes a slightly different interpretation. He suggests that the Buddha images are used here not so much to tame Uppakhut as to lure him out of the water, because Upagupta has an intense desire to see the physical form of the Buddha. That is what prompted him originally to ask Māra to take on the aspect of the rūpakāya, and that is what "captivates" him here.[27]

Neither of these interpretations, however, adequately accounts for why two images are used to accomplish this, or for why these images are placed in the monk's alms bowl for the return to the monastery. Some clues to these puzzles may come from a consideration of two analogous rituals that were observed in Laos by Charles Archaimbault. In Tambiah's account, no mention is made of any stones being taken from the pond; instead, Uppakhut's symbolic presence apparently rests with a "kettle" that is filled with water and taken back to the wat, along with the Buddha images in the alms bowl. In a swamp near Wat Phu in Bassak (Southern Laos), Archaimbault observed a similar but simpler invitation of Uppakhut in which no images or kettle were involved; instead, an Uppakhut stone was placed in an alms bowl, which was then filled with water and taken in procession back to the monastery.[28] This at least raises the possibility that the Buddha images in the bowl in Tambiah's account may be viewed as substitutes for or anthropomorphizations of the stones which in other rituals represent Upagupta.[29]

The other analogous ritual observed by Archaimbault—also in Bassak, but at Wat Thong—is even more suggestive along these lines. On this occasion, Uppakhut was to be invited to protect the annual Mahā Vessantara recitation, and *three* small Buddha images—all in the posture of subduing Māra—were taken down to the river on an offering tray. These images, however, were not ordinary Buddha images, for they were each given a specific identity. The two larger ones, placed side by side on the tray, were said to represent Śākyamuni and Maitreya, while the third, smaller and placed between them and slightly to the fore, *was said to be Uppakhut.*[30] But there was more to the rite than this. After a brief ceremony of invitation conducted by a few old laymen, three stones were placed in the water, and the three Buddha images on their tray-stand were put on some bricks in the shallows by the shore and left there. Everyone was then told to go away, and only three hours later did the ritual resume. At that point, the three stones were placed with the images, and the whole tray was taken back in a procession to the wat.[31]

No one could ever tell Archaimbault why the stones and images were left, why there was this ritual delay, and why the privacy of this moment seemed to be necessary. He speculates that the three Buddha images were to gradually imbibe the powers of the water (i.e., Uppakhut).[32] In a different vein, one might hypothesize that the image of the Buddha alone by the riverside recalls the Laotian myth of his fathering of Uppakhut—his ejaculation into the stream. For this, privacy would be appropriate, and time would be needed for Uppakhut to be "born."

In either case, it seems clear that these images are being used not so much to tame or lure Uppakhut as to give him an identity. One of Upagupta's chief epithets, as we know, specifies that he is a "Buddha without the marks," an alakṣaṇaka Buddha. It would appear that we have in this Bassak example a ritual bifurcation of this epithet: as a stone, Uppakhut remains featureless, alakṣaṇaka; as a statue, he is shown to be a Buddha—not quite as big or established, perhaps, as Śākyamuni and Maitreya, but a Buddha nonetheless.

A number of other points about this identification need to be made. First of all, the positioning of the Phra Uppakhut/Buddha statue between Śākyamuni and Maitreya is significant, for it makes perfect ritual and mythological sense. As a "Buddha for a Buddhaless age," as an arhat who has extended his lifetime to protect Śākyamuni's Dharma until the coming of Maitreya, this is exactly where he belongs.

Second, the placing of the Buddha images on the tray on the bricks in the water exactly corresponds to the way Uppakhut images are often treated. In Burma, as we have seen, they are usually found on platforms or on rafts in tanks, and in Thailand, as we shall see, people who have small Uppakhut images at home keep them on stands placed in the midst of basins of water.

Finally, there are ample precedents for the confusion of Upagupta and the Buddha in the Upagupta legend itself. In Burma, in fact, Upagupta is sometimes called the "little Buddha,"[33] a title which appears to reflect his being the smallest of the statues in this Wat Thong ritual. In Mathurā, it will be recalled, Māra himself proclaimed to all that, if they had never seen the Tathāgata during his lifetime, they should look upon the elder Upagupta. More significantly, in the *Divyāvadāna* story of Aśoka's invitation to Upagupta to come downriver to Pāṭaliputra (a story which forms a backdrop to the Thai rituals we have been considering), Aśoka's first words to the elder upon helping him onto the shore were, "Looking at you today I see the incomparable Self-existent Pure One [the Buddha] even though he is gone beyond."[34]

The Buddhist Nature of the Ritual

The symbolic associations of Upagupta with the Buddha and the Sangha also serve another purpose: they affirm the Buddhist nature of this ritual of invitation and make it clear that Uppakhut—a stone taken from the water—is a Buddhist figure and not some indigenous spirit (phī) or Brahmanical divinity.

We have already given a number of Southeast Asian examples in which stones were used to symbolize the presence of indigenous spirits. These spirits' overlaps with Upagupta are real, and the need to distinguish Uppakhut from, for instance, the phī ban, the protective spirit of the village (who, like him, may be represented by a stone) is also real. For example, in Laos, at certain rocket festivals, both Uppakhut and the phī ban are invited to attend and protect the ceremonies, and two identical temporary altars are built for them on the grounds of the wat, side by side, facing the display of rockets.[35] The principal characteristic that distinguishes Uppakhut from the phī ban in this context is the fact that he is a Buddhist monk, and this is asserted by the alms bowl, seat, and robes that are placed on his altar.

The same distinction is reinforced by the ritual recognition of Upagupta's vegetarianism. At Ban Huay Cho, as we have seen, no meat was given to the saint; the food offerings made to him consisted almost entirely of rice and fruits—items whose purity is uncontested. Although vegetarianism is by no means the norm for monks in Southeast Asia, it is a recognized Buddhist ascetic ideal, and it thus can help distinguish Buddhist from non-Buddhist supernatural beings and deities, who might normally receive meat offerings. In South and Southeast Asia, the higher the status of a divinity, the purer the food given to him or her. Thus, while demons may get flesh and alcohol, higher divinities and the Buddha will not. In Northern Thailand, these lines are fairly precisely drawn: forest spirits, field spirits, witch spirits, and village spirits are commonly offered whiskey and chickens, while, for the more significant town spirits (phī muang), annual buffalo sacrifices were traditionally held.[36] Vegetarian offerings, however, are associated with the figures of the Buddha and with such guardian divinities as Indra, the four lokapālas, and the earth goddess Nang Thoranī.[37] The giving of rice and fruits to Uppakhut thus helps distinguish him from some spirits with whom he might be confused and, at the same time, helps associate him with others who might perhaps be termed more Buddhistic—or, at least, less in need of taming.

Reasons for Inviting Uppakhut

The formulae of invitation generally make it clear why Uppakhut is invited to a festival: he is to prevent Māra from disrupting the occasion. This, as we have seen, is in perfect harmony with the whole Southeast Asian and Indian legendary tradition. Something more needs to be said, however, about the specific ways in which Māra is thought to interfere in Southeast Asia, for these reflect the more down-to-earth context of present-day Buddhist festivals.

In the *Divyāvadāna*, it will be remembered, Māra disrupted Upagupta's preaching by creating showers of precious goods and shows of dancing girls. In the *Lokapaññatti*, he took on various forms (bull, nāga, yakṣa) and engaged Upagupta in a struggle of magical powers in his attempt to thwart Aśoka's stūpa festival. In Thailand today, Māra is less dramatic, and he interferes primarily in two ways: first, he causes villagers to drink too much and to become rowdy or otherwise disrupt the proceedings; and second, he brings bad weather, specifically rain, which likewise wrecks the festivities.[38]

As Mr. Mūn put it in Ban Huay Cho, there are three kinds of Māras: drunks, irreverent youths, and people who fight. This interpretation is, in fact, a common one in Northern Thailand, where drunkenness especially is emphasized and is usually blamed for other things that go wrong, such as quarrels, thievery, licentious behavior, and disrespect for one's elders. Uppakhut is invited because he can deal with all of this; he is, in the words of one informant, "like a policeman."[39]

As is commonly acknowledged, in many parts of Northern Thailand and Laos, Buddhist festivities—whatever they may be celebrating—are also a prime occasion for drinking. Richard Davis, who was familiar with most aspects of Northern Thai life, went so far as to state that "drink is the *sine qua non* of any festival. A festival without drink is pointless, for alcohol is one of the cements that bind Northern Thai society."[40] It can also, of course, become one of the solutions that dissolves it. Drunkenness is associated with the untamed forest and the spirits of the wild, and so it is opposed to the ideal of domesticated order, whose primary representative is supposed to be the Buddhist monk.[41] Buddhist festivals thus tend to be times when the struggles of cosmos and chaos—culture and nature, village and forest—are most clearly in evidence. It makes sense to enlist the help of Uppakhut on such occasions; as the offspring of the Buddha and a fish princess, as a wild child of the woods brought up by a princess and an ṛṣi only to become a monk—a forest monk—he bridges in more ways than one the two poles here in play.

Uppakhut makes things seem right regardless of how they work out. His presence is thought to have a calming, ordering effect. As one informant, a professor of philosophy at Chiang Mai University, put it: "In my own experience, regardless of the facts of the matter, it makes for a very different feeling in the festival when Phra Uppakhut is invited. When he is there, there is a self-fulfilling confidence in the peaceful and orderly conduct of the ceremony. When he is not invited, there is a tendency for trouble."[42] Indeed, believers are full of stories of tragic accidents that happened when, for one reason or another, they failed to invite Uppakhut.[43]

Drunkenness, disorderly conduct, and accidents are not the only reasons for inviting Uppakhut, however. Throughout Northern Thailand, it is generally agreed that rainstorms, especially violent downpours during a Buddhist festival, are one of the primary forms of Māra-caused chaos that Upagupta is good at combatting. In some places, in fact, this view has led to a rereading of the *Lokapaññatti* legend in this light. Thus, as one monk in Mae Hong Son put it: "Long ago, King Aśoka wanted to celebrate the dedication of eighty-four thousand stūppas, but the rain came. So he called on Uppakhut, and when Uppakhut came, the rain stopped. Nowadays there is a tradition to call Uppakhut to stop the rain whenever there is a big ceremony."[44]

Much the same belief may be found in Burma. A recent book on the worship of Shin Upago, for instance, contains a foreword by "a materialist agnostic," who explains that one night he was going to a Buddhist initiation (shin byu) ceremony where a dance troupe was going to perform. It was the monsoon season. A large crowd had gathered. The sky was overcast. It was raining nearby, but it never rained on the place of the ceremony. Wondering how this could be, the agnostic shared his amazement with the person sponsoring the ordination—who revealed to him that he had invoked Shin Upago to assure there would be no rain.[45]

In fact, there exists in Burma a well-established rite involving Upagupta which closely resembles the Northern Thai invitations we have been describing and which is specifically intended to prevent rainstorms. As Maung Kin describes it:

> This *Kadaw Pwe* has for its object the production of fine weather, and is generally resorted to by the believers in Upagutta's power, whenever they are about to give any theatrical entertainment or other festival for the success of which fine weather is

necessary. The rite is performed as follows: a cocoanut, two bunches of plantains, betel-leaves and betel-nuts are placed upon a stand; and, after a petition in Burmese to Upagutta, two candles,—which must burn for the whole time for which the fair weather is needed—are set alight in the midst of the offerings.[46]

Sometimes, in this ceremony, an image of Upagupta is used, in which case it is "immersed up to its neck in water." This apparently is intended as a statement that enough rain has fallen—as a veiled threat to the saint that he will be returned completely to his underwater abode were any more to come down.[47]

All of this evidence of Upagupta's ability to prevent rain is of some significance, since a number of scholars have concluded that Upagupta's chief function is quite the opposite—to bring rain rather than prevent it. Some have even called him a "rain god,"[48] a spirit of the waters, or "un génie de la pluie"[49] and have seen his primary function as ensuring the regularity and plenitude of the monsoon.

To be sure, divinities who can stop the rain are usually also able to make it fall, and in this Upagupta is no exception. Certain ritual details, certain precautions that one must take reflect this fact. Thus, it is commonly said that the white-robed acharn inviting Uppakhut should not himself bathe until the end of the ceremony lest this cause the rain to fall.[50] There would appear to be a recognition that Uppakhut can make it rain, but that he does so *only if something goes wrong with the ritual.* If the ceremony is carried out correctly, it will instead prevent the showers that might plague the people.

Nonetheless, there is one occasion on which Upagupta's rainmaking powers may be invoked. Our saint, it should be recalled, can stop the sun; and thus, in the case of a prolonged period of too much sun (i.e., no rain), he may be called upon. Indeed, the Northern Thai "Formula for Inviting Mahā Upagrutta" recorded by Richard Davis specifies that he can not only prevent "rainstorms in the case of a festival," but also the "broiling sun in the case of a drought."[51] In such instances, however, Upagupta is not invited to come from a river or swamp, nor is he asked to be present at a major festival. Instead, a statue of him (and not a stone) may be taken out of the wat and showered with water in the hopes of making it rain. This, in my view, would appear to be an extension to Upagupta of what might be called the Songkran mentality, the traditional celebration of New Year's in which the aspersion of Buddha images, of venerated monks, and indeed of friends and neighbors plays a major role and is likewise intended to bring on the forthcoming monsoon.[52]

In any case, such instances involving Upagupta are rare. The only one that I ever learned of occurred at a wat in Mae Hong Son during a dry spell in 1981. Moreover, the abbot of a neighboring wat was very critical of it; in his monastery, he told me, they never use an Upagupta image to make it rain, only to ensure good weather. When they want rain, they use an image of Pong Ta U.[53] Finally, it is important to realize that such rare occasions when Upagupta may be invoked to bring rain are significantly different from the ones we have been considering in this chapter, for they occur in a different context. As a provider, Upagupta may sometimes be asked to bring rain when it is desperately needed; as a protector, he is expected to prevent it from falling.

CHAPTER THIRTEEN

Personal Rewards and Domestic Rites

THE INVITATION of Upagupta to ensure the orderly success of communal festivals is perhaps the most prominent aspect of his cult in Thailand and Laos, but it is not its only feature by any means. Even on these public occasions, the saint's powers may be tapped for other, more personal reasons. As an arhat still involved in this world, Upagupta is not just a guardian against malevolent forces, but potentially also a more positive benefactor, a rewarder of meritorious actions, willing and able to respond to the individual offerings made to him.

At Ban Huay Cho, as we have seen, considerable attention was directed towards Uppakhut in the form of food offerings early on the morning of the festival day. To some extent, these offerings may be merely part of the bribe—a fulfillment of the promise made to Uppakhut at the time of his invitation at the river. Alternatively, they may be seen as intended to fortify the saint for his struggle against Māra. This, it will be recalled, was one of Aśoka's concerns in the *Lokapaññatti*. At the same time, however, a number of other motivations may be found here. These offerings are not just token rituals made only to secure the presence and powers of the arhat, but genuine acts of dāna performed by villagers for their own purposes.

The food offerings made to Uppakhut at Ban Huay Cho, in fact, fit into a larger pattern of Upagupta worship according to which Upagupta, when he is present, is a particularly effective field of merit. There are several reasons for this, but basically they all rest in the fact that he is not just an ordinary monk, but a symbol of the Sangha at its best, an arhat, a potent substitute for the Buddha in a Buddhaless age. Thus, offerings to him are likely to result in the personal reaping of great merit and good fortune.

In Buddhism, there are two basic forms of karmic rewards for meritorious action: fruits that are harvested in some future rebirth, and benefits that are experienced more immediately, in this very lifetime. It is results of this latter type that appear to be most emphasized in the case of offerings made to Uppakhut.

According to a recent Burmese paperback on Shin Upago, worship of the saint, if done properly and regularly, will without fail result in twelve benefits: Long life, good health, freedom from danger, success in whatever is proposed, obtaining whatever is wanted, increase in moral integrity, having a large retinue of dependents, good physical strength, getting a lot of presents, wealth, intellectual prowess, and being loved by humans and gods.[1] Less formally, these assertions are reinforced by stories that emphasize Upagupta's wealth-granting powers and recount examples of persons who have struck it rich soon after making offerings to him. For instance, one rumor a few years ago was that the owner of Tiger Balm Gardens in Hong Kong owed his fortune to Upagupta; and, in Burma today, it is commonly claimed that the saint rewards sailors with government permits to go abroad, thus enabling them to import Japanese pickup trucks that can be transformed into Rangoon jitneys, resulting in quick profits.[2]

Sightings of Upagupta

Often, such stories are connected with tales of actual "sightings" of Upagupta. We saw in chapter 11 that the saint is thought to be able—especially on full-moon Wednesdays—to appear in person to some of his devotees. The experience or the recounting of such appearances has the effect of reaffirming the merit maker's faith in the saint's effectiveness. Indeed, throughout Burma and Northern Thailand, testimonials abound of persons who claim to have actually seen Upagupta in the flesh and to have reaped the rewards thereof.

In Northern Thailand, such stories often feature merchants as the individuals who happen to encounter the saint. More specifically, they may emphasize the good fortunes of the so-called overland (as opposed to overseas) Chinese—the Haw merchants who used to ply the trade routes to and from Yünnan. The man who founded Wat Uppakhut in Chiang Mai, for instance, is said to have been a Haw trader named "Red Dog" who, many years ago, got up very early (2:00 A.M.) on a full-moon Wednesday and happened to see a monk all alone. He gave him some food; soon thereafter, the trader became rich, and he realized that the monk must have been Phra Uppakhut.[3]

A more complicated tale was narrated by Acharn Pannya at Ban Huay Cho. It also involves Chinese Haw merchants, but this time, they do not end up with the goods:

> Early one morning, a very poor man in a small village happened to see a dark-skinned, ugly monk crossing the river by walking on the water. Impressed by this, he gave all the food he had to the monk, who then, to his astonishment, disappeared. Some days later, a caravan of Haw merchants with thirty-one mules arrived in the poor man's village and deposited their goods in his house, announcing that they would come back to retrieve them in seven days' time. But they never returned, and, when the man opened the sacks, he found in them gold, silver, and precious stones. He believed these caravaneers were deities who had been sent by Uppakhut to reward him.[4]

Similar stories are told of mysterious appearances that occur even today in Burma. For instance, a bookshop owner in Rangoon recalled for me the tale of a sweets vendor in his neighborhood who, early one morning by the river, saw a monk gradually emerging from the water. His robes were dripping wet and he was very ugly. The vendor thought he had been frolicking in the river, which he should not have been doing, as it is against the Vinaya. Nonetheless, she offered some sweets to him. Soon her income increased, and eventually she became very rich.[5]

Also in Rangoon, quite by happenstance, I met a fifty-two-year-old layman who had lost both of his hands in an accident but who attributed his subsequent good fortune to a personal encounter with Upagupta. Things were pretty grim, he explained, when in his youth an explosion blew off his two hands. But then, at age forty-one, he met Shin Upago on the road early one morning. He appeared as a tall, ugly, very dark-skinned and very strong monk, alone on his begging round. The layman made an offering to him, and shortly thereafter he received a new pair of artifical limbs (made in America) and has since enjoyed a successful career as an astrologer and a practitioner of Burmese medicine.[6]

Sometimes, these tales emphasize Upagupta's ability not only to appear (and disappear) mysteriously, but also to take on many different forms. According to one such tale, there once was a man in Northern Thailand who was very poor and had very little to eat. One day, he came across an old monk on his begging round. He saw that there was nothing in the monk's bowl, so he shared with him the little that he had. The monk suddenly disappeared. About a kilometer away, there was a man who was carrying some rice straw. He met a young novice. As the peasant had no food, he gave him some betel, and the novice suddenly disappeared. Soon thereafter, the poor man and the peasant met and told each other what had happened. The first said, "It was an old monk." The second said, "It was a young monk." But they both said he had disappeared, so they knew it was the same person: Uppakhut.[7]

In most of these stories, Upagupta is encountered quite by chance, when the donor or devotee is not expecting it. In other instances, however, he is actually being sought. At the turn of the century, for example, Maung Kin wrote that the "belief that Upagutta does sometimes appear on earth was responsible for much [miniature] monastery building and alms giving some twelve years ago in Rangoon; for someone had dreamed, three nights in succession[,] . . . that the Great Thera had appeared to him and asserted that he would visit Rangoon on a specified date. Many small monasteries were put up, in the hope that Shin Upagutta might be pleased to take his matutinal meal therein; and the credulous invited set numbers of Monks to take their meal there that day."[8]

The last statement is a reference to a custom that is still practiced in Burma today, that of asking several different monasteries to send a determined number of monks to one's Upagupta festival to receive alms. Then, when one more than that set number of monks arrives, the "extra monk" (whose identity remains a secret, since no one knows which monks were sent by which monasteries) is believed to be Upagupta.[9]

A number of themes emerge from these various "personal" accounts. First, it is once again clear that Upagupta's prime identity is that of a monk. Whenever he appears to devotees in person, he is dressed in robes, with bowl in hand. And this, in fact, corresponds exactly to his depiction in his iconography and to the legendary stories about him. More intriguing, however, is the question of just what kind of a monk he is, and here several new points can be made.

(1) He is a tall, ugly, strong, dark-skinned monk.[10] This fits in with the tradition touched on in chapter 10 that, raised in the forest by the hermit and the fish princess, Upagupta was ugly and wild; but it contradicts the *Lokapaññatti* tale of his apparent weakness as a skinny nāga who needs fortifying, as well as the *Divyāvadāna*'s assertion of his physical beauty. One of the points being made here, however, is that Upagupta, though a monk, does not appear as someone to whom one would readily wish to give alms. One must overcome this reluctance in order to reap the rewards of one's good deed.

(2) He is a monk who can take on many forms. Though often ugly and dark-skinned, he can appear in other guises, as an old bhikkhu or a young novice—a fact which may again emphasize his dual identity as a great elder and as a young novice. In terms of merit making, however, the message is again obvious: when in doubt, give. Otherwise, one can never be sure what opportunity, what field of merit, one might be missing.

(3) He is a monk who can disappear. Whatever form he takes, his ability to vanish suddenly without a trace is thought to be one of the clues to his identity.

(4) He is a wet monk. Often, his robes are clinging to him or still dripping. This, of course, makes perfect sense in view of his watery abode, and it is another telltale sign of his identity.

(5) He is a lone monk. He is rarely encountered in the company of other bhikkhus, and never in the setting of a monastery.[11] This fits in with the tradition of his failing to participate in the regular activities of the Sangha, of his living apart in his underwater palace.

(6) He is a monk who likes to appear early in the morning, and especially on full-moon Wednesdays.

(7) Finally, and perhaps most significantly in the context of our present discussion, he is a monk whom one encounters when one is by oneself. In none of these stories is the merit maker with anyone else when he or she meets Upagupta, on the road or by the river or the seaside, early in the morning. Rather, these are all personal experiences which bring about personal rewards. In this light, they reveal a rather different aspect of the cult of Upagupta than the ritual of inviting him to come and act as a protector of communal festivals.

Upagupta Amulets

Another aspect of this personal dimension of the cult of Upagupta may be found in his representation in the form of medallions or amulets, which individuals may sometimes carry on their persons to protect themselves from bodily harm.

The popularity and use of a bewildering variety of amulets in Thailand (as in other parts of Southeast Asia) are well known.[12] Today, Thais of all ages and both sexes commonly wear on their persons charms for protection, good luck, or other boons. These may be medallions struck with the likeness of a Buddhist saint (living or dead), small images of the Buddha to be worn around the neck, or a host of other, often crudely molded miniature representations of divinities, animals, magical diagrams, phallic symbols, mythological creatures, etc.

Phra Uppakhut amulets come in at least two types. One is an oval medallion about three centimeters long, showing on one side Upagupta looking up at the sun with his hand in his bowl, and on the other side a magic square. This type was distributed by the Burmese abbot of Wat Amarawat in Mae Sariang, who had decided to have them made.

The other type is more difficult to describe. It is also a sort of medallion intended to be hung around the neck, but, rather than being oval and flat, it is bent over into a semicircular concave shape (see fig. 15). The image is on the

Fig. 15. Upagupta Amulet, Private Collection

concave inner side, but, because of the general crudeness of the mold and because the image is almost doubled over, it is difficult to discern the saint's features. His brow and eyes are well delineated and quite prominent, but his nose is close to his chest and feet, and his mouth is usually indistinguishable. He is by no means looking up in the air, and there is no sign of a monk's bowl. It is difficult to determine specifically what features of Phra Uppakhut's cult are being emphasized here; however, because the saint appears almost hidden in their concave sides, such amulets are often related to the Upagupta "shells," which we shall consider below.

Such Upagupta medallions, like other amulets in general, are intended to be worn on one's person to guarantee one's own safety and protection against all sorts of mishaps. For instance, it is claimed that in former times generals with small images of the saint on their persons were never injured and always won resounding victories.[13] And today, similar testimonials about their effectiveness are still told: "Once there was a boat full of people crossing a river. The boat capsized and everyone aboard was lost except for one young man—the only one who was wearing an Uppakhut amulet."[14]

Upagupta charms thus tend to operate at a personal level in the same way that the saint in other guises (stones, statues) does at the level of communal festivals: he protects against mishaps of various sorts. The same powers, in fact, may be invoked in the absence of actual amulets by the use of the mantra "Upaguttena badho Māro" (by Upagutta Māra was bound). As Richard Davis has pointed out, in its Northern Thai form—"Uppakhut mat Maan"—this is "one of the most common spells which a [sūkhwan] specialist recites when he is binding the wrists of a patient [with a protective thread]."[15]

Domestic Cults and Iconography

In between the strictly personal and the communal contexts of the cult of Upagupta, there is another level at which the saint may be venerated: in the home. Indeed, throughout northern Southeast Asia, there are families who keep private images of Upagupta on their household altars, where they remain the object of domestic cults intended both to make merit and to safeguard the prosperity and well-being of the family. The amount of attention paid to such images varies greatly from one home to the next and from one member of the family to another.

In Thailand, as we shall see, there exist a variety of ways of representing the saint in one's home, but in Burma, images depicting him in the fashion that we have described—gazing upwards, hand in bowl—are more or less standard and fairly common. On household altars, they are always subordinate to the Buddha and tend to share their rank with other effective saints such as Shin Thiwali (Sīvalī) or with absorbed divinities such as Sarasvatī. Such images are readily available in any "pagoda shop," or, alternatively, they can be carved or cast at home. We have already considered Saya Zagaru's rules for making an Upagupta image at the time of an eclipse. Another authority stresses the importance of one's personal horoscope in this enterprise, specifying that care should be taken to see that the wood selected for carving the image matches the day of birth of the person hoping to gain some benefit out of its veneration.[16]

No consecration ceremony (such as that performed for new Buddha images) is necessary for an Upagupta statue,[17] but, before it is gilded, the following verse (in Pali) should be inserted into a cavity in its back: "The dispassionate Completely Enlightened One [predicted]: 'in the future, the great elder Upagutta will tame Māra and his army.'"[18] After that, the image should be worshipped every morning and *every evening* with vegetarian food offerings, water, flowers, and lamps.[19] Some authorities object to the making of food offerings in the evening on the grounds that they are unorthodox. As a monk, Upagupta should, of course, not be receiving a meal after noon; yet, according to a popular tradition, the best time for invoking him and presenting such meals to his image is around 6:00 or 7:00 P.M.[20] No justification is given for this belief, and it may be that the practice is dying out; but, as we have already seen in a number of contexts, Upagupta would appear to have questionable eating habits. He stops the sun so as to pretend it is still morning; he goes on his begging round in the middle of the night. Here, we may have another instance of this unorthodoxy, and, in light of it, it is worth recalling that in certain nonorthodox circles—for example, among the Ari monks associated with Mahākassapa and in the "unreformed Mahānikay tradition"—the practice of taking an evening meal was commonplace.[21]

In any case, after the "meal" is served to the saint, the Shin Upago paritta, should be recited. Unlike most paritta, which are usually verses taken from canonical sources, these potent formulae have been made up by various ritual specialists. They are in (sometimes corrupt) Pali; there are various versions of them, but, for the most part, they revolve around the theme of the saint's ability to subdue Māra. Here is one example:

> The Buddha, the Enlightened One, predicted: "Upagutta the Arhat will, in time to come, subjugate Māra and his army."
>
> The Buddha, the Enlightened One, predicted: "Upagutta the Arhat will subdue Māra and his impediments."
>
> May the great saint dispel all calamities, all without exception.
>
> May the great saint be here, poised on my head, and may he repel all misfortunes let loose by Māra.
>
> I now pay my respects to the powerful Reverend Upagutta with my head bowed down. May he grant us protection and repel all maladies.[22]

Upagupta Shells

In addition to such Upagupta images, a bewildering variety of other representations of the saint are kept by some Thais in their homes. These include, first of all, what might be called Upagupta shells. Closely related to Upagupta amulets but intended to be kept at home rather than worn on one's person, these are small (three centimeters long) metallic reproductions of conchlike seashells in the openings of which is seated a figure said to be Phra Uppakhut (see fig. 16). Sometimes he is holding a lotus flower, sometimes his head is covered with a lotus leaf, sometimes he has his hand in an alms bowl, sometimes only his face can be seen peering out from the inside of the shell. Depending on the alloy used in casting, these shells vary in color, and accordingly some are called "silver bronze," others "golden bronze," and still others "copper bronze."[23] Sometimes these figurines are portrayed as sitting not in shells, but in other aquatic surroundings—on the underside of turtles, in the corollas of flowers, or between the leaves of plants. Pierre Lefèvre-Pontalis gives several illustrations of these, calling them all "Phi-out-ta-krout" (Phī Uppakhut) and misunderstanding them, as well as the Upagupta shells, as representing malignant rather than benevolent spirits.[24] The common belief, however, is that if such shells or other Upagupta objects are kept at home, immersed in water as though they were under the sea, they will bring as much good luck as Sīvalī.

Thai folklore contains a number of stories about supernatural beings who

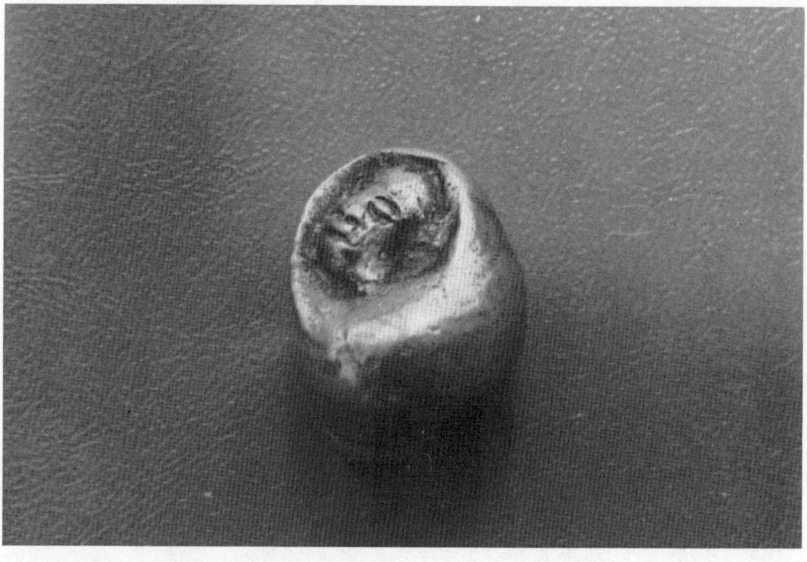

Fig. 16. Upagupta Shell, Private Collection

hid in seashells,[25] and we have already examined the Palaung myth of White Water Snail. Iconographically, however, these Upagupta shells might be said to fall somewhere in between the stones used in the ritual invitations of Upagupta and the full anthropomorphic images (generally Burmese) of Upagupta looking up at the sky and sitting in his brazen pavilion. The common element that holds all of these representations together, of course, is their situation in water. Like the stones on the riverbed, and like Upagupta in his underwater palace, the shells lie at the bottom of a tank. There is a further sense, however, in all of these representations: that Upagupta is a saint who is somehow hidden, but hidden nearby, ready to emerge when needed. This is a theme of some importance, for it reinforces the fact that Upagupta is a figure who may be mysterious and couched in esoterism, but who is in no way otiose.[26]

Phra Bua Khem

The Upagupta figures in the shells are often referred to by the name of another Thai Buddhist saint: Phra Bua Khem, or, more fully, "Phra Bua Khem in the Māra-subduing avatar."[27] This identification is significant, for in other, fuller iconographic forms Phra Bua Khem is sometimes—much like Uppakhut—revered by Thai people in their homes, where he, too, is thought to have protective powers. Indeed, stereotyped stories proving his effectiveness are also told: "Once there was a major fire in a town and all the houses were burnt to the ground, all except that in which they regularly made offerings to the statue of Phra Bua Khem."[28]

The confusion between Bua Khem and Uppakhut would appear to be especially prevalent in Central Thailand, where the Northern Thai and Laotian rituals we described in chapter 12 are virtually unknown. Thus, at the amulet market in Bangkok, the names Phra Bua Khem and Phra Uppakhut seem to be used interchangeably, not only for Upagupta shells, but for Upagupta medallions, for small images of saints looking up in the air, and for other figurines as well. A leading authority on Thai folklore, in fact, has gone so far as to equate the two saints.[29]

Even in Northern Thailand, there may be a great deal of confusion on this matter. A senior monk at Wat Chedi Luang in Chiang Mai assured me, for instance, that the two saints are one and the same; it is just that they have different forms![30] Part of the mix-up, obviously, rests in the fact that both figures are associated with water and that both are thought to have great magical powers. In homes, statuettes said to be Phra Bua Khem by some and Phra Uppakhut by others are likely to be kept in basins of water, either on a small "island," such as an overturned dish, or with their bases actually immersed. On the bottom sides of these images, one often finds depictions of fish, lotuses, and/or seashells, and it is argued that all of these things should properly be kept wet, in their natural habitat. At the same time, of course, these symbols can be related to myths about Upagupta's birth or to the Upagupta shells we have just described. Phra Bua Khem's name further recalls this aquatic imagery by associating him with the lotus (bua).

Nevertheless, it is possible—and necessary for the sake of clarity—to make certain distinctions between these two saints. In order to do so while still recognizing the genuine fluidity of the traditions about them in the minds of many informants, I shall, in what follows, speak of Phra Uppakhut/Bua Khem, when referring to images which I think are generally identified as Uppakhut by a majority of informants; and of Phra Bua Khem/Uppakhut when referring to images which seem to be chiefly thought of as Bua Khem.

Images of Phra Uppakhut/Bua Khem we have already touched upon. These statues are the ones that show the saint in his characteristic "Burmese" posture of looking up in the air while holding his hand in his bowl on his lap. As we have seen, they are far more common in Burma than in Thailand or Laos. In fact, Northern Thais who have such images in their homes usually admit that they came from Burma, and they sometimes call them "Burmese Uppakhuts."

On the other hand, statues of Phra Bua Khem/Uppakhut, while of roughly the same size as those of Phra Uppakhut/Bua Khem, are usually found in the earth-touching (bhumisparśa) mudra signalling the defeat of Māra. They are further distinguished by an iconographic particularity which is reflected in their name: the needlelike protuberances (*khem* means "needle") that are supposed to be imbedded in the image.[31] These figures, it should be specified, are usually made of compounded materials—scented wood powders, the seeds and petals of certain flowers, crumbled old palm-leaf manuscripts, dead leaves and twigs of Bodhi trees—mixed together with gum or resin. Before this compound sets, five or sometimes nine khems—tiny metal tubes about a centimeter long—are inserted, usually one in the forehead (at the point of the ūrṇā), two at the shoulders, and two at the knees.[32] After the image is lacquered or gilded, the khems can still be seen as small protuberances at these points. These are said to be the lakkhana (characteristic bodily marks) of Bua Khem/Uppakhut. They are thought to impart great magical powers to the image and to strengthen in particular the saint's sensory perceptions (such as the divine eye and divine ear). One informant added that the khems served to reinforce the image's powers of mettā (loving-kindness), whose primary function, it was understood, was to protect against threatening forces.[33]

The khems are not visible on all Bua Khem/Uppakhut images; but, whether they are or not, statues of this saint may be found in one of two forms: as a figure wearing a lotus-leaf hat (which further emphasizes its connection with water) or as a figure which is more or less faceless, because its brow, eyes, nose, ears, and mouth are masked by what is said to be a piece of cloth (part of the statue) pulled down over its head (see fig. 17). Two explanations are usually given for this curious facelessness.

The first is that the covering of all facial features with the robe—that is, the

Fig. 17. Phra Bua Khem/Uppakhut with Face Masked, Wat Chedi Luang, Chiang Mai, Thailand

closing of eyes, ears, nose, and mouth—is symbolic of the state of samādhi. Simply put, it means Phra Bua Khem/Uppakhut is in a meditative trance.[34] One informant, who appeared knowledgeable on this subject, added that this was the way the saint closed himself off for meditation underwater.[35] One can readily see here the connections with the myth of Upagupta, who, as we know, is also thought to spend most of his time at the bottom of the sea in a meditative trance.

The second explanation for Phra Bua Khem/Uppakhut's cloth-covered face is a ritual-devotional one. Long ago, it is claimed, villagers worshipping him covered his images with so much gold leaf that his face and other features were obliterated. Nowadays, nobody can remember what he looked like, and so he is portrayed in this fashion.[36]

Much the same story is told in Burma and in parts of Northern Thailand about yet another saintly image, that of Phra Pong Ta U, whose chief center of worship is in the Shan States at Inle Lake. Images of Pong Ta U, which generally come in sets of six or five, are supposed to represent the Buddha surrounded by his first five disciples at the time of his first sermon in the deer park in Sarnath,[37] but, in fact, there is hardly any anthropomorphism left in these images. So covered are they by gold leaf that they are even more featureless than the faceless Phra Bua Khem/Uppakhut; they might best be described as amorphous gilded globules. Yet their connections with Phra Bua Khem/Uppakhut are clear: the original Pong Ta U image is said to have been made from the prow of a great king's magical barge, and in Burma today such images are taken on rafts at festival time and worshipped successively at different villages along the shore. Moreover, like Upagupta, Pong Ta U is said to have the power to make or to prevent rain; and, similarly, his veneration is credited with the magical protection of sites: I was assured by a Burmese monk in Mae Hong Son that during the Second World War, no bombs fell on towns in Burma that honored Pong Ta U.[38]

Upagupta Associations

We have so far, in this chapter, been considering a variety of Upagupta images in both Northern Thailand and Burma that are the focus of individual or family rites, whether the images remain at home on household altars, are carried on one's person, or are set up in special shrines. It may happen, however, that devotees, wishing to share their enthusiasm and practice, band together to form an organized group dedicated to the worship of the saint. Such associations vary greatly in their purposes; some are specifically focussed on Upagupta, while others are simply in the habit of invoking his aid in pursuing other goals (such as meditation). There is also a good deal of variety in the degree of organization of such groups; some of them are rather loose associations of persons of a particular community, while others are established societies with clear-cut expectations for members.

All such groupings, however, are associations of laypersons, whose attention to and veneration of Upagupta are carried on outside of the context of Buddhist monastic establishments and outside of the framework of regular communal festivals. Many of the groups, moreover, are involved in the practice of meditation. This is significant, for it reflects an additional dimension of the private cult of Upagupta in Southeast Asia: he is called on not only to guard against Māra and to be a great field of merit, but also to assist devotees in their spiritual endeavors. In this, perhaps, we have an echo, a distant recognition, of his qualities as a teacher (see chapter 6) and of the fact that one of his epithets in India was that he was the "foremost of those disciples who are instructors in meditation."

There is nothing particularly new about such devotional-meditation groups. Maung Kin, writing in 1903, mentions one association "founded some twenty years ago at Akyab in Arakan, and now possessing many adherents in Moulmein, Rangoon, and other parts of Burma."[39] Its main purpose seems to have been the practice of a particular kind of śamatha meditation in which Upagupta was supposed to be of some support. It met regularly in the homes of members, and all sessions began with the invocation "Upagutta-mahātherena Mābadana Hari," which Maung Kin compares to "the mystic mantras of the Tibetans" and says is interpreted by members of the group as meaning "O Upagutta, Great Thera, bind for us Māra, and shew us the Way to Nibbāṇa."[40] In what follows, I would like to describe three somewhat similar but more contemporary associations of Upagupta devotees—two in Burma and one in Northern Thailand.

The first of these is an organization of lay meditators that meets in a small shrine on the northeast side of the main terrace of the Shwe Dagon pagoda in Rangoon. The hall is especially designed for meditators, who can come and sit there singly or together in front of several altars, one of which features an image of Shin Upago. This statue is somewhat unusual in that, unlike most depictions of the saint, it portrays him not with his hand in his bowl, but with it raised halfway to his mouth and holding a rather large lump of food. Once every three years, the meditation group sponsors the floating of this image and then replaces it with another. In the meantime, they invoke his aid in their meditational endeavors, as well as for more material benefits.

The involvement of this group with the saint is further emphasized by the fact that its building stands very near a votive pillar about thirty feet in height, on the top of which is a larger and more standard image of Upagupta sitting in a small pavilion. This undoubtedly is one of the most unusual votive pillars on the whole of the Shwe Dagon terrace. According to the lay leader of the meditation group, it was built around 1953. The donor had intended to erect an ordinary votive pillar, but one night had been told in a dream to put an image of Shin Upago on top of it. As a result, the niches around the bottom of the obelisk which had been intended for Buddha images now stand empty, as it would not do to have the Buddha in a position inferior to that of the arhat. This expression of piety, however, is in contrast to the most striking thing about the image on top of the pillar, namely, that it "faces away from the Buddha," that it has its back turned to the main spire of the Shwe Dagon. The lay leader who pointed it out to me gave no explanation for this almost-blasphemous posture (except that it was also a result of the donor's dream); but, once again, we might have here an example of Upagupta's ambiguous relationship to the Blessed One and of the theme that he is one who has never seen the Buddha.[41]

The second group of Upagupta enthusiasts I want to describe is associated with a pagoda in a suburban neighborhood about seven miles northeast of Rangoon. There, a self-styled Shin Upago Committee, headed by a number of nationally prominent and well-to-do laypersons, annually organizes a great merit-making and money-raising tour in which a large statue of the saint is taken to spend a day or two at the homes of various members of the group in

Rangoon. The first time this was done, in 1981, the "tour" lasted eighty-one days, and the image visited no fewer than sixty-three homes.[42]

The committee has printed up a formal "Rules and Regulations of the Association" instructing members on their duties as potential hosts. On the day they are to receive the image in their home, they are to prepare, by 7:00 A.M., special altars and offering tables for it. They must also arrange for the transportation of the image (by car) from the previous host family's house. If they cannot do so, they must ask the committee ahead of time to make alternate arrangements. They should fly the Buddhist flag in front of their home. The image should arrive by 9:00 A.M. As soon as it comes, it should be installed on the altar, and the family should light candles for it and make offerings of an umbrella, a fan, and other paraphernalia of a monk. Also, they should offer several trays bearing nine kinds of fruits and nine kinds of flowers—one tray for the Buddha, one tray for Shin Upago, and one tray for each member of the host family. They should serve Shin Upago breakfast and a midday meal, taking care that both be strictly vegetarian. They should receive guests wishing to pay their respects to the image from 4:00 P.M. to 9:00 P.M., at which time they should start the prayers and recite the paritta texts that are printed on an accompanying leaflet. The following day, they should be ready to give the image over to the next host family.[43]

The prayers and paritta prescribed by this association are not unlike others we have examined. Written in a mixture of Pali and Burmese, they recount the prediction that the Buddha made about Upagupta (that he would be "a victor over King Māra"), and they call upon the saint to extend his "protection from all kinds of danger, from the evils of government, fire, thieves, storms, ill-wishers, and from the sixteen types of anxiety and disease." In addition, however, they invoke the saint's help in developing in the devotee the powers of mettā (loving-kindness), meditation on which forms one of the practices of the group.[44]

Mettā also forms part of the practice of a third group of Upagupta devotees, a group composed of a number of laypersons connected with one of the major wats of Mae Sariang in Northern Thailand. There, the meditation on loving-kindness is advocated not only as a way to develop a positive attitude towards others and as a defensive technique for warding off wild animals and spirits, but also as something which, if practiced regularly by laypeople, will result in long life, health, good fortune, and, after death, heaven and/or Nirvāṇa.[45] More significantly for our purposes, however, its practice is also highlighted in an annual festival held by lay members of the wat involving the home worship of their monastery's image of Phra Uppakhut, as well as of one of its Buddha statues.

The ceremony was described to me by the abbot of the wat, who advertised it as "something you won't find in Chiang Mai." It begins with a complex method of selecting the households which are to "host" the images of Phra

Uppakhut and the Buddha. Two sets of cards are placed in two separate bowls. On one set are written the names of all the monks and novices in the wat; in the other set, two cards are inscribed with the names of Uppakhut and the Buddha, while the others are left blank. Laypersons draw from the first bowl the name of a cleric. Monks and novices draw from the second bowl; one of them gets the card "Uppakhut" and another gets the card "the Buddha." The two statues are then taken to the homes of the two laypersons who drew the names of the two clerics who got the cards marked "Uppakhut" and "the Buddha."[46] As in the *Lokapaññatti* tale of Aśoka's invitation of the saint, access to Upagupta here is only through the Sangha.

The lucky winners are then expected to host their respective images for three days and two nights, arranging for their worship and for the entertainment of all devotees who come to make offerings. On the third day, the two images are brought together again, being taken in procession back to the wat. That night, devotees go down to the river and make food offerings to Uppakhut (bananas, sweets, etc.), which they place on a small offering raft that is set adrift. According to the abbot, this is thought to be a type of exorcism, a way of "getting rid of the bad." Then everyone retires to the wat; there they practice the meditation on mettā, which is thought to be a way of "bringing in the good."[47]

Wat Uppakhut

Finally, in addition to these various lay associations, mention should be made here of one Thai monastery that is particularly connected to the worship of Upagupta. This is Wat Uppakhut, located in the heart of downtown Chiang Mai.

According to its abbot, the present site of Wat Uppakhut used to be a cremation ground. In those days, monks would come there to perform meditations on impurity, and eventually some people built a shelter for them nearby on the site of what is now the Buddhist Association lecture hall. By and by, that shelter came to be called Wat Uppakhut. When the Burmese ruled over the Northern Thai,[48] however, some Burmese monks came to live there, and the Northern Thai monks were forced to move over onto the old cremation ground. Thereafter, people said there were two Wat Uppakhuts—a Thai one and a Burmese one. But now there is only one, and the old Burmese wat has been replaced by the Buddhist Association lecture hall.[49]

Today, there are fourteen monks resident at Wat Uppakhut, but the place is most famous as the locale for elaborate Chinese funerals. These are held in a building just off the front courtyard, which itself is rented out as a car park. About thirty years ago, the abbot decided to have a statue of Phra Uppakhut made. People were always asking what the wat's namesake saint looked like, and he felt it would be helpful for them to be able to see for themselves. Also,

Fig. 18. Upagupta Image at Wat Uppakhut,
Chiang Mai, Thailand

he needed a place where the Chinese could easily come to shake their divination sticks. He originally wanted to put the image in an open shrine on the sidewalk out in front of the wat, but there was no room on the busy street, so he had it installed inside the compound.

According to the abbot, Wat Uppakhut's image is the only one of its kind in Thailand, and it is indeed anomalous. It shows the saint not looking up in the air, but in the act of getting ready to bind Māra (see fig. 18). He is supposed to be either still in meditation or just awakening from it; he is seated cross-legged and his left hand is in his lap, but his right hand is raised. He holds in it the end of his monastic belt, which he will use to tie Māra to the mountain. This intriguing depiction was the result of community consensus. When he decided to have the image made, the abbot asked the old laypeople of the wat what Uppakhut looked like. Some thought he looked like the Buddha, others said he was more like Maudgalyāyana or Śāriputra; but still others knew the Uppakhut legend, and that, in the end, determined what they agreed to depict.

Today, this almost life-size image sits on a high altar-throne in an open three-sided pavilion to the rear of the main hall of the wat, not far from the shrine for the guardian phī of the locality. The statue has been much garlanded with flower chains and haphazardly plastered with gold leaf by devotees. In front of the statue, but not part of it, sits an alms bowl with the name "Phra Uppakhut" written on it. On the altar to one side of the image, someone has placed a small statue of Khrūba Sīwichai, a famous Northern Thai saint.[50] On the wall is a sign reading, "The kuṭī of the Elder, the luang phau Uppakhut."[51]

Devotees applying gold leaf appear to have paid particular attention to the monastic belt in Uppakhut's right hand—the item which most clearly symbolizes the saint's protective powers. On the wall to the left of the image, however, a handwritten notice reminds the devotee of the saint's role as a provider: "You are invited," it proclaims, "to bow to ask for anything that is good from Luang phau Uppakhut. This old image has been here a long time, so this place is called Wat Uppakhut." And underneath that are two quotes: "A person who does not try for something he wants will never know. . . ." and "Have good luck wherever you travel." On the floor in front of the altar is a large covered water jar with a small cup provided for the benefit of worshippers who wish to transfer merit. Nearby there are also two divination-stick shakers and a board with printed fortunes numbered to correspond to the divination sticks. Near the entrance, an old gasoline can painted bright red with a slot in it is ready to receive cash contributions to pay for the shrine's upkeep.

All told, this appears to be a fairly well maintained and frequented shrine which is obviously used now for many purposes. Syncretism and innovation are clearly at work here, combining an unusual iconography and calling on the practices of merit making, private divination, asking for special boons and protection, and general respect for saintly Thai monks.

We have, in these last two chapters, examined a bewildering variety of ritual and iconographic traditions involving Upagupta. Though these may operate at different levels (communal, personal, and domestic) and focus on different representations of the saint, it is nevertheless possible to distinguish in them certain continuities of theme.

Upagupta may primarily be thought of as a saint who is protective of merit makers and productive of merit. He acts especially as a guardian against Māra, who himself may be thought of as taking on different forms (rain, drunks, thieves). Clearly, all of these characteristics are part of the Southeast Asian cult's inheritance from India and from the *Lokapaññatti*, and they are most evident in the invitation of Uppakhut to come to communal festivals at Buddhist monasteries. Yet, to some extent, the same desire for protection also governs his worship in private households and his cult in the form of amulets worn on one's person.

As a producer of merit, Upagupta is also able, more positively, to speed up karmic rewards for the offerings made to him and to bring his devotees tangible benefits in this very lifetime. In this, he would seem to be most effective when he appears and receives offerings in person. Generally, he may be called upon to bring long life, good health, and other boons, but especially wealth and worldly success. At the same time, he may assist devotees in their practice of mettā and other forms of meditation, so as to increase both their spiritual achievements and their mental and magical powers.

Much of Upagupta's own power lies in the fact that he is an arhat who has *not* "gone beyond." This is something that is emphasized in his legend and in the stories about his appearances, but it is also found in his iconography. His residence in the depths of the water or on board a raft reflects the notion that, like a bodhisattva or a lo-han, he has crossed over the stream or ocean of saṃsāra while still remaining in it. The same theme may be detected, perhaps, in some of the other iconographic depictions of him that we have examined in this chapter. The Upagupta shells and the association with Phra Bua Khem and with lotuses show him as having emerged from the waters, yet still connected to them—a representation that also reflects the Southeast Asian legends of his descent from a nāgī or a fish.

Conspectus and Conclusion

One of the benefits of the study of sacred biography is the multiplicity of themes that are often brought to life in the focus on the figure of a single saint. Hagiographies intersect not only with each other, but with a host of different contexts—social, doctrinal, mythic, cultic, artistic, and literary—and these all inform the world of meaning of those who worship a saint and listen to or tell stories about him or her.

If I may transform the image of a Buddhist act of merit into a metaphor, I have, in this study of the traditions about Upagupta, sought to free a multiplicity of birds from one cage, to release many fish in one pond. It is not my purpose to recapture all of these birds and fishes in this conclusion, but it might be useful to start by recapitulating some of our findings. In Part One, we focussed on the Mathuran cycle of stories dealing with Upagupta. We first examined, in chapter 1, the prediction that the Buddha made about him, and we saw how it not only set the major themes for the saint's own life at Mathurā, but also addressed right away a crucial post-parinirvāṇa problem: what happens to Buddhism in the absence of its departed Master? In chapter 2, we touched on the karmic antecedents to Upagupta's career by examining various accounts of his previous lives in Mathurā and elsewhere. By raising the issue of his relationship to the future Buddha Maitreya, we also suggested that one further aspect of the post-parinirvāṇa problem is that Upagupta—and, indeed, all present-day Buddhists—find themselves in a liminal situation, caught between two Buddhas: too late to have seen Gautama and too early to meet Maitreya. In chapter 3, we examined Upagupta's connections to the tradition of the Masters of the Dharma, and we saw how that lineage—especially the figure of Mahākāśyapa—also represents one attempt at dealing with this liminal situation. At the same time, we noted connections between the Masters of the Dharma themselves and the tradition of forest-dwelling meditating monks. In chapter 4, we returned to Mathurā to continue tracing Upagupta's career there, a career which bridged both lay and monastic life and in which the event of ordination, interpreted as a ritualized realization of the end of death and rebirth, played a crucial role in accelerating his attainment of arhatship.

In chapter 5, we focussed on one of the major events in Upagupta's life: his dealings with Māra. We noted how his binding of Māra with corpses had certain affinities with the ritual of ordination, and we highlighted the importance of bhakti both in Māra's change of heart and in Upagupta's own emotions. Then we examined the story of Upagupta's veneration of Māra in the guise of the Buddha and saw it as a paradigm of present-day image worship, a practice which we interpreted, in turn, as a ritual realization of the truth of impermanence. In chapter 6, we recounted stories of Upagupta's dealings with his own disciples, and we examined traditions about his death and about the veneration of him at Mount Urumuṇḍa, interpreting the main feature of this cult—the tossing of a śalākā into his cave—as a testimonial to his powers in controlling Māra and the forces of evil. Finally, in chapter 7, we turned to various aspects of Upagupta's relationship with King Aśoka, and in this we found ourselves looking ahead to later traditions that were to evolve in Southeast Asia.

In Part Two, we moved to a consideration of these Southeast Asian materials, examining first, in chapter 8, the Burmese and Thai context of Theravāda orthodoxy into which Upagupta's legend and cult came to fit. In chapter 9, we considered the legend of the saint as it was established in the *Lokapaññatti*, relating the legend to ritual traditions when appropriate and highlighting Upagupta's role as a protector of Buddhist festivals. In chapter 10, we looked at some of the Southeast Asian mythic elaborations on the tradition of Upagupta's residence in the midst of the waters, and we saw how these were connected to the theme of his being a son of the Buddha. In chapter 11, we traced his relationship to other arhat cults as these originated in India and developed in Burma. Finally, in chapters 12 and 13, we turned more specifically to an examination of the different cults of Upagupta in Southeast Asia, seeing various transformations of his role as protector against Māra and a new emphasis on his abilities as a provider of material benefits in this day and age.

Obviously, there is no single conclusion to be reached from all of this, but it is possible to isolate a few significant, interrelated themes. In shorthand fashion, these might be summarized as (1) Māra, (2) bhakti, (3) ordination, (4) nāga, and (5) water.

(1) In both India and Southeast Asia, the taming of Māra is Upagupta's most famous act. We have seen it highlighted in his career at Mathurā; we have read it into his role as a narrator of avadāna texts; we have found it in the Pali grammars; we have seen it featured in the battle scenes of the *Lokapaññatti*; and we have noted it in the Thai and Burmese ritual traditions of inviting Upagupta to come to one's festival, or one's home, to prevent the rain from falling or fights from occurring.

Insofar as Māra represents the forces of saṃsāra, of life and death, the message here is clear: Upagupta helps keep those forces at bay. He does in this day and age what the Buddha did in former times. Thus, the taming of Māra is closely connected to the theme of the continuing effectiveness of the Buddha. Simply put, when Upagupta is present, Māra is tamed; when Māra is tamed, the Buddha is present. Conversely, when Upagupta is absent, Māra is abroad; when Māra is abroad, the Buddha is not present. This logic, perhaps more than anything, helps explain the curious confusions we have seen throughout this book between Upagupta and the Buddha—but it also raises directly the basic question of the nature of final Nirvāṇa. What does it mean to say the Buddha is present when by definition he is not?

A popular understanding of the Sarvāstivādin system, we have seen, enables us to say that he is somehow "present," that is, that he can be cognized as existing, in the past. This argument no doubt is debatable, and perhaps ultimately philosophically untenable; but it is the solution assumed by the literature we are dealing with, and it carries with it an important corollary: Upagupta's taming of Māra does not so much make the Buddha "present" as it makes us "past." With his mastery over time (in which he resembles Rāhu), Upagupta enables us to see past and future dharmas. The vision of the Buddha that is explicit or assumed in Buddhist festivals of all sorts thus involves a pilgrimage into former times, a recapturing or visualizing of the Blessed One's past glory. But, like all such pilgrimages, this journey is not complete without a return to the present; and with this return comes a renewed realization of the Buddha's absence, of the truth of impermanence, non-self, and suffering. Upagupta thus must be dismissed at the end of the festival, Māra must be released, the Buddha must be let go. Were they not, we would continue to exist only in the past.

(2) The same dynamic process also characterizes the worship of the Buddha image. In one fashion or another, the realization of the past presence of the Buddha in an object of devotion is ritually coupled to a realization of his present absence. In this sense, all image worship in Buddhism takes as its model the pattern that was eventually to become established in Tantric visualizations, where the evocation of a Buddha or bodhisattva or other deity is always followed by its eventual "deconstruction." The same paradigm, perhaps, may be found in Buddhist pilgrimage, where the devotee retraces the whole of the life of the Buddha but terminates with his parinirvāṇa and his relics. And the same demand helps explain why representations of Upagupta in Southeast Asia are not kept permanently present; at festivals in Thailand and Laos, he is fetched from the river or swamp, but then returned to it; and at shrines and pagodas and homes in Burma, he is venerated for a while, but then sent on his way, floating downstream.

What this implies is that bhakti in Buddhism, whether directed towards a Buddha or an arhat, is closely linked to the realization of the Dharma. Far from being a concession to the emotional needs of the masses or a deviation from monastic norms brought about by the demands of the laity, Buddha bhakti is a powerful way in which to come to an understanding of the truth of impermanence.

(3) It is not the only way, however. Other forms of meditation were also advocated by Upagupta and by the tradition that he represents; and, in chapter 6, we saw some of these being followed by the forest monks who became his

disciples at the Naṭabhaṭika on Mount Urumuṇḍa. Moreover, as we argued, the event of ordination itself can have soteriological effects, speeding up one's final liberation from saṃsāra.

In several chapters of this book, we encountered the Buddhist ritual of higher ordination in a number of different contexts. We saw that the whole invitation of Upagupta from the river and the procession accompanying him to the wat had certain affinities with the preliminary parades in the upasampadā rite. We saw how that rite, related to the tradition of cemetery meditations, could lead to a realization of the end of rebirth and of death. We argued, in turn, that this could amount to a speeding up of the liberation process, a switch from a slow to a fast track, a transformation of a bodhisattva into an arhat, of a Maitreya into a Gautama.

Ordination, then, is significant not only as a ritual, but also for its symbolic associations and repercussions. Like all rites of passage, it accomplishes something; but it is also fraught with liminality. It is important to remember that in many parts of northern Southeast Asia, monkhood is not a permanent state; it is a stage in the lives of men. In Northern Thailand, at least, it is rare for anyone to remain in the Sangha forever. What this means is that ordination is almost always followed, at some point, by defrocking, the less ceremonial but equally important return to lay life. In this, we have a further parallel with the cult of Upagupta: his being brought from the river represents his upasampadā, and his return to the water—less emphasized, though just as significant—is his defrocking.

(4) The same liminality may be found in the claim that Upagupta is a nāga. This association, we argued, is related first and foremost to the tradition of calling candidates for ordination nāgas. There has always been a fundamental paradox, however, in this use of the word. In the Vinaya legend, the nāga who became a monk was made to defrock when it was discovered that he was a nāga. To remain a monk, therefore, a candidate for ordination (nāga) has to cease being a nāga.

This scenario makes sense in terms of the transformative effectiveness of ordination as a rite of passage, and it may also be applied to the ritual invitations of Upagupta. As a resident of the waters (river, pond, or ocean), Upagupta is also associated with the nāgas; but when he is asked to come to protect a festival, he emerges from the waters and leaves behind his nāga connections. By the time he takes up residence in his miniature vihāra, he has fully become a monk, and more: he is an ideal member of the Sangha, an arhat, a Buddha. The same sequence of events may be found in the Indian legend meticulously describing Aśoka's welcome of the elder at the riverside, as well as in the Burmese film describing his emergence as a fully grown bhikkhu from the pond where he is dunked as a boy. In all of these instances, however, Upagupta eventually returns to the water, where he regains his domicile among the nāgas.

(5) This theme of Upagupta's temporary emergence from the waters is an important one, for it is found in several other dimensions of his cult and legend. The Southeast Asian legends of his birth from the princess who smelled like a fish and of his eventual residence on a raft in the midst of the waters (whence he occasionally pays visits to this world, as a monk, still dripping wet) reflect this theme. So, too, does the iconographic tradition of representing him as a seashell or some other aquatic figure. The tradition that portrays him as residing in a magically maintained palace in the depths of the sea clearly shows him as able, while residing in the waters, to hold the waters at bay; and the same skill may be reflected in his reputation in Burma and Thailand as one who can keep the rain from falling, even in the midst of the monsoon.

In the history of religions, of course, the waters are broadly symbolic of the forces of chaos and death which need to be parted and contained. More specifically in a Buddhist context, the waters are associated with the sea of saṃsāra in which we are all submerged. And here their symbolic relation to Upagupta becomes clear: as an arhat who has put off parinirvāṇa for the sake of the Buddha Dharma, he has mastered the waters of saṃsāra, though he still dwells in their midst. Like a bodhisattva, he has emerged from this world, only to remain in it; and, like Rāhula (the Buddha's son, whom he resembles), he has crossed over the stream of life and death, only to return from the other side.

If there is anything that holds all of these themes together, it is perhaps this: that the presence of Upagupta forms, for a given time and place—for the duration of a festival, for the length of a text, in the confines of a home or a monastery—a sort of protective cocoon in the midst of saṃsāra, in which the forces of chaos are kept at bay and the truth and reality of the Buddha, the Dharma, and the Sangha can shine forth unimpeded. We began this book by seeing that this is what the Buddha predicted Upagupta would do, long ago at Mathurā; and it is perhaps fitting that we end it with the same note.

Notes

PREFACE

1. Finot 1917:41–60.
2. Ibid., pp. 61–174.
3. Hawley 1987:xi.
4. See, for example, the works of Wendy Doniger (O'Flaherty) and her statement that "stories reveal things that are not easily gleaned from the harder disciplines" (1988: 2).
5. See Reynolds and Capps 1976; Hawley 1987; Kieckhefer and Bond 1988; and Granoff and Shinohara 1988.
6. Bastide (1965:2).
7. The term *Hīnayāna*, meaning the "Lesser Vehicle [of Buddhism]," is generally thought to be pejorative, in contrast to *Mahāyāna* (the "Greater Vehicle"). For lack of a good substitute, however, I continue to use it, though with no derogatory intent.
8. See Mus 1928, 1935, and 1939.

INTRODUCTION

1. On forest-dwelling as opposed to town-dwelling monks, see chapter 3.
2. In *AbhK.*, p. 71 (Fr. trans. of Chinese, La Vallée Poussin 1923–31, 1:205; Eng. trans., Pruden 1988:226), reference is made to Upagupta's *Netrīpada śāstra.*
3. *T.* 2087, 51:890b (Eng. trans., Beal [1884] 1968, 1:181–82).
4. See, for example, Tambiah 1970:168–78; Davis 1984:223–36; Maung Kin 1903:219–42; Archaimbault 1966:32n.26; and Condominas 1973:82–83.
5. See, for example, Przyluski 1923a; Waddell 1897; Dutt and Bajpai 1956:257–66; Yamazaki 1975; and Yamazaki 1979:187–211.
6. The only Pali text of any antiquity in which the story of Upagupta is told is the eleventh- to twelfth-century *LP.* (see chapter 9). There is also a passing reference to Upagupta in the preface to the Siamese edition of the *Mil.*, where it is stated that the Buddha made a prediction about Nāgasena and Milinda "just as, long ago, he made a prediction about the elders Moggaliputta Tissa and Upagutta" (see Yamazaki 1979: 200). A similar sentence is found in the Pali Text Society edition of the *Mil.*, but without any mention of Upagupta, while the Chinese version of the text omits any reference to either Upagupta or Moggaliputta Tissa. Yamazaki (ibid.) concludes that the Siamese edition's reference to Upagupta must have been added in Southeast Asia. There is, furthermore, a reference to an elder named Upalagutta in *PJāt.* (2:474) who, Jaini speculates, might possibly be related to "the celebrated Sthavira Upagupta" (*PJāt.* 2:xxxiv–v).
7. On this tradition, see Ray 1936:19–39; and Guillon 1985:24–26.
8. *GilgMss.* 3, pt. 1:14–15. See also Jaini 1989:21; and Dutt and Bajpai 1956:261.

Much the same list of drawbacks of the city may be found in *A.* 3:256–57 (Eng. trans., Woodward and Hare 1932–36, 3:188).

9. *M.* 2:83–90 (Eng. trans., Horner 1954–59, 2:278). See also *A.* 1:67 (Eng. trans., Woodward and Hare 1932–36, 1:62). The *MSV.* (*GilgMss.* 2:35–36) also recounts two cures effectuated in Mathurā by the Buddha's lay disciple, the physician Jīvaka.

10. *GilgMss.* 3, pt. 1:8–14.

11. *GilgMss.* 3, pt. 1:16–17. See also Jaini 1989:218–19.

12. Hofinger 1946:191. According to *T.* 1545, 27:510c (Fr. trans., Lamotte 1958:304), Mahādeva, the propounder of the Five Theses on arhats that may or may not have been the cause of the Council of Vaiśālī, was a native of Mathurā. See also Demiéville 1931–32:33.

13. See Lamotte 1949–80, 3:xvii.

14. In *AbhK.*, p. 71 (Fr. trans. of Chinese, La Vallée Poussin 1923–31, 1:205; Eng. trans., Pruden 1988:226), the elder Upagupta's *Netrīpada śāstra* is quoted as asserting the view that the Tathāgata attains first the trance of cessation (nirodha samāpatti) and then the knowledge of decay (kṣayajñāna). This is said to be the position of "Western" Sarvāstivādins, the Paścātyas (on whom see Pruden 1988:344n.235), and it is denied by the Vaibhāṣikas of Kashmir. On this debate, see also Lin 1949:14n.1. The *Netrīpada* is also apparently quoted in a nonorthodox Pali text, the *Vimuttimagga* (see Ehara, Soma, and Kheminda 1977:166).

15. Bareau 1955:36. For a useful summary of the relevant epigraphical evidence in Lüders 1961, see Jaini 1989:215n.

16. On early-second-century inscriptional evidence for the cult of Amitābha in Mathurā, see Huntington 1989:86; and Sharma 1989:313–14.

17. Legge 1886:12–14 (text), 42–47 (Eng. trans.).

18. On the Sarvāstivādin canon, see Lamotte 1949–80, 3:xiv–xxii; and Banerjee [1957] 1979. On the Abhidharma of the school, see Takakusu 1905; Frauwallner 1964:59–99; Frauwallner 1973; and, for further references, Nakamura 1980b:105–13.

19. The largest of these, the *Mahāvibhāṣā* (*T.* 1545; partial Fr. trans., La Vallée Poussin 1930–37), is a monumental commentary on the chief book of the Sarvāstivādin Abhidharma, the *Jñānaprasthāna*. Disagreeing with this basic Vaibhāṣika text on a number of points, but equally informative on Sarvāstivādin views, is the *Abhidharmakośa*, which itself spawned a number of commentaries. On the relationships among these and other texts, see Pruden 1988:xxxvi–lxi; Griffiths 1986:44–58; and Frauwallner 1971.

20. Bareau 1955:137–40.

21. This and what follows hardly do justice to the complexities of the Sarvāstivādin position. For further details and translations of relevant sources, see La Vallée Poussin 1925; La Vallée Poussin 1930–37:7–187 (esp. 128–34); and Stcherbatsky [1923] 1970:76–91. For recent helpful studies, see Williams 1981 and Kajiyama 1977.

22. La Vallée Poussin 1930–37:126–29.

23. For the positions of the four masters Dharmatrāta, Ghoṣaka, Vasumitra, and Buddhadeva, see ibid., pp. 89–92.

24. Ibid., p. 119.

25. *Kvu.* 1:115–43 (Eng. trans., Aung and Davids 1915:84–110). See also *KvuA.*, pp. 43–49 (Eng. trans., Law [1940] 1969:52–60).

26. Bareau 1955:132, 155.

27. For two opposing views, see Lamotte 1958:191–92; and Frauwallner 1956:24–41.

28. Bareau 1955:154.

29. A still-valuable survey of avadāna literature may be found in Winternitz 1933, 2:277–94. For a bibliographically rich analysis of the stories in the Tibetan *MSV*., see Panglung 1981.

30. The avadānas are part of the twelvefold (dvādaśānga) categorization of the Buddha's Teaching that originated with the Sarvāstivādins. They are not part of the ninefold (navānga) listing of the Pali texts. On this, see Thomas 1933.

31. *Div*., pp. 348–418. These two chapters form part of the four that together have come to be known as the *Aśokāvadāna*. A more recent edition of this same material may be found in *Aśokāv*., pp. 1–28, 75–93 (Eng. trans., Strong 1983b:173–97, 238–56; partial Fr. trans., Burnouf 1876:336–50). On the relationship of the *Div*. to the *MSV*., see Huber 1906 and Lévi 1908.

32. *Avś*., pp. 260–63 (Fr. trans., Feer 1891:430–35). For problems in dating the hundredth story of the text, see chapter 9.

33. *T*. 2042, 50:99a–131a (Fr. trans., Przyluski 1923a:225–427).

34. *T*. 2043, 50:131b–70a (partial Ger. trans. by Ernst Waldschmidt in Lüders 1926:77–83).

35. *T*. 99, 2:161b–70c (partial Fr. trans., Przyluski 1914:558–59).

36. *GilgMss*. 3, pt. 1:3–7; *T*. 1448, 24:41c–42b (Fr. trans., Przyluski 1914:518–22; partial Eng. trans. of Tibetan, Rockhill 1907:164–70); see also Panglung 1981:29.

37. For a summary of the debate which once raged over the titles and authorships of this work (or these works), see Tomomatsu 1931; for a more recent bibliography on the question, see de Jong 1979a:340.

38. *T*. 201, 4:307c–9b (Fr. trans., Huber 1908:263–73). See also Huber 1904:700–719.

39. *T*. 202, 4:442b–43c (Ger. trans. of Tibetan, Schmidt 1843, 2:382–91; Eng. trans. of Mongolian, Frye 1981:231–36). For an edition of the Tibetan text with Jap. trans. and Eng. notes, see Takahashi 1969:547–58.

40. On the composition of the *Hsien yü ching* and relations between the Chinese and Tibetan texts, see Takakusu 1901; Lévi 1925; and, for further bibliography, de Jong 1979a:98.

41. *T*. 2087, 51:890b–c, 937b (Eng. trans., Beal [1884] 1968, 1:181–82, 2:273). See also Watters [1904] 1961, 1:306, 2:91, 252.

42. *Avk*. 2:449–53. There is also a passing reference to Upagupta in chapter 73 (ibid., 2:456).

43. Chimpa and Chattopadhyaya [1970] 1980:34–44. See also Roerich [1949] 1976, 1:23–24.

44. See chapter 7.

45. See, for example, the anecdote in *T*. 1509, 25:129c (Fr. trans., Lamotte 1949–80, 1:572–73). See also the various lists that pause long enough in their enumerations of Buddhist patriarchs to provide some details about the life of each master. One that does so for Upagupta is *T*. 2058, 50:304cff. (Fr. summary, Maspero 1911:139–41; see also Edkins 1893:67–70). Other listings of patriarchs may be found in Lamotte 1958:772–73; and in McRae 1986:79–82. Also of note is *T*. 2145, 55:66c–67a (Fr. trans., Lin 1949:348n.6). Similarly, some Upagupta stories were picked up in various

Transmission of the Lamp histories of the Ch'an (Zen) school (see McRae 1986, ch. 4), and some have survived in Japanese anthologies of Buddhist tales, e.g., *Konjaku*, pp. 277–82; and *Uji shūi*, pp. 383–85 (Eng. trans., Mills 1970:396–97).

46. Przyluski 1923a:8.

47. *Avś.*, pp. 260–63 (Fr. trans., Feer 1891:430–35).

48. *T.* 202, 4:442b–43c (Ger. trans. of Tibetan, Schmidt 1843, 2:382–91; Eng. trans. of Mongolian, Frye 1981:547–58).

49. This is the case, for example, in the *Divyāvadāna.*

50. See chapter 6.

51. Or dharmabhāṇaka, according to Dantinne 1983:40–41n.

52. On this, see chapter 3.

53. On all of these comparisons, see chapter 7.

54. Luce 1964, 1:76, 376.

55. Ibid., p. 378; see also Luce and Ba Shin 1961:385; and Guillon 1985:75.

56. *Sdn.* 3:691.

57. Mason 1868:160. There is some dispute about Kaccāyana's date (see Norman 1983a:163).

58. *LP.*, 1:162–74 (Fr. trans., Denis 1977, 2:144–52). See also Duroiselle 1904.

59. On the parallels between the *LP.* and the *Lokaprajñapti* (*T.* 1644), see Denis 1977, 2:xix–xxviii, 253–88; and Mus 1939:126–27.

60. See chapter 9.

61. *LP.* 1:165 (Fr. trans., Denis 1977, 2:147).

62. Eng. trans., Reynolds and Reynolds 1982; Fr. trans., Coedès and Archaimbault 1973.

63. Kala 1960:80–91. I remain grateful to the late U Ko Ko for his help with these and the following Burmese sources.

64. A portion of this text has been translated in Pe Maung Tin and Luce [1923] 1960, but not the section on Upagupta.

65. *HmanNanY.*, pp. 163–64.

66. Kin 1957:109–20.

67. Kin 1981:793–808.

68. Ohn Maung 1973; Zagaru 1977; Min Kyi Hlaing 1986; Aung Myint 1983.

69. *PSK.*, pp. 522–56. In this work, the Upagupta story is called the Mārabandhana chapter. For a discussion of the work, see Coedès 1968b. There is also a modern work in Laotian on Upagupta which I have been unable to consult: Viravong 1966.

70. In the catalogue of Northern Thai palm-leaf manuscripts thus far microfilmed by scholars at Chiang Mai University, at least four are identified as dealing with Upagupta.

71. On these myths, see chapter 10.

72. Przyluski 1925:267.

73. Ibid., p. 281.

74. Ibid., p. 268.

75. Davis 1984:227.

76. Ibid., p. 229.

77. Tambiah 1970:170.

78. Ibid., p. 173.

79. Ibid., p. 171.

80. Ibid.

81. Ibid., p. 172.
82. Field notes, Chiang Mai, 4 March 1983.
83. Field notes, Rangoon, 16 October 1982.
84. On this tradition, see chapter 11.
85. For some of these stories, see chapter 13.

Chapter One
Provisions for the Buddha's Absence

1. *Div.*, pp. 348–49 (Eng. trans., Strong 1983b:174).
2. See *Avś.*, pp. 28, 73 (Fr. trans., Feer 1891:49, 109).
3. See *GilgMss.* 3, pt. 1:2; and *T.* 1448, 24:41b (Fr. trans., Przyluski 1914:517).
4. *Div.*, p. 348.
5. *T.* 99, 2:165b (Eng. trans., Soper 1949–50, pt. 1:276; Fr. trans., Przyluski 1914:558; Fr. trans., Lamotte 1949–80, 1:548n).
6. *T.* 2043, 50:135b, 149b (Eng. trans., Soper 1949–50, pt. 1:276; Fr. trans., Przyluski 1923a:246n; Fr. trans., Lamotte 1949–80, 1:548n).
7. *T.* 2042, 50:102b (Eng. trans., Soper 1949–50, pt. 1:276; Fr. trans., Przyluski 1923a:245–46; Fr. trans., Lamotte 1949–80, pt. 1:548n). Soper's "ox Nāga" reflects what may be an incomplete Chinese transliteration of Gopālanāga as "Gonāga."
8. On the journey to South India, see Lamotte 1949–80, 1:548. On that to Sri Lanka, see *Mhv.*, pp. 3–11 (Eng. trans., Geiger [1912] 1960:1–10). On various visits to sites in Burma, Thailand, and Laos, see Shorto 1970:16–17; Swearer 1976b:7–8; and Pruess 1976:177.
9. Lamotte 1966–74, 1:133–34.
10. *T.* 1448, 24:37c–39c (Fr. trans., Przyluski 1914:495–507). The Sanskrit texts of the conversions of the Brahmins of Hastināpura and of Śrughnā may be found in *Div.*, pp. 72–80.
11. Vajrapāṇi, the "thunderbolt-wielder," is a being who has close associations with the figure of Indra but is generally thought to be distinct from him. Scantily clad and robust, he is often portrayed as a sort of bodyguard or henchman of the Buddha. See Lamotte 1966–74; Foucher 1905–18, 2:48–69; and Sénart 1906.
12. *T.* 1448, 24:39c (Fr. trans., Przyluski 1914:507); *GilgMss.* 3, pt. 1:2. See also *T.* 1448, 24:41c (Fr. trans., Przyluski 1914:517).
13. On these two towns, see Lamotte 1947–50.
14. *GilgMss.* 3, pt. 1:2–3; *T.* 1448, 24:41c (Fr. trans., Przyluski 1914:517–18). From Mathurā, the Buddha goes on to Otalā, Vairambhā, and Ayudhya and eventually leaves the Northwest.
15. See Frauwallner 1956:31; and Przyluski 1923a:4.
16. This, to a large extent, is Lamotte's endeavor (see Lamotte 1966–74, 1:133–34). See also the proposed identifications in Lévi 1915a:35–40; and in Tucci 1958:285, 288, 325n.12, 327.
17. For depictions of this episode in art, see Foucher 1905–18, 1:544–54; Marshall 1960:51–52, pl. 69; and Facenna 1962, pl. 107.
18. For a listing of these, see Ch'en 1945–47:279–80. The story was not unknown in late Pali sources, e.g., *Thūpavaṃsa*, p. 233 (Eng. trans., Jayawickrama 1971:116).
19. *T.* 1507, 25:51c–52a (Fr. trans., Przyluski 1914:559–62). The story is also told

by Hsüan-tsang (*T.* 2087, 51:882b–c; Eng. trans., Watters [1904] 1961, 1:229) and by Fa-hsien (*T.* 2085, 51:858a; Eng. trans., Legge 1886:29).

20. *T.* 1448, 24:40b–c (Fr. trans., Przyluski 1914:510–12). It is interesting to contrast the centripetality of the events here with the centrifugality of the Buddha's chasing away of the yakṣas in his conquest of Sri Lanka. See *Mhv.*, p. 5 (Eng. trans., Geiger [1912] 1960:4).

21. See *T.* 1507, 25:51c–52a (Fr. trans., Przyluski 1914:559–62). See also Lamotte 1966–74, 1:132.

22. For a study of this famous episode, see Foucher 1917:147–84.

23. *T.* 202, 4:363a (Fr. trans., Lévi 1925:312); *T.* 211, 4:598c–99a (Fr. trans., Lamotte 1966–74, 1:122–24).

24. *T.* 1451, 24:332c (Fr. trans., Lamotte 1966–74, 1:125–26). See also the brief account of the storm recorded in Kṣemendra's *Avk.* (1:115), the edited text of which has been corrected by Lévi in Foucher 1917:175n.

25. *Div.*, pp. 163–64 (Fr. trans., Lamotte 1966–74, 1:125–26).

26. Lamotte 1966–74, 1:157.

27. Soper 1949–50, pt. 2:318. For a different approach to this whole question, see Bloss 1973.

28. On this myth, see O'Flaherty 1975:56–90.

29. Soper 1949–50, pt. 1:263–72.

30. Saṃsāra is often compared to a flood or stream that must be crossed in order to escape. On the simile of fire for this world of suffering, see Lamotte 1949–80, 2:934.

31. The *MSV.*'s lack of attention to this story is noteworthy and perhaps may be explained by its concentration instead on the nāga of Nandivardhana, whose tale may be found in *GilgMss.* 3, pt. 1:xvii (Fr. trans. of Chinese in Przyluski 1914:515).

32. *T.* 2087, 51:879a (Eng. trans., Watters [1904] 1961, 1:198).

33. *T.* 643, 15:679b–81b (Fr. trans., Przyluski 1914:565–68). The reconstructed Sanskrit title used here is not listed in Lancaster 1979, but is commonly found in discussions of this text.

34. *Avk.*, 2:338–40 (Eng. trans., M. Das 1894).

35. *T.* 2087, 51:879a (Eng. trans., Watters [1904] 1961, 1:198). The site of the cave, in present-day Afghanistan, has perhaps been identified (see Cospani 1945 and Foucher 1925:278).

36. In *Avk.* 2:338, Gopāla is said to dwell on a rocky hill near Hinguvardana, where he does harm to people, beasts, and crops.

37. *T.* 643, 15:679b–81a (Fr. trans., Przyluski 1914:565–67). In *Avk.* 2:338–39, the Buddha turns the hailstones into blossoms, and sylvan deities convince Gopāla to surrender.

38. *T.* 643, 15:681a (Fr. trans., Przyluski 1914:567–68).

39. *Avk.*, 2:339 (Fr. trans., Lévi 1915a:82).

40. *T.* 2087, 51:879a–b (Eng. trans., Beal [1884] 1968, 1:94).

41. *Div.*, pp. 547–49 (Ger. trans., Grünwedel 1924, 2:6–9). See also Ger. trans. of Tibetan in Nobel 1955:52–55.

42. *T.* 643, 15:681a (Fr. trans., Przyluski 1914:568).

43. Even the earliest Chinese pilgrims seem to have visited it (see Petech 1966–74, 1:179–80). On the other pilgrims' journeys there, see below and Soper 1949–50, pt. 1:273–74.

44. *T.* 2053, 50:229b–30a (Eng. trans., Li 1959:61–62).

45. Grousset 1971:102–3.

46. *T.* 2085, 51:859a (Eng. trans., Legge 1886:39).

47. *T.* 2092, 51:1021c–22a (Eng. trans., Wang 1984:244). See also Chavannes 1903:428.

48. *T.* 643, 15:681b–c (Eng. trans., Zürcher 1959:224–25).

49. Mus 1935, 1:62–63.

50. *T.* 2085, 51:859a (Eng. trans., Legge 1886:39).

51. Ware 1933:156.

52. Soper 1949–50, pt. 1:282. See also Zürcher 1959:224–25.

53. *T.* 2059, 50:358b (Eng. trans., Zürcher 1959:242).

54. Eng. trans., Zürcher 1959:242–43. On the importance of the Buddha's shadow image for Hui-yüan and on its fame in China, see also Tsukamoto 1985:885–89.

55. See in particular the intriguing story of the nāgas of Nandivardhana which is recounted in *GilgMss.* 3, pt. 1:xviii.

56. The *Div.* presents the variant *kumbhakārī*, "the woman-potter."

57. *GilgMss.* 3, pt. 1:xviii.

58. It is true that, at the very end of the story, the Buddha resumes his own form; but no hint of his glory is given, and this occurs only after the potter has become favorably disposed to the Teaching.

59. The word *Dharma* has a multiplicity of meanings in the Indian context, and the texts we are dealing with often seem to play on its various connotations.

60. *M.* 3:238 (Eng. trans., Horner 1954–59, 3:293).

61. DeSilva 1986:6.

62. *Aṣṭa*, p. 513 (Eng. trans., Conze 1973:291).

63. *GilgMss.* 3, pt. 1:xviii–1. Compare *T.* 1448, 24:41a–b (Fr. trans., Przyluski 1914:515–17).

64. See Introduction.

65. Soper 1949–50, pt. 1:278; Péri 1917:44.

66. The chief source for the legend of Hārītī is the *MSV.* (*T.* 1451, 24:361ff.; Fr. trans., Péri 1917:3–14). Other important sources include I-ching's *Record* (Eng. trans., Takakusu [1896b] 1966:37–38); *Avk.* 1:107–10 (Eng. trans., Vidyābhūṣaṇa 1897:26–29); *T.* 203, 4:492a (Fr. trans., Chavannes 1934, 3:115); and *T.* 1262, 21:290c ff. (Fr. trans., Péri 1917:16–21). For discussions of these sources, see Péri 1917 and Dhirasekera 1976.

67. Foucher 1905–18, 2:130; Auboyer and Mallmann 1950:225; Péri 1917:38. For an attempt to relate Hārītī's cult to a datable smallpox epidemic, see Aivar 1970:10–21.

68. In some places, this function of hers was filled by Avalokiteśvara/Kuan-yin (see Péri 1917:65ff).

69. *Div.*, p. 349. Compare *GilgMss.* 3, pt. 1:3.

70. *GilgMss.* 3, pt. 1:xvii.

71. Aśokāv., p. 34 (Eng. trans., Strong 1983b:203).

72. *Div.*, pp. 386–87 (Eng. trans., Strong 1983b:241).

73. *T.* 1435, 23:130b–c (Fr. trans., Lamotte 1949–80, 1:286n).

74. See *T.* 1509, 25:164c (Fr. trans., Lamotte 1949–80, 2:874); and *T.* 2087, 51:900a (Eng. trans., Beal [1884] 1968, 2:8).

75. *Div.*, p. 356.

76. Windisch 1895:163n.4.

77. Burnouf 1876:337n.1.

78. *Div.*, p. 349.

79. *GilgMss.* 3, pt. 1:3. See also *T.* 1448, 24:42a (Fr. trans., Przyluski 1914:519).

80. *A.* 1:19–23 (Eng. trans., Woodward and Hare 1932–36, 1:16–25).

81. See Przyluski 1923a:559. There is a cryptic reference in a Mathurā inscription to teachers (ācārya) who were great preachers (mahopadeśaka). Lüders (1961:123) interprets this as referring not to "great teachers," but to an otherwise-unknown Buddhist school called the Mahopadeśakas (but see K. Das 1980:97).

82. On each of these masters, see chapter 3.

83. *T.* 1425, 22:548b (Eng. trans., Beal [1883] 1975:xi–xii; Fr. trans., Lamotte 1958:190).

84. *T.* 2145, 55:20a (Fr. trans., Lamotte 1958:192).

85. *Div.*, p. 349.

86. Mus 1935, 1:9.

Chapter Two
Monk and Monkey: Upagupta's Karmic Past

1. See *Div.*, p. 349 (Eng. trans., Strong 1983b:174); *T.* 2042, 50:111b (Fr. trans., Przyluski 1923a:309); and *T.* 2043, 50:149c. In the *MSV.*, the request is made more generally by "the monks"; see *GilgMss.* 3, pt. 1:4; *T.* 1448, 24:42a (Fr. trans., Przyluski 1914:519).

2. *GilgMss.* 3, pt. 1:4–7.

3. For two examples of this, see the stories in chapter 10 about the bodhisattva as a rapist-thief and about the bodhisattva seduced. For others, see Strong 1983c:503–18.

4. *Div.*, p. 349. See also *T.* 2042, 50:111c (Fr. trans., Przyluski 1923a:310).

5. *T.* 1448, 24:42a (Fr. trans., Przyluski 1914:520). The same is true in the Tibetan version (see Panglung 1981:29).

6. On this topic, see Strong 1983a.

7. See Strong 1979b.

8. In some versions, he is reborn as a monk. On the gift of honey by the monkey, see Foucher 1963:16–18. For other stories of frolicking monkeys and the preaching of the Dharma, see Mair 1989:51–52.

9. On pratyekabuddhas, see R. Kloppenborg 1974, Norman 1983b, and La Vallée Poussin 1918.

10. *Div.*, p. 428.

11. They might thus be said to embody two of the refuges of the Triple Gem—the Buddha and the Sangha. In this they would differ from full Buddhas, who embody all three refuges (Buddha, Dharma, and Sangha), as well as from śrāvakas (disciples), who embody only the refuge of the Sangha.

12. *Sn.*, vv. 35–75 (Eng. trans., R. Kloppenborg 1974:81ff.).

13. *AbhK.*, p. 183 (Fr. trans. of Chinese, La Vallée Poussin 1923–31, 3:194–95).

14. *GilgMss.* 3, pt. 1:5; see also *T.* 1448, 24:42a (Fr. trans., Przyluski 1914:520). The *Div.* does not specify this.

15. *Vin.* 1:225 (Eng. trans., Horner 1938–52, 4:306); *M.* 1:13, 207 (Eng. trans., Horner 1954–59, 1:17, 259). On *not* making use of such water, see *Vin.* 4:125 (Eng. trans., Horner 1938–52, 3:3).

16. See Gombrich 1971:122. Today, food given to monks is sometimes shared, though not that given to the Buddha. See Yalman 1973.

17. *Sn.*, p. 15 (Eng. trans., Saddhatissa 1985:9; see also Norman 1984:13).

18. According to Buddhaghosa, the gods did this on several other occasions; see Bareau 1971:4. On this subtle nutritive essence, see also *M.* 1:245 (Eng. trans., Horner 1954–59, 1:300).

19. *SnA.* 1:154 (Fr. trans., Bareau 1971:4). See also *S.* 1:167–69 (Eng. trans., Davids and Woodward 1917–30, 1:209–13).

20. *Sn.*, p. 15 (Eng. trans., Norman 1984:13). *Mil.*, pp. 258–62 (Eng. trans., T. W. Rhys Davids [1890–94] 1963, 2:85–91) has a long discussion of boiling water, elaborately proving that its "hissing and bubbling" does not mean that it contains "living creatures".

21. Apparently, we are dealing here with a polemical situation that seeks to distinguish Buddhist from non-Buddhist practice; food offered to the Buddha cannot be eaten as prasāda, as can food offered to Hindu gods. On this, see Gombrich 1971:120.

22. Takakusu [1896b] 1966:24–26.

23. *Vin.* 1:223–24 (Eng. trans., Davids and Oldenberg [1882–85] 1975, 2:94). When there is yet again some sugar left, the Buddha tells Kaccāna to throw it away in some water where there are no living creatures. He does so, and it hisses and bubbles as in the case of the other leftovers.

24. See *S.* 1:181 (Eng. trans., Davids and Woodward 1917–30, 1:230); *Mtu.* 2:209–31 (Eng. trans., Jones 1949–56, 2:199–218); and *J.* 6:70 (Eng. trans., Cowell [1895–1907] 1969, 6:39).

25. *DhA.* 2:85 (Eng. trans., Burlingame 1921, 2:151). The text presents this as a pregnancy longing and interprets it as a sign that her son will become a monk (which he does).

26. On the *MSV.* version of this story, see Banerjee [1957] 1979:179. For a Pali version, see Davids and Oldenberg [1882–85] 1975, 1:204–5.

27. See Terwiel 1975:65–68. The degwads have canonical roots in the paścācchramaṇa, on which see chapter 3.

28. Terwiel 1975:207. Some laypersons suppose such food to be especially imbued with power from having been in the monks' bowls; see Khantipalo 1979:118.

29. Takakusu [1896b] 1966:24; on feeding pets and strays in present-day monasteries, see also Terwiel 1975:205; and Gombrich 1971:119.

30. On the mystical/buddhological implications of such a commensal community, see MacDonald 1955 and Mus 1935, 1:263–65.

31. For descriptions of this hierarchical seating, see Takakusu [1896b] 1966:37; and *Div.*, p. 404 (Eng. trans., Strong 1983b:266–67).

32. *Div.*, p. 349 (Eng. trans., Strong 1983b:175).

33. *T.* 202, 4:442b (Ger. trans. of Tibetan, Schmidt 1843, 2:382; Eng. trans. of Mongolian, Frye 1981:211). Much the same story is preserved in *T.* 2145, 55:52b–53a (Fr. trans., Lin 1949:348n.6); see also Lévi 1927:119–20.

34. *T.* 202, 4:443c. Compare Schmidt 1843, 2:390–91. This is not the only story in which an individual suffers rebirth as a monkey for insulting an enlightened monk by mocking his simian characteristics. For references, see Malalasekera [1938] 1974, 2:846–47; and Durt 1980:98.

35. *Mtu.* 3:249 (Eng. trans., Jones 1949–56, 3:239). See also *T.* 190, 3:670a (Eng. trans., Beal [1875] 1985:14); and La Vallée Poussin 1923–31, 4:229.

36. *T.* 643, 15:679b (Fr. trans., Przyluski 1914:566).

37. See La Vallée Poussin 1928 and Lamotte 1958:252n.

38. *Avś.*, p. 251 (Fr. trans., Feer 1891:412–14). It is not insignificant to find this story in a Sarvāstivādin text. Jan Nattier (1988:36) has argued that the whole Maitreya myth has its origins among Sarvāstivādins.

39. Seeking to explain this, the *Mahāprajñāpāramitā śāstra* states that Śākyamuni fell karmically behind the beings he was destined to convert because he was very concerned about the well-being of others and little concerned about himself, whereas Maitreya somehow got ahead of those he was to convert because he was very concerned about himself and less about others. This crediting (by a Mahāyānist author) of Śākyamuni with more bodhisattva-like compassion than his rival Maitreya (who ends up looking somewhat like a Hīnayānist arhat) is interesting. See *T.* 1509, 24:87c (Fr. trans., Lamotte 1949–80, 1:255).

40. This detail does not appear in the *Avś.*, but it figures in *T.* 1509, 24:87c (Fr. trans., Lamotte 1949–80:253) and in *T.* 1545, 27:890b (Fr. trans., La Vallée Poussin 1928:19).

41. For a similar tale, see *Ratnamālāv.*, p. 365; and Feer 1901:296–98 (where, however, the story concludes with a different account of the hero's past life).

42. This is according to the *Vibhāṣa* (see La Vallée Poussin 1928:19). The *Avś.* claims that he was searching for "roots and fruits" on the mountain when he came across Puṣya in his cave.

43. *Avś.*, p. 251 (Fr. trans., Feer 1891:413). See also Lamotte 1949–80, 1:253.

44. On Candraprabha, see the bibliography in Lamotte 1949–80, 1:144.

45. *Div.*, p. 326 (Eng. trans., Jaini 1988:58).

46. For a bibliography, see Lamotte 1949–80, 1:143.

47. There are several versions of this tale. See *Suvarṇabhāsottamasūtra*, pp. 208–12 (Eng. trans., Emmerick 1970:87–88); *JM.*, pp. 1–6 (Eng. trans., Speyer [1895] 1982:2–8); and *T.* 202, 4:352b–53b (Ger. trans. of Tibetan, Schmidt 1843, 2:21–26; Eng. trans. of Mongolian, Frye 1981:13–16). For a Pali variant, see Jayawickrama 1968: 5–6.

48. A reflection, perhaps, of this association of Maitreya and Upagupta may be found in a very different context: the Mādhyamika philosopher Candrakīrti cites Upagupta and Maitreya as examples of beings who are contemporaries, though not of the same continuum. I would like to thank Jeffrey Hopkins for this reference (see Hopkins 1983:184; and Wilson 1980:50).

Chapter Three
Birth and Lineage, Patriarchs, and the Forest-Monk Tradition

1. *Avk.* 2:449.

2. The name is variously spelled Śāṇakavāsin, Śāṇavāsin, and Śanakavāsin. In any case, it means "wearer of hempen cloth." Hemp was one of the materials allowed for robes (see *Vin.* 3:256; Eng. trans., Horner 1938–52, 2:143), but, as a coarse cloth, it was generally associated with the garb of the more ascetically inclined monks (see T. W. Rhys Davids 1899–1924, 1:230; 3:38).

3. *Div.*, pp. 351–52 (cf. Eng. trans., Strong 1983b:176–78).

4. *A.* 3:137 (Eng. trans., Woodward and Hare 1932–36, 3:106). See also *Div.*, pp.

95, 433; *Avś.*, pp. 204, 240; and Banerjee [1957] 1979:142–47. Other names for this kind of servant/disciple appear to have been antevāsika, sārdhaṃvihārika (Pali: saddhivihārika), and śramaṇoddeśa(ka) (Pali: samaṇuddesa).

5. See chapter 6. See also Edkins 1893:70.

6. Feer 1901:65.

7. *Div.*, p. 204 (Fr. trans., Burnouf 1876:280). For a similar example, see *Catuṣ* 2:194 (Eng. trans., R. Kloppenborg 1973:38).

8. This story is found in slightly different versions in *Avś.*, pp. 203–5 (Fr. trans., Feer 1891:309–12); the *Kalpadrumāvadāna* (see Feer 1891:312); and the *Karmaśataka* (Fr. trans., Feer 1901:76).

9. This practice was, in fact, common enough to give rise to a scholastic debate about its legitimacy. See *T.* 1545, 27:178c (Fr. trans., La Vallée Poussin 1932:84).

10. See, for example, *T.* 1448, 24:38c (Fr. trans., Przyluski 1914:500–502); and, more generally, Bareau 1976.

11. Davis 1984:226.

12. See Bareau 1970–71, 2:136–37.

13. See *Vin.* 5:2–3 (Eng. trans., Horner 1938–52, 6:4–5); *Dpv.*, pp. 32–33, 40 (Eng. trans., Oldenberg [1879] 1982, pp. 136–37, 145); *Mhv.*, pp. 38–43 (Eng. trans., Geiger [1912] 1960:34–39); and *VinA.*, pp. 32–33 (Eng. trans., Jayawickrama 1962: 28–29). See also Lamotte 1958:223–25.

14. On the Masters of the Dharma, see *T.* 2042, 50:112a–21b (Fr. trans., Przyluski 1923a:311–69); *T.* 2043, 50:150a–62c (partial Fr. trans., Przyluski 1926:23ff); *T.* 1451, 24:408c–11b (Fr. trans., Przyluski 1914:522–37; Eng. trans. of Tibetan, Rockhill 1907:161–70). See also Chimpa and Chattopadhyaya [1970] 1980:22–49; and especially Lamotte 1958:226–32.

15. See Lamotte 1958:770–75.

16. For example, see the list of twenty-four patriarchs in *T.* 2058, 50:297–322 (Eng. trans., Edkins 1893:60–86); on the Ch'an lineage list of twenty-eight Indian patriarchs in the *Transmission of the Lamp* and elsewhere, see McRae 1986:73–97.

17. See *T.* 2042, 50:112a ff.; and *T.* 2043, 50:150a ff. The easiest place to follow both texts at once is in the Fr. trans. in facing columns in Przyluski 1926:23ff.

18. The four lokapālas (or mahārājas) are: Dhṛtarāṣṭra (and the gandharvas) in the east, Virūḍhaka (and the kumbhāṇḍas) in the south, Virūpākṣa (and the nāgas) in the north, and Vaiśravaṇa (and the yakṣas) in the west.

19. Przyluski 1926:24–25.

20. See Bareau 1970–71, 2:223–30. The same figure is called Subhadda in Pali sources (not to be confused with the Subhadda who was the last person ordained by the Buddha); see Malalasekera [1938] 1974, 2:1231.

21. See, besides the *Aśokarājāvadāna* and the *Aśokarājasūtra*, *T.* 2027, 49:4b (Fr. trans., Przyluski 1926:3); *T.* 1451, 24:402c (Fr. trans., Lamotte 1949–80, 1:89n; Eng. trans. of Tibetan, Obermiller 1931, 2:73–91); and *T.* 1509, 25:67b (Fr. trans., Lamotte 1949–80, 1:90–91).

22. *T.* 2043, 50:150c (Fr. trans., Przyluski 1926:31). The full legend of Gavāṃpati is more complex than this; as we shall see, eventually he becomes the converter of Suvarṇabhūmi (Burma), where he is regarded as the patron saint of the Mon.

23. *T.* 2043, 50:151a (Fr. trans., Przyluski 1926:33).

24. *T.* 1509, 25:67c (Fr. trans., Lamotte 1949–80, 1:91).

25. As Williams (1989:52–54) has pointed out, however, the claim that Mahāyāna bodhisattvas postpone their entry into Nirvāṇa for the sake of others is fraught with complications.

26. Przyluski 1926:36–53.

27. For textual references to the First Council, see Lamotte 1949–80, 1:88; for secondary studies, see Lamotte 1958:136.

28. *T.* 2042, 50:114a (Fr. trans., Przyluski 1923a:327). See also Rockhill 1907:161; and *T.* 1451, 24:408c (Fr. trans., Przyluski 1914:522).

29. Ajātaśatru is asleep when this message arrives and is consequently late for Mahākāśyapa's parinirvāṇa. By the time he gets there, the saint's body has already been miraculously immured in the mountain, although the peak reopens temporarily to give the king one last chance to venerate the body. See *T.* 2042, 50:115a (Fr. trans., Przyluski 1923a:332–34). Ajātaśatru is similarly late for Ānanda's parinirvāṇa.

30. The mountain is also called Gurupadaka (see *Div.*, p. 61; and Watters [1904] 1961, 2:143). For other variants, see Lamotte 1949–80, 1:192n.1.

31. According to *T.* 2042, 50:114c (Fr. trans., Przyluski 1923a:331), the robe which the Buddha had shared with Mahākāśyapa was a pāṃśukūla (ragheap robe). Alternatively, it is called a saṃghāṭī (*T.* 2042, 50:115a [Fr. trans., Przyluski 1923a:334]) or simply a white or faded robe (śvetacivāra; see *Aśokāv.*, p. 90 [Eng. trans., Strong 1983b:254]).

32. This legend was not unknown in the late Pali tradition. See the reference to the *Mahāsampiṇḍanidāna* in Saddhatissa 1975:43–45 (where Mahākāśyapa is actually cremated in Maitreya's hand). See also G. Martini 1973:73. Similar cases (see Brock 1988:237–39) may be found in the legend of the Mādhyamika scholar Bhāvaviveka, who, according to Hsüan-tsang, entered a cave at the end of his life in order to keep his body until the advent of Maitreya; and in the legend of the Japanese saint Kūkai, who even today is said to be in samādhi, awaiting the arrival of Maitreya on Mount Kōya.

33. *T.* 2042, 50:115a (Fr. trans., Przyluski 1923a:333). By Maitreya's time, Mahākāśyapa's body will appear to be very small, since people then will be much taller than they are now. Maitreya's disciples consequently will be contemptuous of it.

34. On this concept in a different context, see Hori 1962.

35. *T.* 1451, 24:409a (Fr. trans., Przyluski 1914:527–28).

36. *Div.*, p. 6l. See also Fa-hsien's account of his visit to the mountain in *T.* 2085, 51:863c (Eng. trans., Legge 1886:92–93; Beal [1884] 1968, 1:lxvi–lxvii).

37. *T.* 2087, 51:919b–c (Eng. trans., Beal [1884] 1968, 2:142–44; Watters [1904] 1961, 2:143–46). Compare *T.* 1509, 25:9a (Fr. trans., Lamotte 1949–80, 1:195); and *T.* 1545, 27:698b (Fr. trans., Lamotte 1949–80, 1:191–92n).

38. *T.* 456, 14:433b (Ger. trans., Watanabe in Leumann 1919:276–78; partial Fr. trans., Lamotte 1949–80, 1:191n). Even then his relics will be heard to preach one more sermon.

39. *Maitreya samiti*, pp. 73–74 (Ger. trans., Leumann 1919:107–10; Eng. trans., Emmerick 1968:333).

40. On the sixteen arhats, see Lévi and Chavannes 1916, De Visser 1918–23, and chapter 11.

41. *T.* 2042, 50:114b (Fr. trans., Przyluski 1923a:328–29). On the quinquennial festival, see Strong 1990.

42. Moggaliputta Tissa says the same thing to Aśoka in *Mhv.*, p. 47 (Eng. trans.,

Geiger [1912] 1960:43), except that there the gift of Dharma is described as Aśoka giving his son Mahinda to the Sangha as a monk.

43. *T.* 2042, 50:115a–b (Fr. trans., Przyluski 1923a:335).

44. *T.* 2042, 50:115b (Fr. trans., Przyluski 1923a:336). The correct version of the verse may be found in *T.* 213, 4:789a (Eng. trans., Willemen 1978:102). My translation is an attempt to restore a pun only partially preserved in the Chinese. The Sanskrit original is a matter of speculation.

45. *T.* 2042, 50:115b (Fr. trans., Przyluski 1923a:336).

46. *T.* 2042, 50:115c (Fr. trans., Przyluski 1923a:337).

47. *T.* 2042, 50:115c–16b (Fr. trans., Przyluski 1923a:337–40). For other versions, see Przyluski 1914:533–34; Rockhill 1907:166; Legge 1886:75–77; and, with some variation in details, *DhA.* 2:99 (Eng. trans., Burlingame 1921, 2:160–61).

48. On Madhyāntika, see *T.* 2042, 50:116b–c (Fr. trans., Przyluski 1923a:340–42). It should be pointed out that, according to one passage of the *MSV.* (*GilgMss.* 3, pt. 1:3; *T.* 1448, 24:41c [Fr. trans., Przyluski 1914:519]), it is Madhyāntika who converts Upagupta. The text, however, does not follow through on this theme. For a Pali version of Madhyāntika's (Majjhantika's) conversion of Kashmir (very similar to that found in the *Aśokarājāvadāna*), see *VinNid.*, pp. 182–83 (Eng. trans., Jayawickrama 1962:57–58).

49. It is worth noting that Śāṇakavāsin, like Madhyāntika, is not unknown in the Pali tradition, where he is identified with Sambhūta Sāṇavāsī—an elder who, like him, wore a robe made of hemp (sāṇa). Sambhūta Sāṇavāsī is also said to have been ordained by Ānanda and to have lived until about one hundred years after the Buddha's parinirvāṇa, at Mount Ahogangā on the upper Ganges, a place which has been identified with Mount Urumuṇḍa. See chapter 7.

50. On mahallas, see below.

51. *T.* 2042, 50:117b (Fr. trans., Przyluski 1923a:346).

52. *T.* 2042, 50:121a (Fr. trans., Przyluski 1923a:368–69).

53. *T.* 2042, 50:121a (Fr. trans., Przyluski 1923a:367).

54. Przyluski 1923a:368n.1.

55. *T.* 2042, 50:121a (Fr. trans., Przyluski 1923a:368). Much the same message can be found in *T.* 1545, 27:79b (Fr. trans., Lamotte 1958:179). See also La Vallée Poussin 1923–31, 2:245n; and Obermiller 1931, 2:169–71.

56. *T.* 1509, 24:129c (Fr. trans., Lamotte 1949–80, 1:572–74). See also *T.* 2058, 50:306a.

57. Durt 1980:98.

58. *Div.*, p. 520. On the Mākandika story, see also Huber 1906:21–27; and *DhA.* 1:199–202 (Eng. trans., Burlingame 1921, 1:274–77).

59. *GilgMss.* 3, pt. 1:44–45.

60. *Div.*, p. 329 (Eng. trans. by Cowell and Neil in ibid., pp. 707–8n; and by Ware 1938:65). On these bhikṣus, see Dhirasekera 1970.

61. *MPS.*, p. 423.

62. *T.* 2042, 50:120c–21a (Fr. trans., Przyluski 1923a:366–67).

63. *Div.*, p. 427 (Eng. trans., Strong 1983b:231–32).

64. *T.* 2042, 50:121b–c (Fr. trans., Przyluski 1923a:371–72). See also chapter 6.

65. See below; and see G. Martini 1973:68.

66. Somewhat amused at being considered a heretic merely because of his appear-

ance, Mahākāśyapa wanders off to beg his meal among the poor. He accepts an offering of rice-water from a leprous washerwoman and is not in the least perturbed when one of her diseased fingers falls off and lands in his bowl; he drinks the gruel nonetheless. See *GilgMss.* 3, pt. 1:80–81.

67. Field notes, Mae Hong Son, 9 October 1982. I never encountered this opinion elsewhere.

68. See Duroiselle 1915–16; Bizot 1976:36–42; Than Tun 1959b; and Finot 1912.

69. On this practice and others akin to it, see chapter 8.

70. Than Tun 1959b:117.

71. Duroiselle 1915–16:92n; Bizot 1976:36. Incidentally, Davids and Stede suggest ([1921–25] 1975:525) that the word *mahallaka* also comes from *ariya* to which has been added the prefix *mahā-*, "great."

72. See Huber 1909; Finot 1912:123; and Than Tun 1959b:99.

73. Than Tun 1959b:99.

74. See Przyluski 1923a:311, 363.

75. *Div.*, p. 426 (Eng. trans., Strong 1983b:229).

76. *GilgMss.* 3, pt. 1:80.

77. On forest monks in India and Thailand, see Tambiah 1984.

78. The legend of Ānanda is a bit of an anomaly in this regard. Further evidence of Sarvāstivādin affinities with the forest-monk tradition may be found in Chau 1964a:29–30.

79. *T.* 2042, 50:120b (Fr. trans., Przyluski 1923a:364). This life-style recalls the meditational practice of gTummo advocated in Tibet by such "cotton-clad" saints as Milarepa. Śāṇakavāsin's fondness for wearing coarse hempen robes (hence his name) stems from his admiration, in a previous life, of a pratyekabuddha who was so dressed.

80. *Aśokāv.*, p. 3 (Eng. trans., Strong 1983b:174); see also Przyluski 1923a:363. Note that the form of meditation stressed here is śamatha (trance) and not vipāśyanā (insight).

81. See the stories of Upagupta's disciples in chapter 6.

82. *T.* 2042, 50:120b (Fr. trans., Przyluski 1923a:363).

83. *GilgMss.* 3, pt. 1:80.

84. *A.* 1:23 (Eng. trans., Woodward and Hare 1932–36, 1:16). For Mahākāśyapa's aspiration to this status, see *AA.* 1:162–63.

85. See *S.* 2:202, 222 (Eng. trans., Davids and Woodward 1917–30, 2:136–37, 149).

86. It is significant that, in "orthodox" circles, the ascetic practices came to be associated with the figure of Devadatta, the archfoe of the Buddha. On this question, see Bareau 1988–89:545; and Mukherjee 1966:146.

87. Edition and Fr. trans. in G. Martini 1973:67–76. As Martini points out (ibid., pp. 55–60), ānisaṃsas, which are better known to ordinary Buddhists than the texts of the canon, often show signs of Sanskrit Buddhist avadāna influence. On ānisaṃsas (Laotian: sōn.), see also Finot (1917:72–74), who lists over one hundred such texts. For other genres reflecting forest-monk concerns, see Bapat 1984; Ehara, Soma, and Kheminda 1977; and Woodward [1916] 1970.

88. A similar story is told in *Lal.*, p. 265 (Fr. trans., Foucaux 1884:229). G. Martini (1973:59) sees this as another evidence of Sanskrit influence in Southeast Asia "before the great wave of Theravāda Buddhism covered over everything."

89. *Brapaṃsukūla.*, p. 67 (Fr. trans., G. Martini 1973:71).

90. *Brapaṃsukūla.*, p. 68 (Fr. trans., G. Martini 1973:72).

91. *Brapaṃsukūla.*, p. 69 (Fr. trans., G. Martini 1973:74).

92. On the Paṃsukūlika, Āraññika, and related "sects" in Sri Lanka and Southeast Asia, see Tambiah 1984:55–77; for the modern period, see Carrithers 1983 and Yalman 1962.

93. The list of twenty-three paṃsukūlas may also be found in the *Vsm.* 1:62 (Eng. trans., Ñyāṇamoli [1956] 1976, 1:63).

94. *Brapaṃsukūla.*, p. 68 (Fr. trans., G. Martini 1973:73). This is not the usual Pali story of the ordination of Mahākassapa, who is generally said to have wandered forth in the prime of life (see Malalasekera [1938] 1974, 2:477). In fact, Mahākassapa is here echoing a line in *DhA.* 1:8 (Eng. trans., Burlingame 1921, 1:149) which features the monk Mahāpāla, who makes much the same choice. For other examples of old men entering the Sangha and opting for the path of meditation, see W. Rahula 1956:160.

95. *T.* 2087, 51:873b–c (Eng. trans., Beal [1884] 1968, 1:52–53). Hsüan-tsang also saw Śāṇakavāsin's quite large bowl.

96. Tambiah 1984:293–320.

Chapter Four
Lay Life, Ordination, and Arhatship

1. *Div.*, p. 352 (Eng. trans., Strong 1983b:178). In *T.* 2042, 50:117c (Fr. trans., Przyluski 1923a:348), Māra merely encourages people to go to buy perfumes.

2. *Div.*, p. 352 (Eng. trans., Strong 1983b:178).

3. *T.* 2042, 50:117c (Fr. trans., Przyluski 1923a:348). This definition is not specified in the Sanskrit.

4. It is not clear of what these "strips" (paṭṭikā) were made. *T.* 2042, 50:117c (Fr. trans., Przyluski 1923a:348) has "black and white stones"; so, too, does *T.* 202, 4:442c (Ger. trans. of Tibetan, Schmidt 1843, 2:384; Eng. trans. of Mongolian, Frye 1981:232). Durt (1979:451) compares these paṭṭikā to śālakā.

5. *Div.*, p. 352 (Eng. trans., Strong 1983b:179).

6. On the practice of mindfulness within the Theravāda tradition, see Conze 1956:62–107; and Nyanaponika 1969. For a Sarvāstivādin perspective, see Lin 1949.

7. *Avś.*, p. 304 (Fr. trans., Feer 1891:3).

8. *Div.*, p. 352 (Eng. trans., Strong 1983b:179).

9. *T.* 2042, 50:118a (Fr. trans., Przyluski 1923a:348).

10. *Div.*, p. 352 (Eng. trans., Strong 1983b:179).

11. See *Div.*, pp. 353–56 (Ger. trans., Zimmer 1925:186–94; Eng. trans., Strong 1983b:179–84); *T.* 2042, 50:118a–b (Fr. trans., Przyluski 1923a:349–52); *T.* 202, 4:442c–43a (Ger. trans. of Tibetan, Schmidt 1843, 2:385–86; Eng. trans. of Mongolian, Frye 1981:232–33); and *Avk.* 2:449–51. Cf. Huber 1908:105–16. The tale was reworked in modern times into a short story by Rabindranath Tagore (1937:154–55).

12. *Avk.* 2:449.

13. Ibid.

14. According to the *Pañcatantra*, perfumers in ancient India did not enjoy a reputation for honesty (see Gode 1951:1).

15. Jaini (1989:217) suggests translating the pieces of money involved here (purāṇas) as "old" coins.

16. *Div.*, p. 353 (Eng. trans., Strong 1983b:179–80).

17. For other stories of merchants who "arrive in Mathurā with five hundred horses," see Jaini 1989:216, 219.

18. *Div.*, p. 353 (Eng. trans., Strong 1983b:179–80); cf. *T.* 2043, 50:118a (Fr. trans., Przyluski 1923a:349). *Avk.* 2:449–50 provides some amplifications to this passage. It features a long reflection by Vāsavadattā, in which she tries to justify her action; in the end, she personally poisons the caravaneer with the approval of her mother.

19. *Avk.* 2:450.

20. *Div.*, p. 354 (Eng. trans., Strong 1983b:181).

21. *Avk.* 2:450.

22. See Horner 1938–52, 1:49; she indicates most of these passages with asterisks, leaving them untranslated and providing only the Pali text of them at the back of the book (p. 341).

23. See *VinA.* 1:262–68; Bapat and Hirakawa 1970:199–204.

24. *Vsm.* 1:180 (Eng. trans., Ñyānamoli [1956] 1976, 1:187).

25. *Avk.* 2:450.

26. *Div.*, p. 354 (Eng. trans., Strong 1983b:182).

27. *Div.*, p. 355 (Eng. trans., Strong 1983b:182).

28. *Avk.* 2:451. *T.* 202, 4:442c (Eng. trans. of Mongolian, Frye 1981:233; Ger. trans. of Tibetan, Schmidt 1843, 2:385–86) is equally explicit.

29. *Div.*, p. 356 (Eng. trans., Strong 1983b:183). On the srotāpanna and anāgāmin stages, see below.

30. According to the Vinaya, parental consent was one of the prerequisites for ordination.

31. *Div.*, p. 356 (Eng. trans., Strong 1983b:185–86); compare *T.* 2042, 50:118b–c (Fr. trans., Przyluski 1923a:353).

32. Masefield's work (1986) is based entirely on Pali canonical materials, and we shall see how the Sanskrit tradition will force us to deviate from it; it is useful, however, in setting up a number of issues.

33. Pali: putthujana (often translated "ordinary folk," but defined by Masefield [1986:175] as anyone not possessing insight into the Four Truths).

34. Pali: sotāpanna, sakadāgāmin, anāgāmin, and arahant. For a bibliography of textual reference to all of these, see Dantinne 1983:255–59. Masefield (1986:133–34) disputes the usual translation of *sotāpanna*, but I shall retain "stream-winner," with the understanding that the stream is equivalent not to saṃsāra, but to a salvific current within it that will result in liberation in seven more lifetimes.

35. *D.* 1:156 (Eng. trans., T. W. Rhys Davids 1899–1924, 1:200–201). See also Horner [1936] 1979:213n.1.

36. Already Horner ([1936] 1979:225) raised questions about it.

37. Masefield 1986:71–93.

38. Oversimplifying a complex issue, we may find it useful to think of the stream-winner and once-returner as still subject to death and rebirth (several times or just once); of the nonreturner as still subject (once more) to death but *not* to rebirth; and of the arhat as no longer subject to either death or rebirth. This scheme, however, is complicated by the fact that there are several different types of once-returners and that certain schools were unwilling to accept the notion of an intermediate state between lives or between death and final liberation. See Masefield 1986:105f.; and La Vallée Poussin 1923–31, 3:210f.

39. Masefield 1986:136.

40. The paradigmatic model for these two events is, of course, the life of the Buddha, whose enlightenment at Bodhgaya and parinirvāṇa at Kuśinagarī are well known.

41. According to Masefield (1986:71), initial enlightenment destroys a considerable amount of old karma, but not all of it.

42. Masefield 1986:142, 136ff. For Masefield, after the Buddha's death, beings can no longer embark on the Path. The only persons to attain final liberation are those few once-returners and stream-winners who previously had entered their tracks under the Buddha and have now finally exhausted their karma. Everyone else will simply have to wait for the next Buddha, Maitreya.

43. He dismisses as aberrations those few cases in which, it is said, some of the Buddha's disciples, such as Śāriputra, led others to enlightenment (see Masefield 1986:136–44).

44. *S.* 3:120 (Eng. trans., Davids and Woodward 1917–30, 3:103); *Itv.*, p. 91 (Eng. trans., Woodward 1948:181); *Mil.*, p. 73 (Eng. trans., T. W. Rhys Davids [1890–94] 1963, 1:114). For Mahāyāna citations of the same passage, see Wayman 1970:28.

45. *Div.*, p. 356 (Eng. trans., Strong 1983b:183). We should not be surprised that Upagupta is here preaching the Dharma as a layman; the practice was not uncommon. See, for example, *S.* 4:282–304 (Eng. trans., Davids and Woodward 1917–30, 4:190–212). See also Hecker 1967:1–13 for an account of the householder Citta Macchikāsaṇḍika, whom the Buddha extolled as "foremost among those laymen who are teachers of the Dharma."

46. See chapter 6.

47. *Mil.* 1:15–16 (Eng. trans., T. W. Rhys Davids [1890–94] 1963, 1:25–26). For a variant on this story, see Demiéville 1924:88–89.

48. *Div.*, p. 355 (Eng. trans., Strong 1983b:182–83).

49. *Vsm.* 1:178–79 (Eng. trans., Ñyāṇamoli [1956] 1976, 1:185–86).

50. See the discussion of the variants on this list in Lamotte 1949–80, 3:1312–14; and Edgerton 1953, 2:80.

51. *Vsm.* 1;194–95 (Eng. trans., Ñyāṇamoli [1956] 1976, 1:201).

52. *Div.*, p. 354 (Eng. trans., Strong 1983b:182).

53. The most famous example of this genre is the story of the Buddha's transformation of Māra's daughters into old hags at the time of his "temptation." See Rockhill 1907:31; and Karetzky 1982:85.

54. *T.* 2042, 50:124a (Fr. trans., Przyluski 1923a:386–87). This story recalls the famous tale of the elder Mahātissa in *Vsm.* 1:21 (Eng. trans., Ñyāṇamoli [1956] 1976, 1:22).

55. See Huber 1908:105–16.

56. See, for example, *Avś.*, pp. 258, 260–61, 263, 265, etc. (Fr. trans., Feer 1891:239, 242, 244, 246, 248, etc.). In some stories, Feer has mistakenly reversed the order of events, having ordination come before stream-winning. The same pattern (*pace* Masefield) is typical in the Pali canon (see Davids and Oldenberg [1882–85] 1975, 1:97–102).

57. Masefield 1986:11. See also Bareau 1955:218.

58. Bareau 1955:247. On the Uttarāpathakas, see also Bareau 1957:247–49; and Malalasekera [1938] 1974, 1:363.

59. *Mil.*, p. 20 (Eng. trans., T. W. Rhys Davids [1890–94] 1963, 1:31–32);

Demiéville 1924:94–95. Much the same argument is still in use today in Sri Lanka (see Southwold 1983:72).

60. See Takakusu 1896a (Fr. trans., Chavannes 1934, 3:120–24).

61. He is not actually named in the text.

62. Chavannes 1934, 3:123. See also *Mil.*, pp. 242–44 (Eng. trans., T. W. Rhys Davids [1890–94] 1963, 2:56–59).

63. See Malalasekera [1938] 1974, 1:1059; 2:975, 1163.

64. For various descriptions and interpretations, see Holt 1981b:106–24; Lévy [1957] 1968; Mendelson 1965; Seneviratne 1973; and Bunnag 1973:165–79. For a summary of the upasampadā from the *MSV.*, see Banerjee [1957] 1979:114–47.

65. For two canonical versions of this episode, see *M.* 1:242–47 (Eng. trans., Horner 1954–59, 1:297–301); and *T.* 1428, 22:780c–81a (Fr. trans., Bareau 1963:45–48).

66. Bareau 1963:50.

67. See *M.* 1:245–46 (Eng. trans., Horner 1954–59, 1:300).

68. *Sanghbhv.*, 1:107.

69. In *Sanghbhv.* 2:119, too, the double news is sent that the Buddha is dead, the Buddha is alive. See Strong, forthcoming.

70. *M.* 1:245 (Eng. trans., Horner 1954–59, 1:299); emphasis added.

71. Horner 1954–59, 1:299n.1.

72. See the *Upasampadā-kammavācā* (Eng. trans., Dickson 1874:7; reprinted in Warren 1922:396) and the *Upasampadāvidhi* (Eng. trans., Vajirañāṇavarorasa 1973: 23). See also Seneviratne 1973:254; and Wells 1960:142.

73. Warren 1922:396. The same formula was used at ordinations into the novitiate. See Bizot 1988:26; and, for literary references, *J.* 1:116 (Eng. trans., Cowell [1895–1907] 1969, 1:15) and *DhA.* 1:243; 2:87, 140, 242 (Eng. trans., Burlingame 1921, 1:301; 2:152–53, 185, 239).

74. Burlingame 1921, 2:153.

75. For examples of monks who attain arhatship in the midst of ordination—the moment the razor touches their hair—see Horner [1936] 1979:221.

76. For sources relevant to South Asia, see Hara 1986:84–85n, to which should be added Obeyesekere 1981:33–51.

77. Obeyesekere 1981:45.

78. Dubois 1906:484; Monier-Williams 1885:281.

79. Bizot 1981:13–32; G. Martini 1973. See also the story of the first paṃsukūla in chapter 3, and in *Lal.*, p. 265 (Fr. trans., Foucaux 1884:229).

80. On the parallelism between the ritual treatment of the Sangha and of the dead, see Holt 1981a.

81. Van Gennep 1960.

82. Eliade 1958:53–54. See also Holt 1981b:108–9.

83. Like any other performative action, ritual may fail to be effective. Hence, not all ordained monks were arhats (although, according to accounts of the early days of the Sangha, a remarkably high number of those ordained seem to have been).

84. In a different context, Hawley (1987:xvii) has shown that "lay audiences are expected to react one way to the example of the saints, clerical or religious audiences in another."

85. On ornaments concealing the marks of the Mahāpuruṣa and the association of this with Maitreya, see Mus 1928:262–72.

Chapter Five
Upagupta and Māra: Bhakti and the Buddha Body

1. For general works on Māra, see Windisch 1895, Boyd 1975, Ling 1962, and Przyluski 1927; for textual references, see Dantinne 1983:142–44; and Lamotte 1949–80, 1:339–40. On Māra as Death-and-life, see also Malalasekera [1938] 1974, 2:613; Wayman 1959:113; Boyd 1971:63; and Karetzky 1982:77. For more on the relation of Māra and Kāma, see Fischer 1980.

2. Among these, the following will be referred to in this chapter: (1) *Div.*, pp. 356–64 (Ger. trans., Windisch 1895:161–76; Eng. trans., Strong 1983b:185–97); (2) *T.* 201, 4:307c–9b (Fr. trans., Huber 1908:263–73; Skt. fragments in Lüders 1926:166–69); (3) *T.* 202, 4:442b–43c (Ger. trans. of Tibetan, Schmidt 1843, 2:382–91; Eng. trans. of Mongolian, Frye 1981:233–35); (4) *T.* 2042, 50:118c–20b (Fr. trans., Przyluski 1923a:353–62); (5) *T.* 2043, 50:159a–61a (Ger. trans., Waldschmidt in Lüders 1926:77–83); (6) Kumārajīva's version of the story contained in a note to his translation of the *Vimalakīrti nirdeśa* (Fr. trans., Lévi 1927:119–25); (7) Tāranātha's synopsis of the story (Eng. trans., Chimpa and Chattopadhyaya [1970] 1980:35–37); (8) *LP.* 1:170–74 (Fr. trans., Denis 1977, 2:150–52); and (9) *Avk.* 2:451–53. For other references, see Lamotte 1976:100n. For a study of this episode as a whole, see Bloss 1979.

3. *Div.*, pp. 356–57 (Eng. trans., slightly altered, from Strong 1983b:185–87).

4. *LP.* 1:156–57 (Fr. trans., Denis 1977, 2:139). A similar story may be found, without reference to Upagupta, in *S.* 1:113 (Eng. trans., Davids and Woodward 1917–30, 1:143–44).

5. Indeed, in the *LP.*, as we shall see, Māra takes a vow to become a Buddha, and a prediction is made that, in a future life, he will attain that goal. Other Pali evidence of Māra's future Buddhahood may be found in the *DBK.* (See F. Martini 1936:292–93, 310–13, 347–50; though in another edition of this text [Saddhatissa 1975:15], Māra is replaced by a figure called Abhibhū Devarāja.)

6. See *T.* 2042, 50:118c (Fr. trans., Przyluski 1923a:353); *T.* 2043, 50:159a (Ger. trans., Waldschmidt in Lüders 1926:78); *Avk.* 2:451; Chimpa and Chattopadhyaya [1970] 1980:35; and *T.* 202, 4:443a (Eng. trans. of Mongolian, Frye 1981:233; Ger. trans. of Tibetan, Schmidt 1843, 2:386–87), where we find interruptions featuring blue elephants from whose six tusks flow streams of sparkling water in which crystal maidens bathe and sing. Interestingly, the *LP.* (1:147–51; Fr. trans., Denis 1977, 2:131–34) does not attribute the interruptions to Māra; instead, it recounts a similar story featuring the Buddha and the god Śiva (Pali: Mahissara). On the parallels between Māra and Śiva, see also O'Flaherty 1976:213.

7. For references to Sanskrit and Pali sources, see Lamotte 1976:46n, to which should be added *Śāyanāsav.*, p. 17.

8. Lamotte 1958:84.

9. For a prime example, see *Śāyanāsav.*, p. 17 (Eng. trans., R. Kloppenborg 1973:33).

10. *Mil.*, p. 16 (Eng. trans., T. W. Rhys Davids [1890–94] 1963, 1:25). See also the similar story in Demiéville 1924:86.

11. See Huber 1908:150–57. For a similar story, see Przyluski 1923a:412–13. On the preaching of the Dharma to women, see Dantinne 1983:134–35.

12. The terms are Melford Spiro's (1982), but the tendency is more widespread.

13. *T.* 201, 4:307c (Fr. trans., Huber 1908:263). See also Lévi 1927:121.

14. See Horner 1938–52, 4:105. In *Vin.* 2:123 (Eng. trans., Horner 1938–52, 5:170), monks are allowed to accept flowers from the laity, but not to wear them.

15. In *T.* 202, 4:443a (Eng. trans. of Mongolian, Frye 1981:234; Ger. trans. of Tibetan, Schmidt 1843, 2:387), Māra does not garland Upagupta with flowers, but crowns him with a jewelled diadem—a symbol of kingship epitomizing lay life.

16. See Lévi 1927:121.

17. See Strong 1977.

18. Pali text and Eng. trans. (here slightly altered) in DeSilva 1980:85.

19. Structurally, as we shall see, this tale foreshadows the story of Upagupta's worship of Māra in the guise of the Buddha.

20. Lévi 1927:121.

21. *T.* 201, 4:307c (Fr. trans., Huber 1908:263) also speaks of three corpses but does not specify which kind.

22. *Div.*, p. 358 (Eng. trans., Strong 1983b:187).

23. Lévi 1927:120–21; *T.* 202, 4:443a–b (Eng. trans. of Mongolian, Frye 1981:234; Ger. trans. of Tibetan, Schmidt 1843, 2:387).

24. See Przyluski 1926:102–3. In another tale, the Buddha refers to a time when he personally bound Māra with a corpse (see Huber 1908:110).

25. *GilgMss.* 4:51.

26. See *Śīkṣ.*, p. 92 (Eng. trans., Bendall and Rouse [1902] 1971:161).

27. *T.* 642, 15:637b–c (Fr. trans., Lamotte 1965:193–97).

28. *A.* 1:141 (Eng. trans., Woodward and Hare 1932–36, 1:124); *M.* 3:166, 183 (Eng. trans., Horner 1954–59, 3:212, 227); *Div.*, p. 376 (Eng. trans., Strong 1983b:213). For further discussion of this form of torture, see Przyluski 1923a:159–60.

29. *LP.* 1:172 (Fr. trans., Denis 1977, 2:151).

30. *PSK.*, frontispiece illustration to chapter 28.

31. Lévy 1957:9, 17, 32. For Burma, see Ananda Maitreya 1903:277. The same ritual is also found in Sri Lanka (Mahinda Deegalle, personal communication, Kandy, 1 July 1987).

32. deYoung 1963:120–22.

33. *GilgMss.* 4:51.

34. *LP.* 1:172 (Fr. trans., Denis 1977, 2:151).

35. *Div.*, p. 358 (Eng. trans., Strong 1983b:188).

36. Chimpa and Chattopadhyaya [1970] 1980:37. See also *Div.*, pp. 358–59 (Eng. trans., Strong 1983b:189–90); and *T.* 202, 4:443b (Ger. trans. of Tibetan, Schmidt 1843, 2:388; Eng. trans. of Mongolian, Frye 1981:234). See also *Avk.* 2:452.

37. *Div.*, pp. 359–60 (Eng. trans., Strong 1983b:191).

38. *Div.*, p. 360 (Eng. trans., Strong 1983b:191).

39. See Lévi 1927:123; Denis 1977, 3:201n.30; and Mus 1939:297.

40. Frye 1981:234. See also *T.* 202, 4:443b.

41. See Lévi 1927:122.

42. *LP.* 1:173 (Fr. trans., Denis 1977, 2:151).

43. Eliade 1938:202, quoted in Ling 1962:25.

44. O'Flaherty 1976:7.

45. Ibid., p. 95.

46. Ibid., p. 98.

47. Ibid., chaps. 5–6.

48. Ibid., p. 134.

49. Ibid., p. 213.

50. Indeed, in the *Śūraṃgamasamādhi sūtra* (*T.* 642, 15:638b [Fr. trans., Lamotte 1965:200–201]), Māra fakes a vow for Buddhahood simply in order to free himself from the five fetters. Wonderfully, his vow is willy-nilly effective, and the Buddha predicts Māra's future Buddhahood over his protestations.

51. *Div.*, p. 360 (Eng. trans., Strong 1983b:192).

52. Lévi 1927:119. See also *T.* 642, 15:637b (Fr. trans., Lamotte 1965:193). Some art historians (Karetzky 1982:90) have pointed to an eclipse of Māra in iconography with the rise of the Mahāyāna.

53. *T.* 310, 11:571a (Eng. trans., Chang 1983:35).

54. See Lévi 1927:122.

55. *Avk.* 2:452.

56. *Bhūtikāya* in *LP.* 1:173 (Fr. trans., Denis 1977, 2:152).

57. *Div.*, p. 360 (Eng. trans., Strong 1983b:192).

58. Bareau (1980:1) has stressed the importance, in the development of Buddha bhakti, of disciples who never knew the Master. For other examples of Buddhists who, born "one hundred years after the parinirvāṇa" like Upagupta, nonetheless yearned for a vision of the Buddha's body, see *Div.*, pp. 390, 392 (Eng. trans., Strong 1983b:245, 249); and *Mhv.*, pp. 37–38 (Eng. trans., Geiger [1912] 1960:33–34).

59. On the two-body theory, see Lancaster 1974; Demiéville 1934:176; F. E. Reynolds 1977:377; and La Vallée Poussin 1928–29, 2:766.

60. On the various correspondences between different eyes and different bodies, see Falk 1943:114–15. For complications, see Wayman 1970.

61. *Div.*, p. 19. On Śroṇa Koṭikarṇa, see Lamotte 1949–80, 1:546–47n; Lévi 1915b:401–17; and Waldschmidt 1967.

62. *Itv.*, p. 91 (Eng. trans., Woodward 1948:181). See also *Aṣṭa.*, p. 514 (Eng. trans., Conze 1973:292).

63. This would seem to be the assumption in *D.* 2:141 (Eng. trans., T. W. Rhys Davids 1899–1924, 2:154).

64. *Div.*, p. 362.

65. *Div.*, p. 29.

66. *LP.* 1:173 (Fr. trans., Denis 1977, 2:152). See also *T.* 202, 4:43b (Eng. trans. of Mongolian, Frye 1981:234; Ger. trans. of Tibetan, Schmidt 1843, 2:388–89).

67. *Avk.* 2:453. See also Lévi 1927:122.

68. *Div.*, pp. 360–61 (Eng. trans., Strong 1983b:192–93). Compare Przyluski 1923a:359–60. Much the same details are found in *T.* 201, 4:308c–9a (Fr. trans., Huber 1908:269–70).

69. *Mtu.* 2:26 (Eng. trans., Jones 1949–56, 2:23).

70. *Mtu.* 3:114 (Eng. trans., Jones 1949–56, 3:114). For a list of canonical passages recounting similar incidents, see Durt 1972 and Lamotte 1949–80, 1:1346–47n.1.

71. *Div.*, p. 361 (Eng. trans., Strong 1983b:193).

72. *A.* 1:26 (Eng. trans., Woodward and Hare 1932–36, 1:23).

73. See Huber 1908:230–36.

74. *AA.* 1:396–98 (partial Eng. trans., Hardy 1902:952–53). The same story may be found in *DA.* 3:864.

75. *AA*. 1:397–98 (Eng. trans., E. Hardy 1902:952).

76. Hardy 1902:954.

77. See Huber 1908:235.

78. Note should be made of the theatrical metaphors in the text that follows. See also Dutt 1957:236; and, on the relation of theater and magic, see Mair 1989:57.

79. *Div*., pp. 360–63 (Eng. trans., Strong 1983b:192–96).

80. The various versions of the story are quite explicit about this: see *Div*., p. 362 (Eng. trans., Strong 1983b:195); *T*. 2042, 50:120a (Fr. trans., Przyluski 1923a:361); and *T*. 201, 4:309b (Fr. trans., Huber 1908:272).

81. See Myer 1986:107; and Gangoly 1938:49–50. Dutt (1957:236) notes that, in the *Div*., no mention is actually made of Buddha images (only images of the gods), and he concludes that "the spirit of image-worship has effloresced—but without the image." Other versions of the story, however, do mention images of the Buddha (see Przyluski 1923a:361–62; and Huber 1908:272).

82. Coomaraswamy 1927; Van Lohuizen-De Leeuw 1949:171; Dutt 1962:189. On this much debated issue, see, more recently, Narain 1985 and Van Lohuizen-De Leeuw 1979.

83. See, for examples of both views, Southwold 1983:167. For the connection between the making of early Buddha images and the desire to see the Buddha, see Huntington 1985.

84. Gombrich 1971:4–10, 142.

85. Tambiah 1984:4, 132. Tambiah is here adapting notions borrowed from Arthur Burks and Roman Jakobson.

86. See Conze 1967:139.

87. Ver Eecke 1980:iii. Phussadeva also figures in the *Vsm*., in the *Sahassavatthu*, and in later anthologies such as the *Sārasangaha* and the *Saddharmaratnākara*. See *T*. Rahula 1984:179; and W. Rahula 1956:xxxiii.

88. *Sīhaḷav*., p. 19 (Fr. trans. [omitting one verse], Ver Eecke 1980:22). In these multiple transformations of Māra, there is an interesting parallel to the *LP*. story of Upagupta and Māra (see chapter 12).

89. *Sīhaḷav*., p. 20 (Fr. trans., Ver Eecke 1980:23). Phussadeva is here recollecting the past lives of the Buddha when he devoted himself to the practice of various perfections.

90. *Sīhaḷav*., p. 21 (Fr. trans., Ver Eecke 1980:23). I have corrected "amicca" to "anicca" and "kayam" to "khayam."

91. *Sīhaḷav*., p. 21 (Fr. trans., Ver Eecke 1980:24); emphasis added.

92. *Sīhaḷav*., p. 21 (Fr. trans., Ver Eecke 1980:24).

93. Chimpa and Chattopadhyaya [1970] 1980:37.

94. Mus 1935, 2:282–83.

95. Much the same dynamic may be found in some of the meditations on devices (kasiṇa) in the Theravāda tradition.

96. Dutt 1962:134, 192.

97. Vogel 1930, pl. LVI, a and b. See also Van Lohuizen–De Leeuw 1949:171; and Gangoly 1938:45.

98. Dutt 1962:191–92.

99. Ibid., p. 192.

100. One might also note a tradition that has lasted until the present day of inserting relics into images of the Buddha, for, "without them, an [image] is of little or no religious value" (W. Rahula 1956:126).

101. Conze 1959a:144–60; Gokhale 1980; W. G. Weeraratne 1966:397.

102. Lamotte 1958: 434.

103. Herman 1983:255. Some scholars deny that bhakti has any role in the Theravāda path (see Jayatilleke [1963] 1980:384).

104. Warder (1970:259) speaks of bhakti as "mere devotion" which is "better than nothing . . . for the weakest."

105. Dutt 1962:116, 193; Gokhale 1980:22.

106. Herman 1983:259. See also Dayal [1932] 1970:31.

107. Text and Eng. trans. in Van Buitenen 1981:104–5.

108. On Buddhānusmṛti more generally, see Lamotte 1949–80, 3:1340–61.

109. In some ways, as we have seen, the stūpa is a "safer" object of worship than the Buddha image because it contains within it the reminder of the Buddha's impermanence. As Lamotte (1958:482) notes, in the Pali commentaries, the destruction of a caitya containing relics is considered to be a grave sin, but "nowhere is there a condemnation of an offense to an image." On the crucial importance of the cult of the stūpa, see Hirakawa 1963.

110. Dutt 1962:116.

111. Lamotte 1958:437, 474ff.

Chapter Six
Master-Disciple Relations

1. *Div.*, p. 363 (Eng. trans., Strong 1983b:196).

2. *Div.*, p. 364 (Eng. trans., Strong 1983b:197–98).

3. *Div.*, p. 364 (Eng. trans., Strong 1983b:197).

4. Przyluski (1923a:370–98) has translated in full over twenty of the stories (*T.* 2042, 50:121b–26b). In what follows, I shall summarize these but, for purposes of discussion, rearrange their order and introduce a few additional tales of Upagupta's disciples found in other sources.

5. On guru pūjā and the importance of the teacher in the Tibetan tradition, see Dhargyey 1982:100–139; and Snellgrove 1987:176–80.

6. *T.* 2042, 50:121b (Fr. trans., Przyluski 1923a:370–71). See also *T.* 2043, 50:162c–63a.

7. *T.* 2042, 50:125b (Fr. trans., Przyluski 1923a:392). See also *T.* 2043, 50:168b.

8. *T.* 2042, 50:122b–c (Fr. trans., Przyluski 1923a:377–78). See also *T.* 2043, 50:164b–c.

9. *T.* 2042, 50:122c–23a (Fr. trans., Przyluski 1923a:378–79). See also *T.* 2043, 50:164c–65a.

10. For various accounts of this event, see Przyluski 1926:36, 67, 140, 143, 175, 208. The significance of the circumstances of Ānanda's enlightenment lies in the fact that he becomes an arhat while *not* in any of the four modes of meditation: sitting, standing, walking, and lying down.

11. *T.* 2042, 50:120c (Fr. trans., Przyluski 1923a:366). See also *T.* 2043, 50:162a.

It may be that here the text wishes to distance Upagupta from another reputed matricidal fornicator, the great heretic Mahādeva, who is sometimes said to have been from Mathurā. On him, see *T.* 1545, 27:510c–12a (Fr. trans., Lamotte 1958:303–5); Watters [1904] 1961, 1:267–69; and Demiéville 1931–32:23–24.

12. *T.* 2042, 50:122b (Fr. trans., Przyluski 1923a:376–77). See also *T.* 2043, 50:164a–b.

13. *T.* 2042, 50:123c (Fr. trans., Przyluski 1923a:384). See also *T.* 2043, 50:166a. A similar story may be found in *T.* 1509, 25:173c (Fr. trans., Lamotte 1949–80, 2:943–44).

14. *T.* 2042, 50:123a (Fr. trans., Przyluski 1923a:380). See also *T.* 2043, 50:165a.

15. See *Vsm.* 1:341–47 (Eng. trans., Ñyāṇamoli [1956] 1976, 1:372–80).

16. *T.* 2042, 50:123c (Fr. trans., Przyluski 1923a:383–84). See also *T.* 2043, 50:166a.

17. *T.* 2042, 50:123a–b (Fr. trans., Przyluski 1923a:380–81). See also *T.* 2043, 50:165a–b.

18. *T.* 2042, 50:124b (Fr. trans., Przyluski 1923a:387–88). See also *T.* 2043, 50:167a.

19. *Sanghbhv.* 2:31. See also *T.* 1450, 24:159a–b (Fr. trans., Lamotte 1949–80, 2:1003–4n). For discussions of this episode, see Bareau 1982:42–43; and Péri 1918: 4–5.

20. For versions of this well-known story, see *Saund.* (Eng. trans., E. H. Johnston [1928] 1975); *Avk.* 1:85–95 (Eng. trans. [except for verses deemed obscene], Anonymous 1896); *T.* 1451, 24:260c–61c (Fr. trans., Lamotte 1949–80:288n–92n); *T.* 203, 4:485c–86c (Fr. trans., Chavannes 1934, 3:87–94); and *T.* 190, 3:911b–14b (Eng. trans., Beal [1875] 1985:369–78). For a Pali version, see *DhA.* 1:115–25 (Eng. trans., Burlingame 1921, 1:217–25).

21. *T.* 2042, 50:125b–c (Fr. trans., Przyluski 1923a:393–95). See also *T.* 2043, 50:168b–c. The first part of this story recalls the tale in *Vin.* 3:11–20 (Eng. trans., Horner 1938–52, 1:23–38) of Sudinna, who, unlike Upagupta's disciple, succumbs to the wiles of his wife and parents.

22. *T.* 2042, 50:125a–b (Fr. trans., Przyluski 1923a:391–92). See also *T.* 2043, 50:168a–b.

23. *T.* 2042, 50:123b–c (Fr. trans., Przyluski 1923a:382–83). See also *T.* 2043, 50:165c–66a. This story recalls the tale in *DhA.* 4:62 (Eng. trans., W. Rahula 1976: 299) of the acrobat who attains arhatship while standing on top of a pole.

24. I have here combined three versions of this tale. See *T.* 1509, 25:148c (Fr. trans., Lamotte 1949–80, 2:738–40); *T.* 208, 4:531c–32a (Fr. trans., Chavannes 1934, 2:72–74); and *T.* 2042, 50:123b (Fr. trans., Przyluski 1923a:381–82).

25. *T.* 2042, 50:122b (Fr. trans., Przyluski 1923a:375–76). See also *T.* 2043, 50:164a.

26. *T.* 2042, 50:123c–24a (Fr. trans., Przyluski 1923a:385–86). See also *T.* 2043, 50:166a–c. Virtually the same tale is found again in *T.* 2042, 50:124b–c (Fr. trans., Przyluski 1923a:388–89). See also *T.* 2043, 50:167a–b.

27. More specifically, they are sometimes said to have confused the first four levels of dhyāna with the four tracks to final nirvāṇa (stream-winner, once-returner, nonreturner, and arhat).

28. This equanimity (upekṣa), which is one of the four sublime attitudes (brahmavihāra), is so similar to the equanimity that comes with Nirvāṇa that confusion may arise as to what one has attained. Nonetheless, the two types of equanimity are distinct (see Aronson 1980:86–89; Griffiths 1986:58, 121; and Masefield 1983:81).

29. For this rule, see Prebish 1975:50–53; Conze 1959b:73–74; and Horner 1938–52, 1:151–90.

30. *T.* 2042, 50:125b (Fr. trans., Przyluski 1923a:392–93). See also *T.* 2043, 50:168b.

31. The last portion of it was included in the twelfth-century Japanese collection of Buddhist tales, the *Konjaku monogatari* (1:277–79), and retold in the thirteenth-century *Uji shūi monogatari* (pp. 383–85; Eng. trans., Mills 1970:396–97). The story is also cited by Dōgen in his *Shōbōgenzō* (Eng. trans., Nishiyama 1977–85, 4:8). Dōgen is here quoting Chih I's *Mo-ho-chih-kuan*. I would like to thank Karen Jagielski for these latter references.

32. *T.* 2042, 50:124c–25a (Fr. trans., Przyluski 1923a:390–91). See also *T.* 2043, 50:167c–68a. The end of the Japanese version (see Mills 1970:397) is even more graphic; as the monk is about to rape the woman (who here is not consenting), she turns into Upagupta. The monk tries to pull away, but Upagupta holds him fast between his legs and demands, "Why do you torment an aged priest in such a manner?"

33. *T.* 2042, 50:125c–26a (Fr. trans., Przyluski 1923a:395–96). See also *T.* 2043, 50:168c–69a.

34. The particulars of this story are noteworthy in view of Upagupta's later reputation in Southeast Asia as an arhat who is capable of controlling the rain.

35. *T.* 2042, 50:126a (Fr. trans., Przyluski 1923a:396–97). See also *T.* 2043, 50:169a–b.

36. *T.* 2042, 50:124c (Fr. trans., Przyluski 1923a:389–90). See also *T.* 2043, 50:167b–c.

37. On this famous verse, which was recited by Indra right after the death of the Buddha, see Bareau 1970–71, 2:162.

38. *T.* 2042, 50:120b–c (Fr. trans., Przyluski 1923a:364). See also *T.* 2043, 50:161b–c.

39. *T.* 2042, 50:121b–22b (Fr. trans., Przyluski 1923a:371–75). See also *T.* 2043, 50:163a–64a. The nun in this story reminds Lamotte (1949–80, 1:573n) of the old bhikṣuṇī who embarrassed Upagupta when he spilled the bowlful of oil she had placed at her door.

40. *T.* 2042, 50:126a–b (Fr. trans., Przyluski 1923a:397–98). See also *T.* 2043, 50:169b–70a. Tāranātha (Chimpa and Chattopadhyaya [1970] 1980:45–49) gives a different and more developed version of the Dhītika story.

41. We assume, of course, that all his disciples have made merit at some point in their present and/or past lives. Otherwise, they would not be where they are.

42. Story 5 was omitted from this table, as its protagonist was refused as a disciple by Upagupta.

43. For the five Vinaya accounts of this rule, see Lévi and Chavannes 1916:233–47. For the Buddha's statement that the rule was made for his monks but not for himself, see *DhA*. 3:204 (Eng. trans., Burlingame 1921, 3:39); and Strong 1979a:71–75.

44. Griffiths 1986:13–27.

45. Griffiths 1986:14–16. Simplistically put, the one practice deals with the problem of ignorance, while the other attacks the problem of desire. For a different perspective on this whole question, see La Vallée Poussin 1929 and 1937.

46. Mus 1935, 1:12, 56–57. For a different angle, see Masefield 1983.

47. Griffiths 1986:16.

48. I do not mean to suggest by this that hearing the Dharma and meditating are not also meritorious practices; clearly they are, and they could be analyzed as such.

49. *T.* 2042, 50:126b (Fr. trans., Przyluski 1923a:398). See also *T.* 2043, 50:170a.

50. *GilgMss.* 3, pt. 1:4. See also *T.* 1448, 24:2a (Fr. trans., Przyluski 1914:519).

51. On the varying dimensions this cave is said to have had, see Durt 1979:450.

52. *T.* 2087, 51:890b (Eng. trans., Watters [1904] 1961, 1:306–7). See also Li 1959:77.

53. The name is mentioned in an inscription on the Lion Pillar at Mathurā that also records the deposit of a Buddha relic at this Sarvāstivādin monastery. See Sircar 1942, 1:114–18; and the discussion in K. Das 1980:94. See also Bühler 1894:526.

54. *T.* 2087, 51:890b (Eng. trans., Watters [1904] 1961, 1:306).

55. Watters [1904] 1961, 1:307.

56. One might note a passage in a Maitreyist sūtra that tells of ninety-nine hundred million great arhats all taking a śalākā in hand as a sign of their willingness to remain in the world and protect the Dharma. See *T.* 1634, 32:39b (Fr. trans., Lévi and Chavannes 1916:203).

57. On the connection between śalākās and bodhisattva vows, see Durt 1979:451.

58. It could also be made of other materials (Durt 1979:433).

59. Ibid., pp. 433–43; see also Durt 1974.

60. Durt 1979:452. In the Jain context, the epithet "śalākā-puruṣa" was reserved for the sixty-three great beings.

61. *A.* 1:24 (Eng. trans., Woodward and Hare 1932–36, 1:18).

62. This story is found in many sources. In Sanskrit, see *Sumāg.*, p. 12; *Avk.* 2:529; and *Div.*, p. 44 (Fr. trans., Burnouf 1876:231–32). See also *T.* 1448, 25:13c–14a; *T.* 130, 2:47a (Eng. trans., Iwamoto 1968:142); *T.* 128, 2:836c (Eng. trans., Tokiwai 1898:57–58), where it is the novice Cuṇḍa who acquires magical powers by taking a śalākā; and *T.* 125, 2:662a (Eng. trans., Tokiwai 1898:25–26). In Pali, see, inter alia, *SA.* 2:374–79 (Fr. trans., Duroiselle 1905:164).

63. *Div.*, pp. 184–85. For the *MSV.* version of this story, see *T.* 1442, 23:858c (Eng. trans., Ch'en 1945–47:238).

64. *Div.*, pp. 184–85.

65. *T.* 1451, 24:220b (Fr. trans., Durt 1979:450). See also *Vin.* 2:125 (Eng. trans., Horner 1938–52, 5:173), where Vaḍḍha has imposed on him the "exclusion from eating with the community." This would imply, as Durt notes, that the śalākā is being considered here above all as a meal token.

66. *T.* 1425, 22:492a–b (Fr. trans., Przyluski 1926:214–15); *T.* 1451, 24:404c–5c (Fr. trans., Durt 1979:446).

67. See Hofinger 1946:114–25. Interestingly, when Devadatta instigates the heterodoxy of the Vajjis, he has five hundred of them *take up* śalākās to indicate their secession. See *Vin.* 2:199 (Eng. trans., Horner 1938–52, 5:279).

68. Mair 1983:74.

69. Durt 1979:454.

70. *T.* 1421, 22:123a (Fr. trans., Durt 1979:434).

71. *Vin.* 1:204 (Eng. trans., Davids and Oldenberg [1882–85] 1975, 2:53). The context of this rule is different, as it concerns śalākās that were used for applying ointment to the eyes; still, the worry about not letting them fall on the ground is intriguing.

72. *T.* 1899, 45:892b (Fr. trans., Durt 1979:453).

73. Watters [1904] 1961, 1:302. On the possible meanings of the "three longs" when these festivals took place, see ibid., pp. 304–5.

74. Legge 1886:14, 44–46.

75. *A.* 1:24 (Eng. trans., Woodward and Hare 1932–36, 1:20).

76. Ānanda's action in convincing the Buddha to allow for the ordination of women is well known.

77. Śāriputra and Maudgalyāyana were renowned for the qualities mentioned. Sīvalī, who in Burma is often paired with Upagupta, was foremost among those who receive offerings; Bakkula was foremost of those of good health (see *A.* 1:24; Eng. trans., Woodward and Hare 1932–36, 1:18).

Chapter Seven
Upagupta and Aśoka

1. For editions and translations of the edicts, see Bloch 1950 and Nikam and McKeon 1959.

2. For a recent presentation and discussion of Aśoka's Dharma, see Tambiah 1976:9–72.

3. For different views on this dispute, see Gokhale 1949:65; Smith [1909] 1964:35; and Dikshitar 1932:258, 288.

4. See Strong 1983b:15.

5. Przyluski 1923a:8.

6. *Avś.*, p. 262 (Fr. trans., Feer 1891:434). Przyluski (1920:7), unwilling to have Upagupta reside anywhere but Mathurā, claims that this episode must have been a late interpolation into the *Avś.* written in Gandhāra or Kashmir, a point which is disputed by Iwamoto (see de Jong 1979a:331).

7. See Huber 1902:257.

8. Waddell 1897:80.

9. Watters [1904] 1961, 2:91, 252. Hsüan-tsang here seems to confuse Upagupta both with the figure of Samudra (who, in the Sanskrit tradition, is usually the converter of Aśoka) and with the arhat Yaśas (who is involved in the construction of the stūpas).

10. *T.* 202, 4:42b (Ger. trans. of Tibetan, Schmidt 1843, 2:383; Eng. trans. of Mongolian, Frye 1981:231).

11. Chimpa and Chattopadhyaya [1970] 1980:34.

12. *Div.*, p. 385 (Eng. trans., Strong 1983b:238). The gift of dirt was Aśoka's most famous act of merit in a past life when, as a young boy, he placed some dust into the Buddha's bowl. It is noteworthy that, in Burmese tradition, Upagupta came to be associated with the gift of dirt, the claim being made either that he was Aśoka's companion on that occasion and so a sort of karmic fellow traveller of the king, or that he was

actually the one who made the offering of dirt. See Ohn Maung n.d.:1–3 and note facing p. 1.

13. *Div.*, p. 385 (Eng. trans., Strong 1983b:239–40).

14. *Div.*, p. 386 (Eng. trans. Strong 1983b:240). The implication seems to be that, if Upagupta should refuse the royal summons, nothing could be done to force him to comply. In *T* 2042, 50:102b (Fr. trans., Przyluski 1923a:247), Aśoka declares that he must go to see Upagupta because he himself does not yet have a vajra-like mind. For other variants, see Przyluski 1923a:247n.1.

15. *Div.*, p. 386 (Eng. trans., Strong 1983b:240). Contrast Przyluski 1923a:247.

16. *Mhv.*, pp. 53–54 (Eng. trans., Geiger [1912] 1960:47–48). See also *VinNid.*, pp. 177–79 (Eng. trans., Jayawickrama 1962:50–53).

17. Waddell 1897:77.

18. Smith 1903:365.

19. Wayman 1981. On this connection, see also Yamazaki 1982.

20. Waddell 1899.

21. Sambhūta, it will be recalled, was one of Moggaliputta Tissa's predecessors in the lineage of Theravādin masters and has been convincingly identified with Upagupta's teacher, Śāṇakavāsin (see Hofinger 1946:208).

22. Tambiah 1984:274–80. On the use and distribution of Upagupta amulets, see chapter 13.

23. Tambiah 1984:93–99, 280–83. On the correlation of heavens and meditation states, see Kloetzli 1983:34; and Masefield 1983:78.

24. *Div.*, p. 385 (Eng. trans., Strong 1983b:239).

25. *T.* 2043, 50:169b. In brief, the story is as follows: Due to Upagupta's popularity at Mathurā, many temples were erected in that country. But a faithless lord came to rule there and oppressed the monks in various ways. Upagupta, therefore, used his supernatural powers, flew to Pāṭaliputra, and complained to Aśoka. The latter quickly issued an edict ordering the local lord to cease his persecution and assigning the revenue of one country to the Naṭabhaṭika. Upagupta then returned in the manner in which he had come.

26. *Mhv.*, pp. 52–53 (Eng. trans., Geiger [1912] 1960:47). See also *VinNid.*, p. 177 (Eng. trans., Jayawickrama 1962:50–51).

27. Tambiah 1984:81–110.

28. *Mhv.*, pp. 52–53 (Eng. trans., Geiger [1912] 1960:47). See also *VinNid.*, p. 178 (Eng. trans., Jayawickrama 1962:51). For a monk to ride in a palanquin would be a dukkaṭa offense (see *Vin.* 1:191 [Eng. trans., Davids and Oldenberg [1882–85] 1975, 2:24]).

29. *Div.*, p. 386 (Eng. trans., Strong 1983b:240). We shall encounter another *nausaṃkrama* in chapter 10, where it appears to mean a large raft planted with trees to make it look like a park. On this term, see also *Aśokāv.*, p. 170n.77; *Div*, p. 683; Edgerton 1953, 2:313; Jayawickrama 1962:51; and Przyluski 1923a:247. On the raft's possible construction, see *Avk.*, 2:416.

30. See chapter 10 for details of one such ceremony in Rangoon.

31. Thus, in Thailand, Buddha images found in the water or transported by boat are called Gangā images (see G. Martini 1969:135n.2).

32. Thus Upagupta on shipboard is called "the helmsman of the Teaching . . . standing at the head of [those] who have crossed over to the other shore of the stream

of existence" (*Div.*, p. 386 [Eng. trans. Strong 1983b:240]). For other interpretations along this line, see Przyluski 1923a:248n.

33. See, however, the comments on the relationship in Hinduism between "fording" and "descent" in Eck 1981:336.

34. See Eck 1982:211–20. See also Darian 1978.

35. Zimmer 1955, 1:88.

36. Mention could be made here of another "descent" of the Buddha—that of his coming down from heaven to be born in the womb of his mother.

37. Foucher 1963:205.

38. In another version of the story, it is King Udrāyaṇa who welcomes the Buddha (see Lamotte 1949–80, 2:634n.1).

39. *DhA*. 3:222 (Eng. trans., Burlingame 1921, 3:51) specifies that when the Buddha had to go on his alms round, he would leave a double of himself in the heaven to preach the Dharma in his place so that his sermon would continue uninterrupted.

40. See Lamotte 1949–80, 2:634n.1; and *DhA*. 3:224 (Eng. trans., Burlingame 1921, 3:52) for the use of these two terms.

41. Lamotte 1949–80, 2:635. The commingling of gods and humans was also a feature of the Pure Lands (see Dantinne 1983:239, 264).

42. *Div.*, p. 401 (Eng. trans., Strong 1983b:262). The term has various connotations such as prosperity, achievement, wholeness, and accomplishment. Burnouf (1876:355) calls it "the brilliant festival of gods and men." See also Edgerton 1953, 2:575.

43. *DhA*. 3:218 (Eng. trans., Burlingame 1921, 3:48).

44. Field notes, Chiang Mai, 7 October 1982. Elsewhere, images of the Buddha may be lowered from the top of a caitya. At this time, the Devorohana Sutta is recited, sometimes dramatically by three monks taking on the roles of the Buddha, Sāriputta, and Moggallāna (see Wells 1960:104). On the connection between the Buddha's descent from Trāyastriṃśa and the festival of lights in Burma, see Brohm 1957:159ff.

45. Field notes, Mae Hong Son and Khun Yuam, 9–10 October 1982.

46. *Div.*, p. 387 (Eng. trans., Strong 1983b:241–42).

47. When he first meets Piṇḍola Bhāradvāja, for example, Aśoka prostrates himself and announces, "By looking at you, I can, even today, see the Tathāgata" (see *Div.*, p. 400; Eng. trans., Strong 1983b:261). This same thing is recalled in *Avk.* 2:456, where Kṣemendra states, "The sight of the Jina hidden in parinirvāṇa being hard to obtain, [Aśoka] listened to Upagupta, who is like the Sugata in qualities." (On the Tibetan version of this passage, see Tucci 1949, 2:512.)

48. *Mhv.*, p. 53 (Eng. trans., Geiger [1912] 1960:47–48).

49. *VinNid.*, p. 178 (Eng. trans., Jayawickrama 1962:52); *ExtMhv.*, p. 87. In these texts, this story is presented as the fulfillment of a dream that Aśoka had of a great white elephant who came and held him by the right hand with his trunk. The elephant (hatthināga) is said to presage the coming of Tissa, an ascetic monk (samaṇanāga).

50. Filliozat 1967:45–47.

51. Such a breakdown may, in fact, have been historically a part of Aśoka's program; in one of his edicts, Aśoka declares that, as a result of his zeal towards the Sangha, "devas and humans who formerly were not mingled, have now become mingled" (see Bloch 1950:146; Nikam and McKeon 1959:49; and Filliozat 1967).

52. See Przyluski 1936; T. W. Rhys Davids 1907; and Strong 1983b:109–19. This story corresponds to the building and dedication of eighty-four thousand monasteries (vihāras) in the Pali tradition (see *Mhv.*, p. 36; Eng. trans., Geiger [1912] 1960:32).

53. See, for example, Watters [1904] 1961, index, s.v. "Asoka topes."

54. On this line of interpretation, see Mus 1935, 1:245; and Strong 1983b:116–17.

55. Watters [1904] 1961, 2:91. See also Beal [1884] 1968, 2:88–90.

56. *Div.*, p. 381 (Eng. trans., Strong 1983b:220). On the confusion of Yaśas and Upagupta, see also Yamazaki 1979:192–96.

57. *Mhv.*, p. 45 (Eng. trans., Geiger [1912] 1960:41).

58. See Eggermont 1956, supplement 4. Eggermont chooses 4 May 249 B.C.E., the date on which a partial solar eclipse was visible in Northern India. For other possibilities, see Lamotte 1958:262n.

59. The standard list of ṛddhi has been preserved in many texts. For Sanskrit and Pali versions, see *Pañca.*, pp. 83–84 (Eng. trans., Conze 1975:79–80); and *D.* 1:78 (Eng. trans., T. W. Rhys Davids 1899–1924, 1:88–89). On Buddhist ṛddhi, see also Eliade 1969:177–85.

60. See *Vsm.* 1:398 (Eng. trans., Conze 1959b:126–27).

61. Sanskrit fragments edited in Waldschmidt 1977 (Fr. trans. of Tibetan, Feer 1883:411–13); Pali text in *S.* 1:50 (Eng. trans., Davids and Woodward 1917–30, 1:71–72). For Chinese versions, see *T.* 99, 2:155a–b (Fr. trans., Lamotte 1949–80, 1:610–11n); and *T.* 1509, 25:135b (Fr. trans., Lamotte 1949–80, 1:610–12).

62. See Malalasekera [1938] 1974, 2:735–37.

63. Plenge 1976:118–19.

64. Ibid., p. 120.

65. *A.* 2:17 (Eng. trans., Woodward and Hare 1932–36, 2:17). See also Malalasekera [1938] 1974, 2:735–37.

66. *A.* 3:243 (Eng. trans., Woodward and Hare 1932–36, 3:178).

67. See chapter 12.

68. On full-moon Wednesday rituals, see chapter 11.

69. This is the case, for instance, in the Burmese film on Shin Upago, which we shall analyze in chapter 10.

70. Two additional interpretations are suggested by other Indian traditions. According to one story also recounted by Hsüan-tsang (Beal [1884] 1968, 2:305), the sight of the shining sun is the signal for arhats who spend their time in meditative ecstasy to awaken from their trance. The arhat who gazes up at the sun is thus one who is about to emerge from meditation, ready for action in this world. According to another tradition preserved in *T.* 1509, 24:79c (Fr. trans., Lamotte 1949–80, 1:201), as well as in *S.* 3:239 (Eng. trans., Davids and Woodward 1917–30, 3:190), monks who eat looking up at the sun and the moon are thought to be involved in astrology and thus are seen as impure.

71. *Mhv.*, p. 45 (Eng. trans., Geiger [1912] 1960:41). On the office of superintendent of construction, see Njammasch 1974.

72. *VinA.* 1:49 (Eng. trans., Jayawickrama 1962:43). The same details are found in *Thūp.*, p. 188 (Eng. trans., Jayawickrama 1971:52).

73. Witanachchi 1976:355. He fails, however, to note some points of discrepancy (on which see Malalasekera [1938] 1974, 2:1337).

74. *Mhv.*, pp. 228, 243 (Eng. trans., Geiger [1912] 1960:193, 208). See also *Dpv.*,

p. 100 (Eng. trans., Oldenberg [1879] 1982:208–9). In *MhvṬ.*, 2:524–25, Indagutta is listed as one of twelve elders at the Mahāthūpa dedication ceremony and plays a crucial role in the design of the relic chamber (p. 548).

75. *Mhv.*, p. 253 (Eng. trans., Geiger [1912] 1960:216). For a similar story about the monk Tuvaṭakanāga, who was asked to prevent Māra from marring the stūpa pūjā of Duṭṭhagāmaṇī's successor Saddhātissa, see *Sīhaḷav.*, p. 130 (Fr. trans., Ver Eecke 1980:144).

76. It is noteworthy that Indagutta bears in his name a reminder of the god Indra, who figures in this Mathuran Kṛṣṇa legend. On the ritual connections of this legend, see Vaudeville 1980.

77. According to *Avk.* 2:456, it was specifically for this reason that Aśoka sent for "him who abides at Urumuṇḍa."

78. See the colophon of the *Kalpadrumāvadāna* (in Mitra [1882] 1981:303). A similar term, *Aśoka-Upagupta-saṃvāda*, occurs in the *Bhadrakalpāvadāna* (see Matsunami 1965:219).

79. *S.* 1:67–102 (Eng. trans., Davids and Woodward 1917–30, 1:93–127).

80. *A.* 3:57–60 (Eng. trans., Woodward and Hare 1932–36, 3:48–51).

81. Hahn 1985:11. On the problematic date of its last chapter, however, see below.

82. For an analysis of the contents, see Feer 1891:xiv–xvi.

83. Burnouf 1876:385–88; Przyluski 1920:5–46; Speyer 1899.

84. For references to Kuṇāla (also spelled Kunāla), whose legend may be found in *Div.*, pp. 405–19, see Strong 1983b:151n.32.

85. *Avś.*, pp. 260–63 (Fr. trans., Feer 1891:430–35). For a striking interpretation of this story, see Vaudeville 1964.

86. *T.* 200, 4:203a–57a (partial Eng. trans., Fa Chow 1945). See also Bagchi 1945.

87. See Fa Chow 1945:53–55; Bagchi 1945:60; and Vaudeville 1964:88.

88. It was first presented in Feer 1879, then again in Feer 1891:xix. See also *Ratnamālāv.*, p. viii–ix. Recently, however, Feer's stress on the systematicity of the selection scheme has been called misleading (see Zimmermann 1975:9).

89. On the *Kalpadrumāvadānamālā.*, see Mitra [1882] 1981:293; and Bendall 1883:15. One chapter edited by Speyer has been reprinted in *Avś.*, pp. 265–96; another may be found in de Jong 1979b (summarized Eng. trans., de Jong 1979a:363–64). See also Feer 1895.

90. See Feer 1891:xxvi.

91. See *Ratnamālāv.*, p. viii.

92. On this anthology, see Mitra [1882] 1981:6–17; and Bendall 1883:110–14. Various chapters have been edited in Zinkgräf 1940:91; Handurukande 1984:218; and Iwamoto 1978:217–30. For the chapter on Kunāla (which does *not* feature Upagupta as narrator), see Bongard-Levin and Volkova 1965:8.

93. Feer 1891:xxvii. See also Mitra [1882] 1981:85–89; Turner 1913; and Zimmermann 1975. According to Hahn (1985:18), the work has been edited by Mamiko Okada in her Ph.D. dissertation (Bonn, 1985). One tale is translated in Feer 1883:544–52.

94. Edited by P. L. Vaidya in appendix to *Avś.*, p. 265.

95. *Ratnamālāv.*, p. 1n.

96. See, for example, ibid., pp. 20, 36, 53, 69.

97. Mitra [1882] 1981:6–17. On these tales, see Strong 1983b.

98. See Handurukande 1984:218; Iwamoto 1978:219; and Zinkgräf 1940:91.

99. For examples, see the *Vicitrakarṇikāvadāna* (Iwamoto 1978:188–95); the *Maṇiśailāvadāna* (Handurukande 1976a:187); the *Saptakumārikāvadāna* (Handurukande 1970, 1976b; Dargyay 1978); the *Saṃbhadrāvadānamālā* (Handurukande 1984:187); and the *Śasajātakāvadāna* (Bendall 1883:104).

100. On this text, see Mitra [1882] 1981:102–4, 275–80. For editions of various chapters, see *Lakṣacait.*, 1:130–57 (Eng. trans., Rajapatirana 1974, 3:107–38); and Iwamoto 1978:48–112, 231–46.

101. *Lakṣacait.*, 1:130 (Eng. trans., Rajapatirana 1974, 3:107).

102. Bendall 1883:89. See also Mitra [1882] 1981:42–47.

103. Sastri 1894:33. See also La Vallée Poussin 1894 and Handurukande 1967: 147ff.

104. On this text, see Hahn 1985; Handurukande 1976a:265–201 [*sic*]; Handurukande 1984:196; and Lang 1912, where two chapters have been translated into French.

105. *MJM.*, pp. 5–17.

106. Ibid., p. 18.

107. The Hindu tradition distinguished between *śruti* (what was "heard" or "revealed") and *smṛti* (what was "remembered" or "passed on"). The Buddhist distinction between "Thus have I heard" and "Thus it has been repeated" might be thought of in similar terms, except that it is typical of Buddhist one-upsmanship to have preserved the crucial root *śru* ("to hear") to designate both of their categories.

108. Strong 1985. See the *Kalpadrumāvadānamālā* passage in *Avś.*, pp. 272, 275.

109. For example, the dīghabhānakas, who were specialists in the recitation of the *Dīgha Nikāya*, did not accept the canonicity of the *Apadāna* (see Malalasekera [1938] 1974, 1:1082–83).

110. The nine genres generally listed in Pali texts are sutta, geyya, veyyākaraṇa, gāthā, udāna, itivuttaka, jātaka, abbhutadhamma, and vedalla. Listings do not all agree with one another, however. Moreover, some Sanskrit texts (e.g., the *Lotus Sūtra*) have a nine-limb listing which includes the avadāna. See Lamotte 1958:157–59.

111. This scheme, generally speaking, adds to the Pali listing the nidāna, the avadāna, and the upadeśa. But variations are common (see Lamotte 1958:159–61).

112. This event is said to have taken place at the time of Upagupta (see Lamotte 1958:191).

113. *MJM.*, pp. 34ff.

114. Hurvitz 1976:52.

115. Kern [1884] 1963:63–64.

116. See, for example, Lévi and Chavannes 1916:203.

117. *Div.*, p. 389 (Eng. trans., Strong 1983b:244).

118. For a list of all thirty-two sites, see Strong 1983b:142–43n.

119. See, for example, Foucher 1963.

120. See *Div.*, pp. 390, 392 (Eng. trans., Strong 1983b:246, 249).

121. Ibid. He takes similar action after listening to the testimony of the nāga Kālika on the road to Bodhgaya.

122. See discussion in Strong 1983b:125–27.

123. *Div.*, p. 394 (Eng. trans., Strong 1983b:251).

124. Shulman 1985:40. On viraha in the Hindu tradition, see also O'Flaherty 1980:122–24; and Dimock [1966] 1971.

125. Shulman 1985:41.

126. *Div.*, p. 394 (Eng. trans., Strong 1983b:252).

127. *A.* 1:23–27 (Eng. trans., Woodward and Hare 1932–36, 1:16–25). For the legends of each of these individuals, see *AA.* 1:136–458 (Eng. trans. of pp. 337–81, Bode 1893).

128. *Div.*, p. 397 (Eng. trans., Strong 1983b:256).

Chapter Eight
The Southeast Asian Context: Upagupta and Theravāda Orthodoxy

1. Porée-Maspero (1962–69, 2:391) does cite a manuscript from a Phnom Penh collection that gives the gist of the Upagupta story, but there is little widespread knowledge of the saint in Cambodia. In Central Thailand, as we shall see, he is sometimes confused with and replaced by the figure of Phra Bua Khem.

2. The first term is Spiro's, the second Tambiah's. Other variants (e.g., animism and magical-animism) are sometimes used.

3. The expression is borrowed from Tambiah 1970, ch. 20.

4. Spiro 1967:3.

5. Brohm 1963:167.

6. See Tambiah 1970:338, where the picture presented is, however, more profound than this. See also Htin Aung [1962] 1978.

7. N. Ray 1946:263.

8. Ames 1964:22–23; King 1964:72.

9. See also Mendelson 1961b:560; and Mendelson 1961a:231.

10. Spiro 1967:44n, citing Duroiselle 1922–23.

11. It may be that the cult of Upagupta, like that of other saints, fluctuates in popularity and that it is more prevalent now than it was during Spiro's stay in Burma. A number of Upagupta shrines I visited were of fairly recent vintage. The large Upagupta shrine in Rangoon, however, dates from 1955, and the Upagupta pillar at the Shwe Dagon is even older.

12. See Terwiel 1975:5; M.A.G.T. Kloppenborg 1979; and, for a somewhat different perspective, Obeyesekere 1963.

13. Ferguson and Mendelson 1981:62.

14. N. Ray 1936; Luce 1964, 1:ch. 10; Aung-Thwin 1985:32–46.

15. Aung-Thwin 1985:17. N. Ray (1936, ch. 1) has likewise stressed the Sarvāstivādin connections of Śrī Kṣetra, based primarily on testimony of the Chinese pilgrim I-ching.

16. See Coedès 1967:68; and LeMay 1954:46.

17. This is Luce's (1964, 1:202) assessment of the evidence presented in Dupont 1959. Mon presence in Haripuñjaya (Lamphun) lasted until the end of the thirteenth century and was clearly influential in the development of Northern Thai Buddhism.

18. See Guillon 1985:24–26; Guillon 1983:57; and Shorto 1970.

19. Halliday 1917:78.

20. By the ninth century, Buddhism had become the state religion of the Nanchao kingdom (see Backus 1981:129).

21. Sainson 1904:24–61. See also Chapin and Soper 1971:38.

22. Aung-Thwin 1985:20.

23. Pelliot 1904:157–58. Similarly, Aung-Thwin (1981) has studied the tradition that led Burmese kings to call their kingdom Jambudīpa.

24. This may reflect the Burmese belief that Mahākāśyapa's mountain is somewhere in Northwest Burma (see Ferguson 1977:6).

25. Pelliot 1904:161–62. It will be noted that, despite the identification of Nanchao with Gandhāra, most of these sites appear to be in Magadha. Things may be more complicated, however, because of the tendency to reduplicate Magadha pilgrimage sites in Gandhāra. Indeed, by the sixth century, some pilgrims coming from China did not bother to go all the way to Magadha, since they could see everything they wanted to in Gandhāra (see Chavannes 1903:381–87).

26. As Luce (1964, 1:6l) put it: "[Pagan's] sculpture, votive tablets, bronzes, painting, are all North Indian in origin, based on Gandhāran, Mathuran, and Pāla Bengal models."

27. Aung-Thwin 1985:23.

28. Luce 1964, 1:72.

29. On the Ari, see Duroiselle 1915–16; N. Ray 1936, ch. 4; Htin Aung [1962] 1978, ch. 9; Finot 1912; Bizot 1976:41–42; Pe Maung Tin and Luce [1923] 1960:39, 59, 71; and Than Tun 1959b.

30. Pe Maung Tin and Luce [1923] 1960:39, 59, 71. Obviously, these accusations are not without bias, and we would do well to remember the same text's admission (p. 39) that the doctrine of the Ari was espoused by "thirty generations of kings at Pagan" prior to Aniruddha.

31. Pelliot 1902:153–54.

32. Ibid., pp. 154–55.

33. Ibid., p. 154n.

34. Duroiselle 1915–16:92–93.

35. Wood 1965:151.

36. Bizot 1976:41–42. A modern Burmese equivalent might be found in the girls' ear-boring ceremony, which takes place at the same time as the boys' Buddhist initiation (shin-byu)—a ceremony which, as Spiro (1982:241ff.) has pointed out, is not without its bacchanalian overtones.

37. Than Tun 1959b:107–10.

38. Ibid., p. 117.

39. Ibid., p. 118.

40. On these connections, see Mendelson 1961b:577; and Ferguson and Mendelson 1981:65–69.

41. *Dpv.*, p. 54 (Eng. trans., Oldenberg [1879] 1982:160); *Mhv.*, p. 94 (Eng. trans., Geiger [1912] 1960:82). Thai Buddhists, too, lay claim to the Soṇa and Uttara story in accounting for Buddhism's establishment in their country (see Wells 1960:3).

42. The same myth serves other functions, not the least of which is the attachment of Burmese kingship to the figure of the great emperor Aśoka.

43. Pe Maung Tin and Luce [1923] 1960 :72–73.

44. Ibid., pp. 77–79.

45. See Dupont 1959, 1:14–15.

46. Luce 1964, 1:16. See also Than Tun 1959a.

47. Thus, when the *Glass Palace Chronicle* (Pe Maung Tin and Luce [1923]

1960:143) relates the story of the new official establishment of the Sri Lanka Sīhala Sangha by Uttarajiva and his disciple Chapaṭa, it still stresses their Thaton connection.

48. Guillon 1983:61.

49. Paraphrased from Shorto 1970:16–17. The same story is recalled in Bigandet [1858] 1979, 2:144–45. A somewhat different tale, recorded in Kyanzittha's Shwezigon inscription, associates Gavāṃpati with the foundation of Śrī Kṣetra (see Duroiselle [1919] 1960:114–17; and Pe Maung Tin and Luce [1923] 1960:14). On the scheme of the thirty-three relics, see Shorto 1963.

50. Przyluski 1926:239–56. See also Lévy [1957] 1968:82–96.

51. Przyluski 1926:115–16. A similar case of a monk who had been a cow in a past life and was now a "ruminator" is reported in *Vin.* 2:131 (Eng. trans., Horner 1938–52, 5:183) with, however, a rather different solution: the Buddha simply allows rumination!

52. Shorto 1970:24; Guillon 1983:55; Przyluski 1926:241; Lefèvre-Pontalis 1926:6–9.

53. *Mkv.*, p. 62 (Fr. trans., Lévi 1932:131). The full list of missionaries and the lands they convert is as follows: Mahākātyāyana, the peoples of the west (Avanti); Madhyandina, Kashmir; Gavāṃpati, Suvarṇabhūmi; Piṇḍola, Pūrvavideha; Mahendra, Sri Lanka; and Pūrṇa, Śūrpāraka. For the Pali list, see *Mhv.*, p. 94 (Eng. trans., Geiger [1912] 1960:82).

54. *T.* 1451, 24:228a (Fr. trans., Guillon 1983:55). See also Lamotte 1949–80, 2:629n.

55. Shorto 1970:21, 23.

56. Ibid., p. 22. We shall see this also with Upagupta.

57. Ibid., pp. 18–19. The same story is told of Gavāṃpati in *Sās.*, p. 36ff. (Eng. trans., Law 1952:33f.).

58. Malalasekera [1938] 1974, 1:756–57.

59. See chapter 10 for a discussion of these myths.

60. Luce 1964, 1:373.

61. Luce and Ba Shin 1961:385.

62. Ibid. The frescoes themselves, however, clearly distinguish the story depicted here from that of Aśoka and Moggaliputta Tissa, which is pictured separately on a different wall devoted to the Third Council (see p. 382).

63. The same may be said of the only other scene at the Kubyauk-gyi that has been identified as coming from the *LP.*, the tale of the elephant Rucāgiri. It is located on the lowest row of an outside wall of the hall. See ibid., p. 404; Denis 1977, 2:vii; and Guillon 1985:74–75.

64. Luce and Ba Shin 1961:382; see also Strachan 1989:71–74.

65. Luce 1964, 1:375.

66. *Sdn.* 3:691.

67. See Malalasekera [1938] 1974, 2:1015.

68. Reynolds and Reynolds 1982:46, 350.

69. Bode [1909] 1965:104.

70. Kala 1960:80–81.

71. *PSK.*, pp. 422–46.

72. Pe Maung Tin and Luce [1923] 1960:ix.

73. *HmanNanY.*, pp. 163–64. Eng. trans. courtesy U ko ko.

74. Thus we now have two versions of the *PSK.*, one demythologized, another uncensored. See Coedès 1968b:218; and M.L.M. Jumsai 1980:80. On Mongkut's reformist attitudes, see Griswold 1957; Moffat 1961:15–19; and, on Mongkut's son, C. J. Reynolds 1979.

75. Maung Kin 1903:219–20.

76. Ibid., pp. 241–42.

77. Bizot 1976:32. See also Bizot 1980a and 1981.

78. Bizot 1976:27.

Chapter Nine
The *Lokapaññatti* Legend

1. Duroiselle 1904:414. See also Mus 1939:37, 131n. Other names for this monk include Saghosa, Asmaghosa, and Assaghosa, all of which reflect an association, real or contrived, with the figure of Aśvaghoṣa, whom some would like to credit with the Sanskrit original of at least part of the *LP*. Debates about Aśvaghoṣa preoccupied a whole generation of buddhologists; their relevance to the *LP.* has been summarized by Denis (1977, 2:ii–v) (who, it should be pointed out, disputes the assignation of the text to Saddhammaghosa and prefers to label it anonymous). Lin (1949:132), through a series of identifications (Saddhammaghosa = Mou-lien = Moggaliputta Tissa = Upagupta), claims that Upagupta himself was the real author of the *LP.*—so that the part of the text that deals with him is, in fact, autobiographical!

2. There is also some debate about the place of the *LP.*'s compilation, but Mus (1939:37) and Denis (1977, 2:v) have convincingly argued for Thaton over the other contenders (India and Sri Lanka).

3. *T.* 1644, 32:173a–226a. On the concordances between this text and the *LP.*, see Mus 1939:125–27; and Denis 1977, 2:xix–xxviii; 3:253–88. On the relation of this text to the "Lokaprajñapti" that constitutes the first section (missing in Chinese but extant in Tibetan) of the *Prajñaptiśāstra* (*T.* 1538; one of the books of the Sarvāstivādin Abhidharma piṭaka), see Mus 1939:120–25; Banerjee [1957] 1979:68–69; and Takakusu 1905. See also La Vallée Poussin 1914–19. For a bibliography on a Sanskrit fragment of a *Lokaprajñapti* which includes a noteworthy genealogy of King Aśoka, see Bechert 1985:55n.

4. This text also appears to be founded on Sanskrit materials, although it has close affinities with a Pali cosmological treatise, the commentary on the *Chagatidīpanī* (Explanation of the Six Realms of Existence). See Mus 1939:27; and Denis 1977, 2:ii.

5. See, for example, *DA.* 2:612–15; *Thūp.*, pp. 189–90 (Eng. trans., Jayawickrama 1971:53–54); and Przyluski 1923a:425–26.

6. See Denis 1976. The saga of the robots was picked up by several later Burmese texts, e.g., Kin 1957:108–9; and Kala 1960, 1:75–77.

7. Summarized from *LP.* 1:162–64 (Fr. trans., Denis 1977, 2:144–45).

8. On the theme of the magically potent young novice, see *Div.*, p. 404 (Eng. trans., Strong 1983b:266–67); *T.* 2042, 50:128c–29a (Fr. trans., Przyluski 1923a:413–14); and Huber 1908:25.

9. *LP.* 1:164–65 (Fr. trans., Denis 1977, 2:147).

10. On nāgas in Hinduism and Buddhism, see Vogel 1926.

11. Denis 1977, 2:lxv.

12. Tambiah 1970:172.

13. Wells 1960:113.

14. Lamotte 1949–80, 1:212.

15. This story is given to explain the origin of the Vinaya rule forbidding nonhumans from becoming bhikṣus. See Banerjee [1957] 1979:182; and Davids and Oldenberg [1882–85] 1975, 1:217–19.

16. Davis 1984:340.

17. For slightly different versions of this tale, see *T.* 1509, 25:181c (Fr. trans., Lamotte 1949–80, 2:994–95); *T.* 206, 4:511c–12a (Fr. trans., Chavannes 1934, 1:358–60); and *T.* 208, 4:533c–34a (Fr. trans., Chavannes 1934, 2:87–88).

18. Kala 1960, 1:82; *HmanNanY.*, p. 160; and Kin 1957:114. See also Maung Kin 1903:237; and Witanachchi 1976:353.

19. Warren 1922:398–99.

20. Field notes, Rajamaha Viharaya (Peradeniya, Sri Lanka), 1 July 1987.

21. Tambiah (1970:109) gives a list of eight that are recognized in Northeastern Thailand, but variants are common.

22. Lafont and Bitard 1957. See also Tambiah 1970:109–15; Lévy [1957] 1968:34–36; Condominas 1973:79; Archaimbault 1966:42–44n; Zago 1972:65–68; and Gabaude 1988:248n, 260–63.

23. Lafont and Bitard 1957:201–2. The "wrong" candidates sitting in the first two hermitages are identified as Asita (the sage who foretold the Buddha's future Buddhahood at his birth) and Mahākāśyapa.

24. Ibid., p. 202.

25. A different explanation was given by monk informants.

26. Lafont and Bitard 1957:204n. This back-and-forth jostling of the palanquin recalls a similar movement that is imparted to coffins of abbots and other monastic dignitaries at the time of their funerals. Keyes (1975) interprets this as involved in death and rebirth symbolism.

27. Lafont and Bitard 1957:204. This is an aspect of the Buddha Jayanti that Theravāda officialdom managed to cover up in its twenty-five-hundredth-anniversary celebrations, although various aspects of these celebrations (e.g., the "Sixth" Council held in Burma) might be seen as desperate attempts to stave off the decline of the Dharma. On the Buddha Jayanti, see also Coedès 1956.

28. Lafont and Bitard make no mention of the nāga shape of this shower head, but it is clearly indicated in Condominas 1973:77, fig. a. See also Tambiah 1970:112 for an interpretation of its significance; and Archaimbault 1966:44 for its relation to the bamboo rockets set off at rocket festivals (Bun Bang Fai).

29. Lafont and Bitard 1957:208–9.

30. Ibid., pp. 212, 221.

31. *LP.* 1:165–66 (Fr. trans., Denis 1977, 2:147–48).

32. For somewhat similar invitations aimed at bringing the elders Nāgasena and Moggaliputta Tissa to the aid of the Sangha, see *Mil.*, pp. 5–14 (Eng. trans., Davids [1890–94] 1963, 1:10–23); Demiéville 1924:75–88; Chau 1964b:36–46; *VinNid.*, pp. 160–65 (Eng. trans., Jayawickrama 1962:31–37); and *T.* 1462, 24:678b–79c (Eng. trans., Bapat and Hirakawa 1970:20–25). For a comparison of the two invitations, see Durt 1963.

33. This story is strongly reminiscent of that of the Buddha utterly outpacing the long-haired ascetic Uruvilvā Kāśyapa in a race to the latter's hermitage, on which see *Sanghbhv.* 1:224–25 (Eng. trans., R. Kloppenborg 1973:59–61); and *Vin.* 1:29–31 (Eng. trans., Davids and Oldenberg [1882–85] 1975, 1:127–29). See also Bareau 1963:287–90.

34. *Vin.* 1:105 (Eng. trans., Davids and Oldenberg [1882–85] 1975, 1:247–48). See also *DhA.* 2:112–26 (Eng. trans., Burlingame 1921, 2:167–76); *AA.* 1:318–24; *ThagA.* 2:230–36; *Avś.*, pp. 219–23 (Fr. trans., Feer 1891:336–40); and *GilgMss.* 3, pt. 1:266. The parallelism between Upagupta and Mahākappina is reinforced by the fact that, in *A.* 1:25 (Eng. trans., Woodward and Hare 1932–36, 1:20), Kappina is called the foremost of the Buddha's disciples who are instructors of monks (bhikkhu-ovādakānam aggo). The word *ovādaka* (Buddhist Sanskrit: avavādaka) recalls the *Div.*'s designation of Upagupta as the foremost of the disciples who are instructors (avavādakānām agro).

35. Others include a call from the Buddha, the sound of a gong (ghaṇṭā), the light of the sun, and the moment of death. See *Mhv.*, pp. 40–41 (Eng. trans., Geiger [1912] 1960:37); and Beal [1884] 1968, 2:305.

36. *LP.* 1:166–68 (Fr. trans., Denis 1977, 2:148–49).

37. See chapters 12 and 13.

38. *LP.* 1:169–70 (Fr. trans., Denis 1977, 2:149–50).

39. For the well-known tale of the Buddha's taming of the mad elephant Nālāgiri (alias Dhanapālaka) that Devadatta sent charging after him, see *Sanghbhv.* 2:186–92; Feer 1891:122–23; *J.* 5:333–37 (Eng. trans., Cowell [1895–1907] 1969, 5:175–78); and *Vin.* 2:194–95 (Eng. trans., Horner 1938–52, 5:273–74). The *Rasavāhinī* has preserved the story of an elder intriguingly named Tissamahānāga who subdues a wild elephant and then takes shelter underneath it during a storm (see Malalasekera [1938] 1974, 2:1348).

40. In the oral tradition collected by Tambiah (1970:170), the elephant is let loose not by Aśoka but by King Pasenathikosol (Prasenajit), when Upagupta (here confused with Moggaliputta Tissa) is on his way to the Third Council.

41. Ibid., p. 171.

42. One might further argue that such a demonstration is necessary only when royal power (like the elephant) has gone amuck.

43. *LP.* 1:170–71 (Fr. trans., Denis 1977, 2:150). The text then goes on to recount the binding of Māra and eventually his taking on the body of the Buddha at Upagupta's request. Porée-Maspero (1962–69, 2:391) cites a Cambodian variant of this story, according to which Māra hampers work on the Great Stūpa by making the construction workers ill. When the chief of the builders tells Obbakot (Upagupta) about this, the elder realizes that the trouble is due to Māra, and he chants paritta, sprinkles holy water, and distributes cotton threads for protection. Then Māra disguises himself as a man wishing to become a monk; Upagupta agrees to ordain him but declares that if his heart is not pure, his monastic robes will change into the corpse of a dog. This indeed happens, and Māra, after trying in vain to remove the corpse, is forced to return to Upagupta and promise never to disrupt any festivals again.

44. This is not the first time Māra has taken on these forms. In *Div.*, p. 359 (Eng. trans., Strong 1983b:189–90), he himself recalls confronting the Buddha as a bull and as a snake; and, as we shall see, he is also sometimes likened to a yakṣa.

45. *T.* 202, 4:418b–20c (Eng. trans., Mair 1989:53–55). For a much-abbrevi-

ated version, see *Sanghbhv.* 1:174–75; for a much-expanded one, see Mair 1983:76–81.

46. In a manuscript version of the story translated by Davis (1984:335–36), Upagupta catches the showers of rain, stones, and coals in a giant sheet of gold and diverts them outside the universe.

47. Davis 1984:330; Wells 1960:112; Denis 1982:49; Anuman Rajadhon n.d.:37–44. Compare Gode 1960 and Eberhard 1968:198–201.

48. Hall 1914:167–68.

49. Ibid., p. 168. In saying this, he may be reflecting a common "noninterpretation" of Loi Krathong, that is, the attitude that it has no meaning, or that its meaning has been lost (see Denis 1982:49). This view was perhaps first put forth by King Chulalongkorn, who called the ceremony "merely a matter of rejoicing" (see Anuman Rajadhon n.d.:40). The romance of the festival is reinforced by one explanation that it originated with Nang Nophamat, a beautiful and learned concubine at the Sukhothai court, who instituted it to please the king (see ibid., pp. 40–41).

50. See Mus 1931:115; Lévy 1942:13; and Archaimbault 1972:100.

51. See Nginn 1956a.

52. See Wells 1960:113; Denis 1982:50; and Anuman Rajadhon n.d.:44.

53. Wells 1960:113; this was also Notton's conclusion (1930, 2:81). On the connection between Loi Krathong and Upagupta in Burma, see Maung Kin 1903:221; and Duroiselle 1904:415. For Laos, see Archaimbault 1972:54. Attagara (1967:485–87) reports the perhaps aberrant tradition that the lamp at the top of the pole in a temple at Loi Krathong represents the eyes of the elder Upagupta.

54. Anuman Rajadhon n.d.:39. See also Zago 1972:321n.137; and Archaimbault 1972:30.

55. This tale, recounted in the commentary on the *Samyutta Nikāya* (text and Fr. trans., Duroiselle 1905:157–66), was retold in various Southeast Asian vernacular histories of the sacred footprint (on which see ibid., pp. 147–51; Alabaster 1871:245–310; and Archaimbault 1966:15).

56. Archaimbault 1972:30; Porée-Maspero 1962–69, 2:389; Nginn 1956a:961; Davis 1984:331–34.

57. Davis 1984:331–32.

58. In Pali, these associations are reinforced by a series of rather weak puns. The wild rooster (vanakukkuṭa) will be *Kukku*sandha (Kakusandha); the *nāga*rāja will be Ko*nāga*mana; the tortoise (*kacchapa*) will be *Kassapa*; the great bull (usabharāja) will be Gotama (go means "cow"). The punning appears to break down with the lion (rājasiṃha) and Ariya Metteyya, which may account for the large number of variations on the identity of this fifth animal. In some accounts he is a lion, in others a tiger, a human, or another nāga.

59. I have here amalgamated several versions of this tale, the basic one being the *Pañcabuddhabyākaraṇa* (Pali ed. and Fr. trans. of Thai version in G. Martini 1969). For Laotian, Northern Thai, and Khmer versions of the mother-crow story, see Nginn 1956a:961; Davis 1984:333–34; and G. Martini 1969:129n. See also Porée-Maspero 1962–69, 2:366–67. As G. Martini (1969:127) has pointed out, the worship of the five Buddhas in Southeast Asia is much more widespread than is commonly thought. Indeed, we shall see that in some places five candles lit for Upagupta are said to symbolize the five Buddhas.

60. Ritual worship of riverine Buddha's footprints in Southeast Asia (see Archaimbault 1966, fig. 4) sometimes involves the building of sand stūpas, which, as Gabaude (1979:37–41) has shown, are powerful symbols both of the Buddha and of his impermanence.

61. It might be noted, however, that in the opposition bull-tiger we have the same pairing that, in the myth of the white mother crow, distinguished Gautama (the bull) from Maitreya (the lion, alias tiger).

62. See Davis 1984:344; and Zimmer 1946:74–75.

63. Davis 1984:344. See also Tambiah 1970:175.

64. For a photograph of the image, see the plates in Davis 1984.

65. Davis 1984:229.

66. Ibid., pp. 229–30.

67. Field notes, Saa, 10 March 1983. The manner in which Uppakhut as garuḍa here grasps the nāga is, moreover, similar to the way in which this same scene is depicted in a mural illustrating the *Lokapaññatti* legend at Wat Bunnyavat in Lampang.

68. *Dāṭh.*, pp. 29–32 (Eng. trans., Law 1925:37–39).

69. Coomaraswamy [1928–31] 1971.

70. *Div.*, p. 434 (Eng. trans., Strong 1983b:294).

71. For different versions of it, see *Div.*, pp. 433–34 (Eng. trans., Strong 1983b:292–94); *T.* 2042, 50:111a–b (Fr. trans., Przyluski 1923a:301–3); *T.* 1465, 24:800a–b (Fr. trans., Lamotte 1958:427–29); and *T.* 99, 2:181b–82c (partial Fr. trans., Demiéville 1924:45–46). For an interesting variant, see also the *Mahāvibhāṣā* (*T.* 1545, 27:655b–c [Fr. trans., Lamotte 1958:425]).

72. It is interesting to note that, in the *Mañjuśrīmūlakalpa* (see Jayaswal 1934, v. 538), the "good king" who restores Buddhism after Puṣyamitra's death is named Mahāyakṣa ("Big Yakṣa").

73. Attagara 1967:485–87.

74. *LP.* 1:174 (Fr. trans., Denis 1977, 2:152).

75. For similar stories, see *Sdmp.*, pp. 405–8 (Eng. trans., Kern [1884] 1963:377–80); *J.* 1:31 (Eng. trans., T. W. Rhys Davids 1880:33–34); *BuvA.*, pp. 143–44 (Eng. trans., Horner 1978:206–7); Lamotte 1949–80, 2:688–91; and *GilgMss.* 2, pt. 3:455–67. For discussions, see Gernet 1960 and Filliozat 1963.

Chapter Ten
Mythic Elaborations and Ritual Developments

1. *LP.* 1:165 (Fr. trans., Denis 1977, 2:147).

2. See Ohn Maung n.d., page "nya." I have never found out who these "scientists" were, nor the newspaper from which this account was purportedly taken.

3. Ohn Maung n.d.:62–63.

4. Waddell 1897:83. See also Beal [1884] 1968, 2:273.

5. Shway Yoe [1882] 1963:228; Brown 1908:146. Similar tales of the "Theft of Clothes" are well known in both Kṛṣṇaite and Buddhist legend—where, however, they are told to very different ends.

6. Brown 1908:146.

7. Ohn Maung n.d.:4–12; Min Kyi Hlaing 1986:3–6; Zagaru 1977, passim. See also Maung Kin 1903:225–26. A Shan version of the story (published in Rangoon, 1968)

was summarized for me by the abbot of a monastery near Mae Hong Son, 9 October 1982.

8. In Maung Kin (1903:225), the king is not the ruler of Rājagṛha, but Brahmadatta of Benares, and Macchadevī's presentation to him is the result of his ritual attempts to get an heir.

9. The river was the Ganges, according to Maung Kin (1903:225).

10. In Maung Kin (1903:126), Upa, on the riverbank, asks Macchadevī to take him across the stream on her raft. She tells him it would be improper for her, a lone woman, to do so; but he, knowing nothing of distinctions of caste or sex, insists. She therefore ferries him across, and, as they get to the other side, their eyes meet. This is the moment of conception. The Shan version (field notes, Mae Hong Son, 9 October 1982) has impregnation occur when Upa gets sick and Macchadevī is nursing him. All of these accounts, however, are careful to stress that no physical sexual union takes place between Upagupta's parents.

11. The Shan version adds that, as a child, Upagupta climbs trees like a wild animal (field notes, Mae Hong Son, 9 October 1982).

12. We encountered this well-known formula in chapter 5, where it was used by Śūra in chasing away Māra.

13. In the Shan version (field notes, Mae Hong Son, 9 October 1982), it is not a deva who makes off with Upagutta, but the king's men. Intent on doing him harm, they throw him up into the air, where he realizes arhatship and remains aloft.

14. Ohn Maung n.d.:4–12.

15. Unfortunately, despite several attempts, I was unable to see this film myself. My knowledge of it is based on a detailed twenty-page plot synopsis provided to me by the late U Ko Ko, who kindly viewed the film for me and took notes.

16. On the Indian implications of not passing through the birth canal, see Hara 1980.

17. See Ohn Maung n.d., page "nga." According to U Ko Ko, the whole film is based on older stage presentations of the drama, but I am not aware of any such plays being performed recently.

18. For a diagram of this scheme, see Becker 1975:116. As Becker points out, the "Buddha category" not only stands in the middle of this system of orbits but pervades the whole of it as well.

19. Ibid., p. 116. Specifically, the terms *kaung*, *yau?*, *'u*, *'pa*, and *shu* are employed to designate beings and things in orbits 4, 3, 2, 1, and the center.

20. Ibid., p. 115.

21. Rhum 1987:92.

22. Davis 1974:13–14.

23. See below, this chapter.

24. *LP*. 1:165 (Fr. trans., Denis 1977, 2:147).

25. Tambiah 1970:169.

26. Rhum 1987:104n. I was told the same story by a novice in a village north of Chiang Mai.

27. On the tour of the Buddha and his disciples to Laos and Northeastern Thailand, see Pruess 1976:177.

28. Archaimbault 1972:55.

29. See Davids and Oldenberg [1882–85] 1975, 1:7; and, for the Sarvāstivādin ruling, *T*. 1435, 23:344b (Latin trans., Lamotte 1949–80, 2:807n). Perhaps for this rea-

son, the abbot of Wat Uppakhut in Chiang Mai, in recounting this story, specified that the Buddha had an involuntary nocturnal emission of semen which wet his robes. When these were washed, his sperm got into the water (field notes, Chiang Mai, 4 October 1982). Such wet dreams are not violations of the monastic code. The same justification is recalled by Attagara (1967:485).

30. Denis 1977, 2:lxiv. On Skanda, see Dimmitt and Van Buitenen 1978:185–88; and O'Flaherty 1973:103–7.

31. See Van Buitenen 1973:132–34. Vyāsa's grandfather, a king named Uparicara, spills some semen that eventually winds up in the Yamunā River, where it is swallowed by a fish. The fish then "gives birth" to a boy and a girl. The latter smells like a fish and is condemned to plying a ferry on the river. There she has sex with an ascetic and conceives Vyāsa, i.e., Kṛṣṇa Dvaipāyana, who is born on an island in midstream. See also Przyluski 1925:265–66.

32. The mythic motif of a sage's seed inadvertently engendering a son is very widespread. See motifs B631.3 ("Fish bears men children after swallowing man's rinsing") and T549.3 ("Boy born from fish") in Thompson 1955–58, 1:465; 5:399.

33. Tambiah 1970:171.

34. *Sanghbhv.* 1:81. See also Péri 1918:3.

35. See *Sanghbhv.* 2:31; 1:120. See also *T.* 1450, 24:158c (Fr. trans., Lamotte 1949–80, 2:1003n.1). A similar tale, more influenced perhaps by the legend of Rāma and Sītā, is found in *T.* 203, 4:496b (Fr. trans., Chavannes 1934, 3:136–37).

36. *Sanghbhv.* 2:31–32. See also *T.* 1450, 24:158c (Fr. trans., Lamotte 1949–80, and 2:1003n.1); *T.* 203, 4:496b (Fr. trans., Chavannes 1934, 3:136); and *T.* 1509, 25:182b–c (Fr. trans., Lamotte 1949–80, 2:1005). In *Mtu.* 3:142–43 (Eng. trans., Jones 1949–56, 3:137–38), the Buddha's multiplication of his body is missing. In later tradition, Rāhula comes to be thought of as a patron saint of novices.

37. *Sanghbhv.* 2:32–36. Like many jātakas, this was a well-travelled piece of folklore. For other versions, see Herodotus 1942:174–77; Tawney 1924–28, 2:93; Schiefner and Ralston 1893:37–43; and Huber 1904:704–7.

38. *Sanghbhv.* 2:38–40. The hermit is also called Riṣyaśṛnga or Ekaśṛnga, and, in Pali, Isisinga. There are many versions of this legend in Buddhist, Hindu, Jain, and Western lore. For studies of it, see Lüders 1897, 1902; and O'Flaherty 1973:40–42.

39. This point is especially brought out in the Ṛṣyaśṛnga jātaka.

40. Przyluski 1925:273–84. These included (1) the legend of Kauṇḍinya, who, by virtue of his relation with the nāgī Somā, founds the dynasty of Funan (Coedès 1968a:37–38; Porée-Maspero 1950; Christie 1970); (2) a similar story in a seventh-century Champa inscription (Finot 1911:206); (3) Khmer traditions associated with the king of Angkor (Pelliot 1902:145); (4) the story of the foundation of Thaton by the son of a wizard and a nāgī (Shorto 1970:16–19); (5) the Thai story of King Phra Ruang, the offspring of Abhayagamuni and a nāgī (Pallegoix [1854] 1976:215–16); (6) several versions of the South Indian tale of the establishment of the Pallava dynasty (Coedès 1911 and Goloubew 1924); (7) various Yünnanese stories that feature the impregnation of a widow by a floating log (Sainson 1904:25–26, 86); and (8) an assortment of other Indian, Bengali, and Chinese traditions.

41. Przyluski 1925:281–82. For a recent reassertion of this view, see S. Jumsai 1988.

42. The Palaung, a Mon-Khmer-speaking people, have settled in hilltop villages in the Shan States and parts of Yünnan. See Milne 1924.

43. Summarized from Milne 1921:146–87.

44. In a passage not summarized here, he is clearly considered a freakish being, making his living by always winning at a gambling game of beans. See Milne 1921: 165–69.

45. See ibid., p. 171.

46. Milne 1924:44–45.

47. Maung Kin 1903:221; Hall 1914:167.

48. There are less dramatic expressions of this rite. Devotees making offerings to Upagupta images kept on rafts in small tanks of water sometimes float their donations over to him in small dishes. More commonly, they will try to toss coins in such a way that they land on the raft and not in the water.

49. Here, as elsewhere, rites and ceremonies involving Upagupta are entirely in the hands of the laity.

50. Field notes, Rangoon, 16 October 1982, 19 February 1983. Photographs of the festivities show crowds of considerable size.

51. Field notes, Rangoon, 24 February 1983.

52. Field notes, Rangoon, 24–26 February 1983. Sadly, my Burmese visa expired on the twenty-sixth, the day the raft was to be launched, so that I was not able to see the end of the ceremony. According to Min Kyi Hlaing (1986:29), the following is a standard ritual formula for sending off a raft: "A person who, the Buddha predicted, would destroy all dangers and evils, and bring blessings: his name is Upagutta. To him we make our offerings. He will be leaving the monastery erected for him for his own vihāra in the south. He will enter a trance and go away from our human world, back to his brazen pavilion. O Lord, you may now return to your palace."

53. Brown 1908:146.

54. Field notes, Rangoon, 25 February 1983. Such stories are not at all unusual.

55. Tambiah 1970:366. See also ibid., p. 307.

56. Ibid., p. 302.

57. Davis 1984:288; Davis 1974:22.

58. Przyluski mentions Skeat 1900:191; and Tawney 1924–28, 1:103. For Northern Thailand, see Wood 1965:107; photo, p. 51.

Chapter Eleven
Upagupta and the Arhat Cults

1. *D.* 2:115–19 (Eng. trans., T. W. Rhys Davids 1899–1924, 2:121–26).

2. See *T.* 125, 2:789a (Fr. trans., Lévi and Chavannes 1916:192–93); *T.* 1465, 24:902a (Fr. trans., Lévi and Chavannes 1916:193–94); and *T.* 453, 14:422b (Ger. trans., Leumann 1919:250).

3. Strong 1979a:76–77. Involvement in the world as penance is also a theme found in the *LP.* with reference to Upagupta.

4. *Lakṣacait.* 1:130 (Eng. trans., Rajapatirana 1974, 3:107). The nine are Ānanda, Mahākāśyapa, Ājñātakauṇḍinya, Gayā Kāśyapa, Uruvilvā Kāśyapa, Mahāmaudgalyāyana, Śāriputra, Subhūti, and Rāhula.

5. See Lévi and Chavannes 1916; De Visser 1918–23; Shan Shih Buddhist Institute 1961; Watters 1898; and Tucci 1949, 2:550–70.

6. For lists of the sixteen arhats, see Lévi and Chavannes 1916:292–93; and Lamotte 1958:768–70.

7. See *T.* 2030, 49:13a (Fr. trans., Lévi and Chavannes 1916:10). Variants associate Piṇḍola with other places.

8. See Strong 1979a:77; and Lessing 1954.

9. See Lévi and Chavannes 1916:8–9.

10. For astrological purposes, in Burma, Wednesday is divided into two days, one lasting until noon, the other from noon to midnight.

11. On this scheme, see Shway Yoe [1882] 1963:8; Wales 1983:40–50; and Schober 1980:49. For an Indian analog, see Dubois 1906:379–82.

12. See, for example, Schober 1980:45.

13. Htin Aung [1962] 1978:11.

14. This was the case, for instance, at a Burmese-style monastery in Thailand (field notes, Mae Sariang, 8 October 1982).

15. On the connotations of sīmā stones in Buddhist monasteries and the many rituals associated with them, see Giteau 1969 and Wijeyewardene 1982:91–118.

16. Htin Aung [1962] 1978:17.

17. On occasion, five "Hindu" deities are set up in a row facing this model monastery: Sarasvatī, Caṇḍī (Durgā), Śiva, Ganeṣa, and Viṣṇu. Sometimes, two others—Kālī and Lakṣmī—are added to the row. On the hybrid beast on which Ketu, the "king of the planets," rides, see Htin Aung [1962] 1978:12.

18. *DhA.* 2:237 (Eng. trans., Burlingame 1921, 2:236–37). The protective screen formed by the Buddha and his disciples, along with the paritta texts which they recite, is also featured in the "Jinapañjara" (the Cage of the Conqueror), a noncanonical paritta text which, despite its lack of orthodoxy, is recited at major pirit ceremonies in Thailand, Burma, and Sri Lanka today. See DeSilva 1981:9; and Sivaraksa 1987.

19. Davis 1984:225.

20. Field notes, Ban Huay Cho, 1 October 1982; Mae Sariang, 8 October 1982. On the number nine, see Schober 1980:50.

21. Tambiah 1970:171.

22. Duroiselle 1922–23:174. See also Dowling 1982.

23. Duroiselle 1922–23:175.

24. *A.* 1:24 (Eng. trans., Woodward and Hare 1932–36, 1:18). See also the story of Sīvalī in *DhA.* 2:192–95 (Eng. trans., Burlingame 1921, 2:211–14).

25. Duroiselle 1922–23:175–76.

26. For Pali sources, see Malalasekera [1938] 1974, 1:22–23; and Hecker 1984. For Sanskrit and Chinese sources, see Lamotte 1949–80, 1:260–63. For a more general perspective, see Watanabe 1909.

27. *M.* 2:103–4 (Eng. trans., Horner 1954–59, 2:288–89).

28. Duroiselle 1922–23:176.

29. See DeSilva 1981:10; and Schalk 1972:38–40.

30. Duroiselle 1922–23:176.

31. Duroiselle 1922–23:176; Finot 1924:264. It may be that, in Burma, Piṇḍola has been replaced in this capacity by the arhat Bakkula, the "foremost of those of good health."

32. See Lévi and Chavannes 1916:216–47; and Strong 1979a:71–77.

33. See *T.* 1689, 32:784b–c (Fr. trans., Lévi and Chavannes 1916:216–20). He is also the patron saint of the monks' bathhouse.

34. See Strong 1979a:57. Images of Binzuru, much worn from centuries of rubbing,

can still be seen on the porch of the Tōdaiji in Nara and at the Daiunji in Iwakura, north of Kyoto.

35. Duroiselle 1922–23:174–75.

36. On the four cosmic continents, see Kloetzli 1983:23–31.

37. Alternative transliterations or versions of these names include Saradatta (also Radutta), Sakkosara (also Sakkosakkara), and Medhara. See Zagaru 1977:34; Min Kyi Hlaing 1986:49; and Ferguson 1977:17n. I have been given oral versions of these lists by monks in Rangoon, Mae Sariang, Mae Hong Son, and Chiang Mai. The same scheme is found among the Lü (see Archaimbault 1966:32n).

38. Unfortunately, I was unable to observe this rite, although I did see the labyrinth set up. For something similar, see Bizot 1981:26–31; and Ferrars 1900:185–87. The labyrinth is connected to the story of Vessantara; the platform in the middle is equated with Vankagiri, the mountain to which Vessantara is banished. Its name seems to refer to the crooked (vanka; i.e., labyrinthine) path leading to the mountain (giri). Perhaps this ritual should also be related to the Sri Lankan giribhaṇḍa pūjā, which has interesting parallels with the *LP*. story of Upagupta and Aśoka's stūpa festival (see Malalasekera [1938] 1974, 1:770).

39. Field notes, Rangoon, 26 February 1983.

40. Sometimes, the two groups together are called the eight Upaguptas.

41. Zagaru 1977:35; Min Kyi Hlaing 1986:53; Ferguson 1977:17n. Variants exist for all these names.

42. Ferguson 1977:7.

43. Than Tun 1959b:107–10.

44. A famous image of Mahākassapa/Kāśyapa is still to be seen at Mount Popa (see Ferguson 1977:6–7; and Mendelson 1963:791).

45. Ferguson (1977:7), citing an unpublished paper by Henry Nodder. There, the two lists are quite different, the four living arhats being Mahākassapa, Sāriputta, Moggallāna, and Ānanda; and the four dead ones being Anuruddha, Revata, Kondañña, and Mahākissi(?).

46. On weikzas, see Mendelson 1961a, 1961b, 1963; Ferguson and Mendelson 1981; Spiro 1982:162–87; and Htin Aung [1962] 1978:41–60.

47. Ferguson and Mendelson 1981:65–69. On the connection of weikzas and the Ari, see Mendelson 1961b:576–77.

48. See Mendelson 1961b.

49. Spiro 1982:164.

50. See Mendelson 1975:145.

51. See Mendelson 1963:797.

52. See Przyluski 1923b.

53. Mendelson 1961b:580n.1. See also Ray, forthcoming.

54. Field notes, Rangoon, 25 February 1983.

55. Field notes, Rangoon, 26 February 1983. Similarly, at one of Bo Min Gaung's putative residences—at Taungalat Hill near Mount Popa—one finds an Upagupta image (see Mendelson 1963:792; photo, p. 795). Mount Popa itself, of course, is famed as the shrine of the Mahāgiri nats.

56. See chapter 13.

57. As one Northern Thai informant put it, if you do not invite Phra Uppakhut, you should make offerings to Phra In, the four lokapālas, and Nang Thoranī (the

earth goddess) (field notes, Mae Sariang, 8 October 1982). See also Davis 1984: 105–6.

58. See Lévi and Chavannes 1916:13–15.

59. Field notes, Ban Huay Cho, 1 October 1982.

60. Field notes, Mae Sariang, 8 October 1982. This, of course, is an unorthodox view, since official Theravāda doctrine does not recognize any more Buddhas in our kalpa after Maitreya.

61. Field notes, Chiang Mai, 4 October 1982.

62. Field notes, Mae Sariang, 8 October 1982.

63. Lafont and Bitard 1957:213.

64. Ibid., p. 200.

65. Anonymous 1982:25. Much the same account is found in Pannya Nantha 1971:109–11. I would like to thank Sud Chonchirdsin of Payap College, Chiang Mai, for these references.

66. Field notes, Chiang Mai, 4 March 1983. On domestic images of Uppakhut, see chapter 13.

67. Halliday 1923:62.

68. Wales 1983:41.

69. Reynolds and Reynolds 1982:330–31. On the tradition that one should not cut one's hair on a Wednesday because that was the day on which the Buddha wandered forth (and cut his own hair), see Davis 1976:9; and Nginn 1956b:893.

70. Zagaru 1977:115–16.

Chapter Twelve
Communal Cults: Upagupta as Protector of Festivals

1. Ohn Maung n.d.:47–48.

2. Min Kyi Hlaing 1986:26. For a more formulaic invitation, see Ohn Maung n.d.: 49–50.

3. On the acharn wat's role in Northern Thailand, see Swearer 1976a.

4. The relative youth of the abbot is not atypical of Northern Thai Buddhism, where comparatively few monks remain in robes very long and where, consequently, abbots tend to be quite young.

5. This wish, though directly referring to Upagupta, is nonetheless a formulaic one. See Zago 1972:125.

6. This pattern is confirmed by Charles Archaimbault (personal communication, 12 October 1982). Similarly, Condominas (1973:83n) reports on his experience that, the day after Bun Phra Vet, Upagupta was simply asked to go back to the river, despite earlier assurances that he would be returned there with pomp and procession.

7. For applications of this scheme to Burma and Thailand, see Nash 1966; Spiro 1982:206–8; and Davis 1984:13–22.

8. Donald Swearer (personal communication, 8 April 1990) indicates that a formulaic "Incantation to Invite Upagutta" is used in Northern Thai Buddha-image consecration rites.

9. Field notes, Mae Sariang, 8 October 1982; Archaimbault 1966:32n.26; field notes, Amphur Saa, 10 March 1983; Zago 1972:292n.38; Condominas 1973:83.

10. Mus 1933:376–77. In Thailand, moreover, smooth, round, fist-size river stones

are sometimes kept in the rice-storage hut so as to propitiate the rice goddess (see Terwiel 1976:397–98; and Terwiel 1975:94).

11. Lévy 1943:316. See also Wijeyewardene 1982:76–78.

12. Maspero 1950:174. In a broader Indian context, mention might also be made of the Vaishnavite worship of the śālagrāma—the stones or fossilized shells taken from water (ideally the Gaṇḍakī River) and kept in Brahmin households, where they are thought to represent Viṣṇu (see Dubois 1906:648–49).

13. Davis 1984:235–36. See also Mahāprīcha Prinyāno 1967:31; and Tambiah 1970:171.

14. See, for example, Tambiah 1970:163.

15. Field notes, Mae Sariang, 8 October 1982. See chapter 9.

16. Condominas 1973:83. Here it is specified that no other novice or monk should be present for the invitation, which itself is pronounced by a lay elder. A garbled myth recorded by Condominas (ibid., p. 82) states that once, long ago, some villagers were having trouble building a wat because of interference from the spirits (phī). Finally, one day, a devatā appeared to the villagers in the form of a young novice and told them how to invoke the aid of Phra Uppakhut, whom he had once served.

17. Tambiah 1970:169.

18. Ibid., p. 163.

19. Tambiah 1970:162–63.

20. Mahāprīcha Prinyāno (1967:29) says the following are needed: umbrella, monk's bowl, betel, teapot, monk's robe, and iron walking stick. At Ban Huay Cho, when pressed to say what items were most essential, Acharn Pannya specified monk's fan, monk's bowl, and monk's robes. See also Davis 1984:235.

21. Tambiah 1970:163.

22. See Archaimbault 1966:32n.26. Here, the words of invitation are very simple: "I invite you to come and protect the region. We are going to celebrate the ceremony of the Holy T'at. May everyone remain healthy" (see Archaimbault 1959:388).

23. The same theme is found in the Burmese film on Shin Upago, which tells of the magic pond that immediately transforms one into what one is destined to become. Upagutta, dipped into it as an ambiguous infant, comes out as a fully ordained monk.

24. Davis 1984:225.

25. This was described also as a standard practice in Mae Sariang (field notes, 8 October 1982). On the invocation of the eight planetary deities at the time of the invitation of Uppakhut, see also Tambiah 1970:171.

26. Tambiah 1970:171. These images, it should be specified, are by no means universally used in rites of invitation for Uppakhut.

27. Denis 1977, 2:lxiii.

28. Archaimbault, personal communication, 12 October 1982.

29. A monk's bowl is hardly an appropriate place in which to put the Buddha; it is, however, a recognized receptacle for a nāga who has just been tamed. See *Sanghbhv.* 1:217 (Eng. trans., R. Kloppenborg 1973:50–51); and *Vin.* 1:24ff. (Eng. trans., Davids and Oldenberg [1882–85] 1975, 1:119ff.).

30. This information comes from Archaimbault's extensive and exact field notes, which he kindly shared with me at his home in Bangkok. In a published reference to this ritual (1966:32), he was forced to omit many of these details due to lack of space.

31. Archaimbault, personal communication, 12 October 1982.

32. Archaimbault 1966:32.

33. Bernot 1971:314–15.

34. See chapter 7. Similarly, in Laos, Suzanne Karpelès (1931) was once told that Upagupta was the "spirit of the Buddha" invited to come to the festival.

35. Archaimbault, personal communication, 12 October 1982. See also Archaimbault 1966:32n. On the spirit of the village, see Condominas 1975. Tambiah (1970:300) has also tried to specify the relationship of Uppakhut and the village guardian spirits.

36. Davis 1984:157–281. On the annual rite for the guardian spirits of Chiang Mai, see Kraisri Nimmanhaeminda 1967.

37. Davis 1984:105–6; and Wijeyewardene 1970.

38. These concerns are often reflected in the formulae of invitation. At one wat in Mae Sariang, for instance, the opening words addressed to Uppakhut were said to be: "We are having a big ceremony today; please come and protect it from the rain, drunks, thieves, and bandits" (field notes, 8 October 1982).

39. Field notes, Amphur Saa, 10 March 1983.

40. Davis 1984:191. See also Durrenberger 1983:70–71.

41. See Rhum 1987 and Davis 1984:81.

42. Field notes, Chiang Mai, 8 March 1983.

43. Thus, I was told at a wat in Mae Sariang (field notes, 3 October 1982) that one year they "forgot" to invite Uppakhut to the Bang Fai rocket festival; when one of the bamboo rockets exploded, a person was killed by a sliver that pierced his heart.

44. Field notes, Mae Hong Son, 10 October 1982.

45. Min Kyi Hlaing 1986:1–2. The same book goes on to present several formulaic invocations of Shin Upago to keep the rain from falling (pp. 55–56). See also the similar "prayer to prevent wind" on pp. 57–59.

46. Maung Kin 1903:222.

47. The words "immersed up to its neck in water" (Maung Kin 1903:223) were unfortunately mistranslated as "lui plonger la tête dans l'eau" (plunging its head in water) in a note gratuitously added to Duroiselle's article (1904:414n.3) by one of the editors of the *BEFEO*. As a result, the rite has been misrepresented by several scholars reading Duroiselle (e.g., Przyluski 1925:267; and Tambiah 1970:178).

48. Tambiah 1970:178. Tambiah, of course, also offers other interpretations of Uppakhut, who is for him a more complex figure than this epithet indicates.

49. Porée-Maspero 1962–69, 2:391.

50. Ibid.; field notes, Mae Sariang, 8 October 1982; field notes, Saa, 10 March 1983.

51. Davis 1984:236.

52. Wells 1960:85–94. See also Archaimbault 1968:205, 210.

53. Field notes, Mae Hong Son, 9 October 1982. On Pong Ta U, see chapter 13.

Chapter Thirteen
Personal Rewards and Domestic Rites

1. Min Kyi Hlaing 1986, cover and pp. 6, 25–26.

2. Field notes, Rangoon, 19 February 1983. For this reason, a number of Shin Upago shrines in Rangoon are especially frequented by sailors, who also find the saint's domicile in the water attractive. One informant maintained that some Burmese sailors,

before they go to sea, make wharfside offerings to Shin Upago, who fits into a "sailor's pantheon" that includes also the Buddha, Sīvalī, Maṇimekhalā (the sea goddess), and a delta-area nat called U Shingyi. In Northern Thailand, another informant reports that Upagupta images are sometimes used in ceremonies for blessing boats (field notes, Chiang Mai, 3 March 1983).

3. Field notes, Chiang Mai, 4 October 1982. On the Haw trade, see Moerman 1975 and Mote 1967. Mention might also be made here of a curious habit among the muleteers plying the overland trade routes between Burma, Thailand, and Yünnan. According to C. P. Fitzgerald, they used to get up in the middle of the night about two o'clock, cook a large meal of rice and vegetables, and then go back to sleep. "They never satisfactorily explained this custom" ([1941] 1973:196).

4. Field notes, Ban Huay Cho, 25 September 1982.

5. Field notes, Rangoon, 25 February 1983. See also the report by a friend of Maung Kin (1903:224) of the mysterious appearance of the saint emerging from the waters.

6. Field notes, Rangoon, 26 February 1983.

7. Field notes, Chiang Mai, 25 September 1982.

8. Maung Kin 1903:224.

9. This was the case at the Shin Upago floating in Rangoon described in chapter 10.

10. One informant in Northern Thailand said that he has on occasion heard Uppakhut called a nakleng (champion), a term that is applied to rough types who are both feared and admired. On nakleng, see D. B. Johnston 1980.

11. When he is with other monks, as when an extra bhikkhu comes uninvited to a lay-sponsored meal, nobody knows who he is.

12. On this subject, see Tambiah 1984:195–289; Anuman Rajadhon n.d.:268–95; Terwiel 1975:75–95; Lefèvre-Pontalis 1926; Peltier 1977:50–57; Peltier 1982; Coedès 1925; Filliozat 1954; and Bizot 1980b.

13. Field notes, Chiang Mai, 6 March 1983.

14. Field notes, Mae Sariang, 8 October 1982.

15. Davis 1984:224n.25. On sūkhwan rites, see Heinze 1972; and Tambiah 1970, ch. 13.

16. Ohn Maung n.d.:53.

17. Ibid., p. 55. On the Buddha-image consecration ceremony, see Gombrich 1966; Tambiah 1984:243–57; and Ruelius 1978.

18. Maung Kin 1903:222. See also Zagaru 1977:116.

19. Zagaru 1977:116.

20. Ohn Maung 1973:47.

21. Bizot 1976:6.

22. Zagaru 1977:117–19. See also Maung Kin 1903:223.

23. Varaman n.d.:231–32. I would like to thank Louis Gabaude for this reference and translation.

24. Lefèvre-Pontalis 1926:16; plates xi, xii, xiii.

25. See, for example, Sibunruang 1976:201–31.

26. It might be pointed out here that one literal interpretation of Upagupta's name is that he is someone who is "concealed [gupta] hereabouts [upa]."

27. Varaman n.d.:231.

28. Field notes, Chiang Mai, 3 March 1983.

29. Phya Anuman Rajadhon, cited in Davis 1984:228.

30. Field notes, Chiang Mai, 4 March 1983.

31. Some people, however, point out that *bua khem*, as a distinct term, may refer to a kind of lotus.

32. When nine khems are used, the additional ones are put in the sides of the torso.

33. Field notes, Chiang Mai, 6 March 1983. The insertion of khem into the saint's body may be related to the practice of inserting needles under the skin as a magical protective act. As Wood (1965:89) observes: "Another [Shan] charm . . . is often used by Siamese and Laos—usually by rather tough customers. This consists in inserting needles under the skin. [These, in time,] work their way to the surface. Some of them form a small ulcer and come out, but others remain for years just under the skin, forming small lumps, faintly sensitive to the touch. Bullets or blades of weapons are supposed to be drawn to one of these magic lumps, from which they glance harmlessly off."

34. Field notes, Chiang Mai, 4 March 1983; field notes, Nan, 9 March 1983.

35. Field notes, Chiang Mai, 4 March 1983. We may recall here a curious detail in the story given in chapter 9 of the monk who wished to become a nāga: just prior to entering the waters of the lake, he covered his head with his monastic robe.

36. Field notes, Mae Hong Son, 9–10 October 1982.

37. Sometimes only four other images surround the central one.

38. Field notes, Mae Hong Son, 9 October 1982. This same informant explained that there are five different images that belong together in the same group: Bua Khem, Uppakhut, Pong Ta U, Sīvalī, and Dakhiṇa Sākhā (an image made from the south branch of a Bodhi tree). On the importance of the Bodhi tree's southern bough, see *Mhv*., pp. 143–44 (Eng. trans., Geiger [1912] 1960:124–25).

39. Maung Kin 1903:220.

40. Ibid., p. 221.

41. Field notes, Rangoon, 19 February 1983.

42. Field notes, Rangoon, 24 February 1983. The tour began on 9 August 1981 and ended eighty-one (nine times nine) days later, on 28 October 1981. The association's emphasis on the traditionally lucky number nine is reflected in this schedule. In 1982, the tour lasted only forty-five days (from 2 November to 16 December), a sign, perhaps, of the dampening of the group's initial enthusiasm.

43. Field notes, Rangoon, 24 February 1983.

44. Anonymous 1981 (Eng. trans., Maung Maung Gyi).

45. Field notes, Mae Sariang, 8 October 1982. Information about this practice and the one that follows came from an untitled Lanna Thai manuscript read to me by the abbot of Wat Sribunryung.

46. Field notes, Mae Sariang, 8 October 1982. A somewhat similar method of selection is found in the so-called label-eating festival described by Davis (1984:190–99).

47. Field notes, Mae Sariang, 8 October 1982.

48. Chiang Mai was more or less under Burmese rule from 1556 to 1728 (see Wood n.d.:230).

49. Field notes, Chiang Mai, 4 October 1982. It is not clear where the tale of the Haw merchant "Red Dog" fits into this history.

50. On Phra Sīwichai, see Keyes 1981:154–64; and Tambiah 1984:302–7.

51. It is noteworthy that Uppakhut is here called "luang phau" ("royal father"), a title given to respected elder monks. On this notion, see Peltier 1977 and Tambiah 1984:200.

Glossary

The following list does not give all the possible meanings for each term, but only the ones relevant to our discussion of the legend and cult of Upagupta. All terms are Sanskrit unless otherwise indicated.

Abhidharma — Scholastic elaborations on the Teaching of the Buddha; also, one of the major divisions of the Buddhist canon.

acharn wat (Thai) — A leading lay elder of a congregation; usually a former monk, he may take on certain ritual responsibilities.

alakṣaṇaka — An epithet meaning "without the [thirty-two bodily] marks [of the Mahāpuruṣa]"; applied to Upagupta, who is called an alakṣaṇaka Buddha.

anāgāmin — A "nonreturner"; an enlightened person who has no more rebirths to suffer before final liberation.

anātman (Pali: *anattā*) — The Buddhist doctrine that there is no real permanent unchanging self within individuals.

ānisaṃsa (Pali) — A genre of text comprising stories that extoll the advantages of meritorious deeds.

anitya (Pali: *anicca*) — The Buddhist doctrine of impermanence.

añjali — A salutation of respect and subservience consisting of cupping the hands and raising them in the direction of the respected person.

anupūrvikathā — In a sermon, a preliminary discourse on merit making prior to the preaching of the Dharma proper.

āraṇyaka (Pali: *āraññaka*) — A forest-dwelling monk, often devoted to meditative endeavors, contrasted to the town-dwelling grāmavāsin.

arhat — A Buddhist saint; one who has attained enlightenment and is no longer subject to death and rebirth.

ārya — A "noble one"; a person who has attained enlightenment and is no longer a pṛthagjana.

āśrama — Any one of the four stages of life in Hinduism (student, householder, forest dweller, renunciant).

aśubhabhāvanā — "Contemplation of the impurities [of a corpse]"; a cemetery meditation.

asura — One of a class of supernatural beings whose fate is constantly to wage war against the devas (gods). The asura gati is one of the realms of rebirth.

ātman — The Upaniṣadic doctrine that there is a real permanent unchanging self within individuals.

avadāna (Pali: *apadāna*) — Often translated as "legend"; a genre of Buddhist story usually showing the workings of karma through the deeds of ordinary individuals.

Bhadanta — "Venerable one"; an appellation used in addressing Buddhist monks.

bhakti — Devotion, adoration directed towards the Buddha or a divine figure.

bhikṣu (Pali: *bhikkhu*) — Literally, a "beggar"; a Buddhist monk.

bhikṣuṇī (Pali: *bhikkhunī*) — Literally, a "beggar"; a Buddhist nun.

bodhisattva (Pali: *bodhisatta*) — Anyone who has taken a vow to become a Buddha and who will attain that goal, but who, in the meantime, compassionately engages in assisting others.

brahmacārin — The first of the four Hindu stages of life (āśramas), characterized by study and celibacy.

Buddhānusmṛti — Meditative recollection of the person and qualities of the Buddha.

caitya (Pali: *cetiya*; Thai: *cedi*) — A monument or sanctuary that brings to mind the person of the Buddha or an event in his life.

cakravartin — A "wheel-turning" monarch; a great king who rules the world according to Dharma.

dāna — The practice of giving, of making donations, especially to the Sangha; one of the principal ways of making merit.

Daśabala — An epithet of the Buddha; literally, the "Ten-powered One."

deva — A god; also, a king. The deva gati is one of the realms of rebirth.

Dharma (Pali: *Dhamma*) — The Teaching of the Buddha, Truth, Law, Doctrine; a basic element of reality (in the latter sense, usually written *dharma*). The word has many meanings, but they mostly revolve around the notion of anything that is fundamentally true or real.

Dharmakāya (Pali: *Dhammakāya*) — The corpus of the Buddha's Teaching, but identified with his person; his "Truth body."

dhūtaguṇa (Pali: *dhutānga*) — Literally, the "qualities of a purified person"; a set of ascetic practices not usually expected of Buddhist monks but followed by bhikṣus who are so inclined.

dhyāna (Pali: *jhāna*) — Meditation; more specifically, one of four or eight levels of trancelike meditative absorption.

gaing (Burmese) — A voluntary association of devotees, often followers of a particular weikza.

gandharva — One of a class of minor divinities, often in attendance on other gods, sometimes portrayed as celestial musicians.

ganthadhura (Pali) — The vocation of books; one of two life-styles in the Sangha, the other being the more meditatively inclined vipassanādhura.

gati — A realm of rebirth. There are classically five gatis: those of the gods, humans, animals, hungry ghosts, and hellbeings. Later a sixth gati, that of the asuras, was added to the scheme.

grāmavāsin (Pali: *gāmavāsin*) — A town-dwelling monk, often devoted to pastoral and scholarly endeavors, contrasted to the forest-dwelling monk (āraṇyaka).

Hīnayāna — The "Lesser Vehicle"; one of the major divisions of Buddhism, the other being the Mahāyāna, or "Greater Vehicle."

jñāna — Salvific knowledge.

kalpa — An aeon; the largest imaginable unit in the cycle of time.

kāma — Physical love, desire, sensuality; sometimes personified as a deity.

kāmadhātu — The "realm of desire," presided over by Māra; the lowest of the three layered divisions of the Buddhist cosmos, the others being the rūpadhātu (realm of form) and the arūpadhātu (the formless realm).

karma — Literally, "action," especially ritual, moral action; any deed which will bring about certain corresponding effects in this or a future lifetime; also, the law or principle governing these cause-and-effect relationships.

kāyabandhana — The belt of a monk's robe.

khem (Thai) — A "needle"; a small piece of metal inserted into certain images.

kuṭī — The "hut" or private cell of a monk.

lo-han (Chinese) — An arhat, especially one who has extended his life span to remain in this world to protect the Dharma.

lokapāla — A guardian deity of one of the four quarters.

mahalla/mahallaka — An epithet applied, often pejoratively, to monks who were ordained late in life.

mahānāyaka — Literally, a "great leader"; the chief monk of a given region or sect.

Mahāpuruṣa — A "Great Man"; one who is endowed with thirty-two characteristic bodily marks and who can be either a Buddha or a cakravartin.

mettā (Pali) — Loving-kindness; a topic of a particular kind of meditation.

muang (Thai) — A town, a center of civilized order.

nāga — A male snake or snakelike supernatural being often associated with water; a candidate for Buddhist ordination; an elephant.

nāgī — A female snake or snakelike supernatural being often associated with water.

nat (burmese) — An indigenous spirit or divinity.

Nirvāṇa (Pali: *Nibbāna*) — The soteriological goal in Buddhism, characterized by the cessation of desire, ignorance, and hatred. Sometimes *Nirvāṇa* is used to mean enlightenment, other times as equivalent to *parinirvāṇa*.

Org Phansa (Thai) — The end of the rains retreat; a major annual Buddhist festival.

pāṃśukūla — A robe made of discarded rags and worn especially by ascetically inclined monks. The wearing of such a robe is the first of the dhūtaguṇa.

pāṃśukūlika — One who makes a practice of wearing a pāṃśukūla.

pañcabandhana — A "fivefold fetter," used to bind and punish various beings.

pañcavārṣika — A quinquennial festival held periodically by kings or rich laypersons during which great donations are made to the Sangha.

parinirvāṇa — The final Nirvāṇa occurring at the death of the Buddha or any enlightened being, after which there is no more rebirth.

paritta (Pali) — Any text chanted for its magical, protective efficacy, generally by monks.

paścācchramaṇa — A junior monk who attends to the needs of a senior one.

phī (Thai) — An indigenous spirit or divinity.

phī ban (Thai) — The protective spirit of a village.

piṇḍa — A food offering given in Buddhism to Buddhist monks, and in Hinduism to deceased ancestors.

piṇḍapatha — The alms round of a Buddhist bhikṣu.

Piśāca — A threatening, frightening, ogrelike supernatural being.

piṭaka — See *Tripiṭaka.*

prasāda — In Hinduism, the sacred "leftovers" of the food offered to the gods, consumed by devotees.

pratyekabodhi — The enlightenment of a pratyekabuddha.

pratyekabuddha — One who, like the Buddha, attains enlightenment on his own, without the immediate help of a teacher, but who then, unlike the Buddha, does not share his enlightenment with others by preaching or founding a community.

preta — A hungry ghost whose chief suffering is that of hunger and thirst. The preta gati is one of the realms of rebirth.

pṛthagjana — An unenlightened person who is not yet on the Buddhist Path.

pūjā — An act of worship or reverence performed in front of a divinity or great saint or their images.

rākṣasī — A malevolent and threatening supernatural being, a demoness, an ogress.

ṛddhi (Pali: *iddhi*) — Supernormal magical powers thought to be attained by advanced meditators.

ṛṣi — A seer, a sage, an ascetic.

rūpadhātu — The "realm of form"; the second of the three layered divisions of the Buddhist cosmos.

rūpakāya — The "body of form"; the physical body of the Buddha.

ṣaḍvārgika (Pali: *chabbaggiya*) — A group of six monks and their followers renowned for their heteropraxy.

sakṛdāgāmin — A "once-returner;" an enlightened person who has to suffer only one more life before final liberation.

śalākā — A tally stick used for various purposes in Buddhist monastic life.

samādhi — Meditative concentration; a trance state attained through yoga.

śamatha (Pali: *samatha*) — Meditation, especially enstatic absorption involving trances; sometimes contrasted to vipāśyanā.

saṃsāra — The flow of death and rebirth, characterized by suffering, in which all beings are caught.

Sangha — The Buddhist community of monks and nuns; one of the Three Refuges of Buddhism.

sannyāsin — The last of the four Hindu stages of life (āśramas); a person who has completely renounced the world.

setsuwa (Japanese) — A Buddhist legend of a particular genre.

skandha (Pali: *khandha*) — The five "aggregates" that constitute what is usually thought of as an individual self.

śramaṇa — Literally, a "striver"; one who has abandoned the householder's life and embarked on a religious quest.

śrāvaka — A disciple; one who hears the Dharma from a teacher; in Mahāyāna texts, a follower of the Hīnayāna.

srotāpanna — A "stream-winner"; an enlightened person who has only seven more rebirths to suffer before final liberation.

stūpa — A moundlike monument containing relics of the Buddha or some other object of veneration.

Sugata — An epithet of the Buddha; literally, the "Well-gone One."

sūtra (Pali: *sutta*) — Any doctrinal discourse attributed to the Buddha; also, one of the major divisions of the Buddhist canon.

tacapañcaka (Pali) — A fivefold formula of meditation on the impermanence of the human body.

Tathāgata — An epithet of the Buddha often used by the Buddha in referring to himself; literally, the "Thus-gone (or come) One."

Trichiliomegachiliocosm — English neologism for Trisāhasramahāsāhasralokadhātu; the largest imaginable unit in the expanse of space: a world system consisting of three thousand great thousand worlds.

Tripiṭaka (Pali: *Tipiṭaka*) — Literally, the "three baskets"; the Buddhist canon, consisting of Vinaya, Sūtra, and Abhidharma texts.

upadhyāya — The preceptor of a candidate for Buddhist ordination.

upāsaka — A practicing Buddhist layman.

upasampadā — The ritual of higher ordination that makes a person into a bhikṣu or bhikṣuṇī.

upāsikā — A practicing Buddhist laywoman.

upāyā — "Expedient means" in teaching the Dharma; good didactic strategy.

upoṣadha (Pali: *uposatha*) — A weekly assembly of the Sangha which all residents of a monastery are expected to attend, and on which laypersons may undertake to observe certain extra precepts.

ūrṇā — The whorl of hair located between the eyebrows of the Buddha; one of the thirty-two signs of the Great Man (Mahāpuruṣa).

uṣṇīṣa — The protuberance on top of the Buddha's head; one of the thirty-two signs of the Great Man (Mahāpuruṣa).

vargacārin — A pratyekabuddha who "lives in a group"; contrasted to the more solitary pratyekabuddha who is "like a rhinoceros" (khaḍgaviṣāṇakalpa).

vidyādhara (Pali: vijjādhara) A being having great magical powers; a sorcerer.

vihāra — A Buddhist monastery, especially the residence halls of its monks.

Vinaya — The discipline or code of conduct for monks; also, one of the major divisions of the Buddhist canon.

vipassanādhura (Pali) — The vocation of meditation; one of two divisions of the Sangha, the other being the ganthadhura.

vipāśyanā (Pali: *vipassanā*) — Meditation, especially insight meditation; sometimes contrasted to śamatha.

wat (Thai) — A Buddhist monastery.

weikza (Burmese) — A charismatic master, possessed of esoteric knowledge and thought to be endowed with supernatural powers.

yakṣa (Pali: *yakkha*) — One of a class of supernatural beings, generally thought of as powerful and demonic, but capable of being tamed and converted to the cause of Buddhism.

yakṣiṇī — A female yakṣa, often associated with disease and infant deaths.

Bibliography of Works Cited

Abhidharmakośabhāṣyam of Vasubandhu. 1975. Edited by Prahlad Pradhan. Patna.

Aivar, A. D. H. 1970. "Hārītī and the Chronology of the Kuṣanas." *Bulletin of the School of Oriental and African Studies* 33:10–21.

Alabaster, Henry. 1871. *The Wheel of the Law*. London.

Ames, Michael M. 1964. "Magical-Animism and Buddhism: A Structural Analysis of the Sinhalese Religious System." In *Religion in South Asia*, edited by Edward B. Harper, pp. 21–52. Seattle.

Ananda Maitreya. 1903. "In the Shadow of the ShweDagon II: The Going-Forth from Home." *Buddhism* (Rangoon) 1:267–88.

Anguttara Nikāya. 1885–1900. 5 vols. Edited by R. Morris and E. Hardy. London.

Anonymous. 1896. "The Story of Sundarī and Nanda." *Journal of the Buddhist Text Society* 4:20–28.

Anonymous. 1981. *Shin Upagutta Paritta*. Pamphlet printed by Shin Upago Committee of the Yan Myo Aung pagoda, Thingan Town. Rangoon.

Anonymous. 1982. [Interview with Pannya Nantha, August 19, 1982.] *Siamrat* 29 (no. 11): 25.

Anuman Rajadhon, Phya. N.d. *Essays on Thai Folklore*. Bangkok.

Archaimbault, Charles. 1959. "L'histoire et l'organisation rituelle de Basak-Campasak." Ph.D. thesis, Université de la Sorbonne.

———. 1966. "La fête du T'at à Luang Prabang." In *Essays Offered to G. H. Luce*, edited by Ba Shin, Jean Boisselier, and A. B. Griswold, 1:5–47. Ascona.

———. 1968. "Les rites pour l'obtention de la pluie à Luong P'rabang (observés en juillet 1954)." *Bulletin de la Société des Etudes Indochinoises*, n.s., 43:199–217.

———. 1972. *La course de pirogues au Laos*. Ascona.

Aronson, Harvey. 1980. *Love and Sympathy in Theravāda Buddhism*. New Delhi.

Aśokāvadāna. 1963. Edited by Sujitkumar Mukhopadhyaya. New Delhi.

Aṣṭasāhasrikā-prajñāpāramitā-sūtra. 1888. Edited by Rajendralal Mitra. Calcutta.

Attagara, Kingkeo. 1967. *The Folk Religion of Ban Nai*. Bloomington.

Auboyer, Jeannine, and Marie-Thérèse de Mallmann. 1950. "Sītalā-la-froide." *Artibus Asiae* 13:207–27.

Aung, Shwe Zan, and C. A. F. Rhys Davids. 1915. *Points of Controversy*. London.

U Aung Myint. 1983. *Shin Upagut* [The Venerable Upagupta]. Rangoon.

Aung-Thwin, Michael. 1981. "Jambudīpa: Classical Burma's Camelot." *Contributions to Asian Studies* 16:38–61.

———. 1985. *Pagan: The Origins of Modern Burma*. Honolulu.

Avadānakalpalatā of Kṣemendra. 1959. 2 vols. Edited by P. L. Vaidya. Darbhanga.

Avadāna-śataka. 1958. Edited by P. L. Vaidya. Darbhanga.

Backus, Charles. 1981. *The Nan-chao Kingdom and T'ang China's Southwestern Frontier*. Cambridge.

Bagchi, P. C. 1945. "A Note on the Avadānaśataka and Its Chinese Translation." *Visva-Bharati Annals* 1:56–61.

———. 1946. "Krimiśa and Demetrius." *Indian Historical Quarterly* 22:81–91.

Banerjee, Anukul Chandra. [1957] 1979. *Sarvāstivāda Literature*. Reprint. Calcutta.

Bapat, P. V. 1984. *Vimuktimārga-Dhūtaguṇa-Nirdeśa*. Bombay.

Bapat, P. V., and A. Hirakawa.1970. *Shan-Chien-P'i-P'o-Sha: A Chinese Version by Sanghabhadra of Samantapāsādikā*. Poona.

Bareau, André. 1955. *Les sectes bouddhiques du petit véhicule*. Paris.

———. 1957. "Les controverses relatives à la nature de l'arhant dans le bouddhisme ancien." *Indo-Iranian Journal* 1:241–50.

———. 1963. *Recherches sur la biographie du Buddha dans les sūtrapiṭaka et les vinayapiṭaka anciens I: De la quête de l'éveil à la conversion de Śāriputra et de Maudgalyāyana*. Paris.

———. 1970–71. *Recherches sur la biographie du Buddha dans les sūtrapiṭaka et les vinayapiṭaka anciens II: Les derniers mois, le parinirvāṇa et les funérailles*. 2 vols. Paris.

———. 1971. "La transformation miraculeuse de la nourriture offerte au Buddha par le Brahmane Kasibhāradvāja." In *Etudes tibétaines dédiées à la mémoire de Marcelle Lalou*, pp. 1–10. Paris.

———. 1974a. "La jeunesse du Buddha dans les sūtrapiṭaka et les vinayapiṭaka anciens." *Bulletin de l'Ecole Française d'Extrême-Orient* 61:199–274.

———. 1974b. "Le parinirvāṇa du Buddha et la naissance de la religion bouddhique." *Bulletin de l'Ecole Française d'Extrême-Orient* 61:275–99.

———. 1976. "Les réactions des familles dont un membre devient moine selon le canon bouddhique pali." In *Malalasekera Commemoration Volume*, edited by O. H. deA. Wijesekera, pp. 15–22. Colombo.

———. 1980. "The Place of the Buddha Gautama in the Buddhist Religion during the Reign of Aśoka." In *Buddhist Studies in Honour of Walpola Rahula*, edited by Somaratna Balasooriya et al., pp. 1–9. London.

———. 1982. "Un personage bien mystérieux: l'épouse du Buddha." In *Indological and Buddhist Studies: Volume in Honour of Professor J. W. de Jong on His Sixtieth Birthday*, edited by L. A. Hercus et al., pp. 31–59. Delhi.

———. 1988–89. "Etude du bouddhisme." *Annuaire du Collège de France*, pp. 533–47. Paris.

Bastide, Roger. 1965. *Réincarnation et vie mystique en Afrique noire*. Paris.

Beal, Samuel. [1875] 1985. *The Romantic Legend of Śākya Buddha*. Reprint. Delhi.

———. [1883] 1975. *The Fo-Sho-Hing-Tsan-King: A Life of Buddha*. Reprint. Delhi.

———. [1884] 1968. *Si-Yu-Ki: Buddhist Records of the Western World*. 2 vols. Reprint. New York.

Bechert, Heinz. 1961. *Bruchstücke buddhistischer Verssammlungen, I: Die Anavataptagāthā und die Sthaviragāthā*. Berlin.

———. 1985. *Die Lebenszeit des Buddha: das älteste feststehende Datum der indischen Geschichte*. Göttingen.

Becker, Alton L. 1975. "A Linguistic Image of Nature: The Burmese Numerative Classifier System." *International Journal of the Sociology of Language* 5:109–21.

Bendall, Cecil. 1883. *Catalogue of the Buddhist Sanskrit Manuscripts in the University Library, Cambridge*. Cambridge.

Bendall, Cecil, and W. H. D. Rouse. [1902] 1971. *Śikshā-samuccaya: A Compendium of Buddhist Doctrine Compiled by Śāntideva*. Reprint. Delhi.

Bernot, Denise. 1971. "Le monde des Nats." In *Génies, anges et démons*, pp. 295–342. Paris.

Bigandet, P. [1858] 1979. *The Life or Legend of Gaudama, the Buddha of the Burmese.* 2 vols. Reprint. Varanasi.

Bizot, François. 1976. *Le figuier à cinq branches: Recherches sur le bouddhisme khmer*. Paris.

———. 1980a. "La grotte de la naissance: Recherches sur le bouddhisme khmer II." *Bulletin de l'Ecole Française d'Extrême-Orient* 67:221–73.

———. 1980b. "Notes sur les yantra bouddhiques d'Indochine." In *Tantric and Taoist Studies in Honour of R. A. Stein*, edited by Michel Strickmann, 1:155–91. *Mélanges chinois et bouddhiques*, vol. 20. Brussels.

———. 1981. *Le don de soi-même: Recherches sur le bouddhisme khmer III.* Paris.

———. 1988. "Les traditions de *pabbajjā* en Asie du Sud-Est." *Abhandlungen der Akademie der Wissenschaften, Göttingen, Philologisch-Historische Klasse*, ser. 3, 169:24–48.

Bloch, Jules. 1950. *Les inscriptions d'Asoka*. Paris.

Bloss, Lowell. 1973. "The Buddha and the Nāga: A Study in Buddhist Folk Religiosity." *History of Religions* 13:36–53.

———. 1979. "The Taming of Māra: Witnessing to the Buddha's Virtues." *History of Religions* 18:156–76.

Bode, Mabel. 1893. "Women Leaders of the Buddhist Reformation." *Journal of the Royal Asiatic Society*, pp. 517–66, 763–98.

———. [1909] 1965. *The Pali Literature of Burma*. Reprint. Rangoon.

Bongard-Levin, G. M., and O. F. Volkova. 1965. *The Kunāla Legend and an Unpublished Aśokāvadānamālā Manuscript*. Calcutta.

Boyd, James. 1971. "Symbols of Evil in Buddhism." *Journal of Asian Studies* 31:63–75.

———. 1975. *Satan and Māra: Christian and Buddhist Symbols of Evil*. Leiden.

Brapaṃsukūlānisaṃsaṃ. See G. Martini. 1973.

Brock, Karen L. 1988. "Awaiting Maitreya at Kasagi." In *Maitreya the Future Buddha*, edited by Alan Sponberg and Helen Hardacre, pp. 214–47. Cambridge.

Brohm, John. 1957. "Burmese Religion and the Burmese Religious Revival." Ph.D. dissertation, Cornell University.

———. 1963. "Buddhism and Animism in a Burmese Village." *Journal of Asian Studies* 22:155–67.

Brown, R. Grant. 1908. "Rain-Making in Burma." *Man* 80:145–46.

Buddhacarita. See E. H. Johnston, [1936] 1978.

Bühler, G. 1894. "Dr. Bhagvānlāl Indrājī's Interpretation of the Mathurā Lion Pillar Inscription." *Journal of the Royal Asiatic Society*, pp. 525–40.

Bunnag, Jane. 1973. *Buddhist Monk, Buddhist Layman*. Cambridge.

Burlingame, E. W. 1921. *Buddhist Legends*. 3 vols. Cambridge, Mass.

Burnouf, Eugène. 1876. *Introduction à l'histoire du buddhisme indien*. 2d ed. Paris.

Carrithers, Michael. 1983. *The Forest Monks of Sri Lanka*. Delhi.

Das Catuṣpariṣatsūtra. 1956. Edited by Ernst Waldschmidt. Berlin.

Chang, Garma C. C. 1983. *A Treasury of Mahāyāna Sūtras*. University Park.

Chapin, Helen B., and Alexander Soper. 1971. *A Long Roll of Buddhist Images*. Ascona.

Chau, Thich Minh. 1964a. *The Chinese Madhyama Āgama and the Pāli Majjhima Nikāya (A Comparative Study)*. Saigon.

———. 1964b. *Milindapañha and Nāgasenabhikshusūtra (A Comparative Study)*. Calcutta.

Chavannes, Edouard. 1903. "Voyage de Song Yun dans l'Udyana et le Gandhara." *Bulletin de l'Ecole Française d'Extrême-Orient* 3:379–441.

———. 1934. *Cinq cent contes et apologues extraits du Tripiṭaka chinois*. 4 vols. Paris.

Ch'en, Kenneth K. S. 1945–47. "A Study of the Svāgata Story in the *Divyāvadāna* in Its Sanskrit, Pāli, Tibetan and Chinese Versions." *Harvard Journal of Asiatic Studies* 9:207–314.

Childers, Robert C. 1909. *A Dictionary of the Pali Language*. London.

Lama Chimpa and Alaka Chattopadhyaya. [1970] 1980. *Tāranātha's History of Buddhism in India*. Reprint. Calcutta.

Christie, Anthony. 1970. "The Provenance and Chronology of the Early Indian Cultural Influence in South-East Asia." In *R. C. Majumdar Felicitation Volume*, edited by Himansu Bhusan Sarkar, pp. 1–14. Calcutta.

Coedès, Georges. 1911. "Etudes cambodgiennes: la légende de la nāgī." *Bulletin de l'Ecole Française d'Extrême-Orient* 11:391–93.

———. 1925. "Tablettes votives bouddhiques du Siam." In *Etudes asiatiques* 1:145–67. Paris.

———. 1956. "The Twenty-Five Hundredth Anniversary of the Buddha." *Diogenes* 15:95–111.

———. 1967. *The Making of South East Asia*. Translated by H. M. Wright. Berkeley.

———. 1968a. *The Indianized States of Southeast Asia*. Translated by Susan Brown Cowing. Honolulu.

———. 1968b. "Une vie indochinoise du Buddha: la Pathamasambodhi." In *Mélanges d'indianisme à la mémoire de Louis Renou*. Paris.

Coedès, Georges, and Charles Archaimbault. 1973. *Les trois mondes (Traibhūmi Brah R'van)*. Paris.

The Commentary on the Dhammapada. 1906–15. 5 vols. Edited by H. Smith and H. C. Norman. London.

Condominas, Georges. 1973. "Notes sur le bouddhisme populaire en milieu rural lao." *Bulletin des Amis du Royaume Lao* 9:27–118.

———. 1975. "Phībān Cults in Rural Laos." In *Change and Persistence in Thai Society*, edited by G. William Skinner and A. Thomas Kirsch, pp. 252–73. Ithaca.

Conze, Edward. 1956. *Buddhist Meditation*. London.

———. 1959a. *Buddhism: Its Essence and Development*. New York.

———. 1959b. *Buddhist Scriptures*. Harmondsworth.

———. 1967. *Buddhist Thought in India*. Ann Arbor.

———. 1973. *The Perfection of Wisdom in Eight Thousand Lines and Its Verse Summary*. Bolinas, Calif.

———. 1975. *The Large Sutra on Perfect Wisdom*. Berkeley.

Coomaraswamy, Ananda. 1927. "The Origin of the Buddha Image." *The Art Bulletin* 9:1–43.

———. [1928–31] 1971. *Yakṣas*. Reprint. New Delhi.

Cospani, E. 1945. "The Cave of the Shadow of the Buddha at Nagarahara." *Journal of the Asiatic Society of Bengal* (Letters) 11:49–52.

Cowell, E. B. [1895–1907] 1969. *The Jātaka or Stories of the Buddha's Former Births*. 6 vols. Reprint. London.

Dantinne, Jean. 1983. *La Splendeur de l'Inébranlable (Akṣobhyavyūha)*. Vol. 1. Louvain-la-neuve.

Dargyay, Lobsang. 1978. *Die Legende von den sieben Prinzessinnen (Saptakumārikā-Avadāna)*. Vienna.

Darian, Steven G. 1978. *The Ganges in Myth and History*. Honolulu.

Das, Kalyani. 1980. *Early Inscriptions of Mathurā—A Study*. Calcutta.

Das, Mahendra Lal. 1894. "Story of the Conversion of Gopāla Nāga." *Journal of the Buddhist Text Society* 2, pt. 1:5–7.

Das, Nobin Chandra. 1893. "Ekasringa." *Journal of the Buddhist Text Society* 1, pt. 2:1–12.

Dasabodhisattuppattikathā. See Saddhatissa 1975.

Dāṭhavaṃsa. See Law 1925.

Davids, C. A. F. Rhys. 1909. *Psalms of the Early Buddhists: I. Psalms of the Sisters*. London.

Davids, C. A. F. Rhys, and F. L. Woodward. 1917–30. *The Book of Kindred Sayings*. 5 vols. London.

Davids, T. W. Rhys. 1880. *Buddhist Birth Stories*. London.

———. [1890–94] 1963. *The Questions of King Milinda*. 2 vols. Reprint. New York.

———. 1899–1924. *Dialogues of the Buddha*. 3 vols. London.

———. 1907. "Aśoka and the Buddha Relics." *Journal of the Royal Asiatic Society*, pp. 297–410.

Davids, T. W. Rhys, and Hermann Oldenberg. [1882–85] 1975. *Vinaya Texts*. 3 vols. Reprint. Delhi.

Davids, T. W. Rhys, and William Stede. [1921–25] 1975. *Pali-English Dictionary*. Reprint. New Delhi.

Davis, Richard. 1974. "Tolerance and Intolerance of Ambiguity in Northern Thai Myth and Ritual." *Ethnology* 13:1–24.

———. 1976. "The Northern Thai Calendar and Its Uses." *Anthropos* 71:1–32.

———. 1984. *Muang Metaphysics: A Study of Northern Thai Myth and Ritual*. Bangkok.

Dayal, Har. [1932] 1970. *The Bodhisattva Doctrine in Buddhist Sanskrit Literature*. Reprint. Delhi.

de Jong, J. W. 1979a. *Buddhist Studies*. Edited by Gregory Schopen. Berkeley.

———. 1979b. "The Sanskrit Text of the Ṣaḍantāvadāna." *Indologica Taurinensia* 7:281–97.

Demiéville, Paul. 1924. "Les versions chinoises du Milindapañha." *Bulletin de l'Ecole Française d'Extrême-Orient* 24:1–258.

———. 1931–32. "L'origine des sectes bouddhiques d'après Paramārtha." *Mélanges chinois et bouddhiques* 1:15–64.

———. 1934. "Busshin." In *Hōbōgirin*, edited by S. Lévi, J. Takakusu, and P. Demiéville, pp. 174–85. Tokyo.

Denis, Eugène. 1976. "La *Lokapaññatti* et la légende birmane d'Aśoka." *Journal Asiatique* 264:97–116.

Denis, Eugène. 1977. *La Lokapaññatti et les idées cosmologiques du bouddhisme ancien*. 3 vols. Lille.

———. 1982. "A propos de 'Loy Krathong'." In *Bicentenaire de Bangkok*, pp. 49–54. Bangkok.

DeSilva, Lily. 1981. *Paritta: The Buddhist Ceremony for Peace and Prosperity in Sri Lanka*. Vol. 36, pt. 1 of *Spolia Zeylanica*. Colombo.

———. 1986. "Buddhist Attitude to Other Religions." *Ceylon Studies Seminar* (University of Peradeniya), ser. 2, no. 106:1–12.

DeSilva, Lynn. 1980. *Buddhism: Beliefs and Practices in Sri Lanka*. 2d ed. Colombo.

De Visser, M. W. [1913] 1969. *The Dragon in China and Japan*. Reprint. Wiesbaden.

———. 1918–19, 1920–22, 1922–23. "The Arhats in China and Japan." Parts 1–3. *Ostasiatische Zeitschrift* 7:87–102, 221–31; 9:116–44; 10:60–102.

deYoung, John E. 1963. *Village Life in Modern Thailand*. Berkeley.

Dhammapada. See Nārada 1972.

Dhammapadaṭṭhakathā. See *The Commentary on the Dhammapada*.

Dhargyey, Ngawang. 1982. *An Anthology of Well-Spoken Advice*. Edited by Alexander Berzin. Dharmsala.

Dhirasekera, J. D. 1970. "The Rebels against the Codified Law in Buddhist Monastic Discipline." *Bukkyō kenkyū* 1:77–90.

———. 1976. "Hāritī and Pāñcika: An Early Buddhist Legend of Many Lands." In *Malalasekera Commemoration Volume*, edited by O. H. deA. Wijesekera, pp. 61–70. Colombo.

Dickson, J. F. 1874. "Ordination in Theravada Buddhism." *Journal of the Royal Asiatic Society*, pp. 1–16.

Dīgha Nikāya. 1911. 3 vols. Edited by J. Estlin Carpenter. London.

Dikshitar, V. R. Ramachandra. 1932. *The Mauryan Polity*. Madras.

Dimmitt, Cornelia, and J. A. B. Van Buitenen 1978. *Classical Hindu Mythology*. Philadelphia.

Dimock, Edward C. [1966] 1971. "Doctrine and Practice among the Vaiṣṇavas of Bengal." In *Krishna: Myths, Rites and Attitudes*, edited by Milton Singer, pp. 41–63. Reprint. Chicago.

———. 1982. "A Theology of the Repulsive: The Myth of the Goddess Śītalā." In *The Divine Consort: Rādhā and the Goddesses of India*, edited by John Stratton Hawley and Donna Marie Wulff, pp. 184–203. Berkeley.

Dīpavaṃsa. See H. Oldenberg. [1879] 1982.

Divyāvadāna. 1886. Edited by E. B. Cowell and R. A. Neil. Cambridge.

Dowling, Nancy H. 1982. "Burmese Lokapalas: A Problem of Identification." *Journal of the Siam Society* 70:86–100.

ḥDsangs blun. See Schmidt 1843 and Takahashi 1969.

Dubois, J. A. 1906. *Hindu Manners, Customs, and Ceremonies*. 3d ed. Edited and translated by Henry K. Beauchamp. Oxford.

Dupont, Pierre. 1959. *L'archéologie mōne de Dvāravatī*. 2 vols. Paris.

Duroiselle, Charles. 1904. "Upagutta et Māra." *Bulletin de l'Ecole Française d'Extrême-Orient* 4:414–28.

———. 1905. "Notes sur la géographie apocryphe de la Birmanie: à propos de la légende de Pūrṇa." *Bulletin de l'Ecole Française d'Extrême-Orient* 5:146–67.

———. 1915–16. "The Ari of Burma and Tantric Buddhism." *Annual Report of the Archaeological Survey of India*, pp. 79–93.

———. [1919] 1960. "Mon Inscriptions." *Epigraphia Birmanica* 1, pt. 2:69–168. Reprint.

———. 1922–23. "Four Burmese Saints." *Annual Report of the Archaeological Survey of India*, pp. 174–76.

Durrenberger, E. Paul. 1983. "The Shan Rocket Festival: Buddhist and Non-Buddhist Aspects of Shan Religion." *Journal of the Siam Society* 71:63–74.

Durt, Hubert. 1963. "La vocation de Moggaliputta Tissa et de Nāgasena." *Miscellanea Indologica Kiotiensia/Indogaku shironshu*, nos. 4–5:16–28.

———. 1972. "Note sur l'origine de l'*Anavalokitamūrdhatā*." *Samādhi* 6:24–26.

———. 1974. "The Counting Stick (Śalākā) and the Majority/Minority Rule in the Buddhist Community." *Indogaku bukkyōgaku kenkyū/Journal of Indian and Buddhist Studies* 23:470–64 (sic).

———. 1979. "Chū." In *Hōbōgirin*, edited by Jacques May, pp. 431–56. Tokyo.

———. 1980. "Mahalla/Mahallaka et la crise de la communauté après le parinirvāṇa du Buddha." In *Indianisme et bouddhisme*, pp. 79–99. Louvain.

Dutt, Nalinaksha, and Krishna Datta Bajpai. 1956. *The Development of Buddhism in Uttar Pradesh*. Lucknow.

Dutt, Sukumar. 1957. *The Buddha and Five After-Centuries*. London.

———. 1962. *Buddhist Monks and Monasteries of India*. London.

Eberhard, Wolfram. 1968. *The Local Cultures of South and East China*. Translated by Alide Eberhard. Leiden.

Eck, Diana L. 1981. "India's Tīrthas: 'Crossings' in Sacred Geography." *History of Religions* 20:323–44.

———. 1982. *Banaras, City of Light*. Princeton.

Edgerton, Franklin. 1953. *A Buddhist Hybrid Sanskrit Grammar and Dictionary*. 2 vols. New Haven.

Edkins, Joseph. 1893. *Chinese Buddhism*. London.

Eggermont, P. H. L. 1956. *The Chronology of the Reign of Asoka Moriya*. Leiden.

Ehara, N. R. M., Soma Thera, and Kheminda Thera. 1977. *The Path of Freedom (Vimuttimagga)*. Kandy.

Eliade, Mircea. 1938. "Notes de démonologie." *Zalmoxis* 1:197–203.

———. 1958. *Rites and Symbols of Initiation*. New York.

———. 1969. *Yoga, Immortality and Freedom*. 2d ed. Princeton.

Emmerick, R. E. 1968. *The Book of Zambasta*. London.

———. 1970. *The Sūtra of Golden Light*. London.

Extended Mahāvaṃsa. 1937. Edited by G. P. Malalasekera. Colombo.

Fa Chow. 1945. "Chuan Tsi Pai Yuan King and the Avadānaśataka." *Visva-Bharati Annals* 1:35–55.

Facenna, D. 1962. *Sculptures from the Sacred Area of Butkara I, Part 2*. Rome.

Falk, Maryla. 1943. *Nāma-Rūpa and Dharma-Rūpa*. Calcutta.

Feer, Léon. 1879. "Etudes bouddhiques: le Livre des cent légendes." *Journal Asiatique* 14:283ff.

———. 1883. *Fragments extraits du Kandjour*. Paris.

———. 1891. *Avadāna-çataka: cent légendes (bouddhiques)*. Paris.

Feer, Léon. 1895. "Le Chaddanta-jātaka." *Journal Asiatique*, pp. 31–85.

———. 1901. "Le Karma-çataka." *Journal Asiatique* 17:53–486.

Ferguson, John P. 1977. "The Arahat Ideal in Modern Burmese Buddhism." Paper presented at annual meeting of the Association for Asian Studies, March. New York.

Ferguson, John P., and E. Michael Mendelson. 1981. "Masters of the Buddhist Occult: The Burmese Weikzas." *Contributions to Asian Studies* 16:62–80.

Ferrars, Max and Bertha. 1900. *Burma*. London.

Filliozat, Jean. 1954. "Les usages des tablettes bouddhiques aux Saintes Empreintes." *Arts Asiatiques* 1:309–16.

———. 1963. "La mort volontaire par le feu et la tradition bouddhique indienne." *Journal Asiatique* 251:21–51.

———. 1967. "The Devas of Aśoka: 'Gods' or 'Divine Majesties'?" In *Studies in Aśokan Inscriptions*, translated by Mrs. R. K. Menon, pp. 35–53. Calcutta.

Finot, Louis. 1911. "Sur quelques traditions indochinoises." In *Mélanges d'indianisme offerts par ses élèves à M. Sylvain Lévi*, pp. 193–212. Paris.

———. 1912. "Un nouveau document sur le bouddhisme birman." *Journal Asiatique* 20:121–36.

———. 1917. "Recherches sur la littérature laotienne." *Bulletin de l'Ecole Française d'Extrême-Orient* 17:1–218.

———. 1924. "[Review of] Report of the Superintendent of the Archaeological Survey, Burma for the Year Ending 31st March 1923." *Bulletin de l'Ecole Française d'Extrême-Orient* 24:263–64.

Fischer, Klaus. 1980. "Hidden Symbolism in Stūpa-Railing Reliefs: Coincidentia Oppositorum of Māra and Kāma." In *The Stūpa: Its Religious, Historical and Archaeological Significance*, edited by Anna Libera Dallapiccola, pp. 90–99. Wiesbaden.

Fitzgerald, C. P. [1941] 1973. *The Tower of Five Glories: A Study of the Min Chia of Ta Li, Yunnan*. Reprint. Westport, Conn.

Foucaux, Edouard. 1884. *Le Lalita vistara: développement des jeux*. Paris.

Foucher, Alfred. 1905–18. *L'art gréco-bouddhique du Gandhara*. 2 vols. Paris.

———. 1917. *The Beginnings of Buddhist Art*. Paris.

———. 1925. "Notes sur l'itinéraire de Hiuan-tsang en Afghanistan." In *Etudes asiatiques*, pp. 257–84. Paris.

———. 1963. *The Life of the Buddha*. Translated by Simone Boas. Westport, Conn.

Frauwallner, Erich. 1956. *The Earliest Vinaya and the Beginnings of Buddhist Literature*. Rome.

———. 1964. "Abhidharma Studien II." *Wiener Zeitschrift für die Kunde Süd- und Ost-Asiens* 8:9–99.

———. 1971. "Abhidharma Studien III." *Wiener Zeitschrift für die Kunde Süd- und Ost-Asiens* 15:69–121.

———. 1973. "Abhidharma Studien V." *Wiener Zeitschrift für die Kunde Süd- und Ost-Asiens* 17:97–121.

Frye, Stanley. 1981. *The Sūtra of the Wise and the Foolish (mdo bdzans blun) or the Ocean of Narratives (üliger-ün dalai)*. Dharmsala.

Gabaude, Louis. 1979. *Les cetiya de sable au Laos et en Thaïlande*. Paris.

———. 1988. *Une herméneutique bouddhique contemporaine de Thaïlande: Buddhadasa Bhikkhu*. Paris.

Gangoly, O. C. 1938. "The Antiquity of the Buddha-Image: The Cult of the Buddha." *Ostasiatische Zeitschrift* 14:41–59.

Geiger, Wilhelm. [1908] 1984. *The Dīpavaṃsa and Mahāvaṃsa and Their Historical Development in Ceylon.* Translated by Ethel Coomaraswamy. Reprint. Colombo.

———. [1912] 1960. *The Mahāvaṃsa or the Great Chronicle of Ceylon.* Reprint. Colombo.

Gernet, Jacques. 1960. "Les suicides par le feu chez les bouddhistes chinois du Ve au Xe siècle." In *Mélanges publiés par l'Institut des hautes études chinoises* 2:527–58. Paris.

Gilgit Manuscripts. 1939–59. 9 vols. Edited by Nalinaksha Dutt. Srinagar and Calcutta.

The Gilgit Manuscript of the Sanghabhedavastu. 1977–78. 2 vols. Edited by Raniero Gnoli. Rome.

The Gilgit Manuscript of the Śāyanāsavastu and the Adhikaraṇavastu. 1978. Edited by Raniero Gnoli. Rome.

Giteau, Madeleine. 1969. *Le bornage rituel des temples bouddhiques au Cambodge.* Paris.

Gjertson, Donald E. 1981. "The Early Chinese Buddhist Miracle Tale: A Preliminary Survey." *Journal of the American Oriental Society* 101:287–301.

Gode, P. K. 1951. "Indian Science of Cosmetics and Perfumery." *The International Perfumer* 3:1–9.

———. 1960. "Some Notes on the History of Divālī Festival." *Studies in Indian Cultural History* 2:187–260. Poona.

Gokhale, Balkrishna Govind. 1949. *Buddhism and Aśoka.* Baroda.

———. 1980. "Bhakti in Early Buddhism." *Journal of Asian and African Studies* (Toronto) 15:16–28.

Goloubew, Victor. 1924. "Les légendes des nāgī et de l'apsaras." *Bulletin de l'Ecole Française d'Extrême-Orient* 24:501–10.

Gombrich, Richard. 1966. "The Consecration of a Buddhist Image." *Journal of Asian Studies* 26:23–26.

———. 1971. *Precept and Practice: Traditional Buddhism in the Rural Highlands of Ceylon.* Oxford.

Granoff, Phyllis, and Koichi Shinohara. 1988. *Monks and Magicians: Religious Biographies in Asia.* Oakville, Ont.

Griffiths, Paul J. 1986. *On Being Mindless.* LaSalle, Ill.

Griswold, A. B. 1957. "King Mongkut in Perspective." *Journal of the Siam Society* 45:1–41.

Grousset, René. 1971. *In the Footsteps of the Buddha.* Translated by J. A. Underwood. New York.

Grünwedel, Albert. 1924. *Die Teufel des Avesta und ihre Beziehungen zur Ikonographie des Buddhismus Zentral-Asiens.* 2 vols. Berlin.

Guillon, Emmanuel. 1983. "Notes sur le bouddhisme Mōn." *Nachrichten der Akademie der Wissenschaften Göttingen, Philologisch-Historische Klasse*, pp. 43–63.

———. 1985. *L'armée de Māra: Au pied de l'Ānanda (Pagan-Birmanie).* Paris.

Hahn, Michael. 1977. *Haribhaṭṭa and Gopadatta. Two authors in the Succession of Āryaśūra: On the Rediscovery of Parts of Their Jātakamālās.* Tokyo.

Hahn, Michael. 1985. *Der grosse Legendenkranz (Mahajjātakamālā). Asiatische Forschungen*, vol. 88. Wiesbaden.

Hall, H. Fielding. 1914. *The Soul of a People*. London.

Halliday, R. 1917. *The Talaings*. Rangoon.

———. 1923. "Slapat Rājāwan Datow smin ron—A History of Kings." *Journal of the Burma Research Society* 13:5–67.

Handurukande, Ratna. 1967. *Maṇicūḍāvadāna and Lokānanda*. London.

———. 1970. "The Story of the Shell Maidens." In *Añjali: Papers on Indology and Buddhism Presented to O. H. deA. Wijesekera*, pp. 46–49. Peradeniya.

———. 1976a. "The Maṇicūḍa Study." *Bukkyō kenkyū* 5:309–168 [*sic*].

———. 1976b. "A Propos Kṛkin's Daughters." In *Malalasekera Commemoration Volume*, edited by O. H. DeA. Wijesekera, pp. 116–27. Colombo.

———. 1984. *Five Buddhist Legends in the Campū Style from a Collection Named Avadānasārasamuccaya*. Bonn.

Hara Minoru. 1980. "A Note on the Buddha's Birth Story." In *Indianisme et bouddhisme*, pp. 142–57. Louvain.

———. 1986. "The Holding of the Hair (Keśa-grahaṇa)." *Acta Orientalia* 47:67–92.

Hardy, Edmund. 1902. "Māra in the Guise of Buddha." *Journal of the Royal Asiatic Society*, pp. 951–55.

Hardy, Friedhelm. 1983. *Viraha-Bhakti: The Early History of Kṛṣṇ a Devotion in South India*. Delhi.

Hawley, John Stratton. 1987. *Saints and Virtues*. Berkeley.

Hecker, Hellmuth. 1967. *Lives of the Disciples I*. Wheel Publication, no. 115. Kandy.

———. 1984. *Angulimala: A Murderer's Road to Sainthood*. Wheel Publication, no. 312. Kandy.

Heinze, Ruth-Inge. 1972. *Tham Khwan: How to Contain the Essence of Life*. Singapore.

Herman, A. L. 1983. *An Introduction to Buddhist Thought*. Lanham, Md.

Herodotus. 1942. *The Persian Wars*. Translated by George Rawlinson. New York.

Hirakawa Akira. 1963. "The Rise of Mahāyāna Buddhism and Its Relationship to the Worship of Stūpas." *Memoirs of the Research Department of the Toyo Bunko* 22:57–106.

Hman-Nan-Yazawindawgyi [Glass Palace Chronicle]. 1883. Mandalay.

Hofinger, Marcel. 1946. *Etude sur le concile de Vaiśālī*. Louvain.

———. 1954. *Le congrès du lac Anavatapta (vies de saints bouddhiques) extrait du Vinaya des Mūlasarvāstivāda Bhaiṣajyavastu*. Louvain.

Holt, John. 1981a. "Assisting the Dead by Venerating the Living." *Numen* 28:1–28.

———. 1981b. *Discipline: The Canonical Buddhism of the Vinayapiṭaka*. Delhi.

Hopkins, Jeffrey. 1983. *Meditation on Emptiness*. London.

Hori Ichiro. 1962. "Self Mummified Buddhas in Japan." *History of Religions* 1:222–42.

Horner, I. B. [1936] 1979. *Early Buddhist Theory of Man Perfected*. Reprint. New Delhi.

———. 1938–52. *The Book of the Discipline*. 6 vols. London.

———. 1954–59. *The Collection of the Middle Length Sayings*. 3 vols. London.

———. 1975. *Minor Anthologies of the Pali Canon, Part 3*. London.

———. 1978. *The Clarifier of the Sweet Meaning*. London.

Htin Aung, Maung. [1962] 1978. *Folk Elements in Burmese Buddhism*. Reprint. Westport, Conn.

Huber, Edouard. 1902. "L'itinéraire du pélerin Ki Ye dans l'Inde." *Bulletin de l'Ecole Française d'Extrême-Orient* 2:256–59.

———. 1904. "Etudes de littérature bouddhique." *Bulletin de l'Ecole Française d'Extrême-Orient* 4:698–726.

———. 1906. "Les sources du Divyāvadāna." *Bulletin de l'Ecole Française d'Extrême-Orient* 6:1–37.

———. 1908. *Sūtrālaṃkāra*. Paris.

———. 1909. "[Review of] The Report of the Superintendent, Archaeological Survey, Burma, for the Year Ending 31st March 1908." Bulletin de l'Ecole Française d'Extrême-Orient 9:584.

Huntington, John C. 1985. "The Origin of the Buddha Image: Early Image Traditions and the Concept of Buddhadarśanapunyā." In *Studies in Buddhist Art of South Asia*, edited by A. K. Narain, pp. 23–58. New Delhi.

———. 1989. "Mathurā Evidence for the Early Teachings of Mahāyāna." In *Mathurā: The Cultural Heritage*, edited by Doris Meth Srinivasan, pp. 85–92. New Delhi.

Hurvitz, Leon. 1976. *Scripture of the Lotus Blossom of the Fine Dharma*. New York.

Itivuttaka. 1890. Edited by E. Windisch. London.

Iwamoto Yutaka. 1968. *Sumāgadhāvadāna*. Kyoto.

———. 1978. *Bukkyō setsuwa kenkyū josetsu* [An introduction to studies in Buddhist legends]. Tokyo.

Jaini, Padmanabh S. 1988. "Stages in the Bodhisattva Career of the Tathāgata Maitreya." In *Maitreya the Future Buddha*, edited by Alan Sponberg and Helen Hardacre, pp. 54–90. Cambridge.

———. 1989. "Political and Cultural Data in References to Mathurā in the Buddhist Literature." In *Mathurā: The Cultural Heritage*, edited by Doris Meth Srinivasan, pp. 214–22. New Delhi.

The Jātaka Together with Its Commentary. 1877–96. 6 vols. Edited by V. Fausbøll. London.

Jātakamālā by Ārya Śūra. 1959. Edited by P. L. Vaidya. Darbhanga.

Jayaswal, K. P. 1934. *An Imperial History of India in a Sanskrit Text*. Lahore.

Jayatilleke, K. N. [1963] 1980. *Early Buddhist Theory of Knowledge*. Reprint. Delhi.

Jayawickrama, N. A. 1951. *The Nidānakathā of the Jātaka Commentary*. Colombo.

———. 1962. *The Inception of Discipline and the Vinaya Nidāna*. London.

———. 1968. *The Sheaf of Garlands of the Epochs of the Conqueror Being a Translation of Jinakālamālīpakaraṇam*. London.

———. 1971. *The Chronicle of the Thūpa and the Thūpavaṃsa*. London.

Johnston, David B. 1980. "Bandit, Nakleng, and Peasant in Rural Thai Society." *Contributions to Asian Studies* 15:90–101.

Johnston, E. H. [1936] 1978. *Aśvaghoṣa's Buddhacarita or Acts of the Buddha*. Reprint. Delhi.

———. [1928] 1975. *Saundarananda of Aśvaghoṣa*. Reprint. Delhi.

Jones, J. J. 1949–56. *The Mahāvastu*. 3 vols. London.

Jumsai, M. L. Manich. 1980. *Understanding Thai Buddhism*. Bangkok.

Jumsai, Sumet. 1988. *Naga: Cultural Origins in Siam and the West Pacific*. Oxford.

Kajiyama Yuichi. 1977. "Realism of the Sarvāstivāda School." In *Buddhist Thought and Asian Civilization*, edited by Leslie S. Kawamura and Keith Scott, pp. 114–31. Emeryville, Calif.

U Kala. 1960. *Mahāyazawingyi* [The Great Chronicle]. Edited by U Pwa. Rangoon.

Karetzky, Patricia Eichenbaum. 1982. "Māra, Buddhist Deity of Death and Desire." *East and West* 32:75–92.

Karmavibhangopadeśa. See Lévi 1932.

[Karpelès, Suzanne]. 1931. "Chronique—Laos." *Bulletin de l'Ecole Française d'Extrême-Orient* 31:331–32.

Kathāvatthu. 1894–97. 2 vols. Edited by A. C. Taylor. London.

Kathāvatthuppakaraṇa-aṭṭhakathā. 1899. Edited by J. P. Minayeff. In *Journal of the Pali Text Society 1899*, pp. 1–199.

Kern, Hendrik. [1884] 1963. *Saddharma-Puṇḍarīka or The Lotus of the True Law*. Reprint. New York.

———. 1898. *A Manual of Indian Buddhism*. Strassburg.

Keyes, Charles F. 1975. "Tug-of-War for Merit: Cremation of a Senior Monk." *Journal of the Siam Society* 63:44–62.

———. 1981. "Death of Two Buddhist Saints in Thailand." *Journal of the American Academy of Religion, Thematic Studies* 48:149–80.

Khantipalo Bhikkhu. 1979. *Banner of the Arahants*. Kandy.

Kieckhefer, Richard, and George D. Bond. 1988. *Sainthood: Its Manifestation in World Religions*. Berkeley.

U Kin. 1957. *Maha-win wutthu*. Reprint. Rangoon.

———. 1981. *Jinathapakāsini*. Reprint. Rangoon.

King, Winston L. 1964. *A Thousand Lives Away: Buddhism in Contemporary Burma*. Cambridge, Mass.

Kloetzli, Randy. 1983. *Buddhist Cosmology*. Delhi.

Kloppenborg, M. A. G. T. 1979. "Some Reflexions on the Study of Sinhalese Buddhism." In *Official and Popular Religion*, edited by Pieter Hendrik Vrijhof and Jacques Waardenburg, pp. 487–513. The Hague.

Kloppenborg, Ria. 1973. *The Sūtra on the Foundation of the Buddhist Order*. Leiden.

———. 1974. *The Paccekabuddha: A Buddhist Ascetic*. Leiden.

Konjaku monogatari shū [Tales of times now past]. 1959. Vol. 1. Edited by Yoshio Yamada et. al. Tokyo.

Kraisri Nimmanhaeminda. 1967. "The Lawa Guardian Spirits of Chiangmai." *Journal of the Siam Society* 55:185–226.

Lafont, Pierre Bernard, and Pierre Bitard. 1957. "Ordination de deux dignitaires bouddhiques 'Tay Lu'." *Bulletin de la Société des Etudes Indochinoises*, n.s., 32:199–220.

Lakṣacaityasamutpatti. See Rajapatirana 1974.

Lalitavistara. 1902. Edited by S. Lefmann. Halle.

Lamotte, Etienne. 1947–50. "Alexandre et le bouddhisme." *Bulletin de l'Ecole Française d'Extrême-Orient* 44:147–62.

———. 1949–80. *Le traité de la grande vertu de sagesse*. 5 vols. Louvain.

———. 1958. *Histoire du bouddhisme indien*. Louvain.

———. 1965. *La concentration de la marche héroïque (Śūraṃgamasamādhisūtra)*. *Mélanges chinois et bouddhiques*, vol. 13. Brussels.

———. 1966–74. "Vajrapāṇi en Inde." In *Mélanges de sinologie offerts à Monsieur Paul Demiéville*, 1:113–59. Paris.

———. 1976. *The Teaching of Vimalakīrti*. Translated by Sara Boin. London.

Lancaster, Lewis R. 1974. "An Early Mahāyāna Sermon about the Body of the Buddha and the Making of Images." *Artibus Asiae* 36:287–91.

———. 1979. *The Korean Buddhist Canon: A Descriptive Catalogue*. Berkeley.

Lang, M. E. 1912. "Le Mahajjātakamālā." *Journal Asiatique*, pp. 511–50.

La Vallée Poussin, Louis de. 1894. "Maṇicūḍāvadāna as Related in the Fourth Chapter of the Svayambhūpurāṇa." *Journal of the Royal Asiatic Society*, pp. 297–319.

———. 1905. "Les deux premiers conciles." *Le Muséon* 6:213–323.

———. 1914–19. "Bouddhisme: Etudes et matériaux. Cosmologie: le monde des êtres et le monde réceptacle." *Mémoires de l'Académie royale de Belgique* 6:295–350.

———. 1918. "Pratyekabuddha." In *Encyclopaedia of Religion and Ethics*, edited by James Hastings, 10:152–54. Edinburgh.

———. 1923–31. *L'Abhidharmakośa de Vasubandhu*. 6 vols. Paris.

———. 1925. "La controverse du temps et du pudgala dans le Vijñānakāya." In *Etudes asiatiques*, 1:343–76. Paris.

———. 1928. "Les neuf kalpas qu'a franchis Śākyamuni pour devancer Maitreya." *T'oung pao* 26:17–24.

———. 1928–29. *Vijñaptimātratāsiddhi, la siddhi de Hiuan-tsang*. 2 vols. Paris.

———. 1929. "Extase et spéculation." In *Indian Studies in Honor of Charles Rockwell Lanman*, pp. 135–36. Cambridge.

———. 1930, 1932, 1937. "Documents d'Abhidharma." Parts 1–5. *Bulletin de l'Ecole Française d'Extrême-Orient* 30:1–28; *Mélanges chinois et bouddhiques* 1:65–125; *Mélanges chinois et bouddhiques* 5:7–187.

———. 1937. "Musila et Narada: le chemin du Nirvāṇa." *Mélanges chinois et bouddhiques* 5:189–222.

Law, B. C. 1925. *The Dāṭhāvaṃsa: A History of the Tooth-Relic of the Buddha*. Lahore.

———. [1940] 1969. *The Debates Commentary*. Reprint. London.

———. 1952. *The History of the Buddha's Religion*. London.

Lefèvre-Pontalis, Pierre. 1926. *Notes sur des amulettes siamoises*. Paris.

Legge, James. [1886] 1965. *A Record of Buddhistic Kingdoms*. Reprint. New York.

LeMay, Reginald. 1954. *The Culture of South East Asia*. London.

Lessing, Ferdinand. 1954. "The Eighteen Worthies Crossing the Sea." In *Contributions to Ethnography, Linguistics and History of Religion*, pp. 111–28. Sino-Swedish Expedition Publication, no. 38. Stockholm.

Leumann, Ernst. 1919. *Maitreya samiti, das Zukunftsideal der Buddhisten*. Strassburg.

Lévi, Sylvain. 1908. "Eléments de formation du Divyāvadāna." *T'oung pao* 8:105–22.

———. 1915a. "Le catalogue géographique des yakṣa dans la Mahāmāyūrī." *Journal Asiatique* 5:19–138.

———. 1915b. "Sur la récitation primitive des textes bouddhiques." *Journal Asiatique* 5:401–47.

———. 1925. "Le sūtra du sage et du fou dans la littérature de l'Asie Centrale." *Journal Asiatique* 2:305–32.

———. 1927. "La Dṛṣṭāntapankti et son auteur." *Journal Asiatique* 211:95–127.

———. 1932. *Mahākarmavibhanga et Karmavibhangopadeśa*. Paris.

Lévi, Sylvain, and Edouard Chavannes. 1916. "Les seize arhat protecteurs de la loi." *Journal Asiatique* 8:5–48, 189–304.

Lévy, Paul. 1942. "Quand le ciel touche la terre: le mois des Phis au Laos." *Cahiers de l'Ecole Française d'Extrême-Orient* 30:13–14.

———. 1943. "Le sacrifice du buffle et la prédiction du temps à Vientiane." *Bulletin de l'Institut Indochinois pour l'Etude de l'Homme* 6:301–33.

———. [1957] 1968. *Buddhism: A Mystery Religion?* Reprint. New York.

Li Yung-hsi. 1959. *The Life of Hsüan-tsang Compiled by Monk Hui-li.* Peking.

Lin Li-kouan. 1949. *L'aide-mémoire de la vraie loi.* Paris.

Ling, Trevor. 1962. *Buddhism and the Mythology of Evil.* London.

Lokapaññatti. See Denis 1977.

Luce, Gordon H. 1964. *Old Burma, Early Pagan.* 3 vols. Artibus Asiae, suppl. 25. New York.

Luce, Gordon H., and Bohmu Ba Shin. 1961. "Pagan Myinkaba Kubyauk-gyi Temple of Rājakumār." *Bulletin of the Burma Historical Commission* 2:277–416.

Lüders, Heinrich. 1897. "Die Sage von Ṛṣyaśṛnga." *Nachrichten von der Königlichen Gesellschaft der Wissenschaften, Göttingen, Philologisch-Historische Klasse,* pp. 87–135.

———. 1902. "Zur Sage von Ṛṣyaśṛnga." *Nachrichten von der Königlichen Gesellschaft der Wissenschaften, Göttingen, Philologisch-Historische Klasse,* pp. 28–56.

———. 1926. *Bruchstücke der Kalpanāmaṇḍitikā des Kumāralāta.* Kleinere Sanskrit-texte aus den Turfanfunden, no. 2. Leipzig.

———. 1961. *Mathurā Inscriptions.* Göttingen.

MacDonald, Alexandre. 1955. "La notion du sambhogakāya à la lumière de quelques faits ethnographiques." *Journal Asiatique* 243:228–39.

McRae, John R. 1986. *The Northern School and the Formation of Early Ch'an Buddhism.* Honolulu.

Madhuratthavilasinī. 1946. Edited by I. B. Horner. London.

Mahajjātakamālā. See Hahn 1985.

Mahākarmavibhanga. See Lévi 1932.

Das Mahāparinirvāṇa Sūtra. 1950. Edited by Ernst Waldschmidt. Abhandlungen der deutschen Akademie der Wissenschaften. Berlin.

Phra Mahāprīcha Prinyāno. 1967. *Prapheni boran—Thai Isan* [Ancient traditions of the Northeast]. Ubon Ratchathani.

The Mahāvaṃsa. 1908. Edited by Wilhelm Geiger. London.

Le Mahāvastu. 1882–97. 3 vols. Edited by Emile Sénart. Paris.

Mair, Victor. 1983. *Tun-huang Popular Narratives.* Cambridge.

———. 1989. *T'ang Transformation Texts.* Cambridge, Mass.

Maitreya Samiti. See Leumann 1919.

Majjhima Nikāya. 1888–99. 3 vols. Edited by V. Trenckner and R. Chalmers. London.

Majumdar, R. C. 1948. "The Karaṇḍavyūha: Its Metrical Version." *Indian Historical Quarterly* 24:293–99.

Malalasekera, G. P. [1938] 1974. *Dictionary of Pāli Proper Names.* 2 vols. Reprint. London.

Manorathapūraṇī: Buddhaghosa's Commentary on the Anguttara Nikāya. 1924–30. 4 vols. Edited by M. Walleser and H. Kopf. London.

Marshall, John. 1960. *The Buddhist Art of Gandhāra*. Cambridge.

Martini, François. 1936. "Dasa-bodhisatta-uddesa." *Bulletin de l'Ecole Française d'Extrême-Orient* 36:287–413.

Martini, Ginette. 1969. "Pañcabuddhabyākaraṇa." *Bulletin de l'Ecole Française d'Extrême-Orient* 55:125–44.

———. 1973. "*Brapaṃsukūlānisaṃsaṃ*." *Bulletin de l'Ecole Française d'Extrême-Orient* 60:55–76.

Masefield, Peter. 1983. "Mind/Cosmos Maps in the Pāli Nikāyas." In *Buddhist and Western Psychology*, edited by Nathan Katz, pp. 69–93. Boulder.

———. 1986. *Divine Revelation in Pali Buddhism*. London.

Mason, Francis. 1868. *Kachchāyano's Pali Grammar*. Bibliotheca Indica, vol. 59. Toungoo.

Maspero, Henri. 1911. "Sur la date et l'authenticité du Fou fa tsang yin yuan tchouan." In *Mélanges d'indianisme offerts par ses élèves à M. Sylvain Lévi*, pp. 129–49. Paris.

———. 1950. "La société et la religion des Chinois anciens et celles des Tai modernes." In *Les religions chinoises*, pp. 139–94. Paris.

Matsunami Seiren. 1965. *A Catalog of the Sanskrit Manuscripts in the Tokyo University Library*. Tokyo.

Maung Kin. 1903. "The Legend of Upagutta." *Buddhism* (Rangoon) 1:219–42.

Mendelson, E. Michael. 1961a. "The King of the Weaving Mountain." *Journal of the Royal Central Asian Society* 48:229–37.

———. 1961b. "A Messianic Buddhist Association in Upper Burma." *Bulletin of the School of Oriental and African Studies* 24:560–80.

———. 1963. "Observations on a Tour in the Region of Mount Popa." *France-Asie* 179:786–807.

———. 1965. "Initiation and the Paradox of Power: A Sociological Approach." In *Initiation*, edited by C. J. Bleeker, pp. 214–22. Leiden.

———. 1975. *Sangha and State in Burma: A Study of Monastic Sectarianism and Leadership*. Edited by John P. Ferguson. Ithaca.

Milindapañha. 1880. Edited by V. Trenckner. London.

Mills, D. E. 1970. *A Collection of Tales from Uji*. Cambridge.

Milne, Mary Lewis. 1921. *An Elementary Palaung Grammar*. Oxford.

———. 1924. *The Home of an Eastern Clan: A Study of the Palaungs of the Shan State*. Oxford.

Min Kyi Hlaing. 1986. *Shin Upago Mahāthera Therupatti nee parittaw* [The Venerable elder Upagupta—hagiography and magical formulae], edited by Shin Narada. Syriam.

Minakata Kumagusu. 1899. "The Wandering Jew." *Notes and Queries* 4:121–24.

Mitra, Rajendralal. [1882] 1981. *The Sanskrit Buddhist Literature of Nepal*. Reprint. New Delhi.

Moerman, Michael. 1975. "Chī angkham's Trade in the 'Old Days.'" In *Change and Persistence in Thai Society*, edited by G. William Skinner and A. Thomas Kirsch, pp. 151–71. Ithaca.

Moffat, Abbot Low. 1961. *Mongkut the King of Siam*. Ithaca.

Monier-Williams, Monier. 1885. *Religious Thought and Life in India*. London.

Mote, F. W. 1967. "The Rural 'Haw' (Yunnanese Chinese) of Northern Thailand." In *Southeast Asian Tribes, Minorities, and Nations*, edited by Peter Kunstadter, 2:487–524. Princeton.

Mukherjee, Biswadeb. 1966. *Die Überlieferung von Devadatta, dem Widersucher des Buddha in den kanonischen Schriften*. Munich.

Mus, Paul. 1928. "Le Buddha paré: son origine indienne. Śākyamuni dans le Mahāyānisme moyen." *Bulletin de l'Ecole Française d'Extrême-Orient* 28:153–278.

———. 1931. "Les religions de l'Indochine." In *Indochine*, edited by Sylvain Lévi, pp. 103–56. Paris.

———. 1933. "Cultes indiens et indigènes au Champa." *Bulletin de l'Ecole Française d'Extrême-Orient* 33:367–410.

———. 1935. *Barabuḍur: esquisse d'une histoire du bouddhisme fondée sur la critique archéologique des textes*. 2 vols. Hanoi.

———. 1939. *La lumière sur les six voies*. Travaux et mémoires de l'Institut d'ethnologie, no. 35. Paris.

Myer, Prudence R. 1986. "Bodhisattvas and Buddhas: Early Buddhist Images from Mathurā." *Artibus Asiae* 47:107–42.

Nakamura Hajime. 1980a. "The Aṣṭamahāsthānacaityastotra and the Chinese and Tibetan Versions of a Text Similar to It." In *Indianisme et bouddhisme*, pp. 259–65. Louvain.

———. 1980b. *Indian Buddhism: A Survey with Bibliographical Notes*. Hirakata City.

Nārada Thera. 1972. *Dhammapada: Pali Text and Translation with Stories in Brief*. New Delhi.

Narain, A. K. 1985. "First Images of the Buddha and Bodhisattvas: Ideology and Chronology." In *Studies in Buddhist Art of South Asia*, edited by A. K. Narain, pp. 1–21. New Delhi.

Nash, Manning. 1966. "Ritual and Ceremonial Cycle in Upper Burma." In *Anthropological Studies in Theravāda Buddhism*, edited by Manning Nash, pp. 97–115. New Haven.

Nattier, Jan. 1988. "The Meanings of the Maitreya Myth: A Typological Analysis." In *Maitreya the Future Buddha*, edited by Alan Sponberg and Helen Hardacre, pp. 23–47. Cambridge.

Nginn, Pierre S. 1956a. "Le carême et la fête des eaux." *Présence du Royaume Lao*, pp. 959–61. *France-Asie*, special nos. 118–19.

———. 1956b. "Le code des bons usages." *Présence du Royaume Lao*, pp. 891–93. *France-Asie*, special nos. 118–19.

Nikam, N. A., and Richard McKeon. 1959. *The Edicts of Aśoka*. Chicago.

Nishiyama Kōsen. 1977–85. *Dōgen's Shōbōgenzō*. 4 vols. Tokyo.

Njammasch, Marlene. 1974. "Der Navakammika und seine Stellung in der Hierarchie der buddhistischen Klöster." *Alt-orientalische Forschungen* 1:279–93.

Nobel, Johannes. 1955. *Udrāyaṇa, König von Roruka*. Wiesbaden.

Norman, K. R. 1983a. *Pāli Literature*. Wiesbaden.

———. 1983b. "The Pratyeka-Buddha in Buddhism and Jainism." In *Buddhist Studies Ancient and Modern*, edited by Philip Denwood and Alexander Piatigorski, pp. 92–106. London.

———. 1984. *The Group of Discourses*. London.

Notton, Camille. 1930. *Annales du Siam.* 3 vols. Paris.

Ñyāṇamoli Bhikkhu. [1956] 1976. *The Path of Purification.* 2 vols. Reprint. Berkeley.

Nyanaponika Thera. 1969. *The Heart of Buddhist Meditation.* New York.

Obermiller, E. 1931. *History of Buddhism (Chos-hbyung) by Bu ston.* 2 vols. Heidelberg.

Obeyesekere, Gananath. 1963. "The Great Tradition and the Little in the Perspective of Sinhalese Buddhism." *Journal of Asian Studies* 22:39–53.

———. 1981. *Medusa's Hair.* Chicago.

O'Flaherty, Wendy Doniger. 1973. *Asceticism and Eroticism in the Mythology of Śiva.* Oxford.

———. 1975. *Hindu Myths.* Harmondsworth.

———. 1976. *The Origins of Evil in Hindu Mythology.* Berkeley.

———. 1980. *Women, Androgynes, and Other Mythical Beasts.* Chicago.

———. 1988. *Other Peoples' Myths.* New York.

U Ohn Maung. N.d. [1973?] *Shin Upagut: Therupatti nee kogwe puzaw nee mya* [Biography and worship of the Venerable Upagupta]. Rangoon.

Oldenberg, Hermann. [1879] 1982. *The Dīpavaṃsa: An Ancient Buddhist Historical Record.* Reprint. New Delhi.

d'Oldenburg, Serge. 1893. "On the Buddhist Jātakas." Translated by H. Wenzel. *Journal of the Royal Asiatic Society*, pp. 301–56.

Pallegoix, Jean-Baptiste. [1854] 1976. *Description du Royaume Thai ou Siam.* Abridged reprint. Bangkok.

Pañcaviṃśatisāhasrikā prajñāpāramitā. 1934. Edited by N. Dutt. Calcutta.

Panglung, Jampa Losang. 1981. *Die Erzählstoffe des Mūlasarvāstivāda Vinaya analysiert auf Grund der tibetischen Übersetzung.* Tokyo.

Paññāsa-Jātaka or Zimme Paṇṇāsa (in the Burmese Recension). 1983. 2 vols. Edited by P. S. Jaini. London.

Pannya Nantha [Bhikkhu]. 1971. *Chiwit Khong Khapachao* [My life]. Bangkok.

Paramaṭṭha-dīpanī Therāgātha-Aṭṭhakathā. 1940–59. 3 vols. Edited by F. L. Woodward. London.

Pe Maung Tin and Gordon H. Luce. [1923] 1960. *The Glass Palace Chronicle of the Kings of Burma.* Reprint. Rangoon.

Pelliot, Paul. 1902. "Mémoires sur les coutumes du Cambodge." *Bulletin de l'Ecole Française d'Extrême-Orient* 2:123–77.

———. 1904. "Deux itinéraires de Chine en Inde à la fin du VIIIe siècle." *Bulletin de l'Ecole Française d'Extrême-Orient* 4:131–413.

Peltier, Anatole-Roger. 1977. *Introduction à la connaissance des hlvn ba¹ de Thaïlande.* Paris.

———. 1982. "Les amulettes dans la vie quotidienne." In *Bicentenaire de Bangkok*, pp. 89–94. Bangkok.

Péri, Noël. 1917. "Hārītī la mère-de-démons." *Bulletin de l'Ecole Française d'Extrême-Orient* 17:1–102.

———. 1918. "Les femmes de Śākya-muni." *Bulletin de l'Ecole Française d'Extrême-Orient* 18:1–37.

Petech, Luciano. 1966–74. "La description des pays d'occident de Che Tao-Ngan." In *Mélanges de sinologie offerts à Monsieur Paul Demiéville* 1:167–90. Paris.

Phra Paṭhamasambodhikathā. 1978. Bangkok.

Plenge, Vagn. 1976. "The Sun, the Moon and Rāhu—and Other Tai Tales and Stories Recorded in Northern Thailand." In *Lampang Reports*, edited by Søren Egerod and Per Sørensen, pp. 111–32. Copenhagen.

Porée-Maspero, Eveline. 1950. "Nouvelle étude sur la nāgī Somā." *Journal Asiatique* 238:237–67.

———. 1962–69. *Etude sur les rites agraires des Cambodgiens*. 3 vols. Paris.

Prebish, Charles. 1975. *Buddhist Monastic Discipline*. University Park.

Pruden, Leo. 1988. *Abhidharmakośabhāṣyam by Louis de La Vallée Poussin*. Vol. 1. Berkeley.

Pruess, James B. 1976. "Merit-Seeking in Public: Buddhist Pilgrimage in Northeastern Thailand." *Journal of the Siam Society* 64:169–206.

Przyluski, Jean. 1914. "Le Nord-ouest de l'Inde dans le Vinaya des Mūlasarvāstivādin et les textes apparentés." *Journal Asiatique* 4:493–568.

———. 1920. *Le parinirvāṇa et les funérailles du Buddha*. Paris.

———. 1923a. *La légende de l'empereur Açoka (Açokāvadāna) dans les textes indiens et chinois*. Paris.

———. 1923b. "Les Vidyārāja: contribution à l'histoire de la magie dans les sectes mahāyānistes." *Bulletin de l'Ecole Française d'Extrême-Orient* 23:301–68.

———. 1925. "La princesse à l'odeur de poisson et la nāgī dans les traditions de l'Asie orientale." In *Etudes asiatiques* 2:265–84. Paris.

———. 1926. *Le Concile de Rājagṛha*. Paris.

———. 1927. "La place de Māra dans la mythologie bouddhique." *Journal Asiatique* 210:115–23.

———. 1936. "Le partage des reliques du Buddha." *Mélanges chinois et bouddhiques* 4:341–67.

Rahder, J. 1931–32. "La satkāyadṛṣṭi d'après Vibhāṣā 8." *Mélanges chinois et bouddhiques* 1:227–39.

Rahula, Telwatte. 1984. "The *Rasavāhinī* and the *Sahassavatthu*: A Comparison." *Journal of the International Association of Buddhist Studies* 7:169–84.

Rahula, Walpola. 1956. *History of Buddhism in Ceylon*. Colombo.

———. 1976. "Zen and the Taming of the Bull." In *Malalasekera Commemoration Volume*, edited by O. H. deA. Wijesekera, pp. 292–303. Colombo.

Rajapatirana, Tissa. 1974. "*Suvarṇavarṇāvadāna* and the *Lakṣacaityasamutpatti*." 3 vols. Ph.D. dissertation, Australian National University, Canberra.

Ratnamālāvadāna: A Garland of Precious Gems. 1954. Edited by Kanga Takahata. Tokyo.

Ray, Nihar-Ranjan. 1936. *Sanskrit Buddhism in Burma*. Amsterdam.

———. 1946. *An Introduction to the Study of Theravada Buddhism in Burma*. Calcutta.

Ray, Reginald. Forthcoming. *Mahāsiddhas: A Study in the Hagiography and Tradition of the Tantric Buddhist Saints in India*.

Reynolds, Craig J. 1979. *Autobiography: The Life of Prince-Patriarch Vajirañāṇa of Siam, 1860–1921*. Athens, Ohio. 1979.

Reynolds, Frank E. 1977. "The Several Bodies of the Buddha: Reflections on a Neglected Aspect of Theravāda Tradition." *History of Religions* 16:374–89.

Reynolds, Frank E., and Donald Capps. 1976. *The Biographical Process*. The Hague.

Reynolds, Frank E., and Mani B. Reynolds. 1982. *Three Worlds According to King Ruang*. Berkeley Buddhist Series, vol. 4. Berkeley.

Rhum, Michael. 1987. "The Cosmology of Power in Lanna." *Journal of the Siam Society* 75:91–107.

Rockhill, W. Woodville. 1907. *The Life of the Buddha*. London.

Roerich, George N. [1949] 1976. *The Blue Annals*. 2 vols. Reprint. Delhi.

Ruelius, Hans. 1978. "Netrapratiṣṭhāpana—eine singhalesische Zeremonie zur Weihe von Kultbildern." In *Buddhism in Ceylon and Studies on Religious Syncretism in Buddhist Countries*, edited by Heinz Bechert, pp. 304–34. Göttingen.

Saddanīti: la grammaire palie d'Aggavaṃsa. 1928–66. 5 vols. Edited by Helmer Smith. Lund.

Saddharmapuṇḍarīka Sūtra. 1908–12. Edited by Hendrik Kern and Bunyo Nanjo. St. Petersburg.

Saddhatissa, H. 1975. *The Birth-Stories of the Ten Bodhisattas and the Dasabodhisattuppattikathā*. London.

———. 1985. *The Sutta-Nipāta*. London.

Sainson, Camille. 1904. *Nan-tchao Ye-che: histoire particulière du Nan-tchao*. Paris.

Samantapāsādika: Buddhaghosa's Commentary on the Vinaya Piṭaka. [1924–1947] 1968. 7 vols. Edited by J. Takakusu and M. Nagai. Reprint. London.

Samyutta Nikāya. 1884–98. Edited by Léon Feer. 5 vols. London.

Sanghabhedavastu. See *The Gilgit Manuscript of the Sanghabhedavastu*.

Sāratthappakāsinī. 1929–37. 3 vols. Edited by F. L. Woodward. London.

Sāsanavaṃsa. 1897. Edited by Mabel Bode. London.

Sastri, Haraprasad. 1894. "Notes on the Svayambhū Purāṇaṃ" *Journal of the Buddhist Text Society* 2, pt. 2:33–37.

Saundarananda. See E. H. Johnston [1928] 1975.

Śāyanāsavastu. See *The Gilgit Manuscript of the Śāyanāsavastu and the Adhikaraṇavastu*.

Schalk, Peter. 1972. *Der Paritta-Dienst in Ceylon*. Lund.

Schiefner, F. Anton von, and W. R. S. Ralston. 1893. *Tibetan Tales Derived from Indian Sources*. London.

Schmidt, I. J. 1843. h.*Dsangs blun oder der Weise und der Thor*. 2 vols. St. Petersburg.

Schober, Juliane. 1980. "On Burmese Horoscopes." *The South East Asian Review* 5:43–56.

Sénart, Emile. 1906. "Vajrapāṇi dans les sculptures du Gandhāra." In *Actes du XIVe congrès des orientalistes, Alger, 1905* 1:121–31. Paris.

Seneviratne, H. L. 1973. "L'ordination bouddhique à Ceylan." *Social Compass* 20:251–56.

Shan Shih Buddhist Institute. 1961. *The Sixteen and the Eighteen Arhats*. Peking.

Sharma, R. C. 1989. "New Inscriptions from Mathurā." In *Mathurā: The Cultural Heritage*, edited by Doris Meth Srinivasan, pp. 308–15. New Delhi.

Shorto, H. L. 1963. "The Thirty-two Myos in the Medieval Mon Kingdom." *Bulletin of the School of Oriental and African Studies* 26:572–91.

———. 1970. "The Gavampati Tradition in Burma." In *R. C. Majumdar Felicitation Volume*, edited by Himansu Bhusan Sarkar, pp. 15–30. Calcutta.

Shulman, David Dean. 1985. *The King and the Clown in South Indian Myth and Poetry*. Princeton.

Shway Yoe [James George Scott]. [1882] 1963. *The Burman: His Life and Notions*. Reprint. New York.

Sibunruang, Jit-Kasem. 1976. *Contes et légendes de Thaïlande*. Bangkok.

Sīhaḷavatthuppakaraṇa. See Ver Eecke 1980.

Śikṣāsamuccaya. 1961. Edited by P. L. Vaidya. Darbhanga.

Sircar, D. C. 1942. *Select Inscriptions Bearing on Indian History and Civilization*. 2 vols. Calcutta.

Sivaraksa, S. 1987. "*Jīnapañjaragāthā*." *Journal of the Siam Society* 75:299–302.

Skeat, W. W. 1900. *Malay Magic*. New York.

Smith, Vincent. 1903. "Aśoka's Father Confessor." *Indian Antiquary* 32:365–66.

———. [1909] 1964. *Aśoka, the Buddhist Emperor of India*. Reprint. Delhi.

Snellgrove, David. 1987. *Indo-Tibetan Buddhism: Indian Buddhists and Their Tibetan Successors*. London.

Soper, Alexander C. 1949–50. "Aspects of Light Symbolism in Gandhāran Sculpture." Parts 1–3. *Artibus Asiae* 12:252–83, 314–30; 13:63–85.

Southwold, Martin. 1983. *Buddhism in Life: The Anthropological Study of Religion and the Sinhalese Practice of Buddhism*. Manchester.

Speyer, J. S. [1895] 1982. *The Jātakamālā or Garland of Birth-Stories of Āryaśūra*. Reprint. Delhi.

———. 1899. "Buddhas Todesjahr nach dem Avadānaśataka." *Zeitschrift der Deutschen Morgenländischen Gesellschaft* 53:120–24.

———. 1902. "Critical Remarks on the Text Divyāvadāna." *Wiener Zeitschrift für die Kunde des Morgenlandes* 16:344–59.

Spiro, Melford E. 1967. *Burmese Supernaturalism*. Englewood Cliffs, N.J.

———. 1982. *Buddhism and Society: A Great Tradition and Its Burmese Vicissitudes*. 2d ed. Berkeley.

Stcherbatsky, Theodore. [1923] 1970. *The Central Conception of Buddhism and the Meaning of the Word "Dharma"*. Reprint. Delhi.

Strachan, Paul. 1989. *Pagan: Art and Architecture of Old Burma*. Edinburgh.

Strong, John S. 1977. "Gandhakuṭī: The Perfumed Chamber of the Buddha." *History of Religions* 16:390–406.

———. 1979a. "The Legend of the Lion-Roarer: A Study of the Buddhist Arhat Piṇḍola Bhāradvāja." *Numen* 26:50–88.

———. 1979b. "The Transforming Gift: An Analysis of Devotional Acts of Offering in Buddhist Avadāna Literature." *History of Religions* 18:221–37.

———. 1983a. "Filial Piety and Buddhism: The Indian Antecedents to a 'Chinese' Problem." In *Traditions in Contact and Change*, edited by Peter Slater and Donald Wiebe, pp. 171–86. Waterloo, Ont.

———. 1983b. *The Legend of King Aśoka*. Princeton.

———. 1983c. "Wenn der magische Flug misslingt." Translated by Udo Rennert. In *Sehnsucht nach dem Ursprung: zu Mircea Eliade*, edited by Hans Peter Duerr, pp. 503–18. Frankfurt.

———. 1985. "The Buddhist Avadānists and the Elder Upagupta." In *Tantric and Taoist Studies in Honour of R. A. Stein*, edited by Michel Strickmann, *Mélanges chinois et bouddhiques*, vol. 22. 3:862–81. Brussels.

———. 1990. "Rich Man, Poor Man, Bhikkhu, King." In *Ethics, Wealth, and Salvation: A Study in Buddhist Social Ethics*, edited by Russell F. Sizemore and Donald K. Swearer, pp. 107–23. Columbia, S.C.

———. Forthcoming. "A Family Quest: The Buddha, Yaśodharā, and Rāhula in the *Mūlasarvāstivāda Vinaya*."

Sumangalavilāsinī: Buddhaghosa's Commentary on the Dīgha Nikāya. 1971. 2d ed. 3 vols. Edited by William Stede. London.

Suttanipāta. 1913. Edited by Dines Andersen and Helmer Smith. London.

Sutta Nipāta Commentary Being Paramatthajotika II. 1916–18. 2 vols. Edited by Helmer Smith. London.

Suvarṇabhāsottamasūtra: das Goldglanz Sūtra, ein Sanskrittext des Mahāyāna Buddhismus. 1937. Edited by Johannes Nobel. Leipzig.

Swearer, Donald K. 1976a. "The Role of the Layman *Extraordinaire* in Northern Thai Buddhism." *Journal of the Siam Society* 64:151–68.

———. 1976b. *Wat Haripuñjaya*. Missoula.

Tagore, Rabindranath. 1937. *The Collected Poems and Plays of Rabindranath Tagore*. New York.

Taishō shinshū daizōkyō [New Taishō era edition of the Buddhist canon]. 1924–29. 55 vols. Edited by J. Takakusu and K. Watanabe. Tokyo.

Takahashi Moritaka. 1969. *Ḥdsaṅs Blun or the Sūtra of the Wise and the Foolish*. Osaka.

Takakusu Junjiro. 1896a. "Chinese Translations of the Milindapañha." *Journal of the Royal Asiatic Society*, pp. 17–21.

———. [1896b] 1966. *A Record of Buddhistic Religion as Practiced in India and the Malay Archipelago*. Reprint. Delhi.

———. 1901. "Tales of the Wise Man and the Fool in Tibetan and Chinese." *Journal of the Royal Asiatic Society*, pp. 447–60.

———. 1905. "On the Abhidharma Literature of the Sarvāstivādins." *Journal of the Pali Text Society*, pp. 67–146.

Tambiah, Stanley J. 1970. *Buddhism and the Spirit Cults in North-east Thailand*. Cambridge.

———. 1976. *World Conqueror and World Renouncer*. Cambridge.

———. 1984. *The Buddhist Saints of the Forest and the Cult of Amulets*. Cambridge.

Tawney, C. H. 1924–28. *The Ocean of Story*. 10 vols. London.

Terwiel, B. J. 1975. *Monks and Magic: An Analysis of Religious Ceremonies in Central Thailand*. Lund.

———. 1976. "A Model for the Study of Thai Buddhism." *Journal of Asian Studies* 35:391–403.

Than Tun. 1959a. "Religion in Burma, A.D. 1000–1300." *Journal of the Burma Research Society* 42, pt. 2:47–69.

———. 1959b. "Mahākassapa and His Tradition." *Journal of the Burma Research Society* 42, pt. 2:99–118.

Thomas, E. J. 1933. "Avadāna and Apādana." *Indian Historical Quarterly* 9:32–36.

Thompson, Stith. 1955–58. *Motif-Index of Folk-Literature*. 6 vols. Bloomington.

Thūpavaṃsa. See Jayawickrama 1971.

Tokiwai Tsurumatsu. 1898. *Studien zum Sumāgadhāvadāna*. Darmstadt.

Tomomatsu Entai. 1931. "Sūtrālaṃkāra et Kalpanāmaṇḍitikā." *Journal Asiatique* 219: 164–74.

Tsukamoto Zenryū. 1985. *A History of Early Chinese Buddhism*. Translated by Leon Hurvitz. Tokyo.

Tucci, Giuseppe. 1949. *Tibetan Painted Scrolls*. 3 vols. Rome.

———. 1958. "Preliminary Reports and Studies on the Italian Excavations in Swāt (Pakistan)." *East and West* 9:285–327.

Turner, R. 1913. "Notes on the Language of the Dvāviṃśatyavadānakathā." *Journal of the Royal Asiatic Society*, pp. 289–304.

Uji shūi monogatari shū [A collection of tales from Uji]. 1960. Edited by Tsunaya Watanabe and Kōichi Nishio. Tokyo.

Upasampadāvidhi. 1936. Bangkok.

[Prince] Vajirañāṇavarorasa. 1973. *Ordination Procedure*. Bangkok.

Vaṃsatthappakāsinī: Commentary on the Mahāvaṃsa. 1935. 2 vols. Edited by G. P. Malalasekera. London.

Van Buitenen, J. A. B. 1973. *The Mahābhārata I: The Book of the Beginning*. Chicago.

———. 1981. *The Bhagavadgītā in the Mahābhārata*. Chicago.

Van Gennep, Arnold. 1960. *The Rites of Passage*. Translated by Monika B. Vizedom and Gabrielle L. Caffee. Chicago.

Van Lohuizen–De Leeuw, J. E. 1949. *The "Scythian" Period*. Leiden.

———. 1979. "New Evidence with Regard to the Origin of the Buddha Image." *South Asian Archaeology*, pp. 377–400.

Varaman, Shanna. N.d. *Damrab Kueng Rang-Khong Khang* [Stories of magical things]. Bangkok.

Vaudeville, Charlotte. 1964. "La légende de Sundara et les funérailles du Buddha." *Bulletin de l'Ecole Française d'Extrême-Orient* 52:73–91.

———. 1980. "The Govardhana Myth in Northern India." *Indo-Iranian Journal* 22:1–45.

Ver Eecke, Jacqueline. 1980. *Le Sīhaḷavatthuppakaraṇa: texte Pāli et traduction*. Paris.

Vidyābhūṣaṇa, Satīśa Chandra. 1897. "The Story of Hārītikā." *Journal of the Buddhist Text Society* 5, pt. 1:26–29.

Vinaya Nidāna. See Jayawickrama 1962.

The Vinayapiṭakam. 1879. 5 vols. Edited by Hermann Oldenberg. London.

Viravong, Sila. 1966. *Ruang Phra Upakhuta Thera*. Vientiane.

Visuddhimagga. 1920–21. 2 vols. Edited by C. A. F. Rhys Davids. London.

Vogel, J. Ph. 1926. *Indian Serpent-Lore or the Nāgas in Hindu Legend and Art*. London.

———. 1930. *La sculpture de Mathurā*. Paris.

Waddell, L. A. 1897. "Upagupta, the Fourth Buddhist Patriarch and High Priest of Açoka." *Journal of the Asiatic Society of Bengal* 66:76–84.

———. 1899. "Identity of Upagupta, the High-priest of Açoka with Moggaliputta Tisso." *Proceedings of the Asiatic Society of Bengal*, pp. 70–75.

Waldschmidt, Ernst. 1967. "Zur Śroṇakoṭikarṇa-Legende." In *Vom Ceylon bis Turfan*, pp. 203–25. Göttingen.

———. 1977. "Buddha Frees the Disc of the Moon." *Bulletin of the School of Oriental and African Studies* 33:179–83.

Wales, H. G. Quaritch. 1983. *Divination in Thailand: The Hopes and Fears of a Southeast Asian People*. London.

Wang Yi-t'ung. 1984. *A Record of Buddhist Monasteries in Lo-Yang by Yang Hsüan-chih*. Princeton.

Warder, A. K. 1970. *Indian Buddhism*. Delhi.

Ware, James. 1933. "Weishou on Buddhism." *T'oung pao* 30:100–181.

———. 1938. "The Preamble to the *Saṃgharakṣitāvadāna*." *Harvard Journal of Asiatic Studies* 3:47–67.

Warren, Henry Clarke. 1922. *Buddhism in Translations*. Cambridge, Mass.

Watanabe, K. 1909. "The Story of Kalmāṣapāda and Its Evolution in Indian Literature." *Journal of the Pali Text Society*, pp. 236–310.

Watters, Thomas. 1898. "The Eighteen Lohan of Chinese Buddhist Temples." *Journal of the Royal Asiatic Society*, pp. 329–47.

———. [1904] 1961. *On Yuan Chwang's Travels in India*. 2 vols. Reprint. Delhi.

Wayman, Alex. 1959. "Studies in Yama and Māra." *Indo-Iranian Journal* 3:4–73, 112–31.

———. 1970. "The Buddhist Theory of Vision." In *Añjali—Papers on Indology and Buddhism: A Felicitation Volume Presented to Oliver Hector DeAlwis Wijesekera*, pp. 27–32. Peradeniya.

———. 1981. "Aśoka and Upagupta-Moggaliputta." In *K. P. Jayaswal Commemoration Volume*, pp. 300–307. Patna.

Weeraratne, Amarasiri. 1972. "The Chabbagiyas—Miscreant Monks of the Buddha's Time." *Mahābodhi* 80:471–74.

Weeraratne, W. G. 1966. "Avadāna." In *Encyclopaedia of Buddhism*, edited by G. P. Malalasekera, 2:395–98. Colombo.

Wells, Kenneth E. 1960. *Thai Buddhism, Its Rites and Activities*. Bangkok.

Wijeyewardene, Gehan. 1970. "The Still Point and the Turning World: Towards the Structure of Northern Thai Religion." *Mankind* 7:247–55.

———. 1982. *Place and Emotion in Northern Thai Ritual Behavior*. Bangkok.

Willemen, Charles. 1978. *The Chinese Udānavarga. Mélanges chinois et bouddhiques*, vol. 19. Brussels.

Williams, Paul M. 1981. "On the Abhidharma Ontology." *Journal of Indian Philosophy* 9:227–57.

———. 1989. *Mahāyāna Buddhism: The Doctrinal Foundations*. London.

Wilson, Joe. 1980. *Chandrakirti's Sevenfold Reasoning*. Dharmsala.

Winternitz, Maurice. 1933. *A History of Indian Literature*. 3 vols. Translated by Mrs. S. Ketkar. Calcutta.

Windisch, Ernst. 1895. *Māra und Buddha*. Leipzig.

Witanachchi, C. 1976. "Upagupta and Indagutta." In *Malalasekera Commemoration Volume*, edited by O. H. DeA. Wijesekera, pp. 353–62. Colombo.

Wood, W. A. R. 1965. *Consul in Paradise: Sixty-Nine Years in Siam*. London.

———. N.d. *A History of Siam*. Bangkok.

Woodward, F. L. [1916] 1970. *Manual of a Mystic*. Reprint. London.

———. 1948. *The Minor Anthologies of the Pali Canon II: Udāna—Verses of Uplift and Itivuttaka—As It Was Said*. London.

Woodward, F. L., and E. M. Hare. 1932–36. *The Book of the Gradual Sayings*. 5 vols. London.

Yalman, Nur. 1962. "The Ascetic Buddhist Monks of Ceylon." *Ethnology* 1:315–28.

Yalman, Nur. 1973. "On the Meaning of Food Offerings in Ceylon." *Social Compass* 20:287–302.

Yamazaki Gen'ichi. 1975. "Upagupta densetsu kō" [On the legend of Upagupta]. In *Enoki Hakushi kanreki kinen Tōyōshi ronsō* [A collection of essays on East Asian history in commemoration of Dr. Enoki's sixtieth birthday], pp. 465–81. Tokyo.

———. 1979. *Ashoka ō densetsu no kenkyū* [The legend of Aśoka: a critical study]. Tokyo.

———. 1982. "The Spread of Buddhism in the Mauryan Age with Special Reference to the Mahinda Legend." *Acta Asiatica* 43:1–16.

[Saya] Zagaru. 1977. *Shin Upagutta Yahanta* [The arhat Upagupta]. Rangoon.

Zago, Marcel. 1972. *Rites et cérémonies en milieu bouddhiste lao*. Rome.

Zimmer, Heinrich. 1925. *Karman: ein buddhistischer Legendenkranz*. Munich.

———. 1946. *Myths and Symbols in Indian Art and Civilization*. New York.

———. 1955. *The Art of Indian Asia*. 2 vols. Princeton.

Zimmermann, Heinz. 1975. *Die Subhāṣita-ratna-karaṇḍaka-kathā (dem Āryaśūra zugeschrieben) und ihre tibetische Übersetzung*. Wiesbaden.

Zinkgräf, Willi. 1940. *Vom Divyāvadāna zur Avadāna-Kalpalatā: ein Beitrag zur Geschichte eines Avadāna*. Heidelberg.

Zürcher, Erik. 1959. *The Buddhist Conquest of China*. 2 vols. Leiden.

Index

A-yü wang ching, 9. See also *Aśokarājasūtra*
A-yü wang chuan, 9. See also *Aśokarājāvadāna*
Abhayā, 108
Abhibhū Devarāja, 315n.5
Abhidharma, 7, 8, 62, 131, 143, 151, 163, 298n.18, 332n.3
Abhidharmakośa, 48, 298n.19
abhijñā, 53
abhiśeka, 193, 194
ācārya, 45
acharn wat, 254–55, 257, 264
Acintyabuddhaviṣayānirdeśa sūtra, 104
act of truth, 221, 241
Ādirajya, 25
Aggavaṃsa, 12, 182
Agnidatta, 68
Ahogangā, 147, 148, 309n.49
Ajanta, 115
Ajātaśatru, 62, 63, 66, 187, 308n.29
Akha, 177
alakṣanaka Buddha, 39–40, 131, 267
Ālikavendā, 6
amulets, 16, 148, 180, 225, 277, 278, 280, 281, 289
anāgāmin, 78, 79, 312n.34. *See also* nonreturners
Ānanda, 11, 23, 25, 28, 41, 44, 50, 60, 62–67, 99, 110, 122, 135, 139, 141–44, 162, 166, 175, 236, 239–40, 308n.29, 309n.49, 310n.78, 319n.10, 323n.76, 339n.4, 341n.45
Anāthapiṇḍada, 70. *See also* Anāthapiṇḍika
Anāthapiṇḍika, 41. *See also* Anāthapiṇḍada
anātman, 85, 128, 129. *See also* non-self
Angkor, 176, 338n.40
Angulimāla, 238, 241, 247
Anguttara Nikāya, 41, 58, 108, 141, 144, 166
animals, 51; in astrology, 238–40; identified with various Buddhas, 203; realm of, 54, 93, 130; Upagupta's association with, 213, 218, 254, 337n.11
animism, 172–73, 263
Aniruddha (disciple of the Buddha), 59, 110
Aniruddha (king), 175–76, 178–80, 182, 330n.30
ānisaṃsa, xi, 72, 310n.87
anitya, 85, 165. *See also* impermanence
anupūrvikathā. *See* pūrvakālakaraṇīyā kathā
Anurādhapura, 157
Apadāna, 163, 328n.109
Apalāla, 23–29, 32, 35, 37, 39
Aparagodānīya, 237
apsāras, 94
Arahan, 178
āraṇyaka, 70, 177
Archaimbault, Charles, 220–21, 266–67
arhatī, 158
arhatology, 167
arhats, 52, 65, 85–92, 145–47, 158, 175, 181–82, 190–93, 285, 298n.12, 306n.39, 326n.70; cult of; 14, 19, 51, 143–44, 166–67, 236–248, 253, 273; and the First Council, 61–62; four dead, 238, 242, 245, 341n.45; four living, 56, 238, 242, 244–46, 341n.45; sixteen, 64, 149, 237–38, 240–41, 247, 286, 308n.40, 339n.6; Upagupta as, 52, 150, 184, 209, 213, 227, 258–59, 279, 290. *See also* arhatship; lohan
arhatship, 18, 47, 59, 66, 84, 88, 113, 159, 183, 314n.75, 320n.23; confused with fourth trance level, 130–33; and the laity, 85–86, 96; and merit making, 120–22; and ordination, 86–90; track to, 79–80, 89–91, 107, 312n.38; of Upagupta, 78–79, 93, 213, 216, 291; of Upagupta's disciples, 23, 24, 41, 81, 118–43. *See also* arhats
Ari, 70, 176–78, 244, 279, 330n.30, 341n.47
Aṣāḷha, 69, 134
ascetic, 16, 44–45, 48, 52, 66, 68–73, 76, 268, 325n.49, 337n.31; Upagupta as, 53, 181, 191, 199, 201; Upagupta's father as, 16, 181, 212, 217, 219. *See also* asceticism; ṛṣis
asceticism, 16, 18, 45, 70, 73, 87, 88
Asita, 54, 333n.23

226, 249, 254, 261–66, 268–69, 273, 282, 293, 301n.8, 335n.53, 337n.27, 344n.34
laukika, 244
Lefèvre-Pontalis, Pierre, 180, 280
leftovers, 37, 48–52, 305nn. 16, 21, 23, and 28. *See also* food offerings
Lévi, Sylvain, 234, 237
Lévi-Strauss, Claude, 234
Lévy, Paul, 100, 180, 263
lo-han, 64, 245, 247, 290. *See also* arhats: sixteen
Loi Krathong, 150, 202–4, 206, 261, 335n.49. *See also* festival of lights
lokapālas, 61, 307n.18
Lokapaññatti, 12–13, 95, 99, 101–2, 104, 107, 149, 155, 172, 175, 182–83, 186–208, 214, 236, 255, 264, 266, 269–70, 273, 276, 287, 289, 292, 336n.67
Lokaprajñapti, 12, 300n.59, 332n.3
lokottara, 244
Lotus Sūtra, 40, 164, 328n.110
loving kindness, 26–27, 67, 260, 282. *See also* mettā
luang phau, 289
Luce, Gordon, 12, 179, 182–83
Lumbinī, 105, 165

Ma Huan, 177
Macchadevī, 16, 212–14, 229, 254, 337n.10
Madhyāntika, 11, 38, 41, 60–61, 66, 180, 308n.48. *See also* Majjhantika
Mae Hong Son, 152, 243, 270–71, 284
Mae Sariang, 249, 262, 264, 277, 286
Maedara, 243–44
Magadha, 5–6, 145, 330n.25
magical powers, 4, 14, 25–27, 32, 35, 41, 52–53, 64, 84, 98, 123, 125–29, 131–37, 141–42, 144, 149, 151, 155–57, 177, 187, 189, 195, 209, 213, 222, 236, 242, 247, 257, 260, 264, 269, 281–82, 290, 322n.62. *See also* ṛddhi; supernatural powers
Maha-win wutthu, 13
Mahābhārata, 220
Mahādeva, 298n.12, 319n.11
Mahajjātakamālā, 161, 164
Mahākaccāna, 6. *See also* Mahākātyāyana
Mahākappina, 195–96, 334n.34
Mahākarmavibhanga, 180
Mahākassapa, 70, 72, 177–78, 244, 279, 311n.94, 341n.45. *See also* Mahākāśyapa
Mahākāśyapa, 11, 28, 41, 60–65, 70–71, 74, 90–91, 99, 110, 139, 142, 159, 175, 196, 237–38, 245, 247, 291, 308nn. 29 and 31–33, 310n.66, 330n.24, 333n.23. *See also* Mahākassapa
Mahākātyāyana, 28, 331n.53. *See also* Mahākaccāna
mahalla, 66, 68–71
mahallaka, 68–70, 73, 90, 149, 310n.71
Mahāmaudgalyāyana, 28–29, 110, 166, 339n.4. *See also* Maudgalyāyana; Moggallāna
Mahāmuni Temple, 173
Mahānikay tradition, 185, 279
Mahāpāla, 311n.94
Mahāparinibbāna Sutta, 236
Mahāparinirvāṇa sūtra, 69
Mahāprajñāpāramitā śāstra, 62, 129
Mahāpuruṣa, 39, 106, 108, 165, 314n.85. *See also* Great Man; marks of the Great Man
Mahāsaṃghikas, xii
Mahāsamnipāta ratnaketu dhāraṇī sūtra, 99, 101
Mahāsampiṇḍanidāna, 307
Mahāsubhara, 244
Mahātissa, 313n.54
Mahāvaṃsa, 13, 153, 155, 157, 182
Mahāvastu, 54
Mahāvibhāṣā, 8, 298n.19, 306n.42
Mahāvihāra, 174
Mahāyāna, xii, 6, 8, 19, 40, 82, 85, 90, 99, 102, 104, 106, 112, 116–17, 131, 161, 164, 175–76, 182, 184, 236–37, 242, 297n.7, 306n.39
Mahāyāzawin-gyi, 13, 183
Mahendra, 101, 180, 331n.53
Mahinda, 178, 180, 309n.42
Mahīśāsakas, 61, 142
Mahissara, 186, 315n.6. *See also* Śiva
mahopadeśaka, 304n.81
Maitreya, 14, 18, 68, 71, 73–74, 140, 203, 211, 237, 244–48, 306nn. 38 and 48, 313n.42, 314n.85, 342n.60; and Mahākāśyapa, 63–64, 71, 166, 308n.32; and Śākyamuni, 54–56, 90–92, 107, 194, 267, 291, 294, 306n.39, 308n.32
Maitreya samiti, 63
Maitreyāvadāna, 63
Majjhantika, 180, 308n.48. *See also* Madhyāntika
Majjhima Nikāya, 87